NOUVELLE THÉOLOGIE AND
SACRAMENTAL ONTOLOGY

Nouvelle Théologie and Sacramental Ontology

A Return to Mystery

HANS BOERSMA

OXFORD
UNIVERSITY PRESS

OXFORD
UNIVERSITY PRESS

Great Clarendon Street, Oxford OX2 6DP

Oxford University Press is a department of the University of Oxford.
It furthers the University's objective of excellence in research, scholarship,
and education by publishing worldwide in

Oxford New York

Auckland Cape Town Dar es Salaam Hong Kong Karachi
Kuala Lumpur Madrid Melbourne Mexico City Nairobi
New Delhi Shanghai Taipei Toronto

With offices in

Argentina Austria Brazil Chile Czech Republic France Greece
Guatemala Hungary Italy Japan Poland Portugal Singapore
South Korea Switzerland Thailand Turkey Ukraine Vietnam

Oxford is a registered trade mark of Oxford University Press
in the UK and in certain other countries

Published in the United States
by Oxford University Press Inc., New York

British Library Cataloguing in Publication Data

Data available

Library of Congress Cataloging in Publication Data
Library of Congress Control Number: 2008943931

Typeset by SPI Publisher Services, Pondicherry, India
Printed in Great Britain
on acid-free paper by the
MPG Books Group, Bodmin and King s Lynn

ISBN 978–0–19–922964–2

To Linda

sacramentum caritatis

To recognize creatureliness as creatureliness means to recognize God immediately in it. To perceive the limit of worldly truth means to apprehend
concomitantly and tacitly what lies beyond it.

Hans Urs von Balthasar, *Theo-Logic*

Preface

The opportunity to spend an entire sabbatical year reading the theology of the *ressourcement* movement has been a sacramental gift. It has served as a foretaste of the eternal Sabbath rest, and I am most grateful to Regent College in Vancouver for allowing me a year away from my teaching responsibilities, even though I had spent only two years at this wonderful evangelical graduate school of theology. I also express my sincere thanks to the Association of Theological Schools and to the Henry Luce Foundation for their gracious support for this research project by appointing me Henry Luce III Fellow in Theology for 2007–8. It has been a joy to attend Luce conferences in Pittsburgh together with my dear colleague from Regent College, Bruce Hindmarsh, and also to engage there in fruitful dialogue with the convener for my session, Thomas G. Guarino. The generous Luce Fellowship made it possible for me to spend the summer of 2007 as Visiting Scholar at the Katholieke Universiteit in Louvain, Belgium (KUL). I have fond and lasting memories of the unequalled Flemish hospitality—particularly in the form of great discussions over lunch—which Lieven Boeve, Coordinator of the Research Unit, Systematic Theology at KUL, extended to me over these summer months. It was a privilege to get to know some of the colleagues at the Evangelical Theological Faculty in Louvain (ETF). Their kind invitation for me to come back in May 2008 to teach a course for them has meant a lot to me. I want to thank especially Andreas Beck, Ron Michener, and Patrick Nullens, who ensured that I immediately felt at home at ETF.

Although much of the sustained work for this book took place over the last couple of years—and especially this past year—I none the less have the sense that the project has been with me much longer. About eight years ago, I joined a few friends and colleagues from Trinity Western University, at Langley, British Columbia in an ecumenical reading group called 'Paradosis' (Tradition). One of the books we discussed during our informal conversations was Yves Congar's *Tradition and Traditions*. The huge tome was impressive not just in its scholarship but also in the opening that it created for Catholic–Protestant dialogue. As a Protestant, I sensed that I was in the presence of a Catholic scholar who truly understood non-Catholics and, what is more, who had a great deal of appreciation for them. Congar had a way of dissolving false dilemmas with regard to the Scripture–Tradition relationship. One of the things he made clear was that in an important sense Tradition was simply the Church's authoritative interpretation of Scripture itself. Around the same time—perhaps partially through the reading of Congar—I stumbled across a small essay by de Lubac on spiritual interpretation. From a different angle than Congar, de Lubac too conveyed to me the importance of reading Scripture through the lens of the Church. When my friend Jamie Smith invited me to speak on Radical Orthodoxy at a conference at Calvin

College, Grand Rapids, Michigan in 2003, I started reading John Milbank, and I soon noticed his dependency on *nouvelle théologie* and on de Lubac, in particular. Milbank's insistence that theology not be afraid to assume her proper role as queen of the sciences was an inspiration for me to start taking *nouvelle théologie* more seriously.

One of the reasons why, by now, *nouvelle théologie* had become quite appealing to me was its character as a movement of *ressourcement*. My reading had convinced me that both Protestants and Catholics needed the pre-modern inspiration of the Church Fathers and of medieval theology. Thus, when I joined Regent College in 2005, my inaugural lecture dealt with the anthropology of St Irenaeus and Henri de Lubac, and in the process I raised a few questions about evangelical accommodation to contemporary culture. *Ressourcement* of the 'great Tradition' had become an obvious requirement for me. The basic reason was the traditional 'Platonist–Christian synthesis' (a term I sometimes use, only in part to watch the reaction of my dear friends and colleagues) which had constituted a sacramental view of reality—a sacramental ontology—that recognized the mystery inherent in the created order. *Ressourcement* of this sacramental ontology was necessary, so it seemed to me, for authentic ecumenical dialogue. So, when in 2006 I had the opportunity to join Bill Cavanaugh from the University of St Thomas in one of Calvin College's Seminars in Christian Scholarship, I decided to do a research project on de Lubac's ecclesiology. A larger book project on *nouvelle théologie* seemed to be the logical next step.

The cover of this book contains Fra Angelico's mystic wheel (*c.*1450). I explain the details of the painting in Chapter 5 (n. 46). The mystic wheel depicts Ezekiel's vision of the four living creatures, each accompanied by a wheel, 'their construction being as it were a wheel within a wheel' (Ezek. 1: 16). Fra Angelico's painting is based on a homily that St Gregory the Great (*c.*540–604) had written on this same vision. Pope Gregory had regarded the outer and inner wheels as referring to the Old and New Testaments, respectively. Analogously, the outer and inner wheels could refer to the literal and spiritual meanings of the Scriptures, to secular and sacred history, to human discourse and divine reality, to the original deposit of faith and its later development in the Tradition of the Church, to the structure and the life of the Church, and, ultimately, to nature and the supernatural. In each case, the *nouvelle* theologians discussed in this book regarded the 'outer wheel' as sacramentally containing the 'inner wheel', or the sacrament (*sacramentum*) as making present the reality (*res*) of the mystery of God. Fra Angelico's painting of Ezekiel's vision thus depicts the key to what I will argue—that the *ressourcement* movement was an attempt to recover a sacramental ontology and so was a return to mystery.

It has been a privilege to be able to present, on different occasions, some of the material that has found its way into this book. I am grateful for the fellowship and the interaction in connection with presentations for the Evangelical Theology

Group and for the Christian Systematic Theology Group at annual meetings of the American Academy of Religion; for the Research Unit Systematic Theology at KUL; for the Graduate Program of Theology and the Aquinas Center for Theological Renewal at Ave Maria University in Ave Maria, Florida; and for the Canadian Evangelical Theological Association. Some of the material in this book has been published before, and I appreciate the permissions for republication given by the following journals: *International Journal of Systematic Theology, New Blackfriars, Calvin Theological Journal, Louvain Studies, and Heythrop Journal.* My essays in these journals are listed in the bibliography. I also need to make a small comment about the translations used in this book. Where English translations are available, I have made use of them; when I quote from a foreign language directly, the translation is mine.

I am thankful for the many people who have surrounded me with advice, encouragement, and care. William T. Cavanaugh, Dennis R. Danielson, Augustin Laffay, OP, Joseph G. Mueller, SJ, and James K. A. Smith have all been very gracious in responding to my calls for help. Others have read and commented extensively on parts of the book; I much appreciate the wisdom of Fritz Dewit, Adam English, Gabriel Flynn, Thomas G. Guarino, John M. McDermott, SJ, Jürgen Mettepenningen, Bert Moes, Dick Moes, Placidus Sander, OSB, and Myles Werntz. It was a special joy to discuss with my son Gerald—who also indexed the book for me—many of the issues that came up through his reading of the manuscript. Fergus Kerr, OP, Matthew Levering, Richard Mouw, and John Stackhouse were most kind to heed my rather late request to go through the manuscript. Some of them were actually foolhardy enough to *offer* to read it. None of these careful scholars bears any blame for blemishes that still remain. The interaction with the students of my *nouvelle théologie* seminar was not just a lot of fun; it also helped me to get a better grasp of some of the material that I was working on. I much appreciate Chad Raith's bibliographical research at the early stages of the project. I am especially grateful for the unstinting support—by way of research, editing, and the compilation of the bibliography—rendered by my research assistant, Tora Klassen. Finally, it has been a pleasure to work with the editorial staff at Oxford University Press. I especially want to thank Charlotte Green, Michael Janes, Tom Perridge, Lizzie Robottom, and Paul Smith for their support and punctual attention to detail.

I am a slow learner; I still am not quite sure what the 'profound mystery' is of which St Paul speaks in Ephesians 5: 32. What has become clear to me, however, is that not only marriage, but also one's spouse, is a 'mystery'—in the ancient, sacramental sense of the term. Beyond doubt, my wife Linda is a sacrament of love. I dedicate this book to her, since her loving support and faithfulness make present to me the very love of God.

H.B.

Langley, British Columbia
2008

Contents

Abbreviations

AAS	*Acta apostolicae sedis*
AER	*American Ecclesiastical Review*
Ang	*Angelicum*
APC	*Annales de philosophie chrétienne*
ArchPhil	*Archives de philosophie*
ASS	*Acta sanctae sedis*
ATh	*L'Année théologique*
ATR	*Anglican Theological Review*
BETL	Bibliotheca ephemeridum theologicarum Lovaniensium
Bib	*Biblica*
Bijdragen	*Bijdragen: International Journal in Philosophy and Theology*
BLE	*Bulletin de littérature ecclésiastique*
BM	*Bulletin des missions*
BT	*Bulletin thomiste*
Cath	*Catholica*
CC	*Cross Currents*
Comm	*Communio: International Catholic Review*
Conc	*Concilium: Revue internationale de théologie*
CTJ	*Calvin Theological Journal*
DownR	*Downside Review*
DS	Henricus Denzinger and Adolfus Schönmetzer (eds), *Enchiridion symbolorum: Definitionum et declarationum de rebus fidei et morum* (34th edn, Barcelona: Herder, 1967).
DViv	*Dieu vivant: Perspectives religieuses et philosophiques*
Eccl	*Ecclesiology*
ECT	Evangelicals and Catholics Together
ETL	*Ephemerides theologicae Lovanienses*
EvQ	*Evangelical Quarterly*
FHS	*French Historical Studies*
FrR	*The French Review*
Greg	*Gregorianum*
HeyJ	*Heythrop Journal*
Integr	*Integration*

Irén	*Irénikon*
IJST	*International Journal of Systematic Theology*
IPQ	*International Philosophical Quarterly*
JOC	*Jeunesse Ouvrière Catholique*
JR	*Journal of Religion*
Jur	*The Jurist*
LMD	*La Maison-Dieu*
LouvStud	*Louvain Studies*
LS	*Letter & Spirit*
LTP	*Laval théologique et philosophique*
MSR	*Mélanges de science religieuse*
MTh	*Modern Theology*
MTZ	*Münchener Theologische Zeitschrift*
NBl	*New Blackfriars*
NRT	*Nouvelle revue théologique*
NV Eng	*Nova et Vetera,* English edn
OiC	*One in Christ*
PG	*Patrologia Graeca,* ed. J.-P. Migne, 166 vols (Paris: Migne, 1856–66)
PL	*Patrologia Latina,* ed. J.-P. Migne, 221 vols (Paris: Migne, 1844–64)
PT	*Philosophy and Theology*
RCF	*Revue du clergé français*
RCIF	*Revue catholique des idées et des faits*
RHE	*Revue d'histoire ecclésiastique*
RPh	*Revue de philosophie*
RSPT	*Revue des sciences philosophiques et théologiques*
RSR	*Recherches de science religieuse*
RT	*Revue thomiste*
RTL	*Revue théologique de Louvain*
RTP	*Revue de théologie et de philosophie*
ScEs	*Science et esprit*
SJT	*Scottish Journal of Theology*
SL	*Studia liturgica*
ST	Thomas Aquinas, *Summa Theologica,* 5 vols (1948; repr. Notre Dame, Ind.: Ave Maria, 1981)
TD	*Theology Digest*
Thomist	*The Thomist: A Speculative Quarterly Review*

TQ	*Theologische Quartalschrift*
TS	*Theological Studies*
TTod	*Theology Today*
TZ	*Theologie der Zeit*
USCath Hist	*US Catholic Historian*
VC	*Vigiliae christianae*
VE	*Vox Evangelica*
VInt	*La Vie intellectuelle*
VSpir	*La Vie spirituelle*
ZKT	*Zeitschrift für Katholische Theologie*

1

Introduction: The Rupture between Theology and Life

The Church is not a special little group, isolated, apart, remaining untouched amidst the changes of the world. The Church is the world as believing in Christ, or, what comes to the same thing, it is Christ dwelling in and saving the world by our faith.

Yves M.-J. Congar[1]

JEAN DANIÉLOU'S PROGRAMMATIC STATEMENT

In a spirited, programmatic 1946 essay, Jean Daniélou (1905–74), student of Henri de Lubac (1896–1991) and patristic scholar at the Institut Catholique in Paris, outlined what he saw as the main characteristics of the growing French theological trend to 'return to the sources'.[2] The essay, entitled 'Les Orientations

---

[1] Yves M.-J. Congar, 'The Reasons for the Unbelief of Our Time: A Theological Conclusion', *Integr* (Dec. 1938), 21.

[2] For helpful (auto)biographical accounts on the most significant theologians dealt with in this book, see the following: On Chenu: Marie-Dominique Chenu, *Un théologien en liberté: Jacques Duquesne interroge le Père Chenu* (Paris: Centurion, 1975); Christophe F. Potworowski, *Contemplation and Incarnation: The Theology of Marie-Dominique Chenu* (Montreal: McGill–Queen's University Press, 2001), passim; Fergus Kerr, *Twentieth-century Catholic Theologians: From Neoscholasticism to Nuptial Mysticism* (Malden, Mass.: Blackwell, 2007), 17–21. On Congar: Congar, *Une passion; L'Unité: Réflexions et souvenirs 1929–1973* (Paris: Cerf, 1974); id., *Une vie pour la vérité: Jean Puyo interroge le Père Congar*, ed. Jean Puyo (Paris: Centurion, 1975); id., *Journal d'un théologien (1946–1956)*, ed. Étienne Fouilloux (Paris: Cerf, 2000); Jean-Pierre Jossua, *Yves Congar: Theology in the Service of God's People* (Chicago, Ill.: Priory, 1968), 11–37; Aidan Nichols, *Yves Congar* (Wilton, Conn.: Morehouse/Barlow, 1989), 1–13; Étienne Fouilloux, 'Friar Yves, Cardinal Congar, Dominican: Itinerary of a Theologian', *USCath Hist* 17/2 (1999), 63–90; Elizabeth Teresa Groppe, *Yves Congar's Theology of the Holy Spirit* (Oxford: Oxford University Press, 2004), 15–27; Fergus Kerr, *Twentieth-century Catholic Theologians*, 34–8. On de Lubac: Henri de Lubac, *At the Service of the Church: Henri de Lubac Reflects on the Circumstances that Occasioned his Writings*, trans. Anne Elizabeth Englund (San Francisco, Calif.: Ignatius, 1993); Jean-Pierre Wagner, *Henri de Lubac* (Paris: Cerf, 2001), 9–46; Georges Chantraine, *Henri de Lubac*, i, *De la naissance à la démobilisation (1896–1919)* (Paris: Cerf, 2007); Kerr, *Twentieth-century Catholic Theologians*, 67–77; Rudolf Voderholzer, *Meet Henri de Lubac: His Life and Work*, trans. Michael J. Miller (San Francisco, Calif.: Ignatius, 2008), 19–103. On Bouillard: Michel Castro, 'Henri Bouillard (1908–1981): Éléments de biographie intellectuelle', *MSR* 60/4 (2003), 43–58; 63/2 (2006), 47–59. On Daniélou: Jean Daniélou, *Et qui est mon prochain? Mémoires* (Paris: Stock, 1974); Paul Lebeau, *Jean Daniélou*

présentes de la pensée religieuse', proved to be controversial, and for the public eye it served to identify the group of theologians that became known as *nouvelle théologie* or the movement of *ressourcement*.[3] Daniélou observed that the 'Modernist Crisis', which had been the cause of great upheaval in the Catholic Church forty years earlier, remained unresolved. While Daniélou himself criticized Modernism's 'agnosticism' and 'abuse of critical exegesis', the Jesuit patrologist none the less insisted that the condemnation of Modernism should not be the final word on the matter. While Modernism had rightly been rejected, the central theological problem continued to plague the Catholic world. There still existed, in Daniélou's day, a 'rupture between theology and life'.[4] The Modernists had rightly sensed that this rupture, reinforced by the dominance of neo-Thomism since the late nineteenth century, needed to be bridged.[5] Daniélou was convinced that contemporary thought would no longer be satisfied with the unresolved dualism: 'The theoretical speculations, separated from action while not engaging life, have had their day.'[6]

Daniélou maintained that contemporary theology could overcome the rupture between theology and life by meeting three conditions. First, it would have to 'treat God as God, not as an object, but as the Subject *par excellence*'.[7] To do this, a 'return to the sources' would be necessary. The *ressourcement* Daniélou advocated was a return to the Bible, the Church Fathers, and the liturgy.[8] Biblical *ressourcement* meant a reappraisal of the 'increasing rupture between exegesis and theology', ever since the thirteenth century.[9] While Daniélou believed a great deal of work had already been done in terms of the 'restoration of the Bible to its central function in Christian thought', until now theological thought had insufficiently benefited from the advances in biblical scholarship. Of particular importance, Daniélou insisted, was the theological appropriation of the Old

(Paris: Fleurus, 1967); Jemima Rosario Sullivan, 'The Contribution of Jean Daniélou to an Understanding of Biblical and Liturgical Typology in Liturgical Catechesis' (PhD diss., Catholic University of America, Washington, DC, 1999), 68–104. On Balthasar: Peter Henrici, 'Hans Urs von Balthasar: A Sketch of His Life', in David L. Schindler (ed), *Hans Urs von Balthasar: His Life and Work* (San Francisco, Calif.: Communio/Ignatius, 1991), 7–43.

[3] Daniélou, 'Les Orientations présentes de la pensée religieuse', *Études*, 249 (1946), 5–21. Cf. the response of Marie-Michel Labourdette, 'La Théologie et ses sources', *RT* 46 (1946), 353–71. The debate is reviewed in Philip J. Donnelly, 'On the Development of Dogma and the Supernatural', *TS* 8 (1947), 471–7. For further analysis of Daniélou's essay, see John Auricchio, *The Future of Theology* (Staten Island, NY: Alba, 1970), 265–72.

[4] Daniélou, 'Les Orientations', 6.

[5] Neo-Thomist theology strongly opposed Kantian subjectivism and insisted that human experience should not influence theology. This explains Daniélou's complaint about a 'rupture between theology and life'.

[6] Daniélou, 'Les Orientations', 7.

[7] Ibid.

[8] For historical accounts of this threefold *ressourcement*, see Roger Aubert, *La Théologie catholique au milieu du XXe siècle* (Tournai: Casterman, 1954); James M. Connolly, *The Voices of France: A Survey of Contemporary Theology in France* (New York: Macmillan, 1961), 30–69.

[9] Daniélou, 'Les Orientations', 8.

Testament. He insisted that one could learn a great deal from the Church Fathers' willingness to look to the Old Testament for types of Christ, while also keeping in mind the new insights of scientific exegesis.[10]

With these comments, Daniélou moved on to the necessity of a *ressourcement* of the Church Fathers, whose work had been 'in large part a vast commentary on Holy Scripture'.[11] Noting the recent initiatives of the monograph series Théologie and of the republication of the Church Fathers in the Sources chrétiennes series (which he had initiated together with de Lubac), Daniélou explained that the Fathers 'are not just genuine witnesses to a past state of affairs; they are still the most timely nourishment for people today'.[12] Persuaded that the notion of history was 'alien to Thomism', Daniélou wished to restore to theology a sense of historical development, and he looked to Church Fathers like Irenaeus (d. *c.*202), Origen (*c.*185–*c.*254), and Gregory of Nyssa (*c.*334–*c.*395), for assistance in this endeavour.[13] Convinced that 'the West since Saint Augustine' (354–430) had viewed salvation as an individual matter Daniélou believed that the Greek Fathers could assist in bringing the collective understanding of salvation back into focus.[14]

In addition to biblical and patristic *ressourcement*, the reintroduction of earlier patterns of liturgical celebration also ranked high in Daniélou's programme. He was convinced that liturgical *ressourcement* would allow for the retrieval of 'contemplation of realities hidden behind the sacramental signs'.[15] A shift in focus from the efficacious character of the liturgy to the actual contents of its teaching would draw attention to the fact that the liturgy first of all signified something; only then was it also efficacious. The liturgy, Daniélou maintained, should more clearly take the form of a human encounter with the mystery of God.[16]

Daniélou's return to biblical, patristic, and liturgical resources was fuelled by the conviction that such a renewal fit the demands of the time. The second condition to overcome the rupture between the theology and life, therefore, was that theology would have to enter into dialogue with contemporary philosophical developments. It should respond to the 'modern spirit' (*l'âme moderne*) and take into account the 'new dimensions' that science and history had provided for time and space and that literature and philosophy had given to the soul as well as to society.[17] *Ressourcement* theology would battle the neo-scholastic rupture between theology and life by means of dialogue with contemporary philosophy, most notably Marxism and existentialism: 'It is the proper function of the theologian to go back and forth, like the angels on Jacob's ladder, between heaven and earth and to weave continually new connections between them.'[18] Although he remained critical both of Marxism and of existentialism, Daniélou none the

[10] Ibid. 9.   [11] Ibid.   [12] Ibid. 10.
[13] Ibid.   [14] Ibid. 11.   [15] Ibid.
[16] Ibid. 12.   [17] Ibid. 7.   [18] Ibid. 13.

less argued that the significance of history in the former and the role of human subjectivity in the latter allowed for dialogue with these philosophical movements. Particularly helpful in Søren Kierkegaard's (1813–55) existentialism, for example, was the affirmation of the mystery of a personal God as opposed to a theology that treated God as an object.[19]

Third, in order to overcome the separation between theology and life, it was necessary for theology to function as a concrete attitude, as 'a response that engages the entire person, an interior light of an action where life unfolds in its entirety'.[20] This meant that theology and spirituality, as well as constructive and moral theology, should be reintegrated.[21] Here Daniélou commented positively on recent theological exploration of the vocation of individual lay people, the spirituality of marriage, and temporal (especially political) activities. Theology was in need of a universal perspective, and it was called to become 'incarnate' in the great cultures of the world, those of India, China, and Africa. Although revelation had come to an end with Christ's redemptive work, the incarnation of the Christian faith in different cultures would enable 'a progress of dogma'.[22] The forms of each cultural mindset would highlight 'new aspects of the inexhaustible treasure of Christ'.[23]

RESSOURCEMENT AND THE RETURN TO MYSTERY

The Shared Sensibility of *Nouvelle Théologie*

Daniélou's essay was not appreciated by the neo-Thomists. Their scholasticism had dominated the theological landscape since Pope Leo XIII's revival of Thomism in the late nineteenth century.[24] The theological manuals of the neo-Thomist scholastic theologians tried to be faithful to the theology of Thomas Aquinas (1224/5–74), and they believed that this could be done only by maintaining a strict separation between the natural and supernatural realms. In the natural realm, the rational 'preambles to the faith' (*praeambula fidei*) presented arguments for the existence of God and demonstrated the reliability of divine revelation by pointing to divine miracles and prophetic fulfilment. Once these preliminary natural steps had been taken, the supernatural truth of the gospel presented itself. In the supernatural realm, faith accepted the Church's teaching as divine revelation coming from the outside or from above. Daniélou regarded this strictly extrinsic character of the supernatural in neo-Thomism as the reason for the rupture between theology and life. He believed that theology had the duty to connect with the experiences of people's actual day-to-day lives. Nature and the

[19] Daniélou, 'Les Orientations', 16.   [20] Ibid. 7.   [21] Ibid. 17.
[22] Ibid. 20.   [23] Ibid. 21.
[24] For more detailed discussion of neo-Thomism, see Chap. 2, sect.: Nineteenth-century 'Footnotes' to Kant.

supernatural had to be reconnected, if theology was to restore its meaningful role in people's actual lives. At the heart of *nouvelle théologie*'s sacramental ontology was, therefore, the desire to reconnect nature and the supernatural. The *nouvelle* theologians were convinced that God had created the human person with a supernatural end, so that the supernatural was not a strictly extrinsic divine imposition on nature. Such a separation of nature and the supernatural would render the realm of nature (as well as people's day-to-day lives) strictly autonomous or secular, while theology and faith would become privatized and disconnected from life in the natural realm. In other words, according to Daniélou and the other *nouvelle* theologians, neo-Thomism ended up endorsing modernity's acceptance of the autonomy of nature as well as the Enlightenment belief in human progress in this independent (or immanent) realm of nature. In the eyes of the *nouvelle* theologians, this was a deeply ironic situation, considering neo-Thomist distrust of the Enlightenment and the secularism that it had brought.

Nouvelle théologie wished to reconnect nature and the supernatural, so as to overcome the rupture between theology and life. Only in this way could faith and theology be meaningful in contemporary society. The result of this desire to reconnect nature and the supernatural was a strong Christological focus. Hans Urs von Balthasar (1905–88) used the image of an 'hourglass', whose two contiguous vessels (God and the creature) met at the narrow passage at the centre (Jesus Christ). Revelation was primary, was supernatural in character, and did come from above. At the same time, the gift of supernatural revelation through Christ made it legitimate to turn the hourglass upside down, so that nature, too, made its genuine contribution, in and through Christ.[25]

In his essay, Daniélou did not just express a few marginal reservations about neo-Thomism and its dry, intellectual manuals of theology; he seemed to take issue with the entire system. His article touched on many of the main issues that the *nouvelle* theologians would take up over the years. Of particular significance was his allusion to the sacramental mindset of the *ressourcement* movement, expressed in his insistence that the liturgy should be an encounter with the 'mystery' of God. All of the other *nouvelle* theologians would agree with Daniélou that the focus of theology should be the contemplation of the realities behind the sacramental signs rather than the latter's legitimacy or efficacy.

For the *nouvelle* theologians, 'mysteries' did not simply refer to unknown or obscure divine truths that rational, discursive thought would gradually be able to uncover. An intellectualist approach like this implied that theology's task was to grasp and overcome mystery. According to *nouvelle théologie*, however, the purpose of theology was rather to enter into mystery's hidden depths. Truth was the dynamic realization of existential, loving engagement of the known

---

[25] Hans Urs von Balthasar, *The Theology of Karl Barth*, trans. Edward T. Oakes (San Francisco, Calif.: Communio/Ignatius, 1992), 197. Cf. Chap. 4, sect.: Karl Barth: Christ as the Hourglass.

object rather than abstract, objective analysis. As Balthasar put it in his 1947 *Wahrheit der Welt*:

In the end, only something endowed with mystery is worthy of love. It is impossible to love something stripped of mystery; at best it would be a thing one uses as one sees fit, but not a person whom one could look up to. Indeed, no progress in knowledge, not even when it occurs in love, may lift the veil from the beloved. Love itself demands, not only possession and unveiling, but just as forcefully reverence and, therefore, veiling.[26]

Truth, according to Balthasar, required unveiling *and* veiling, simultaneously. Truth was a trusting, loving, and hence dialogical entry into the mystery of life. This implied a much more experiential than just intellectual view of theology.

An epistemology that focused on mystery had implications throughout the theological spectrum, and it necessitated a return to a patristic and medieval mindset that had been sacramental in character. *Mysterium*—a term that had sometimes been regarded as identical to the material *sacramentum* and at other times had pointed beyond it to the intended spiritual reality itself—had been central throughout the earlier Tradition.[27] *Nouvelle théologie* was keen to recover 'mystery' as a central theological category serving an overall sacramental ontology.[28] Thus, in his discussion of the mystery of the Eucharist, Henri de Lubac, Daniélou's mentor and colleague, maintained that for the Church Fathers and medieval theologians, the term 'mystery' 'conveys dynamism and synthesis. It focuses less on the apparent sign, or rather the hidden reality, than on both at the same time: on their mutual relationship, union and implications, on the way in which one passes into the other, or is penetrated by the other.'[29] Turning to the interpretation of Scripture, de Lubac reiterated that '[i]n Latin *mysterium* serves as the double for *sacramentum*. For Saint Augustine, the Bible is essentially

---

[26] Id., *Theo-Logic: Theological Logical Theory*, trans. Adrian J. Walker and Graham Harrison, 3 vols (San Francisco, Calif.: Ignatius, 2000–5), i (*Truth of the World*), 209. Balthasar published *Wahrheit der Welt* (Einsiedeln: Benziger, 1947) as the first volume of a planned series entitled *Wahrheit*. He republished the book in 1985 as the first volume of *Theologik*, the third part his trilogy.

[27] Cf. the discussions of the term 'mystery' in de Lubac, *Corpus Mysticum: The Eucharist and the Church in the Middle Ages: Historical Survey*, trans. Gemma Simmonds, Richard Price, and Christopher Stephens and ed. Laurence Paul Hemming and Susan Frank Parsons (London: SCM, 2006), 37–54; id., *Medieval Exegesis: The Four Senses of Scripture*, trans. Marc Sebanc and E. M. Macierowski, 2 vols (Grand Rapids, Mich.: Eerdmans, 1998–2000), ii. 19–27; Congar, *Un peuple messianique: L'Église, sacrement du salut: Salut et libération* (Paris: Cerf, 1975), 47–55.

[28] A quick survey of some of the *nouvelle* theologians' titles serves to illustrate the centrality of 'mystery'. See de Lubac, *Le Mystère du surnaturel* (Paris: Aubier/Montaigne, 1964); id., *Paradoxe et mystère de l'Église* (Paris: Aubier/Montaigne, 1967); Daniélou, *Le Mystère du salut des nations* (Paris: Seuil, 1948); id., *Le Mystère de l'avent* (Paris: Seuil, 1948); id., *Culture et mystère* (Brussels: Éditions universitaires, 1948); id., *Mythes païens, mystère chrétien* (Paris: Fayard, 1966); id., *Essai sur le mystère de l'histoire* (Paris: Cerf, 1982); Congar, *Esquisses du mystère de l'Église* (Paris: Cerf, 1953); id., *Le Mystère du temple, ou, L'Économie de la présence de Dieu à sa créature de la Genèse à l'Apocalypse* (Paris: Cerf, 1958); Balthasar, *Mysterium Paschale: The Mystery of Easter*, introd. Aidan Nichols (1990; repr. San Francisco, Calif.: Ignatius, 2000); English trans. of *Theologie der drei Tage* (Einsiedeln: Benziger, 1970).

[29] De Lubac, *Corpus Mysticum*, 51.

the "writing of mysteries," and its books are the "books of the divine sacra-ments".'[30]

The sacramental ontology of *nouvelle théologie* meant that the relationship between the sacramental sign (*signum*) and the reality (*res*) of the mystery served as the key to questions concerning the nature–supernatural relationship, the historical and spiritual meanings of Scripture, secular and sacred history, the development of doctrinal truth in human language, and the Eucharistic character of the Church.[31] Theological truth always aimed at the dynamic purpose of entering into the mysteries of sacramental realities. Throughout this book, therefore, I will highlight the sacramental ontology of *nouvelle théologie* and its focus on theology as arising from and leading to an experiential entry into the divine mystery. Historical realities of the created order served, according to *nouvelle théologie*, as divinely ordained, sacramental means leading to eternal divine mysteries. The interpenetration of *signum* and *res* meant that the external, temporal appearances already contained the spiritual, eternal realities which they represented and to which they dynamically pointed forward. The sacramental interpenetration of sign and reality could also be applied to the relationship between nature and the supernatural. For the *nouvelle* theologians, nature was inherently oriented to the supernatural. God had created the natural world in such a way that at its depth it bore the supernatural stamp of its divine origin and end. The created order—and the spirit of the human person, in particular—sacramentally represented the supernatural reality of the mystery of God.

Speaking of sacramental ontology as the key to understanding *nouvelle théologie* may give the impression that the *nouvelle* theologians formed a clearly identifiable school of thought with a sharply delimited system of theological convictions. This is hardly the case. The expressions '*nouvelle théologie*' and '*ressourcement* movement' may perhaps convey more cohesion or unanimity than history actually warrants. Yves Congar (1904–95), in his 1950 *Vraie et fausse réforme dans l'Église*, insisted that the first condition for successful reform was that the pastoral needs of the Church rather than an intellectual system would form the impetus. It was important, he maintained, that a prophet's discernment 'not develop in an abstract fashion, in a system; that it not become a tradition or a school by itself and for itself'.[32] Congar argued that

---

[30] Id., *Medieval Exegesis*, ii. 20.

[31] My interpretation of *nouvelle théologie* as primarily interested in returning to a sacramental ontology is in line with a recent trend in *ressourcement* studies. Cf. John M. McDermott, *Love and Understanding: The Relation of Will and Intellect in Pierre Rousselot's Christological Vision* (Rome: Universitá Gregoriana Editrice, 1983); Susan K. Wood, *Spiritual Exegesis and the Church in the Theology of Henri de Lubac* (Grand Rapids, Mich.: Eerdmans, 1998); Cornelis Th. M. van Vliet, *Communio sacramentalis: Das Kirchenverständis von Yves Congar–genetisch und systematisch betrachtet* (Mainz: Matthias-Grünewald, 1995); Kevin Mongrain, *The Systematic Thought of Hans Urs von Balthasar: An Irenaean Retrieval* (New York: Crossroad/Herder, 2002); Brian E. Daley, 'The *Nouvelle Théologie* and the Patristic Revival: Sources, Symbols and the Science of Theology', *IJST* 7 (2005), 362–82.

[32] Congar, *Vraie et fausse réforme dans l'Église* (Paris: Cerf, 1950), 249.

if prophet–reformers based themselves on an intellectual system of thought, they would end up absolutizing their theories, thereby ignoring the requirement that reform should occur *within* the Church.[33] *Nouvelle théologie*, by seeking an alternative to the dominant intellectualist approach of neo-Thomism, did not want to establish another school of thought.[34] Instead, the *ressourcement* project was based on the conviction that the Church's living Tradition provided the criteria and parameters for doctrinal development.

We need to keep in mind, therefore, that the '*nouvelle théologie*' label was not one that the movement chose for itself. The term was first used in a negative sense by its detractors, for whom any innovative departure from the neo-Thomist system was deeply problematic.[35] The Jesuit theologian from the Gregorium in Rome, Charles Boyer (1884–1965), used the adjective '*nouvelle*' no fewer than six times in a 1940 essay dealing with recent theological trends.[36] Pietro Parente (1891–1986), Rector of the seminary in Naples, made reference to '*nouvelle théologie*' in a sharply critical 1942 article in *L'Osservatore Romano*.[37] Next, the term was picked up by Pope Pius XII in 1946 in a presentation to the General Congregation of the Jesuits.[38] Réginald Garrigou-Lagrange (1877–1964), the indomitable scholar from the Angelicum in Rome, ensured that the '*nouvelle théologie*' designation became the standard term for the theologians under discussion, when he published a rebuttal of the recent theological trends in a 1946 essay entitled 'La Nouvelle Théologie, où va-t-elle?'[39] Many of the *ressourcement* scholars themselves, however—Henri de Lubac, Jean Daniélou, Henri Bouillard (1908–81), Hans Urs von Balthasar, and Yves Congar—questioned the appropriateness of the term. Intent on a *ressourcement* of the Tradition, they did not regard their theology as new; nor had they any intention of starting a distinct

---

[33] Cf. Congar, *Vraie et fausse réforme*, 251: 'We must not make *another Church* [*une autre Eglise*] and we must make, to some degree, a *different Church* [*une Eglise autre*]'.

[34] A. N. Williams agrees with the objections to the term *nouvelle théologie*—namely, 'that those designated by the term had never constituted themselves as any kind of group, did not espouse any common system, and perhaps most significantly, that what any of them was about was precisely not "new" ' ('The Future of the Past: The Contemporary Significance of the *Nouvelle Théologie*', *IJST* 7 (2005), 348).

[35] Thus, by using the term *nouvelle théologie* in this book I am not expressing the idea of a distinct school of thought; I am simply adapting to the common use of the word in most of the secondary literature.

[36] Charles Boyer, 'Qu'est-ce que la théologie: Réflexions sur une controverse', *Greg* 21 (1940), 255–66. I owe the reference to the sixfold use of '*nouvelle*' to Jean-Claude Petit, 'La Compréhension de la théologie dans la théologie française au XXᵉ siècle; Vers une nouvelle conscience historique: G. Rabeau, M.-D. Chenu, L. Charlier', *LTP* 47 (1991), 229.

[37] Pietro Parente, 'Nuove tendenze teologiche', *L'Osservatore Romano* (9–10 Feb. 1942), 1.

[38] Cf. Étienne Fouilloux, *Une Église en quête de liberté: La pensée catholique française entre modernisme et Vatican II (1914–1962)* (Paris: Desclée de Brouwer, 1998), 193.

[39] Réginald Garrigou-Lagrange, 'La Nouvelle Théologie, où va-t-elle?' *Ang* 23 (1946), 126–45. For Garrigou-Lagrange, see Richard Peddicord, *The Sacred Monster of Thomism: An Introduction to the Life and Legacy of Reginald Garrigou-Lagrange* (South Bend, Ind.: St Augustine's, 2005); Aidan Nichols, *Reason with Piety: Garrigou-Lagrange in the Service of Catholic Thought* (Naples, Fla.: Sapientia Press of Ave Maria University, 2008).

theological school.[40] Indeed, *nouvelle théologie* is less a school of thought than a common sensibility—namely, a shared sacramental ontology.[41]

Accommodation versus Sacramental Ontology

The shared sensibility of a sacramental ontology did not prevent the various theologians from developing their own distinct directions and emphases. Daniélou's 1946 essay alluded to quite a variety of issues that he believed required attention. It was one thing to assert that the Modernist Crisis had raised issues that were waiting to be addressed. It was quite another to indicate precisely how to deal with these issues, and different theologians might well deal with them in different ways. Daniélou's allusion to the demands of his cultural context—mentioning specifically Marxism and existentialism—raised numerous and difficult questions regarding the relationship between faith and culture, without spelling out in detail how to resolve them. Daniélou's appeal to the Incarnation to deal with the question of the enculturation of the gospel was theologically promising, but it did not address practical implications. Talk of the vocation of lay people might be suggestive of a new way forward, but it raised the question of the relationship between hierarchy and laity without in any way resolving it. And accentuating history as a theological category by itself did not provide clarity on how doctrine might develop without endangering the continuity of the Tradition. This broad scope of Daniélou's essay did not detract from its value. But it did mean that when the *nouvelle* theologians actually addressed the wide spectrum of issues that were at stake, they did so in a variety of ways. The *ressourcement* movement was home not just to a shared sacramental sensibility, but to some extent also to theological tensions, contradictory viewpoints, and direct personal disagreements.

---

[40] See de Lubac, *A Brief Catechesis on Nature and Grace*, trans. Richard Arnandez (San Francisco, Calif.: Ignatius, 1984), 251; id., *De Lubac: A Theologian Speaks*, trans. Stephen Maddux and ed. Angelo Scola (Los Angeles, Calif.: Twin Circles, 1985), 3; Henri Bouillard, *Vérité du christianisme*, ed. Karl H. Neufeld (Paris: Desclée de Brouwer, 1989), 406; Balthasar, *Test Everything; Hold Fast to What Is Good: An Interview with Hans Urs von Balthasar*, ed. Angelo Scola and trans. Maria Shrady (San Francisco, Calif.: Ignatius, 1989), 11–12; Congar, *A History of Theology*, trans. and ed. Hunter Guthrie (Garden City: Doubleday, 1968), 8. Cf. Marcellino G. D'Ambrosio, 'Henri de Lubac and the Recovery of the Traditional Hermeneutic' (PhD diss., Catholic University of America, Washington, DC, 1991), 20–1; Wood, *Spiritual Exegesis*, 13–14; Rudolf Voderholzer, 'Die Bedeutung der so genannten "Nouvelle Théologie" (insbesondere Henri de Lubacs) für die Theologie Hans Urs von Balthasars', in *Logik der Liebe und Herrlichkeit Gottes: Hans Urs von Balthasar im Gespräch*, ed. Walter Kasper (Ostfildern: Matthias-Grünewald, 2006), 206; Jürgen Mettepenningen, 'Truth as Issue in a Second Modernist Crisis? The Clash between Recontextualization and Retrocontextualization in the French-speaking Polemic of 1946–47', in M. Lamberigts, L. Boeve, and T. Merrigan (eds), *Theology and the Quest for Truth: Historical and Systematic Theological Studies* (Louvain: Leuven University Press, 2006), 126–7.

[41] My use of the word 'sensibility' has been triggered by Graham Ward's use of the term to describe the movement of Radical Orthodoxy. Cf. James K. A. Smith, *Introducing Radical Orthodoxy: Mapping a Post-secular Theology* (Grand Rapids, Mich.: Baker Academic, 2005), 63–70.

One of the most significant points of tension arose from the combination of two distinct parts of Daniélou's programmatic appeal. The Parisian theologian had highlighted both the necessity of a return to the ancient sources and the need to take seriously the demands of the times by means of an incarnational approach to theology. To Daniélou, it seemed natural to keep one eye on the past and another on the contemporary context. Both of these worlds, after all, were wary of scholastic abstractions, and both could contribute to a renewed integration of theology with people's actual life experiences. Although there was a degree of validity to this assessment, the congruity between a return to the sources and enculturation depends in large part on the situation of any given culture. Some cultures may be more open to the gospel than others.[42] The *nouvelle* theologians by and large came to a rather negative evaluation of modernity's compatibility with the gospel. Daniélou, too, later became more cognizant of areas where gospel and modern culture were at odds.[43]

Theology has long lost its status as queen of the sciences.[44] It may be tempting, therefore, to interpret the developments of the pre-Second Vatican Council period primarily through a political or sociological lens, by means of left–right or progressive–conservative polarities. As a result, one might wish to portray *nouvelle théologie* as a group of theologians dedicated to theological diversity, freedom of expression within the Church, and adaptation to modern culture and scientific developments. One might regard *nouvelle théologie* as a movement that enabled critical biblical scholarship to take its proper place in the Catholic Church.[45] *Ressourcement* would then appear as code for a renewal of Modernism, in which inward experience, rather than extrinsic revelation, served as the ultimate normative source for theology. *Nouvelle théologie*, as the progressive wing of the Church, would then finally have managed to secure its legacy by means of the Second Vatican Council (1962–5). Such an interpretation would require us to understand the disappointment—perhaps even consternation—of some of the *nouvelle* theologians with regard to post-conciliar developments as a conservative retrenchment into pre-conciliar modes of thought. This reading would also imply that the recent pontificates of John Paul II and Benedict XVI have been conservative setbacks to *nouvelle théologie*'s original quest for freedom and to Pope John XXIII's attempt to bring the Church up to date (*aggiornamento*).

There is a degree of truth to this socio-political genealogy of contemporary Catholicism. Rome's drastic measures against some of the theologians from

---

[42] Joseph Ratzinger rightly emphasizes the providential entry of the Christian faith in the Greek world (*Truth and Tolerance: Christian Belief and World Religions*, trans. Henry Taylor (San Francisco, Calif.: Ignatius, 2004), 90–5; id., *Introduction to Christianity*, trans. J. R. Foster (rev. edn, San Francisco, Calif.: Communio/Ignatius, 2004), 78).

[43] Cf. Chap. 5, sect.: Typology as Doctrine of Analogy.

[44] Cf. Hans Boersma, 'Theology as Queen of Hospitality', *EvQ* 79 (2007), 291–310.

[45] Of course, Pius XII had already accepted critical scholarship in his 1943 encyclical, *Divino afflante*.

Louvain, Fourvière, and Le Saulchoir stirred a desire among the *ressourcement* scholars to be able to speak their mind freely, without fear of repercussions from the neo-Thomist establishment. The wish to 'adapt' the Church and her theology to the needs of contemporary society was integral to the original aim of *nouvelle théologie*, as was evident from Daniélou's 1946 essay. Marie-Dominique Chenu (1895–1990) and Yves Congar, the two Dominicans from Le Saulchoir, believed it was important for the Church to read the 'signs of the times' and to 'adapt' to contemporary philosophical and cultural developments. Chenu was deeply involved in the post-war worker–priest movement, and issues of social and economic justice were important both to him and to Congar. Both theologians also regarded the post-conciliar changes in the Church generally as positive.

To view adaptation or accommodation as the driving force behind *nouvelle théologie*, however, would be seriously to misrepresent the movement. First, the desire for cultural accommodation was not universal. The Jesuits from Fourvière—de Lubac, Daniélou, and Bouillard (as well as Balthasar)—were much more sceptical about the compatibility of modern culture with the programme of *ressourcement* than the Dominicans from Le Saulchoir—Chenu and Congar.[46] The *nouvelle* theologians who were disappointed with the initial results of the Second Vatican Council did not suddenly lapse into a more conservative theological mindset. De Lubac, Daniélou, Bouillard, Balthasar (as well as Ratzinger) were all concerned about what they regarded as horizontalizing (the exclusion of a vertical relationship with God) or immanentizing (the rejection of any transcendent impact on historical cause and effect) ecclesial and cultural developments, especially since the mid-1960s.[47] It would stretch credibility to think that each of these insightful scholars made a radical turn when faced with the consequences of their own theology. Indeed, I will make the case that they largely remained true to the sacramental cast of their overall theology and became convinced that the culture of modernity was beginning to set the agenda for the Church's future.

Second, to the extent that cultural accommodation was of interest to *nouvelle théologie*, it was theologically motivated. Although Daniélou's essay did apply the language of 'incarnation' to the need for enculturation, the Saulchoir theologians Chenu and Congar were much more enamoured with such discourse than Daniélou or any of the other Jesuits from Lyons-Fourvière. This difference between the Jesuit and the Dominican theologians may point, on the one hand, to a predilection among the Fourvière Jesuits for the Greek Fathers with their Neoplatonic inclinations; and, on the other hand, to a more pronounced interest among the Dominicans from Le Saulchoir in St Thomas with his

[46] Chenu and Congar both signed the controversial 1969 manifesto on theological freedom of expression, while none of the other *ressourcement* scholars did ('Déclaration sur la liberté et la fonction des théologiens dans l'Église', *Conc* 41 (1969), 147–51).
[47] For the connection between Pope Benedict XVI and *nouvelle théologie*, see Tracey Rowland, *Ratzinger's Faith: The Theology of Pope Benedict XVI* (Oxford: Oxford University Press, 2008), 17–29.

Aristotelian background. Thus, for de Lubac—with his upward 'natural desire' (*desiderium naturale*) for a supernatural end—the sacramental reality (*res*) was the focus; while for Chenu—with his downward 'law of the Incarnation'—the this-worldly historical realities themselves (*sacramentum*) remained much more central. The relative autonomy of the created order, as well as the need to adapt to modern culture, was felt more keenly by the Saulchoir theologians than among the scholars from Lyons-Fourvière.[48] These relative differences were emphatically theological in nature, and we cannot reduce them to a conservative (Fourvière)–progressive (Le Saulchoir) divide.

Third, and most importantly, by exaggerating the significance of cultural accommodation for *nouvelle théologie*, we may lose sight of its most significant theological motivation: a return to mystery by means of the sacramental ontology that had stamped the Christian tradition until the High Middle Ages. *Nouvelle théologie* was first and foremost a movement concerned with *ressourcement*. Marcellino D'Ambrosio, while acknowledging that terms like *incarnation, présence, engagement*, and *adaptation* functioned as pastoral buzzwords among the *nouvelle* theologians,[49] none the less maintains that *ressourcement* theology was not

driven by any desire to 'adapt' theology to contemporary thought and values. Rather their goal was to break the 'fortress mentality' and compel Catholic theology to engage in a critical dialogue with twentieth-century thinkers, a dialogue that would send theologians back to the sources with new questions, provoking the rediscovery of forgotten or neglected dimensions of the tradition.[50]

In this book, I will argue that the purpose of this *ressourcement* was to revitalize the sacramental ontology that had been obscured by the neo-scholastic separation between nature and the supernatural.

NOUVELLE THÉOLOGIE AND CATHOLIC–PROTESTANT DIALOGUE

Part of my motivation for writing this book has been ecumenical in nature. As a Protestant theologian, my interest in *nouvelle théologie* is tied in with the growing

[48] These broad strokes do need qualifications in all sorts of ways. St Thomas had been influenced not just by Aristotle but also by Denys's Neoplatonism. We will see that for Balthasar (whom we may count among the Fourvière theologians) history and the goodness of the created order were central to the Christian faith. Bouillard, teacher at Fourvière, shared Chenu's and Congar's interest in Thomas's approach, while Karl Barth's Christological emphasis also influenced his thinking. Finally, we need to keep in mind that mystical theology was important to Chenu and that Congar's ecclesiology focused more on the sacramental reality of the Church than on its external, juridical framework.

[49] Marcellino D'Ambrosio, '*Ressourcement* Theology, *Aggiornamento*, and the Hermeneutics of Tradition', *Comm* 18 (1991), 534.

[50] Ibid. 549.

conviction that Protestants need to take the Catholic tradition more seriously than they sometimes do. My reading of the *ressourcement* theologians has also reinforced my belief that, intramural debates notwithstanding, Catholics and Protestants largely face a common theological task. It may seem to some that a reading of *nouvelle théologie* as reconnecting with pre-modern sacramental sensibilities will do little to stimulate my ecumenical motivation. After all, sacramental sensibilities may precisely be the feature that distinguishes the Catholic imagination from the Protestant mindset. In *The Catholic Imagination* Andrew Greeley argues that

Catholic theologians and artists tend to emphasize the presence of God in the world, while the classic works of Protestant theologians tend to emphasize the absence of God from the world. The Catholic writers stress the nearness of God to His creation, the Protestant writers the distance between God and His creation; the Protestants emphasize the risk of superstition and idolatry, the Catholics the dangers of a creation in which God is only marginally present. Or, to put the matter in different terms, Catholics tend to accentuate the immanence of God, Protestants the transcendence of God.[51]

Greeley makes a valid point. A sacramental imagination differs from a rational mindset, and the differences largely result from the way in which narratives, symbols, and practices function within the respective communities.[52] Protestants have traditionally focused on the Word rather than on the sacraments and as a result rational confessional truth claims have often taken centre stage. Catholics may conclude that for Protestants truth appears to trump unity.[53] My focus on *nouvelle théologie*'s 'sacramental ontology' may, therefore, well seem to accentuate rather than to overcome Catholic–Protestant differences.

There are several reasons, however, why a study of *nouvelle théologie* holds ecumenical promise. First, *nouvelle théologie* has contributed significantly to Catholic interest in ecumenical dialogue. Beginning with his 1937 *Chrétiens désunis*, Yves Congar, in particular, devoted himself tirelessly to the cause of Christian unity.[54] The *ressourcement* scholars were keenly interested in Protestant thought. Balthasar and Bouillard both wrote large tomes on the theology of Karl

---

[51] Andrew Greeley, *The Catholic Imagination* (Berkeley, Calif.: University of California Press, 2000), 5. Greeley draws especially on David Tracey, *The Analogical Imagination: Christian Theology and the Culture of Pluralism* (New York: Crossroad, 1981). I want to thank Prof. Richard Mouw for drawing my attention to this book.

[52] Cf. N. T. Wright, *Christian Origins and the Question of God*, i, *The New Testament and the People of God* (Minneapolis, Minn.: Fortress, 1992), 215–43.

[53] This apprehension with regard to the Reformation was evident in Congar's *Vraie et fausse réforme*. As a result, the entire third part of the book (pp. 353–536) was dedicated to a refutation of Protestant views of reform.

[54] Congar, *Chrétiens désunis: Principes d'un 'oecuménisme' catholique* (Paris: Cerf, 1937); English trans.: *Divided Christendom: A Catholic Study of the Problem of Reunion*, trans. M. A. Bousfield (London: G. Bles, 1939). Cf. Monika-Maria Wolff, *Gott und Mensch: Ein Beitrag Yves Congars zum ökumenischen Dialog* (Frankfurt: Knecht, 1990).

Barth (1886–1968).[55] As we will see, Barth's Christological focus influenced both his Catholic interlocutors. Furthermore, since the *nouvelle* theologians sought to regain history as a theological category, they came into contact with the Protestant focus on salvation history. Jean Daniélou, for instance, was deeply influenced by the theology of the Lutheran theologian, Oscar Cullmann (1902–99). In a number of other areas, too, the interests of *nouvelle théologie* and the Reformation coincided. Both shared an emphasis on the vocation of the laity, both advocated a return to the Bible, both rejected the view that Scripture and Tradition formed two separate sources of authority, and both took issue with the neo-scholastic separation between nature and the supernatural. Most significantly, like *nouvelle théologie*, the Reformation could also be described as a movement of *ressourcement*. This is not to deny significant differences between the two movements, even within the very areas that I have just mentioned, and the remainder of this book will discuss some of these differences. It remains true, none the less, that *nouvelle théologie* opened up avenues of dialogue that previously had been unthinkable.

Second, over the past few decades, Protestant theologians, particularly evangelicals, have increasingly turned to dialogue with Catholic theology and to a *ressourcement* of the 'great Tradition'—the common theological heritage of East and West as embodied in the Creeds and the theology of the Church Fathers. In North America, the dialogue spearheaded by Richard John Neuhaus and Charles Colson—Evangelicals and Catholics Together (ECT)—is significant in its own right, as well as in creating an opening for Catholics and evangelicals to engage in theological discussion and cooperation.[56] This cooperation is particularly evident in biblical interpretation.[57] Protestant sensitivity towards the authority of Tradition is further evidence that a project of *ressourcement* may echo across ecclesial boundaries.[58] A number of evangelical Christians have embarked on explicit

---

[55] Balthasar, *Karl Barth: Darstellung und Deutung seiner Theologie* (Cologne: Hegner, 1951); English trans.: *The Theology of Karl Barth*, trans. Edward T. Oakes (San Francisco, Calif.: Communio/Ignatius, 1992); Bouillard, *Karl Barth*, i, *Genèse et évolution de la théologie dialectique*; ii, *Parole de Dieu et existence humaine* (Paris: Aubier/Montaigne, 1957).

[56] For a discussion of the various ECT statements, see Mark A. Noll and Carolyn Nystrom, *Is the Reformation Over? An Evangelical Assessment of Contemporary Roman Catholicism* (Grand Rapids, Mich.: Baker Academic, 2005), 151–83. For recent evangelical interaction with Catholic theology, see e.g. Tim Perry, *Mary for Evangelicals: Toward an Understanding of the Mother of Our Lord* (Downers Grove, Ill.: InterVarsity Press, 2006); id. (ed.), *The Legacy of John Paul II: An Evangelical Assessment* (Downers Grove, Ill.: InterVarsity Press, 2007).

[57] Cf. Chap. 5, sect.: Spiritual Interpretation and Ecumenical Dialogue.

[58] See e.g. James S. Cutsinger (ed.), *Reclaiming the Great Tradition: Evangelicals, Catholics, and Orthodox in Dialogue* (Downers Grove, Ill.: InterVarsity Press, 1997); Christopher A. Hall, *Reading Scripture with the Church Fathers* (Downers Grove, Ill.: InterVarsity Press, 1999); id., *Learning Theology with the Church Fathers* (Downers Grove, Ill.: InterVarsity Press, 2002); D. H. Williams, *Retrieving the Tradition and Renewing Evangelicalism: A Primer for Suspicious Protestants* (Grand Rapids, Mich.: Eerdmans, 1999); Craig D. Allert, *A High View of Scripture? The Authority of the Bible and the Formation of the New Testament Canon* (Grand Rapids, Mich.: Baker Academic, 2007). For a fascinating intra-Protestant discussion on the relationship between Scripture and Tradition,

attempts at evangelical *ressourcement* of the great Tradition, taking their cue directly from the Catholic movement of *nouvelle théologie*.[59] My study of *nouvelle théologie* ties in, therefore, with a growing interest in *ressourcement* and in ecumenical discussion between Catholic and Protestant theology.

Third, this book will make clear that the recovery of a sacramental ontology is incumbent not only on Protestants but also on Catholics. They owe their common task to a shared intellectual history that has caused problems on both sides of the ecclesiastical divide. Protestants may be characterized by a rational mindset more than by a sacramental imagination. But the argument of the *ressourcement* theologians was that a sacramental ontology had been declining also in Catholicism. Their *ressourcement* of patristic and medieval theology implied a negative evaluation of later theological approaches. The immediate object of *nouvelle théologie*'s critique was the manualist theology—the systematic theology handbooks or manuals—of contemporary Thomist thought. But the *nouvelle* theologians were agreed that the problems went back much further than the nineteenth-century rise of neo-Thomism. This is particularly clear from the historical account of the desacramentalizing of the West that emerges from the work of Henri de Lubac and Yves Congar.[60] Interestingly, their genealogy of modernity partially overlaps with the negative accounts that Louis Dupré and the 'Radical Orthodoxy' group are presenting today.[61] According to the assessment of all of these scholars, sixteenth-century Protestants and Catholics were both heirs to the problematic ramifications of the decline of mystery.

De Lubac pointed to several key historical developments that had caused difficulties. He was convinced that the neo-scholastic separation of nature and the supernatural had already entrenched itself in the sixteenth and seventeenth centuries and that part of the problem was a Catholic overreaction against the

---

see Heiko A. Oberman, '*Quo vadis, Petre?* Tradition from Irenaeus to *Humani generis*', in *The Dawn of the Reformation: Essays in Late Medieval and Early Reformation Thought* (Edinburgh: T. & T. Clark, 1986), 269–96; A. N. S. Lane, 'Scripture, Tradition and Church: An Historical Survey', *VE* 9 (1975), 37–55.

[59] I am thinking here of Baker Academic's 'Evangelical *Ressourcement*' series (ed. D. H. Williams) and of Robert E. Webber's 2006 'Call to an Ancient Evangelical Future', which has led to annual conferences aimed at the promotion of a *ressourcement* of the Fathers among evangelicals.

[60] Chenu's evaluation of medieval developments was markedly different from that of de Lubac and Congar. Chenu was quite taken by what he saw as the desacralization and desacramentalizing of the twelfth and thirteenth centuries. This coincided with his more optimistic attitude towards modernity and towards Catholic developments after the Second Vatican Council. Cf. Chap. 4, sect.: Desacralization and Signs of the Times.

[61] See Louis Dupré, *Passage to Modernity: An Essay in the Hermeneutics of Nature and Culture* (New Haven, Conn.: Yale University Press, 1993); id., *Religion and the Rise of Modern Culture* (Notre Dame, Ind.: University of Notre Dame Press, 2008). For Radical Orthodoxy, see John Milbank, *Theology and Social Theory: Beyond Secular Reason* (Oxford: Blackwell, 1990); Catherine Pickstock, *After Writing: On the Liturgical Consummation of Philosophy* (Oxford: Blackwell, 1998); Milbank, Catherine Pickstock, and Graham Ward (eds.), *Radical Orthodoxy: A New Theology* (London: Routledge, 1999); Connor Cunningham, *Genealogy of Nihilism* (London: Routledge, 2002). For a helpful analysis of Radical Orthodoxy's genealogy of modernity, see Smith, *Introducing Radical Orthodoxy*, 87–122. I have followed a similar line of thought in Boersma, 'Theology as Queen'.

radical Augustinianism of Michael Baius (1513–89) and of the Protestant Reformers.[62] De Lubac also took issue with the increasing fixation on real presence and on the legitimacy of the sacraments at the expense of the spiritual reality to which the sacraments pointed. He traced this development back to the twelfth-century Berengarian controversy on the nature of Christ's presence in the Eucharist. As a result of these medieval developments, the sacramental unity between the Eucharistic and the ecclesial body of Christ had already disintegrated by the time of the Reformation, so that the loss of a sacramental ontology had affected both sides of the Reformation debate. De Lubac was convinced that these developments were tied in with an increasingly rationalist approach to theology—which was not the exclusive domain of Protestantism.[63]

Although Congar's focus was slightly different, he also understood the loss of a sacramental ontology to be rooted in the Middle Ages. He pointed repeatedly to the Gregorian Reform of the eleventh century, as he was convinced that the decline of the laity's role in the Church and the juridicizing of ecclesial authority could be traced to the attempt of Pope Gregory VII to establish the priority of papal supremacy over the state. As a result, authority came to be viewed as something extraneous to the sacramental life of the Church. For Congar, this initial desacralizing of the medieval imagination had additional consequences. The juridicized authority of the Church could now be played off against the authority of Scripture. Conflict between Church and Scripture had become a real possibility by the twelfth and thirteenth centuries. The two sides of the Reformation debate had opted for opposite sides of an altogether mistaken dilemma. Again, it appeared that the decline of a sacramental ontology affected Catholics as well as Protestants, and Congar had particularly harsh words for the role played by post-Tridentine ecclesiology.[64]

Nouvelle théologie's return to mystery does present a challenge to Protestant thought, in particular to its abandonment of a sacramental ontology. One of my hopes for this book is that it will contribute to a Protestant re-evaluation of the nominalist fragmentation of the created order, which regards sensible objects as separate from one another and from their transcendent origin. In line with the participatory or sacramental ontology of the great Tradition, this book is based on the conviction that appearances signify and make present a mystery that they do not possess of themselves.[65] While some may fear that such a return to Platonic sensibilities may surrender the value of the created order, this fear seems to me entirely unwarranted.[66] The opposite is, in fact, the case. Created

---

[62] See Chap. 3, sect.: Pure Nature and Natural Desire.
[63] See Chap. 7, sect.: The Eucharist Makes the Church.
[64] See Chap. 6, sect.: Scripture, Tradition, and Church: The History of Juridicizing.
[65] Cf. Balthasar's excellent reflections on the world of images in *Theo-Logic*, i. 132–79.
[66] To be sure, an uncritical acceptance of Neoplatonism would be problematic. The Christian Tradition has largely recognized that the Platonic tradition had serious faults and shortcomings. Creation *ex nihilo*, the doctrine of the Trinity (which implied plurality at the heart of being itself),

objects derive their value from sacramental participation in their transcendent ground. As Balthasar put it: 'In order to be really significant, what expresses itself in the image must be nonidentical with the image itself.'[67] The world of images or appearances derives its value from a transcendent source. This book is an attempt to re-source the sacramental ontology of *nouvelle théologie*, and in so doing it urges Protestant theology to re-evaluate the abandonment of a pre-modern sacramental ontology.

At the same time, *nouvelle théologie* represents a challenge to Catholic theology. The *ressourcement* project was not simply a protest against neo-Thomist intellectualism—though it was that, too. The purpose of the protest was to re-appropriate the mystery of being. An interpretation of the Second Vatican Council that primarily focuses on the gain of theological freedom and on *aggiornamento* (or accommodation to contemporary culture) overlooks the deepest intentions of the *ressourcement* project of the preceding decades.[68] The Second Vatican Council may well have opened up genuine possibilities for dialogue with Protestant thought. But it did not do so by embracing secular modernity's adherence to a radical autonomy of the natural order. Rather, *nouvelle théologie* was concerned to reintegrate nature and the supernatural by way of a sacramental ontology. The post-conciliar period will be amenable to ecumenical dialogue only to the extent that Catholics and Protestants are both willing to accept the challenge of a genuine return to mystery, which was implied in the *ressourcement* of the pre-modern period.[69]

CONTROVERSIES OVER *NOUVELLE THÉOLOGIE*

Modernism's Non-sacramental Mindset

If we interpret the *nouvelle* theologians as primarily concerned with a sacramental ontology, this allows us to take seriously their disavowals of the Modernist theology of the turn of the twentieth century. Of course, we have already seen that Daniélou believed that the Modernist Crisis had left unfinished business for

and the goodness of the created order (along with the resurrection of the body) were essential to the Christian faith and, to a large extent, incompatible with the Platonic tradition. Cf. Andrew Louth, *The Origins of the Christian Mystical Tradition: From Plato to Denys* (Oxford: Oxford University Press, 1981), 78; Dupré, *Passage to Modernity*, 168.

[67] Balthasar, *Theo-Logic*, i. 139.

[68] Cf. Boersma, 'Accommodation to What? Univocity of Being, Pure Nature, and the Anthropology of St Irenaeus', *IJST* 8 (2006), 266–93.

[69] Cf. the 'Final Report' of the 1985 extraordinary Synod of Bishops: 'Despite secularism, signs of a return to the sacred also exist. Today, in fact, there are signs of a new hunger and thirst for the transcendent and divine. In order to favor this return to the sacred and to overcome secularism, we must open the way to the dimension of the "divine" or of mystery and offer the preambles of faith to mankind today' (*Origins*, 15 (1985), 446). This remark about signs of a return to mystery rings even more true today than it did in 1985.

the Church to deal with, particularly in terms of a reintegration of theology and life. This was obviously a controversial assessment. Modernism had, after all, caused great consternation in the Catholic Church, both because of its embrace of historical critical exegesis and because of its neo-Kantian focus on subjective experience rather than propositional truth.[70] Modernism may not have been the well-coordinated, concerted attempt to overturn Catholic doctrine that some of its critics, notably Pope Pius X, thought it was; a number of theologians were none the less simultaneously engaged in a rather drastic reworking of Catholic doctrine. The Modernist movement included Italian thinkers like Ernesto Buonaiuti (1881–1946) and Antonio Fogazzaro (1842–1911); Germans such as Joseph Schnitzer (1858–1939) and Thaddäus Engert (1875–1945); the Frenchmen Alfred Loisy (1857–1940), Edouard Le Roy (1870–1954), and Lucien Laberthonnière (1860–1932); as well as the Irish-born British theologian, George Tyrrell (1861–1909). This international scope of the movement contributed to the sense that the Church was under serious attack. The Modernist Crisis came to an abrupt end, however, when, in July 1907, Pius X's decree *Lamentabili sane exitu* condemned sixty-five Modernist propositions. Two months later, the Pope published the encyclical *Pascendi dominici gregis* in which he unequivocally condemned the agnosticism, immanentism, and relativism of Modernism as the 'synthesis of all heresies'.[71] Pius X subsequently enforced the condemnation of Modernism by forcing all clergy to swear allegiance to the so-called 'anti-Modernist oath' of 1910.[72]

A brief look at the Modernist theologians Alfred Loisy and George Tyrrell will make clear that the Modernist agenda was fundamentally different from that of *nouvelle théologie*.[73] Loisy was a Hebrew and Assyrian scholar. He initially taught at the Parisian Institut Catholique, but lost his position in 1893 as a result of controversy over exegetical freedom. Loisy's dismissal from the Institut Catholique was immediately followed by Pope Leo XIII's encyclical *Providentissimus*

---

[70] For more detailed expositions on the Modernist Crisis, see Gabriel Daly, *Transcendence and Immanence: A Study in Catholic Modernism and Integralism* (Oxford: Clarendon Press, 1980); Marvin R. O'Connell, *Critics on Trial: An Introduction to the Catholic Modernist Crisis* (Washington, DC: Catholic University of America Press, 1994); Pierre Colin, *L'Audace et le soupçon: La Crise du modernisme dans le catholicisme français 1893–1914* (Paris: Desclée de Brouwer, 1997); Darrell Jodock (ed.), *Catholicism Contending with Modernity: Roman Catholic Modernism and Anti-modernism in Historical Context* (Cambridge: Cambridge University Press, 2000).

[71] *ASS* 40 (1907), 593–650, at 632; English trans.: *Pascendi dominici gregis*, 39 <http://www.vatican.va>.

[72] The oath remained in force until 1966. Cf. Fergus Kerr, 'A Different World: Neoscholasticism and its Discontents', *IJST* 8 (2006), 134–6.

[73] For the controversy surrounding Loisy, see esp. Émile Poulat, *Critique et mystique: Autour de Loisy ou la conscience catholique et l'esprit moderne* (Paris: Centurion, 1984); id., *Histoire, dogme et critique dans la crise moderniste* (3rd edn, Paris: Albin Michel, 1996). For Tyrrell, see Ellen Leonard, *George Tyrrell and the Catholic Tradition* (London: Darton, Longman and Todd, 1982); David G. Schultenover, *George Tyrrell: In Search of Catholicism* (Shepherdstown, W.Va.: Patmos, 1981); Aidan Nichols, *From Newman to Congar: The Idea of Doctrinal Development from the Victorians to the Second Vatican Council* (Edinburgh: T. & T. Clark, 1990), 114–35.

Deus, in which he issued a stern warning against a historical critical approach to exegesis that questioned the teachings of the Church and challenged the trustworthiness of Scripture. Loisy, who subsequently took up a position as spiritual director at a girls' boarding school, continued to explore questions surrounding critical scholarship. In his book *L'Évangile et l'église* (1902), he opposed the claim that Adolf von Harnack (1851–1930) had put forward in *Das Wesen des Christentums* (1900): that the eternal, unchanging essence of the Christian faith consisted of the union between God and the soul of the individual Christian.[74] Over and above Harnack's Liberal Protestantism, Loisy defended the social character of Catholicism. Despite his disapproval of Harnack's approach, however, Loisy was sharply critical of Catholicism's developments towards a centralizing hierarchy. As a result, his orthodoxy quickly became suspect. His attempt to clarify his position in *Autour d'un petit livre* (1903) did little to allay the magisterium's concerns.[75] In the end, his disagreements with the Church led to his excommunication in 1908.

Loisy's Modernism was predicated on a separation between history and theology. Continuously insisting that he was merely engaging in historical research, Loisy was reluctant to acknowledge the significant doctrinal implications of the exegetical and historical work he was doing. To his critics, however, it seemed clear that his rejection of later hierarchical developments in the Church was based on his historical exegesis. Bernard Reardon explains: '[A]lways his personal concern was to claim autonomy for the critical exegete. What he could not allow was that the scope of criticism should be determined by the theologians. History was history, he insisted— *Was ist geschehen*, in Ranke's phrase—and had every right to be pursued independently of a theological *a priori*.'[76] Loisy was reluctant to admit that his insistence on exegetical autonomy was theologically motivated. He realized that Harnack's book on the essence of the Christian faith had theological underpinnings, and he objected to the German theologian's confusion between historical scholarship and theology.[77] Thus, Loisy's insistence on the radical autonomy of history and of critical exegesis was the motivating factor behind his opposition to Harnack.

George Tyrrell was an Irish priest and Thomist scholar who had converted from Anglicanism to Catholicism. Baron Friedrich von Hügel (1852-1925), a well-connected and influential Catholic lay theologian from England, drew

---

[74] Alfred Loisy, *L'Évangile et l'église* (Paris; Picard, 1902); Adolf von Harnack, *Das Wesen des Christentums: Vorlesungen vor Studierenden aller Fakultäten im Wintersemester 1899/1900 an der Universität Berlin gehalten* (Leipzig: Hinrichs, 1900).

[75] Loisy, *Autour d'un petit livre* (Paris: Picard, 1903).

[76] Bernard M. G. Reardon, 'Roman Catholic Modernism', in Ninian Smart et al. (eds), *Nineteenth-century Religious Thought in the West*, ii (Cambridge: Cambridge University Press, 1985), 153.

[77] For Loisy's insistence on the autonomy of historical scholarship, see Harvey Hill, 'Loisy's "Mystical Faith": Loisy, Leo XIII, and Sabatier on Moral Education and the Church', *TS* 65 (2004), 73–94; id., 'Loisy's *L'Évangile et l'église* in Light of the "Essais"', *TS* 67 (2006), 73–98.

Tyrrell's attention to the work of John Henry Newman (1801–90), and particularly to the latter's organic approach to doctrinal development. Tyrrell's thought, however, soon turned into a direction that was different from that of Hügel and Newman, when he separated the prayerful experience of faith from subsequent theological exposition. In his books *L'Église et l'avenir* (1903) and *Through Scylla and Charybdis* (1907) Tyrrell took his starting-point unambiguously in the practical purpose of Christian doctrine, identifying revelation with experience rather than with propositional truth.[78] Revelatory experience, which he regarded as ongoing throughout history, was independent of theoretical truth and transcended the theological concepts that surrounded the experience. Edward Schillebeeckx helpfully summarizes Tyrrell's position: 'The two aspects of the act of faith—the aspect of experience and the conceptual aspect—were . . . according to Tyrrell, completely separate. The conceptual aspect was simply an extrinsic, symbolic, and pragmatic protection for the real core of faith (the so-called revelation in time consisting in this conceptual aspect).'[79] This separation between revelatory experience, on the one hand, and theological concepts, on the other hand, caused the neo-Thomists to fear that Tyrrell had lapsed into agnosticism: it was no longer clear that theological concepts were connected to a particular reality. Tyrell's radical focus on human piety and experience led to his expulsion from the Society of Jesus in 1906 and to his exclusion from the sacraments several years later.

Undoubtedly, there is overlap between Modernism and *nouvelle théologie*. Both reacted against neo-Thomist theology with its conceptualist understanding of Christian doctrine, its rational apologetic, its logical view of doctrinal development, and its juridical, perhaps even authoritarian ecclesiology. Most importantly, both wanted theology to take subjective experience much more seriously than scholastic theology had been willing to do. It would be erroneous, however, to look to Modernism as one of the main precursors to *nouvelle théologie*.[80] The fundamental difference between Modernism and *nouvelle théologie* lay precisely in the latter's sacramental ontology. Despite their strong disagreement with neo-Thomism, Loisy's view of history and Tyrrell's approach to theology presupposed the same gap between nature and the supernatural on which the manualist tradition insisted. Loisy considered history and theology as separate from one

[78] George Tyrrell [Hilaire Bourdon], *L'Église et l'avenir* (priv. pub., 1903); id., *Through Scylla and Charybdis; or, The Old Theology and the New* (London: Longmans, Green, and Co, 1907). Tyrrell wrote the former pseudonymously in French and had it privately published.

[79] Edward Schillebeeckx, *Revelation and Theology,* ii *The Concept of Truth and Theological Renewal*, trans. N. D. Smith (London: Sheed & Ward, 1968), 12. Cf. Nichols, *From Newman to Congar*, 132–5. Allessandro Maggiolini makes the interesting observation that Tyrrell 'could not admit that our statements about God have an authentically analogical character. In this way, *Pascendi's* charge of agnosticism does indeed apply to Tyrrell' ('Magisterial Teaching on Experience in the Twentieth Century: From the Modernist Crisis to the Second Vatican Council', trans. Andrew Matt and Adrian Walker, *Comm* 23 (1996), 235–6).

[80] For this reason, I deal with Modernism in this chapter, rather than in the next, which discusses nineteenth- and twentieth-century precursors to the sacramental ontology of *nouvelle théologie*.

another, while Tyrrell divided human discourse and divine revelation. Both Modernist scholars evinced the modern incapacity to reach beyond the natural horizons. In terms of history (biblical exegesis) as well as human discourse (theology), *nouvelle théologie* took a much bolder approach because of its sacramental reintegration of nature and the supernatural. Rather than focusing on historical critical exegesis, *nouvelle théologie* presented a plea for a *ressourcement* of pre-modern spiritual interpretation, a method that had been based on the conviction that historical appearances contained spiritual, eternal realities.[81] And, rather than collapsing revelation into mystical experience, *nouvelle théologie* saw doctrinal statements as sacramentally (or analogically) conveying the divine truth that infinitely surpassed human language.[82] The Modernists were largely uninterested in *ressourcement*; by contrast, *ressourcement* of the Tradition was indispensable for *nouvelle théologie*, since this allowed for the recovery of sacramental ontology and thus for the reconnection of theology and life.

Controversy over the Nature of Theology (1937–42)

The neo-Thomist theologians, perhaps blindsided by the fact that their position was again coming under attack, were convinced that the *ressourcement* movement was Modernism in disguise.[83] In an essay that carried as its title the probing question, 'La Nouvelle Théologie, où va-t-elle?' ('*Nouvelle théologie*: Where is it Headed?'), Réginald Garrigou-Lagrange answered his own question with the now legendary response, 'It goes back to Modernism.'[84] Beyond question, it was the perceived affinity between Modernism and *nouvelle théologie* that led to the repeated stifling of the voices associated with *nouvelle théologie*. These attempts to silence the *nouvelle* theologians caused immense personal suffering, which eventually came to an end in the 1960s. The announcement of the Second Vatican Council—when John XXIII appointed de Lubac and Congar to the preparatory Theological Commission in 1960—was the beginning of an exoneration that climaxed under the papacies of Paul VI and John Paul II, who elevated several of the *nouvelle* theologians to the position of cardinal.[85]

[81] Cf. the discussion of spiritual interpretation in Chap. 5. We will see in Chap. 2 (sect.: Overcoming the Doctrine of Immanence) that Maurice Blondel, who exerted tremendous influence on *nouvelle théologie*, was never convinced of Loisy's Modernism, precisely because of the latter's isolating of history from faith.

[82] Cf. Chap. 2, sect.: The Sacramental Character of Analogical Predication; Chap. 3, sect.: Bouillard, Le Blond, and the 'Analogy of Truth'; Chap. 6, sects: Marie-Dominique Chenu: Development and the Theandric Mystery; and Louis Charlier: Growth of the Revealed Deposit.

[83] For historical overviews of the controversies surrounding *nouvelle théologie*, see esp. Jacques Guillet, *La Théologie catholique en France de 1914 à 1960* (Paris: Médiasèvres, 1988); Fouilloux, *Une Église*. Cf. also below, nn. 100, 122.

[84] 'Où va la nouvelle théologie? Elle revient au modernisme' (Garrigou-Lagrange, 'La Nouvelle Théologie', 143).

[85] The following *ressourcement* theologians were appointed cardinal: Jean Daniélou (1969), Henri de Lubac (1983), Hans Urs von Balthasar (1988), and Yves Congar (1994). Balthasar died on 26 June 1988, two days before he was to be elevated to the College of Cardinals.

Nouvelle théologie is commonly associated with the study centres of Le Saulchoir and Lyons-Fourvière.[86] The Dominican studium of Le Saulchoir was Marie-Dominique Chenu's initial training ground for ordination, and he returned there after finishing his doctorate at the Angelicum in Rome, in 1920. Interestingly, the supervisor for his dissertation was Garrigou-Lagrange. After completing his doctorate, Chenu returned to Le Saulchoir, where in 1932 he was appointed as Regent of Studies, following in the footsteps of his illustrious predecessor, Ambroise Gardeil (1859–1931). Although Gardeil had remained within the neo-scholastic tradition, his theology did prepare the way for *nouvelle théologie*. He had stressed the continuity (*homogénéité*) between the supernatural origin of faith and people's actual lives and had emphasized that faith was not blind obedience to the Church's external authority. Gardeil, explains Potworowski, had erected a bridge 'between the data of revelation and the believing subject'.[87] Chenu's 1937 *Une école de théologie: Le Saulchoir* radicalized his predecessor's approach.[88] The book approvingly quoted George Tyrell, and Chenu made clear that his theological direction would not fit the neo-scholastic mould: 'Theological systems', he insisted, 'are simply the expression of spiritualities... A theology worthy of the name is a spirituality that has found rational instruments suitable to its religious experience.'[89] Chenu's insistence that theology was connected to experience caused apprehensions in Rome that Le Saulchoir's Regent was advocating theological relativism. As a result, Chenu was ordered to appear the next year before his erstwhile doctoral supervisor in Rome and was forced to sign ten propositions, designed to exclude any possible relativism.[90]

In 1931, Yves Congar, one of Chenu's former students at Le Saulchoir, joined him there as a colleague. Chenu and Congar together with church historian Henri-Marie Féret (1904–92) embarked on a programme of renewal that they believed was required for the Church's well-being. Congar was passionate about the unity of the Church and was deeply troubled by the growing signs of French indifference towards the Church and the Christian faith. In 1928, Chenu had given him a copy of Johann Adam Möhler's (1796–1838), *Einheit in der Kirche* (1825), and Congar was impressed with the organic ecclesiology and the

[86] The Dominican Centre had been located in the Dominican Province of Paris since 1865. It was renamed Le Saulchoir in 1903, when it was expelled from Paris and moved to Kain-Lez-Tournai in Belgium. In 1937, the studium returned to Étiolles near Paris, where it remained until it moved to the Dominican convent of St Jacques in Paris in 1971.

[87] Potworowski, *Contemplation and Incarnation*, 45.

[88] Chenu, *Une école de théologie: Le Saulchoir* (Kain-Lez-Tournai: Le Saulchoir, 1937). For analysis of the book and its historical context, see Potworowski, *Contemplation and Incarnation*, 46–55; Fergus Kerr, 'Chenu's Little Book', *NBl* 66 (1985), 108–12. See also Chap. 4, sect.: Chenu's Programme of *ressourcement*.

[89] Chenu, *Une école de théologie: Le Saulchoir*, with contributions by Giuseppe Alberigo, Étienne Fouilloux, Jean-Pierre Jossua, and Jean Ladrière (Paris: Cerf, 1985), 148–9. Cf. Kerr, 'Different World', 144.

[90] The first proposition stated: 'Dogmatic formulations express absolute and immutable truth'. For a helpful account, see Kerr, 'Different World', 128–48.

appreciation for the Church Fathers that he found in the German Romantic theologian. He began a French translation of the book, which he published in 1937 in Unam sanctam, a new series that he had initiated two years earlier.[91] In 1935, the Parisian publisher *Les Éditions du Cerf* invited Congar to write a theological conclusion to a three-year-long inquiry into the causes of unbelief in France.[92] Congar published his findings in an essay in the journal *La Vie intellectuelle*.[93] He identified a 'hiatus between faith and life' as the root cause of the spreading problem of unbelief.[94] Congar's diagnosis was, of course, nearly identical to that of a 'rupture between theology and life', which Daniélou would lament just over a decade later. Both were concerned with the Church's retreat into the private domain, which was contributing to the secularizing of society.[95] The Unam sanctam series was Congar's attempt to relate ecclesiology to the lived needs of society and so to contribute to a solution to the 'problem of unbelief'. The first volume of the new series was Congar's own *Chrétiens désunis* (1937), which broached the sensitive topic of ecumenical dialogue.[96] The second volume, his translation of Möhler's *Einheit der Kirche*, was soon followed by Henri de Lubac's *Catholicisme* (1938), which de Lubac wrote at Congar's request.[97] Congar's overtures to Orthodoxy and Protestantism caused such concern that Mariano Cordovani, Master of the Sacred Pontifical Palace, criticized his *Chrétiens désunis* in *L'Osservatore Romano*. The result was that the Dominican Master General, Martin Stanislas Gillet (1875–1951), summoned Congar to Paris for a reprimand.[98]

Around the same time, controversy erupted over the nature of the theological discipline. In 1937, the Franciscan scholar Jean-François Bonnefoy (1887–1958) published a series of essays on St Thomas's understanding of theology which departed significantly from the common approach of the neo-Thomists.[99] Then

[91] Möhler's work was published as *L'Unité dans l'Église ou Le principe du Catholicisme d'après l'esprit des Pères des trois premiers siècles de l'Église*, trans. André de Lilienfeld (Paris: Cerf, 1938).

[92] For Congar's findings surrounding the inquiry, see esp. Gabriel Flynn, 'The Role of Unbelief in the Theology of Yves Congar', *NBl* 85 (2004), 426–43.

[93] Congar, 'Une conclusion théologique à l'enquête sur les raisons actuelles de l'incroyance', *VInt* 37 (1935), 214–49; English trans.: 'The Reasons for the Unbelief of Our Time: A Theological Conclusion', *Integr* (Aug. 1938), 13–21; (Dec. 1938), 10–26.

[94] Id., 'Reasons for the Unbelief' (Aug. 1938), 14; (Dec. 1938), 26.

[95] Congar warned against 'the principle of immanence implying the sufficiency of reason and the possibility of an indefinite progress in the world' (ibid. (Dec. 1938), 13).

[96] Owing to translation problems with Möhler's *Einheit der Kirche*, Congar's own book *Chrétiens désunis* (1937) became the first in the Unam sanctam series. See Congar, *Une vie pour la vérité: Jean Puyo interroge le Père Congar*, ed. Jean Puyo (Paris: Centurion, 1975), 48.

[97] De Lubac, *Catholicisme: Les Aspects sociaux du dogme* (Paris: Cerf, 1938); English trans.: *Catholicism: Christ and the Common Destiny of Man*, trans. Lancelot C. Sheppard and Elizabeth Englund (San Francisco, Calif.: Ignatius, 1988).

[98] Congar, *Une vie pour la vérité*, 100. In 1950, Congar was unable to obtain permission for a second edition of *Chrétiens désunis* from the new Master General, Manuel Suárez (ibid. 107).

[99] Jean-François Bonnefoy, 'La Théologie comme science et l'explication de la foi selon Thomas d'Aquin', *ETL* 14 (1937), 421–46, 600–31; 15 (1938), 491–516. This material was republished as *La Nature de la théologie selon saint Thomas d'Aquin* (Paris: Vrin, 1939).

Louis Charlier (1898–1981), a Louvain Dominican, published a book entitled *Essai sur le problème théologique* (1938) which set off a storm of controversy because it rejected the neo-scholastic conceptualist view of theology—according to which divine truth could be adequately accessed by human concepts—and because it insisted that the revealed deposit of faith continued to grow through the development of doctrine.[100] René Draguet (1896–1980), who taught at the Catholic University of Louvain, wrote a review of the book in which he explained that, unbeknownst to him, Charlier had taken much of the book from Draguet's lectures, but in which he then expressed his general agreement with Charlier's anti-intellectualist approach.[101] Earlier, in 1936, Draguet himself had already published a series of articles on the nature of theology, as well as on the development of doctrine, in which the Louvain patrologist had distanced himself from the neo-scholastic approach.[102] By associating himself directly with Charlier's position, Draguet implicated himself even more in the crisis that ensued.

By the time Draguet brought up the topic of doctrinal development again, in his 1941 *Histoire du dogme catholique*, the lines had already been drawn in the sand.[103] Marie-Rosaire Gagnebet (1904–83), a Dominican from the Angelicum in Rome, reacted strongly and in detail to the publications of Charlier and Bonnefoy.[104] Congar wrote a review essay in which he discussed several of the positions that had recently been expressed. Interestingly, while he was relatively sympathetic to Charlier, he showed himself rather critical of Bonnefoy's position, convinced that the Franciscan scholar had insufficiently acknowledged the rational character of theology.[105] Henri-Dominique Simonin wrote an article expressing strong disagreement with Charlier.[106] Charles Boyer then entered

---

[100] Louis Charlier, *Essai sur le problème théologique* (Thuillies: Ramgal, 1938). Cf. Chap. 6, sect.: Louis Charlier: Growth of the Revealed Deposit. For the controversies from 1937 to 1942, see Robert Guelluy, 'Les Antécédents de l'encyclique "Humani Generis" dans les sanctions Romaines de 1942: Chenu, Charlier, Draguet', *RHE* 81 (1986), 421–97; Jean-Claude Petit, 'La Compréhension de la théologie', 215–29; Étienne Fouilloux, 'Autour d'une mise à l'index', in Joseph Doré and Jacques Fantino (eds), *Marie-Dominique Chenu: Moyen-âge et modernité* (Paris: Cerf, 1997), 25–56; Jürgen Mettepenningen, 'L'Essai de Louis Charlier (1938): Une contribution à la *nouvelle théologie*', *RTL* 39 (2008), 211–32.

[101] Draguet characterized Charlier's borrowing from his lectures as 'a simple omission, which will eventually be fixed in the preface to the second edition' (René Draguet, review of Louis Charlier, *Essai sur le problème théologique*, in *ETL* 16 (1938), 143).

[102] René Draguet, 'Méthodes théologiques d'hier et d'aujourd'hui', *RCIF* 15/42 (10 Jan. 1936), 1–7; 15/46 (7 Feb. 1936), 4–7; 15/47 (14 Feb. 1936), 13–17; id., 'L'Évolution des dogmes', in Maurice Brillant and Maurice Nédoncelle (eds), *Apologétique: Nos raisons de croire, réponses aux objections* (Paris: Bloud et Gay, 1937), 1166–92. This work on doctrinal development was republished as *L'Évolution des dogmes* (Saint-Dizier: Brulliard, 1937).

[103] René Draguet, *Histoire du dogme catholique* (Paris: Michel, 1941).

[104] Marie-Rosaire Gagnebet, 'Un essai sur le problème théologique', *RT* 45 (1939), 108–45.

[105] Congar, review of R. Draguet, 'Méthodes théologiques d'hier et d'aujourd'hui'; J.-F. Bonnefoy, 'La Théologie comme science et l'explication de la foi selon saint Thomas d'Aquin'; L. Charlier, *Essai sur le problème théologique;* and R. Gagnebet, 'La Nature de la théologie spéculative', in *BT* 5 (1937–9), 490–505.

[106] Henri-Dominique Simonin, 'De la nécessité de certaines conclusions théologiques', *Ang* 16 (1939), 72–82. Simonin had also written an earlier essay on the topic: ' "Implicite" et "explicite" dans le développement du dogme', *Ang* 14 (1937), 126–45.

the fray by writing in opposition to the 'new interpretation' of St Thomas, which he believed undermined the Angelic Doctor's intellectualist position. He challenged not only Draguet, Charlier, and Bonnefoy, but also implicated Congar in his attack on the new experience-based theology.[107] In the end, the heated controversy brought about a formal condemnation from Rome. In February 1942, Charlier's book, along with Chenu's *Une école de théologie*, was placed on the *Index Librorum Prohibitorum*, and by July of the same year, Chenu, Charlier, and Draguet had all been removed from their teaching positions.[108] Pietro Parente (1891–1986), Professor at the Lateran University in Rome, explained the theological rationale behind the decisions in an article in *L'Osservatore Romano*.[109] Parente's criticism was that Chenu and Charlier had substituted religious experience for rational arguments and had created room for the growth of divine revelation through the development of Christian doctrine.[110] It was clear that Rome suspected the *nouvelle théologie* of Le Saulchoir and Louvain of a return to Modernism.[111]

Controversy over *Ressourcement* (1944–50)

De Lubac, Professor of Fundamental Theology at the Catholic University of Lyons, moved into the nearby Jesuit scholasticate up the hill in Fourvière in 1934. Although he taught only one regular course for the Jesuits, his presence none the less ensured that he had a profound impact on theologians such as Daniélou, Bouillard, and Balthasar. De Lubac was no more impressed with the theological manuals of the neo-Thomists than were the Dominicans from Le Saulchoir and Louvain. De Lubac, however, did not focus directly on the experiential character of theology. Instead, he began with a sustained reading of the Church Fathers and medieval theologians, focusing particularly on the nature–supernatural relationship, the spiritual interpretation of Scripture, and the relationship between Eucharist and Church. De Lubac's intense reading programme led to his prodigious output between 1944 and 1946.[112] One of the results was his wide-ranging book, *Catholicisme* (1938), which he published in Congar's Unam sanctam series. De Lubac's manuscript on the relationship between Eucharist and Church, *Corpus mysticum*, had also been completed

---

[107] Charles Boyer, 'Qu'est-ce que la théologie: Réflexions sur une controverse', *Greg* 21 (1940), 255–66.

[108] Chenu moved to the École des Hautes Études in Paris and returned to Le Saulchoir in 1962. After being dismissed in 1942, Charlier returned to the Dominican studium of La Sarte in 1953. Draguet was moved from the theological faculty to that of philosophy and literature and was allowed to return to the theological faculty in 1948.

[109] Parente, 'Nuove tendenze', 1.

[110] Cf. Mettepenningen, 'L'Essai de Louis Charlier', 229.

[111] Robert Guelluy describes the dominant mindset of the early 1940s in Rome as 'traumatized by modernist immanentism' ('Les antécédents', 430).

[112] For a careful account, see Étienne Fouilloux, 'Henri de Lubac au moment de la publication de *Surnaturel*', *RT* 101 (2001), 13–30.

around 1938, although he had to wait for its publication until 1944 as a result of the war.[113] De Lubac's controversial *Surnaturel* did not get published until 1946, but de Lubac had been working on it for years and had finished much of the writing by the late 1930s.[114] This book went to the heart of his disagreement with neo-scholastic theology: its separation between nature and the supernatural. De Lubac argued, in uncompromising fashion, that nature and the supernatural were not two parallel orders, running alongside one another, each with its own, distinct end. Instead, he argued that God had created nature in such a way that from the beginning it had a supernatural goal for its purpose. The natural desire (*desiderium naturale*) for the beatific vision that this implied seemed, to the neo-Thomists at least, to endanger the gratuity of divine grace: if human beings contributed a natural desire, the process of salvation did not seem to be originating only with God. De Lubac's *Surnaturel* was the cause of serious controversy. Angelicum scholars Réginald Garrigou-Lagrange, Louis-Bertrand Gillon (1901–87),[115] and Marie-Rosaire Gagnebet, as well as Gregorium theologian, Charles Boyer, all weighed in on de Lubac's startling thesis.[116] Bernard Sesboüé rightly notes that de Lubac was suspected of being a 'neo- or crypto-modernist'.[117] Asked by the General of the Society of Jesus not to respond immediately, de Lubac waited until 1949 before finally publishing an essay in self-defence.[118]

De Lubac's open challenge of the neo-Thomist hegemony had been preceded by a similarly startling publication from his younger colleague in Fourvière, Henri Bouillard. In 1941, Bouillard had joined the Fourvière faculty, and his theological position fit with de Lubac's general approach. Bouillard published his

---

[113] De Lubac, *Corpus mysticum; L'Eucharistie et l'Église au moyen âge: Étude historique* (Paris: Aubier, 1944); English trans.: *Corpus Mysticum*. Already in 1939 and 1940 de Lubac published several articles on the relationship between Eucharist and Church ('Corpus mysticum: Étude sur l'origine et les premiers sens de l'expression', *RSR* 29 (1939), 257–302, 429–80; 30 (1940), 40–80, 191–226).

[114] De Lubac, *Surnaturel: Études historiques* (Paris: Aubier, 1946). De Lubac wrote his first sketch for *Surnaturel* in the late 1920s while still a theology student. He published the first three chapters, on Baius and Jansenius in a 1931 essay ('Deux Augustiniens fourvoyés: Baius et Jansénius', *RSR* 21 (1931), 422–43, 513–40). He also wrote an article on the history of the word 'supernatural' in 1934 ('Remarques sur l'histoire du mot "surnaturel"', *NRT* 61 (1934), 225–49, 350–70). In 1939, he published an initial sketch of the second part of *Surnaturel* ('Esprit et liberté dans la tradition théologique', *BLE* 40 (1939), 121–50, 189–207). Owing to circumstances of the war, de Lubac was unable to continue working on his manuscript until 1943. See de Lubac, *At the Service of the Church*, 28–9, 34–6.

[115] I am much indebted to Fr Augustin Laffay, OP for providing me with valuable information on Gillon from the archives of the Toulouse Dominicans.

[116] Réginald Garrigou-Lagrange, 'La Nouvelle Théologie'; Louis-Bertrand Gillon, 'Aux origines de la "puissance obédientielle"', *RT* 55 (1947), 304–10; Boyer, 'Nature pure et surnaturel dans le *Surnaturel* du Père de Lubac', *Greg* 28 (1947), 379–96; Gagnebet, 'L'Amour naturel de Dieu chez saint Thomas et ses contemporains', *RT* 56 (1948), 394–446; 57 (1949), 31–102. Cf. Bruno de Solages' defence of de Lubac in 'Pour l'honneur de la théologie, les contre-sens du R. P. Garrigou-Lagrange', *BLE* 48 (1947), 64–84.

[117] Bernard Sesboüé, 'Le Surnaturel chez Henri de Lubac: Un conflit autour d'une théologie', *RSR* 80 (1992), 387. The article provides a careful account of the entire controversy.

[118] De Lubac, 'Le Mystère du surnaturel', *RSR* 36 (1949), 80–121.

dissertation in 1944, three years after he had obtained his doctorate at the Gregorium under Charles Boyer. The dissertation, *Conversion et grâce chez s. Thomas d'Aquin*, was the first volume in the new Théologie series, another significant plank in Fourvière's *ressourcement* platform.[119] Bouillard's book so emphasized the human role in conversion that to the neo-Thomists it seemed to call into question God's assistance in the process. The supernatural gratuity of grace seemed to be at stake, and Bouillard also appeared to relativize Thomas's theology as well as human truth claims in general.[120] Bouillard's book, which appeared two years prior to de Lubac's *Surnaturel*, caused a great deal of discussion. Numerous authors entered the fray to oppose Bouillard's perceived betrayal of Thomism: Michel-Louis Guérard des Lauriers (1898–1988) from the Pontifical Lateran University, Garrigou-Lagrange and Gillon from the Angelicum, and Garrigou's former student Marie-Michel Labourdette (1908–90), who taught at the Dominican studium of Saint-Maximin and served as editor of the *Revue thomiste*.[121] Of course, the controversy around Bouillard's dissertation did little to ease the reception of de Lubac's book when it came out in 1946. The debate surrounding Bouillard became part of a more general debate on the position of the Fourvière theologians, including de Lubac's approach to the nature–supernatural relationship.[122]

Jean Daniélou was also included in the barrage of criticism.[123] Although he taught at the Institut Catholique in Paris, he was one of the Fourvière theologians. During his three years of theological studies in Lyons-Fourvière (1936–9), he took de Lubac's history of religions course, and it was de Lubac who directed

---

[119] Bouillard, *Conversion et grâce chez s. Thomas d'Aquin: Étude historique* (Paris: Aubier, 1944). For more on the Théologie series, see Guillet, *La Théologie catholique*, 42–3; Fouilloux, *Une Église*, 187–91.

[120] Cf. Chap. 3, sect.: Fear of Relativism.

[121] Michel-Louis Guérard des Lauriers, 'La Théologie de s. Thomas et la grâce actuelle', *ATh* 6 (1945), 276–332; Louis-Bertrand Gillon, 'Théologie de la grâce', *RT* 46 (1946), 603–13; Labourdette, 'La Théologie et ses sources', 353–71; Garrigou-Lagrange, 'La Nouvelle Théologie'; id., 'Vérité et immutabilité du dogme', *Ang* 24 (1947), 124–39; id., 'Les Notions consacrées par les Conciles', *Ang* 24 (1947), 217–30; id., 'Nécessité de revenir à la définition traditionnelle de la vérité', *Ang* 25 (1948), 185–8; id., 'L'Immutabilité du dogme selon le Concile du Vatican, et le relativisme', *Ang* 26 (1949), 309–22; id., 'Le Relativisme et l'immutabiltité du dogme', *Ang* 27 (1950), 219–46; id., 'La Structure de l'encyclique "Humani generis"', *Ang* 28 (1951), 3–17. Cf. the common response of the Fourvière theologians to Labourdette: 'La Théologie et ses sources: Réponse', *RSR* 33 (1946), 385–401. The debate between Labourdette and the *nouvelle* theologians was republished in M. Labourdette, M.-J. Nicolas, and R.-L. Bruckberger, *Dialogue théologique: Pièces du débat entre 'La Revue Thomiste' d'une part et les RR PP de Lubac, Daniélou, Bouillard, Fessard, von Balthasar, SJ, d'autre part* (St-Maximin: Arcades, 1947). For Labourdette, see esp. Henry Donneaud, 'Une vie au service de la théologie', *RT* 92 (1992), 17–51. This entire issue of *RT* is devoted to Labourdette.

[122] The controversy is traced in Karl-Heinz Neufeld, 'Fundamentaltheologie in gewandelter Welt: H. Bouillards theologischer Beitrag', *ZKT* 100 (1978), 417–40; Fouilloux, 'Dialogue théologique? (1946–1948)', in Serge-Thomas Bonino, et al. (eds), *Saint Thomas au XXe siècle* (Paris: St-Paul, 1994), 153–95; Aidan Nichols, 'Thomism and the *Nouvelle Théologie*', *Thomist*, 64 (2000), 1–19; Peddicord, *Sacred Monster*, 146–60; Jürgen Mettepenningen, 'Truth as Issue in a Second Modernist Crisis?'. Cf. Étienne Fouilloux, 'La "Dialogue théologique" selon Marie-Joseph Nicolas', *BLE* 103 (2002), 19–32.

[123] Cf. above, n. 3.

him to the Church Fathers and encouraged him to work on St Gregory of Nyssa.[124] This resulted in Daniélou's 1943 *Platonisme et théologie mystique*, which he wrote in Paris at the Institut Catholique.[125] Around this same time, he joined forces with de Lubac to publish scholarly editions of the Church Fathers—particularly the Eastern theologians—in a series called the Sources chrétiennes. Daniélou edited the very first volume, which was, not surprisingly, Gregory of Nyssa's *The Life of Moses*.[126] Clearly, Daniélou owed his lifelong interest in *ressourcement* to de Lubac. What is more, Daniélou also shared de Lubac's and Bouillard's desire for reform in the Church. When, two years after the publication of Bouillard's book, Daniélou published his programmatic essay, 'Les Orientations présentes de la pensée religieuse', it was becoming obvious that dissent was fomenting among the Fourvière theologians.

Hans Urs von Balthasar, too, had a great deal at stake in the debate. He had studied theology at the Fourvière scholasticate from 1933 till 1937. And, although he had never taken courses from de Lubac, Balthasar left no doubt about his indebtedness to the patristic scholar. Looking back on his years at Fourvière, Balthasar commented that

fortunately Henri de Lubac was in residence, and he referred us beyond scholasticism to the Church Fathers, generously making his notes and excerpts available to us. So it came about that while the others were playing soccer, I studied with Daniélou, Bouillard and a number of others (Fessard was no longer there), and I wrote books about Origen, Gregory of Nyssa and Maximus.[127]

De Lubac was a source of inspiration to Balthasar. The latter's *ressourcement* of the Fathers, his opposition to neo-Thomism, and his interest in spiritual interpretation can all be traced to de Lubac. Despite de Lubac's influence, Balthasar stayed out of the Fourvière debates, except that he was briefly mentioned in Labourdette's essay.[128]

The Fourvière debates climaxed in the appearance of Pius XII's 1950 encyclical *Humani generis*. In the time leading up to its publication, a number of the faculty lost their positions and were exiled from Fourvière, including de Lubac and Bouillard, who ended up as neighbours in Paris.[129] De Lubac had three of his books removed from circulation: *De la connaissance de Dieu*,[130] *Corpus mysticum*,

---

[124] Daniélou, *Et qui est mon prochain?*, 92.

[125] Id., *Platonisme et théologie mystique: Doctrine spirituelle de Saint Grégoire de Nysse* (Paris: Aubier, 1944).

[126] Gregory of Nyssa, *La Vie de Moïse ou Traité de la perfection en matière de vertu*, ed. and trans. Jean Daniélou, Sources chrétiennes, 1 (Paris: Cerf, 1942). In 2000, Cerf republished the corrected 3rd edn. For the origin of the Sources chrétiennes, see Fouilloux, *La Collection 'Sources chrétiennes': Editer les Pères de l'Église au XXᵉ siècle* (Paris: Cerf, 1995).

[127] Balthasar, *Test Everything*, 11–12. Cf. Henrici, 'Sketch', 13.

[128] Labourdette also briefly referred to Gaston Fessard and Pierre Teilhard de Chardin.

[129] Cf. de Lubac, *At the Service of the Church*, 67–8. De Lubac took up his teaching responsibilities again towards the end of 1953. Also removed from their faculty positions were Alexandre Durant, Pierre Ganne, Emile Delaye, and the Prefect of Studies, Henri Rondet.

[130] De Lubac, *De la connaissance de Dieu* (Paris: Témoignage chrétien, 1941); English trans.: *The Discovery of God*, trans. Alexander Dru, et al. (Grand Rapids, Mich.: Eerdmans, 1996).

and, of course, *Surnaturel*. The encyclical appeared to take direct aim at the Fourvière *ressourcement* scholars, even though it did not mention any of them by name.[131] The encyclical rejected the view that 'the mysteries of faith are never expressed by truly adequate concepts but only by approximate and ever change-able notions, in which the truth is to some extent expressed'.[132] The view that was here repudiated closely echoed comments Bouillard had made in *Conversion et grace*. The encyclical reacted against the *ressourcement* of patristic interpret-ation, warning against a 'new exegesis, which they are pleased to call symbolic or spiritual'.[133] De Lubac and Daniélou were clearly the targets. And de Lubac's *Corpus mysticum* seemed referenced when the encyclical argued that some theo-logians regarded the consecrated species merely as 'efficacious signs of the spiritual presence of Christ and of His intimate union with the faithful members of His Mystical Body'.[134] Even if de Lubac was not quoted directly, the reference to the Fourvière Jesuit seemed clear enough when the encyclical stated: 'Others destroy the gratuity of the supernatural order, since God, they say, cannot create intellectual beings without ordering and calling them to the beatific vision.'[135] The shake-up at Fourvière, along with the publication of *Humani generis*, was the most serious setback that the *ressourcement* movement experienced.

Controversy over Worker–Priests (1943–54)

The events of 1950 were soon followed by a similar suppression of the Domin-ican studium of Le Saulchoir. The issue here was quite different in character. It concerned primarily the involvement of the Saulchoir faculty with the worker–priest movement.[136] The worker–priest movement was a post-war response of clerics and theologians to the growing secularization and de-christianizing of France. Prior to the war, Chenu had been involved with the *Jeunesse Ouvrière Catholique* (JOC).[137] Henri Godin and Yvan Daniel, chaplains of the JOC, had

---

[131] Cf. Gustave Weigel, 'The Historical Background of the Encyclical *Humani Generis*', *TS* 12 (1951), 208–30; id., 'Gleanings from the Commentaries on *Humani Generis*', *TS* 12 (1951), 520–49.

[132] *AAS* 42 (1950), 566; English trans.: *Humani generis*, 15 <http://www.vatican.va>.

[133] Ibid. 570 (*Humani generis*, 23).

[134] Ibid. 571 (*Humani generis*, 26).

[135] Ibid. 570 (*Humani generis*, 26). De Lubac displayed remarkable ingenuity, actually claiming that the encyclical had called for a renewal that would support his theological conclusions (*Augus-tinianism and Modern Theology*, trans. Lancelot Sheppard (New York: Crossroad/Herder, 2000), 274–5; cf. also id., *De Lubac: A Theologian Speaks*, trans. Stephen Maddux; ed. Angelo Scola (Los Angeles, Calif.: Twin Circles, 1985), 4). For the question of de Lubac's relation to *Humani generis*, see also Schindler, Introduction to id., *The Mystery of the Supernatural*, trans. Rosemary Sheed (New York: Crossroad/Herder, 1998), pp. xxii–xxiii.

[136] For the worker–priest movement and Chenu's involvement in it, I rely on Oscar Arnal, *Priests in Working-class Blue: The History of the Worker–Priests (1943–1954)* (New York: Paulist, 1986); and id., 'Theology and Commitment: Marie-Dominique Chenu', *CC* 38 (1988), 64–75.

[137] The *jocistes* (deriving from JOC) were lay Catholic Action groups involved in mission work among the working classes. Cf. Chenu's 1936 essay, 'La JOC au Saulchoir', in *La Parole de Dieu*, ii *L'Évangile dans le temps* (Paris: Cerf, 1964), 271–4.

drawn the Church's attention to the problem of secularization in a 1943 book, *France, pays de mission?*[138] As a result, priests began to enter the factories to join the workers there. They saw this involvement as part of their missionary apostolate. Chenu was a strong supporter of this worker–priest movement. His understanding of the 'law of the Incarnation' was that it called for the involvement (*engagement*) of the Church and her priests in the actual lives of the working people, and so he supported dialogue with Marxism, and later on also wrote in support of liberation theology. 'Chenu', comments Oscar Arnal, 'saw the organized working class, even with its atheistic and Marxist ideology, as the force which under the hand of God could liberate the proletariat and create a more humane world for all'.[139] These convictions led to Chenu's direct involvement in the experimental seminary of Mission de France, which since 1942 had trained priests to work among the working classes. Chenu also joined Father Henri Godin in establishing the Mission de Paris, which became the centre for many of the worker–priests.

All this involvement came to an end in the first two months of 1954. Many Catholics, both in France and in Rome, had been looking askance at the worker–priest movement. The apprehensions were that the priests were abandoning their proper calling in their parishes and that the Church might be converting to the (socialist) world rather than the other way around. The clampdown finally came when, at Rome's direction, the French bishops called on the worker–priests to leave the factories. Overnight, the worker–priest movement came to an end.[140] Chenu was told to leave Paris and to move to Rouen.

Chenu's younger colleague, Congar, had not been involved in the worker–priest movement. His publications had none the less caused a great deal of anxiety in Rome. The first signs of concern had already been expressed after he had published his book on ecumenical dialogue (*Chrétiens désunis*, 1937). He had subsequently published major books on two other controversial topics: Church reform and the role of the laity.[141] Thus, when the Dominican Master General, Emmanuel Suárez, visited France to ensure that the study houses would comply with the new measures, he removed not only Chenu, but he also exiled Congar, who from then on would have to submit his writings to his superiors for approval prior to publication.[142] After brief stays in Jerusalem, Rome, and

[138] Henri Godin and Yvan Daniel, *La France, pays de mission?*, Rencontres, 12 (Paris: L'Abeille, 1943); English trans.: *France Pagan? The Mission of Abbé Godin*, trans. Maisie Ward (New York: Sheed & Ward, 1949).

[139] Arnal, 'Theology and Commitment', 74.

[140] Cf. Oscar L. Arnal, 'A Missionary "Main Tendue" towards French Communists: The "Témoignages" of the Worker–Priests, 1943–1954', *FHS* 13 (1984), 529.

[141] Congar, *Vraie et fausse réforme*; id., *Jalons pour une théologie du laïcat* (Paris: Cerf, 1950); English trans.: *Lay People in the Church: A Study for a Theology of the Laity*, trans. Donald Attwater (rev. edn 1965; repr. London: Chapman, 1985).

[142] On Suárez' visit to Paris, see Thomas O'Meara, ' "Raid on the Dominicans": The Repression of 1954', *America*, 107/4 (5 Feb. 1994), 9–18. Also removed from Paris were Henri-Marie Féret, the

Cambridge, Congar moved to Strasbourg, where the city's Bishop, Jean Weber, had kindly invited him. Congar stayed there to preach and write until 1960, when the preparations for the Second Vatican Council suddenly and radically changed his position in the Church.

OUTLINING THE SACRAMENTAL SENSIBILITY

The remainder of this book will not be limited to the immediate controversies that I have just described. Instead, I will focus on various theological themes as they were expressed in the most significant works of the *ressourcement* movement, written both during and after the immediate controversies. The main disadvantage of this approach is that it is impossible to do full justice to each of the writings of the authors under discussion. For most of these theologians, the primary as well as secondary literature is vast; comprehensive discussion is thus out of the question. I have been inspired, however, by Yves Congar, who, when faced with a similar predicament, commented: 'It is permissible not to say all that can be said on a topic, but to deal with it from one particular standpoint.'[143] The particular standpoint of this book is the theological return to mystery, which the *nouvelle* theologians advocated by means of their sacramental ontology. We can clearly identify this shared sensibility only by means of a wide-ranging analysis of the overall thought patterns of the various *nouvelle* theologians.

Nouvelle théologie has its place within the larger context of nineteenth- and early twentieth-century theology. In Chapter 2, I will discuss the scholars who were most influential for the movement of *nouvelle théologie*. By way of backdrop, I will deal with some dominant nineteenth-century Catholic schools of thought, including neo-Thomism, which became especially influential towards the end of the century, and against which *nouvelle théologie* reacted. Four scholars in particular proved influential among the *nouvelle* theologians. Johann Adam Möhler's *ressourcement* of the Church Fathers, his Romantic priority of experience over intellect, his pneumatological ecclesiology, and his organic approach to doctrinal development, made him a source of inspiration for *nouvelle théologie*. The attempt of Maurice Blondel (1861–1949), a philosopher from Aix-en-Provence, to reintegrate nature and the supernatural by means of the Church's Tradition, as well as the significance that he accorded to the action of lived human lives (rather than to rational apologetics), turned him into a towering figure for some of the Fourvière theologians, particularly de Lubac and Bouillard. Joseph Maréchal (1878–1944), a philosopher from the Higher Institute of

---

church historian from Le Saulchoir, and Pierre Boisselot, the director at large of the Parisian publisher Cerf.

[143] Congar, *The Mystery of the Temple, or, The Manner of God's Presence to His Creatures from Genesis to the Apocalypse*, trans. Reginald F. Trevett (London: Burns & Oates, 1962), p. xi.

Philosophy in Louvain, wanted to get beyond a traditional metaphysical approach, by adding elements of the transcendental method of Immanuel Kant. Finally, the Jesuit theologian, Pierre Rousselot (1878–1915), interpreted St Thomas through the lens of a chastened intellectualism. Several of the *nouvelle theologians* drew on his conviction that 'eyes of faith' were required for true understanding. Each of these precursors to *nouvelle théologie* maintained that a supernatural ground and purpose enveloped the natural order.

The sacramental ontology of *nouvelle théologie* was essentially an attempt to rework the relationship between nature and the supernatural. Chapters 3 and 4, therefore, will deal with this issue specifically. Chapter 3 will focus on the theology of de Lubac and of Bouillard. They both drew on the Neoplatonic tradition in order to recover a sense of mystery. Thus, they both emphasized the 'upward' direction of the natural world as it pointed towards the supernatural. We will see that de Lubac's insistence on a natural desire for the vision of God, as well as his opposition to the notion of 'pure nature', served to overcome neo-Thomism's dualism between nature and the supernatural. In this way, he wanted to recover a sense of the mystery that constituted the core of each human being. Bouillard opposed neo-Thomism both in his doctrine of grace (his questioning of Thomas's 'elevating grace') and in his epistemology (human language as analogical in character). Thus, for de Lubac the human spirit could serve as a sacramental mystery, and for Bouillard human discourse was able to draw human realities into the mystery of God.

Among the *ressourcement* scholars, Balthasar and Chenu were particularly insistent on the goodness of the created order. In Chapter 4, I will discuss their sacramental approach, which centred on the Incarnation and as a result highlighted the 'downward' direction of grace. Because Balthasar and Chenu were more insistent than de Lubac and Bouillard on the relative autonomy of the created order, they approached the sacramental character of reality from a different angle. Whereas de Lubac and Bouillard highlighted the upward movement of divine ascent, the incarnational approach of Balthasar and Chenu emphasized divine descent into the created realities of this-worldly time and space. I will focus on Balthasar's reading of Irenaeus, Denys, and Maximus. Balthasar understood the doctrine of 'analogy of being' (*analogia entis*) as the key to their theology. His defence of this doctrine in dialogue with Karl Barth allowed him to maintain the goodness of creation. At the same time, Balthasar appreciated Barth's Christological approach and was convinced that Christ was the centre and norm for the doctrine of analogy. Chenu's theology, too, had a sacramental cast. In his case, it stemmed from an appreciation for the contemplative character of theology, as well as from his reliance on the symbolical theology of Denys, for whom mystery had permeated the created order. At the same time, Chenu's sacramental ontology was not always consistent. He accentuated the autonomy of the created order and positively evaluated the desacralizing that he observed in the High Middle Ages. Thus, he placed a stronger emphasis on nature itself than did the other *nouvelle* theologians.

In Chapter 5, I will turn to de Lubac's and Daniélou's recovery of spiritual interpretation. Their *ressourcement* of pre-modern methods of exegesis relied on a sacramental understanding of Scripture. De Lubac and Daniélou believed that the salvation–historical events recorded in Scripture contained deeper, spiritual levels of meaning. Thus, just as nature and the supernatural did not constitute two separate orders of being, so spiritual interpretation was not just an unrelated addition to an already historically established meaning of the text. De Lubac and Daniélou did differ on some points. De Lubac's appreciation for allegorical exegesis meant that the purpose of spiritual interpretation was, ultimately, to move beyond history. Daniélou placed greater emphasis on the historical progression of typological exegesis, which made him wary of allegory. Their differences notwithstanding, both Jesuit scholars looked to Old Testament types as sacraments that pointed beyond themselves to their spiritual fulfilment in the New Testament and in Jesus Christ.

Unlike neo-Thomist scholasticism, the *nouvelle* theologians introduced history as a category that carried theological significance. Remarkably, it was their sacramental ontology that enabled them to recognize this significance. In Chapter 6, I will first discuss Daniélou's approach to history. He regarded the relationship between cosmic and Christian revelation, secular and sacred history, as well as earthly and heavenly cities as sacramental in character. Christian revelation, sacred history, and heavenly city were the final end or sacramental reality to which all of history pointed. Since doctrinal development was one of the main areas of disagreement between the manualist neo-Thomists and the *ressourcement* theologians, I will next focus on the so-called 'theological' theory of doctrinal development in Chenu, Charlier, and de Lubac. They were able to combine historical development (the horizontal element) with continuity of doctrine (the vertical element) because they regarded doctrinal development as the outworking of the Incarnation. The last section of this chapter will focus on Congar's understanding of Tradition as 'the transmission of the reality that is Christianity'.[144] For Congar, the 'time of the Church' was sacramental in character: the eschatological end was already virtually present in the Christological beginning. This meant that later development (plenitude) and original deposit (purity) joined, in sacramental fashion, in the 'time of the Church'. Development of doctrine was thus based on a sacramental ontology.

The seventh chapter of this book will discuss the connection between sacrament and Church in the theology of de Lubac and Congar. For both theologians,

---

[144] Id., *The Meaning of Tradition*, trans. A. N. Woodrow (San Francisco, Calif.: Ignatius, 2004), 44. Throughout this book, I use 'Tradition' (upper case T) to describe the transmission of the living reality of the gospel itself. My use of 'traditions' (lower case t) indicates either distinct ecclesial groupings (such as the Reformation tradition) or the numerous customs and rites within the Church.

ecclesiology was central to their thought. Also, both developed an ecclesiology that was sacramental in character and that shaped the communion ecclesiology of the Second Vatican Council and the period beyond the Council. De Lubac emphasized the reciprocal relationship between Eucharist and Church. On the one hand, the Eucharist made the Church: the Eucharistic body had for its aim the realization of the communion of the ecclesial body. On the other hand, the Church also made the Eucharist, in the sense that clergy were required to produce the Eucharist. De Lubac went on to argue that the Church herself was the sacrament of Christ's presence. Convinced that Christ was sacramentally present in the world through the Church, de Lubac believed that he had overcome the neo-scholastic separation between nature and the supernatural. Congar's approach was quite similar to that of de Lubac. He distinguished between the Church as structure or institution and the Church as life or community, and posited a sacramental relationship between the two. Congar saw the Church's structure as the sacrament (*sacramentum*) that served as the means to bring about life as the reality (*res*) of the Church. Whereas the juridicizing of neo-scholastic ecclesiology had focused on the Church's structure, Congar believed it was time to pay attention to her life. He developed a sacramental understanding of the 'time of the Church' as the 'in between time' (*entre-deux*), and he argued that an undue focus on Christ's Pasch and on the Church's institution would result in a lack of appreciation for the degree to which the sacramental reality of the Church had already been accomplished. By looking only to the Parousia and the Church's life, however, one would undermine the historical provision of the visible sacrament. Over time, de Lubac and Congar developed different ecclesiological emphases. None the less, both intended to restore a sacramental view of the Church by paying attention not just to the properly administered sacrament (*sacramentum*) but also to the mystery of the intended reality (*res*): the unity of the Church in Christ.

In the concluding chapter, I will summarize the sacramental vision that I believe motivated *nouvelle théologie*. At this point, it will be clear that the movement is best interpreted not as a stepping stone between Modernism and post-Second Vatican Council pluralism but as an attempt to recover the mystery of God by means of a sacramental ontology. I will briefly outline some of the significant ecumenical implications of this understanding of the *ressourcement* movement.

2

Eyes of Faith:
Precursors to a Sacramental Ontology

Love, the free homage to the supreme Good, gives us new eyes. Being,
become more visible, delights the beholder.

Pierre Rousselot[1]

In order to understand what motivated *nouvelle théologie*, we need to explore in
some detail the intellectual currents of the nineteenth and twentieth centuries.
Dissatisfied with the dominant, neo-scholastic mindset in the Church, the
nouvelle theologians looked further back. Throughout the nineteenth century,
Catholic theologians had attempted to come to terms with the challenge of the
Kantian turn to the human subject. The *nouvelle* theologians were much more
attracted to some of these nineteenth-century approaches than to contemporary
neo-scholastic attempts at outmanoeuvring Kant's subjectivism by means of
human reason. Other, more recent, scholars had also been turning their backs
on the newer scholastic commentators of St Thomas. They, too, returned to the
kind of questions that neo-scholastics hoped had been settled for good. Together
with several nineteenth-century theologians—in particular the Tübingen
school—these early twentieth-century scholars, too, influenced the movement
of *nouvelle théologie*.

In this chapter, therefore, I will begin with a brief description of the various
nineteenth-century Catholic schools of thought and of the neo-scholastic reaction to these attempts at charting a new path for theology. Next, I will discuss
four individual theologians who, to varying degrees and in different ways, each
impacted the movement of *nouvelle théologie*. Here I will first go back to the first
half of the nineteenth century, to the Romanticism of Johann Adam Möhler
(1796–1838). Then I will look at several late nineteenth- and early twentieth-
century scholars, each of whom deeply influenced *nouvelle théologie*: Maurice
Blondel, Joseph Maréchal, and Pierre Rousselot.

This chapter makes no claim to a complete theological sketch of these various
scholars. I will highlight aspects of their thought that especially influenced
nouvelle théologie. For each of the authors discussed, I hope to make clear that

---

[1] Pierre Rousselot, *The Eyes of Faith*, trans. Joseph Donceel; id., *Answer to Two Attacks*, trans.
Avery Dulles (New York: Fordham University Press, 1990), 56.

there were elements in their theology that later enabled *nouvelle théologie* to develop a theology characterized by a sacramental ontology. It will become clear that what attracted the *nouvelle* theologians to these four authors was their common rejection of an apologetic based on 'pure reason' in favour of an approach that took more seriously the historical and experiential conditions of human existence, so that, to use Pierre Rousselot's expression, 'eyes of faith' were necessary to detect the sacramental connection between nature and the supernatural.

NINETEENTH-CENTURY 'FOOTNOTES' TO KANT

The impact of Immanuel Kant (1724–1804) on modern theology has been profound. This is not to say that Kant is a modern-day Church Father. The most influential Catholic schools of thought in the nineteenth century expressed strong disagreement with the philosopher of Königsberg, as they attempted to uphold the objectivity of divine revelation in the face of the immanentism and subjectivism that gained ground in the modern period following Kant. Modern theology's critical interaction with Kant has thus been different from the medieval appropriation of St Augustine; the oft-quoted statement of Jaroslav Pelikan that we must write the history of Western theology as a 'series of footnotes' to Augustine is not directly applicable to the impact that Kant has had on modern theology.[2] But, of course, footnotes do not just contain references of approbation or even disapprobation; they also signal a critical interaction with their sources. And there is little doubt that Catholicism in the nineteenth and twentieth centuries was engaged in a struggle to come to grips with the challenges that Kant had posed. In that sense it is true that modern Catholic (as well as Protestant) thought heavily footnotes Kant.

The problem that Kant posed for nineteenth-century theology concerned the possibility of divine revelation. Accepting the scepticism of David Hume (1711–76) with regard to the limited abilities of natural reason, Kant appeared to pull the rug from under the traditional Thomist arguments for the existence of God. If it was true, as Kant maintained, that theoretical or pure reason was limited to observable phenomena and that only moral or practical reason was able to posit the existence of God, then how was it still possible to retain the notion of supernatural revelation? An approach to religion that took its starting-point in the natural, subjective, immanent, and moral needs of human beings seemed diametrically opposed to a theology that began with supernatural, objective, external, and propositional revelation. Religion could be based either

---

[2] Cf. Jaroslav Pelikan, *The Christian Tradition: A History of the Development of Doctrine,* i *The Emergence of the Catholic Tradition (100–600)* (Chicago, Ill.: University of Chicago Press, 1971), 330.

on immanent experience or on external revelation. While Kant's *Critique of Practical Reason* (1788) might appear to have salvaged religion in some sense, it certainly was difficult to reconcile the immanentism of the Kantian moral universe with the Catholic demand for divine revelation. In the period that followed, the question would be how to deal with the modern, Kantian interest in the subjective, experiential element of faith without losing the objective character of divine revelation.

In this context, three distinct Catholic schools of thought emerged in the nineteenth century: traditionalism, semi-rationalism, and ontologism.[3] Traditionalism dealt with the post-Kantian situation by acknowledging that pure reason was unable to prove the existence of God. It went beyond Kant by arguing that one could not even insist on the existence of God as a moral postulate that made sense of human existence. Rather than begin with human reason—whether it be pure or practical in character—traditionalism insisted that one had to take one's starting-point in a divine, paradisal revelation and in the Tradition that had passed on this primitive revelation. This traditionalist viewpoint became popular because it dovetailed with Romantic inclinations that were fashionable in the first half of the nineteenth century. In France, Joseph de Maistre (1753–1821), Louis de Bonald (1754–1840), Félicité de Lamennais (1782–1854), and Louis Bautain (1796–1867) were the most well-known advocates of the traditionalist position. And the German Tübingen school of Johann Sebastian Drey (1777–1853), Johann Adam Möhler, and Johann Evangelist Kuhn (1806–87), made common ground with traditionalism in its anti-rationalist tendencies, its appeal to Tradition, as well as in its assertion that it was the organic and linguistic unity of society rather than the individual quest of deductive reason that enabled one to make truth claims.[4] Pope Gregory XVI condemned Lamennais in 1834 for his acceptance of democratic liberalism as much as for his traditionalist epistemology[5] while the Bautain affair came to an end in 1844 when Bautain gave up his combination of traditionalism and Neoplatonic illuminationism after attending

---

[3] For the next few paragraphs, I am indebted especially to the excellent introduction of Gerald A. McCool, *Catholic Theology in the Nineteenth Century: The Quest for a Unitary Method* (New York: Crossroad/Seabury, 1977). McCool's book has been republished as *Nineteenth-century Scholasticism: The Search for a Unitary Method* (New York: Fordham University Press, 1989).

[4] This is not to say that the Tübingen school can be classified as traditionalist in the same sense as people like Lamennais and Bautain. Michael J. Himes points out that Möhler became concerned that Bautain did not sufficiently distinguish between a natural 'intellectual faith' (*Vernunftglaube*) and the faith that flows from grace and that Möhler insisted that the discursive reason of the preambles of the faith did serve a positive role, even though he would grant Bautain that the inner intuition of divine existence should be acknowledged (*Ongoing Incarnation: Johann Adam Möhler and the Beginnings of Modern Ecclesiology* (New York: Crossroad, 1997), 231–41).

[5] For Lamennais, see Alec R. Vidler, *Prophecy and Papacy: A Study of Lamennais, the Church, and the Revolution* (London: SCM, 1954); W. G. Roe, *Lamennais and England: The Reception of Lamennais's Religious Ideas in England in the Nineteenth Century* (Oxford: Oxford University Press, 1966); Louis Le Guillou, *Lamennais* (Paris: Desclée de Brouwer, 1969).

the lectures of the Jesuit Thomist scholar, Giovanni Perrone (1794–1876) at the Roman College.[6]

Like the traditionalist position, the semi-rationalist approach responded to the Kantian critique by accepting Kant's argument that speculative reason was incapable of reaching beyond the phenomenal world. While Georg Hermes (1775–1831) and Anton Günther (1783–1863) sharply differed on some points, from the neo-scholastic perspective their semi-rationalism created a basic kinship.[7] Hermes, following Kant, insisted that absolute certainty resulted from the moral categorical imperative—namely, the need to establish and preserve human dignity. One had to accept as true any statement that was necessary in support of this categorical imperative.[8] Thus, while pure reason could not provide a foundation for the Christian faith, practical reason did provide that basis. Hermes's position, whose Kantian moral categorical imperative appeared to obviate the need for divine revelation, was condemned shortly after his death, in 1837. This condemnation of Hermes's Kantian take on theology was an indication of neo-Thomism's growing influence in Rome.

Its influence became even more apparent twenty years later, when the teachings of Anton Günther were also condemned and his writings were placed on the *Index Librorum Prohibitorum*.[9] Günther, a private scholar from Vienna, employed the distinction of Friedrich Heinrich Jacobi (1743–1819), popular among the Romantics, between *Vernunft* and *Verstand*, the former referring to intuitive, the latter to discursive, knowledge. Günther saw the emphasis on *Verstand*, both in Aristotle and in G. W. F. Hegel (1770–1831), as inevitably leading to pantheism.[10] Strongly opposing Hegelian pantheism, Günther insisted on a metaphysical dualism between finite spirits and infinite Spirit, and on a dualism within the world between spirit and nature.[11] The charge of semi-rationalism inevitably entered the picture when Günther took his metaphysical dualism as the starting-point for his argument that the human awareness of its own finite nature caused the intuition of faith (*Vernunftsglaube*) to posit the necessity of the existence of a God whom one could rationally demonstrate to be triune.[12] Each in his own way, then, Hermes and Günther took on the challenge that Kant had posed to human reason, the former by adopting the Kantian moral

---

[6] McCool, *Catholic Theology*, 48, 54. For Bautain, see Walter Marshall Horton, *The Philosophy of the Abbé Bautain* (New York: New York University Press, 1926); Paul Poupard (ed.), *L'Abbé Louis Bautain* (Paris: Bloud et Gay, 1964).

[7] For Hermes, see Karl Eschweiler, *Die zwei Wege der neueren Theologie: Georg Hermes–Matt. Jos. Scheeben: Eine kritische Untersuchung des Problems der theologischen Erkenntnis* (Augsburg: Filser, 1926); Thomas Fliethmann, *Vernünftig Glauben: Die Theorie der Theologie bei Georg Hermes* (Würzburg: Echter, 1997). For Günther, see Joseph Pritz, *Glauben und Wissen bei Anton Günther: Eine Einführung in sein Leben und Werk mit einer Auswahl aus seinen Schriften*, Wiener Beiträge zur Theologie, 4 (Vienna: Herder, 1963); Karl Beck, *Offenbarung und Glaube bei Anton Günther*, Wiener Beiträge zur Theologie, 17 (Vienna: Herder, 1967).

[8] McCool, *Catholic Theology*, 62–3.   [9] Ibid. 130.

[10] Ibid. 91–3.   [11] Ibid. 93–5.   [12] Ibid. 96, 104, 109–10.

method, the latter by taking recourse to human intuition rather than to discursive reason in arguing for the existence of God.

Vincenzo Gioberti (1801–52) and Antonio Rosmini (1797–1855) were the main theologians associated with what Gioberti called 'ontologism', a school of thought that for a while was rather influential in Europe, partially because of Gioberti's influence at the University of Louvain.[13] While accepting the traditionalist notion of a primitive revelation that was communicated in history through the gift of human language, Gioberti and Rosmini combined this notion with Augustinian illuminationism. Divine ideas illuminated the human *Vernunft*, so that intuitive knowledge of God was possible as a result of divine illumination. This meant, at least for Gioberti, that direct contact between God and the human mind was possible. The divine Idea of Being was directly present to the human mind. As a result, one did not need to rely on sense experience in order to arrive at a discursive argument for the existence of God. Ontologism's moderate traditionalism and its rejection of discursive rational arguments for the existence of God proved to be obstacles to the ever stronger party of the neo-scholastic interpreters of St Thomas, who secured the ontologists' demise by means of two subsequent condemnations, in 1861 and 1866.[14]

The neo-Thomists were concerned about the proliferation of theological novelties during much of the nineteenth century, and they were determined to prevent post-Kantian idealism from setting the theological agenda. They were particularly agitated by the seemingly cavalier way in which the various nineteenth-century schools of thought appeared to follow Kant in casting aside Aristotelian appeals to sense experience and to discursive reason. While traditionalism, semi-rationalism, and ontologism certainly differed from each other in terms of how they dealt with the post-Kantian situation, according to the neo-Thomist view, all of these approaches failed to make the appropriate distinction between nature and the supernatural. To put it differently, the lines separating the two realms appeared to get blurred, either by nature overtaking the supernatural, as in the case of traditionalism and ontologism, or by the natural gift of practical reason determining the actual contents of the Christian faith, as in the case of semi-rationalism. The neo-Thomists were convinced that by confusing nature and the supernatural, their theological opponents mixed supernatural grace with natural human striving, thereby undermining the gratuity of grace.[15]

The neo-Thomist movement originated with Luigi Taparelli (1793–1862) and Serafino Sordi (1793–1865), and it became influential in part due to the Jesuit journal, *Civiltà Cattolica*, founded in 1850 by the Jesuit theologian, Carlo Maria Curci (1810–91). The 1878 papal election of Leo XIII, a former student

---

[13] Cf. ibid. 113–28.   [14] Ibid. 129–32.

[15] For a helpful brief overview of the neo-Thomist views on fundamental or apologetic theology, see Gabriel Daly, *Transcendence and Immanence: A Study in Catholic Modernism and Integralism* (Oxford: Clarendon Press, 1980), 7–25.

of Taparelli, secured the long-term success of the movement.[16] Other theologians, such as Alberto Lepidi (1838–1925), Louis Billot (1864–1931), and Réginald Garrigou-Lagrange strengthened the renown of neo-Thomist scholasticism throughout the early twentieth-century Modernist controversy and beyond. The most famous of the neo-Thomists, however, were Joseph Kleutgen (1811–83) and Matteo Liberatore (1810–92). Kleutgen took on traditionalism as well as Günther's semi-rationalism, while Liberatore was especially influential in the condemnation of ontologism. By 1866, the enemies of the neo-Thomist scheme had been soundly defeated. As McCool puts it: 'Rome was determined to carry through the course of action that it had undertaken; and, in the momentous years between 1855 and 1870 the majority of the bishops and the mass of pious Catholics stood behind Rome and the pope. Rome's intervention was also amazingly far-reaching. Almost every major force in Catholic theology had been condemned except scholasticism.'[17]

The neo-Thomist domination received official sanction when, in 1870, the First Vatican Council issued the apostolic constitution *Dei Filius* and when, nine years later, Pope Leo XIII published his encyclical *Aeterni Patris*. Joseph Kleutgen's hand could be observed in both these documents. In the face of post-Kantian idealism, they reasserted the ability of discursive reason to prove the existence and some of the attributes of God. In one of its best-known statements, *Dei Filius* maintained that God, as the source and end of all things, could be 'known with certitude by the natural light of human reason from created things'.[18] Furthermore, the apostolic constitution insisted, in typically neo-Thomist fashion, that miracles and prophecies, 'demonstrating as they do the omnipotence and infinite knowledge of God, are the most certain signs of revelation and are suited to the understanding of all'.[19] Likewise, according to Leo's encyclical, 'reason declares that the doctrine of the Gospel has even from its very beginning been made manifest by certain wonderful signs, the established proofs, as it were, of unshaken truth'.[20] After having carefully explained the relationship between philosophy and theology, *Aeterni Patris* held up St Thomas as a continuous source of inspiration. Speaking of the medieval scholastic theologians, the Pope commented, 'The doctrines of those illustrious men, like the scattered members of a body, Thomas collected together and cemented, distributed in wonderful order, and so increased with important additions that he is rightly and deservedly esteemed the special bulwark and glory of the Catholic faith.'[21] *Dei Filius* and *Aeterni Patris* firmly ensconced the neo-Thomist quest for a unitary method within the Catholic Church, both in philosophy and theology. Neo-Thomism's avoidance of the human subject, its lack of a historical

---

[16] McCool, *Catholic Theology*, 84.   [17] Ibid. 132.
[18] *Dei Filius*, chap. 2.1 (DS 3004).   [19] Ibid. 3009.
[20] *ASS* 12 (1879), 101; English trans.: *Aeterni Patris*, 5 <http://www.vatican.va>.
[21] Ibid. 108 (*Aeterni Patris*, 5).

method, and its reliance on discursive reason would dominate Catholic theology until the rise of *nouvelle théologie* and its sacramental ontology.

ECCLESIOLOGY AND DOCTRINAL DEVELOPMENT IN JOHANN ADAM MÖHLER

A *Ressourcement* Project

It is not surprising that in its reaction to neo-scholasticism, *nouvelle théologie* found in the nineteenth-century Tübingen school, and particularly in Johann Adam Möhler, a source of inspiration. Henri de Lubac was convinced that with regard to ecclesiology Möhler had reopened 'a great traditional path'.[22] Like Möhler, de Lubac turned to the Fathers and to their emphasis on the unity of the Church to inform his ecclesiology.[23] De Lubac adopted Möhler's notion of the Church as 'continued Incarnation'.[24] He also appealed to Möhler's understanding of the interpretation of Scripture, especially as the German Romantic theologian had expounded it in one of the appendices to *Einheit in der Kirche* (1825).[25] And, although de Lubac never appealed to Möhler in terms of the latter's understanding of the nature–supernatural relationship, their anthropology was none the less remarkably similar.[26]

---

[22] De Lubac, *The Splendor of the Church*, trans. Michael Mason (1956; repr. San Francisco, Calif.: Ignatius, 1999), 92. Cf. ibid. 266 n. 114; id., *The Motherhood of the Church Followed by Particular Churches in the Universal Church and an Interview Conducted by Gwendoline Jarczyk*, trans. Sergia Englund (San Francisco, Calif.: Ignatius, 1982), 278–9, 310.

[23] The notion of the unity of the Church as opposed to individualist piety is present throughout de Lubac's writings, perhaps most prominently in *Catholicism: Christ and the Common Destiny of Man*, trans. Lancelot C. Sheppard and Elizabeth Englund (San Francisco, Calif.: Ignatius, 1988); and id., *Corpus Mysticum; The Eucharist and the Church in the Middle Ages: Historical Survey*, trans. Gemma Simmonds, Richard Price, and Christopher Stephens and ed. Laurence Paul Hemming and Susan Frank Parsons (London: SCM, 2006).

[24] See e.g. de Lubac, *The Church: Paradox and Mystery*, trans. James R. Dunne (New York: Ecclesia, 1969), 24. Cf. Susan K. Wood, *Spiritual Exegesis and the Church in the Theology of Henri de Lubac* (Grand Rapids, Mich.: Eerdmans, 1998), 83. The influence of Möhler is also noted in Austin J. Lindsay, 'De Lubac's Images of the Church: A Study of Christianity in Dialogue' (PhD diss., Catholic University of America, Washington, DC, 1974), 28–33.

[25] Johann Adam Möhler, *Die Einheit in der Kirche oder das Prinzip des Katholizismus, dargestellt im Geiste der Kirchenväter der drei ersten Jahrhunderte* (Tübingen: Laupp, 1825); English trans.: *Unity in the Church, or The Principle of Catholicism: Presented in the Spirit of the Church Fathers of the First Three Centuries*, ed. and trans. Peter C. Erb (Washington, DC: Catholic University of America, 1996), 289–96. Cf. de Lubac, *History and Spirit: The Understanding of Scripture according to Origen*, trans. Anne Englund Nash and Juvenal Merriell (San Francisco, Calif.: Ignatius, 2007), 13, 42, 431–2.

[26] Michael J. Himes argues throughout his book that the nature-supernatural relationship lay at the heart of Möhler's search for an adequate ecclesiology. Himes makes clear that Möhler rejected the notion of 'pure nature' (i.e., nature apart from any consideration of a supernatural end) and insisted on a 'natural desire' for the vision of God (*Ongoing Incarnation*, 113–14, 195–8, 235, 250). Thus, while de Lubac did not indicate his awareness of the fact, his position was similar to that of Möhler. For further discussion of 'pure nature' and natural desire, and for de Lubac's position on this, see Chap. 3, sect.: Pure Nature and Natural Desire.

Even more so than de Lubac, Yves Congar was influenced by Möhler.[27] Congar became enamoured with Möhler from the time that his teacher Marie-Dominique Chenu encouraged him to read the Tübingen theologian, in 1928.[28] It is not clear why exactly Chenu recommended Möhler to Congar, but we do know that Chenu himself was also attracted to Möhler's Romantic emphasis on experience rather than theological concepts as the starting-point for theology.[29] Congar's reading resulted in a number of early essays on Möhler,[30] and he planned a French translation of Möhler's *Einheit in der Kirche* as the first volume of Unam sanctam, with the distinct purpose 'to provide the spirit of the series'.[31] We could justifiably say that no theologian had as lasting an impact on Congar as did Möhler. 'That which Möhler did in the nineteenth century', commented Congar, 'has become for me an ideal by which I wanted to be inspired to guide my own thinking in the twentieth century'.[32] Intrigued with Möhler's pneumatocentric ecclesiology, Congar made the doctrine of the Spirit central also to his own ecclesiology.[33] Furthermore, the Dominican theologian found in Möhler the view that Tradition was not merely a static deposit but was a living and developing organic whole. As a result, Möhler also influenced Congar's understanding of the development of doctrine.

[27] See Johannes Bunnenberg, *Lebendige Treue zum Ursprung: Das Traditionsverständnis Yves Congars*, (Mainz: Grünewald, 1989), 66–71; Monika-Maria Wolff, *Gott und Mensch: Ein Beitrag Yves Congars zum ökumenischen Dialog* (Frankfurt: Knecht, 1990), 36–9; Pablo Sicouly, 'Yves Congar und Johann Adam Möhler: Ein theologisches Gespräch zwischen den Zeiten', *Cath* 45 (1991), 36–43; Cornelis Th. M. van Vliet, *Communio sacramentalis: Das Kirchenverständis von Yves Congar–genetisch und systematisch betrachtet* (Mainz: Matthias-Grünewald, 1995), 54–60; Thomas F. O'Meara, 'Beyond "Hierarchology": Johann Adam Möhler and Yves Congar', in Donald J. Dietrich and Michael J. Himes (eds), *The Legacy of the Tübingen School: The Relevance of Nineteenth-century Theology for the Twenty-first Century* (New York: Crossroad, 1997), 173–91; Gabriel Flynn, *Yves Congar's Vision of the Church in a World of Unbelief* (Burlington, Vt.: Ashgate, 2004), 90–2; Elizabeth Teresa Groppe, *Yves Congar's Theology of the Holy Spirit* (Oxford: Oxford University Press, 2004), 40–3.

[28] Congar, 'Johann Adam Möhler: 1796–1838', *TQ* 150 (1970), 47; id., *Une vie pour la vérité: Jean Puyo interroge le Père Congar*, ed. Jean Puyo (Paris: Centurion, 1975), 48.

[29] This is clear especially in Chenu, 'Position de la théologie', *RSPT* 24 (1935), 232–57; repr. id., *La Parole de Dieu*, i *La Foi dans l'intelligence* (Paris: Cerf, 1964), 115–38; English trans.: 'What is Theology?', in *Faith and Theology*, trans. Denis Hickey (New York: Macmillan, 1968), 15–35. Chenu also repeatedly alluded to the Tübingen theologians in the third chap. of *Une école de théologie: Le Saulchoir* (Paris: Cerf, 1985). See Chap. 6, sect.: Chenu: Development and the Theandric Mystery.

[30] Congar, 'La Pensée de Möhler et l'ecclésiologie orthodoxe', *Irén* 12 (1935), 321–9; id., 'La Signification œcuménique de l'œuvre de Moehler', *Irén* 15 (1938), 113–30; id., 'Sur l'évolution de l'interprétation de la pensée de Moehler', *RSPT* 27 (1938), 205–12; id., 'L'Esprit des Pères d'après Moehler', *VSpir* suppl., 55 (1938), 1–25; id., 'L'Hérésie, déchirement de l'unité', in Pierre Chaillet (ed.), *L'Eglise est une: Hommage à Moehler* (Paris: Bloud et Gay, 1939), 255–69.

[31] Congar, *Une vie pour la vérité*, 48.

[32] Ibid.

[33] To be sure, Congar did criticize Möhler's early work as too focused on pneumatology and insufficiently recognizing the need for the connection between Christology and ecclesiology. See Congar, 'Johann Adam Möhler', 50. The notion of a 'continued Incarnation' also influenced Marie-Dominique Chenu and Yves Congar. See Chap. 4, sect.: Desacralization and Signs of the Times; and Chap. 7, sect.: Church as Return to the Trinity.

To understand why Möhler's theology was so attractive to *nouvelle théologie*, we need to analyse several aspects of his theology in more detail. In what follows, I will focus mainly on Möhler's early work, especially on his 1825 book *Einheit in der Kirche*. As we will see, the distinctive elements of his theology were most pronounced in this early work. While one might argue that his later theology provided a necessary balance to his earlier thought, the impact of Möhler on *nouvelle théologie* came mostly through *Einheit in der Kirche*. The sacramental cast of Möhler's first book appealed to Congar: 'This priority of the realities of grace, and even of uncreated grace, made Möhler get back to the inspiration of the early ecclesiology, which one may characterize, in terms inspired by St Augustine, by attention paid to the *res* [reality], more than to the *sacramentum* [sacrament], to the interior reality of life more than to the mediations and to the external structures.'[34]

Möhler intended *Einheit in der Kirche* as a project of *ressourcement*. As the subtitle indicated, he presented here the 'principle of Catholicism' in 'the Spirit of the Church Fathers of the First Three Centuries'. His enthusiasm for the Church Fathers, he indicated in a letter to his friend, Joseph Lipp, stemmed from the fact that in the Fathers he 'discovered for the first time a living, fresh, full Christianity'.[35] As a result, his argument for the unity of the Church was supported by continuous references to the ante-Nicene Fathers, to whose views he appealed with the obvious intent of drawing normative ecclesiological conclusions. Consequently, we find Möhler looking wistfully to the situation prior to the Constantinian settlement in an 1823 review of a volume on the early Church by the Münster church historian Theodor Katerkamp (1764–1834). Reflecting on the forced secularization of German Catholicism after the 1794 French Rhineland occupation, Möhler commented,

In all the calamities which we bemoan, if we look to what is essential, things have never been better for the Catholic Church than at the present. We have been forced to look to ourselves for help; previously we looked to external circumstances for it. Riches and pomp have never been healthy for the church, otherwise the ancient church would have been most unfortunate.[36]

Möhler's turn to the early Church as a source of inspiration coincided with the general tendency among the Tübingen theologians to advocate a separation between Church and state. Möhler's teacher, Johann Sebastian Drey, held to a similar view on the Church–state relationship, and he, too, appreciated the spiritual benefits that might come with the secularization of the Church.[37]

---

[34] Congar, 'Johann Adam Möhler', 47–9.
[35] Quot. Peter C. Erb, Introduction, Möhler, *Unity*, 1.
[36] Johann Adam Möhler, review in *TQ* 5 (1823), 486 (quot. Himes, *Ongoing Incarnation*, 64).
[37] James Tunstead Burtchaell, 'Drey, Möhler and the School of Tübingen', in Ninian Smart et al. (eds), *Nineteenth-century Religious Thought in the West*, ii (Cambridge: Cambridge University Press, 1985), 118–19.

Möhler was particularly interested in the pre-Nicene period because of the flexibility he observed there in terms of church polity and because of the early Church's willingness to follow the leading of the Spirit. It was the presence of the Spirit in the Church that he wanted to take as the starting-point of his own ecclesiology. He divided *Einheit in der Kirche* into two parts, the first dealing with the 'unity of the Spirit of the Church' and the second with the 'unity of the Body of the Church', thus moving from the internal principle of the Spirit to external ecclesial forms. Adopting the sacramental language that we noted in Congar, we might say that Möhler wanted to start with the sacramental reality (*res*), in order to discuss next the outward sacramental forms (*sacramentum*). In his preface, Möhler acknowledged that his pneumatological starting-point might 'appear strange', but he explained it by expressing his desire to begin 'with what is temporally first in our becoming Christians'.[38] The mystical unity of the Church, Möhler argued at the outset of his book, was the result of 'the Spirit *essentially* (*ousiōdōs*) communicating itself to believers'. Quoting the first-century Pope, St Clement of Rome, Möhler insisted that Christ was the 'life-giving and life-forming principle to which his true disciples are related, as the spirit in a person is to the body',[39] implying that all believers 'through the Spirit' 'are held and bound together as a whole so that the *one* spirit of believers is the action of the *one* divine Spirit'.[40] Möhler's ecclesiology thus moved from the inside out. With the Spirit first communicating a new 'life principle' (*Lebensprinzip*) to the apostles, 'the new divine life is to flow out from those already made alive. Such begetting is to bring about further begetting.'[41]

Two aspects are of particular significance in connection with these appeals to the Spirit's presence in the Church. First, in no way did Möhler mean to imply that the Spirit was the possession of individual Christians by themselves. Influenced as he was by Romantic idealism, and particularly by F. W. J. Schelling (1775–1854), Möhler was convinced that the Spirit provided the foundation for communal, ecclesial unity. For the Church Fathers, it was impossible, he insisted, that a self-taught individual could declare the Christian faith on his own. 'No one since the beginning of the Church' has ever been self-baptized, offered Communion to himself or laid hands upon himself.[42] It was 'impossible', he maintained, 'for an individual to form doctrines by himself or herself'.[43] Inveighing against 'egotistical' Christianity throughout his work,[44] Möhler declared the focus on the individual at the cost of the community as the basic ingredient of heresy: 'This is the essence of every heresy and the basis of its nothingness: it wishes to raise the limited individuality of its master to

---

[38] Möhler, *Unity*, 77.   [39] Ibid. §1, p. 82.
[40] Ibid. §1, p. 83.   [41] Ibid. §3, p. 85.
[42] Ibid. §3, p. 86.   [43] Ibid. §10, p. 102.
[44] e.g., ibid. §11, p. 104; §13, p. 110; §17, p. 120; §18, p. 124; §27, p. 143; §31, pp. 152–3; §34, pp. 162, 164.

generality.'⁴⁵ Protestantism, Möhler believed, went wrong precisely by consistently carrying through the 'egotistical principle'.⁴⁶

Second, the pneumatological starting-point implied a priority of experience over doctrine. Without meaning to denigrate the importance of the latter, Möhler none the less believed that Christian experience lay at the root of Christian doctrine, which really was the expression of the experiential life of faith. At times, this made him sound like Friedrich Schleiermacher (1768–1834), who appears to have influenced him especially during this early period of his life. Möhler commented, for example:

All the apostles together obtained the Holy Spirit before they proclaimed their inner stirrings, their inner faith. Like the apostles, we must say of ourselves in every case that we do not understand the doctrine, the intelligible expression of the new life communicated through the Holy Spirit, before we have received the life principle itself.⁴⁷

Möhler described the unity of Christian doctrine as 'the utterance of one inner religious life, as well as the expression of one and the same Spirit'.⁴⁸ 'Christianity', he typically insisted, 'is no mere concept but a matter to be understood as grasping the whole person and having rooted itself in that person's life.'⁴⁹ In line with this view of doctrine, Möhler interpreted heresy as 'the attempt to discover Christianity by mere thought (we are speaking here especially of the mystical separatists), without consideration for the common Christian life and that which arises from it.'⁵⁰ Understandably, Möhler's starting-point in the Christian life meant that he had little confidence in the convincing power of the rational proofs of the preambles of the faith (*praeambula fidei*).⁵¹

---

⁴⁵ Ibid. §44, p. 190. Cf. ibid. §18, p. 124. Since he regarded heresy as inherently divisive, and thus as mere negation, Möhler denied it proper being and regarded it as outside the Kingdom of God (ibid. §32, p. 158).

⁴⁶ Ibid. 30, p. 152.

⁴⁷ Ibid. §8, pp. 96–7. Cf. ibid. §13, p. 111: 'Christianity does not consist in expressions, formulae, or figures of speech; it is an inner life, a holy power, and all doctrinal concepts and dogmas have value only insofar as they express the inner life that is present within them. Indeed, as a concept, which is always confined, dogma does not embrace and create life, the unspeakable, and it is always defective. However, as life, it is also not communicable and cannot be fixed; this occurs through explanations in concepts, through expressions.'

⁴⁸ Ibid. §9, p. 99. Himes describes Möhler's affinity to Schleiermacher's panentheism during this period, and he explains Möhler's later work as a move away from Schleiermacher's near-pantheist implications. Himes also points out, however, that from the outset, Möhler had reservations with regard to Schleiermacher's lack of a theology of the Fall and with his identification of the Holy Spirit as the communal Spirit (*Gemeingeist*) of the community (*Ongoing Incarnation*, 88, 115). George B. Gilmore also highlights Möhler's differences with Schleiermacher and Hegel ('J. A. Möhler on Doctrinal Development', *HeyJ* 19 (1978), 383–98).

⁴⁹ Möhler, *Unity*, §4, p. 89. Cf. ibid. §5, p. 91.

⁵⁰ Ibid. §18, pp. 123–4.

⁵¹ Himes, *Ongoing Incarnation*, 76.

Development of Doctrine

Möhler was too careful a theologian, however, simply to buy into a 'fall para-digm' of historiography by interpreting later ecclesial developments as a disas-trous betrayal of the purity of early Christianity.[52] The pre-Nicene period was not simply a golden age to which one had to call the Church to return. When describing the changing role of the bishop in the early church, Möhler accepted the inevitability of these developments. While at first the bishop had simply been an expression of the love and unity of the Church, 'considered part of the congregation' and 'not raised above the others',[53] this had begun to change once people started coming to the Church 'out of impure motives'.[54] Now, the bishop had come to represent the 'law' to those who were weak and unholy.[55] As a result, the bishop had 'seemed to act often *without* and *against* the will of the majority of the congregation'. Möhler refused to condemn the increasing con-centration of power in the person of the bishop: 'How can a poor historical [*historisch*] judgement now conclude that it was the pride and search for power on the part of the bishops that changed their relationship to the people? It was not characteristically the bishops who raised themselves up, but the people who sank, and as a result the bishops obviously appeared higher and more powerful than earlier.'[56]

Likewise, Möhler believed that the centralizing developments—from bishop, via metropolitan and entire episcopate, to papacy—had been inevitable and needed to be accepted as positive.[57] It had been 'Christianity's inner forming impulse' that had been 'the true basis for the union of the metropolitanate'.[58] And, while Möhler admitted he had doubted for 'a long time' whether the primacy of one Church was characteristic of Catholicism,[59] he none the less had come to accept it because of his organic view of history: 'In the succession described a member is lacking, the keystone of the whole. In a complete organism, as in the universal whole, individual parts are organic so that each member is seen as a type of the whole, and the power forming the whole repeats its basic form within individual parts.'[60] To look, therefore, to the early

---

[52] Cf. Henry Raphael Nienaltowski, *Johann Adam Möhler's Theory of Doctrinal Development: Its Genesis and Formulation* (Washington, DC: Catholic University of America Press, 1959), 14–16. For a helpful analysis and critique of the 'fall paradigm', see D. H. Williams, *Retrieving the Tradition and Renewing Evangelicalism: A Primer for Suspicious Protestants* (Grand Rapids, Mich.: Eerdmans, 1999).

[53] Möhler, *Unity,* §55, p. 226.

[54] Ibid. §55, p. 227.

[55] Ibid.

[56] Ibid. §55, p. 228 (square brackets in original).

[57] At the same time, Möhler's organic approach, starting with the experience of the Spirit in the community faith, was a reaction against the common medieval, juridical ecclesiology. See Dennis M. Doyle, 'Möhler, Schleiermacher, and the Roots of Communion Ecclesiology', *TS* 57 (1996), 469, 479.

[58] Möhler, *Unity,* §56, p. 231.   [59] Ibid. §67, p. 255.   [60] Ibid.

Church for evidence in support of papal primacy would be to ignore the proper development of the ecclesial organism. Such a quest would be to desire 'something excessive', which 'was not possible according to the law of true development'.[61]

Clearly, then, Möhler's project of *ressourcement* did not imply a simple repristination of pre-Nicene Christianity. He even went so far as to say that 'the majority of heretics designated *primitive Christianity* as the point to which one must return'.[62] Such an idealizing of the early Church resulted from the heretical view of Christianity 'not as something living, but as a dead, conceptual matter that needed, and was capable of, no development, and could be returned to in a mechanistic way'.[63] Möhler instead attempted to balance the need for *ressourcement* with his belief in a Tradition whose ongoing development one had to accept as essentially positive.

The notion of the Church as an organism that grows and develops over time raises the question how exactly Möhler balanced the conserving and forward-looking elements that were both inherent in the Tradition. He first introduced the notion of Tradition in *Einheit in der Kirche* by commenting: 'This spiritual power of life that perpetuates and transmits itself in the Church is tradition, the inner, mysterious aspect of the Church that draws back from all scrutiny.'[64] Tradition, for Möhler, was a function of the Holy Spirit, whose unifying presence guaranteed the continuation of the truth in the Church. This meant that the conserving aspect of the Tradition was dear to Möhler's heart. Searching for truth was a matter of inquiring after the Tradition: 'The question "What is Christian doctrine?" is completely historical [*historisch*]. It asks, "What has always been taught in the Church from the time of the apostles? What does the *common, enduring* transmission say?".'[65] As a result, the mere occurrence of doctrinal novelty had been sufficient indication to believers in the early Church that they were facing false teaching. Demonstration of the 'continuing faith' of the Church 'occurred by means of the unbroken episcopal succession from the time of the apostles'.[66] While an appeal to Tradition could not provide 'proof' of any individual Christian doctrine, none the less, the presence of 'novelties' was adequate within the Church 'to refute those who establish foreign developments in the territory of the Church'.[67] J. R. Geiselmann sums up Möhler's insistence on the unchangeable character of Christian doctrine by commenting:

For how could a later time know better than an earlier what it is that has been inherited and that constitutes the apostolic doctrine which has been handed down? A change is excluded also because the determinations regarding the inherited doctrine take place

---

[61] Ibid. §68, p. 257.   [62] Ibid. §18, p. 126.
[63] Ibid. §18, p. 127.   [64] Ibid. §3, p. 86.
[65] Ibid. §10, p. 102 (square brackets in original).
[66] Ibid. §11, p. 104.   [67] Ibid. §12, p. 108.

under the guidance of the Holy Spirit. If the later pronouncement about this would contradict an earlier one, the Holy Spirit would contradict himself.[68]

Clearly, Möhler inherited from the Church Fathers a sense of the 'unchangeable' character of the faith throughout the Christian Tradition.[69]

At the same time, we have already seen that Möhler's acceptance of an increasingly centralized church polity was predicated on his belief that genuine historical developments had taken place. How was one to explain them? In line with his understanding of doctrine as the expression of the inner life of the Church, Möhler did not adopt the logical explanation of development that would gain currency especially later on in the nineteenth century through the impact of the Leonine neo-Thomist revival. According to this 'intellectual' or 'logical' view, later doctrinal developments were largely the logical conclusions drawn from original divine revelation along with non-revealed premises.[70] The advantage of this view was that it made it easy to combine continuity of identity with development: on the one hand, logical conclusions did not go beyond their premises, thus safeguarding the unchangeable character of doctrine; on the other hand, the new insight gained by the conclusions explained why they had not been noted before. Möhler was far too Romantically inclined, and his understanding of the nature of theology far too experience based, to allow for such an explanation. This meant, of course, that he was forced to look for a different answer to the question of how to combine the unchangeable character of the faith with true development.

Möhler found the solution in his understanding of the Holy Spirit within the community as the impetus for the life of the Church. As a result, he distinguished between the Christian consciousness of the Church and the doctrinal expressions of this consciousness:

Since Christianity is seen as a new divine life given to people, not as a dead concept, it is capable of development and cultivation... The identity of the consciousness of the Church in the various moments of its existence thus in no way needs a mechanistic protection: *The inner unity of life must be preserved or it will not always be the same Christian Church; but the same consciousness develops, the same life unfolds itself ever more; is always more specific; makes itself always clearer. The Church attains to the humanity of Christ.* These forms are the characteristic *developments of the life* of the Church, and tradition

---

[68] Josef Rupert Geiselmann, *Die katholische Tübinger Schule: Ihre theologische Eigenart* (Freiburg: Herder, 1965), 75.

[69] Möhler, *Unity,* §12, p. 109. Cf. ibid. §35, p. 168.

[70] For the many nuances within the neo-Thomist perspective on this point, see Gezinus Evert Meuleman, *De ontwikkeling van het dogma in de Rooms Katholieke theologie* (Kampen: Kok, 1951), 31–51; Herbert Hammans, *Die neueren katholischen Erklärungen der Dogmenentwicklung* (Essen: Ludgerus-Verlag Hubert Wingen KG, 1965), 119–73; Owen Chadwick, *From Bossuet to Newman: The Idea of Doctrinal Development* (2nd edn, Cambridge: Cambridge University Press, 1987), 21–48; Aidan Nichols, *From Newman to Congar: The Idea of Doctrinal Development from the Victorians to the Second Vatican Council* (Edinburgh: T. & T. Clark, 1990), 136–94.

contains these successive unfoldings of the higher seed of life by protecting the inner unity of life itself.[71]

Möhler's distinction between a common Christian spirit (*Gemeingeist*) and specific Christian doctrines might appear to introduce a thoroughgoing subjectivism. And it is certainly true he was wary of doctrinal abstractions. His sharp denunciation of a 'dead concept' type of Christianity went hand in hand with an equally vehement rejection of the Protestant *sola scriptura* position. Scripture and Tradition, Möhler insisted, were not to be regarded as two distinct sources but were inseparable. This meant that 'the Scriptures, composed only in the Church and intended for the Church, are only understood in her and cannot be set in contradiction to the living gospel'.[72] Scripture was, in fact, 'the first member in the written tradition'.[73] It was his conviction that Tradition functioned as the expression of the Spirit that led Möhler to his rejection of the *sola scriptura* principle.[74] And, as we have just seen, it is also true that for Möhler development was far more than drawing logical conclusions from revealed principles. Although he did not explicitly confront himself with the logical explanation of the scholastic tradition, his prioritizing of 'life' over 'ideas' was at odds with such a viewpoint. For Möhler, this position was no less rationalist in its basic principles than the Protestant view. His Romanticism, taking its cue from the continuous presence of the Spirit in history, clashed with rationalist presuppositions, whether they were Protestant or Catholic in provenance.

Already in *Einheit in der Kirche* Möhler nevertheless also tried to guard against an overly subjectivist understanding of doctrine. It is true that in this book the magisterium appeared mostly as the focal point of the unity of the Church and thus as the supreme instance of the Christian *Gemeingeist*. Or, as Hammans puts it, for Möhler the Church was built up 'from the inside to the outside'.[75] As a result, the consent of the faithful (*consensus fidelium*) was crucial to Möhler, certainly at this stage of his thinking. But he did accept at least some kind of determining role for the magisterium, even if he did not place a great deal of emphasis on it. We have already seen that he believed that bishops in the early Church had not been afraid to oppose themselves to the majority of their congregations. Furthermore, already at this point in his career Möhler expressed

---

[71] Möhler, *Unity*, §13, pp. 111–12 (emphasis in original). Möhler similarly explained that Christians' 'intuited, living' consciousness yielded material for their 'intuiting, reflecting' consciousness (ibid. §19, p. 127).

[72] Ibid. §15, p. 114. Cf. ibid. §16, p. 117.

[73] Ibid. §16, p. 117.

[74] Cf. ibid.: 'If it is said that Scripture alone is enough for the Christian, one is justified in asking the meaning of this assertion. Scripture alone, apart from our apprehension, is nothing at all; it is a dead letter. Only the product, which comes into light by the direction of our spiritual activities from the Scripture, is something.'

[75] Hammans, *Die neueren katholischen Erklärungen*, 29.

his apprehension of the idea of a purely invisible Church.[76] While he did not employ sacramental language to describe it, it would be fair to conclude that Möhler did not neglect objective ecclesial structures as sacramental means to obtain the internal grace of the Holy Spirit.

Beyond *Einheit*: Christology and Human Responsibility

Möhler became increasingly concerned about the subjectivist pitfalls to which his strictly pneumatological starting-point might lead. Soon after the publication of *Einheit in der Kirche*, two significant new elements—Christology and human responsibility—made their way into his writing.[77] Möhler's two next major books, *Athanasius der Grosse* (1827) and *Symbolik* (1832), gave increasing evidence of his new insights.[78] Both new elements would strengthen the sacramental pattern of his ecclesiology and of his understanding of doctrinal development. First, he began to recognize the need for a Christological ingredient to his ecclesiology. This had the effect of countering any possible pantheist implications that his earlier emphasis on the spiritual life-principle of the community might have had. The Church, he now maintained, had its origin not simply in Pentecost, but first of all in the Incarnation.

This new Christological element in no way lessened his emphasis on the divine character of the Church. In fact, Möhler came boldly to identify Christ and the Church by speaking of the latter as a continuation of the Incarnation. Insisting that the visibility of the Church had to be grounded in the doctrine of the Incarnation, Möhler commented in an oft-quoted passage: 'Thus, the visible Church, from the point of view here taken, is the Son of God himself, everlastingly manifesting himself among men in a human form, perpetually renovated, and eternally young—the permanent incarnation of the same, as in Holy Writ, even the faithful are called "the body of Christ".'[79]

---

[76] Thus, Möhler commented: 'The thought of an invisible Church founded on earth by Christ is so completely opposed to Christianity, however, that only the visible Church was assumed by Jesus Christ, by his apostles, and by the early Church' (*Unity*, §49, p. 211). Gustav Voss points out that already at this point Möhler was convinced that without the magisterium 'there would be neither tradition nor the true Catholic *Gemeinsinn*' ('Johann Adam Möhler and the Development of Dogma', *TS* 4 (1943), 441).

[77] The changes are generally recognized. They are most carefully documented, also with reference to Möhler's other publications, in Himes, *Ongoing Incarnation, passim*. For a helpful brief outline of the changes, see Geiselmann, *Die katholische Tübinger Schule*, 76–84. Yves Congar was quite aware of Möhler's changing views, highlighting the latter's increasingly combative stance towards Protestantism. See Congar, 'Sur l'évolution'.

[78] Johann Adam Möhler, *Athanasius der Grosse und die Kirche seiner Zeit, besonders im Kampfe mit dem Arianismus* (Mainz: Kupferberg, 1827); id., *Symbolik oder Darstellung der dogmatischen Gegensätze der Katholiken und Protestanten nach ihren öffentlichen Bekenntnisschriften* (Mainz: Kupferberg, 1832); English trans.: *Symbolism: Exposition of the Doctrinal Differences between Catholics and Protestants as Evidenced by their Symbolical Writings*, trans. James Burton Robertson (New York: Crossroad, 1997).

[79] Möhler, *Symbolism*, §36, p. 259.

Second, Möhler moved away from Schleiermacher's influence on his earlier theology (with the Spirit directly providing the inner life principle for the believers) by insisting more strongly on the human aspect of the Church (with the Spirit working mediately through created realities). The new incarnational bent of his ecclesiology was able to do justice to this human aspect. Möhler started patterning his ecclesiology on the Chalcedonian formula of a union without confusion of the two natures of Christ. The Church, as his continuing Incarnation, was both divine and human: 'Nay, as in Christ the divinity and the humanity are to be clearly distinguished, though both are bound in unity; so is he in undivided entireness perpetuated in the Church.'[80] Michael J. Himes comments on the theological significance of this new theological understanding:

The classic christological formula from the council of Chalcedon, one person and two natures, inseparably united but never confused, answers the need for a new pattern of the God–world relation. Möhler specifically notes that God and humanity are kept clearly distinguished even though Christ is called 'the unity of all the faithful'. Here is a principle of unity for the church which avoids the divinization of the community, the result of basing an ecclesiology on a panentheist model, which ends by deifying the human pole of the God–humankind relation.[81]

If the early Möhler's Romanticism had unduly focused on divine immanence, the use of a Christological prism for his ecclesiology entailed a more robust sacramental position: Möhler no longer just insisted on the divine character of the Church, but he now accepted, at the same time, the intrinsic value of the Church's human character.

This recognition of the human pole resulted in a much stronger focus on the role of the magisterium in the development of doctrine and in a clearer recognition of the significance of the doctrinal contents of the Christian faith.[82] With regard to the magisterium, Möhler now recognized the validity of the questions that *Einheit in der Kirche* was bound to raise: in the face of heresy, how could one discern the organic life of the Spirit in the Church? How could one make binding decisions if one did not sufficiently distinguish the Holy Spirit from the spirit of the community? Much more unequivocally than *Einheit in der Kirche* did *Symbolik* assert the authoritative role of the magisterium. Discussing the fact that the Church had come to a deeper consciousness of the truth as the result of contest and struggle, Möhler commented: 'It explains the necessity of a living, visible authority which in every dispute can, with certainty, discern the truth, and separate it from error. Otherwise, we should have *only* the variable—the disputed—and at last Nihilism itself.'[83] Even more strongly than in his earlier

---

[80] Ibid.
[81] Himes, *Ongoing Incarnation*, 189–90. Cf. ibid. 201, 260, 307.
[82] Cf. Nienaltowski, *Johann Adam Möhler's Theory of Doctrinal Development*, 27–32.
[83] Möhler, *Symbolism*, §40, p. 292.

work did Möhler assert the ecclesial context for the interpretation of Scripture.[84]
As Hammans puts it, for Möhler, the development of doctrine is 'tied to contest
and struggle, to history. Here the dialectic shows itself again. This fact explains
the necessity of a visible, living authority, which recognizes in every contest the
truth and distinguishes it from error'.[85]

   In *Symbolik*, Möhler also articulated more precisely what it was that developed
in Christian doctrine. The reader of *Einheit in der Kirche* might easily conclude
that Möhler believed that the only factor that was constant in the development of
doctrine was the organically developing *Gemeingeist*, while particular doctrines
continuously changed.[86] In *Symbolik*, however, Möhler made crystal clear that
Christian doctrines themselves contained changeable *and* unchangeable aspects.
As a result, he paid more attention to the unchangeable character of Christian
doctrine.[87] He distinguished between the 'substance' of Christian doctrine and
the 'form' in which it was passed down through the centuries. The 'form' of
doctrine, Möhler argued, developed and changed. As a result, the original
doctrine 'remained the original, and yet did not; it was the same in substance,
and yet differed as to form'.[88] To be sure, he still explained the changes in 'form'
in a way that could not but unnerve theologians with an 'intellectual' or 'logical'
view of development (for whom development could never move beyond the
conclusions of rational argumentation). 'This form', claimed Möhler, 'is in itself
the human, the temporal, the perishable element, and might be exchanged for
a hundred others'.[89] As we will see in the next chapter, a very similar approach
would cause a great deal of trouble for Henri Bouillard in the 1940s. Considering, however, Möhler's earlier work, his distinction between 'substance' and
'form' implied a clear nod in the direction of the integrity of Christian doctrine.

MAURICE BLONDEL AND THE 'METHOD OF IMMANENCE'

The Dynamism of Human Action

If the Romantically inclined Möhler stressed the immanence of the Spirit, the
subjective nature of the Christian faith, and the historical character of developing
doctrine, the focus on 'human action' in Maurice Blondel resulted in similar

---

    [84] Möhler, *Symbolism*, §38, p. 278; §39, pp. 282–8. To be sure, Möhler had already maintained
the ecclesial framework for biblical interpretation in *Unity*, §18, p. 126. Cf. Hammans, *Die neueren
katholischen Erklärungen*, 32–3. Cf. Voss, 'Johann Adam Möhler', 441–3.
    [85] Hammans, *Die neueren katholischen Erklärungen*, 32–3.
    [86] In fairness, in *Unity*, Möhler's first addendum had cautioned against a pantheist understanding
of the role of the Spirit (*Unity*, 269–72).
    [87] Hammans, *Die neueren katholischen Erklärungen*, 32.
    [88] Möhler, *Symbolism*, §40, p. 289.
    [89] Ibid. §40, p. 290.

emphases. As a result, the philosopher from Aix-en-Provence found avid readers among the *nouvelle* theologians, particularly in the two Fourvière scholars, Henri de Lubac and Henri Bouillard.[90] Blondel had a great impact on Henri de Lubac, perhaps more so than anyone else. Étienne Fouilloux goes so far as to describe de Lubac's work as, 'in large measure, the theological extension of the philosophy of action' that Blondel had advocated.[91] De Lubac mentioned him, along with Joseph Maréchal and Pierre Rousselot, as the contemporaries to whom he owed 'a particular debt'.[92] Blondel's notion of Tradition as he had developed it in his 1904 *Histoire et dogme* presented to de Lubac a way forward in a theological climate dominated by neo-scholasticism. Furthermore, for Blondel, as for de Lubac, the Eucharist lay at the centre of his life and thought.[93]

Most significantly, perhaps, Blondel's insistence on an organic relationship between nature and the supernatural profoundly shaped de Lubac's approach.[94] In his *Petite catéchèse sur nature et grace* (1980), de Lubac looked back to his early discovery of Blondel. Blondel, de Lubac explained, was 'the one who launched the decisive attack on the dualist theory which was destroying Christian thought. Time after time he demonstrated the deficiencies of the thesis of the "extrinsicist" school'.[95] Blondel's opposition both to what he called 'extrinsicism' (the neo-Thomist outside imposition of divine grace on the realm of nature) and to what he termed 'historicism' or 'immanentism' (the Modernist and secular exclusion of any supernatural impact on historical cause and effect) provides, I believe, the key to de Lubac's sacramental ontology.

At least partially as a result of his reading of Blondel, Henri Bouillard acquired a passion for finding a point of contact for divine grace in the actual lives and realities of the people whom God addressed with his revelation and grace. Perhaps no one exercised as decisive an influence on Bouillard's thought as the philosopher from Aix. Bouillard remarked that he recognized in Blondel's

[90] Blondel's influence on the Jesuits of Lyons-Fourvière dates from around 1901, when Auguste Valensin, a student of Blondel at Aix, introduced him to the Jesuit scholasticate, then located on the Isle of Jersey. Blondel would have a profound impact not only on de Lubac and Bouillard, but also on Gaston Fessard and Yves de Montcheuil. See Étienne Fouilloux, *Une Église en quête de liberté: La pensée catholique française entre modernisme et Vatican II (1914–1962)* (Paris: Desclée de Brouwer, 1998), 174–81.

[91] Ibid. 178.

[92] De Lubac, *At the Service of the Church: Henri de Lubac Reflects on the Circumstances that Occasioned his Writings*, trans. Anne Elizabeth Englund (San Francisco, Calif.: Ignatius, 1993), 19.

[93] Paul McPartlan, *The Eucharist Makes the Church: Henri de Lubac and John Zizioulas in Dialogue* (Edinburgh: T. & T. Clark, 1993), 13.

[94] When he studied philosophy (1920–3), de Lubac had already read, 'with enthusiasm', Blondel's *L'Action* (1893) and his *Lettre d'apologétique* (1896). During this time, in 1922, de Lubac had also paid Blondel a visit. See de Lubac, *At the Service of the Church*, 18–19. For a detailed account of Blondel's influence on de Lubac, see Antonio Russo, *Henri de Lubac: Teologia e dogma nella storia: L'Influsso di Blondel* (Rome: Edizioni Studium, 1990). See also Kevin L. Hughes, 'The "Fourfold Sense": De Lubac, Blondel and Contemporary Theology', *HeyJ* 42 (2001), 451–62. Cf. also de Lubac, *A Brief Catechesis on Nature and Grace*, trans. Richard Arnandez (San Francisco, Calif.: Ignatius, 1984), 37–8.

[95] De Lubac, *Brief Catechesis*, 37–8.

doctoral dissertation, *L'Action* (1893), a masterpiece.[96] There is little doubt that part of the reason why the neo-Thomists came to suspect Bouillard of relativism was the fact that Blondelian traces could be found throughout his writings.[97] While it was only in 1961 that Bouillard wrote his book, *Blondel et le christianisme*, he already published two key essays on Blondel's philosophy in 1949 and 1950, both of which he would later incorporate in his book.[98] In fact, Bouillard indicated that it was around 1930, long before his doctoral work on Thomas Aquinas, that he had first read Blondel's *L'Action*.[99] A careful reading of Bouillard's 1941 dissertation on St Thomas Aquinas makes clear that, even if Bouillard did not yet overtly appeal to Blondel, the latter's 'logic of action', with its focus on human action and experience, none the less already influenced Bouillard's approach.[100] Blondel was clearly an influential figure among the *nouvelle* theologians.

Interestingly, John Milbank maintains that Blondel, 'more than anyone else, points us beyond secular reason'.[101] This verdict sounds, at least initially, counter-intuitive. Didn't Blondel's philosophy collude with nearly all the failures of modernity? His apparent neo-Kantianism, his rejection of a realist epistemology, his consequent moral pragmatism, his prioritizing of action over being, his 'method of immanence', his voluntarism, and his inability to ground the Christian faith rationally all seemed to indicate to his neo-Thomist contemporaries that Blondel pointed *to* rather than *beyond* secular reason.

It is none the less warranted to take a closer look at the French philosopher, whose 'logic of action' would have such a profound influence on *nouvelle théologie*. Blondel looked to the logic of the lived lives of human beings—action—as the place where philosophy should begin. He opened his 1893 dissertation in a direct, perhaps even strident, fashion:

Yes or no, does human life make sense, and does man have a destiny? I act, but without even knowing what action is, without having wished to live, without knowing exactly either who I am or even if I am ... The problem is inevitable; man resolves it inevitably; and this solution, true or false, but voluntary at the same time as necessary, each one bears it in his actions. That is why we must study *action*: the very meaning of the word and the richness of its contents will unfold little by little.[102]

[96] Bouillard, *Blondel and Christianity*, trans. James M. Somerville (Washington, DC: Corpus, 1969), 5. Bouillard referred to Blondel, *L'Action: Essai d'une critique de la vie et d'une science de la pratique* (Paris: Alcan, 1893); English trans.: *Action (1893): Essay on a Critique of Life and a Science of Practice*, trans. Olivia Blanchette (Notre Dame, Ind.: University of Notre Dame Press, 1984).
[97] By protesting 'I make no profession of being a Blondelian' Bouillard made clear, in fact, how deeply his sympathies ran (*Blondel and Christianity*, 102).
[98] Bouillard, 'L'Intention fondamentale de Maurice Blondel et la théologie', *RSR* 36 (1949), 321–402; id., 'Maurice Blondel et la théologie', *RSR* 37 (1950), 105–12.
[99] Id., *Blondel and Christianity*, p. ix.
[100] Cf. Karl-Heinz Neufeld, 'Fundamentaltheologie in gewandelter Welt: H. Bouillards theologischer Beitrag', *ZKT* 100 (1978), 428.
[101] John Milbank, *Theology and Social Theory: Beyond Secular Reason* (Oxford: Blackwell, 1990), 219.
[102] Blondel, *Action*, 3.

The inevitability of human action and, at the same time, its inability to arrive at its true goal lay, Blondel averred, at the root of the human predicament. Whenever our will imposed itself on a particular object, it turned out that our will actually transcended that object, so that a will disproportionally emerged between the simple object of our will—that is, the 'willed will' (*la volonté voulue*)—and the underlying spiritual dynamism—the 'willing will' (*la volonté voulante*)—which lay at the basis of our action. The immanent dynamism of human action was thus unable to find true satisfaction.

According to Blondel, our acting and desiring were attempts to reach beyond what we actually encountered in any of the objects that we willed. We were ultimately faced, therefore, with a 'supreme option'—that of acknowledging what Blondel called the transcendent 'one thing necessary' (*l'unique nécessaire*). Only this supernatural 'one thing necessary' corresponded fully to everything contained in the desire of the 'willing will'. Thus, the 'one thing necessary' allowed the will to will itself. This dynamic élan of human action took its starting-point in the realization of the inadequacy of every human act and in the yearning for full correspondence (*adaequatio*) between mind and life—that is to say, between what we will and what, in fact, we accomplish in our actions. Needless to say, this approach implied a radical departure from the Thomist understanding of truth as correspondence between mind and reality.[103] With good reason, then, does Wayne Hankey recognize in Blondel's thought a kinship to Neoplatonism that the traditional rational metaphysics of neo-Thomism had been unable to accommodate.[104]

When, after a lengthy account of the ultimately ineffective immanent journey of the human will, Blondel arrived at the fifth and final part of *L'Action*, he commented: '[A]ll that has gone before results in making us conscious of an incurable disproportion between the *élan* of the will and the human end of action.'[105] In other words, immanent human action itself turned out to be incapable of uniting the *volonté voulue* with the *volonté voulante*. For Blondel, this meant that philosophy was in need of theology:

They want philosophy to have its proper and independent domain. Theology wants the same with and for philosophy. Both the one and the other demand a separation of competences; they remain distinct from one another, but distinct in view of an effective

---

[103] Cf. Blondel's comment: 'The abstract and fanciful *adaequatio rei et intellectus* gets replaced by the legitimate methodical investigation, the *adaequatio realis mentis et vitae*' ('Le Point de départ de la recherche philosophique', *APC* 152 (1906), 235; cf. also id., *Action*, 283). On this point, Bouillard took his cue from Blondel. See below in Chap. 3, sect.: Fear of Relativism.

[104] Wayne J. Hankey, *One Hundred Years of Neoplatonism in France: A Brief Philosophical History* (Louvain: Peeters, 2006), 131–41. Hankey points out that the connection between Blondel and Neoplatonism was noted both by Henry Duméry and by Jean Trouillard, who drew their inspiration from him. See Henry Duméry, *La Philosophie de l'action: Essai sur l'intellectualisme blondélien* (Paris: Aubier/Montaigne, 1948), 114; Jean Trouillard, 'Pluralité spirituelle et unité normative selon Blondel', *ArchPhil* 24 (1961), 21–8.

[105] Blondel, *Action*, 358.

cooperation: *non adjutrix nisi libera: non libera nisi adjutrix philosophia* (philosophy is not a helper unless it is free and not free unless it is a helper). The fullness of philosophy consists, not in a presumptuous self-sufficiency, but in the study of its own powerlessness and of the means which are offered from elsewhere to supply for its powerlessness.[106]

By insisting that philosophy could not reach its own completion, Blondel paved the way for positing the hypothesis of Christian revelation. The mediation of the logic of action had prepared the move from unbelief to Christian faith.[107]

Integrating Nature and the Supernatural

The neo-Thomist opposition to Blondel stemmed, in large part, from a desire to uphold a purely rational apologetic. For neo-Thomism, the task of fundamental (or apologetic) theology was not a negative one—namely, to show up the inadequacy of all human willing—but rather a positive one: to prove the fact of divine revelation by means of signs and miracles.[108] Blondel objected that divine revelation did not come 'entirely from the outside like a completely empirical datum'.[109] Taking a swipe at the manualist tradition, he insisted that signs and miracles were in themselves not sufficient to prove the reality of revelation. The meaning of signs and miracles was always a matter of discussion: 'It is the interpretation, it is the interior need, that is everything, because upon this preparation depends whether the light will be blinding or whether the darkness will bring out the brilliance more vividly.'[110] In a biting critique of a retrograde move to thirteenth-century Thomism, Blondel's 1896 *Lettre d'apologétique* rejected the scholastic separation between nature and the supernatural: 'We must not exhaust ourselves refurbishing old arguments and presenting an *object* for acceptance while the *subject* is not disposed to listen.'[111] Thus, like some of the nineteenth-century schools of thought, Blondel, with his philosophy of action, attempted to reintegrate nature and the supernatural. One needed eyes of faith in order to see the brilliance of the light. Blondel's overall intent was to oppose a natural order that would yield the *praeambula fidei* in a purely rational

[106] Blondel, *Action*, 361–2.

[107] It is impossible, within the confines of this chapter, to do justice to the intricacies of the various steps that Blondel traced. They are carefully outlined in Bouillard, *Blondel and Christianity*, 60–77.

[108] For a helpful introduction to the contrast between Blondel's thought and that of neo-Thomist apologetics, see Gregory Baum, 'The Blondelian Shift', in *Man Becoming: God in Secular Experience* (1970; repr. New York: Crossroad/Seabury, 1979), 1–36.

[109] Blondel, *Action*, 363. Comments like this, which appeared not just to *connect* revelation with experience, but to *identify* the two to some extent, seemed to do at least some justice to the charges of neo-Kantianism.

[110] Ibid. 365.

[111] Id., *The Letter on Apologetics and History and Dogma*, trans. and ed. Alexander Dru and Illtyd Trethowan (Grand Rapids, Mich.: Eerdmans, 1994), 146. The French original was published as 'Lettre sur les exigences de la pensée contemporaine en matière d'apologétique et sur la méthode de la philosophie dans l'étude du problème religieux', APC 131 (1896), 337–47, 467–82, 599–616; 132 (1896), 131–47, 225–67, 337–50.

fashion, as though experiential and participative elements did not contribute to conversion.[112]

It is particularly this attack on the neo-Thomist configuration of the *praeambula fidei* that set into motion the opposition, notably through the sharp pens of Marie-Benoît Schwalm (1860–1908) and Hippolyte Gayraud (1856–1911).[113] 'Is there not in the miracle a *special intervention* of God's grace from which reason is to demonstrate divine revelation and the divinity of Christ?' asked Gayraud in exasperation.[114] In rejecting miracles as conclusive evidence, Blondel did not, however, mean to advocate a separation between phenomena and being, as Schwalm maintained. Quite the contrary was, in fact, the case. As Michael Conway puts it: 'At no point in a critical phenomenology would Blondel accept the absolute separation of the phenomena and being, since this would be to go against the very principles of a positive method. In an article published in 1906, he categorically states: "Nothing is more artificial than the claim to distinguish and to absolutely oppose being and the phenomenon".'[115]

To be sure, Schwalm and Gayraud were correct in their assessment that Blondel took a different approach to theology. What they failed to realize, however, was how much of their purely rational apologetic was itself the embodiment of modern positivism. It was an apologetic that failed to recognize that the dynamic movement of historical action could function as a sacramental realization of the supernatural presence of God in time and in space. Blondel, in contrast, sought a way to combine the transcendence of God with the belief that the contingency of human action mattered. Jacob Schmutz rightly insists that Blondel called for 'unification with the principle of thought which is itself *beyond* every intellectual comprehension. This goes back to the clearest criticism: we are not in the presence of a metaphysics of understanding or speculation, but in a metaphysics of union with the very first principle. We are closer to Neoplatonism than to Aristotelianism.'[116] Blondel, it would seem, drew on a mystical Neoplatonism for inspiration in his attempt to avoid the modern separation between nature and the supernatural.[117]

---

[112] Cf. Blondel's comment that 'we cannot arrive at God, affirm him truly...have Him for ourselves, except by belonging to Him and by sacrificing all the rest to Him' (*Action*, 404).

[113] Marie-Benoît Schwalm, 'Les Illusions de l'idéalisme et leurs dangers pour la foi', *RT* 4 (1896), 413–41; Hippolyte Gayraud, 'Une nouvelle apologétique chrétienne', *APC* 35 (1896–7), 257–73, 400–8. Cf. Jean Caron, 'La Discussion entre le P. Schwalm et Maurice Blondel à propos de la méthode d'immanence en apologétique (1895–1898)', in Serge-Thomas Bonino et al. (eds), *Saint Thomas au XXᵉsiècle* (Paris: St-Paul, 1994), 41–52.

[114] Gayraud, 'Une nouvelle apologétique', 260.

[115] Michael A. Conway, 'A Positive Phenomenology: The Structure of Blondel's Early Philosophy', *HeyJ* 47 (2006), 595. Conway refers here to Maurice Blondel (alias François Mallet), 'La Foi et la science', *RCF* 47 (1906), 599 n. 1.

[116] Jacob Schmutz, 'Escaping the Aristotelian Bond: The Critique of Metaphysics in Twentieth-century French Philosophy', *Dionysius* 17 (1999), 184–5. Cf. Hankey, *One Hundred Years*, 140.

[117] Blondel discussed the continuity and discontinuity implied in the distinction between natural and mystical knowledge in 'Le Problème de la mystique', in Maurice Blondel et al. (eds), *Qu'est-ce*

In some of his later writings, Blondel expressed this mystical tendency by his use of the term 'transnatural state' (*état transnaturel*).[118] Speaking of the transnatural state of human beings was a way of saying that all human beings had an innate desire—Thomas's 'intention'—for the vision of God, which came with their being created in the very image of God. Blondel thus avoided a separation between nature and the supernatural, as he argued that, in their actual state, human beings were drawn to God from the beginning. Adam English describes the reality of a transnatural world, as Blondel viewed it, as follows:

> It is not centrifugal, or efferent, spinning beings away from their source into darkness and chaos, turning and turning in the widening gyre, to employ the metaphor of W. B. Yeats. It acts centripetally, like a whirlpool draining everything into its eye. The direction of the movement in the transnatural state is afferent, gravitating all life to the center of the universe, which is, metaphysically speaking, God's own self. It is 'natural to the "transnaturalized" (*transnaturé*) human being to be ordered to "divine beatitude", because there is no other'. By the very nature of reality, men and women are drawn towards relationship with the Father even while the triune God reaches out for them.[119]

To be sure, the mystery of the Christian faith implied, also for Blondel, that it was only by means of a divine rebirth from above that a person would join the divine life. He always remained careful to uphold the gratuity of grace.[120] It was none the less important for Blondel not just to escape the dangers of a pantheist human identification with God, but also those of a deist separation between nature and the supernatural. It seemed to him that the concept of the 'transnatural' avoided a separation between nature and the supernatural and so provided a way of sailing between two equally dangerous cliffs.

Overcoming the Doctrine of Immanence

More was at stake in the controversy surrounding Blondel's work than merely his rejection of a completely self-contained and autonomous philosophical system. The charge of Blondel's collusion with modernity also has to do with the fact that he turned to the human will and thus to the subject as the starting-point for a Christian philosophy. Moreover, his rejection of the traditional correspondence view of truth added fuel to the fire. Blondel appeared to be diametrically opposed

---

que la mystique? Quelques aspects historiques et philosophiques du problème (Paris: Bloud et Gay, 1925), 2–63. Cf. George S. Worgul, 'M. Blondel and the Problem of Mysticism', *ETL* 61 (1985), 100–22.

[118] For the following paragraph, I am indebted especially to Adam C. English, *The Possibility of Christian Philosophy: Maurice Blondel at the Intersection of Theology and Philosophy* (London: Routledge, 2007), 48–52.

[119] English, *Possibility of Christian Philosophy*, 49. English's brief quotation is from Blondel, 'The Third "Testis" Article', trans. Peter J. Bernardi, *Comm* 25 (1999), 869.

[120] Cf. Koen Boey's comment: 'Blondel does not argue that *God must* give himself to man, but does argue that *man must* take into himself the gift—gratuitous from God's point of view—with which Christian revelation is concerned' ('Blondels metafysica van de wil', *Bijdragen* 62 (2001), 336).

to the intellectualism of St Thomas. To theologians like Schwalm, Blondelian philosophy seemed like a neo-Kantian Trojan horse: 'Mr Blondel is neo-Kantian. For him, the "philosophical method" is the Kantian method, pushed to its ultimate phenomenist consequences: [for Blondel] speculative reason knows that we have ideas; it does not know whether these ideas correspond to anything that might be outside us. It is practice, action, which teaches it the objective truth of what it thinks.'[121]

Blondel never accepted the charges of idealism and neo-Kantianism.[122] To be sure, there is no denying that he was influenced by the idealist tradition. But at the heart of his philosophy lay the concern to reach beyond it. Unlike Modernists such as George Tyrrell and Lucien Laberthonnière, Blondel remained convinced of the need for divine revelation coming from the outside. As John McNeill puts it, '[T]he consistent application of the principle [of immanence] must "open an access to the transcendent". Kant, by contrast, had believed that his immanent critical method resulted in an exclusion of all transcendent reality from speculative thought.'[123]

Blondel's insistence on divine revelation and on the need for theology represented, in the words of Adam English, 'a bold but perilous move'.[124] It certainly offended the Sorbonne philosophers. When Blondel first published *L'Action*, they opposed it by reason of its emphasis on transcendence and the literal practice of Catholicism with which the dissertation concluded. Blondel's secular peers recognized that a strong insistence on divine transcendence provided the context and aim of his dynamism of human action. Theology appeared to encapsulate philosophy.[125] Unlike Blondel, the modern rationalism of the Sorbonne faculty took for granted 'the notion of immanence as the basis and very condition of all philosophical doctrine'.[126]

There is little doubt that Blondel's secular critics were correct in their perception. This is precisely why Milbank is convinced that Blondel points beyond secular reason. In Milbank's words, 'The task of philosophy, for Blondel, its truly *scientific* task, is to acknowledge its own inadequacy: for the least thought, as action, escapes it, in (implicitly) acknowledging the plenitude of supernatural super-addition, and the ever-renewed mediation of love.'[127] In an interesting

---

[121] Schwalm, 'Les Illusions de l'idéalisme', 413.

[122] It seems to me that Peddicord misses this important nuance in his discussion of the disagreement between Garrigou-Lagrange and Blondel (*The Sacred Monster of Thomism: An Introduction to the Life and Legacy of Reginald Garrigou-Lagrange* (South Bend, Ind.: St Augustine's, 2005), 74–9).

[123] John J. McNeill, *The Blondelian Synthesis: A Study of the Influence of German Philosophical Sources on the Formation of Blondel's Method and Thought* (Leiden: Brill, 1966), 60. For a similar assessment, see Boey, 'Blondels metafysica', 326, 332–3, 336.

[124] English, *Possibility of Christian Philosophy*, 14.

[125] Cf. Bouillard, *Blondel and Christianity*, 16.

[126] Quot. ibid.   [127] Milbank, *Theology and Social Theory*, 215.

statement regarding the opposition between modern immanentism and Christian supernaturalism, Blondel commented, also in his 1896 *Lettre d'apologétique*:

[M]odern thought, with a jealous susceptibility, considers the notion of *immanence* as the very condition of philosophizing; that is to say, if among current ideas there is one which it regards as marking a definite advance, it is the idea, which is at bottom perfectly true, that nothing can enter into a man's mind which does not come out of him and correspond in some way to a need for development and that there is nothing in the nature of historical or traditional teaching or obligation imposed from without which counts for him, no truth and no precept which is acceptable, unless it is in some sort autonomous and autochthonous. On the other hand, nothing is Christian and Catholic unless it is *supernatural*, not only transcendent in the simple metaphysical sense of the word, because there could be truth or beings superior to ourselves which we could nevertheless affirm immanently by the use of our own powers, but strictly supernatural, that is to say, beyond the power of man to discover for himself and yet imposed on his thought and on his will.[128]

While Blondel was willing to accept a method of immanence—as opposed to a *doctrine* of immanence—he realized that the Christian faith demanded an unambiguous affirmation of the supernatural.[129] Both in *L'Action* and in *Lettre d'apologétique*, Blondel showed himself keenly aware that contemporary idealism was captivated by immanence and unable to overcome subjectivism.

Blondel's appropriation of the phrase 'method of immanence' in his second book, *Lettre d'apologétique*, was no doubt a move to make clear to the philosophical guild that the dynamism of human action was true to actual human experience, regardless of a person's religious convictions. The expression may well sound like a capitulation to a subjectivist epistemology. But the above quotation makes clear that this would be a misinterpretation.[130] Blondel presented his argument as a theologian, and he remained convinced that only divine revelation would provide the answer to the human quest for meaning. Hans Urs von Balthasar rightly points out, therefore, that Blondel did not intend to 'immanentize' revelation. Instead, his 'purpose was to burst the bonds of the whole sphere of nature to reach that of revelation—which had already occurred in fact and which indeed was the very foundation of the whole sphere of nature in the first place'.[131] Thus, when in his *Lettre d'apologétique* Blondel introduced the phrase 'method of immanence' he was hardly substituting immanence for transcendence. Instead, he was insisting that Christian revelation needed to touch

[128] Blondel, *Letter*, 151–2. Bouillard quotes this passage in *Blondel and Christianity*, 51.
[129] Daly suggests that the passage just quoted appeared 'virtually to commit [Blondel] to an acceptance not only of the *method* but also of the *principle* of immanence' (*Transcendence and Immanence*, 39). This overlooks the fact that in this very quotation Blondel affirms the human need for the supernatural. Cf. also the clarification offered in Blondel, *Letter*, 153 n. 1.
[130] Conway indicates that in related matters of significance, Bouillard seemed deliberately to equivocate in his use of terminology ('Positive Phenomenology', 583–6).
[131] Balthasar, *The Theology of Karl Barth*, trans. Edward T. Oakes (San Francisco, Calif.: Communio/Ignatius, 1992), 341.

base with the dynamic realities of people's daily lives. For Blondel's logic of action, it seems, historical developments themselves were both a manifestation and an anticipation of the reality of God.

Blondel made this particularly clear in his 1904 essay *Histoire et dogme*. Here he expounded on his differences with the Modernist approach to biblical scholarship, especially with that of Alfred Loisy.[132] Without mentioning Loisy by name, Blondel indicated that the controversial biblical scholar had fallen prey to what Blondel termed 'historicism'. Blondel explained his disagreements with Loisy, and at the same time he made clear that his own 'method of immanence', which he had advocated in his 1896 *Lettre d'apologétique*, should not be confused with 'historicism' or 'immanentism'. While the historian indeed had a 'relative autonomy' in relation to Christian doctrine,[133] and 'while the historian has, as it were, a word to say in everything concerning man, there is nothing on which he has the last word'.[134] The difficulty with historicism, Blondel maintained, was that it did not recognize the spiritual reality that influenced historical research. Satisfied with the logical development of mechanical explanations, historicism, insisting on a purely phenomenological approach, ignored the deeper, non-intellectual realities that shaped people's actions.[135] The only way for historians to remain properly in their own field was, paradoxically,

to open all the doors and windows on to horizons other than one's own; never to lose sight of the essential truth that 'technical and critical history', in the precise and scientific sense of the words, is not 'real history', the substitute for the life of humanity, the totality of historical truths, and that between these two histories, of which one is a science and the other a life, one resulting from a phenomenological method and the other tending to represent genuine reality, there is an abyss.[136]

In short, while Blondel was willing to acknowledge a 'relative autonomy' for historical research, he rejected absolute 'self-sufficiency'.[137]

Blondel did not restrict himself, however, to assailing historicism. An equally serious problem was that of neo-scholastic extrinsicism. Critiquing the notion that empirically observed historical facts functioned to establish the reality of Christian revelation, Blondel maintained:

Thus the relation of the sign to the thing signified is extrinsic, the relation of the facts to the theology superimposed upon them is extrinsic, and extrinsic too is the link between

---

[132] For a helpful discussion of Blondel's disagreement with Loisy, see Nichols, *From Newman to Congar*, 136–54.

[133] Blondel, *History and Dogma*, 232.

[134] Ibid. 236.

[135] Ibid. 241.

[136] Ibid. 238.

[137] Ibid. For a solid discussion of autonomy, see Anton Losinger, *Relative Autonomy: The Key to Understanding Vatican II* (Frankfurt: Lang, 1997). Losinger argues that the Pastoral Constitution *Lumen gentium* (36. 1) advocates only a *relative* autonomy in speaking of a 'rightful autonomy of earthly affairs' (*iusta rerum terrenarum autonomia*) and that it thus rejects the modern tendency towards individual autonomy.

our thought and our life and the truths proposed to us from outside. Such, in its naked poverty, is extrinsicism—it lacks the strength to make life circulate between faith and dogma or between dogma and faith, and allows them turn by turn to fall tyran[n]ically one upon the other.[138]

Using sacramental language, Blondel insisted here that for the neo-Thomist tradition 'the sign' (*signum*) and the 'the thing signified' (*res significata*) remained extrinsic to one another. Although the historicism of Modernism and the extrinsicism of neo-Thomism appeared to be each other's opposites, Blondel was convinced that both in fact assumed the same rationalist separation between *signum* and *res*, history and faith, philosophy and theology.

Blondel attempted to overcome this separation by arguing that the great Tradition of the Church had served as a sacramental connection that allowed history and faith, as well as philosophy and theology to penetrate each other. We do not simply look to a historical Jesus but instead, argued Blondel, to Christ as the Church has come to understand him through the centuries.[139] Thus, the philosopher from Aix presented a plea for an 'intermediary' between history and dogma[140] located in the reality of a Tradition that developed 'as the result of a sort of rumination, by grasping what had first of all escaped us'.[141] Modernist historicism and neo-Thomist extrinsicism, based as they were on a positivist view of rationality, both rejected the idea that a developing Tradition shaped the contents of the Christian faith.[142] For Blondel, then, the supernatural was not a heterogeneous *superadditum* but was rather 'a love-relationship which insinuates a new order into the normal order'.[143] As the next chapters will make clear, it was this sacramental view of the nature–supernatural relationship that would endear Blondel to the movement of *nouvelle théologie*.

JOSEPH MARÉCHAL'S QUEST FOR THE ABSOLUTE

Completing Kant through Intellectual Dynamism

Joseph Maréchal may not have been quite as influential among the *nouvelle* theologians as Maurice Blondel. It is none the less difficult to understand the movement without gaining a sense of Maréchal's philosophy. We have noted the impact of (Neo) Platonism, in the common use of Jacobi's distinction between *Verstand* and *Vernunft* among the Romantics, in the impact of Augustinian illuminationism among the traditionalists and ontologists, as well as in Blondel's mystical understanding of the nature of truth claims. Within this general context, it is not surprising that also Maréchal's thought echoed among the *nouvelle*

---

[138] Blondel, *History and Dogma*, 228.   [139] Ibid. 244–5.   [140] Ibid. 264.
[141] Ibid. 273.   [142] Ibid. 278.   [143] Ibid. 283.

theologians. Henri Bouillard, in particular, appealed to the Belgian biologist and philosopher for a more apophatic approach with regard to the adequacy of human truth claims.[144] Maréchal had authored a six-volume history of metaphysics, a work which he had been unable to complete, owing to his untimely death at the age of sixty-six. The most significant of the six volumes was the fifth, entitled *Le Thomisme devant la philosophie critique*. In this 1926 publication, the Jesuit from Louvain outlined his own Thomist position in the face of the challenges raised by the Kantian turn to the human subject.[145] Maréchal was not satisfied with simply rejecting the Kantian starting-point in the subject and countering it with the bare assertion of metaphysical realism. Strict realism was, of course, the standard approach of neo-Thomism. Its metaphysical epistemology, Maréchal explained, was grounded in the 'absolute value of the "first principle" in its application' to the data of human consciousness.[146] This objective metaphysical critique of knowledge had been common in ancient philosophy in general, and Maréchal agreed that it had 'reached its peak in the Aristotelianism of St. Thomas'.[147]

In the earlier volumes of his series, Maréchal had described both the historical development of this metaphysical approach and what he regarded as its later dissolution in Western thought, first through the attacks of Ockhamism in the fourteenth century, and then through the empiricism of Locke and Hume and the rationalism of Descartes and Leibniz in the seventeenth and eighteenth centuries.[148] To be sure, Maréchal made clear that he did not mean to discount the neo-scholastic reliance on metaphysical realism. He went so far as to express his essential agreement with it, by stating that 'the permanent value of ancient realism remains solidly established in our eyes'.[149] What he attempted to show in his fifth volume, however, is that even if we were to take our starting-point in the human subject rather than in absolute first principles, we could *still* demonstrate the reality of transcendentals and arrive, through intellectual abstraction, at the existence of God. In other words, Maréchal aligned himself with Kant by starting out with the human subject in order to show that the philosopher from Königsberg had none the less erroneously stopped short of affirming pure reason's capacity to transcend the natural realm. As the title of Anthony Matteo's *Quest*

[144] Bouillard, *Karl Barth*, ii *Parole de Dieu et existence humaine* (Paris: Aubier/Montaigne, 1957), 198, 202–3. For Maréchal's understanding of analogy, see also Gerald A. McCool, *From Unity to Pluralism: The Internal Evolution of Thomism* (New York: Fordham University Press, 1989), 87–113.

[145] Joseph Maréchal, *Le Point de départ de la métaphysique: Leçons sur le développement historique et théorique du problème de la connaissance*, v *Le Thomisme devant la philosophie critique* (Louvain: Museum Lessianum, 1926). For the most prominent passages in English, see Joseph Donceel (ed.), *A Maréchal Reader* (New York: Herder & Herder, 1970).

[146] *Maréchal Reader*, 68 (*Le Point de départ*, v. 13–14).

[147] Ibid. (*Le Point de départ*, v. 13).

[148] For a most helpful discussion of the development of Maréchal's argument in *Le Point de départ*, see Anthony M. Matteo, *Quest for the Absolute: The Philosophical Vision of Joseph Maréchal* (DeKalb, Ill.: Northern Illinois University Press, 1992), 3–63.

[149] *Maréchal Reader*, 66 (*Le Point de départ*, v. 9).

for the Absolute indicates, for Maréchal the human quest could still legitimately be regarded as a search for God.

Maréchal insisted, therefore, that Kant's 'transcendental critique would be legitimately completed only by the rational admission of finality which reveals to us the existence of an Absolute Being. Kant, the patient pioneer, would be completed rather than contradicted'.[150] In short, the metaphysical and transcendental approaches, the ancient and the modern, were not simply contradictory. They could be complementary, if only the modern approach were tempered by the recognition that the mind possessed an inherent drive to surmount the finality of being. In doing so, the modern approach could accommodate the adequacy of classical metaphysical claims. Anthony Matteo summarizes it well: 'Maréchal wishes to indicate that the metaphysical critique of knowledge embodied in the work of Thomas Aquinas can be justified in the light of Kantian criticism.'[151] Maréchal's project was thus quite similar to that of Blondel. While Maréchal did not share Blondel's focus on human action and was much more sympathetic to Thomas's intellectualism, both were convinced that Kantianism could function as preparation for the gospel (*praeparatio evangelii*) because of the inherent and dialectical human dynamism towards the supernatural.

Maréchal then set out to demonstrate why Kant's starting-point in the subject should have led him to the acceptance of metaphysical claims, despite his resistance to them. The reason, Maréchal argued, in typically Thomist fashion, lay in the human mind's tendency to abstract from individual material objects. The intellect made sense of particular objects by means of universal forms or essences of concepts. This dynamic activity of the mind, as it always went beyond the object in order to understand it, constituted what one scholar has termed 'the dynamics of longing'.[152] The permanent process of abstraction constituted a continuous dialectical attempt at better understanding in order to achieve its goal: intellectual union with God. It was a simple fact, for Maréchal, that the dynamism of the human mind was ever restless and always strove for further intellectual abstraction:

> As long as any condition whatsoever will look to us as 'limiting', we shall be certain that the absolutely last end of our intelligence lies beyond it, or, which amounts to the same, that the formal object of our intelligence extends beyond this limitation. For the awareness of a limit as limit contains logically, within the very order where the limit occurs, the knowledge of a further possibility.[153]

Maréchal was headed for an affirmation of traditional Thomist metaphysical realism, in which the human mind had an inherent desire to go beyond the

---

[150] *Maréchal Reader*, 84 (*Le Point de départ*, v. 30).

[151] Matteo, *Quest for the Absolute*, 89.

[152] Jan Verhoeven, *Dynamiek van het verlangen: De godsdienstfilosofische methode van Rahner tegen de achtergrond van Maréchal en Blondel* (Amsterdam: Thesis Publishers, 1996).

[153] *Maréchal Reader*, 163–4.

limitations of material objects. The very human capacity and observable desire to reject all limits implied that we had to move beyond finite existence. 'To such formal capacity', concluded Maréchal, 'can only correspond one absolutely last and saturating end: the *infinite* Being'.[154]

The Sacramental Character of Analogical Predication

The dynamic movement of the human intellect towards the infinite God implied, for Maréchal, that we could never, in totalizing fashion, grasp the essence of God. The dynamics of the desiring intellect always continued, precisely because it was through material objects that we could come to an analogical knowledge of God. It is at this point that Maréchal appealed to Thomas's distinction between representation and affirmation. The two had to be clearly distinguished, argued Maréchal, if we wished to maintain that knowledge of God was merely analogical. St Thomas, therefore, had insisted that the names of God *signified* the divine substance and were predicated of God substantially, but none the less fell short in their representation of him. Thus, concluded Maréchal, the 'signification of those divine attributes, that is to say, the objective value that the affirmation confers on them in its judgement, relies on a conceptual "representation" that is very inadequate, because it is borrowed from our experience of creatures'.[155] This analogical predication, according to Maréchal, involved the same kind of distancing as did the human process of abstracting that allowed knowledge of material objects in the first place.[156]

One may well wonder whether such an approach to knowledge in general, as well as to the knowledge of God, allowed for trustworthiness of human understanding. This was the fear of relativism that led Réginald Garrigou-Lagrange and others to oppose the turn to 'neo-Kantianism'. Maréchal explained, however, that the ontological distance, involved both in the human process of abstraction and in analogical predication, in no way jeopardized the abiding significance of human concepts:

No, the proper mode of the understanding reflects both aspects of our composite nature—spiritual and material—at the same time: the understanding is immaterial, but extrinsically dependent on the sensibility. This twofold characteristic is passed on to the result of the understanding, i.e., the concept: universality of the concept, because the unity of the understanding is immaterial; and numerical multiplicity of the concept by virtue of the necessary reference of the universal to the phantasm. The abstract form

---

[154] Ibid. 165.

[155] Maréchal, *Le Point de départ*, v. 234. Thomas Aquinas had stated that the divine names 'signify the divine substance, and are predicated substantially of God, although they fall short of a full representation of Him' (*ST* I Q. 13, art. 2).

[156] As we will see in the next chapter (sects: Fear of Relativism; and Bouillard, Le Blond, and the 'Analogy of Truth'), Henri Bouillard and Jean-Marie Le Blond would appeal to St Thomas in a quite similar fashion.

floats, uncertain, as it were, between two planes of being: the adjudicating affirmation inclines it decidedly to the one side or to the other; but by taking on (under the affirmation) transcendental form (e.g., God is 'living', 'acting'), the abstract form remains no less 'represented', in our spirit, as numerically multipliable; just as by taking on (under the affirmation) individual form in matter (Peter is 'living', 'acting'), it remains no less present to the understanding as universal.[157]

Maréchal, in this somewhat abstruse statement, refused to let go of the tension that is involved both in the process of abstraction and in the doctrine of analogy of being. He wanted to maintain, on the one hand, that an affirmation implied a dynamic process moving away from material limitations towards the infinite and, on the other hand, that the affirmation retained its connection to the contingent and material world. Hence, he evoked the interesting metaphor of an uncertain abstract form floating, as it were, between two planes of being.[158] The material world was not left behind in the search for the infinite. Rather, perhaps counter-intuitively, Maréchal insisted that as our understanding of the material world becomes deeper by way of conceptual abstraction the dynamism of the mind leads us on to the spiritual realm of God.

Maréchal believed that doctrine of analogy provided him with the key to the relationship between nature and the supernatural. Because of the somewhat counter-intuitive move that he made—greater knowledge of the material order brings us closer to the supernatural order—he was able to affirm both a fairly radical apophaticism and the importance of the material world. Precisely because he did not give up on the link between our affirmations and material reality, Maréchal retained his reservations with regard to the Platonic tradition.[159] He resisted monism, and he was able to do this by positing an analogous relationship between God and the created order. For the Platonic tradition, the material order was ultimately redundant; for Maréchal, in contrast, the mind's engagement with the material order was essential for progress in the dynamism of the intellect towards the infinite. In short, it seems Maréchal arrived at an ontology that

[157] Maréchal, *Le Point de départ*, v. 235.

[158] One is reminded of the title of Milbank's book on Henri de Lubac. See John Milbank, *The Suspended Middle: Henri de Lubac and the Debate Concerning the Supernatural* (Grand Rapids, Mich.: Eerdmans, 2005).

[159] 'At the base of Platonic ontologism, St. Thomas denounces the misunderstanding in that regard between the universal representation and the object that is really affirmed: "Now it seems that Plato strayed from the truth because, having observed that all knowledge takes place through some kind of similitude, he thought that the form of the thing known must of necessity be in the knower in the same manner as in the thing known" (*ST* I. 84.1, c; cf. I. 85.3, ad 4). The "similitude" between the knowing subject and the exterior object is the last word of our knowledge: "So also the intellect, *according to its own mode*, receives under conditions of immateriality and immobility, the species of material and mobile bodies: for the received is in the receiver according to the mode of the receiver" (ibid.)' (Maréchal, *Le point de départ*, v. 235). Matteo points out the difference on this score between Aristotle and Plato. Plato held to a direct, intuitive grasp of the forms, whereas for Aristotle our intellect, engaging the material world, intervenes; and for Plato, we can reach the forms by leaving behind uncertain sense experiences, while for Aristotle the forms exist only as material entities in the world (*Quest for the Absolute*, 95; cf. ibid. 102).

attributed a sacramental function to the created order, since the created order enabled the human mind to channel its desire for the infinite.

PIERRE ROUSSELOT

Unity of the Intellect: Reinterpreting St Thomas Aquinas

His life cut short at the age of thirty-six on the battlefield of the Eparges in 1915, Pierre Rousselot's impact on developments in later twentieth-century French Catholicism is nothing short of remarkable.[160] Ordained as a priest in 1908 and appointed the next year to teach theology at the Parisian Institut Catholique, the young theologian had only a few years to make a theological contribution. At the heart of the Jesuit theologian's work lay a sacramental vision of reality. Rousselot believed that this sacramental vision provided the key to epistemology, the place of doctrine, Christology, and the nature–supernatural relationship. 'The Incarnation', John M. McDermott explains, 'guaranteed a sacramental understanding of reality by which the material world serves as a communicator of God to man and as a means enabling him to attain the beatifying possession of God in His kingdom'.[161] Considering the influence of Rousselot's theology on *nouvelle théologie*, McDermott's claim is highly significant. A brief look at Rousselot's three main publications will suffice both to provide support for McDermott's analysis and to give an indication of some of the significant theological implications of this sacramental approach.

Rousselot's major thesis, *L'Intellectualisme de saint Thomas*, written in 1908 at the Sorbonne, presented a defence of Thomas Aquinas's intellectualism.[162] But it

---

[160] For an account of Rousselot's life, see Élie Marty, *Le Témoignage de Pierre Rousselot, SJ, 1878–1915: D'après ses écrits et sa correspondence* (Paris: Beauchesne, 1940). Several *nouvelle* theologians of the 1940s and 50s readily acknowledged Rousselot's impact. Henri de Lubac emphasized his indebtedness to Rousselot as one of the theologians shaping him the most (*At the Service of the Church*, 19). In 1965, de Lubac published Rousselot's 1909 essay on doctrinal development (Rousselot, 'Petite théorie du développement du dogme', ed. Henri de Lubac, *RSR* 53 (1965), 355–90). See further John M. McDermott, 'De Lubac and Rousselot', *Greg* 78 (1997), 735–59; Aidan Nichols, 'Henri de Lubac and Pierre Rousselot', in *From Newman to Congar*, 195–213. For Rousselot's influence on Henri Bouillard, see Thomas G. Guarino, 'Fundamental Theology and the Natural Knowledge of God in the Writings of Henri Bouillard' (PhD diss., Catholic University of America, Washington, DC, 1984), 256–70. For Rousselot's influence on Marie-Dominique Chenu, see Christophe F. Potworowski, *Contemplation and Incarnation: The Theology of Marie-Dominique Chenu* (Montreal: McGill–Queen's University Press, 2001), 9–12. Balthasar acknowledged his debt to Rousselot in *The Glory of the Lord*, i *Seeing the Form*, trans. Erasmo Leiva-Merikakis, ed. John Riches (Edinburgh: T. & T. Clark, 1982), 173–7.

[161] John M. McDermott, *Love and Understanding: The Relation of Will and Intellect in Pierre Rousselot's Christological Vision* (Rome: Università Gregoriana Editrice, 1983), 299. Cf. ibid. 54, 75, 140, 161, 285, 291. While I will not emphasize the centrality of Christology in Rousselot, I appreciate McDermott drawing my attention to this significant aspect of Rousselot's thought.

[162] According to custom, Rousselot presented both a major and a minor thesis. He published his major thesis as *L'Intellectualisme de saint Thomas* (Paris: Alcan, 1908); English trans.: *Intelligence:*

was a defence that must have looked to neo-Thomist readers as very nearly the opposite—namely, a betrayal of the value of the intellect. After all, Rousselot's Angelic Doctor was one who rejected the notion of truth as correspondence between object and intellect,[163] who cautioned strongly against identifying intellectualism with human abstraction and dogmatism,[164] and who looked on propositionalism as idolatry.[165] Indeed, Rousselot argued, interpretations of Thomas's theology as fundamentally a form of rationalism, whether they came from his voluntarist detractors or from his would-be neo-scholastic disciples, missed what St Thomas's intellectualism had set out to do.

Against Thomas's voluntarist detractors, the young Parisian doctor maintained that the will could not be the highest faculty which was capable of attaining to the beatific vision. The intellect, Rousselot argued, along with St Thomas's intellectualism, in some sense *became* the object of its understanding; the intellect had the ability to enter into the object, to become immanent in it. With the object united to the intellect, the intellect grasped not just the object, but in doing so grasped itself at the same time. Knowledge of another object implied an increase in self-understanding. Rational human beings were, therefore, the only creatures (in addition to angels) capable of truly apprehending 'otherness' and so also of self-reflection.[166] The will, however, was a faculty that resisted this kind of immanence of knowledge. According to Rousselot, the will lacked the unifying capacity that only the grasp of knowledge could provide: 'The real reason for its [i.e., the intellect's] superiority over will is that "speaking simply and absolutely, it is better to possess in oneself the nobility of another being than to have a relation to a noble being that remains exterior to it".'[167]

In contrast, voluntarism maintained that the intellect always remained extrinsic to the object; the various objects remained separate from the observer as well as from each other. The result was a tendency towards multiplicity rather than unity. This exteriority and multiplicity of voluntarism, Rousselot believed, meant that the dynamic movement between the will and the object of its desire would continue indefinitely. Since the will was a faculty of movement and imperfection, one could not legitimately consider it the faculty that in the hereafter would enjoy the beatific vision. The final state of perfection should, instead, exclude any further movement: 'When the last term of movement has been realized and all potentiality actualized, then movement is no longer conceivable, and the will's

---

Sense of Being, Faculty of God, trans. and ed. Andrew Tallon (Madison, Wis.: Marquette University Press, 1998). Cf. McCool, 'Rousselot's Intellectualism: The Internal Evolution of Thomism', *From Unity to Pluralism*, 39–58; Robert N. St Hilaire, 'Desire Divided: Nature and Grace in the Neo-Thomism of Pierre Rousselot' (PhD diss., Harvard Divinity School, 2008).

163 Rousselot, *Intelligence*, 25–6.
164 Ibid. 1–10.
165 Ibid. 30.
166 Ibid. 24.
167 Ibid. 16. Rousselot's quotation is from Thomas Aquinas, *De veritate*, 22. 11.

remaining act cannot be other than consent [*consentement*] and pleasure.'[168] So, whereas the will could at best strive or tend towards the beatific vision, the intellect could actually attain this ultimate end, because of its ability to enter into God as the object of its knowledge.

Rousselot's opposition to voluntarism was not just a rhetorical device to pre-empt any possible neo-Thomist attacks. Rather, he appeared genuinely to follow St Thomas in his argument against voluntarism, believing that consistent voluntarism 'substitutes becoming—as the supreme good—for the older subsistent absolute, for the immutable God' and that it implied, therefore, an 'absolute dynamism'.[169] Such absolute dynamism, Rousselot realized, would in the end lead one along the path not only of intellectual relativism but also of a moral pragmatism in which the will would be entitled to make its own arbitrary decisions about good and evil.[170] In line with his anti-voluntarist inclinations, Rousselot could on occasion make some remarkably strong statements in defence of conceptual human knowledge, expressing, for example, his 'love of dogma': 'Take away dogma and you take away God; to touch dogma is to touch God; to sin against dogma is to sin against God.'[171]

At the root of Rousselot's position, then, lay an endorsement of Thomas's intellectualism. As indicated, the dissertation as a whole was presented as a defence of Thomas's intellectualist position. None the less, Rousselot's description of intellectualism was such that it was opposed not only to a voluntarist exaltation of the will, but also to neo-Thomist scholasticism. From a historical point of view, the anti-rationalist cast of Rousselot's intellectualism was much more significant than his rejection of the voluntarist option.[172] The conceptualism of neo-Thomism took its starting-point in a common-sense interpretation of Thomas Aquinas, which regarded truth as the proper correspondence between intellect and object. The neo-Thomists, therefore, saw doctrine as providing positive and fully reliable propositional judgements based on correct intellectual assessments. Rousselot modified this approach by presenting Thomas as a theologian whose intellectualism had been quite Neoplatonic and mystical. According to this interpretation of St Thomas, the role of the intellect went well beyond

---

[168] Rousselot, *Intelligence*, 45 (square brackets in original). After discussing the ontological priority of the intellect (ibid. 41–6), Rousselot dealt with the supremacy of love in Thomas's thought (ibid. 46–9). Rousselot tried to reconcile the two by insisting that in the abstract knowledge was superior, while in the concrete love was superior, at least in cases where the object was superior to the human soul (ibid. 46). This comment really does not seem to do a great deal to reconcile the perceived tension in Thomas's thought.

[169] Ibid. 181.

[170] Ibid. 42, 47, 162–3. Rousselot would come back to these apprehensions in *The Problem of Love in the Middle Ages: A Historical Contribution*, trans. Alan Vincelette (Madison, Wis.: Marquette University Press, 2001), 189–96; id., *Eyes of Faith*, 48–9, 55. Cf. McDermott, *Love and Understanding*, 167.

[171] Rousselot, *Intelligence*, 182. Cf. ibid. 8.

[172] Rousselot explicitly distinguished Thomas's 'intellectualism', which he endorsed, from 'rationalism' (ibid. 179).

that of framing rational concepts and judgements. Rousselot set out to prove that for Thomas Aquinas the intellect had been 'essentially for acquiring being [*captatrice d'être*] and not for constructing propositions'.[173] As we have already seen, Rousselot believed that, for Thomas, true knowledge meant an immanent union rather than just an external correspondence between the intellect and the object. As Rousselot put it: 'To know is primarily and principally to seize and embrace within yourself an *other* who is capable of seizing and embracing you: it is to live by the life of another living being. Intelligence is the sens [*sens*] of the divine because it is capable of embracing God in this way'.[174] The corollary of this position was that concepts and judgements, while valuable, did not express knowledge in the full sense of the term. Knowledge was not the result of isolating objects but was instead a matter of uniting to oneself the most intimate aspects of other objects.[175] 'And', concluded Rousselot, 'if the *true* is "being as related to intelligence," then perfect truth does not consist in the immobile link of two concepts; its deep and ultimate notion is less an "adequation of things to the spirit" [*adequatio rei et intellectus*] than the conformity, assimilation, and union of spirit with the things.'[176] Truth was less about correspondence than it was about assimilation.

Rousselot's argument was an extended plea for a chastening of conceptual realism and thus of the overconfidence that informed the manualist tradition. Unlike God and the angels, human beings were endowed with sense perception and so required space and matter to achieve knowledge.[177] St Thomas, after all, had distinguished intellect (*intellectus*) from reason (*ratio*), and had insisted that the latter was a discursive rationality and was the result of the imperfect nature of the human intellect: it could arrive at knowledge only in a mediate or indirect fashion. Whereas in God and the angels the intellect had an immediate unifying grasp of all material objects, human reason was forced to use 'middle terms', which marked 'a defect' in human nature.[178] This requirement of sense perception as a medium for intellectual apprehension made Rousselot come to the same conclusion as St Thomas—the human intellect was rather limited in its current capacities. 'We are the last and lowest in the intellectual order: faced with what nature unfolds with the greatest clarity, we are as blind as bats in the noonday sun'.[179]

Rousselot's *L'Intellectualisme de saint Thomas* essentially provided a commentary on the abilities and limitations of the various modes of human speculation.

---

173 Rousselot, *Intelligence*, 12 (square brackets in original).
174 Ibid. 7 (square brackets in original). Cf. ibid. 2, 57, 182–83.
175 Ibid. 22, 26.
176 Ibid. 26 (square brackets added).
177 Ibid. 52, 54–5.
178 Ibid. 53. For St Thomas, Rousselot pointed out, infallibility characterized the intellect as such. Human error stemmed from (1) the connection of human knowledge with the senses; and (2) the multiplicity involved in discursive reasoning (ibid. 64–8).
179 Ibid. 50.

Or, to put it differently, Rousselot outlined the various ways in which discursive reasoning was, for St Thomas, a deficient and imperfect mode of arriving at intellectual knowledge. The instruments of human reason—concepts, sciences, systems, and symbols—were simply means by which the intellect tried to deal with its own deficiencies.[180] These instruments of reason were merely 'substitutes' for pure ideas.[181] In providing a detailed analysis of Thomas's understanding of concepts, sciences, systems, and symbols, Rousselot continuously identified the limitations of each in the Angelic Doctor's theology. With regard to concepts, Rousselot reiterated the Thomist doctrine of analogy, built on the Dionysian threefold method of causality, negation, and eminence.[182] This doctrine should induce in us a certain conceptual humility: 'No notion is truly common to God and creature, so no notion is attributed to God *as is*.'[183] Thomas, explained Rousselot, had recognized that human concepts were unable to grasp the essence of a material object's individual particularity, so that the human intellect was forced to impose general concepts on particular objects.[184] For example, while people might rightly use the general concept of *humanitas* to describe both Socrates and Plato, the human intellect was unable to describe the true essence of Socrates and Plato individually. Strict correspondence between intellect and object remained ultimately elusive, and the noetic principles that Thomas Aquinas had employed in his own speculation illustrated his awareness of this limitation of human concepts.[185] Drawing on what he believed to be Thomas's most genuine insight, Rousselot himself went a step further and concluded that *all* human knowledge—not just knowledge of God and of angels—remained analogical in character.[186]

Human science was similarly limited in its reach, maintained Rousselot. Since Thomas had articulated the notion that the sciences could operate only by taking the conclusions of higher sciences as their starting principles—his theory of subalternation—he had held that the ideal human science would always remain out of reach. In searching for foundational principles to solidify any particular science, one would always and necessarily have recourse to another, higher science, on which the first one had based itself. In fact, the greater the specificity of a particular science, the further one had moved down the hierarchical ladder of

---

[180] Ibid. 55, 70.

[181] In four subsequent chapters, Rousselot discussed the 'substitutes' of the concept, of science, of systems, and of symbols (ibid. 86–167).

[182] Ibid. 69–77.

[183] Ibid. 76.

[184] Ibid. 80–1.

[185] Ibid. 82. Rousselot was forced to recognize that for St Thomas material objects were accessible through concepts and definitions, and that they in fact provided perfect and adequate mental counterparts of the essence of objects (ibid. 82–4). Rousselot concluded from this that Thomas had been inconsistent (ibid. 82–90).

[186] Ibid. 87–8.

sciences and the less certainty one could have. Human sciences, then, merely enjoyed a 'borrowed certitude'.[187]

If human concepts and sciences were already necessarily deficient in character, the limitations were perhaps even more evident with regard to systems and symbols. Much of St Thomas's dialectical method of argumentation, Rousselot insisted, made conscious use of the imagination,[188] and was never intended to set up a system that was true for all times and places. Thomas put his 'artistic' logic on display in theological questions. In rational demonstration, Thomas's reason was informed by faith. His work was 'a logical poem, better at charming someone who already believes than useful for controversy'.[189] Likewise, when in his discussions Thomas used religious symbols, he again did not intend this by way of absolute demonstrative certainty. To say, for example, that the two doves of the Presentation at the temple signified Christ's divinity and humanity was clearly not meant to supply absolute proof for the hypostatic union. Rather, the aim was to *reach* the divine by means of symbols: 'Incapable of demonstration, poetry "charms reason with images." Theology cannot use natural reason to deduce its principles but can use it to fix the imagination.'[190]

The limited character of human reason was thus evident in each of its instruments: concepts, sciences, systems, and symbols. To Rousselot's mind, these limitations stood out all the more if one kept in mind that all this speculation merely served in the 'rank of means', which served to reach the great promise of the beatific vision.[191] Moreover, Rousselot insisted that the true value of human reason in this life was finally a question of how much it affected moral action. The value of intellectual activity, therefore, 'must be directly proportionate to its influence upon voluntary action'.[192] Both the instrumental character of human rationality and its moral purpose put strict limits on the kind of intellectualism that the Jesuit theologian was willing to defend.

Rousselot regarded St Thomas's theology as a remarkable synthesis of intuitive knowledge and discursive reasoning. This theological combination, he argued, 'allows him [i.e., St Thomas] to "Platonize" when he considers the universe as a whole while remaining so Aristotelian in his explanation of the sublunary world'.[193] This combination of Platonism and Aristotelianism gave Rousselot's approach its sacramental flavour. On the one hand, he presented what he termed an 'ontological Platonism'.[194] It was a position based on the primacy of the intellect, a position that looked not simply for correspondence between object

---

[187] Rousselot, *Intelligence*, 113.
[188] Ibid. 123–4.
[189] Ibid. 130.
[190] Ibid. 135.
[191] Ibid. 152.
[192] Ibid. 163–4. Cf. ibid. 178: 'To modify the *other* with the help of our organs is for us to "take" [*prendre*] it otherwise and, in a sense to take [*prendre*] it more really [than] to know it, where knowing it means making it participate in our life' (French in square brackets in original).
[193] Ibid. 54.   [194] Ibid. 181.

and intellect but that aimed at union with the life of another. Thus, it was the unity of the intellect that ultimately concerned Rousselot. True knowledge was more an intuitive grasp of simple knowledge than it was the outcome of discursive argument. The beatific vision of the intellect implied, therefore, that the limitations of matter and of multiplicity had to be overcome. There was more to life than matter and senses alone. Put in sacramental terms: this-worldly discourse, objects, and actions were not curved in upon themselves (*incurvatus in se*). On the other hand, Rousselot was also keenly aware of the Aristotelianism of St Thomas's thought, and he recognized that time and space not only limited the human intellect but at the same time created the necessary conditions for intellectual and moral activity that enabled the intellect's progressive journey towards the beatific vision. Or, put differently, discursive knowledge, multiplicity of matter, and the life of the senses all combined to serve as sacramental means to attain to the beatific vision.

Unity of Love: A Plea for Physical Love

The title of Rousselot's so-called 'minor thesis', on the topic of love in the twelfth and thirteenth centuries, appeared to indicate that it was a historical study without obvious theological concerns.[195] The preface to this book was even more modest, indicating that it did not really present a history of two views of love, but that the intention 'was simply to assemble some material for those who would attempt such a study'.[196] Rousselot's assembly of the historical material none the less gives significant insight into his theology. After all, the two views of love that he discussed in his book were quite different from each other in their respective assessments of the relationship between nature and the supernatural. While the medieval mind took for granted that God alone was the ultimate end of human beings—a rather significant observation in itself—the question that was far from settled in the twelfth and thirteenth centuries was whether love of desire (*amor concupiscentiae*) and love of friendship (*amor amicitiae*) were different from each other or were ultimately reducible to a common principle. According to the former viewpoint, the two loves were clearly distinct, even opposed, so that one was ultimately required to sacrifice the pursuit of personal happiness in favour of a completely disinterested love of God. In contrast, the latter viewpoint insisted that, at a higher level, the two loves were really identical, so that it was quite possible, even required, to pursue love of desire and love of friendship at the same time.

The disagreement in viewpoints centred on the basic question 'whether humans by nature love God more than themselves'.[197] This question was

---

[195] Id., *Pour l'histoire du problème de l'amour au moyen âge* (Münster: Aschendorff, 1908) (English trans.: *The Problem of Love in the Middle Ages: A Historical Contribution*).

[196] Id., *Problem of Love*, 80–1.

[197] 'Utrum homo naturaliter diligat Deum plus quam semetipsum?' (ibid. 76).

answered negatively by those advocating an opposition between the two kinds of love in order to pursue only an 'ecstatic' (self-abandoning) or completely disinterested love. According to this view, one did not naturally love God more than self, so that true love of God required self-sacrifice and an abandonment of the love of desire. Rousselot found this position particularly in the school of Saint-Victor, among the Cistercians, and among the followers of Peter Abelard (1079–1142). According to this medieval school of thought, pure love of friendship was ecstatic in nature. That is to say, it placed the subject outside itself in its self-sacrificial attitude towards the other person. Such an understanding of love, explained Rousselot, had four characteristics: (1) it was dualistic, with two separate persons, both completely sacrificing themselves for the sake of the happiness of the other; (2) it was violent, in the sense that it ran counter to one's natural tendencies and tyrannized the loving subject to the point of self-destruction; (3) it was irrational, since natural reason with its self-interest had to be countered; and (4) it was self-sufficient or free, in that there was no other aim than this self-sacrificial love, so that all personal happiness would have to be sacrificed to the ultimate object of love.[198]

Rousselot rejected this ecstatic approach, asserting instead that the two loves were really identical. To make this point, he put forward the 'physical' (i.e., natural) or 'Greco-Thomist' view of love.[199] For theologians in this tradition, explained Rousselot, there was 'between the love of God and the love of self a fundamental identity'.[200] He traced this approach to some of the writings of Hugh of St Victor (1096–1141) and St Bernard of Clairvaux (1090–1153), and he explained that it also found 'strong backing in the Neoplatonic doctrines of pseudo-Dionysius'.[201] This Neoplatonism had influenced Thomas, in particular.[202] The Angelic Doctor made use of three principles that allowed him to posit a reconciliation between self-love and pure love of the other. The first principle was the 'theory of the whole and the part', which could be traced back to Aristotle's *Nichomachean Ethics*.[203] For Aristotle, altruism both derived from and could be reduced to self-love.[204] Thomas accepted this identification between self-love and altruism, explained Rousselot, by regarding the appetite for one's own happiness as the final end that moved the human will. Thus, love of self was 'the measure of all other loves'.[205] That human beings could none the less love God as their highest end was, in Thomas's words, because 'it is clear that

---

[198] Rousselot, *Problem of Love*, 15–16, 79, 155–211.

[199] Ibid. 78. When Rousselot spoke of 'physical' love he did not have in mind sexual love but love that had its basis in the physical or natural realm.

[200] Ibid. 78.

[201] Ibid. Rousselot indicated that Hugh of St Victor and St Bernard were more ambiguous, and he dealt with them both in his section on physical love and in that on ecstatic love.

[202] Henri de Lavalette goes so far as to suggest, rightly it seems, that Rousselot's 'book is simply a thesis complementary to *L'Intellectualisme de saint Thomas* and all the interest is concentrated on the Thomist theory of love, as Rousselot views it' ('Le Théoricien de l'amour', *RSR* 53 (1965), 464).

[203] Ibid. 82–93, 105–16.   [204] Ibid. 82–4.   [205] Ibid. 85.

God is the common good of the whole universe and of all its parts. Hence each creature in its own way naturally loves God more than itself'.[206] The point Thomas made was that all beings participated in God by way of imitation. Therefore, the nature of things would require greater love of God than of self, while at the same time the love of self was part and parcel of the love of God. The conclusion, Rousselot argued, was that the two loves, those of desire and of friendship, were 'in perfect continuity'.[207]

The second Thomistic principle was that of a 'universal appetite of all things for God'.[208] Everything that existed, according to Thomas, even plants and animals, had an inclination towards God. This natural appetite for the 'acquisition of God' meant that it would be impossible to set the love for something finite in opposition to the love of God. To be sure, people were not necessarily aware that by nature they loved God more than themselves, and they might very well be tempted to subordinate the good of the whole to their 'private' goods. Virtue, however, consisted 'in not proposing as an end any other whole than the complete assemblage of being whose good coincides with the good of God Himself'.[209] If one's desire for God was natural, then clearly to follow one's true desire was to love God. There was continuity rather than antithesis between self-love and love for God.

Thomas's third and final principle was that of the 'coincidence of the spiritual good with the good in itself'.[210] When human beings experienced a conflict between self-love and love of God, the reason, according to St Thomas, was not that the two were opposed, but that human beings were composite or material rather than purely spiritual. Since the spiritual nature of human beings was what made them most authentically human, however, one benefited one's true self by denying the senses.[211] Furthermore, because of the weakness of the human soul, some temporal inclinations of the spirit might have to be prohibited for the sake of eternal life: 'When, after our [earthly] state of wayfaring [*l'état de voie*], we come to exist beyond time, the perception of truth cannot but be excellent in regard to its exercise, just as it was in regard to its "specification".'[212]

These three principles countered the ecstatic concept of love, which answered the question whether humans by nature loved God more than themselves with a resounding 'no'. According to the ecstatic view, humans did not have such a natural inclination for God, and, precisely for that reason, the lover had to overcome nature by denying his personhood in favour of the personhood of the beloved.[213] The difficulty with this answer, from Rousselot's perspective, was the dualism it took as its starting-point:

---

[206] Thomas Aquinas, *Quodl.* 1, a.8 (quot. Rousselot, *Problem of Love*, 88).
[207] Rousselot, *Problem of Love*, 92.
[208] Ibid. 94–8, 117–27.   [209] Ibid. 98.   [210] Ibid. 99–104, 127–33.
[211] Ibid. 101.   [212] Ibid. 101–2 (square brackets in original).   [213] Ibid. 151.

If... one wanted—which our medieval thinkers never did—to bring out its dominant principle, the best course of action to take would most likely be to characterize the ecstatic conception of love by the predominance of the idea of *person* over the idea of *nature*. It is because love is conceived of purely as tending from a *person* to a *person* that it is conceived of as *ecstatic*, as doing violence to innate inclinations, as ignoring natural dissimilarities [*distances*], as a pure affair of freedom. In St Thomas, on the contrary, the individual personhood [*personnalité*] itself is conceived of as a participation of God, and in this way is part of nature.[214]

The notion of ecstatic love took for granted the priority of individual personhood over the commonality of human nature. St Thomas, in contrast, took his starting-point in the commonality of nature and in the person as participating in the life of God. Put differently, for St Thomas, unity, as a transcendental concept, took priority over plurality: 'In the physical conception of love, unity is the *raison d'être* and the ideal of love, as it is, its end. Things are quite different in the ecstatic conception of love: there plurality, or at the very least duality, is presented as an essential and necessary element of perfect love.'[215]

The physical or natural view of love, therefore, answered the much-debated question in the affirmative.[216] The intimate connection between human nature and the love of God as its proper end implied that *amor concupiscentiae* and *amor amicitiae* could not be legitimately opposed to each other.[217] They had to be viewed as connected and, if conceived properly, as ultimately one and the same. Of course, identifying *amor concupiscentiae* and *amor amicitiae* meant that in the end the vexed question would not just have to be answered affirmatively but would be exposed as a false dilemma. Thomas's 'full response', indicated Rousselot, 'would aim at abolishing the problem'.[218] 'Instead of reducing the love of God to a mere form of the love of self, it is the love of self that is reduced to a mere form of the love of God'.[219]

Rousselot was quite aware of the Neoplatonic roots of his physical or natural view of love, and also in his minor thesis he clearly celebrated the influence of Neoplatonism, via Denys, on Thomas. To be sure, St Thomas had maintained a certain reserve with regard to the Areopagite, explained Rousselot, because of the latter's tendency towards an obliteration of the distinction between the finite and the infinite.[220] None the less, Thomas approached Denys 'with all the

---

214   Rousselot, *Problem of Love*, 152 (square brackets in original).

215   Ibid. 155. Rousselot makes clear that the Thomist notion of 'unity' was not an indivisible attribute (ibid. 90).

216   Ibid. 87–9.

217   Cf. McDermott's comment: 'That establishment of a participation metaphysics enabled Rousselot to give a convincing answer to the problem of altruistic love since there could be no ultimate opposition between love of self and love of God, the latter being the former's condition of possibility, the transcendental unity grounding the intelligibility of all participants' (*Love and Understanding*, 291–2).

218   Rousselot, *Problem of Love*, 94.   219   Ibid.   220   Ibid. 118–20.

respect due a person who was the disciple of St Paul'.[221] And Rousselot identified without hesitation with 'the Neoplatonic principle which proclaimed that all things have an appetition for God'.[222] The physical view was, in his opinion, rightly termed 'Greco-Thomist'.[223]

The importance of this Neoplatonic lens, as Rousselot viewed it, was that it enabled a sacramental ontology that emphasized the continuity between nature and the supernatural, something which, to his mind, the West's separation between nature and the supernatural had insufficiently appreciated.[224] Rousselot found in Thomas Aquinas a Neoplatonic emphasis on the innate or natural desire for the vision of God.[225] This principle of a 'universal appetite of all things for God' ran directly counter to the neo-scholastic separation between nature and the supernatural, which held that only the infusion of a supernatural principle (i.e., grace) could cause any kind of appetite for God. It was exactly this issue of a natural desire (*desiderium naturae*) that thirty years later would become the key issue for Henri de Lubac through his reading of the Church Fathers and the theologians of the Middle Ages.[226] Rousselot's consistent emphasis on the continuity—even identity—between love of self and love of God would thus find a clear echo in the *nouvelle théologie* debates of the 1940s and 50s surrounding nature and the supernatural. There seems little doubt as to the reason for *nouvelle théologie*'s attraction to the young Parisian theologian.

Unity of Faith: Judgements of Credibility

Having written his 1908 dissertations on the intellectualism of St Thomas and on the topic of love in the Middle Ages, respectively, Rousselot decided to use his first teaching year at the Institut Catholique (1908–9) to extend his doctoral work by lecturing on the virtue of faith. He subsequently published much of this classroom material in two articles entitled 'Les Yeux de la foi' (1910).[227] These articles not only made much more explicit what in some ways had remained implicit in the dissertations, but they also explicitly entered the fray of contemporary discussion. Rousselot here set himself the major task of reconceptualizing the way in which conversion took place. The intellectualism of *L'Intellectualisme de saint Thomas* had already been fairly chastened, considering its Neoplatonic sensitivities and its rejection of neo-Thomist conceptualism. Now, in the 'Eyes

---

[221] Ibid. 118.   [222] Ibid. 212. Cf. ibid. 117.   [223] Ibid. 78.   [224] Ibid. 93.
[225] Robert St Hilaire's dissertation discusses throughout the question of natural desire and Rousselot's indebtedness to—as well as disagreement with—Blondel ('Nature and Grace').
[226] See Chap. 3, sect.: Pure Nature and Natural Desire.
[227] For a comparative analysis of the classroom material and the published essays, see Henri Holstein, 'Le Théologien de la foi', *RSR* 53 (1965), 422–61. For the essays themselves, see Rousselot, *Eyes of Faith*. They were originally published as 'Les Yeux de la foi', *RSR* 1 (1910), 241–59, 444–75.

of Faith' articles, Rousselot further reinforced the mutuality between intellect and will.

The central thesis was that love for God gave us new eyes enabling us to see the rationality of the faith: 'In the act of faith love needs knowledge as knowledge needs love. Love, the free homage to the supreme Good, gives us new eyes. Being, become more visible, delights the beholder.'[228] Knowledge and love were both involved, in reciprocal fashion, in the act of faith. Because of this reciprocity, Rousselot argued, love allowed us to see things in a way that previously had been impossible. Love 'gives us eyes', he said, and with those new eyes love would move the intellect.[229] The idea of a reciprocal relationship between knowledge and love ran directly counter to the common intellectualist mould: for neo-Thomists, the intellect guided the will, not vice-versa. Not surprisingly, 'Les Yeux de la foi' met with some strongly worded reactions.[230] Judging by the irony and sarcasm with which he responded, Rousselot must have been rather upset with his interlocutors.[231] His essays on conversion, more than his doctoral work, were probably the leading factor in the 1920 decision of the Superior General of the Jesuits, Wlodimir Ledochowski (1866–1942), to prohibit Rousselot's teachings within the Society.[232]

Opposing commonly received opinion, Rousselot was convinced that the rationalism of neo-Thomism needed a bold correction. In his essays, he argued that neither the reasonable character of faith, nor its certainty or the freedom of its commitment, was in any way contrary to the supernatural character of faith.[233] In fact, reasonableness, certainty, and freedom were all implied in and derived from the supernatural character of faith. But, how was one to integrate these elements into a meaningful theological whole? This is precisely where the disagreements came in: Rousselot was convinced that previous theological attempts at integration had been unsuccessful. While his articles were respectful towards well-known contemporary theologians such as Louis Billot (1846–1931), Jean-Vincent Bainvel (1858–1937), and Ambroise Gardeil (1859–1931), the polite tone could not hide the radically new turn that Rousselot advocated in 'Les Yeux de la foi'. It was clear that, in his opinion, neo-Thomism had failed to bring together the human and the divine elements of the act of faith in a consistent and meaningful fashion.

---

[228] Rousselot, *Eyes of Faith*, 56.

[229] Ibid. 61.

[230] There were a number of substantial responses: Réginald Garrigou-Lagrange, 'Les Méthodes de l'apologétique', *RT* 21 (1913), 478–89; Hippolyte Ligeard, 'La Crédibilité de la révélation d'après saint Thomas', *RSR* 5 (1914), 40–57; S. Harent, 'Foi', q.v. A. Vacant, E. Mangenot, and E. Amann (eds), *Dictionnaire théologie catholique*, vi (Paris: Letouzey et Ané, 1920), 260–75.

[231] Rousselot responded to Ligeard and Harent in Pierre Rousselot, 'Réponse à deux attaques', *RSR* 5 (1914), 57-69, which has been translated as *Answer to Two Attacks*, published in one volume together with id., *Eyes of Faith*.

[232] Cf. Rousselot, *Eyes of Faith*, 113-17; Fouilloux, *Une Église*, 23.

[233] Ibid., 45.

In typically scholastic fashion, each of these theologians had insisted on a 'double faith', the one natural, the other supernatural.[234] For example, the Saulchoir theologian Ambroise Gardeil had argued in his 1908 book *La Crédibilité et l'apologétique* that supernatural grace was not required for divine prophecy and miracles to be convincing. Their objective evidence of divine intervention was enough to lead anyone to the rational conclusion that one must accept the teachings of the Church. That conclusion, Gardeil explained, in line with standard neo-scholastic teaching, was a judgement of credibility. This judgement of credibility, arrived at in a purely rational fashion, was something to which Gardeil and others referred as 'scientific faith': 'That is why all theologians admit that a natural belief, a "scientific faith" in the revealed truth, is the normal result, possible in itself, of the search for credibility.'[235] To the question how illiterate people or children could possibly evaluate the rational claims for the truth of the Catholic faith the response was that, in their case, supernatural grace would override the regular requirement for a judgement of credibility and for 'scientific faith'.[236] By distinguishing natural 'scientific faith' (the result of rational demonstration) from supernatural faith in the actual contents of the divine deposit (the gift of grace), Gardeil and other neo-scholastics kept apologetics and theology in two separate domains.

This notion of a twofold faith, the one natural and the other supernatural, meant a certain duplication, since faith operated on two distinct planes. Indeed, as Rousselot commented, the neo-Thomists could 'even acknowledge the possibility of a natural faith that not only is certain but, *psychologically speaking, perfectly resembles supernatural faith*'.[237] Gardeil was well aware that such a separation between natural judgements of credibility (leading to scientific faith) and supernatural belief in the truth of the gospel made it difficult to connect them. He thus inserted the so-called 'judgement of credentity' between the judgement of credibility and supernatural faith. This judgement of credentity was a supernatural element that provided the link between human freedom, on the one hand, and supernatural necessity, on the other. Once someone had made a positive judgement of credentity, divine faith imposed itself on the conscience as something 'absolutely obligatory'.[238] To summarize, the neo-scholastics

---

[234] For Billot's theology, see Roger Aubert, *Le Problème de l'acte de foi* (2nd edn, Louvain: Warny, 1950), 241–55; Daly, *Transcendence and Immanence*, 174–9. For Gardeil's theology, see Aubert, *Le Problème*, 393–450; Petit, 'La Compréhension de la théologie', 379–91. Several of these authors also discuss Bainvel.

[235] Ambroise Gardeil, *La Crédibilité et l'apologétique* (Paris: Gabalda, 1908), 23. Rousselot quoted this passage in *Eyes of Faith*, 39 n. 5.

[236] Ambroise Gardeil spoke here of 'surrogates of credibility' (*suppléances de la crédibilité*) (*La Crédibilité*, 97–130). Cf. Rousselot, *Eyes of Faith*, 24.

[237] Rousselot, *Eyes of Faith*, 23.

[238] Gardeil, *La Crédibilité*, 23–4. Cf. Holstein, 'Le Théologien', 431. Interestingly, with this scholastic nicety, Gardeil moved away from the sharp demarcation between nature and the

argued that the origin of faith involved a number of steps. One moved from rational arguments via a 'judgement of credibility' and perhaps also via a 'judgement of credentity' (as in the case of Gardeil) to the supernatural gift of grace. Where the 'judgement of credibility' implied natural or scientific faith, the gift of grace led to supernatural faith.

This system had two advantages. First, the clear demarcation between nature and the supernatural meant that supernatural faith would retain its thoroughly gratuitous character. Second, Christians did not have difficulties in communicating with outsiders. The communicable nature and rational character of the faith were beyond doubt. Rousselot's doctoral work had convinced him, however, that the position of the neo-Thomist establishment implied a non-sacramental view of reality. What is more, he believed that it was possible to retain both of the advantages of the neo-Thomist position while fully integrating the elements that the manualist scheme had disconnected from each other: reason and faith (credibility and divine grace) as well as intellect and will (certainty and freedom).

Rousselot rejected the idea of a 'twofold faith' in favour of the unity of faith. He maintained that the neo-Thomist focus on providing non-Christians with new evidence—notably of supernatural prophecies and miracles—was foolhardy, because more evidence would not necessarily convince them. Rousselot used the example of two scientists or two detectives, both looking at the same evidence:

It does not follow that both will necessarily arrive at identical conclusions. One of them may immediately leap to certainty, while the other remains in the dark. Yet materially—that is, in its individuality—the new fact is represented in both minds. But one man has perceived it, not as a raw and isolated phenomenon, but *as a clue* pointing to the law or conclusion both were seeking. He has perceived that fact in its connection with the law, made the synthesis of fact with law, and instantly affirmed that connection as real. Not so the other. He 'does not see'.[239]

Rousselot insisted that only some would interpret the evidence appropriately. Therefore, rather than focus on rational arguments, theologians should pay attention to the light of faith (*lumen fidei*), which he insisted was the reason why only some people interpreted the evidence as clues pointing to the Christian faith.[240] Thus, Rousselot could insist that if only the *lumen fidei* allowed for an interpretation pointing to supernatural truth, then there was, in fact, no distinct 'judgement of credibility' separate from the light of faith: 'Perception of credibility and belief in truth are identically the same act.'[241]

Of course, such a bold identification between the reasonable judgement of credibility and the supernatural gift of the light of faith would raise neo-Thomist

supernatural. On the one hand, the judgement of credentity imposed an 'absolute obligation' to which the human will had to respond in freedom. On the other hand, this same judgement of credentity was already the insertion of a supernatural element in human nature.

[239] Rousselot, *Eyes of Faith*, 27–8.   [240] Ibid. 26–9.   [241] Ibid. 31.

eyebrows. To neo-Thomists, it seemed Rousselot had given up on the validity of rational argument. It seemed like a lapse into fideism that hardly did justice to human reason. His reasoning appeared circular, since the 'light of faith' was necessary before one could make the rational argument that would lead to faith. As Rousselot himself intimated:

The clue is really the cause of the assent we give to the conclusion, yet it is the perceived conclusion that sheds light on the clue, that endows it with meaning. The same is true when we come to believe: insofar as it makes the assent reasonable, the perceived clue precedes the assent; insofar as it is supernatural, it follows upon the assent.[242]

Viewed from a supernatural angle, the assent of faith preceded the clue, while from a natural perspective the clue preceded the assent of faith. Rousselot was convinced, however, that in no way did this reciprocity imply a vicious circle. After all, he explained, assent was possible only because of the insertion into the 'circle' of the 'instantaneously acquired habit' of the light of faith.[243] This newly acquired spiritual faculty ensured reciprocity while avoiding a vicious circle.

Rousselot was trying to establish a more sacramental relationship by breaking through the strict separation between rational argument and supernatural faith. After all, the supernatural was now not superimposed, as a distinct entity, onto a separate realm of nature. Instead, the supernatural 'must encompass and transcend the other, deepening and perfecting it *from within*'.[244] Nature and the supernatural did not, as it were, bring two different objects to the table; rather, they were always intimately connected with one another. Using language that hinted at a mysticism based on a sacramental ontology, Rousselot commented: 'In the final analysis the essence of natural being consists in its essential aptitude to serve as a means for created spirits to ascend to God, their final end; the essence of supernatural being, in its aptitude to lead them to God, object of the beatific vision.'[245] The interpretation of signs had now become a spiritual matter, part of the sacramental journey to the beatific vision. In this journey, scholars had no advantage over illiterate people: 'The motives . . . might well seem contemptible to those bereft of the Spirit. But the lover recognizes the Spouse "by a single hair of [his] neck".'[246]

The first of the two articles essentially dismissed universally convincing 'judgements of credibility' and 'double faith', and so parted also with the neatly outlined stages of conversion implied by these notions. In his second article, Rousselot returned to the relationship between intellect and will. He maintained

---

[242] Ibid. 31–32.

[243] The supernatural insertion of the *lumen fidei* provided a marked emphasis on divine gratuity in Rousselot's writing. Maurice Blondel would have his questions about the consistency of Rousselot's position on this score. See Pierre Colin, *L'Audace et le soupçon: La Crise du modernisme dans le catholicisme français 1893–1914* (Paris: Desclée de Brouwer, 1997), 442; Aubert, *Le Problème*, 471. J. Eileen Scully points out that Rousselot was more accommodating than Blondel to both scholastic and intellectualist theology (*Grace and Human Freedom in the Theology of Henri Bouillard* (Bethesda, Md.: Academica, 2006), 31–4).

[244] Rousselot, *Eyes of Faith*, 34. [245] Ibid. 34. [246] Ibid. 35.

that too often the question of certainty and freedom—and their compatibility with faith's supernatural quality—was decided in terms of temporal priority. Voluntarists began with freedom, in the hope of attaining certainty. ('Some say: *Believe blindly first, and afterward you will see.*'[247]) Rationalists began with certainty, in the hope of attaining freedom. ('Others say: *See clearly first, and afterward you will believe.*'[248]) While the former might jettison the intellect, the latter could end up discarding the voluntary nature of faith. Again, Rousselot had recourse to an argument involving reciprocity. Voluntary choice and rational practical judgement could very well influence each other. There was, he argued, a 'kind of circumincession' between the two: 'Love arouses the faculty of knowing, and by the same stroke knowledge justifies that love. Without any preceding "judgment of credibility", the soul instantaneously believes and can exclaim "My Lord and my God!".'[249]

Needless to say, the spectre of voluntarist arbitrariness and pragmatism still hovered over this position. With the love—as voluntary act of the will—arousing the faculty of knowledge, how could one avoid arbitrariness? Rousselot was willing to acknowledge these dangers. Convinced, however, that God had 'made our spirit naturally *sympathetic to being as such*',[250] Rousselot believed that as long as intelligence remained inclined, as it was supposed to, towards the First Truth (i.e., God), it need not fear being goaded by the will. In a tightly worded, significant section, Rousselot explained how this reciprocity of intellect and will could function:

If intelligence is an inclination, every voluntary inclination that would *restrict* it and impose some particular being on it as its norm would be a perversion, a corruption of that nature. But we can also conceive of an inclination that deepens and *expands* it, that enables it better to penetrate its object, derived and secondary being, by making it more deeply enamored of the subsisting Truth, its primary object and ideal. This transformation by love will be identical to an increase of intelligence, and the loving vision it directs will be a more perfect knowledge along the very lines of intellectuality itself.[251]

It is clear what Rousselot was doing. He again rejected the neo-scholastic view of the intellect as merely interested in propositional truth and evidence. By arguing for the intellect as 'inclination', he was subjecting it to legitimate influence by the will.[252] Of course, this was quite in line with his earlier insistence that the

---

[247] Rousselot, *Eyes of Faith*, 46.
[248] Ibid. Rousselot, without actually using the term 'rationalists' himself, clearly had in mind contemporary neo-Thomists.
[249] Ibid. 50.
[250] Ibid. 52.
[251] Ibid. 54–5.
[252] Rousselot discussed at some length Thomas's notion of 'sympathetic knowledge', a knowledge that was immanent to the movement of desire, functioned like a gravitational pull, and so did not go through the regular rational processes of reflection (ibid. 56–60). It is a notion that Rousselot brought out more prominently in another set of two essays. See Rousselot, 'Amour spirituel et synthèse aperceptive', *RPh* 16 (1910), 225–40; id., 'L'Être et l'esprit', *RPh* 16 (1910), 561–74.

intellect naturally progressed towards unity with its object of knowledge. Accepting the need for knowledge and love to cooperate in their search for the beatific vision, Rousselot believed to have found a way to link certainty and freedom in a reciprocal exchange on the wayfarer's pilgrimage. By insisting that the *lumen fidei*, a 'voluntary inclination' of the intellect, allowed us to interpret the clues that in turn gave rise to faith, Rousselot tried to overcome, even more daringly than before, the dilemma of voluntarism versus rationalism. Of course, it meant that love claimed a perhaps even more central role in the knowledge of faith than it had already received in the dissertation.[253] In one of his most mystical moments, Rousselot exclaimed: 'Enchanted, as it were, charmed and fascinated by the God who made it capable of Him, reason itself is nothing other than a pure love of Being.'[254]

CONCLUSION

The theological influences that shaped *nouvelle théologie* were by no means uniform. Each of the scholars discussed in this chapter had his own distinct emphases, and not all of these were compatible with each other. It has not been the burden of this chapter to argue that philosophers and theologians as diverse as Möhler, Blondel, Maréchal, and Rousselot represented a unified school of thought. The sacramental ontology of *nouvelle théologie* did, however, make for a relatively cohesive, shared sensibility, and the thinkers discussed in this chapter did all contribute to the direction of *nouvelle théologie*.

They made contributions in at least four areas. First, *nouvelle théologie* was primarily a movement that attempted a *ressourcement* of the great Tradition. Möhler's nuanced approach to the early Church served as a great model, both for the Jesuits of Fourvière and for the Saulchoir Dominicans. Möhler looked to the Church Fathers for inspiration and for elements of abiding value. At the same time, he recognized that the Spirit continued to work in the Church, so that one had to place the Fathers in their historical context at the origin of the developing Tradition of the Church. As we will see in the remainder of this book, a similar love for the great Tradition, along with an acceptance of the later growth and development of that Tradition, was typical also of *nouvelle théologie*.

Cf. de Lavalette, 'Le Théoricien de l'amour', 474–86. Rousselot's epistemology also opened him up to an understanding of doctrinal development that departed from the common neo-Thomist views and that deeply influenced Henri de Lubac's understanding of development. See Rousselot, 'Note sur le développement du dogme', *RSR* 37 (1950), 113–20; id., 'Petite théorie'. Cf. Maurice Nédoncelle, 'L'Influence de Newman sur les "Yeux de la foi" de Rousselot', *RSR* 27 (1953), 321–32; Andrew Tallon, 'Doctrinal Development and Wisdom: Rousselot on "Sympathetic Knowing" by Connaturality', *PT* 15 (2003), 353–83. I will discuss Rousselot's influence on de Lubac with regard to doctrinal development in Chap. 6, sect.: Henri de Lubac: 'Cashing in' Jesus.

[253] Rousselot, *Eyes of Faith*, 60.
[254] Ibid. 52.

Second, *ressourcement* of the Tradition, and in particular of the Church Fathers, implied a judgement on the failure of neo-Thomism to think in historical categories. History and Tradition had to be taken seriously as theological categories, as especially Möhler, Blondel, and Rousselot were well aware. One could not access truth without taking into account that it was necessarily historically embedded. As a result of this insight, the nineteenth century witnessed a burgeoning of literature on the development of doctrine. Rather than deny that change took place, the question for *nouvelle théologie* was how to reconcile that development with the constancy of truth and with the continuity of Christian doctrine. Whether one reads de Lubac on the development of Eucharistic theology, Congar on the doctrine of the Church or on Tradition, or Chenu on theology in the twelfth and thirteenth centuries, one gets a clear sense of the historical context and its changing character as the framework for these theological ideas.

Third, attention to historical development implied consideration also of the human subject. Möhler, Blondel, Maréchal, and Rousselot each exhibited in their own way the post-Kantian emphasis on human experience. Möhler's ecclesiology was based on a pneumatology that was deeply indebted to Romanticism. Blondel's method of immanence, likewise, wanted to point to divine transcendence by beginning with the experiences of human life (action). And Maréchal's quest for the Absolute consciously began with the Kantian subject, while arguing that this point of view should be complemented by Thomist metaphysical claims. Finally, by drawing attention to the importance of the human will and to the mutuality of knowledge and love, Rousselot made clear that he, too, believed that the human subject and its experiences should not be ignored in one's attempt to make truth claims about God.

Fourth, since these theologians tended to take both history and human experience seriously, these temporal and subjective aspects had to be taken into account also with regard to truth claims. Thus, when Möhler attempted to explain the development of doctrine, he did not simply have recourse to logical arguments based on revealed premises. Instead, he spoke of the Spirit's continuing presence in the Tradition and distinguished between the unchangeable 'substance' and the changing 'forms' of doctrine. Blondel, in line with his insistence on the historical nature of the Tradition, maintained similarly that truth was a matter of correspondence between mind and life rather than between mind and reality. When, in connection with the Thomist doctrine of analogical predication of God, Maréchal insisted on a distinction between inadequate conceptual representations and unchanging eternal affirmations, he also indicated thereby that human truth claims were relative to their contextual situation. And Rousselot's insistence that St Thomas's intellectualism not be confused with a conceptualist or rationalist approach was similarly based on the idea that knowledge had more to do with assimilation than it did with correspondence. As a result, he looked at theology more as poetic than as scientific in character.

Each of these elements ties in with the desire of Möhler, Blondel, Maréchal, and Rousselot to reconfigure the nature–supernatural relationship by taking into account the obstacles that Kant had put in the way of pure reason. Their turn to the Church Fathers, as well as their reassessment of the value of history, the experiences of the human subject, and the nature of truth, served to uphold the claim that only 'eyes of faith' allowed for a proper view of reality. The four scholars were agreed that 'pure reason' did not yield a suitable apologetic to convince the modern world of the truth of the gospel. One needed 'eyes of faith' to appreciate the fact that historical events, human experiences, and linguistic statements participated sacramentally in the transcendent reality of God. Only with 'eyes of faith' was it possible to see the transcendent reality to which the created order witnessed. Thus, by enveloping the natural order in its supernatural ground and purpose, these authors attempted to give meaning to the vicissitudes of the created order while at the same time retaining its subordinate role in a sacramental ontology that retained the priority and ultimacy of the divine life.

3

The Mystery of the Human Spirit: De Lubac and Bouillard on Nature and the Supernatural

Those who think themselves capable of grasping the nature of God would do well to consider whether they have looked into themselves.

St Gregory of Nyssa[1]

INTRODUCTION: *NOUVELLE THÉOLOGIE* AND THE REFORMATION

The conflicts surrounding *nouvelle théologie* centred on its attempts to come to a renewed integration of nature and the supernatural. Each of the issues involved in the controversies of the 1940s and 50s involved the key issue: to what extent are nature and the supernatural distinct from one another? Several other problems, immediately connected, also came to the fore: the relationships between reason and faith, philosophy and theology, history and eternity, experience and revelation, human ability and divine grace, historical and spiritual interpretation were the most evident concerns. Whereas the Leonine Thomist revival of the late nineteenth century had in each case reinforced a more or less strict separation between nature and the supernatural, the *nouvelle* theologians regarded such a separation as the most serious pitfall of the Baroque scholasticism of the sixteenth and seventeenth centuries, with disastrous consequences both in terms of a radicalized autonomy of the realm of nature and in terms of divine grace being isolated from everyday human existence. They were concerned with the rationalism and secularism implied in the immanentism of a purely natural order and with the fideism, spiritualism, and authoritarianism of a strictly other-worldly supernatural order.

When the *nouvelle* theologians tried to reintegrate nature and the supernatural, they took up concerns that had long lain at the heart of the Reformation. The *nouvelle* theologians were like the Reformers in a number of ways. They wanted

---

[1] Gregory of Nyssa, *De hominis opificio*, c. 11 (quot. Henri de Lubac, *The Mystery of the Supernatural*, trans. Rosemary Sheed (New York: Crossroad/Herder, 1998), 210).

to go back beyond scholastic theology to the Church Fathers and place the Scriptures at the centre of the theological enterprise (de Lubac, Daniélou). They were apprehensive of an authoritarian hierarchy and wanted to reintegrate doctrinal authority with the Eucharistic life of the Church and with the active communal participation of the laity (Congar). They insisted that Christ was not just of significance for matters of faith, but that the Incarnation was foundational to every human endeavour (Balthasar). They were interested in recapturing the significance of the ordinary lives of working class people as genuine vocations, worthy of reflection in a theology of work (Chenu). They had questions about the clearly defined sacramental system of Catholicism.[2] Moreover, the focal point of *nouvelle théologie*'s criticism was usually either the scholasticism of the post-Reformation period or the more recent neo-scholasticism of the late nineteenth and early twentieth centuries. Both scholastic periods had reacted against a perceived forswearing of human reason, whether that of the Reformation, with its emphasis on *sola fide* and its protest against Aristotelianism, or that of the nineteenth-century Catholic fideism and traditionalism of Félicité de Lamennais, Louis Bautain, as well as Johann Adam Möhler and others of the Tübingen school.[3] In other words, the approach of *nouvelle théologie* might well be viewed as an olive branch extended to the Reformation, with which it shared an apprehension of rational philosophy setting the theological agenda. Understandably, then, the direction of *nouvelle théologie*, along with its endorsement at the Second Vatican Council, made for a significant ecumenical opportunity.

Although it is true that the *nouvelle* theologians did take up some of the concerns of the Reformation, and while people like Yves Congar and Hans Urs von Balthasar were genuine and passionate in their ecumenical interests, it would be erroneous to view *nouvelle théologie*'s reintegration of nature and the supernatural as a twentieth-century replay of the Reformation. We should keep in mind that the *nouvelle* theologians generally looked beyond nineteenth-century or even sixteenth-century scholasticism to the earlier pre-Reformation period as the source of the problems that would ultimately lead to the rise of neo-Thomism. On this understanding, the Reformation, while correct in some of its observations, was simply one major contributor to a larger shift that had begun in the Middle Ages and would involve both the Catholic Church and the Reformation churches in a gradual drifting apart of nature and the supernatural. In other words, with regard to the central issue of the nature–supernatural relationship, *nouvelle théologie* did not see itself as taking up the Reformation concerns. Rather, *nouvelle théologie* offered a challenge to both neo-Thomism and the Protestant Reformation. Indeed, *nouvelle théologie*'s

---

[2] Cf. Marie-Dominique Chenu's comment that the twelfth-century 'operation of delimiting the seven major sacraments sufficed by itself' to manifest a tendency of 'desacralization' (*Nature, Man, and Society in the Twelfth Century: Essays on New Theological Perspectives in the Latin West*, trans. and ed. Jerome Taylor and Lester Little (Toronto: University of Toronto Press, 1998), 127).

[3] Cf. Chap. 2, sect.: Nineteenth-century 'Footnotes' to Kant.

sacramental readjustment of the nature–supernatural relationship implied the *ressourcement* of a period preceding the deplorable break of the Reformation. *Nouvelle théologie* does offer a genuine possibility of true ecumenical dialogue. But the ecumenical landscape is a complex one, with Catholicism and Protestantism both implicated, although perhaps in different ways, in the loss of a sacramental ontology. Both Catholic and Protestant traditions need the courage to reappraise the problematic history of the split between nature and the supernatural, resulting in the descramentalized universe of modernity.

In this chapter and the next, I will trace in some detail the views of Henri de Lubac, Henri Bouillard, Hans Urs von Balthasar, and Marie-Dominique Chenu on this particular contentious issue. It will become clear that the four theologians shared an opposition to what Chenu called the 'Baroque scholasticism' of neo-Thomism and its nature–supernatural divide. We can note in each of the four authors a concern for a sacramental mindset that regarded the created order as symbolic in character, so that it made the supernatural reality present to the realities of time and space. At the same time, however, the various *nouvelle* theologians pursued this sacramental ontology each with their own distinct emphasis. De Lubac and Bouillard tended to draw on the Greek Church Fathers and the Neoplatonic tradition; as a result, they emphasized the sacramental link in its upward direction: nature pointed upward to the supernatural and made it present. Balthasar and Chenu tended to be a great deal more critical of the Platonic tradition and were fearful of an idealism that might undermine the goodness of creation; as a result, they accentuated the sacramental connection in its downward direction: the Incarnation valued the created order and thereby gave it its sacramental character. To be sure, the contrast was in no way absolute. On the one hand, de Lubac was not naive to the real problems inherent in the Platonic tradition, and the Incarnation remained central to his theology, while Bouillard's Thomism gave him a true appreciation for the relative autonomy of the natural order. On the other hand, both Balthasar and Chenu had a high regard for the Greek Fathers, including the Neoplatonism of Denys. The commonalities far outweighed the differences among the *nouvelle* theologians. Most importantly, a sacramental ontology, informed by a *ressourcement* of the Church Fathers, informed all of them.

HENRI DE LUBAC: *DESIDERIUM NATURALE* AS SACRAMENTAL PRESENCE

Neoplatonism and the Gratuity of Grace

On 10 May 1940, Nazi Germany invaded France and quickly set up a puppet regime, under the leadership of France's First World War hero, Marshal Pétain. Exactly two months later, Pétain was appointed Chief of State of the Vichy regime in central France, beginning five long years of oppressive fascism, anti-Semitic legislation, and other forms of collaboration with Nazi Germany. One of the painful memories of this time period is the massive support many in the Catholic Church gave, first to the Fascist party, Action française, in the 1930s, and then to Pétain's Vichy regime during the Second World War itself. Seventy-six thousand Jews were deported from France to Germany between 1941 and 1945; only about 2,500 survived. In 1997, the Catholic Church of France issued an official apology, pronounced by Bishop Olivier de Berranger. Speaking of the silence of the French Church in the face of the Nazis' extermination of the Jews, he acknowledged: 'Today we confess that this silence was a mistake... We beg God's forgiveness and ask the Jewish people to hear this word of repentance.'[4]

The rise of fascism in Europe, particularly in France, and the question of how the Church should respond, was the context in which Henri de Lubac developed his theology.[5] De Lubac realized the temptation that the Vichy regime presented to traditionalist Catholics, attracted as they were to structures of authority. But he also realized that at its heart fascism constituted a different religion: a return to anti-Catholic and anti-Christian neo-paganism.[6] As de Lubac came to see it, the French cultural and political situation was intimately tied up with the theological question of the relationship between nature and the supernatural. The reason, he believed, why so many accommodated uncritically the fascist neo-paganism of the Vichy regime was the long-standing separation between nature and the supernatural, as if the two formed two hermetically sealed compartments. Such separation, de Lubac believed, granted the realm of nature a nearly autonomous status in relation to the supernatural. In no way related to the supernatural, the realm of nature could move in its own, self-chosen direction, unencumbered by a higher call that the gospel, Jesus Christ, or the Church might issue.

De Lubac's opposition to a strictly autonomous natural realm did not mean, however, that he uncritically adopted a Neoplatonic perspective in which the created order emanated in a hierarchically graduated fashion from an eternal Plotinian One. In the concluding chapter of his book, *Le Mystère du surnaturel* (1965), in a chapter entitled 'The Call of Love', de Lubac issued the following words of caution against Neoplatonism:

One must... be careful to correct—if not wholly to avoid—the neo-Platonist metaphors of flux, of gushing, of 'effluence', of emanation, of soaking into things. God is not, as one might think from some Platonist expressions also taken up by Denys, a generosity pouring himself out, it is at best inadequate to see him simply as that 'fundamental

[4] (Quot. *Le Monde* (1 Oct. 1997), B11.) Cf. Patrick Henry, 'The French Catholic Church's Apology', *FrR* 72 (1999), 1099–105.

[5] Cf. de Lubac, *Résistance chrétienne à l'antisémitisme: Souvenirs 1940–1944* (Paris: Fayard, 1988); English trans.: *Christian Resistance to Anti-Semitism: Memories from 1940–1944*, trans. Elizabeth Englund (San Francisco, Calif.: Ignatius, 1990).

[6] Joseph A. Komonchak, 'Theology and Culture at Mid-century: The Example of Henri de Lubac', *TS* 51 (1990), 599.

generosity' which must mean, for the Absolute, simply the fact of being essentially communicable; or that kind of generosity which is no more than a de-sacralized charity. Those who, in order to avoid 'contingentist theories' which might tend to anthropomorphism, accept rather too readily Platonist or Plotinian theories as if despairing in advance of purifying any personalist theory by the laws of analogy, are in danger of steering from Charybdis on to Scylla. No theory will dispense with the need for correction by analogy.[7]

These strongly worded comments may seem to make it difficult to look to de Lubac as a resource for the recovery of a more sacramental ontology that relies in part on the Platonic tradition. And this lengthy quotation was not an isolated instance of anti-Platonic rhetoric. The entire chapter contrasted the call of God's love in Christ with the Platonic absolute, supreme intelligence, 'eternally unaware of us imperfect beings'.[8] We need to take seriously these anti-Platonic comments, found here and elsewhere in de Lubac's writings. His desire to safeguard both the concrete character of the love of the triune God and his freedom in creating and redeeming was unambiguous. And, of course, in this way, de Lubac simply placed himself in the Christian Tradition, which had generally tried to uphold both the Trinitarian love and the freedom of the Creator and Redeemer God in the face of the emanationism and pantheism of the Platonic tradition.

There was more, however, to de Lubac's quotation than met the eye. He accompanied his expressions of reservation regarding the Platonic tradition with several comments indicating that he wished to safeguard the gratuity of divine grace: 'Let us say it once more in conclusion: God could have refused to give himself to his creatures, just as he could have, and has, given himself. The gratuitousness of the supernatural order is true individually and totally. It is gratuitous in regard to what we see as preceding it, whether in time or in logic.'[9] While by no means disingenuous, either in his cautionary comments against Neoplatonism or in his insistence on the gratuity of the gift of sanctifying grace, we none the less do need to notice the defensive posture that de Lubac adopted with these comments. His anti-Platonic discourse served to maintain the gratuity of grace. And his insistence on the freedom of grace served to protect him against the key accusation that he anticipated from the commentatorial Thomist tradition. Or, to put it somewhat differently, precisely because he was aware of being perceived as a closet Neoplatonist, he pulled out all the stops in trying to pre-empt his opponents' attacks.

Pure Nature and Natural Desire

This raises the question why the neo-Thomists were convinced that de Lubac's position, first advanced in 1946 in *Surnaturel*, and then in somewhat modified

---

[7] De Lubac, *Mystery*, 234–5; English trans. of *Le Mystère du surnaturel* (Paris: Aubier, 1965).
[8] De Lubac, *Mystery*, 228.   [9] Ibid. 236.

form again in 1965 in *Augustinisme et théologie moderne* and in *Le Mystère du surnaturel*, would endanger the gratuity of grace.[10] The reason for this lies, partially at least, in the influence that Maurice Blondel exerted on de Lubac.[11] The neo-Thomists saw in de Lubac Blondel's 'method of immanence', along with all of its perceived connections to Modernism. From their perspective, they were right to worry. De Lubac's *Surnaturel* uncompromisingly rejected commentator-ial Thomism and sounded a clarion call for a reintegration of theology and philosophy. De Lubac was convinced that the neo-Thomist tradition had caused a loss of the proper place of theology:

> Theology had reigned as queen of the sciences, and on occasion it had possibly taken unfair advantage of its title. Now it was beginning to lose its position; after dominating the whole of knowledge it was tending to become merely a separate branch. The supernatural end which is, so to say, the keystone of the arch, was no longer that of philosophy. The study of man was cut into two parts.[12]

De Lubac wanted to restore the unity of a Christian anthropology. He objected to two specific developments in the neo-Thomist tradition, in each of which he observed a radical departure from St Thomas himself.[13] First, he lamented the rise of the idea of 'pure nature' (*pura natura*)—that is to say, nature apart from any consideration of grace or of a supernatural end. Initially, the question of *pura natura* had been raised hypothetically in connection with the eternal destiny of unbaptized children. What would be their final end? By way of analogy, the issue was then raised: imagine that *Adam* would have died in a state of pure nature, before receiving sanctifying grace.[14] Thus, the theologoumenon of *pura natura* was, in the neo-Thomist tradition, a state in which God hypothetically could have created Adam. That is to say, according to his absolute power (*potentia absoluta*) God could have created Adam without original justice and sanctifying grace. Such a first creature surely would not have ended up with the same supernatural beatitude that Adam, and all of the saints, did in fact obtain. The later Thomists turned this hypothesis into an elaborate scheme in which two parallel orders ran alongside one another, each perfectly following its own course: the natural and the supernatural orders each leading to its own appropriate connatural end.

---

[10] Cf. de Lubac, *Surnaturel: Études historiques* (Paris: Aubier, 1946); id., *Augustinisme et théologie moderne* (Paris: Aubier, 1965); English trans.: *Augustinianism and Modern Theology*, trans. Lancelot Sheppard (New York: Crossroad/Herder, 2000); id., *Mystery*.

[11] Cf. Chap. 2, sect.: The Dynamism of Human Action.

[12] De Lubac, *Augustinianism*, 214–15.

[13] Interestingly, Henri Bouillard presented a nearly identical analysis of Thomas's position on the nature–supernatural relationship (*Conversion et grâce chez s. Thomas d'Aquin: Étude historique* (Paris: Aubier, 1944), 77–84). The two theological developments, along with their cultural impact, receive careful treatment in Louis Dupré, *Passage to Modernity: An Essay in the Hermeneutics of Nature and Culture* (New Haven, Conn.: Yale University Press, 1993), 167–81.

[14] De Lubac, *Augustinianism*, 110.

Second, inevitably accompanying the notion of *pura natura* was the insistence that human beings were not naturally oriented towards a supernatural end; there was no natural desire (*desiderium naturale*) for the beatific vision. The Aristotelian principle of connaturality meant that every being had an end proportionate to its nature, so that it could attain this end by means of its inherent powers. As Aristotle had argued in Book 2 of *De caelo*, if the stars had had the capacity to move, nature would have given them the appropriate organs to do so.[15] Accordingly, the neo-Thomists argued, it was impossible for human beings to have the innate desire for the supernatural beatific vision without also having the connatural means to attain it. The only conclusion could be that there was no *desiderium naturale* for a supernatural end. The desire for our supernatural end must itself already be a separate supernatural gift of grace. The neo-Thomists thus concluded that human beings had a twofold final end, the one natural and the other supernatural, the latter extrinsically superimposed on the former. De Lubac, however, was not convinced that the Aristotelian principle of connaturality was applicable to faith. The fact that God had given human beings natural desire for the beatific vision did not entail that they could attain their supernatural end by means of their inherent, natural powers.

As a meticulous historian of doctrine, de Lubac carefully traced the rise of the neo-Thomist extrinsicist thought patterns. He concluded that St Thomas had already relied too much on Aristotelian philosophy. This was clear from Thomas's use of the term 'nature'. 'For Aristotle', explained de Lubac, 'nature was a center of properties and a source of activity that was strictly delimited and enclosed within its own order.'[16] According to de Lubac, Thomas Aquinas had borrowed this understanding of 'nature' from Aristotle. Therefore, when fifteenth- and sixteenth-century Thomist thought appealed to the Angelic Doctor for their separation between nature and the supernatural, there was unfortunately some justification for these appeals. De Lubac argued that Thomas's understanding of 'nature' as a distinct domain, unrelated to any supernatural end, had been too Aristotelian and had constituted a deviation from the theology of the Church Fathers. When they had employed the distinction made in Genesis 1: 26 between the image [εἰκών] and the likeness [ὁμοίωσις] of God, this had not been the same as the distinction between the Aristotelian notion of nature and the Christian understanding of grace. Rather, the Church Fathers had distinguished between the mere capacity to see God (the image [εἰκών] of God) and the actual gift of the Holy Spirit communicating life to believers (the likeness [ὁμοίωσις] of God).[17] Aquinas, argued de Lubac, had attempted to integrate two ultimately incompatible notions: the Aristotelian idea of a self-contained 'nature' and the

---

[15] 'Si natura dedisset caelis inclinationem ad motum progressivum, dedisset etiam instrumenta ad talem motum' (quot. de Lubac, *Augustinianism*, 169).
[16] Id., *Surnaturel: Études historiques*, ed. Michel Sales (rev. edn, Paris: Desclée de Brouwer, 1991), 435. Cf. Komonchak, 'Theology and Culture', 587–8.
[17] De Lubac, *Mystery*, 98.

patristic understanding of 'image'.[18] The former had restricted human beings to a natural realm whose ends they could attain by their natural powers. The latter had opened human beings from the outset to the supernatural horizon that they could obtain by the grace of God.

The notion of 'pure nature' itself, however, did not come to the fore until much later. De Lubac traced its origins to the sixteenth century. The first step had been taken by the Louvain theologians John Driedo (1480–1533) and Ruard Tapper (1487–1599), who had insisted that God had not owed human beings the supernatural gift of eternal life and that God could have created Adam without sanctifying grace.[19] The notion of *pura natura* itself had first been used as a polemical tool against the radical Augustinian followers of Michael Baius (1513–89). For Baius, the creation of human nature had necessarily and immediately implied the gift of the Spirit. Thus, Baius had obviated the gratuitous character of the immediate gift of the Spirit in the Garden. God had been obliged to provide Adam in Paradise with eternal life. Prior to the Fall, there had only been merit, no grace.[20] Robert Bellarmine (1542–1621) had defended Catholic doctrine by insisting that God had been under no obligation to give Adam sanctifying grace. Thus, in order to protect the gratuity of grace, Bellarmine had used the term *pura natura*. 'Bellarmine was its creator', insisted de Lubac.[21] The sixteenth-century theologians, however, had remained relatively subdued in their assertions surrounding God's hypothetical use of his absolute power to create a human being in a state of *pura natura*. The notion had served in a purely hypothetical fashion, merely safeguarding the conviction that God had not been obliged to give supernatural grace.

More importantly, none of these theologians had denied that every human being did have a natural desire for the supernatural end of the beatific vision. The Aristotelian principle of connaturality seemed to exclude such an apparent confusion between nature and the supernatural, but de Lubac showed that on this score none of these sixteenth- and seventeenth-century theologians had been impressed with the philosopher. Aristotle had not been a Christian and could not have been expected to speak with authority on the relationship between nature and the supernatural. The Dominican theologian, Dominic Soto (1499–1560), had expressed himself unambiguously: 'Aristotle knew nothing about the supernatural, and he would not have conceded that any matter has a natural inclination towards anything, unless it had the power and natural strengths to obtain it; we, however, do concede that our nature is so sublime that it is inclined towards that end which we cannot obtain except through God's help.'[22] And de Lubac

[18] Komonchak, 'Theology and Culture', 588.
[19] De Lubac, *Augustinianism*, 147–9.
[20] Ibid. 1–30.
[21] Ibid. 152, quoting Fr Smulders.
[22] Soto, *In IV Sent.*, dist. 41, q2, a1 (quot. ibid. 130).

repeatedly pointed out that the belief in an innate *desiderium naturale* had been shared by the various medieval schools of thought. It had been accepted not just by Dominicans like Soto, but also by Scotists, including Duns Scotus (1265/ 6–1308) himself.[23]

Notwithstanding this common acceptance of a *desiderium naturale*, the fifteenth and sixteenth centuries had witnessed a development that would ultimately undermine the notion. Appeals to the Aristotelian principle of connaturality had become increasingly frequent. The application of this principle, along with the implication of the denial of a *desiderium naturale*, had first come to the surface, de Lubac explained, with Denys the Cartusian (1402–71) and then with Thomas Cardinal Cajetan (1469–1534). For both of these theologians, natural power could not have been in vain, so they logically had come to deny that a desire for the vision of God was natural to human beings.[24] Other theologians had supported their denial: Conrad Kroellin (1476–1536), Francis Silvester (Ferrariensis) (1474–1526), and Chrysostom Javelli (1470–1538).[25] Later on in the sixteenth century, other Thomist scholars from Salamanca—Bartholomew of Medina (1527–81) and Dominic Bañez (1528–1604)—had also started to follow the more recent trends.[26] Francisco Suárez (1548–1617), who had introduced the principle of connaturality in his book *De fine ultimo* (1592), had been particularly influential on later theology. De Lubac commented that 'it may well be thought that no one did more to spread it than Suarez'.[27] De Lubac did not hesitate to trace the development of a self-enclosed natural realm through to neo-Thomist luminaries of his own day, scholars such as Ambroise Gardeil, Réginald Garrigou-Lagrange, Joseph de Tonquédec, Blaise Romeyer, Charles Boyer, and Pedro Descocqs.[28]

De Lubac explained that Cajetan and Suárez had been the most influential scholars in promoting the denial of natural desire, both of them insisting that they had been in line with the Angelic Doctor himself. At the same time, however, the Fourvière Jesuit made clear that Suárez, a fellow Jesuit, had not been the first to devise the idea of human nature as a closed, self-sufficient entity: the Dominican theologian 'Cajetan is, if not quite the first initiator of it, at least its patron and leading authority. It was chiefly he who introduced it into Thomism and, more precisely, actually into the exegesis of St Thomas himself, thus conferring upon it a kind of usurped authority'.[29] It was Cajetan, then, whom de Lubac blamed more than anyone else for having introduced an innovation under the guise of merely being a faithful commentator of St Thomas.[30]

[23] De Lubac, *Augustinianism*, 138, 211, 230; id., *Mystery*, 154–5.
[24] De Lubac, *Augustinianism*, 163–5.
[25] Ibid. 125–6, 165–6.   [26] Ibid. 168.
[27] Ibid. 168.   [28] Ibid. 161–2; id., *Mystery*, 149–50.
[29] Id., *Mystery*, 145–6.   [30] Cf. id., *Augustinianism*, 138.

De Lubac was keen to demonstrate that both the notion of pure nature and the denial of natural desire were relatively recent developments, and that they could not possibly boast the support of St Thomas.[31] This is not to say that de Lubac felt equally strongly about both issues. He was willing to recognize that in some sense the notion of *pura natura* might serve a positive purpose, that it might indeed safeguard the gratuity of grace by making clear that divine grace came to us from the outside, and was, in that sense, supernatural or extrinsic. He acknowledged that the idea could serve to keep at bay the Baianist view that God had been obliged to give Adam eternal life.[32] Eager to make clear his differences with Baianism, de Lubac was willing to admit that the hypothetical idea of pure nature could perhaps assist to uphold the priority of grace also in the prelapsarian situation.

But even this admission was mostly a matter of expediency. De Lubac's reservations with regard to *pura natura* remained profound, particularly when this notion was accompanied by the denial of an innate *desiderium naturale*. First, as long as the idea of pure nature functioned at the level of a mere hypothesis, it seemed to him ultimately useless in protecting the gratuity of grace. The question of grace, after all, did not concern a hypothetical human nature, but it concerned *me*, a human being created with a supernatural end:

What can possibly be learnt from the situation of the first, the hypothetical man, in regard to the gratuitousness of the gift given to the second, the man that I am in reality? I can only repeat that ultimately it is solely in relation to me, in relation to our nature as it is, this actual mankind to which we belong, that this question of gratuitousness can be asked and answered.[33]

In other words, even if grace had indeed been gratuitous for a hypothetical person created in a state of pure nature, this in no way provided a guarantee that grace was also gratuitous in our *actual* state.

[31] De Lubac's interpretation of St Thomas continues to be a matter of disagreement. In accord with de Lubac's general position are: Denis J. M. Bradley, *Aquinas on the Twofold Human Good: Reason and Human Happiness in Aquinas's Moral Science* (Washington, DC: Catholic University of America Press, 1997); Éric de Moulins-Beaufort, *Anthropologie et mystique selon Henri de Lubac: 'L'Esprit de l'homme' ou la présence de Dieu en l'homme* (Paris: Cerf, 2003); Stephen Wang, 'Aquinas on Human Happiness and the Natural Desire for God', *NBl* 88 (2007), 322–34. Others express disagreement: Georges P. Cottier, 'Désir naturel de voir Dieu', *Greg* 78 (1997), 679–98; id., *Le Désir de Dieu: Sur les traces de saint Thomas* (Paris: Parole et Silence, 2002); Stephen A. Long, 'On the Possibility of a Purely Natural End for Man', *Thomist* 64 (2000), 211–37; Guy Mansini, 'Henri de Lubac, the Natural Desire to See God, and Pure Nature', *Greg* 83 (2002), 89–109; Lawrence Feingold, *The Natural Desire to See God according to St Thomas Aquinas and his Interpreters* (Rome: Apollinaris, 2001); Reinhard Hütter, '*Desiderium Naturale Visionis Dei—Est autem duplex hominis beatitudo sive felicitas*: Some Observations about Lawrence Feingold's and John Milbank's Recent Interventions in the Debate over the Natural Desire to See God', *NV* Eng 5 (2007), 81–132.

[32] While de Lubac agreed that the notion of pure nature was 'perhaps useful, but recent' (*Augustinianism*, 106), he also made clear that the notion actually did not function a great deal in the Baianist controversy (ibid. 107–9). Elsewhere, de Lubac questioned whether the hypothesis of pure nature was 'really useful' (*Mystery*, 52).

[33] De Lubac, *Mystery*, 60.

Second, over time, the hypothetical character of pure nature had turned out to be not quite so hypothetical. While St Thomas had been content to acknowledge with Aristotle that there were subordinate natural ends of earthly happiness, the new Thomism had gone much further, speaking of a twofold end, the one natural and the other supernatural, even in the hereafter. Soon a twofold beatitude, even a twofold vision of God, had been the result. De Lubac illustrated how the commentatorial Thomists had ended up with the natural realm annexing all the characteristics of grace for itself, including faith, prayer, virtues, disinterested love, etc. 'What remains peculiar to the supernatural order', exclaimed de Lubac, 'except the word?'[34] Once Cajetan and others had denied that from the beginning God had constituted human nature with a supernatural end, the notion of pure nature allowed them to posit two unconnected parallel outcomes to human life.[35] In order to minimize any inherent link between nature and the supernatural, the Thomist tradition had turned *pura natura* from hypothesis into reality.

Third, by a twist of irony, de Lubac believed that the neo-Thomists were the ones endangering the gratuity of grace, while at the same time they were courting secularism. One of de Lubac's deepest motivations came to the surface at this point. Always maintaining that natural desire did not, in fact, undermine the gratuity of grace—the Baianist and Jansenist spectre, which always hovered over his theology—de Lubac pointed to the implication of his opponents' views: the idea of two parallel tracks, the one superimposed on the other, implied strict autonomy for the realm of nature. The neo-scholastic appeal to the gratuity of grace was, de Lubac believed, a mere smokescreen: 'I believe that the profound, and unnoticed, reason is rather the reverse. Towards the end of the fifteenth century, in the first period of the Renaissance, a feverish enthusiasm for philosophy infected certain minds. A large number of Christian thinkers were won over at that time by the renascent naturalism.'[36] Thus, de Lubac repeatedly insisted that the threat to gratuitous grace lay not in the notion of a *desiderium naturale* but in the secularism implicit in the separation of the two realms.[37] As Tracey Rowland comments:

For de Lubac, the idea of a pure nature contained dangerous Pelagian tendencies, since it meant that it would be possible to sever grace from nature and marginalize it under the

---

[34] De Lubac, *Mystery*, 40.

[35] Cf. id., *Augustinianism*, 191–9. Cf. de Lubac's comment that the new model assumed 'that every man, in our world as it is, before having received the grace of baptism or any other enabling grace, was in that state of "pure nature" (at least if one excludes original sin and its consequences). Finality was therefore considered as something fairly extrinsic: not a destiny inscribed in a man's very nature, directing him from within, and which he could not ontologically escape, but a mere destination given him outside when he was already in existence' (id., *Mystery*, 68–9).

[36] Id., *Augustinianism*, 212.

[37] Cf. de Lubac's warnings against secularism in *Augustinianism*, pp. xxxv, 240. Through the events of the Second Vatican Council and beyond, de Lubac became more and more convinced that the threat came less from neo-Thomist extrinsicism than from secular immanentism, though of course he viewed both as based on the same premises. Cf. Chap. 7, sect.: The Church in the World.

category of the 'supernatural'. The supernatural could subsequently be privatized and social life would then proceed on the basis of the common pursuit of goods associated solely with the 'natural' order.[38]

The Mystery of the Human Spirit

The question that remains, of course, is: what was de Lubac positively searching for? Part of the answer lies in Blondel's influence on de Lubac's theology. Blondel's vision of a reintegration of history and faith and of nature and the supernatural coincided with a sacramental ontology that regarded nature as innately or inherently oriented to the supernatural. This natural desire was something on which de Lubac insisted by using terms such as 'appetite', 'imprinted movement', 'innate openness', 'interior aptitude', 'inclination', or 'capacity' for supernatural grace.[39] It was Blondel, along with Joseph Maréchal and Pierre Rousselot, who, in Balthasar's words, gave de Lubac 'the courage to read out of the texts of Thomas Aquinas what he saw in them with evidence: the paradox of the spiritual creature that is ordained beyond itself by the innermost reality of its nature to a goal that is unreachable for it and that can only be given as a gift of grace'.[40] To be sure, it is possible to over-interpret the Neoplatonist tendencies intimated by these comments. We have already seen that de Lubac did not simply want to be a Neoplatonist.[41] And at times he could make concessions to a separation between the two realms that made him sound distinctly modern.[42] De Lubac's tendency towards Neoplatonism always remained tempered, and probably with good reason.[43] It is none the less clear that his arduous insistence on a *desiderium naturale* stemmed from his wish to return to a

[38] Tracey Rowland, *Culture and the Thomist Tradition after Vatican II* (London: Routledge, 2003), 94.

[39] De Lubac, *Mystery*, 130–2, 136–7.

[40] Hans Urs von Balthasar, *The Theology of Henri de Lubac: An Overview*, trans. Joseph Fessio and Susan Clements (San Francisco, Calif.: Communio/Ignatius, 1991), 13.

[41] Cf. also de Lubac, *Mystery*, 119.

[42] Throughout Chap. 5 of *Le Mystère du surnaturel*, de Lubac made some remarkably strong statements limiting the positive character of natural desire, insisting it was no more than a 'passive aptitude' (*Mystery*, 85), which did not even 'initially or distantly' have a participation in our supernatural being (ibid. 84). At one point, he sounded positively neo-scholastic: 'It is as though there were two levels, two floors with no connection between them. For the two orders are incommensurable' (ibid. 81–2). This is exactly the sort of construct de Lubac had been opposing and would continue to oppose throughout his life.

[43] The title of John Milbank's book on de Lubac (*The Suspended Middle*) takes its cue from Balthasar's use of the same phrase (Balthasar, *Theology of Henri de Lubac*, 14–15). See Milbank, *The Suspended Middle: Henri de Lubac and the Debate Concerning the Supernatural* (Grand Rapids, Mich.: Eerdmans, 2005). Milbank is incorrect, however, in assuming that in some sense de Lubac regarded natural desire as already supernatural in character (ibid. 38–40). Balthasar himself pointed out that de Lubac never made this move. For de Lubac there was 'no trace yet of supernatural grace' in the created spiritual nature, which was exactly why he could not agree with Karl Rahner's 'supernatural existential' (Balthasar, *Theology of Henri de Lubac*, 71). Not unfairly, David Lyle Jeffrey points out that 'in *The Suspended Middle*, de Lubac sounds more like Milbank than like himself' (review of *The Suspended Middle*, in *JAAR* 75 (2007), 715).

spirituality that placed mystery and paradox in the centre of its theology.[44] John Milbank rightly points to the fact that the *desiderium naturale* functioned as a 'suspended middle' between nature and the supernatural, something that was reserved for human beings alone. They had a natural desire for God because they were created as spirit,[45] made in the image of God,[46] for the sake of the eternal vision of God.

De Lubac was unyielding on the issue of *desiderium naturale* because it provided an essential theological link with a patristic, more or less Neoplatonic mindset, which had been sacramental in character. De Lubac believed it was necessary to hold together two paradoxical notions: on the one hand, human beings had an innate natural desire for God; on the other hand, this natural desire was unable of itself to attain the beatific vision, so that the human interior aptitude in no way obliged God to give sanctifying grace. The Aristotelian principle of connaturality was, in de Lubac's mind, an unfortunate rejection of paradox and mystery in favour of common sense.[47] Few emphases were as important to him as this acceptance of paradox and mystery, something he had appropriated from his sustained reading of the Church Fathers and the medieval tradition. A purely positivist theology that refused to acknowledge mystery and wished to remove the scandal of apparent contradictions would always end up isolating and rationalizing one side of the equation and would thus become 'heresy properly so called'.[48] The most serious problem with neo-scholastic theology, from de Lubac's perspective, was, therefore, that it seemed like 'a buildup of concepts by which the believer tries to make the divine mystery less mysterious, and in some cases to eliminate it altogether'.[49]

From the outset of his career, de Lubac moved away from what he called the rational 'dialectical' theology that had dominated Catholic thought since the Middle Ages, and turned to what he termed the 'symbolic' theology of the Church Fathers.[50] The Church Fathers had displayed an eye for the mystery of

---

[44] Just a glance at some of the titles of de Lubac's books illustrates the importance of paradox in his thought. See de Lubac, *Paradoxes* (Paris: Éditions du livre français, 1946); English trans.: *Paradoxes of Faith*, trans. Anne Englund Nash (San Francisco, Calif.: Ignatius, 1987); id., *Paradoxe et mystère de l'Église* (Paris: Aubier Montaigne, 1967); English trans.: *The Church: Paradox and Mystery*, trans. James R. Dunne (New York: Ecclesia, 1969); id., *Autres paradoxes* (Namur: Culture et vérité, 1994); English trans.: *More Paradoxes*, trans. Anne Englund Nash (San Francisco, Calif.: Ignatius, 2002).

[45] Cf. de Lubac's historical theological investigations regarding human nature as tripartite, i.e., consisting of body, soul, *and* spirit, the latter being the locale of the *imago dei*. See de Lubac, 'Tripartite Anthropology', in *Theology in History*, trans. Anne Englund Nash (San Francisco, Calif.: Ignatius, 1996), 117–200. Cf. id., *Brief Catechesis*, 26–7 and the reflections on de Lubac's anthropology in Lewis Ayres, 'The Soul and the Reading of Scripture: A Note on Henri de Lubac', *SJT* 61 (2008), 173–90.

[46] Cf. de Lubac, *Mystery*, 98–100, 108.

[47] Ibid. 140–66.

[48] Ibid. 175.

[49] Ibid. 178.

[50] Id., *Corpus Mysticum; The Eucharist and the Church in the Middle Ages: Historical Survey*, trans. Gemma Simmonds, Richard Price, and Christopher Stephens and ed. Laurence Paul Hemming and

God. For them, theology had been much less a rational explanation of matters divine than something that began with faith in Christ and was willing to rest in the unexplained mysteries that this faith relationship with a personal and transcendent God entailed. De Lubac argued that the move from symbolism to dialectic had begun with Anselm (1033–1109) and Aquinas. Theology had become more a form of 'Christian rationalism' than a type of spiritual understanding.[51]

De Lubac's approach took a different starting-point, one that insisted on a return to mystery. Discussing the image of God, de Lubac commented: ' "Who has known the mind of the Lord?" asks St Paul. "For my part", adds St Gregory of Nyssa, "I also ask: Who has known his own mind? Those who think themselves capable of grasping the nature of God would do well to consider whether they have looked into themselves".'[52] God had designated the *desiderium naturale* as an essential aspect of human nature and as the place where he would graciously work an inner transformation. To remove the *desiderium* would be to remove the *mysterium*, which is to say, the sacrament of God's presence in the world.[53] For de Lubac, the historical contingency of the image of God gave it the potential to function as the sacramental means of entering into deifying union with the triune God.

HENRI BOUILLARD: ANALOGY AND SACRAMENTAL ONTOLOGY

Fear of Relativism

Soon after Henri Bouillard joined the faculty at Lyons-Fourvière in 1941, it became evident that his doctoral studies under Charles Boyer had done little to make him fit the neo-scholastic mould. Controversy broke out as soon as he published his *Conversion et grâce chez s. Thomas d'Aquin* (1944). Much of the controversy that ensued resulted from the fear that Modernist relativism was taking root again. Repeatedly, the Dominicans from the St Maximin studium accused Bouillard of falling into this Modernist trap.[54] After all, Bouillard

---

Susan Frank Parsons (London: SCM, 2006), 221–47; English trans. of *Corpus mysticum: L'Eucharistie et l'Église au moyen âge: Étude historique* (Paris: Aubier, 1944). Cf. Komonchak, 'Theology and Culture', 587–90.

[51] Komonchak, 'Theology and Culture,' 589.

[52] Gregory of Nyssa, *De hominis opificio*, c. 11 (quot. de Lubac, *Mystery*, 210).

[53] De Lubac often highlighted the near interchangeability in the great Tradition of the terms *mysterium* and *sacramentum*. See Chap. 5, sect.: A Sacramental Hermeneutic; Chap. 7, sect.: The Eucharist Makes the Church.

[54] e.g., Marie-Michel Labourdette, 'La Théologie et ses sources', *RT* 46 (1946), 364–7. Cf. Thomas Guarino, 'Henri Bouillard and the Truth-status of Dogmatic Statements', *ScEs* 39 (1987), 335.

presented a daring interpretation of St Thomas's views on conversion and grace, in which he placed the Angelic Doctor's theology squarely within the history of the development of doctrine.[55] Such contextualizing of Thomas's theology seemed clearly problematic. First, Bouillard's opponents claimed that an emphasis on the historical context of Thomas's thought could not but relativize his theology. At the very least, Bouillard's book was not just about the conversion of the human person, but also about the conversion of theology.[56] When, in his discussion of St Thomas, Bouillard wrote that a 'theology that is not up to date [*actuelle*] is a false theology', he could hardly expect neo-scholastic theologians to accept his comment without demurral.[57] Understandably, this comment became the most hotly debated line in the entire book. Réginald Garrigou-Lagrange challenged what he saw as Bouillard's dismissal of St Thomas and of the Council of Trent as 'false doctrine'.[58] Bouillard's book was, in the eyes of Garrigou, a disconcerting debut for the new Théologie series that the faculty of Lyons-Fourvière had initiated.

Second, it appeared evident that Bouillard preferred the theology of the earlier tradition—and in particular that of St Augustine—over the Aristotelian scholasticism of Thomas Aquinas. When, for example, Bouillard insisted that Thomas's acceptance of an infused habit (*habitus*) was a novelty (with 'an existence of no more than a century'[59]), or when he highlighted St Augustine's emphasis on spiritual presence over and above the later Aristotelian notion of transubstantiation, it was hard to avoid the impression that Bouillard believed that the achievements of the thirteenth century were up for discussion. And so, when Bouillard's strategy changed from questioning Thomas's hegemony to appealing to his authority in opposition to later neo-Thomist developments, his opponents were not impressed.[60] When, for instance, Bouillard maintained that Thomas Aquinas had never taught the theological notion of 'elevating grace', his

---

[55] Cf. John Auricchio, *The Future of Theology* (Staten Island, NY: Alba, 1970), 277–80.

[56] Cf. Karl-Heinz Neufeld's astute remark: 'At this point, the method and theme of Bouillard's work find themselves combined in a peculiar fashion. Is there not a demand here for a surrender, a repentance, a conversion of theology, through which it might conform to its meaning in today's age?' ('Fundamentaltheologie in gewandelter Welt: H. Bouillards theologischer Beitrag', *ZKT* 100 (1978), 428–9).

[57] Bouillard, *Conversion et grâce*, 219.

[58] Réginald Garrigou-Lagrange, 'La Nouvelle Théologie, où va-t-elle?' *Ang* 23 (1946), 126, 129. Cf. also id., 'Les Notions consacrées par les Conciles', *Ang* 24 (1947), 217–30. Cf. Bouillard's reaction on this point in 'Notions conciliaires et analogie de la vérité', *RSR* 35 (1948), 255–6.

[59] Bouillard, *Conversion et grâce*, 137–8. Cf. ibid. 224. Gillon showed himself particularly outraged by this assertion. See his 'Théologie de la grâce', 46 (1946), 605.

[60] Of course, all the way through, Bouillard insisted that he was merely interested in historical recovery and denied his antagonists' accusations of having a theological agenda, saying he did not mean to take positions on the theology of St Thomas (*Conversion et grâce*, 16; id., 'A propos de la grâce actuelle', 112). Similarly, Bouillard insisted that he had never given his opinion as to whether sanctifying grace was a 'form' and had never denied the existence of habitual grace ('Notions conciliaires', 270, 257 n. 1). Considering the explosive historical context of the controversy, as well as Bouillard's engaged style, this disclaimer seemed somewhat disingenuous.

antagonists were outraged that the Jesuit from Fourvière had dared to oppose the standard interpretation of Thomas Aquinas.[61] One could hardly build on a theology that appeared to deal with the development of doctrine in such a cavalier fashion.

Third, a Kantian epistemology seemed to lie behind Bouillard's emphasis on historical context and his hesitations regarding traditional Thomist theology. In the conclusion of his dissertation, he insisted that it was 'the law of the Incarnation' that permanent divine truth was accessible only by way of contingent human notions.[62] Well aware that this might cause the neo-Thomists to accuse him of relativism, Bouillard clarified by making a distinction between the absolute character of affirmations, on the one hand, and the contingent or relative character of human notions or representations, on the other hand:

History does not, however, lead to relativism. It allows us to know, in the midst of theological evolution, an absolute—not an absolute of representation, but an absolute of affirmation. Whereas notions, methods, and systems change over time, the affirmations that they contain remain, even though they are expressed by means of other categories. Moreover, it is the affirmations themselves that, in order to keep their meaning in a new intellectual universe, determine new notions, methods, and systems in correspondence with that universe... History thus manifests at the same time the relativity of notions, of schemes in which theology takes shape, and the permanent affirmation that governs them. It is necessary to know the temporal condition of theology and, at the same time, to offer with regard to the faith the absolute affirmation, the divine Word that has become incarnate.[63]

Thus, by insisting *both* on the relativity of theological representations and systems with regard to historical contingency *and* on the absolute character of the eternal underlying affirmations, Bouillard wanted to safeguard the validity and significance of both.

Both Garrigou-Lagrange and his student Marie-Michel Labourdette identified in the distinction between affirmation and representation a return to the Kantian subjectivism advocated by the Modernists Alfred Loisy and George Tyrrell.[64] Garrigou-Lagrange was convinced that by insisting that theological notions changed over time Bouillard was giving up on absolute truth and had made it relative to the human subject. Truth, for Bouillard, was no longer a matter of correspondence between reality and intellect (*adaequatio rei et intellectus*). Instead, insisted Garrigou, he had lapsed into a definition that held to a conformity

---

[61] See on this point particularly the criticism of Michel-Louis Guérard des Lauriers, 'La Théologie de s. Thomas et la grâce actuelle', *ATh* 6 (1945), 276–332; and also of Gillon, 'Théologie de la grâce', 609–12.

[62] Bouillard, *Conversion et grâce*, 220.

[63] Ibid. 220–1.

[64] Labourdette was none the less much more nuanced in his criticism than Garrigou. Cf. Agnès Desmazières, 'La "Nouvelle Théologie", prémisse d'une théologie herméneutique? La Controverse sur l'analogie de la vérité (1946–1949)', *RT* 104 (2004), 262–9.

between mind and life (*conformitas mentis et vitae*), a definition borrowed from Maurice Blondel which, to Garrigou's mind, treated truth as the mere expression of human spirituality: 'It is very dangerous to say, "Notions change, affirmations remain." If the notion of truth itself is going to change, the affirmations no longer remain true in the same manner, nor with the same meaning.'[65] Garrigou-Lagrange seemed to have nailed the issue.[66] After all, Bouillard's belief that theological representations could—and at times should—change, allowed him to question the particularities of Thomas's theological system. The apparent doctrinal relativism on display in Bouillard's description of the historical developments leading up to Thomas's doctrine of justification was the result, so Garrigou-Lagrange believed, of a relativist notion of truth itself, one that took its starting-point in the human subject rather than in divine revelation.[67]

Fourth, Bouillard's rejection of 'elevating grace' was perceived as one of the serious doctrinal consequences of this relativism. From the neo-scholastic perspective, the loss of 'elevating grace' turned the preparation for justification (sanctifying grace) into a natural, human affair. Bouillard maintained that 'elevating grace' had not come into the theological mainstream until the rise of nominalism in the fourteenth century. Thomas himself, Bouillard insisted, had

---

[65] Garrigou-Lagrange, 'La Nouvelle Théologie', 130. Maurice Blondel's comment, which Garrigou resurrected in 1946, was the following: 'The abstract and fanciful *adaequatio rei et intellectus* gets replaced by the legitimate methodical investigation, the *adaequatio realis mentis et vitae*' ('Le Point de départ de la recherche philosophique', *APC* 152 (1906), 235; cf. also id., *Action (1893): Essay on a Critique of Life and a Science of Practice*, trans. Olivia Blanchette (Notre Dame, Ind.: University of Notre Dame Press, 1984), 283). For further discussion on this issue, see Garrigou-Lagrange, 'Nécessité de revenir à la définition traditionnelle de la vérité', *Ang* 25 (1948), 185–8; id., *De gratia: Commentarius in Summam Theologicam S. Thomæ I^{ae} II^{ae} q. 109–114* (Turin: Berruti, 1947), 328–9 n. 2; id., *Reality: A Synthesis of Thomistic Thought*, trans. Patrick Cummins (St Louis, Mo.: Herder, 1950), 381. Cf. also Étienne Fouilloux, *Une Église en quête de liberté: La pensée catholique française entre modernisme et Vatican II (1914–1962)* (Paris: Desclée de Brouwer, 1998), 31.

[66] For a recent similar approach to truth and Christian doctrine, highly critical of *nouvelle théologie*, see Ralph McInerny, *Praeambula fidei: Thomism and the God of the Philosophers* (Washington, DC: Catholic University of America Press, 2006).

[67] Bouillard added that he did not believe that theological dogmas were mere representations or that contingent truths were simply adrift in the waves of human experience: 'To avoid all ambiguity let me comment that the absolute affirmations that we oppose to the contingent representations, contain not just defined dogma, that is to say, propositions canonized by the Church, but also everything that is contained explicitly or implicitly in Scripture and the Tradition. [These affirmations] contain also the invariant or the absolute of the human spirit, first principles and acquired truths necessary to imagine dogma. We contrast this ensemble of invariants with that which is contingent in theological concepts. It is essential to understand that these invariants do not subsist *beside* and independent of contingent concepts. They necessarily come about and express themselves *within them*. But when they change, the new constructs contain the same absolute relations, the same eternal affirmations' (*Conversion et grâce*, 221). This comment indicated that Bouillard was no Modernist: (1) he maintained that defined dogmas and canonized propositions—in fact everything contained in one way or another in Scripture or Tradition—were all included in the absolute affirmations; (2) by using the term 'affirmation' rather than 'experience', he made clear that he looked upward rather than inward for the contents of divine revelation; and (3) he refused to separate contingent expressions of truth from the absolute affirmations to which they referred.

still looked to the infused habit (*habitus*) of grace as the object of divine assistance (*secours divin*), so that, for Thomas, God had prepared human beings for conversion by means of this habit of grace. In other words, Thomas had never posited a separate divine act that elevated the human person from the realm of nature into that of grace. The neo-Thomists were convinced that this interpretation of Thomas's view of conversion reduced God's assistance to a bare minimum. Bouillard did not seem to believe in a special divine act of grace in the habit's motion towards conversion, and he appealed to St Thomas for his belief that God did not assist believers beyond the general or natural guidance that he provided to all human beings. The neo-Thomists concluded that Bouillard's rejection of direct divine intervention by means of an 'elevating motion' naturalized or immanentized the process of conversion.

Bouillard's antagonists expressed their concern about this loss of supernatural elevating grace. In self-defence, Bouillard insisted that he did not view this general divine assistance as 'natural', and that he was not at all averse to calling it 'grace', considering it had justification as its supernatural aim.[68] This concession, however, met with scepticism. As far as Bouillard's detractors could see, the question was not about the supernatural finality of this general divine assistance. The real question was who ultimately effected conversion: God or the human person. For Bouillard, while God indeed provided universal assistance, it was the human *habitus* itself that achieved the supernatural act: 'If it [i.e., actual grace] elevates, it is not through itself, but through the form [of the habit] that it acts.'[69] Bouillard insisted that he faithfully followed St Thomas on this score: 'For St Thomas the divine motion, considered in itself as motion, is simply motion to the act; [this motion] merely gives the impetus [*donner le branle*]; it is the infused habits that elevate to the ability to accomplish supernatural acts.'[70] Bouillard concluded that God's movement of the soul was limited to general assistance. The human *habitus* itself had to respond to this general divine impetus.

To neo-Thomists like Louis-Bertrand Gillon this appeared to endanger the gratuitous character of grace. The rejection of a special divine act of elevating grace in favour of a general guidance of the human habit seemed to put into question the distinct character of supernatural conversion: 'With conversion', Gillon countered Bouillard, 'we are in the presence of an absolute beginning, of a first willing that requires a special divine instigation [*instinctus*]'.[71] It was this absolute beginning of supernatural life that Bouillard was accused of endangering. In conclusion, Bouillard's historical contextualization of theology, his return to the Fathers and the earlier medieval tradition, his emphasis on the knowing human subject, and his insistence on the role that the human being played in

---

[68] Bouillard, *Conversion et grâce*, 84; id., 'A propos de la grâce actuelle', 93–4.
[69] Id., 'A propos de la grâce actuelle', 94.
[70] Ibid.
[71] Gillon, 'Théologie de la grâce', 611.

conversion were all indications to the neo-Thomists that Bouillard was reintro-
ducing the relativism of Modernism.

Bouillard, Barth, and the Doctrine of Analogy

Bouillard turned to Karl Barth after being removed from his teaching post in
1950. This gave him the time to reflect more deeply on the significance of the
analogy of being (*analogia entis*). After a seven-year period of silence, Bouillard
published his monumental analysis of Barth's theology.[72] Bouillard's *Karl Barth*
(1957), written as his second dissertation at the Sorbonne and defended in the
presence of the Swiss theologian himself, was, as one Reformed reviewer put it, 'a
turning point in the relations between Catholics and Protestants'.[73] His study of
Barth forced Bouillard to confront issues such as the validity of the traditional
proofs for the existence of God, the value of natural theology, and, underlying
both of these issues, the legitimacy of the traditional doctrine of *analogia entis*.
Barth radically opposed all three by accusing Catholicism of a 'both ... and'
theology (nature *and* grace, faith *and* works, Scripture *and* Tradition; revelation
and reason; revelation *and* history).[74]

Bouillard's mature work on Barth gives clear evidence that in the intervening
years he had thought a great deal more about the problem of the analogy of
being, as well as its connection to the status of human truth claims.[75] Bouillard
was not afraid to voice some serious criticisms in the direction of Barth, and
each time they came from his reading of St Thomas—although his interpretation of the Angelic Doctor was far from neo-scholastic. Bouillard expressed his
reservations regarding Barth's understanding of *analogia entis* as articulated in
the *Church Dogmatics*. Here Barth grounded the analogy entirely in the revelation of God's grace. He did so for understandable reasons, since he reacted

---

[72] Bouillard, *Karl Barth*, i, *Genèse et évolution de la théologie dialectique*; ii, *Parole de Dieu et
existence humaine* (Paris: Aubier/Montaigne, 1957). Bouillard published a number of shorter essays
in which he summarized particularly his disagreement with Barth's rejection of natural theology. See
id., 'La Refus de la théologie naturelle dans la théologie protestante contemporaine', in Henri
Birault, et al., *L'Existence de Dieu* (Tournai: Casterman, 1961), 95–108, 353–8; id., 'La Preuve de
Dieu dans le "Proslogion" et son interprétation par Karl Barth', in *Congrès international du IXe
centenaire de l'arrivée d'Anselme au Bec* (Le Bec-Hellouin: Abbaye Notre-Dame du Bec and Paris:
Vrin, 1959), 190–207; id., *The Logic of the Faith*, trans. M. H. Gill and Son (New York: Sheed &
Ward, 1967), 59–137; id., 'Karl Barth et le catholicisme', in Karl H. Neufeld (ed.), *Vérité du
christianisme* (Paris: Desclée de Brouwer, 1989), 101–16; id., *The Knowledge of God*, trans. Samuel
D. Femiano (New York: Herder & Herder, 1968), 11–62.

[73] Gabriel Widmer, 'Karl Barth vu par le P. Bouillard', *RTP* 3rd ser., 9 (1959), 166.

[74] Cf. J. Eileen Scully, *Grace and Human Freedom in the Theology of Henri Bouillard* (Bethesda,
Md.: Academica, 2006), 93–4. For helpful analyses of Bouillard's nearly 900-page dissertation, see
Guarino, 'Fundamental Theology', 52–212; Scully, *Grace and Human Freedom*, 87–123.

[75] Since Bouillard's second volume of *Karl Barth* consists of two parts, I will refer to these two
parts as *Karl Barth* ii and iii, respectively. Bouillard republished much of *Karl Barth* iii in *La
Connaissance de Dieu: Foi chrétienne et théologie naturelle* (1967), subsequently translated into
English as *The Knowledge of God*. Here see *Karl Barth*, iii. 190–217.

against a view of analogy that he had encountered in the writings of the Lutheran scholastic theologian from Wittenberg, Johannes Andreas Quenstedt (1617–88).[76] Bouillard believed that Barth was correct to reject this view, but erroneous in thinking that St Thomas had held to it, as well. Bouillard explained that one could find Quenstedt's view in the later theology of the Dominican theologian Thomas Cardinal Cajetan, as well as in the Jesuit theologian Francisco Suárez. Their approach was essentially a conceptualist view, according to which human concepts (Bouillard's 'representations') could truly grasp what God was like. To be sure, Cajetan and Suárez still applied human concepts only in an analogous manner, but they none the less believed that to say of God that he was good was to apply to him the ordinary conceptual contents of the term 'good'.[77] Bouillard insisted that Barth was correct in reacting against such a position, because it veered far too much in the direction of univocity—claiming there was no conceptual difference between discourse applied to God and to human beings. Such a view, Bouillard agreed with Barth, tended to undermine the infinite dissimilarity between God and humans, while claiming an untenably close link between God's eternal truth and human theological statements and systems.

In his dissertation on Barth, then, Bouillard engaged in a fascinating dialogue between Thomas Aquinas, on the one hand, and Cajetan and Suárez, on the other.[78] This was anything but a purely academic matter, considering the sharp controversy that had driven Bouillard out of Fourvière seven years earlier. Bouillard insisted that Thomas's view of analogy had been much more restrained than that of Cajetan and especially that of Suárez. For Cajetan and Suárez, Bouillard explained, concepts themselves were analogous, so that they had the ability to give us actual knowledge of the essence of God. An imperfect but none the less direct resemblance existed between human concepts and the essence of God.[79] Suárez even went so far as to speak of a 'division of being between infinite and finite', thereby subjecting both God and humans to 'being' as an overarching category.[80] Such conceptualism, Bouillard explained, was something from which St Thomas had always shied away. When Thomas had discussed the topic, he had never even used the expression *analogia entis*. Bouillard suggested that St Thomas had not seen the concept of being—or any other predication we might make of God—as directly representing the divine essence. It was not the concepts themselves that he had viewed as analogous; instead, it was the mode of signification (*modus significandi*) that had been analogous. That which our concepts signified (*res significata*) had remained beyond our ability to grasp.

[76] See Barth, *Church Dogmatics*, ii, pt 1, *The Doctrine of God*, trans. T. H. L. Parker, et al. and ed. G. W. Bromiley and T. F. Torrance (1957; repr. London: T. & T. Clark, 2004), 237–43. Cf. the analysis of Guarino, 'Fundamental Theology', 170–4.

[77] Cf. Edward Schillebeeckx, *Revelation and Theology*, ii *The Concept of Truth and Theological Renewal*, trans. N. D. Smith (London: Sheed & Ward, 1968), 9–10.

[78] Bouillard, *Karl Barth*, iii. 198–204.   [79] Ibid. 200.   [80] Ibid.

Based on this reading, Bouillard posited that Thomas's position on analogy was closely connected to Denys's apophatic Neoplatonism. Appealing to the sixth-century Syrian monk, Bouillard commented:

The attributes that we borrow from [creatures] to affirm them with regard to God must also be denied being, in order to signify that they do not befit him except in an eminent sense. One will thus say, with pseudo-Denys, 'God is wise', 'God is not wise', 'God is super-wise'. Since wisdom has its source in God, it must be that he possesses it. But it is not in him in the way we conceive it, and in that sense we must deny that attribute of him. This negation does not signify, however, that God lacks in wisdom, but that he possesses it eminently. So, the analogy is the synthesis of a thesis and of an antithesis.[81]

Bouillard's linking of Thomas with Denys sent the not so subtle message that neo-scholasticism, building on the conceptualism of Cajetan and Suárez, had failed to grasp the true meaning of St Thomas and had thereby abandoned the Neoplatonic tradition and had lapsed into a modern form of rationalism. Bouillard explained that Barth had worked with the neo-scholastic misreading of Thomas since he had encountered a similar reading in the Lutheran theologian Quenstedt. As a result, Barth had reacted less to St Thomas himself than to his later scholastic commentators.[82]

Bouillard, Le Blond, and the 'Analogy of Truth'

Bouillard was no doubt pleased to encounter the link between the doctrine of analogy and the nature of the truth claims of Christian doctrine in Jean-Marie Le Blond's 1947 defence on his behalf, in an essay entitled 'L'Analogie de la vérité' ('The Analogy of Truth').[83] This essay provides an interesting entry into the issues at stake in the debate surrounding *nouvelle théologie*. While Le Blond judiciously did not name any of the antagonists by name, he made obvious reference to the difficulties in which Bouillard found himself through the publication of his dissertation on Thomas Aquinas. Le Blond drew a link between the doctrine of analogy of *being* and the notion of analogy of *truth*, a link he believed ought to 'make people guard against hasty judgments and summary condemnations'.[84] Le Blond made the case that if one accepted an

---

[81] Bouillard, *Karl Barth*, iii. 203.

[82] This is not to say that there were no differences between the positions of Bouillard and Barth. Guarino comments, rightly I believe, that Barth's analogy of revelation simply failed to deal with the question that the doctrine of analogy addresses—namely, how it is possible for human beings to speak about God or to receive his revelation ('Fundamental Theology', 200).

[83] Jean-Marie Le Blond, 'L'Analogie de la vérité: Réflexion d'un philosophe sur une controverse théologique', *RSR* 34 (1947), 129–41. For a neo-Thomist response, see Labourdette and Marie-Joseph Nicolas, 'L'Analogie de la vérité et l'unité de la science théologique', *RT* 47 (1947), 417–66. For discussions of Le Blond's essay, see Auricchio, *Future of Theology*, 311–14; Guarino, 'Fundamental Theology', 32–7. For a critical assessment of Le Blond's position, see John F. X. Knasas, *Being and Some Twentieth-century Thomists* (New York: Fordham University Press, 2003), 166–72.

[84] Le Blond, 'L'Analogie de la vérité', 129.

analogy of proportionality between names applied to God and to human beings, then such an analogy had to apply not just to the concept of being, but also to the transcendentals of truth, goodness, and unity, since these transcendentals were 'basically being itself in its relationship to intelligence, appetite, and self-possession'.[85] The result of this identification of truth, goodness, and unity with being itself was that the doctrine of analogy applied to all of them: 'The thesis of the analogy of truth is, in effect, no less compelling than that of the analogy of being. The truth is not univocal; there is, shall we say, a subsistent truth that is absolute, which is God himself in his simplicity, God as he knows himself and knows in himself all things.'[86] All other truths, the Rector of the House of Philosophy at Mongré concluded, had to be 'complex and deficient', just as all human beings were complex and deficient.

By insisting on an 'analogy of truth', Le Blond posited a similarity between ontology and revelation. In both cases, simplicity and fullness could be found only in God. Human being and human truth were always only analogous being and analogous truth. This allowed human theological statements to share in the truth, since they manifested 'a tendency to the absolute'.[87] Le Blond's distinction between absolute, simple truth and contingent, complex truths echoed Bouillard's differentiation between affirmations and representations:

This position of the absolute, which precisely gives our true affirmations their own character, accounts for the *form* of our knowledge, in an affirmation that reaches the infinite and for which the various representations supply the limiting *matter*, the latter unveils the ideal and the domain of the spirit in this fundamental, implicit affirmation of the absolute, which supports all its acts.[88]

Le Blond's essay placed Bouillard's terminology of 'affirmation' and 'representation' within the context of a Thomist doctrine of analogy, which included not just analogy of being but also analogy of truth.[89] And Le Blond did not shy away from the consequences: even the Thomist synthesis itself could not 'be equal to the subsistent Truth, and cash in all [its] riches'.[90] The implication of Le Blond's analysis was, of course, that if one were to make the mistake of identifying the truth with a particular historical theological synthesis, he would fall into the trap of univocity, mistaking limited, historical representations for eternal, absolute affirmations.[91]

---

[85] Ibid. 130.   [86] Ibid.   [87] Ibid. 131.   [88] Ibid.

[89] Bouillard himself appeared to pick up on Le Blond's suggestion, entitling his own article against Garrigou-Lagrange, 'Notions conciliaires et analogie de la vérité', and insisting there that different theological systems (Augustinian, Thomist, Suarezian, etc.) each used analogous notions, expressing in different ways the same reality (Bouillard, 'Notions conciliaires', *RSR* 35 (1948), 254).

[90] Le Blond, 'L'Analogie de la vérité', 133.

[91] Le Blond repeatedly presented the charges of univocity ('L'Analogie de la vérité', 130, 138, 140) and of Cartesian rationalism (ibid. 138, 141). There is little doubt that he had in mind Garrigou-Lagrange and the Dominicans from Toulouse.

This theory of an 'analogy of truth' is intriguing. It allowed Bouillard to overcome both the Scylla of Modernism and the Charybdis of neo-Thomism. On the one hand, Modernism regarded historical or contingent statements as merely the relative expressions of one's ultimately ineffable subjective experience. This implied that for Modernism there were no eternal or absolute truths in which our statements might participate in some fashion.[92] On the other hand, neo-Thomism tended to identify one's particular, contingent theological system of thought with eternal truth in a rather univocal or straightforward fashion. In other words, while Modernism flirted with equivocity, neo-Thomism tended to err on the side of univocity. The doctrine of analogy allowed Bouillard to state that human representations of truth could participate, in some limited fashion, in the eternal and absolute truth of God.[93]

Karl Barth and Relative Autonomy in Bouillard

In his dissertation on Barth, Bouillard, as a Catholic theologian, took position against Barth's apparent fideism. According to Barth, the doctrine of *analogia entis* was the key issue at stake between Protestantism and Catholicism and so formed the basic reason for his rejection of Catholicism.[94] In contrast, Bouillard followed Blondel in acknowledging the significance of human action and agreed with Le Blond that truth claims were analogous in character. Since this implied an ontology that was sacramental in character, Bouillard refused to follow Barth's apparent belittling or disparaging of a relatively autonomous natural realm. According to Bouillard, people came to the knowledge of God in and through the contingencies of historical and material particularity. This led to the repeated refrain in Bouillard, usually against Barth, that *we*, as created human beings, were the ones who knew God, and that we knew him in a creaturely fashion.[95] For Bouillard, this human element prevented faith from turning into something

---

[92] Cf. Chap. 1, sect.: Modernism's Non-sacramental Mindset.

[93] This is not to say that Bouillard managed to iron out all difficulties. He argued that when Trent affirmed that sanctifying grace was the 'formal cause' (*causa formalis*) of justification, it did not mean to insist on this particular Aristotelian category as the object of its affirmation; its real teaching was that justification was an interior renewal and not just an imputation of Christ's merits. Guarino rightly observes, 'It is precisely this "abstraction" which gave rise to Labourdette's bewilderment and the concomitant charge that the invariant affirmation was itself no more than *another* theological notion' ('Fundamental Theology', 36).

[94] Cf. Barth's oft-quoted comment, 'I regard the *analogia entis* as the invention of Antichrist, and I believe that because of it it is impossible ever to become a Roman Catholic, all other reasons for not doing so being to my mind short-sighted and trivial' (*Church Dogmatics*, i, pt 1, *The Doctrine of the Word of God*, trans. G. W. Bromiley and ed. G. W. Bromiley and T. F. Torrance (2nd edn, 1975; repr. London: T. & T. Clark, 2004), p. xiii).

[95] See e.g. Bouillard, *Karl Barth*, iii. 17–19, 103; id., *Knowledge of God*, 27–8, 39, 60, 95. Illustrative is Bouillard's comment: ' "One knows God by God and only by God". Sure; but it is *we* who know him. The grandeur of Barth is to have recalled energetically an essential truth, too often neglected. Far from invalidating or restricting his affirmation, it will become clear that what we add

purely 'arbitrary'.[96] Appealing to Rudolf Bultmann's (1884–1976) notion of pre-understanding (*Vorverständnis*), Bouillard argued that human beings had an original grasp (*saisie originaire*) or natural knowledge of God. This transcendental condition allowed, with regard to the human side at least, for the act of conversion.[97] All of this implied, for Bouillard, that there was some latitude to develop 'proofs' for the existence of God.[98] Bouillard argued that Barth clearly misunderstood the purpose of Anselm's ontological proof: 'The meaning is obvious: Anselm wants to prove *that* God exists, and not just *how* it is true that he exists.'[99]

Despite his disagreements with Barth on the doctrine of analogy, Bouillard's study of the Swiss theologian did affect his own theology. Bouillard found in Barth a congenial discussion partner and perhaps even an ally in his struggles with the neo-Thomist manualist theologians. Their position was that the natural intellect allowed anyone, believer and non-believer alike, to appreciate and be convinced of the classical proofs for the existence of God and to be persuaded, by means of a judgement of credibility, that the Christian gospel could rightly lay claim to the status of divine revelation. This approach assumed a strict separation between nature and the supernatural, according to which human reason—along with proofs and miracles—had its rightful place in the former. The actual dogmatic contents of revelation belonged to the realm of the supernatural. The acceptance in faith of the truth of the gospel was predicated on the authority of the Church. Bouillard came with a fairly drastic reworking of this standard approach, largely due to his reading of Blondel, but also encouraged by the theology of Barth. His reading of Barth allowed him to put forth a sacramental understanding of reality, one in which nature and the supernatural were much more closely connected than was the case among the neo-Thomists.

A look at three areas where Bouillard wanted to appropriate Barth's questioning of a purely autonomous natural realm may serve to illustrate this point. First, when it came to proving God's existence, Bouillard clearly displayed a certain

expresses the condition by which it is true *for us*' (*Karl Barth*, iii. 77). Cf. Guarino, 'Fundamental Theology', 55–7, 68; Scully, *Grace and Human Freedom*, 108. Brian Foley criticizes Bouillard on this point, rejecting the notion that the subjective 'I' must already be *pre*supposed in the act of faith ('The Catholic Critics of Karl Barth: In Outline and Analysis', *SJT* 14 (1961), 147).

[96] Bouillard, *Knowledge of God*, 31, 39, 95. Cf. Scully, *Grace and Human Freedom*, 12.

[97] For an excellent exposition of Bouillard's position on natural knowledge as the transcendental condition for faith, see Guarino, 'Fundamental Theology', 74–92.

[98] Cf. Bouillard's comment: 'The movement by which the original grasp of God, involved in all Christian faith, becomes conscious of itself and explicates its own rational structure, in other words, the process by which the natural knowledge of God becomes "natural theology", constitutes at first the proof of the existence of God' (*Karl Barth*, iii. 141). See also ibid. 177. I am none the less placing the term 'proof' between quotation marks, because, as we will see, Bouillard's emphasis on the *relative* character of human autonomy places the genuine character of this 'proof' in doubt.

[99] Bouillard, *Karl Barth*, iii. 156. Cf. id., *Knowledge of God*, 70, 80. Bouillard outlined his understanding of St Anselm's *Proslogion* in *Karl Barth*, iii. 141–70, and summarized his thought in 'La Preuve de Dieu', 190–207. See also id., *Knowledge of God*, 63–95.

hesitance. Influenced by Blondel, Bouillard was wary of isolating such rational arguments—as if these proofs could be separated from the dynamic action of the people's everyday lives. While approving the well-known affirmation of the First Vatican Council that God could be 'known with certitude by the natural light of human reason from created things',[100] Bouillard none the less also wanted to affirm that this human reason lay embedded within the overall orientation of the desiring subject: 'In reality there is no objective revelation beyond that which is apprehended by human souls, and the divine light in the soul is nothing other than that of the revelation received.'[101] Thus, while not denying the rationality of the proofs as such, Bouillard believed that fundamental theology needed more emphasis on the experience of people's daily existence, within which they could become aware of their still indeterminate or unthematized original grasp of God.[102] Only within such a context could the traditional proofs become convincing. Signs did not offer rational proof in and of themselves, therefore, but only within a subjective attitude of openness to the supernatural.[103] The implication was that for Bouillard the will and the intellect were much more closely connected than the neo-scholastic tradition had recognized. Bouillard, taking his lead from Blondel, looked to the will as the main human factor leading us in our search for understanding.

Second, Bouillard remained unconvinced that believers and unbelievers could grasp the proofs for the existence of God with equal depth. In a careful analysis of St Anselm's *Proslogion*, Bouillard insisted that Anselm had not accepted that the unbelieving fool of Psalm 14 was able fully to understand the conclusion of the ontological argument. To be sure, it was a rational proof, and proof that was accessible to all through a commonly shared language that allowed for reciprocity between believer and unbeliever.[104] Still, Anselm had been fully cognizant of the fact that many would not have grasped his argument and been convinced that it entailed the existence of God. While, at some level, unbelievers could grasp the expression 'that than which nothing greater can be conceived' (*aliquid quo nihil maius cogitari potest*), the fool would not have been persuaded that this in itself implied the real existence of God. Bouillard explained that for Anselm faith had been required to come to this final step and so to understand the full meaning of 'that than which nothing greater can be conceived'. Only faith would acknowledge that *the very expression itself* implied the existence of God. Without the

---

[100] *Dei Filius*, chap. 2.1 (DS 3004).

[101] Bouillard, *Logic of the Faith*, 15–16.

[102] Bouillard preferred the term 'fundamental theology' to apologetics, as this discipline 'would supply the fundamentals to which dogmatic and moral theology must always return' (*Logic of Faith*, 35).

[103] See id., 'L'Idée chrétienne du miracle', *Cahiers Laënnec* 8/4 (Oct. 1948), 25–37; id., *Logic of the Faith*, 16–21. Cf. Guarino, 'Fundamental Theology', 216–19, 231–3, 256–60; Scully, *Grace and Human Freedom*, 26–8.

[104] Bouillard, *Karl Barth*, iii. 155–6.

actual experience of faith, the unbeliever could not grasp the true implication of what he understood merely at a superficial level. Bouillard explained:

This sheds light on the paradox that we pick up in the *Proslogion*. On our reading, the unbeliever, when he *hears* the believer articulate this designation of God—'that than which nothing greater can be conceived'—understands the meaning; yet he does not understand it well, since he does not grasp that the existence of God is necessarily implied here.[105]

This approach committed Bouillard—and, he believed, it had also committed Anselm—to a close connection between faith and reason. Since it was only the believer who could grasp the full implication of the meaning of *aliquid quo nihil maius cogitari potest*, it was only through the experience of faith that reason truly came to its own.

Third, Bouillard believed that St Anselm had rejected a strict separation between philosophy and theology and that this lay behind his conviction that reason flourished more fully within the context of faith. Bouillard agreed with Barth that Anselm had developed his argument as a believer, within the context of prayer, and in the presence of other Benedictine monks. All of this indicated, Bouillard insisted, that the rightful place of the *praeambula fidei* and natural theology was only within the ambit of faith. The proofs for the existence of God and the judgements of credibility could not stand on their own as purely philosophical attempts to arrive at the existence of God and at the reality of divine revelation. Only within a theological context did such attempts truly make sense.[106] Bouillard therefore repeatedly made the case that not only had St Anselm viewed his proof for God's existence as a theological enterprise, but that also Thomas Aquinas, by including his proofs in the *Summa theologica*, had rejected a strict separation between philosophy and theology.[107] Bouillard concluded that natural theology constituted the inside skeleton rather than the outside scaffolding of revealed truth. Natural theology was, in his words, 'the rational *intrastructure*, and not, strictly speaking, the infrastructure, of Christian theology'.[108] The preambles and natural theology had their place only within the context of faith.

These three points, for which he was indebted to Barth's theology, allowed Bouillard to oppose the rationalism of his neo-Thomist adversaries. Divine revelation was no longer completely separate from the existential longings of people in the contemporary world. Instead, fundamental theology's main duty was now to try and show people how divine revelation corresponded to the open questions and experiences of their unfulfilled longings, and thereby to show the 'logic of the faith'. The natural world and its supernatural implications were no

---

[105] Ibid. 166. See on this point the helpful analysis of Guarino, 'Fundamental Theology', 116–22.
[106] Id., *Karl Barth*, iii. 146–52, 166–7; id., *Knowledge of God*, 71–3.
[107] Id., *Knowledge of God*, 77–9; id., *Logic of the Faith*, 114.
[108] Id., *Logic of the Faith*, 114.

longer considered equally intelligible to all. Instead, the divine illumination of faith, through the shaping of both the will and the intellect, would come to take centre stage, not just in the understanding of Christian doctrine, but also in the realm of philosophy and reason. No longer, therefore, would fundamental and speculative theology constitute two hermetically sealed compartments. Bouillard clearly curtailed the neo-Thomist autonomy of nature and assigned it a position of *relative* autonomy only.

Bouillard and the Gratuity of Grace

Bouillard advocated a change from theology as a strictly intellectual endeavour founded on extrinsically construed *praeambula fidei* to a rather more Neoplatonic, sacramental approach in which philosophy served to provide the rational 'intrastructure' within the overall theological discipline. Of course, neo-scholastics were nervous about this reintegration of nature and the supernatural. Particularly, they were concerned that Bouillard would be unable to uphold the distinct character of divine transcendence and the gratuity of divine grace. Bouillard's insistence that there was a correspondence between divine revelation and the inner structure of human experience seemed to them a lapse into semi-Pelagianism. Likewise, Bouillard's emphasis on the human will seemed to imply that human desire *necessitated* supernatural revelation, thus curtailing divine freedom. In short, the neo-Thomist concern was with the implications of Bouillard's sacramental position for the doctrine of grace.

It is true that Bouillard was intent on maintaining the integrity of human freedom.[109] From the outset, one of the concerns about Bouillard's *Conversion et grâce chez s. Thomas d'Aquin* was his rejection of 'elevating grace', since it appeared to imply a naturalizing of grace. In agreement with Blondel, Bouillard insisted that all human beings were faced with the choice 'either to ignore the presence of the Absolute Being within us or to open our hearts to him'.[110] This emphasis on the freedom of human consent stemmed from Bouillard's desire to uphold a correlation between divine revelation and the experience of the natural human question of the supernatural. Bouillard insisted that by freely consenting to the initial option of a still indeterminate supernatural—simply acknowledging in oneself the presence of the Absolute Being—one was already within 'the ambit of the Christian faith'.[111] He so accentuated the inner dynamic of human existence as oriented towards the supernatural that he may inadvertently have excluded some of the mystery involved in the divine–human encounter.

This is not to say, however, that the neo-scholastic objections to Bouillard's theology were largely correct. Clearly, Bouillard passionately insisted both on

---

[109] Scully highlights this point in *Grace and Human Freedom*.
[110] Bouillard, *Logic of the Faith*, 24.
[111] Ibid. 20. Cf. ibid. 25.

divine transcendence and on the gratuitous character of grace, and he refused to regard revelation as the result of human experience or subjective introspection. Bouillard defended Blondel by insisting that the philosopher from Aix had safeguarded the 'transcendence and gratuity' of the supernatural in at least three ways. First, Blondel had highlighted precisely the failure or frustration of the dynamic longing of the human will. This failure would become evident if and when people would recognize that the supernatural was beyond their grasp. Second, Blondel had never introduced the actual contents of Christian theology into his philosophy.[112] He had never gone beyond talking about Christian beliefs as hypotheses, which non-believers should test in order to see whether they could function as answers to the frustrations of the human will. Third, and perhaps most importantly, Blondel had realized that only the experience of faith could discern that the Christian message was the gift of God 'in its ineffable gratuity'.[113]

Bouillard may at times have moved too uncritically on the path of human experience, confident that it would inexorably lead to an affirmation of metaphysics and divine transcendence. He sometimes did come close to confusing divine revelation with human experience. And the human will appeared to receive a great deal of autonomy in Bouillard's theology of conversion. But Bouillard was a theologian willing to take risks. As a result, his theological position neither slid into a rationalist apologetic of signs and miracles, nor into an immanentism that explained the supernatural in terms of human experience. Bouillard's theology was the outcome of a deep desire for a truly sacramental ontology, one that maintained the validity of metaphysical claims, while also recognizing the hermeneutic character of human existence, the dynamism of human experience, and the significance of historical developments. By reading Maurice Blondel and Karl Barth, both through the prism of Thomas's doctrine of analogy, Bouillard became an advocate of a sacramental ontology.

CONCLUSION: *NÉOPLATONISME BELGO–FRANÇAIS*

Nouvelle théologie is sometimes regarded as a movement that was especially intent on adapting Catholicism to modern culture, by paying attention to 'signs of the times'. The term *néoplatonisme belgo–français* may, therefore, not spring readily to mind in relation to the theological movement more commonly known as *nouvelle théologie*. When Fr Louis-Bertrand Gillon, theologian at the Angelicum

---

[112] Thus, Bouillard explained that 'the philosophy of action leads one to take seriously the Christian message. But at the same time it recognizes—and Blondel insists on this—that it cannot affirm their truth. The affirmation can only be attained and posed in the experience of faith' ('The Thought of Maurice Blondel: A Synoptic Vision', *IPQ* 3 (1963), 395).

[113] Bouillard, *Blondel and Christianity*, trans. James M. Somerville (Washington, DC: Corpus, 1969), 83.

in Rome, used the expression *néoplatonisme belgo-français* in 1946, he meant it as
a term of derision, as an attempt to undermine the work of de Lubac and
Bouillard.[114] The dominant Thomist school of thought sought to dismiss *nouvelle théologie* as a group of anti-intellectual radicals who had infested Lyons-
Fourvière in France and Le Saulchoir in Belgium, creating a Belgian–French
Neoplatonism.[115] Ironically, Gillon's caustic comment about *néoplatonisme
belgo-français* highlighted one of *nouvelle théologie*'s most significant emphases:
de Lubac and Bouillard were convinced that the great Tradition, and especially
the Greek Fathers, had held a unified view of reality. This view had not suffered
from the modern extrinsicism characterizing later Thomist thought, as it came to
regard the supernatural as a separate order, superimposed onto the realm of
nature. While Gillon's accusation was an overstatement, his intuition was none
the less correct that *nouvelle théologie* was reacting against the loss of mystery in
theology. *Nouvelle théologie* evaluated as positive the Neoplatonic realization that
the ultimate end of human beings could not possibly lie within the realm of
nature itself.

The neo-Thomist detractors of de Lubac and Bouillard were rightly concerned
to uphold divine transcendence and the freedom of grace. They believed that the
only means at their disposal was to keep the eternal truth of God as far removed
as possible from any human hermeneutic vicissitudes and to hold at bay any sense
of an innate human longing for supernatural beatitude. For them, any link
between divine truth and human existence had to remain strictly extrinsic.
This meant that theological truth systems could be logically deduced from the
deposit of divine revelation and were consequently impervious to historical
development. It also meant that conversion was best described as an unequivocally miraculous intervention, unconnected to innate human desire.

The theologians of Lyons-Fourvière took a vastly different approach. The
struggles of de Lubac and Bouillard gave evidence of a deep underlying commonality between the two Jesuits. De Lubac refused to live in a modern, non-
sacramental world, and he maintained that God drew human beings to himself
by connecting with what was most truly human in them—namely, their natural
desire for the beatific vision. The human spirit could become a sacrament of the
presence of God. Bouillard insisted that human language, embedded within
historical realities and their developments, was able to speak of supernatural,
unchanging truth in an analogical fashion. Human signs could make signified

---

[114] Gillon, 'Théologie de la grâce', 604, 611. Thomas G. Guarino first alerted me to this
reference of Gillon ('Fundamental Theology', 37 n. 58). For Bouillard's response to Gillon, see
Bouillard, 'Précisions', *RT* 47 (1947), 177–83, which is followed by a 'Post-scriptum' by Gillon
(pp. 183–9).

[115] Through circumstances of the anti-Catholic French legislation at the beginning of the early
twentieth century, the scholasticate moved from Flavigny (east of Paris) to Le Saulchoir, Belgium,
where it was located from 1903 to 1937. So, by the time Gillon made his accusation in 1946, all the
main figures connected to *nouvelle théologie* were located in France.

realities present. The human spirit and human discourse could both function as sacraments, drawing human realities into the presence of God. De Lubac and Bouillard thus left a lasting legacy by rediscovering that the contingencies of human existence were sacramental mysteries meant to draw the created order into deifying union with their origin and end, the triune God.

4

The Law of the Incarnation: Balthasar and Chenu on Nature and the Supernatural

God's own creation, which depends for its existence on God's power and art and wisdom, has borne God.

St Irenaeus[1]

The theologians discussed in the previous and present chapters were united in their common rejection of the neo-scholastic separation of nature and the supernatural and their appropriation of a sacramental ontology. Not all of them pursued a sacramental ontology in exactly the same manner or even with the same degree of consistency. The present chapter, therefore, has several aims. First, I wish to make clear that Hans Urs von Balthasar and Marie-Dominique Chenu fit the general mould of *nouvelle théologie*'s sacramental ontology. Second, it will become clear that Balthasar and Chenu stressed the relative autonomy of nature more strongly than Henri de Lubac and Henri Bouillard. Whereas de Lubac and Bouillard highlighted that it was truly supernatural grace in which nature participated (so that they focused on the upward movement of divine ascent), Balthasar and Chenu stressed that it was nature itself that participated in supernatural grace (and thus they emphasized divine descent into created reality).[2] Third, with regard to Chenu, I will question the consistency of his sacramental ontology. His sacramental ontology was based on the Incarnation and was certainly genuine. None the less, his positive appraisal of the desacralizing of the created order in the High Middle Ages raises questions about the consistency of his sacramental approach.

---

[1] Irenaeus, *Against Heresies*, V.18.1 (quot. Hans Urs von Balthasar, *The Scandal of the Incarnation: Irenaeus against the Heresies*, trans. John Saward (San Francisco, Calif.: Ignatius, 1990), 54).

[2] To be sure, the present chapter will qualify this contrast in several ways.

HANS URS VON BALTHASAR: ANALOGY AS SACRAMENTAL PARTICIPATION

Influence of Lubacian *Ressourcement*

Balthasar's theology was characterized by a deep immersion in the Church Fathers.[3] In order to appreciate what he tried to do in this *ressourcement* of the Fathers, it may be helpful to analyse in some detail the profound influence that de Lubac had both in this regard and in terms of Balthasar's overall theology.[4] After all, Balthasar's Fourvière mentor was largely responsible for his patristic explorations. De Lubac's influence made itself felt already in Balthasar's 1939 essay 'Patristik, Scholastik und wir'.[5] Here Balthasar indicated, in line with de Lubac, that the Fathers were of continuing interest because of their determinative impact on the development of Christian doctrine. As we have seen, de Lubac sought to overcome the neo-Thomist intellectualism and turned to the Fathers in order to explore their more direct interaction with Scripture and to recover a sacramental relationship between nature and the supernatural. The same desire motivated Balthasar to explore the Fathers, as well. Balthasar also found in de Lubac and the Fathers support for his opposition to the allegedly 'neutral' character of historical critical exegesis. Balthasar was intrigued with the Fathers'

---

[3] For overviews of Balthasar's main patristic publications, see Charles Kannengiesser, 'Listening to the Fathers', in David L. Schindler (ed), *Hans Urs Von Balthasar: His Life and Work* (San Francisco, Calif.: Communio/Ignatius, 1991), 59–63; Brian E. Daley, 'Balthasar's Reading of the Church Fathers', in Edward T. Oakes and David Moss (eds), *The Cambridge Companion to Hans Urs von Balthasar* (Cambridge: Cambridge University Press, 2004), 193–5. The main publications on the Greek Fathers are the following. On Origen: Balthasar, *Geist und Feuer: Ein Aufbau aus seinen Werken* (Salzburg: Müller, 1938; rev. edn, 1953); English trans.: *Origen: Spirit and Fire: A Thematic Anthology of his Writings*, trans. Robert J. Daly (Washington, DC: Catholic University of America Press, 1984); id., *Parole et mystère chez Origène* (Paris: Cerf, 1957). The last book stems from two earlier essays: 'Le Mysterion d'Origène', *RSR* 26 (1936), 513–62; 27 (1937), 38–64. On Irenaeus: Balthasar, *Irenäus: Geduld des Reifens: Die christliche Antwort auf den gnostischen Mythos des 2. Jahrhunderts* (Basle: Schwabe, 1943; rev. edn, 1956); new edn: *Irenäus: Gott in Fleisch und Blut: Ein Durchblick in Texten* (Einsiedeln: Johannes, 1981); English trans.: *Scandal of the Incarnation*. On Gregory of Nyssa: Balthasar, *Der versiegelte Quell: Auslegung des Hohen Liedes* (Salzburg: Müller, 1939; rev. edn, 1954); id., *Présence et pensée: Essai sur la philosophie religieuse de Grégoire de Nysse* (Paris: Beauchesne, 1942); English trans.: *Presence and Thought: An Essay on the Religious Philosophy of Gregory of Nyssa*, trans. Mark Sebanc (San Francisco, Calif.: Communio/Ignatius, 1995). On Maximus the Confessor: Balthasar, *Kosmische Liturgie: Höhe und Krise des griechischen Weltbildes bei Maximus Confessor* (Freiburg: Herder, 1941); rev. edn: *Die gnostischen Centurien des Maximus Confessor and Das Scholienwerk des Johannes von Scythopolis* (Einsiedeln: Johannes, 1961); English trans.: id., *Cosmic Liturgy: The Universe According to Maximus the Confessor*, trans. Brian E. Daley (San Francisco, Calif.: Ignatius, 2003).

[4] For a brief historical discussion of the link between de Lubac and Balthasar, see Chap. 1, sect.: Controversy over *Ressourcement* (1944–50).

[5] Balthasar, 'Patristik, Scholastik und wir', *TZ* 3 (1939), 65–104; English trans.: 'The Fathers, the Scholastics, and Ourselves', trans. Edward T. Oakes, *Comm* 24 (1997), 347–96. For an analysis of this essay, see Edward T. Oakes, *Pattern of Redemption: The Theology of Hans Urs von Balthasar* (New York: Continuum, 1994), 102–30.

hermeneutic, since it had insisted on Christian experience, on the centrality of Christology, and on the ecclesial context as necessary prerequisites for the interpretation of Scripture.[6]

Particularly significant for understanding Balthasar's *ressourcement* is his adoption of de Lubac's approach to the nature–supernatural relationship, including de Lubac's trepidation regarding the notion of pure nature and his insistence on natural desire for the vision of God. In the first volume of his *Theologik*, first published as a separate volume in 1947, Balthasar presented a discussion on the relationship between philosophy and theology. Here he made a strong case for the reintegration of nature and the supernatural: 'After all, the supernatural takes root in the deepest structures of being, leavens them through and through, and permeates them like a breath or an omnipresent fragrance.'[7] Philosophy, Balthasar insisted time and again, raised theological questions but was unable to provide the answers to its own questions. The relationship between the two disciplines was asymmetrical. While philosophy was in need of theology for its own fulfilment, theology did not need philosophy in the same way. To be sure, theology was impossible without philosophy, and one could say that there was a 'reciprocal interpenetration' between the two.[8] But if inner-worldly structures pointed to the divine Logos, and if revelation elevated and perfected worldly truth,[9] this meant that Christians should 'acknowledge and accept the indelible presence of... theologoumena at the heart of concrete philosophical thinking'.[10] In an important sense, then, theology had priority over philosophy.

In this same context, Balthasar insisted that 'the supernatural has impregnated nature so deeply that there is simply no way to reconstruct it in its pure state (*natura pura*)'.[11] Also here, his approach was obviously Lubacian.[12] Balthasar felt that de Lubac had dealt with the supernatural finality of the created spirit 'so lucidly... that we no longer need to recapitulate the main lines of his argument'.[13] Pure nature seemed to serve little purpose in a world that from the beginning was stamped with a supernatural finality. As a result, Balthasar preferred to speak of the 'formal concept of nature', underlining thereby that

---

[6] For further discussion of de Lubac's influence on Balthasar, see Peter Henrici, 'Hans Urs von Balthasar und der französische Katholizismus', in Walter Kasper (ed.), *Logik der Liebe und Herrlichkeit Gottes: Hans Urs von Balthasar im Gespräch* (Ostfildern: Matthias-Grünewald, 2006), 169–74; Rudolf Voderholzer, 'Die Bedeutung der so genannten "Nouvelle Théologie" (insbesondere Henri de Lubacs) für die Theologie Hans Urs von Balthasars', ibid. 208–12.

[7] Balthasar, *Theo-Logic: Theological Logical Theory*, trans. Adrian J. Walker and Graham Harrison, 3 vols (San Francisco, Calif.: Ignatius, 2000–5), i (*Truth of the World*), 12.

[8] Ibid. 7. Balthasar described the relationship as analogical in character (ibid. 15).

[9] Ibid. 11.

[10] Ibid. 12.

[11] Ibid.

[12] Cf. Chap. 3, sect.: Pure Nature and Natural Desire.

[13] Balthasar, *The Theology of Karl Barth*, trans. Edward T. Oakes (San Francisco, Calif.: Communio/Ignatius, 1992), 267 n. 1.

there had never been a state of pure nature.[14] Nature and the supernatural were not two separate compartments, as the neo-Thomist position appeared to argue.

Balthasar's indebtedness to de Lubac also made him careful, however, not to discard the notion of pure nature altogether. Just as de Lubac occasionally acknowledged the polemical value of a hypothetical *pura natura*, so Balthasar agreed that the notion might serve to safeguard divine grace:

> To pose such a hypothesis, to maintain that a graceless order of nature or creation is at least *possible*, became urgent for theology only when a heretic wanted to make the fluid bond between nature and the supernatural a forced and juridical one. This happened when Baius chose to derive a *de jure* compulsory right to grace understood as a strict requirement (*debitum*) from nature based on the *de facto* configuration of both orders, which were linked because of free grace, not necessity.[15]

Balthasar acknowledged that it might be necessary to speak of a hypothetical notion of pure nature in order to maintain that God was under no necessity or obligation to give divine grace.[16] According to Balthasar, the radical Augustinianism of Michael Baius (1513–89) had uncritically applied Aristotle's philosophical definition of nature to a theological context. Aristotle's philosophy had included the finality of a thing in its nature. Baius, by applying this philosophical approach to theology, had made the mistake of including the supernatural finality of human beings in the very definition of their nature. Balthasar rejected this Baianist 'naturalization' of grace. He insisted it overlooked the fact that in theology one could use the concept of nature only in an analogical fashion.[17] The notion of *pura natura* could thus counter an erroneous inclusion of supernatural finality in the very definition of human nature and, as a result, could safeguard God's freedom in granting supernatural grace. In short, Balthasar appreciated that historically the hypothetical notion of *pura natura* had served to safeguard the theological integrity of divine grace.

Balthasar none the less agreed with de Lubac that the hypothesis of pure nature had never played a role in the theology of St Thomas, and they both regretted that the hypothesis had 'soon managed to develop into a full system detached from its *theological* presuppositions, and on that basis . . . took on a life on its own'.[18] Like de Lubac, Balthasar wanted to root his doctrine of creation in the world as God had actually created it. That world, Balthasar believed, was suffused with grace, both in the form of the free gift of creation itself and in the form of the free gift of supernatural grace.[19] It might perhaps be helpful to 'abstract' or 'subtract' the elements of grace from the totality of this actual created order in

[14] Ibid. 285.

[15] Ibid. 269.

[16] Cf. ibid. 272, where Balthasar commented that the Catholic Church, in opposition to Protestant 'naturalization of grace', had 'to safeguard the purity of the concept of grace'.

[17] Ibid. 273–5, 281.

[18] Ibid. 270.

[19] Cf. Balthasar's discussion on de Lubac (ibid. 295–302).

order to emphasize the contingent and free character of God's grace.[20] But such a hypothetical removal of grace from the created order was by no means an easy or straightforward process. Since the world of people's actual lives was infused with grace from the very outset and was thus a supernatural world, it was almost impossible to describe what a hypothetical pure nature might look like:

> The questions, for example, of how far 'ignorance and hardship belong to natural existence', how much concupiscence, disease, death (and the forms that death takes) are the result of sin or are part of the definition of being human and animal; but also questions about marriage, community, the State, our relation to a God who might not have revealed himself in his personal, interior life, the necessity for prayer in a natural state (which many people deny, for good reasons), the eschatological fate of the soul, resurrection of the body, Last Judgement, eternal bliss: all such questions addressed to pure nature are simply unanswerable.[21]

Balthasar clearly wanted to take his starting-point in theology and in the *de facto* world that God had created. This meant for him that human beings, even after the Fall, or when they rejected God's grace, continued to exist in a world imbued by grace. The world remained supernatural in character. There was, in our actual world, no human being devoid of a supernatural vocation or of divine grace. Balthasar went so far as to say that not only did all human beings have a supernatural goal, they also had the means of grace to attain this goal:

> All, in their own way, share humanity's supernatural goal; hence all somehow share in the supernatural means to attain it. Through Christ, who died for us all, and the Church his Bride, outside of which there is no salvation, all human beings somehow, either openly or hiddenly, partake in the grace of the divine–Christic–ecclesial order, whether they lived before or will have lived after him.[22]

For Balthasar, the supernatural goal of human beings had its counterpart in the supernatural gift of the means to attain this goal.[23]

Not surprisingly, given his reticence with regard to the concept of *pura natura* and his insistence on the supernatural finality of creation as such, Balthasar also agreed with de Lubac that human beings had a natural desire (*desiderium naturale*) for the vision of God. Human nature always had a supernatural end, and human beings were created with more than merely a passive obediential potency (*oboedientia potentialis*). Following one of his mentors, Romano Guardini (1885–1968), Balthasar spoke of this human capacity as a 'third domain' between nature and the supernatural, which he described as 'the depths of nature

---

[20] Balthasar, *Theology of Karl Barth*, 280.

[21] Ibid. 283.

[22] Ibid. 288.

[23] This is not the place to discuss Balthasar's views on universalism, which he discussed especially in his book, *Dare We Hope 'That All Men Be Saved'? With a Short Discourse on Hell*, trans. David Kipp and Lothar Krauth (San Francisco, Calif.: Ignatius, 1988).

that do not emerge into visibility until the light of grace falls on them'.[24] To be sure, this did not mean that human natural desire always attained its appropriate supernatural end. Balthasar agreed with de Lubac that divine grace was needed to attain it, and he expressed himself at times quite strongly: 'Human nature must necessarily retain something of this expectant hovering, insofar as man's ultimate, supernatural destination is beyond the range and scope of nature; consequently, faith is again and again experienced as the unexpected, as something neither deducible from nature nor founded upon it.'[25] Grace was not something that God owed to human beings.

Balthasar's *ressourcement* of the Fathers was thoroughly Lubacian in character. The patristic scholar from Fourvière introduced him to the Church Fathers. De Lubac's recovery of patristic exegesis fuelled Balthasar's scepticism with regard to a historical critical hermeneutic that might wish to claim neutrality for its methodology. Balthasar's understanding of the relationship between philosophy and theology was patterned on de Lubac's attempt to reintegrate nature and the supernatural. And Balthasar also agreed with de Lubac's views on pure nature and natural desire, insisting that the created order was never beyond the pale of God's grace. In each of these ways Balthasar showed himself a true disciple of de Lubac's programme of *ressourcement*.

Irenaeus, Denys, and Maximus: Analogous Participation

Balthasar's understanding of the nature–supernatural relationship was closely modelled after de Lubac's theological approach and displayed the same sacramental structure. Kevin Mongrain turns Balthasar's sacramental sensibility into a central interpretive key for his work: 'God redeems creation *qua* creation, and hence sacramentally infuses and unites worldly beauty, goodness, and truth with supernatural grace.'[26] Mongrain rightly speaks in this connection of a 'sacramental ontology' in Balthasar.[27] De Lubac's and Balthasar's emphases are none the less subtly different from one another. De Lubac used his sacramental ontology in order to highlight that it was truly *supernatural grace* in which nature participated, while Balthasar used the same sacramental ontology to stress that *nature itself* participated in supernatural grace. In other words, de Lubac, ever the Greek patristic scholar, emphasized the upward movement of divine ascent, while

---

[24] Id., *Theo-Logic: Theological Logical Theory*, ii (*Truth of God*), 96. Cf. ibid. i. 13: 'But perhaps we need to go beyond the simple juxtaposition of the natural and supernatural domains and to posit a third domain of truths that genuinely belongs to creaturely nature yet do not emerge into the light of consciousness until they are illumined by a ray of the supernatural.'

[25] Balthasar, *Prayer*, trans. Graham Harrisson (San Francisco, Calif.: Ignatius, 1986), 42.

[26] Kevin Mongrain, *The Systematic Thought of Hans Urs von Balthasar: An Irenaean Retrieval* (New York: Crossroad/Herder, 2002), 61.

[27] Ibid. Mongrain emphasizes Balthasar's sacramental mindset throughout his book. See also Kevin Mongrain, 'Von Balthasar's Way from Doxology to Theology', *TTod* 64 (2007), 58–70.

Balthasar's incarnational approach emphasized divine descent into the created realities of this-worldly time and space.[28]

Balthasar's distinctive emphasis on created realities came to the fore in his writings on the Church Fathers. His 'Patristik, Scholastik und wir' presented a remarkable analysis of the patristic period and its borrowing of Platonic categories. Balthasar did recognize in this essay the Fathers' opposition to Platonic pantheism,[29] and he acknowledged that in many ways the danger of Platonism had been 'hemmed in'.[30] Overall, however, he was convinced that the Fathers had insufficiently recognized the otherness implied in the Creator–creature distinction. He identified this as a 'danger zone', particularly evident in Alexandrian theology.[31] The danger was that 'participation' in God would become natural participation rather than participation by grace and so would turn into pantheism.[32] Balthasar observed the Alexandrian over-reliance on Platonic philosophy in (1) the schema of descent and emanation; (2) the strict monotheism of Denys and Maximus, which had not done justice to the Trinitarian character of God; (3) the docetic and Eutychian tendencies in which the purely spiritual took over from the goodness of the Incarnation; (4) the far-reaching asceticism and mysticism of the patristic epoch; and (5) the tendency to look to the Church's hierarchical structure as symbolic of an inner spiritual hierarchy as its lasting truth.[33]

Balthasar was obviously pleased that the patristic borrowing from the Platonic tradition had later been counterbalanced by the introduction of Aristotelianism in medieval scholastic thought. Its acknowledgement of the goodness of creation had been more congenial to a true mutual otherness between God and creature: 'With the Scholastic concept of nature, the possibility is finally taken seriously that the incarnation can be seriously misinterpreted as a *transitorium* to a purely spiritual condition. The Scholastic concept of nature also obviates every mistrust and hostility towards the material and its natural laws, for with the concept of created nature this danger is avoided in principle.'[34] To be sure, Balthasar

---

[28] Brian Daley also draws attention to Balthasar's quest for a 'sacramental understanding' of the world in his engagement with the Church Fathers, an understanding that does not just press '*through* worldly images' but 'recognizes the presence of transcendent holiness *in* sensible things' ('Balthasar's Reading', 190–1). Cf. also Ben Quash's comment on the 'almost sacramental character' of the mediation of the 'differentiated diversity of material things' ('Hans Urs von Balthasar', in David F. Ford and Rachel Muers (eds), *The Modern Theologians: An Introduction to Christian Theology since 1918* (3rd edn, Oxford: Blackwell, 2005), 111). Rodney A. Howsare also speaks of Balthasar's '"sacramental" sensibilities' (*Hans Urs von Balthasar and Protestantism: The Ecumenical Implications of His Theological Style* (London: T. & T. Clark/Continuum, 2005), 107; and cf. 191 n. 15).

[29] Balthasar, 'The Fathers, the Scholastics, and Ourselves', 377.

[30] Ibid. 378.

[31] Ibid. 372.

[32] Ibid. 273.

[33] Ibid. 374–6.

[34] Ibid. 382. Balthasar made some remarkable un-Lubacian observations. He insisted that the actual dangers of scholasticism came from a residue of Platonism rather than from Aristotelianism. He maintained (1) that Thomas's conception of a 'natural longing' carried 'the danger of interpreting

immediately also recognized the danger of a 'two-storey' universe that might remove the supernatural finality from the realm of nature. He reiterated that he wanted to maintain 'the absolute uniqueness of the ultimate (that is, the supernatural) final goal of this world'.[35] It was none the less clear that Balthasar was not simply looking to the Fathers for a repristination of their sacramental universe.[36] His apprehension of Platonic categories was far too pronounced to allow for such a unilateral retrieval of the patristic period. For Balthasar, by adopting a Platonic ontology one could not do justice to the goodness and beauty of the created order.

Interestingly, however, when Balthasar looked to individual Church Fathers for assistance in developing his own theology of aesthetics, he found a great deal that he could appropriate, and he certainly did not convey the impression of a Platonic patristic universe. Balthasar often emphasized that the Church Fathers had a genuine appreciation for the created order, since it participated by grace in the beauty of God himself. Balthasar's appropriation of Irenaeus (d. *c*.202), Denys (early sixth century), and Maximus the Confessor (*c*.580–662) may illustrate the creation-affirming picture that Balthasar painted. He especially appealed to Irenaeus's anti-Gnostic theology to uphold the goodness and beauty of creation.[37] The second-century Bishop of Lyons had such a great impact on Balthasar's thought that Kevin Mongrain speaks of an 'Irenaean retrieval':

von Balthasar came to see Irenaeus of Lyons's theology of the mutual glorification of God and humanity in Christ as the best articulation of the theological vision presented by de Lubac. Irenaeus, read through de Lubac's lens, therefore became von Balthasar's primary critical resource from the patristic archive for reforming contemporary Catholic theology and challenging various modern intellectual movements in theology, culture, and politics.[38]

Perhaps the most obvious element of Balthasar's *ressourcement* was his celebration of Irenaeus as an anti-Platonic thinker. Gnosticism, Balthasar believed, was a 'regression from Platonic philosophy'.[39] At the outset of his essay on Irenaeus in

the *potentia oboedientialis* as a *potentia naturalis*'; (2) that the doctrine of the 'real distinction' in modern Thomism 'always had to justify itself against the objection of latent pantheism'; and (3) that the doctrine of a *desiderium naturale visionis* was linked with the scholastic tendency to try to ascend the ladder of the hierarchy of being (ibid. 384).

[35] Ibid. 383.
[36] Cf. also Balthasar's cautionary comments about a repristination of the Fathers in *Presence and Thought*, 9–13. Cf. Deirdre Carabine, 'The Fathers: The Church's Intimate, Youthful Diary', in Bede McGregor and Thomas Norris (eds), *The Beauty of Christ: An Introduction to the Theology of Hans Urs von Balthasar* (Edinburgh: T. & T. Clark, 1994), 74–5.
[37] Balthasar not only wrote a chapter on St Irenaeus in the second volume of *The Glory of the Lord* but he also wrote an excursus in the second volume of *Theo-Drama* and published an anthology of Irenaeus's writings (*Scandal*).
[38] Mongrain, *Systematic Thought*, 16. I have drawn theological connections between Irenaeus and de Lubac in Hans Boersma, 'Accommodation to What? Univocity of Being, Pure Nature, and the Anthropology of St Irenaeus', *IJST* 8 (2006), 266–93.
[39] Balthasar, *The Glory of the Lord: A Theological Aesthetics*, ii, *Studies in Theological Style: Clerical Styles*, trans. Andrew Louth, Francis McDonagh, and Brian McNeil, and ed. John Riches (San

The Glory of the Lord, Balthasar drew a direct link between Gnosticism and Platonism, and thus paved the way for a reading of Irenaeus as anti-Platonic theologian *par excellence*.[40]

Balthasar detected this anti-Platonic sentiment in at least three elements of Irenaeus's thought. First, Balthasar noted the Irenaean emphasis on the goodness of created reality. Irenaeus, explained Balthasar, always began with simple observations: 'The two words *videre* [to see] and *ostendere* [to show] fall constantly from Irenaeus' pen. *Videre*, again, is less Plato's contemplation than simply standing before the clear message of the facts.'[41] The beautiful form of created things stemmed from the fact that God created by means of his 'artistic Logos'. Creation was a form of 'divine art'.[42] St Irenaeus's acknowledgement of the beauty of creation was also evident in his eschatology in the last book of his *Contra haereses*. Balthasar thus commented: 'So the physical world is the promise of the supernature which is to follow, because the flesh is itself "not without the artistic wisdom and power of God".'[43] The whole person, body and soul, was a piece of art with an eternal future. Accordingly, it was not only the soul, but also the body that required its own purity.[44] After all, 'for Irenaeus the body does not bear just a trace of God and the soul the image of God, as the Platonising Fathers will later say, but the whole man, made up of body and soul, is created as the image and likeness of God'.[45] Thus, Adam, 'with all his genuine bodiliness', was taken up into Christ through his recapitulation—his faithful retracing and perfecting—of Adamic existence.[46] Balthasar summarized Irenaeus's teaching on the mutual glorification of God and man as follows: 'Man, who preserves God's art in himself and obediently opens himself to its disposing, glorifies the artist and the artist glorifies himself in his work.'[47]

Second, Balthasar noted the significance of time and history in Irenaeus's writings. According to the second-century Church Father, Christ had redeemed

Francisco, Calif.: Ignatius, 1984), 33. Mongrain deals with four elements of Irenaean retrieval in Balthasar: (1) true versus false knowledge (*gnosis*); (2) the theory of the threefold body (*corpus triforme*), with the Word becoming incarnate in the old covenant, in Jesus Christ, and in the new covenant; (3) a depiction of history as divine pedagogy; and (4) a dramatic interpretation of post-Easter history (Mongrain, *Systematic Thought*, 29).

[40] Balthasar assailed Platonism numerous times in his essay on St Irenaeus. See *Glory of the Lord*, ii. 45, 51, 58, 65, 69, 72, 93. But cf. ibid. 89, where in an unencumbered sort of way Balthasar spoke of 'the Platonising perspective of the letter to the Hebrews'. And Cyril O'Regan rightly points out that while for Balthasar, in its genealogical use, the term 'Gnosticism' always functioned as a term of opprobrium, the epithet 'Neoplatonism' did 'not always' function this way ('Balthasar and Gnostic Genealogy', *MTh* 22 (2006), 617).

[41] Balthasar, *Glory of the Lord*, ii. 45.

[42] Ibid. 71.

[43] Ibid. 73.

[44] Ibid. 74.

[45] Ibid. 65.

[46] Ibid. 53. Cf. Balthasar, *Scandal*, 3: 'For [Irenaeus], Christianity is about the divine and spiritual Word becoming flesh and body. The redemption depends on the real Incarnation, the real suffering on the Cross, and the real resurrection of the flesh.'

[47] Id., *Glory of the Lord*, ii. 53.

humanity by means of recapitulation. For Irenaeus, this meant that as humanity's head (*caput*), Christ had retraced all of Adamic existence—without, however, falling into temptation as Adam had done. Balthasar explained that this Irenaean concept of recapitulation meant that Christ bound together the disparate strands of the temporal flow into a unity of essence and meaning: 'Here there is no extraction of a permanent content from lost time as in the Platonists; recapitulation gives time itself validity before eternity.'[48] Every point in the temporal order had its own value and received a 'fullness appropriate to its particular *kairos*'.[49] For Balthasar, recapitulation meant not only that embodied human existence received its value by being included in Christ. It also meant that the particular time (*kairos*) of Christ's actions and sufferings gave value to each moment (*kairos*) in the temporal flow of human history.

Third, Balthasar pointed to the irreducible otherness of the Creator in relation to the creature, which characterized Irenaeus's thought. To be sure, God was the 'One Totality, outside which nothing can exist, no autonomous separate void (*kenōma*)'.[50] The idea that nothing—not even a separate void—could exist outside of God might seem to imply a pantheist identification of God and the world. But for Irenaeus the notion of God's fullness did not 'require him to be at the same time the totality of the world'.[51] Irenaeus did not lapse into pantheism. Instead, for Irenaeus the notion of divine fullness served the opposite purpose: to safeguard divine freedom. In his unbounded freedom, God created the world entirely out of his own goodness, rather than from some pre-existing 'world of ideas as a blueprint'.[52] This one creator God was also the Triune God who revealed himself through his 'two hands', the Son and the Spirit.[53] All of this implied an over-against character in the relationship between the Triune God, on the one hand, and human beings, on the other hand: 'No natural salvation, no "divine core" in man, no overlap between God and the world: Son and Spirit belong unequivocally on the side of the Father.'[54] For Irenaeus, insisted Balthasar, it was the analogy of being (*analogia entis*) that was the 'foundation and background of everything': the ever-greater God grants divine vision to those who love him.[55] In short, Balthasar found in the Irenaean emphasis on the goodness of created reality, on the value of temporal existence, and on the sharp distinction

---

[48] Ibid. 51.
[49] Ibid. 67. Cf. id., *Theo-Drama: Theological Dramatic Theory*, ii, *The Dramatis Personae: Man in God*, trans. Graham Harrison (San Francisco, Calif.: Ignatius, 1990), 148.
[50] Id., *Glory of the Lord*, ii. 58.
[51] Ibid. 59.
[52] Id., *Theo-Drama*, ii. 142 n. 7.
[53] Id., *Glory of the Lord*, ii. 60.
[54] Ibid. 62.
[55] Id., *Theo-Drama*, ii. 141. Cf. ibid. 146. Kevin M. Tortorelli describes Balthasar's analysis of Irenaeus as follows: 'God and the creation are united in a doctrine of analogy of being, in a doctrine of form as the unity both of visible surface and invisible depth, of Irenaean Recapitulation as the unity specific to theological form' ('Balthasar and the Theodramatic Interpretation of St Irenaeus', *DownR* 11 (1993), 122).

between God and creature support for an anti-Platonic *ressourcement* of the Church Fathers.

While Irenaeus's emphases naturally fit Balthasar's paradigm, Denys might initially seem to present more of an obstacle to Balthasar's world-affirming sacramental ontology. Balthasar none the less treated the sixth-century Syrian monk with considerable sympathy, especially in the second volume of *The Glory of the Lord*.[56] Because of this deeply felt bond Balthasar rejected the common scholarly designation 'pseudo-Dionysius'.[57] He perceived in Denys a kindred spirit, based on the latter's aesthetic and liturgical sensibilities. In fact, Balthasar claimed that there had 'hardly been a theology so deeply informed by aesthetic categories as the liturgical theology of the Areopagite'.[58] Denys was far removed from any sort of rational apologetic that might result from a nature–supernatural split, for, in Denys's own words, 'if the truth is rightly developed, it simply offers no opening to any possible attack'.[59] Instead, from beginning to end, this mystical theologian took people on a journey of initiation into the liturgy of praise, so that

where it is a matter of God and the divine, the word *hymnein* [to praise] almost replaces the word 'to say'; for what is at stake is that 'the divine mystery should be honoured by spiritual and invisible knowledge and kept free from any contact with or contamination by the profane'.[60] So it is a matter always and above all of vision, of looking and striving after vision, but ever only (at least on earth) of vision through veils that protect and conceal . . . But it veils only in order to initiate more perfectly, so that ascending the steps of the shrine one can draw yet nearer to the mystery. Theology is essentially initiation, *myesthai* [to be initiated].[61]

Theology was a matter of theurgy: practices of praise causing the initiation of the believer into the divine mystery and ultimately leading to the vision of God. Put differently, theology could be defined as 'the concentric arrangement of heaven and earth, angels and men, in praise around the throne of the Invisible'.[62]

Such a mystical understanding of the nature of theology might seem to endanger a positive appreciation of the created order, the Incarnation, and the structures of the Church. Balthasar insisted, however, that Neoplatonic mysticism and the beauty of creation were not opposed to each other. Balthasar had a remarkably positive assessment of the aesthetic implications of the Platonic

---

[56] Cyril O'Regan points out that Balthasar's earlier text on St Maximus painted Denys in a much less favourable light ('Von Balthasar and Thick Retrieval: Post-Chalcedonian Symphonic Theology', *Greg* 77 (1996), 230–1). While this is true, particularly with regard to Balthasar lamenting Denys's emanationist tendencies in *Kosmische Liturgie*, Balthasar also pointed out, already in this book on Maximus, that in many ways Maximus was able to build on Denys's theology with regard to its emphasis on the autonomy of the finite world (*Cosmic Liturgy*, 49, 55, 94, 107).

[57] Balthasar, *Glory of the Lord*, ii. 144.

[58] Ibid. 154.

[59] Ibid. 149.

[60] Balthasar (quot. Denys, *Ecclesiastical Hierarchy*, I. 1 (372A)).

[61] Balthasar, *Glory of the Lord*, ii. 173.   [62] Ibid.

tradition. While he of course recognized the Plotinian and Procline background of Denys's theology, he gave no intimation that he felt this Neoplatonism stood in the way of the originality or significance of Denys's thought. Balthasar was convinced that Plato was actually an aesthetic thinker, describing him, in fact, as the founder of aesthetics.[63] Likewise, Balthasar was convinced that Plotinian aestheticism did not simply run counter to the Christian faith: 'If Greek thought from Plato to Plotinus has an essentially aesthetic, religious structure—for the cosmos is experienced as the representation and manifestation of the hidden transcendent beauty of God—then it is no sacrilege, but rather a fulfilment, if Christian theology... takes over this aesthetic and metaphysical schema.'[64] We have already seen that Balthasar was not beyond criticizing the Platonic tradition—or the Alexandrian theological tradition where it had followed Neoplatonism too closely—for its spiritualizing tendencies. His essay on Denys none the less revealed that Balthasar believed that a Christian appropriation of the Platonic tradition could incorporate its liturgical and symbolic elements in a theological aesthetics that accepted the created order as a sacramental means of entering the heavenly mysteries. Denys's dependence on Neoplatonic thought patterns illustrated, insisted Balthasar, that the Areopagite did 'not want to borrow, but rather return what has been borrowed to its true owner'.[65] Dionysian theology, in other words, took the form of elevation or fulfilment of an aesthetic Platonic philosophy.

Concretely, this meant according to Balthasar that, for Denys, liturgical initiation took place in what we might term an analogical or sacramental fashion. Speaking of Denys's use of the Neoplatonic movement of procession (*proodos*) and return (*epistrophē*), Balthasar commented that Denys viewed this movement as 'the manifestation of the unmanifest'.[66] The external splendour of beauty, explained Balthasar, was 'the splendour of a mysterious depth' that awakened our sense of reverence.[67] This manifestation of the unmanifest was possible because there was a suitable 'proportion' between spirit and sense.[68] This manifestation in the realm of sensible objects implied that, for Denys, God's descent or revelation in the movement of procession always came first. Referring to the mysticism of Gregory of Nyssa and Augustine, Balthasar commented that it was 'only with Denys' that one saw the ascending movement of negation being kindled by 'God's movement of descent as he imparts himself in manifestations'.[69] This implied that Denys accorded finite realities and ecclesial structures a fundamentally positive role: 'If no one has emphasized so strongly as Denys

---

[63] Id., 'Revelation and the Beautiful', in *Explorations in Theology*, i *The Word Made Flesh*, trans. A. V. Littledale and Alexander Dru (San Francisco, Calif.: Ignatius, 1989), 98–101.

[64] Balthasar, *Glory of the Lord*, ii. 154.

[65] Ibid. 208.

[66] Ibid. 164.

[67] Ibid.   [68] Ibid. 164–5.   [69] Ibid. 165.

the transcendence of God, nor has anyone upheld so decisively the givenness of the essential boundaries and hierarchical ordering of the creation'.[70]

Thus, for Denys, the relationship between the human spirit and the sensible world was based on the sense of proportion or analogy: '[V]iewed from above the relation of likeness and beauty between spirit and the sensible within this world is itself a reflection of the relationship between God and the world (the *analogia entis*).'[71] It was the harmony of analogy, 'a proportion between revelation and the capacity for receiving it',[72] which enabled human beings to contemplate the divine beauty in created realities and so engage in theology: 'Theology is exhausted in the act of wondering adoration before the unsearchable beauty in every manifestation.'[73] Or, as Balthasar put it with a rather pithy saying: 'Things are not simply the occasion for his seeing God; rather, he sees God in things.'[74] Since Denys believed that one could see God *within* created realities, his ana-logical approach was able to value the created order. His great contribution, concluded Balthasar, was to have 'banished definitively' the Alexandrian tendency 'to threaten the Incarnation, the visible Church and the resurrection of the flesh'.[75]

Balthasar insisted that Denys's appreciation of the created order even con-tained the notion that the transcendent God gave 'to the realms of creation a share in himself while safeguarding the immanent order of all things'.[76] Balthasar portrayed Denys as engaged in a careful balancing act. On the one hand, there was true participation of creatures in God, while on the other hand, these creatures retained their ontological difference from the Creator. While Balthasar did not explicitly invoke the 'real difference' between essence and existence, it is clear he had this later Thomist notion in mind when he commented that God allotted 'to each its being and essence "analogously"'.[77] The sharing in God was not a sharing by nature (the way accidents participate in a substance), but it was a sharing by grace: the creature 'participates in God's *allowing* it *to share* and as a creaturely being necessarily possesses within itself the ontological difference between Being and being—put in general terms—or between that in which it participates and that which participates (*metocha* and *metechonta*)'.[78] Thus, the

---

[70] Balthasar, *Glory of the Lord*,166. Cf. ibid. 194–5 on Denys's appreciation of limits and boundaries in the created order.

[71] Ibid. 168.

[72] Ibid. 171.

[73] Ibid. 170.

[74] Ibid. 179.

[75] Ibid. 184.

[76] Ibid. 158.

[77] Ibid. 186.

[78] Ibid. Balthasar made clear that for Denys the Creator–creature distinction was so strong that participating individual essences (*metechonta*) did not participate directly in God. In fact, the *metocha* in which creatures participated were not even hypostasized as 'gods', 'angelic essences', or archetypal 'thoughts' of God. They were simply 'the genuine reality of the world itself, in so far as it consists of principles which share their reality with the individual essences that participate (*metochonta*)' (ibid. 187).

paradox of 'participation while not participating'[79] was a participation in God—a divinization—by means of a participation in the principles or universals of created being, while God himself remained beyond all forms, and so beyond identity and otherness, equality and inequality, likeness and unlikeness.[80] Whatever one may think of the theological consistency of this doctrine of participation, it is clear that Balthasar saw in it a harbinger of the Thomist doctrine of analogy. He believed this doctrine of analogous participation allowed for a sacramental appreciation of the finite structures of the created order within Denys's theology. Thus, Balthasar's Denys was a mystical theologian who could take seriously the structures of the visible Church and who adhered to a sacramental ontology that recognized the 'unmanifest' in the beauty of the manifest.

For Balthasar, the analogy of being was central to his understanding both of Irenaeus and of Denys. In the seventh-century theologian St Maximus the Confessor, however, Balthasar saw the doctrine of analogy come to a fullness of expression that it had not yet attained in either of the earlier two theologians. For Maximus, the analogy between God and creature allowed for true participation without losing sight of the ever-greater dissimilarity between the two. Maximus turned to Chalcedonian Christology to elaborate on the similarity as well as the dissimilarity. Particularly the latter was important to ward off the latent docetism and pantheism of the Alexandrian tradition. Maximus used the dissimilarity of the doctrine of analogy to insist on the full reality of the creaturely character over and above the monothelitism of Severus.[81] Balthasar described the theological accomplishment of Maximus as follows: 'Love, which is the highest level of union, only takes root in the growing independence of the lovers; the union between God and the world reveals, in the very nearness it creates between these two poles of being, the ever-greater difference between created being and the essentially incomparable God.'[82] In other words, for St Maximus, union between God and creature did not exclude their difference, but presupposed and enabled it. 'Union with God', Balthasar summarized, was 'not realized "in spite of" our lasting difference from him, but rather "in" and "through" it'.[83] Chalcedonian Christology had not just insisted that Christ's divine and human natures were undivided, but also that they were unconfused. Balthasar drew the conclusion that the Incarnation, the very place where God fully revealed himself to us, increased rather than removed our ignorance of God.[84]

---

[79] Ibid. 186. [80] Ibid. 188.

[81] Cf. Rodney A. Howsare's comment: 'Maximus is the aesthetic theologian par excellence because he applies the unity of spirit and matter, which occurs in Christ, to his entire worldview' (*Hans Urs von Balthasar*, 116).

[82] Balthasar, *Cosmic Liturgy*, 64. [83] Ibid. 96. [84] Ibid.

Maximus' concern, explained Balthasar, was to safeguard divine transcendence.[85] God remained the wholly other one, so that an encounter with God was
one that took place 'above all conceptual knowing'.[86] An 'unbridgeable chasm'
yawned between God and his creatures.[87] As a result, people were incapable of
grasping the essence of God. Following the tradition from Philo to Gregory of
Nyssa, Maximus affirmed that one could 'only know God's *existence*—know *that*
he is—not his *essence*, or *what* he is'.[88] As a result, Balthasar viewed Maximus as
a strong opponent of univocity of being. God's existence was beyond being.
Even when we employed negative language, saying that God is not-being, we
still used discourse that was not properly applicable to God. God was, in
Maximus' own words, 'exalted beyond all affirmation and denial'.[89] Using
terminology that he often repeated elsewhere in similar terms, Balthasar commented that for Maximus 'no neutral, common "concept" of Being can span the
realities of both God and creature; the analogy of an ever-greater dissimilarity
stands in the way, preventing all conceptualization of the fact and the way
they are'.[90]

Maximus' theology of unity and number displayed the same pattern of
analogy. On the one hand, Balthasar explained, God's unity was the principle
of every created number, so that every number participated in God. On the other
hand, God's unity was beyond all numerical value, so that it was impossible to
add to or take away from the unity of God.[91] 'At this point', commented
Balthasar, 'the whole theory of unity returns to the simple scheme of an analogy
of being between God and the world: to the absolute transcendence of God and
his immanence in created being.'[92] Analogy between God and creature, in other
words, allowed for true participation, while it always remained predicated on the
ever-greater dissimilarity between the two. Both similarity and dissimilarity came
to their fullest expression in the hypostatic union of the Incarnation. '[E]veryone
recognizes', said Balthasar, 'that [Maximus'] ontology and cosmology are exten-
sions of his Christology, in that the synthesis of Christ's concrete person is not
only God's final thought for the world but also his original plan.'[93]

Maximus' doctrine of analogy, Balthasar believed, allowed for the relative
autonomy of the created order that Denys had still found somewhat difficult
to retain. Denys's theology had been troubled by a Neoplatonist emanationism in
which 'potentialities' had seemed to hover in a semi-divine world. In contrast,
Maximus' 'principles' of being (also called 'generalities' or 'universals') clearly had

---

[85] Balthasar, *Cosmic Liturgy*, 95.   [86] Ibid. 92.
[87] Ibid. 95.   [88] Ibid. 88.
[89] Ibid. 89. Balthasar's quotation is from Maximus, *Mystagogia* (*PG* 91, 664AC).
[90] Id., *Cosmic Liturgy*, 89. Cf. id., *Theo-Drama: Theological Dramatic Theory*, iii, *Dramatis
Personae: Persons in Christ*, trans. Graham Harrison (San Francisco, Calif.: Ignatius, 1992), 221;
id., *Theo-Logic*, i. 17.
[91] Id., *Cosmic Liturgy*, 113–14.   [92] Ibid. 114.   [93] Ibid. 207.

their place on this side of the Creator–creature divide.[94] The result, Balthasar insisted, was that the created order finally took on real significance: 'Rather than gazing upward along the straight ladder of being at the choirs of increasingly heavenly spirits, to search for the Divine Reality above the highest movements of the dance, Maximus' eyes look for God in both realms of the world, in sense and intellect, earth and heaven, and meet their limit in both.'[95] The genius of Maximus' defence of orthodox Christology lay in his formulation of the doctrine of analogy, which allowed for a true appreciation of union with God, while at the same time it made possible the relative autonomy of the created order.

Karl Barth: Christ as the Hourglass

Balthasar's immersion in the Church Fathers had fully convinced him of the validity of the doctrine of *analogia entis* as necessary to retain both the goodness of the created order and the complete transcendence of the Creator vis-à-vis the created order.[96] Thus, when Barth opposed his *analogia fidei* to the traditional *analogia entis*, Balthasar was convinced that his Swiss compatriot both misrepresented the notion of *analogia entis* and depreciated the goodness of the created order and the integrity of human action. Often, Balthasar believed, the former was the case. Balthasar insisted that his interlocutor did not appreciate the traditional doctrine for what it really was, thus setting up—in a 'downright fraudulent' manner—a 'straw man'.[97] To be sure, Balthasar observed in Barth an increasing openness to the doctrine of analogy, and also to the reality of the created order and of history.[98] Barth recognized that creation was a 'true sacrament' of the covenant,[99] that it was 'a parable whose final meaning is unlocked when it receives the truth of God's gracious revelation'.[100] But Balthasar, much like Bouillard, believed that Barth misrepresented the Thomist understanding of *analogia entis* when he interpreted Thomas's 'being' as a neutral concept that encapsulated both God and human beings.[101] For Barth, one could 'only know

---

[94] Balthasar's reading of Denys on 'potentialities for being' as located between God and the world (*Cosmic Liturgy*, 83–4) was different from his reading in the second volume of *The Glory of the Lord*, where Balthasar had clearly come to see them as genuine realities of the world (p. 187). The more positive evaluation of Denys in the latter volume hinges on this understanding of universals as fully creaturely in character.

[95] Id., *Cosmic Liturgy*, 84–5.

[96] Cf. Balthasar's appeal to Denys and Maximus in his discussion on *analogia entis* in *Theo-Drama*, iii. 222.

[97] Id., *Theology of Karl Barth*, 382.

[98] Owing to the influential work of Bruce McCormack, many Barth scholars now regard Balthasar's analysis as one-sided. See Bruce L. McCormack, *Karl Barth's Critically Realistic Dialectical Theology: Its Genesis and Development, 1909–1936* (Oxford: Clarendon Press, 1995).

[99] Balthasar, *Theology of Karl Barth*, 124.

[100] Ibid. 125.

[101] Ibid. 130, 162. For Bouillard's views, see above in Chap. 3, sect: Bouillard, Barth, and the Doctrine of Analogy.

what created spirit *really* is from the fact of its being created in Christ'.[102]
Balthasar, however, was not convinced that the doctrine of analogy implied a
neutral concept of being. Marshalling one contemporary Catholic theologian
after the other, Balthasar insisted that all of creation and history centred on
Christ and that one could be 'as radically christocentric as Barth' was 'without
having to go down his "dead end"' of a rejection of *analogia entis*.[103] According
to Balthasar, *analogia entis* did not assume a neutral concept of being; it
merely implied that God's salvation in Christ was the saving of his created
order: '[I]t must be evident to any Protestant not closed off to the most
elementary of insights that the saving event between God and the world is
ontic in character.'[104] For Balthasar, the doctrine of analogy simply served to
defend that there was a natural stability to the created order that God had
redeemed in Christ.

Balthasar made the case, however, that Barth not only misrepresented the
traditional doctrine of *analogia entis*, but that, in spite of his increasing acceptance of analogy, Barth continued to ignore its implications, in particular the
relative autonomy of the created order and the reality of the human response to
divine grace. Balthasar's objections were to the 'over-systematization' of Barth's
Christological starting-point.[105] He was concerned that Barth's rejection of
analogia entis in the name of Christology would result in a loss of the proper
character of creation itself.[106] Barth, he insisted, had not left enough 'breathing
room between creation and covenant. Barth certainly *pre*-supposes creation, but
it is still too much merely a presupposition: he does not give it its proper due.
Though its autonomy is merely relative, it is nonetheless real.'[107] The result,
Balthasar maintained, was that in Barth's approach philosophy could not take on
its appropriate role, without which theology itself could not function properly.[108]

---

[102] Balthasar, *Theology of Karl Barth*, 131.

[103] Ibid. 362. Balthasar provided the quotations in a chapter entitled 'Christocentrism'. Needless
to say, Balthasar's array of Catholic theologians did not include any neo-scholastic Thomists,
which underscores Bouillard's point that it was the later understanding of *analogia entis* in Cajetan
and Suárez that provided the real fodder for Barth's opposition to the notion. Cf. Howsare, *Hans Urs
von Balthasar*, 82.

[104] Balthasar, *Theology of Karl Barth*, 394.

[105] See esp. ibid. 243–5. Balthasar also alluded to even stronger objections regarding Barth's
ecclesiology (ibid. 245–7) but he did not elaborate on these in the remainder of his book.

[106] Balthasar clearly showed, however, that in his *Church Dogmatics* the contents of Barth's
analogia fidei was no different from the scholastic *analogia entis* (ibid. 163–5).

[107] Ibid. 242. Balthasar repeatedly insisted on the 'relative autonomy' of the created order. See
ibid. 120, 336, 351, 362.

[108] Ibid. 243. Cf. ibid. 393. Adrian J. Walker is quite right, therefore, to comment: 'Balthasar is
not a fideist or a theological positivist... Precisely because of his radical Christocentrism, then,
Balthasar is, before anything else, a theologian of the so-called "Catholic 'and' ": of the unity-
without-confusion of the "from above" *and* the "from below"; of grace *and* of nature; of philosophy
and of theology; of the radical following of Christ *and* of passionate love for the world; of tradition
and of the development of doctrine' ('Love Alone: Hans Urs von Balthasar as a Master of
Theological Renewal', *Comm* 32 (2005), 21). Walker's concern also lies at the basis of the fine
study by Howsare, *Hans Urs von Balthasar*.

Balthasar also felt that the creature did not receive is own proper space and freedom.

The consequence of this for the doctrine of grace, Balthasar believed, was that the human pole of the divine–human relationship did not get to play its proper part: 'Barth rejects all discussion of anything in the realm of the relative and temporal that would make for a real and vibrant history of man with his redeeming Lord and God.'[109] As a result, ontological soteriological categories had to make room for purely forensic and cognitive categories. Justification, for Barth, did not include an internal change of heart, but remained instead a mere external verdict. Again, this did not do justice to the reality of our relationship with God: 'God's revelation can only be an event if something actually takes place. And that means once more a genuine ontological transformation, a genuine imparting of divine Being and a genuine sharing of the creature in God's Being that affects the creature's own being as well as the creature's awareness of the world of divine Being.'[110] Balthasar's apprehension of Barth's rejection of *analogia entis* was thus immediately connected with his fear of the latter's understanding of justification. Balthasar concluded that Barth made two mistakes: on the one hand, he did not appreciate the rather limited meaning and function of *analogia entis*; on the other hand, he did not recognize its significance in protecting the relative autonomy of the created order.[111]

At the same time, however, Balthasar had encountered both in de Lubac and in the Greek Fathers (though more obviously in Irenaeus and Maximus than in Denys) the Christological structure of the divine–human relationship. Thus, where Barth's theology was Christocentric, Balthasar agreed without hesitation. Balthasar was convinced that Catholic theology, as it came to grips with its neo-scholastic heritage, needed to re-appropriate the classical theological position, which used to take its starting-point in Christ. He believed that such a Christo-logical approach was possible without repeating Barth's failure to uphold the significance of the created order and of human action. The result was that Balthasar reworked the doctrine of analogy in Christological fashion in a way that was quite out of line with the neo-scholastic approach to analogy.[112] Repeatedly, Balthasar employed the image of an hourglass:

---

[109] Balthasar, *Theology of Karl Barth*, 371.

[110] Ibid. 365.

[111] None of the above should be read as though Balthasar's book was an attack on Barth rather than a sincere attempt at dialogue. Balthasar's theology is impossible to grasp without appreciating the profound impact that Barth had on it. See John Webster, 'Balthasar and Karl Barth', in Oakes and Moss, *Cambridge Companion*, 241–55; John Thompson, 'Barth and Balthasar: An Ecumenical Dialogue', in McGregor and Norris, *Beauty of Christ*, 171–92.

[112] Howsare goes so far as to suggest that Balthasar engaged Barth because he 'recognized in Barth's critique of Liberal Protestantism a concern not unlike de Lubac's critique of neo-Scholastic dualism. In other words, it was not primarily to defend the Catholic understanding of analogy to Barth that Balthasar wrote this study. Rather, it was to show his fellow Catholics the dangers inherent in the doctrine of analogy when it is totally removed from the context of theology proper' (*Hans Urs von Balthasar*, 83).

We could describe this thought as a kind of hourglass, where the two contiguous vessels (God and creature) meet only at the narrow passage through the center: where they both encounter each other in Jesus Christ. The purpose of the image is to show that there is no other point of contact between the two chambers of the glass. And just as the sand flows only from top to bottom, so too God's revelation is one-sided, flowing from his gracious decision alone. But of course the sand flows down into the other chamber so that the sand there can really *increase*. In other words, there *is* a countermovement in the other chamber, but only because of the first movement, the initiative of the first chamber.[113]

For Balthasar, Christ was the narrow passage where God and creature met. Despite the fact that Balthasar particularly objected to Barth's Christological 'narrowing', it was clear that he had learned from the Barthian approach that *analogia entis* could be truly appreciated only when its fulfilment in Christ was taken seriously: 'Karl Barth is absolutely right that the problem of analogy in theology must finally be a problem of Christology.'[114] For Balthasar, the analogy of faith—to which we might also refer as the Christological or theological analogy—was the theological flowering of the philosophical question of similarity, so that the analogy of faith needed the analogy of being as its external basis.[115]

This Christological emphasis became particularly evident where Balthasar identified Christ as the interpretive key to history—both to the salvation history preceding the Incarnation and to the history following the Incarnation.[116] This implied, for Balthasar, that Christ was the 'concrete analogy of being'. Balthasar explained the relationship between *analogia entis* and Christology as follows:

Christ can be called the 'concrete analogy of being', *analogia entis*, since he constitutes in himself, in the unity of his divine and human natures, the proportion of every interval between God and man. And this unity is his person in both natures. The philosophical formulation of the analogy of being is related to the measure of Christ precisely as is world history to his history—as promise to fulfillment, the preliminary to the definitive.[117]

---

[113] Balthasar, *Theology of Karl Barth*, 197. See also ibid. 234, 341; id., *The Theology of Henri de Lubac: An Overview*, trans. Joseph Fessio and Susan Clements (San Francisco, Calif.: Communio/ Ignatius, 1991), 118. Cf. Oakes, *Pattern of Redemption*, 66–7. Balthasar may well have taken the imagery of the hourglass from Oscar Cullmann, who used it to describe salvation history as narrowing in Christ, broadening out from there. See Balthasar, *Theo-Logic: Theological Logical Theory*, iii, *The Spirit of Truth*, 287.

[114] Balthasar, *Theology of Karl Barth*, 55.

[115] Cf. ibid. 261, 382, 286, 396. Bernhard Blankenhorn points to a number of other passages in Balthasar's trilogy ('Balthasar's Method of Divine Naming', *NV* Eng 1 (2003), 250–1).

[116] Cf. Balthasar, *A Theology of History* (San Francisco, Calif.: Communio/Ignatius, 1994), 24: 'The historical life of the Logos—to which his death, Resurrection and Ascension belong—is, as such, that very world of ideas which, directly or reductively, gives the norm for all history; yet not as coming forth from some non-historical height above, but from the living center of history itself. Seen from the highest, definitive point of view, it is the source of history, the point whence the whole of history before and after Christ emanates: its center.'

[117] Ibid. 69–70 n. 5.

For Balthasar the hypostatic union formed the theological fulfilment of the creational *analogia entis*.[118] Because the Incarnation was the climax of history, the Christological analogy not only fulfilled the philosophical analogy, but also provided the norm for it. There was, indeed, no neutral concept of being, Balthasar agreed with Barth. Thomas had never taught it. Balthasar's rejection of a neutral concept of being resulted in a truly sacramental understanding of analogy. He often referred to Christ as the sacrament of the triune God.[119] Analogical doctrine, theologically understood, meant that in Christ both the similarity and the dissimilarity between Creator and creature found their true expression, so that in Christ we could see not only a pointer to God, but could witness to the actual presence of God himself.[120] In the words of Louis Dupré: 'Christ is not a sign pointing beyond itself to an invisible God: he himself, the indivisible God-man, *is* the reality he signifies.'[121]

MARIE-DOMINIQUE CHENU AND THE DIONYSIAN CHARACTER OF THEOLOGY

Chenu's Programme of *Ressourcement*

One of the key characteristics of *nouvelle théologie* was its programme of *ressourcement*, and Marie-Dominique Chenu was no exception in this regard. His groundbreaking work on twelfth- and thirteenth-century theology served to enrich his own contemporary theological and cultural contexts. Chenu was a down-to-earth personality. His activities went well beyond research and writing on medieval theology. *Engagement* with the *jocistes* in the 1930s, with the worker–priest movement in the post-war years, and with Christian–Marxist dialogue throughout much of his career functioned as the heartbeat of Chenu's spirituality.[122] Chenu jokingly recounted that people would sometimes think there were two Chenus, 'one old medievalist, who does palaeography, and a kind of

---

[118] Balthasar made this point consistently. See also id., *Theology of Karl Barth*, 336, 376–7, 383. Cf. Angela Franz Franks, 'Trinitarian *analogia entis* in Hans Urs von Balthasar', *Thomist* 62 (1998), 538–42; Georges de Schrijver, *Le Merveilleux Accord de l'homme et de Dieu: Étude de l'analogie de l'être chez Hans Urs von Balthasar* (Louvain: Leuven University Press, 1983).

[119] Balthasar, *Theology of History*, 75. Cf. Kevin Mongrain's discussion of the 'Christ-form' as the 'permanent, unsurpassable sacramental vehicle of divine grace' ('Von Balthasar's Way', 69).

[120] The sacramental cast of Balthasar's Christological analogy had far-reaching implications, particularly for his doctrine of the Trinity and for atonement theology, since Balthasar insisted that Thomas's 'real distinction' between being and essence in some way went back to the Trinity, so that suffering and other aspects of being human were taken up—in analogical fashion—in the triune God. For further discussion, see Blankenhorn, 'Balthasar's Method'; Matthew Levering, 'Balthasar on Christ's Consciousness on the Cross', *Thomist* 65 (2001), 567–81; Franks, 'Trinitarian *analogia entis*'; Gerard F. O'Hanlon, *The Immutability of God in the Theology of Hans Urs von Balthasar* (Cambridge: Cambridge University Press, 1990).

[121] Louis Dupré, 'Hans Urs von Balthasar's Theology of Aesthetic Form', *TS* 49 (1988), 311.

[122] Cf. Chap. 1, sect.: Controversy over Worker–Priests (1943–54).

scoundrel who runs in the lines of fire of the holy Church'.[123] Chenu clearly believed the two belonged together quite naturally. We should keep in mind, therefore, that Chenu's practical concerns were always intimately connected to his theological programme of *ressourcement*. We will see that Chenu's *ressourcement* was genuinely open to a sacramental ontology, for which the Dominican scholar looked via St Thomas to the sixth-century theologian Denys. At the same time, however, I will argue that Chenu exhibited a great deal of optimism with regard to modernity and that he could be quite outspoken about the autonomy of the natural order. As a result, Chenu's thought was characterized by a degree of ambiguity.

Chenu's dissertation *De contemplatione*, on which he worked from 1914 till 1920 under Réginald Garrigou-Lagrange in Rome, was intended as a work of *ressourcement*.[124] His discussion of the meaning of contemplation in St Thomas Aquinas took place against the twofold backdrop of Thomas's thirteenth-century context and of Chenu's contemporary ecclesial and cultural situation. He insisted on the key principle that Thomas Aquinas be read in his own thirteenth-century context. Explaining, rather agreeably, that he would use a 'scholastic method' in his dissertation, Chenu then continued to insist that, while aware of the novelty of the proposed methodology, he would none the less occasionally use the 'historical method':

It is thus not out of antiquarian interest that I have researched and cited several texts of rather obscure theologians or philosophers of the thirteenth century; but because in order to grasp his thought it is indispensable to resituate the thought of St Thomas in the environment in which it was born or in which it developed, by way of such or such a reaction, under a particular influence.[125]

This plea for a historical reading of the Angelic Doctor must have been somewhat unsettling to Chenu's doctoral supervisor.[126]

---

[123] Chenu, *Un théologien en liberté: Jacques Duquesne interroge le Père Chenu* (Paris: Centurion, 1975), 61. For an analysis of how Chenu regarded the relationship between praxis and theory in an increasingly secularized France, see Christophe Potworowski, 'Dechristianization, Socialization and Incarnation in Marie-Dominique Chenu', *ScEs* 93 (1991), 17–54.

[124] Carmelo Giuseppe Conticello has presented a careful analysis of Chenu's unpublished dissertation, along with lengthy extracts, in ' *De contemplatione* (Angelicum 1920): La Thèse inédite du P. M.-D. Chenu', *RSPT* 75 (1991), 363–422. See also the discussion in Christophe F. Potworowski, *Contemplation and Incarnation: The Theology of Marie-Dominique Chenu* (Montreal: McGill-Queen's University Press, 2001), 5–15.

[125] Conticello, '*De contemplatione*', 387. Jean Jolivet analyses several of Chenu's main publications and also notes the close connection between history and theology in his thought: 'It is always about immersing oneself in the diverse, living, bustling contexts, which give birth to and nourish the theological doctrines, which one suggests to turn into a precise history, neither beyond nor preceding their formulations, but inside their letter as such' ('M.-D. Chenu, médiéviste et théologien', *RSPT* 81 (1997), 386). The entire issue of the journal (pp. 369–437) is devoted to Chenu's work as a medievalist.

[126] In his interview with Jacques Duquesne, Chenu mused that Garrigou-Lagrange 'was a man of two pieces, if I may put it that way. On the one hand, he was a master in spirituality, he read much of Saint John of the Cross, and restored to Rome the great tradition of teaching spiritual theology; his

Chenu's *ressourcement* was not, however, simply a matter of employing the 'historical method' in order to situate St Thomas or other theologians objectively in their original historical contexts. From the beginning, it was clear that for Chenu *ressourcement* deserved the name only if the contemporary social and ecclesial situation entered into dialogue with the text. The topic of contemplation was very much in the forefront of theological discussions in the 1920s, and in the midst of these discussions, Chenu set out to re-appropriate Thomas's understanding of mystical contemplation. Pierre Rousselot's 1908 dissertation on *L'Intellectualisme de saint Thomas* provided much of the interpretive grid for Chenu's own reading,[127] while Chenu also entered into contemporary debates on the relationship between faith and mystical union. Also, in his later writings, Chenu often drew direct parallels between twelfth- and thirteenth-century developments and the changes which had taken place in his own context. In short, Chenu demonstrated, in the words of Jean-Claude Schmitt, a 'continuous interpenetration' (*une constante perméabilité*) between the present and the past.[128] Chenu's *ressourcement* can be understood only if we keep in mind this dual backdrop of the 'historical method', on the one hand, and contemporary theological and social concerns, on the other hand.

In his 1937 *Une École de théologie: Le Saulchoir*—the book for which, a year later, he was summoned by Garrigou-Lagrange and which contributed to his 1942 removal from Le Saulchoir—Chenu reiterated that a programme of *ressourcement* lay at the heart of his approach and that, as Regent of the studium, he intended to promote it zealously.[129] He spoke of an 'appeal' (*recours*) and of a 'return' (*retour*) to the sources,[130] and he again made a plea for the 'historical method'.[131] He did this in a much more outspoken manner, however, than he had done in his formal dissertation. There was never any doubt, neither here nor in his later writings, that St Thomas was Chenu's real and genuine source of inspiration, and he made it apparent that one of the main reasons lay in the Angelic Doctor's daring spirit of renewal that he had displayed in the thirteenth century.[132] Chenu lamented the theological 'system' that had come to dominate scholastic thought in the sixteenth century and that had led to a loss of the

courses were followed by droves of young people. But, on the other hand, he had been fed too much by Aristotle and not enough by the gospel, and his theology always ran the risk of just being a sacred metaphysics—to such an extent that one day I heard him say, certainly in an inordinate manner: "After all, the Incarnation is just a fact." The Incarnation embarrassed him because it could not be metaphysically deduced by starting with God' (*Un théologien en liberté*, 38).

[127] Cf. Conticello, '*De contemplatione*', 367, 401. Potworowski also notes Rousselot's decisive influence on Chenu (*Contemplation and Incarnation*, 9–10, 12, 49).

[128] Jean-Claude Schmitt, 'L'Œuvre de médiéviste du Père Chenu', *RSPT* 81 (1997), 399. Cf. Jacques Guillet, *La Théologie catholique en France de 1914 à 1960* (Paris: Médiasèvres, 1988), 27–8.

[129] Chenu, *Une école de théologie: Le Saulchoir* (Kain-Lez-Tournai: Le Saulchoir, 1937). Chenu's book was republished in 1985 with contributions by Giuseppe Alberigo, Étienne Fouilloux, Jean-Pierre Jossua, and Jean Ladrière (*Une école de théologie: Le Saulchoir* (Paris: Cerf, 1985)).

[130] Chenu, *Une école*, 124, 127. Throughout, I will be quoting from the 1985 edition.

[131] Ibid. 125.   [132] Ibid. 122.

innovative and creative approach that had characterized Thomism itself.[133] Thus, his rejection of the manualist tradition carried more than just a slight edge. Additionally, Chenu made it clear that he did not consider even Thomas's own *philosophia perennis* as a 'definite system of inviolate propositions, but as a body of key intuitions'.[134] Chenu was not afraid to speak of a 'discrete relativism of the framework of the most coherent and most unified systems'.[135] Understandably, then, the kind of *ressourcement* that Chenu set out to practise was a source of serious concern to the neo-Thomist establishment.

Theology as Initiation

The neo-Thomist apprehensions of relativism, spurred by Chenu's turn to history, lead us back to the question of the sacramental character of reality. We have noted its centrality in the theology of several of the *nouvelle* theologians. And I would argue that at its core, also Chenu's theology was concerned to overcome the split between nature and the supernatural—or, as he often put it, between historicism and spiritualism[136]—by way of a sacramental ontology. Chenu, along with de Lubac, Daniélou, Bouillard, Balthasar, and others regarded the neo-scholastic separation between nature and the supernatural, or between faith and history, as seriously problematic. Thus, he continuously inveighed against the rationalism of René Descartes (1596–1650), Gottfried Wilhelm Leibniz (1646–1716), and Christian Wolff (1679–1754), whom he associated with the 'baroque' neo-scholastic tradition.[137] Despite Chenu's appreciation of the medieval flowering of scholasticism, he was apprehensive of the dialectical method with which he maintained Abelard had imprisoned theology in a 'rationalistic cage', thereby undermining the earlier mysticism of the monastic theology still operative in St Anselm.[138] Thus, Chenu's prime concern was to oppose an absolutized neo-Thomist theological system whenever he mentioned his apprehensions of rationalism in the history of Christian thought.

---

[133] Chenu, *Une école*, 123.

[134] Ibid.

[135] Ibid. 125–6. Cf. ibid. 148. Claude Geffré rightly observes, 'In the context of the time, this relativizing of dogma was a real provocation' ('Théologie de l'incarnation et théologie des signes du temps chez le Père Chenu', in Joseph Doré and Jacques Fantino (eds), *Marie-Dominique Chenu: Moyen-âge et modernité* (Paris: Cerf, 1997), 134–5).

[136] Cf. Potworowski, *Contemplation and Incarnation*, 106.

[137] Conticello, '*De contemplatione*', 382–3; Chenu, *Is Theology a Science?* trans. A. H. N. Green-Armytage (New York: Hawthorn, 1959), 92; id., 'Vérité évangélique et métaphysique wolffienne à Vatican II', *RSPT* 57 (1973), 632–40. Chenu took the charge of Wolffian rationalism against neo-Thomism from Étienne Gilson. Cf. Gilson, *Being and Some Philosophers* (2nd edn, Toronto: Pontifical Institute of Mediaeval Studies, 1952), 112–20. For a discussion of the charge, see Fergus Kerr, 'A Different World: Neoscholasticism and its Discontents', *IJST* 8 (2006), 145–7.

[138] Chenu, *Is Theology a Science?* 62. Cf. ibid. 108 n. 4; id., *Toward Understanding Saint Thomas*, trans. Albert M. Landry and Dominic Hughes (Chicago, Ill.: Regnery, 1964), 150, 304; id., *Faith and Theology*, trans. Denis Hickey (New York: Macmillan, 1968), 19, 40–1, 46, 57–8.

His rejection of the dualism between reason and faith implied a deep interest in the experiential character of faith. Faith lay at the root of theology, informing its practice. As a result, Chenu had high regard for the contemplative tradition that Denys had passed on to the West via Thomas Aquinas. Chenu also rejected any notion of theology done outside the context of the Christian faith. Theology without faith was necessarily 'a vicious infiltration of eighteenth-century rationalism into theological method', Chenu insisted.[139] Faith and theology were necessarily connected, for theology was a sharing in divine self-knowledge. Here Chenu was no doubt influenced by Rousselot's reading of Thomas Aquinas. Repeatedly, Chenu returned to this idea of theology as a connatural participation in God's own knowledge of himself.[140] In this context, Chenu often had recourse to the Aristotelian theory of subalternation, which Thomas had adopted as his own. According to this principle, lower (subalternated) sciences could function only if they adopted or 'believed' principles based on the evidence of higher (subalternating) sciences. For example, physics must accept the principles laid out by mathematics, and shipbuilding needed to follow the principles of piloting. Similarly, theology was, as it were, a subalternated science that could operate only on the basis of a higher science.[141] Since theology took its principles from God's self-knowledge, the implication, for Chenu, was that theology operated within faith and involved a participation in God's self-knowledge.

Thus, while agreeing with St Thomas that theology was a science—or, at least, a quasi-science—Chenu wanted to maintain its liturgical setting and its role of initiating people into the mystery of God.[142] Theology, explained Chenu, was 'the science of salvation. One enters it by an "initiation", and for this the liturgy

---

[139] Chenu, *Is Theology a Science?* 23.

[140] Ibid. 24, 89, 122. Chenu first referred to knowledge by connaturality in his 1920 dissertation. See Conticello, '*De contemplatione*', 11–12.

[141] Chenu, *La Théologie comme science au XIIIᵉ siècle* (3rd edn, Paris: Vrin, 1957), 80–5; Chenu, *Is Theology a Science?* 89–92; id., *Aquinas and his Role in Theology*, trans. Paul Philibert (Collegeville, Minn.: Liturgical, 2002), 32–3. Cf. the discussion in Potworowski, *Contemplation and Incarnation*, 62, 72–3.

[142] Chenu was deeply concerned to maintain the connection between theology and faith, and thus strongly qualified the applicability of the Aristotelian theory of subalternation to theology in *La Théologie comme science au XIIIᵉ siècle*. Here he commented: 'The relationship between the believer and God is, epistemologically and really, quite different from the relationship between the physician and the mathematician. The theory of subalternation clarifies the situation admirably; but it only concerns a *quasi*-subalternation, to use St. Thomas's term' (ibid. 83). Chenu's reason for qualifying the applicability of the theory of subalternation was that while the object of an ordinary subalternated science was indeed different from the object of the subalternating science, this was not the case with theology. In theology, it was not the object (God) but the principle (faith) that had been subalternated. Chenu's concern was with a rationalist 'extrinsicism' that would separate theology from faith: 'Beneath the specific difference between the habits of faith and theology, the object of theology is not "other" (i.e., extrinsic) than the object of faith. The continuity between the knowledge of God and the science of the theologian depends on this overall point: *impressio divinae scientiae* [impression of divine knowledge]' (ibid. 81–2). Chenu concluded, therefore, that we could regard theology as a science only in an imperfect sense (*imparfaitement*) (ibid. 84). John I. Jenkins discusses Chenu's qualifications and makes a case for theology as a true science (*Knowledge and Faith in Thomas Aquinas* (Cambridge: Cambridge University Press, 1997), 51–77).

provides both the ritual and the light. Once again we see that theology remains *within* the mystery'.[143] To the chagrin of the neo-scholastics, Chenu went a step further by insisting that various theological systems did not express absolute eternal verities; rather, they were the result of differing spiritualities:

One does not enter into a system because of the logical coherence of its construction or the likelihood of its conclusions; one finds himself here as by birth, through the key intuition that our spiritual life grasps, along with the intelligible scheme that it entails. A theology worthy of the name is a spirituality that has found the rational instruments suitable to its religious experience.[144]

This emphasis on experience and spirituality as foundational for theology was 'original, audacious over against the pseudo-objective neo-scholasticism of the time', and to the neo-Thomists it appeared unnervingly close to the Modernist approach to theology.[145]

Thus, when Chenu insisted on keeping together the notions of 'science' and 'wisdom', he was interested not only in maintaining the scientific character of theology, but also wanted to uphold its experiential or sapiential dimension. Already, in his dissertation, Chenu rejected St Augustine's separation between science and wisdom, and he observed in such a separation the very dualism between nature and the supernatural that he wanted to overcome. Augustine had been erroneous, in his view, to use the term 'wisdom' (*sapientia*) to refer to eternal matters, while restricting the use of the word 'science' (*scientia*) to temporal matters.[146] 'The refusal of the Augustinian point of view regarding two "zones" ', observes Conticelli, 'has remained one of the basic elements of Father Chenu's Thomism'.[147] Theology, while it could indeed be referred to as a 'science', was none the less at its core sapiential in character: 'Theology exists *within* contemplation and within that wisdom which is a participation in the divine knowledge itself—of God and of the world alike.'[148] Thus, while Augustine might have been wrong to separate science and wisdom, Chenu insisted that the African bishop had none the less been correct in his Neoplatonic sensibility that theology was a matter of wisdom.[149]

---

[143] Chenu, *Is Theology a Science?* 46. Cf. ibid. 63, where Chenu insisted that the 'aim of the theologian remains from start to finish the attainment of a beatifying knowledge of God and a full life of grace in the world'.

[144] Id., *Une école*, 148–9.

[145] Jean-Pierre Jossua, 'Théologie et vie spirituelle chez saint Thomas selon le Père Chenu', *VSpir* 147 (1993), 748.

[146] Conticello, '*De contemplatione*', 399. Cf. Potworowski, *Contemplation and Incarnation*, 10.

[147] Conticello, '*De contemplatione*', 399. See e.g. Chenu's exposition in *La Théologie comme science au XIIIᵉ siècle*, 93–100.

[148] Chenu, *Is Theology a Science?* 122.

[149] Ibid. 119–20. Cf. id., *La Théologie comme science au XIIIᵉ siècle*, 97: 'That from which we had to extricate ourselves, in Augustine, was thus not first of all his understanding of wisdom, but the Platonic duality between science and wisdom. Or, better yet: within a superior unity we had to assume the functions of "science", including its value of practical knowledge, which remain adventitious because of its relationship to contemplative faith.'

Dionysian Symbolical Theology

The faith-based, sapiential, and initiatory character of Chenu's approach to theology explains his deep appreciation for Denys, the Neoplatonic mystic. The sixth-century Syrian monk had influenced the theology of St Thomas, and he also served as the main inspiration for Chenu's own mystical-theological programme in *De contemplatione*. In his dissertation, Chenu presented two theories of mystical contemplation:

> The various explanations of contemplative perception can be reduced to a twofold category, in line with a twofold, opposite tendency in theologians. Some appear to reduce the mystical state to the one Christian life in the ordinary grace of the theological virtues, merely varied by way of intensity, without any specific difference. Others, on the contrary, define the mystical act theologically and psychologically in such a way, that it appears entirely beyond the ordinary ways of sanctifying grace, whether in terms of the knowledge of faith or in terms of the affect of charity, and that it seems to pertain to freely given graces [*gratias gratis datas*].[150]

Chenu identified the first position as the 'minimalist explanation' and identified Auguste Saudreau (1859–1946), Joseph Maréchal, Réginald Garrigou-Lagrange, and Anselm Stolz (1900–42) as the position's main representatives. They regarded the mystical state simply as the flourishing of the normal exercise of Christian virtues and tended to look askance at a separation between ascetical and mystical theology, a separation that Chenu explained had first arisen in the seventeenth century.[151] Chenu had a great deal of sympathy for the minimalist position, precisely because it retained the connection between faith and the theological virtues, on the one hand, and mystical contemplation, on the other hand.

In contrast, the 'maximalist explanation' failed to retain this connection. Chenu attributed this second position to the Jesuit theologian Augustin Poulain whose book *Des grâces d'oraison* (1901) had defined the mystical act as an 'immediate intuition or perception of God, in the manner of a certain inchoate beatific vision', and thus qualitatively different from ordinary psychological activities and ordinary grace.[152] If the minimalist perhaps did insufficient justice to the secret, mystical character of contemplation by reducing it to faith and baptismal grace,[153] Chenu was much more fearful of Poulain's 'maximalist' position, because it involved an extra-intellectual human potency for direct contact between God and the mind, and because it posited a purely spiritual perception that avoided recourse to the material world. This, for Chenu, fractured the continuity and homogeneity of the Christian life.[154] In short, it was the

---

[150] Conticello, '*De contemplatione*', 411.

[151] Ibid. 405–6. Despite the major disagreements he had with his former doctoral supervisor, Chenu always remained in agreement with Garrigou-Lagrange that ascetical and moral theology ought not to be separated.

[152] Ibid. 412. [153] Ibid. [154] Ibid. 413.

spiritualizing character of the 'maximalist' position that rendered it suspect to him.

Chenu then turned, via St Thomas, to Denys for an alternative solution to the two positions he considered inadequate. For Denys, mystical contemplation had consisted of 'intellectual passivity', a 'knowledge-experience of God under the influence of divine action by way of connaturality: *pati divina* [suffering divine things]'.[155] With the help of Denys, Chenu maintained, on the one hand, that the gradual ascent to perfection involved an essential moment of discontinuity in faith: a certain habit intervened that, as a species, was different from faith and love. The intervening habit resulted from the distinct, prompting work of the Holy Spirit (*pati divina*) in mystical contemplation.[156] On the other hand, if the passive character of human contemplation was its one, essential element, this also meant for Chenu that, contrary to the quietism of the maximalist position, mystical contemplation was not characterized by immediate spiritual contact by means of an extra-intellectual human potency.[157]

For Chenu, Denys represented the authentic sacramental mindset. In his 1957 publication *La Théologie du douzième siècle* Chenu sharply distinguished between the approach of Augustine and that of Denys. 'It is important', Chenu insisted here, 'to take stock of the difference between the Augustinian "sign" and the pseudo-Dionysian "symbol". Involved were two distinct philosophies, two distinct theologies, of symbolism.'[158] While both were Neoplatonic, the main difference, argued Chenu, was that Denys's mysticism was capable of doing justice to the world of matter, while Augustine's spirituality tended to minimize it. As Chenu viewed it, St Augustine's 'sign' was a psychological category. Here the knower *gave* the 'sign' its value, so that the added 'sacramental' value always remained separate from the nature of things. Augustine's dichotomy between *res et signa* (things and signs) was such that a sign always pointed away from itself, in a more or less arbitrary manner, since a sign was a visible sacrament of an invisible form.[159] As a result, the created order of time and space could never take on a real, sacramental value of its own: 'Exterior objects or events, even those with greatest authority, were but stimulants and aids. Augustine's illumination-ism showed its influence here and, long before *The Imitation of Christ*, a certain individualistic or subjectivist attitude threatened the practice of the sacraments.'[160] Unlike Augustine's 'sign', Denys's 'symbol' did not need the

---

[155] Conticello, '*De contemplatione*', 414.   [156] Ibid. 413, 415.

[157] Ibid. 414.

[158] Chenu, *Nature, Man, and Society in the Twelfth Century: Essays on New Theological Perspectives in the Latin West*, trans. and ed. Jerome Taylor and Lester Little (Toronto: University of Toronto Press, 1998), 124. Cf. ibid. 82: 'The "sign" of Augustine and the "symbol" of pseudo-Dionysius belonged to two quite different Platonisms.'

[159] Ibid. 125–6; id., *Toward Understanding*, 55–6.

[160] Id., *Nature, Man, and Society*, 125.

intervention of human words in order for it to take on a sacramental character: 'In pseudo-Dionysian symbolism, wholly taken up with mystagogy, such conceptualization did not come into play. The symbol was the starting point of knowledge, of "initiation", and it was no more reducible to analysis than the mystery made present.'[161] In short, for Denys, the sacramental mystery inhered objectively in the created reality as such, while St Augustine's notion of human de*sign*ation separated the invisible forms from the visible world. Chenu thus traced the desacralizing of Western society in part to the pervasive influence of St Augustine in the West.[162] While Chenu made the occasional positive reference to St Augustine, the North-African bishop generally served as the historical figure that combined all of the dangers of illuminationism, spiritualism, Neoplatonist idealism, and anthropological dualism.[163] St Augustine's 'sign', Chenu believed, had pointed away from the material world, while Denys's 'symbol' had acknowledged its inherent value, at the same time anagogically leading the believer into mystical contemplation. In Denys, Chenu found what we might call a sacramental ontology, which he thought was capable of overcoming the extrinsicism of the manualist tradition.[164]

Chenu was genuinely interested in recovering a sacramental ontology. Quite often, he would refer to it as the 'incarnational principle' of the divine–human or 'theandric mystery'. Christophe Potworowski has traced this incarnational principle throughout Chenu's writings.[165] This was Chenu's language denoting what I am calling a 'sacramental ontology'. Potworowski puts it well:

It was through a determined and unwavering focus on incarnation that Chenu was able to negotiate successfully the major cultural shift facing the Church at the turn of the previous century. It was by remaining faithful to what he called the law of the Incarnation that Chenu could identify the weakness of 'baroque scholasticism', the urgency of the Modernist questions, as well as the inadequacy of the Modernist solution. He was able to develop the centrality of incarnation in a number of areas, all of them relating to the issue of human history.[166]

---

[161] Ibid. 126–7. Cf. Chenu's comment: 'Dionysius ... holds that of two infirmities in the spirits of earth-bound men the symbol is a medium more apt than the rational concept with which to express the mystery. The symbol may indeed be brought low by the gross weight of our senses, but the concept may lead us into the illusions of idealism' (*Is Theology a Science?* 84). Cf. Chenu's repeated references to Denys, ibid. 23, 33, 38–9, 76.

[162] Id., *Nature, Man, and Society*, 127. At the same time, Chenu did acknowledge that history was more important in Augustine than it was in Denys (ibid. 86, 127–8).

[163] See e.g. Chenu, *Faith and Theology*, 51, 108–9, 111, 121–8, 130, 136. Cf. Potworowski, *Contemplation and Incarnation*, 86–7. Cf., however, Chenu's warm introduction to St Augustine in 'Pour lire saint Augustin', *VSpir* 24 (1930), 135–57.

[164] When stumbling across Chenu's repeated and often unqualified denunciations of Platonic idealism, we need to keep in mind, therefore, that Chenu took aim at the Augustinian tradition, not the Dionysian tradition.

[165] Potworowski, *Contemplation and Incarnation, passim*. See also Claude Geffré, 'Le Réalisme de l'incarnation dans la théologie du Père M.-D. Chenu', *RSPT* 69 (1985), 389–99.

[166] Potworowski, *Contemplation and Incarnation*, 226.

For Chenu, the Incarnation represented the safeguarding of the material, historical, and social realities of the created order and provided the warrant for human
engagement in society at large, including the many social issues that were of
importance to him.[167]

Desacralization and Signs of the Times

Despite Chenu's concern for a sacramental ontology, we need to question the
consistency with which he pursued it. Joseph Komonchak has commented that
there are 'few words that appear more often in these writings of Chenu than the
word *autonomy*'.[168] Even if this is an overstatement, it rightly draws our attention
to a central concern in Chenu's thought. His outlook was fundamentally optimistic about modernity, and rarely, if ever, did he question the positive character
of modern social developments, whether they were economic, social, or technological in nature. For Chenu, the law of the Incarnation meant not just a
celebration of the historical and material character of the created order, but
also an acceptance of cultural shifts that focused increasingly on the natural
realm. As a scholar of twelfth- and thirteenth-century theology, Chenu traced
what he called 'the discovery of nature' among twelfth-century theologians.[169]
He described in rather glowing terms the disintegration of the feudal monopoly
on property, leading to a new mobility of urban artisans, and the rise of the
market economy:[170] 'The encounter between man and nature becomes complete
only when man has subdued nature to his service; the order of nature demands
man's mastery and, for the Christian, so too does the command given man by the
Creator on the first pages of the Bible. The twelfth century followed this
command.'[171] Not only did the twelfth century manage to impose human
control over nature but, at the same time, a new historical awareness came to
the fore.[172] Both the new discovery and mastery of nature and the new emphasis
on history, argued Chenu, had a secularizing effect. The result of these changing
attitudes was that 'the new *homo artifex*, maker of shapes and forms, distinguished between the animate and the mechanical, rid himself of the childish
fancies of animism and of the habit of seeing divinity in the marvels of nature.
The sacred realm which he secularized by this process no longer possessed any
properly religious value for him'.[173] The new appreciation of historical development meant that 'bit by bit was secular history to emerge'.[174] Indeed, throughout

---

[167] Cf. id., 'History and Incarnation in the Theology of Marie-Dominique Chenu', *ScEs* 92
(1990), 237–65.
[168] Joseph A. Komonchak, 'Returning from Exile: Catholic Theology in the 1930s', in Gregory
Baum (ed.), *The Twentieth Century: A Theological Overview* (New York: Orbis, 1999), 41.
[169] Chenu, *Nature, Man, and Society*, 1–48.
[170] Ibid. 39.
[171] Ibid. 38.
[172] Ibid. 162–201.   [173] Ibid. 44–5.   [174] Ibid. 167. Cf. ibid. 200.

his study of the twelfth century, Chenu made reference to the 'desacralizing' of a previously 'sacramentalized' world.[175]

Chenu's positive appreciation of these twelfth-century developments of desacralizing or desacramentalizing reflects his interest in the autonomy of the natural realm. This interest came to the fore when Chenu described the breakdown of the monastic schools that were forced to give way to the scholasticism of the newly established universities. Chenu depicted the monastic schools as bulwarks that had safeguarded the sacred and sacramental universe of the Middle Ages. Their strength dissipated in the twelfth and thirteenth centuries. Chenu made clear that he regarded this as a positive development. Conservative monastic theologians like Rupert of Deutz (*c.*1075–1129) and Stephen of Tournai (1128–1203), whose otherworldly monastic tradition had flourished in the medieval arrangements between bishops and feudal lords, were out of step with their time. Chenu's preference lay with the innovative mendicant orders of the Franciscans and Dominicans, the new masters of theology who had aligned themselves with the burgeoning this-worldly, urban classes. Describing these medieval origins of modernity in theological terms, Chenu commented:

Set apart from the world, yet still present to it: this is the paradox of the Christian in the world. God's presence to the whole of human reality, carnal as well as spiritual, impacts not only the level of actions, both individual and collective; the divine presence extends as well, following the logic of the incarnation and of the Spirit, to the exercise of human reasoning. These evangelical thinkers are deeply involved in the civilization of their time and concern themselves with all kinds of problems: from that of the cities of Lombardy fighting to get their charters of freedom with the help of the mendicants, to that of sharing the exhilarating discovery of Greek thought with the faithful—leading to its exploitation and promotion in theology.

Grace thus allows nature to be free to be itself, and leads it on to its perfection in both communities and individuals, in both action and contemplation.[176]

Chenu not only connected the desacralizing effects of twelfth- and thirteenth-century developments with the 'logic of the incarnation', but he also made clear that his basic reason for applauding these developments was that in the newly developing paradigm grace 'allows nature to be itself'. In other words, what we encounter here is Chenu's interest in the autonomy of the natural realm. It seems difficult to reconcile this interest of Chenu to his more sacramental Dionysian anagogical approach.

As already indicated, Chenu's *ressourcement* was never a purely academic exercise. It served immediate and pressing ecclesial as well as social concerns. Thus, when describing the secularizing tendencies of the twelfth and thirteenth

---

[175] Ibid. 5, 14, 127, 265.
[176] Id., *Aquinas and his Role*, 11. While Chenu traced the developments in technical detail in *Man, Nature, and Society*, he painted a particularly lucid picture in his more popular work on Thomas Aquinas, *Aquinas and his Role in Theology*.

centuries, Chenu was consistently drawn to themes such as the mendicant poverty of the itinerant preachers, the democratic structures of the order of the Friars Preachers, and the involvement of the new orders in the social and political life of society.[177] The concerns of the mendicant orders with socio-economic justice, oppressive authority structures, and Christian political involvement provided a model for engagement with similar concerns in Chenu's own day.[178]

Understandably, then, Chenu often appealed to 'signs of the times', which had to be read carefully and could be ignored only at one's own peril.[179] The origin of this notion in Chenu's theology lay in the idea of a 'continued Incarnation', for which he was indebted to Johann Adam Möhler of the Tübingen school. 'Continued Incarnation' meant that the Incarnation continued in the Church and on into society, in many ways. This notion, combined with Chenu's Thomist appreciation of the created order, enforced his understanding of the autonomy of the natural order. Often, Chenu simply adopted Möhler's approach by speaking of the Church as a continuation of the Incarnation.[180] At other times, the 'law of the Incarnation' meant for Chenu that the Incarnation continued not just in the Church, but also continued wherever redemptive values took shape in human history.[181] Occasionally, Chenu made little distinction between the continuation of the Incarnation and the progressive humanizing of humanity.[182] Claude Geffré summarizes Chenu's position well in his comment that the Dominican theologian 'integrates the "signs of the times" in his vision of the continued Incarnation: they are assimilated to profane values that, despite their ambiguity, are points of contact [*pierres d'attente*], obediential potencies, positive dispositions by way of their recapitulation in Christ'.[183] For

---

[177] See e.g. Chenu, *Aquinas and his Role*, 2–11. Cf. also Chenu's comment on the 'desacralizing of authority' (*Nature, Man, and Society*, 264).

[178] Cf. Chenu's comment: "The mendicants renounced feudalism in the same way that Mission de France has separated itself from capitalism; the same evangelical, rather than ideological, force' (*Aquinas and his Role*, 9; trans. adjusted).

[179] Cf. esp. id., 'Les Signes des temps', in *Peuple de Dieu dans le monde* (Paris: Cerf, 1966), 35–55; id., *La 'Doctrine sociale' de l'église comme idéologie* (Paris: Cerf, 1979), 57–67.

[180] e.g., id., *Faith and Theology*, 152, 155, 167. Cf. Potworowski, *Contemplation and Incarnation*, pp. xi, xiii–xiv.

[181] Cf. Chenu's comment about the lay witness of Christian life being 'a prolongation of the incarnation whereby the full range of human society, all professions and all classes, is assumed in specialized institutional movements—the typical structure of the new Christianity' (*Faith and Theology*, 161; cf. ibid. 58, 94, 164). Chenu made the optimistic comment that the fraternity of the various social classes would 'contribute to the establishment of a "mystical body"—the organic expression of our divine fraternity' (ibid. 196; cf. ibid. 200; id., 'Towards a Theology of Work,' trans. Joseph Cunneen, *CC* 7/2 (1957), 182).

[182] Cf. id., 'Le Message du concile au monde', in *La Parole de Dieu*, ii, *L'Évangile dans le temps* (Paris: Cerf, 1964), 642: 'But this presence of God in the world, this realization of an Incarnation of the divine life, does not take place from the outside, *imposed* on a humanity itself left to its own destiny. Presence, Incarnation: these words themselves rise up against any rupture between grace from on high and earthly nature, in its development as well as in its potency. The scheme of the Incarnation operates up to the outer ranges of humanization.' Cf. Geffré, 'Théologie de l'incarnation', 137.

[183] Geffré, 'Théologie de l'incarnation', 144.

Chenu it was important that theology adapt itself to the points of contact that contemporary culture provided.

Of course, if the 'law of the Incarnation' is not just a general principle based on a Thomist appreciation for the created order but is, at the same time, a continuation of the actual Incarnation of the eternal Word, the question of how to discern such a continued Incarnation becomes crucial.[184] This is where, for Chenu, the 'signs of the times' entered the picture. Theologians had the prophetic task of reading these 'signs of the times'.[185] Potworowski rightly makes the point, however, that one needs criteria to decide whether or not particular historical developments are to be viewed as 'signs of the times': 'Chenu does not offer a prescription for correct interpretations, nor does he develop a system of theological criteria by which signs of the times can be discerned and plans for action followed.'[186] Chenu's optimistic reading of history as 'continued Incarnation' meant that occasionally he was too naive in assuming that, like the Carolingian Renaissance of the ninth, the Aristotelian Renaissance of the thirteenth, and the humanist Renaissance of the sixteenth centuries, so twentieth-century cultural developments should be evaluated positively, and that to criticize them would be to misread the 'signs of the times'.[187]

The lack of criteria to discern 'signs of the times', combined with Chenu's optimistic attitude towards modernity, endangered his own professed interest in a sacramental ontology. If Chenu was correct that the twelfth and thirteenth centuries had desacralized the world in order to appreciate the (perhaps relative) autonomy of the created order, is it not possible that with the loss of the Augustinian 'sign' character of reality the Dionysian 'symbolic' character also disappeared from the once-sacred horizons? Would the result not be a purely natural world, predicated on the very separation between nature and the supernatural that Chenu set out to defeat? One can hardly avoid the impression that his strong emphasis on the autonomy of the natural world led to exactly such a dualism. For example, when applauding the desacralizing effects of technology, Chenu commented that 'in this decidedly technological civilization, a true religious perception accepts and bases itself on the autonomy of the profane. This autonomy is manifested by the growing distinction between the sacred and the profane'.[188] This comment evinced a remarkably positive assessment both of the rise of technology and of its accompanying desacralizing effects, and in order to do so Chenu appeared willing to accept the very separation between nature

---

[184] We might even wish to press the issue and ask to what extent Chenu was able to maintain the distinct character of the Church vis-à-vis society, in which Christians give expression to their faith.

[185] Chenu, 'Les Signes', 41.

[186] Potworowski, *Contemplation and Incarnation*, 180. Cf. ibid. 115.

[187] Chenu uncritically jumped from earlier use of Greek philosophy to the use of contemporary philosophy in *Faith and Theology*, 82. He drew explicit links between the various periods of renewal in *La Théologie comme science au XIII^{e}siècle*, 18–22; id., *Une école*, 117–18; id., *Toward Understanding*, 24–31; id., *Nature, Man, and Society*, 1–4.

[188] Id., *Faith and Theology*, 221.

and the supernatural that he had been critiquing in the Augustinian tradition and in contemporary neo-scholasticism. Similarly, when developing his theology of work, Chenu insisted that work carried its own value and its own, admittedly secondary, end, independent of our spiritual finality.[189] One wonders how such a strong assertion of a natural *telos*, independent of the supernatural end of human beings, could avoid lapsing into the very 'historicism' that Chenu wished to avoid. Nor is it clear how such an approach fit with his Dionysian theurgical and faith-based reading of reality. Sometimes, a closed, natural finality removed Chenu far from the sensibilities of de Lubac, who was able to overcome more consistently the twofold danger of historicism and extrinsicism.[190] Most significantly, Chenu's advocacy of a desacralized universe made it difficult for him to sustain the incarnational or sacramental ontology that he was intent on recovering.

In short, Chenu's theology was marked by a degree of ambivalence. On the one hand, like other *nouvelle* theologians, he sought to overcome the extrinsicism of the neo-scholastic Thomist tradition. This led to a genuine openness towards a sacramental ontology, and to this end Chenu mined the Dionysian strand of Thomas's theology in his *ressourcement* of the Middle Ages. On the other hand, his strong cultural engagement, along with his Thomist emphasis on the autonomy of the natural order, led to an overall theological stance that appeared to reintroduce a certain dualism through the back door. While this would not necessarily play into the hands of his neo-scholastic opponents, it did imply an acceptance of modernity's desacralized secularism that was at odds with Chenu's search for a sacramental ontology.

---

[189] Id., *The Theology of Work*, trans. Lilian Soiron (Chicago, Ill.: Henry Regnery, 1966), 29–31. Cf. Potworowski, *Contemplation and Incarnation*, 136.

[190] Komonchak accurately points out four differences between Chenu and de Lubac: (1) de Lubac was less enthusiastic about the Thomistic achievement, which had made possible a later compartmentalized anthropology; (2) de Lubac insisted less on the autonomy of the created order and more on the supernatural finality of creation; (3) de Lubac placed less emphasis on economic questions and was more reserved about alliances with Marxism; and (4) de Lubac was more critical of the post-conciliar situation than was Chenu ('Returning from Exile', 44–5). Potworowski adds to this that Chenu's approach to 'signs of the times' made him less sensitive than de Lubac to problems associated with the question of evil (*Contemplation and Incarnation*, 178–9).

5

A Wheel within a Wheel: Spiritual Interpretation in de Lubac and Daniélou

The Old and New Law are to be understood as a double wheel: The outside wheel is the covering one, while the second, covered wheel, is the wheel that does the uncovering.

St Gregory the Great[1]

SPIRITUAL INTERPRETATION AND ECUMENICAL DIALOGUE

The debates surrounding *nouvelle théologie* were heated especially because the very character of the theological discipline was at stake. Henri de Lubac, Jean Daniélou, and Hans Urs von Balthasar were all deeply interested in the relationships between theology, spirituality, and Scripture. They insisted not only that theology had for its aim spiritual maturity and ultimately union with God but also that on the path towards it theology was fundamentally a matter of biblical interpretation.[2] This chapter will focus on the nature of biblical interpretation. We find ourselves here at the heart of the sacramental ontology which motivated many of the endeavours of this French renewal movement. We also find ourselves at the place where genuine theological *rapprochement* between Catholicism and Protestantism should originate.

The desire to connect theology closely to biblical interpretation should endear *nouvelle théologie* to a Protestant mindset. This same desire caused debate within the Catholic fold: the spiritual interpretation of the *nouvelle* theologians challenged the neo-Thomist tendency to locate eternal dogmatic truths in the

---

[1] Gregory the Great, *In Ezekiel*, Bk 1, h. 7, n. 15 (*PL* 77, 844–8) (quot. de Lubac, *Medieval Exegesis: The Four Senses of Scripture*, trans. Marc Sebanc and E. M. Macierowski, 2 vols (Grand Rapids, Mich.: Eerdmans, 1998–2000), ii. 257).

[2] The interconnection of theology, spirituality, and Scripture can be found throughout the writings of the *nouvelle* theologians. Particularly clear is Balthasar, 'Theology and Sanctity', in *Explorations in Theology*, i *The Word Made Flesh*, trans. A. V. Littledale and Alexander Dru (San Francisco, Calif.: Ignatius, 1989), 181–209. Cf. Marcellino D'Ambrosio, '*Ressourcement* Theology, *Aggiornamento*, and the Hermeneutics of Tradition', *Comm* 18 (1991), 534–6. For a helpful discussion of the nature of theology in *nouvelle théologie*, see John Auricchio, *The Future of Theology* (Staten Island, NY: Alba, 1970), 117–90.

biblical text by means of a combination of literal exegesis and deductive reason, a process understood to be guided by the magisterium. According to the neo-scholastic view, spiritual interpretation ran the danger of relying too heavily on the subjective disposition of the biblical reader, and implied an abdication of the prima facie literal meaning of the Bible in favour of allegorical or typological speculation.[3] The spiritual interpretation advocated by the *ressourcement* theologians put it on a collision course with commonly accepted Catholic biblical hermeneutic.[4]

At the same time, however, *nouvelle théologie*'s return to spiritual interpretation presented a challenge to Protestants—and it continues to do so today. First, the rationalist systematizing that de Lubac denounced was not the sole prerogative of neo-Thomism. Its scholasticism has also bedevilled post-Reformation Protestantism, and to some extent still does.[5] Moreover, *nouvelle théologie* did not just oppose the abstract theology of neo-Thomism. The typological and allegorical interpretation advocated by *nouvelle théologie* also confronted the historical–critical approach, which had been introduced first of all by nineteenth-century Liberal Protestant scholars, and which had only subsequently been adopted by Modernist Catholics such as Alfred Loisy. The inability of such 'historicism' to take into account the deeply religious motives that often propelled history was anathema to the proponents of *nouvelle théologie*, who worked with the conviction that theology—and thus the interpretation of Scripture—was, above all, an exploration of the divine mystery. For the *ressourcement* theologians, scholasticism and historicism were united in their vehement rejection of pre-modern exegetical methods. It mattered little whether such rejection was Catholic or Protestant. In both ecclesial settings, the decline of pre-modern exegesis was the result of the loss of a sacramental hermeneutic. *Nouvelle théologie*'s recovery of a sacramental approach to interpretation, it seems to me, presents an opportunity for renewed ecumenical discussion.[6]

This chapter, therefore, will discuss spiritual interpretation in the writings of two *ressourcement* theologians who dedicated much of their scholarly attention

[3] See e.g. *AAS* 42 (1950), 561–78, at 570; English trans.: *Humani generis*, 23 <http://www.vatican.va>.

[4] Cf. Walter Burghardt's comment on de Lubac's 1944 introduction to Origen's homilies on Genesis: 'De Lubac's Introduction is born of rebellion. It is a provocative challenge to entrenched ideas and as such fairly courts counter-attack' (review of Louis Doutreleau (ed.), *Origène: Homélies sur la Genèse* in *TS* 9 (1948), 266).

[5] For developments in post-Reformation scholasticism, see Brian G. Armstrong, *Calvinism and the Amyraut Heresy: Protestant Scholasticism and Humanism in Seventeenth Century France* (Madison, Wis.: University of Wisconsin Press, 1969); Stephen Strehle, *Calvinism, Federalism and Scholasticism: A Study of the Reformed Doctrine of the Covenant* (Bern: Peter Lang, 1988); Richard A. Muller, 'Calvin and the "Calvinists": Assessing the Continuities and Discontinuities between the Reformation and Orthodoxy', *CTJ* 30 (1995), 345–75; 31 (1996), 125–60; Carl R. Trueman and R. Scott Clark (eds), *Protestant Scholasticism: Essays in Reassessment* (Exeter: Paternoster, 1998); Willem J. van Asselt and Eef Dekker (eds), *Reformation and Scholasticism: An Ecumenical Enterprise* (Grand Rapids, Mich.: Baker, 2001).

[6] Particularly hopeful is the recovery of 'theological interpretation', which is becoming ever more common among evangelicals in the wake of Barthian and post-liberal attempts to reconnect

it—Henri de Lubac and Jean Daniélou.[7] Both Jesuit scholars advocated a recovery of the sacramental hermeneutic that had been common throughout the patristic and medieval periods.[8] De Lubac, especially, brought to the fore the sacramental dimension of interpretation by insisting that the spiritual meaning constituted a deeper dimension of reality, one that was contained within the historical event conveyed by Scripture. While de Lubac and Daniélou certainly had differences in point of view, both put forth a form of spiritual interpretation that drew on the Church Fathers for a sacramental hermeneutic that was not restricted to just a literal interpretation but instead took seriously a spiritual reading of the text.

HENRI DE LUBAC AND THE FOURFOLD METHOD OF INTERPRETATION

'An Infinite Forest of Meanings'[9]

De Lubac's approach to Scripture appeared like a radical innovation alongside the two dominant alternatives of neo-scholastic and historical–critical interpretation. The neo-scholastic and historical–critical camps strongly opposed one another, yet were both equally startled by de Lubac's unabashed plea for an

theology and biblical studies. Among the many examples are the hugely successful Ancient Christian Commentary series (InterVarsity); the Evangelical Ressourcement series (Baker Academic); the Brazos Theological Commentary series; the *Dictionary for Theological Interpretation of the Bible*, ed. Kevin J. Vanhoozer (Grand Rapids, Mich.: Baker Academic, 2005); and the forthcoming Classical Christianity series on interpretation in the Church Fathers (Brazos).

[7] One could also mine the theology of Hans Urs von Balthasar, who was quite sympathetic to the endeavours of de Lubac and Daniélou. See Balthasar, 'Geleitwort', in de Lubac, *Der geistige Sinn der Schrift*, trans. Martha Gisi (Einsiedeln: Johannes, 1952), 7–12; id., 'Holy Scripture', trans. Jeremy Holmes, *NV* Eng 5 (2007), 707–24. See further Bevil Bramwell, 'Hans Urs von Balthasar's Theology of Scripture', *NBl* 86 (2005), 308–22; W. T. Dickens, *Hans Urs von Balthasar's Theological Aesthetics: A Model for Post-critical Biblical Interpretation* (Notre Dame, Ind.: University of Notre Dame Press, 2003). Marie-Dominique Chenu, in contrast, was much more positive about critical biblical scholarship, while sharply critical of twelfth-century allegorical interpretation. See Chenu, *La Théologie au XIIe siècle* (1957; repr. Paris: Vrin, 2006), 159–209 (chs 7 and 8). The first of these two chapters has been translated as *Nature, Man, and Society in the Twelfth Century: Essays on New Theological Perspectives in the Latin West*, trans. and ed. Jerome Taylor and Lester Little (Toronto: University of Toronto Press, 1998), 99–145. See further id., 'Histoire et allégorie au douzième siècle', in Erwin Iserloh and Peter Manns (eds), *Festgabe Joseph Lortz*, ii (Baden-Baden: Grimm, 1958), 59–71.

[8] Frances M. Young has argued that in the fourth century language was regarded as the sacramental vehicle of truth, as it 'acknowledged the poverty of human language to express the divine reality, yet retained the evocative power of the true metaphor. This was a linguistic possibility, I suggest, because the structure of Christian thought revolved around the notion of a transcendent God choosing to accommodate the divine self to the limitations of the human condition in incarnation and eucharist. Scriptural language, they recognized, belonged to the same fundamental pattern' (*Biblical Exegesis and the Formation of Christian Culture* (Cambridge: Cambridge University Press, 1997), 160). In retrospect, I regret not having done justice to the sacramental character of language in an earlier discussion on metaphors (Hans Boersma, *Violence, Hospitality, and the Cross: Reappropriating the Atonement Tradition* (Grand Rapids, Mich.: Baker Academic, 2004), 99–132).

[9] Jerome, *Epistles* 64, c. 21 (quot. de Lubac, *Medieval Exegesis*, i. 75).

infinite multiplicity of biblical meaning. De Lubac directly opposed the positivist mindset behind historicist exegesis when he opened his discussion on the multiplicity of meaning with a rhetorically powerful string of quotations from patristic and medieval authors:

Scripture is like the world: 'undecipherable in its fullness and in the multiplicity of its meanings'. A deep forest, with innumerable branches, 'an infinite forest of meanings': the more one gets in it, the more one discovers that it is impossible to explore it right to the end. It is a table arranged by Wisdom, laden with food, where the unfathomable divinity of the Savior is itself offered as nourishment to all. Treasure of the Holy Spirit, whose riches are as infinite as himself. True labyrinth. Deep heavens, unfathomable abyss. Vast sea, where there is endless voyaging, 'with all sails set'. Ocean of mystery.[10]

De Lubac made clear that the medieval approach had centred on the infinite fecundity of the divinely inspired Scriptures.[11] The understanding of St Gregory the Great had been common throughout the pre-modern exegetical tradition: 'Scripture, inasmuch as it is inspired by God, surpasses the loftiest minds by the same degree to which these minds are inferior to God.'[12]

De Lubac realized that by excluding this multiplicity of meaning the neo-Thomist essentialist ontology had caused a narrowing and hardening of exegetical methodology. He believed that this recent development was the result of the way biblical interpretation had unwittingly borrowed from the positivism of modernity. The pre-modern exegetical tradition had allowed much more scope for the imagination and thus for a genuine meeting between the text and the human subject. For de Lubac, the Spirit's authorship of Scripture meant that the revelatory and spiritual contents conveyed by the text were much more important than the literal meaning of the words themselves. As a result, he assailed the notion of 'inerrancy', a 'very narrow concept, which bears the mark of a rationalist age', and which 'could just as well be applied to some treatise on chemistry or mathematics'.[13] The inerrantist approach failed to realize that one could only interpret Scripture aright in the awareness of the 'unity of its divine intention', through the process of 'conversion', so that '[t]he Church alone understands Scripture'.[14] Only by joining the merged horizons of Scripture

---

[10] De Lubac, *Medieval Exegesis*, i. 75.

[11] Ibid. 75–82. Based on the fact that rabbinical exegesis also allows for multiple allegorical and spiritual explanations, Michel Fédou argues that de Lubac did not mean to contest the rightful place of Jewish interpretation of Scripture ('"Histoire et esprit": Les Travaux du père de Lubac sur l'interprétation de l'Écriture et leurs apports à la théologie contemporaine', in Jean-Dominique Durand (ed.), *Henri de Lubac: La Rencontre au cœur de l'Église* (Paris: Cerf, 2006), 264–5). De Lubac, however, nowhere acknowledged that Jewish exegesis has a place alongside Christian interpretation. He consistently argued that the only proper spiritual interpretation of the Old Testament Scriptures was one that was stamped by the Christ event.

[12] De Lubac, *Medieval Exegesis*, i. 79.

[13] Id., *History and Spirit: The Understanding of Scripture According to Origen*, trans. Anne Englund Nash and Juvenal Merriell (San Francisco, Calif.: Ignatius, 2007), 341.

[14] Ibid. 347.

and the Church could one arrive at true understanding. Scripture, de Lubac claimed,

> is not a document handed over to the historian or the thinker, even to the believing historian or thinker. It is a word, which is to say, the start of a dialogue. It is addressed to someone from whom it awaits a response. More precisely, it is God who offers himself through it, and he awaits more than a response: a return movement.[15]

For de Lubac, Scripture lay embedded within the Church, and the Church's dialogical and faithful response to the Scriptures opened up endless possibilities of meaning. Both the infinite depth of the Scriptures and the believers' varying circumstances would naturally result in a great diversity of interpretation.

The medieval interpreters had none the less mined the inexhaustible riches of meaning in more or less structured ways, the most common of which was the fourfold method of interpretation, which de Lubac explained with the use of a now well-known distich: *Littera gesta docet, quid credas allegoria, moralis quid agas, quo tendas anagogia* (The letter teaches what took place, the allegory what to believe, the moral what to do, the anagogy what goal to strive for).[16] This fourfold doctrine began with the *littera* or *historia*.[17] As we will see shortly, for polemical reasons, de Lubac emphasized the foundational position of the historical meaning in the pre-modern exegetical tradition. But the historical meaning had never been regarded as the only meaning. The text also carried an allegorical meaning, which gave the believer the doctrine of Christ and of the Church— *quid credas allegoria*—so that allegory pointed to the truth of Christian doctrine, foreshadowed in the Old Testament. The believer was then asked to appropriate the passage by way of tropology. With the word 'tropology' referring to a 'turning', the moral meaning was intended for the reader to turn towards the end that God had appointed for him. In other words, the 'moral' meaning of the text spoke of the life of the soul as well as of one's actions or walk of life. Finally, because the Christian life was always oriented towards the eschatological future, each of the first three levels came to fruition in the life hereafter. The Scriptures

---

[15] Ibid. 346–7. Cf. de Lubac, 'On an Old Distich: The Doctrine of the "Fourfold Sense" in Scripture', in *Theological Fragments*, trans. Rebecca Howell Balinski (San Francisco, Calif.: Ignatius, 1989), 121; English trans. of 'Sur un vieux distique: La Doctrine du "quadruple sens"', in *Mélanges offerts au R. P. Ferdinand Cavallera* (Toulouse: Bibliothèque de l'Institut Catholique, 1948), 347–66. For a superb recent study that does justice to the dialogical character of Scripture in its participatory (or sacramental) dimension, see Matthew Levering, *Participatory Biblical Exegesis: A Theology of Biblical Interpretation* (Notre Dame, Ind.: University of Notre Dame Press, 2008).

[16] De Lubac gave a clear exposition in 'On an Old Distich', 109–27. He explained the origin of the distich in *Medieval Exegesis*, i. 1–2. For a helpful overview of the four senses as given by de Lubac in his *Exégèse médiévale*, see Robert E. McNally, 'Medieval Exegesis', *TS* 22 (1961), 451–3.

[17] Needless to say, the *littera* or *historia* took into account literary conventions, so that the meaning of a parable, proverb, or commandment would have a 'historical' meaning, without implying that the passages conveyed something that actually occurred in time and space. In those cases, the literal and allegorical senses would coincide (de Lubac, 'On an Old Distich', 123; cf. also Daniélou, *Origen*, trans. Walter Mitchell (London: Sheed & Ward, 1955), 179–80).

were meant to 'lead up' (*anagōgē*) to one's final, heavenly end. De Lubac gave a helpful illustration to show how the fourfold doctrine functioned: 'Take the classic example, repeated everywhere, that, by its scope, can be said to contain all others: Jerusalem. It is, first of all, the historical city of the Jews; then the Church, a mystical city; then the Christian soul; and, finally, the heavenly Jerusalem, the triumphant Church.'[18]

A Sacramental Hermeneutic

De Lubac's work prompts us to ask what he positively intended to accomplish with his *ressourcement* of pre-critical interpretation. He unequivocally rejected a straightforward recovery of the doctrine of the fourfold sense: 'No one would seriously dream of that.'[19] De Lubac did not mean to promote 'any sort of archaism, any sort of desire to arrest time or stem its flow'.[20] He realized that higher criticism prevented a simple return to the past, all the more so since doctrinally and liturgically the Church had already gleaned the benefits of the fourfold method.[21] He was also quite aware of limitations inherent in pre-critical exegesis, which also prevented a straightforward retrieval. And de Lubac's view of Tradition and doctrinal development resisted turning one particular moment in the history of Christian doctrine into the sole standard for all subsequent biblical interpretation.[22]

Instead, de Lubac insisted that contemporary exegesis should seek to reproduce the 'spiritual movement' (*mouvement spirituel*) of pre-modern interpretation.[23] As we will see, this 'spiritual movement' was essentially a sacramental hermeneutic. He did not make clear, however, how one might retain this 'spiritual movement' without returning to the traditional doctrine of the fourfold sense. He gave little indication in his writings how contemporary exegesis ought to differ from patristic and medieval interpretation. In one sense, his own work exemplified the use of critical methodology: de Lubac's research in primary and secondary literature was impeccable. In another sense, however, he seemed remarkably uncritical. Throughout his studies on the history of interpretation, de Lubac simply quoted the Alexandrian theologian Origen as well as other authorities, without indicating whether or not he agreed with them. Generally, he

[18] De Lubac, 'On an Old Distich', 115.

[19] Ibid. 124.

[20] De Lubac, *Medieval Exegesis*, i, p. xxi. For similar denials of advocating a simple return to pre-modern exegesis, see id., *History and Spirit*, 450, 489; id., 'Spiritual Understanding', trans. Luke O'Neill, in Stephen E. Fowl (ed.), *The Theological Interpretation of Scripture: Classic and Contemporary Readings* (Malden, Mass.: Blackwell, 1997), 4. This last essay is a translation of 'Sens spirituel', *RSR* 36 (1949), 542–76.

[21] De Lubac, *History and Spirit*, 489. Cf. Bryan C. Hollon, *Everything Is Sacred: Spiritual Exegesis in the Political Theology of Henri de Lubac* (Eugene, Ore.: Cascade-Wipf & Stock, 2008), 192.

[22] Cf. Chap. 6, sect.: Henri de Lubac: 'Cashing in' Jesus.

[23] De Lubac, *History and Spirit*, 450. Cf. id., 'On an Old Distich', 124: 'Preserving or rediscovering its spirit is not the same thing as reestablishing it.'

left the reader with the impression that when he referenced these authors and explained their methodology, he was in agreement with their approach. Marcellino D'Ambrosio rightly observes that 'from beginning to end, de Lubac's writings on the Church's hermeneutical past were intended to impinge upon its hermeneutical present'.[24] Often, de Lubac failed to make clear whether he was presenting his own approach or was merely citing someone else, leaving the reader with the question *how* one should go beyond the Fathers or the Middle Ages while retaining their 'spiritual movement'. De Lubac never provided an answer to this question; I suspect that he would have been uneasy with any approach that deviated considerably from the doctrine of the fourfold sense.

By endorsing the 'spiritual movement' of pre-modern exegesis, de Lubac hinted at a link between spiritual interpretation and a sacramental view of reality. The entire Tradition, he pointed out, had argued for a sacramental understanding of the historical facts related in the Old Testament. De Lubac rallied an impressive array of witnesses—a hallmark of his historical scholarship—and demonstrated that medieval interpreters had equated mystery and allegory;[25] the terms *mysterium* and *sacramentum* had often been used interchangeably, both of them referring to the spiritual, allegorical, or mystical meaning of the Scriptures. As an example, de Lubac quoted Rufinus of Aquileia (*c.*345–410): 'In his Revelation, John reads the things that have been written in the Law according to the history of the divine mysteries and teaches that certain sacraments are contained within them. These truths are both useful and divine, but...have been covered over with sacraments and wound up in mysteries.'[26] At other times, when medieval theologians had distinguished between *sacramentum* and *mysterium*, they had used the former to speak of the exterior facts, reserving the latter for the inner mystery. As de Lubac put it:

In short, in the traditional language as in contemporary French, and in the language of exegesis as in that of liturgy, the sacrament contains the mystery, it relates to the mystery. 'Through the grace of the sacrament the fellowship of the mystery is restored', says Saint Ambrose regarding the pardoned sinner. Consequently, in the relationship between the two Testaments, the *sacramentum* belongs rather to the Old and the *mysterium* to the New. The entire New Testament is a great mystery hidden within this sacrament, or signifies by means of this sacrament which is the Old Testament.[27]

This quotation reflects de Lubac's conviction that in the Middle Ages the relationship between external fact and internal meaning had been patterned on the relationship between Old and New Testaments. In both cases, the point of

[24] Marcellino G. D'Ambrosio, 'Henri de Lubac and the Recovery of the Traditional Hermeneutic' (PhD diss., Catholic University of America, Washington, DC, 1991), 222.
[25] De Lubac, *Medieval Exegesis: The Four Senses of Scripture*, trans. Marc Sebanc and E. M. Macierowski, 2 vols (Grand Rapids, Mich.: Eerdmans, 1998–2000), ii. 19–20.
[26] Ibid. 20. The two sentences of Rufinus are from *In Num.*, h. 20, n. 1, and *In Jos.*, h. 20, n. 4, respectively.
[27] De Lubac, *Medieval Exegesis*, ii. 22.

connection had been the historical fact of the Christ event. Medieval interpreters had understood the events reported in the Old Testament as *futura mysteria* or *futura sacramenta*, referring to Jesus Christ and to the Church.[28] Susan Wood, in her excellent study of de Lubac's understanding of spiritual interpretation, rightly explains that for de Lubac 'the structure of allegory is fundamentally sacramental. That is, the content or signification of both the historical event and the future historical reality of Christ and the Church to which the allegorical meaning refers exceed what is observable within history'.[29]

The fact that the spiritual meaning went beyond history did not imply, however, that de Lubac considered history irrelevant. The fear among historical–critical interpreters was exactly that: a return to pre-modern exegesis would mean the abandonment of history. De Lubac, however, relinquished neither the significance of history nor the valuable contributions made by higher biblical criticism.[30] Marcellino D'Ambrosio has rightly pointed out that it would be erroneous to view de Lubac's *ressourcement* of Origen and the medieval tradition as an attempt to counter the approval of higher criticism in Pius XII's encyclical *Divino afflante Spiritu* (1943).[31] De Lubac frequently expressed the need for critical biblical scholarship. 'My endeavour would be misconstrued', he commented in the introduction to *Histoire et esprit*, 'if ascribed to even a limited or amended "antiscientific reaction", which I am told "is prevalent currently in spiritualist circles".'[32] While de Lubac could at times be uncomplimentary towards historical–critical interpretation, he did believe that it contributed genuine exegetical insights.

Thus, de Lubac was convinced that his hermeneutic upheld the importance of history. The burden of de Lubac's main publications on spiritual interpretation—his lengthy study of Origen, *Histoire et esprit* (1950),[33] and his four

---

[28] De Lubac, *Medieval Exegesis*, ii. 94–6.

[29] Susan K. Wood, *Spiritual Exegesis and the Church in the Theology of Henri de Lubac* (Grand Rapids, Mich.: Eerdmans, 1998), 39.

[30] Cf. the comment of David Lyle Jeffrey: 'The rehabilitation of allegory in the hermeneutic of the *Ressourcement* biblical scholars, so far from displacing the foundation of the literal and historical sense of Scripture, gives back to history the charged sacramental resonance it had for Augustine, Ambrose, and the early church' (*Houses of the Interpreter: Reading Scripture, Reading Culture* (Waco, Tex.: Baylor University Press, 2003), 8).

[31] Marcellino D'Ambrosio, 'Henri de Lubac and the Critique of Scientific Exegesis', *Comm* 19 (1992), 365–88.

[32] De Lubac, *History and Spirit*, 14.

[33] Id., *Histoire et esprit: L'Intelligence de l'Écriture d'après Origène* (Paris: Aubier, 1950). This nearly 450-page study was preceded by lengthy introductions to Origen's commentaries on Genesis and Exodus in the Sources chrétiennes series which formed the basis on which de Lubac then built his book. See id., Introduction to Origen, *Homélies sur la Genèse*, trans. Louis Doutreleau (Paris: Cerf, 1943), 5–62; id., Introduction to Origen, *Homélies sur l'Exode* trans. P. Fortier (Paris: Cerf, 1947), 7–75. For critical assessments of de Lubac's book, see John L. McKenzie, 'A Chapter in the History of Spiritual Exegesis: De Lubac's *Histoire et esprit*', *TS* 12 (1951), 365–81; R. P. C. Hanson, *Allegory and Event: A Study of the Sources and Significance of Origen's Interpretation of Scripture* (London: SCM, 1959), *passim*.

volumes on the Middle Ages, *Exégèse médiévale* (1959–64)[34]—was to demonstrate that Christian allegory did not undermine but rather presupposed the integrity of the historical meaning of the text. To be sure, de Lubac was under no illusion that either Origen or later medieval readers had possessed the kind of historical sense characteristic of the modern age.[35] De Lubac approvingly quoted the medievalist Jean Leclercq (1911–93) and agreed that the 'preoccupation with studying the Old Testament as a historical document for the sake of what it teaches us about the history of the Hebrew people' had been completely 'alien' to the medieval mindset.[36] De Lubac acknowledged that, at times, Origen's theology had led to wrong historical opinions. For example, the Alexandrian Church Father had erroneously believed that the Old Testament patriarchs and prophets had possessed special insight into the spiritual meaning of their actions and proclamation.[37] Nevertheless, Origen had usually presupposed the historicity of the Old Testament events, taking 'meticulous care' to justify the literal meaning of the Flood (Gen. 6–8), of Lot's wife being turned into a pillar of salt (Gen. 19), of the ten plagues against Egypt (Exod. 7–11), of the Balaam narrative (Num. 22–4), and of the miracle of Joshua stopping the sun (Josh. 10).[38] De Lubac noted a certain irony in the fact that while biblical criticism condemned allegorical exegesis for its depreciation of history, it denied the historicity of biblical accounts on a much more regular basis than Origen or later medieval interpreters had done. The only exceptions that the Alexandrian theologian had been willing to make to the literal character of the historical foundation had been texts concerning human origins and the eschaton.[39] 'This whole symbolic construction, with its "allegorizations", its interiorizations, its spiritual consequences', insisted de Lubac, 'does not evacuate history. It is not even indifferent to it, as Philo's allegorism could be. It is built, in principle, on the ground of history.'[40]

De Lubac's recognition of the importance of a historical foundation—both with regard to pre-modern interpretation and in terms of his own views—was much more than a matter of paying lip service to history with a view to silencing potential critics of allegorical exegesis. The genius of his sacramental hermeneutic was that it was predicated on the link between history and spirit and, therefore, on the indispensable significance of historical events. De Lubac was convinced that spiritual or allegorical interpretation was the only way to safeguard the historicity of biblical accounts.[41] Rather than 'thinning out history or seeing it

[34] De Lubac, *Exégèse médiévale: Les Quatre Sens de l'écriture*, 4 vols (Paris: Aubier, 1959–64).
[35] Id., *History and Spirit*, 281–3.
[36] Id., *Medieval Exegesis*, ii. 80.
[37] Id., *History and Spirit*, 295–302.
[38] Ibid. 107.
[39] Ibid. 116, 227.
[40] Ibid. 281. Cf. id., *Catholicism: Christ and the Common Destiny of Man*, trans. Lancelot C. Sheppard and Elizabeth Englund (San Francisco, Calif.: Ignatius, 1988), 166–7.
[41] Matthew Levering makes the same point when he argues that a historical approach to Scripture in no way precludes, but rather requires, participation in the realities of faith. Levering

at most as a simple "support"', Christian allegory gave history its 'value'.[42] The spirit, therefore, for the medieval interpreters, 'ennobles the letter that bears it'.[43] It is important to pause and take note of the radical character of de Lubac's position. He did not just grudgingly acknowledge the significance of the literal or historical meaning of the text, while admitting certain weaknesses in the medieval appreciation for history. Instead, he insisted in the strongest possible terms that for pre-modern exegesis, history had served as the crucial 'foundation' for deeper levels of interpretation. Time and again, de Lubac observed, the term *fundamentum* cropped up in the Middle Ages to describe the indispensable character of sacred history.[44] De Lubac's sacramental understanding of the relationship between history and spirit enabled him to maintain that allegory provided the true warrant for the value of history.

De Lubac often made a point of emphasizing the sacramental interconnectedness of the four levels of biblical meaning—historical, allegorical, tropological, and anagogical. Speaking of the 'dynamic unity' or 'reciprocal interiority' of the various senses, de Lubac commented: 'Just as one ancient author says of the four degrees of contemplation, so ought we to say of these four senses that they are interlinked like the rings of a priceless chain: *concatenati sunt ad invicem* [they have been linked to each other].'[45] De Lubac was particularly fond of expressing this reciprocity of meanings—and in particular of the two main senses, the historical and the spiritual—by alluding to St Gregory the Great's exposition of Ezekiel 1. In his first vision, Ezekiel saw four living creatures, each accompanied by a wheel, 'their construction being as it were a wheel within a wheel' (Ezek. 1: 16). St Gregory explained the wheels as a reference to the unity of Scripture: 'The Old and New Law are to be understood as a double wheel: The outside wheel is the covering one, while the second, covered wheel, is the wheel that does the uncovering.'[46] De Lubac was attracted to this explanation because of the sacramental connection it had posited between historical and spiritual interpretation, as well as between Old and New Testaments. While it was possible, in the light of

---

specifically appeals to de Lubac as the theologian who modelled what he terms 'participatory biblical exegesis' (*Participatory Biblical Exegesis*, 143–5).

[42] De Lubac, *Medieval Exegesis*, ii. 100.

[43] Ibid. 60. Cf. id., *History and Spirit*, 317.

[44] Id., *Medieval Exegesis*, ii. 47–50.

[45] Ibid. 201. De Lubac here refers to Guigues du Chastel (*c.*1083–*c.*1137).

[46] Gregory the Great, *In Ezek.*, Bk. 1, h. 7, n. 15 (*PL* 77, 844–8) (quot. de Lubac, *Medieval Exegesis*, i. 257). Cf. ibid. 246; ii. 26, 111, 201, 207. The 'mystic wheel' painted by Fra Angelico (*c.*1400–55), which I have used as the cover for this book, is part of the 'Armadio degli Argenti' (*c.*1450), held by the Museum of San Marco in Florence. The rim of the outer wheel contains Gen. 1: 1–5, the rim of the inner wheel John 1: 1–3, both from the Vulgate. The outer wheel depicts (clockwise, beginning at the top) Moses, Solomon, Ezekiel, Jeremiah, Micah, Jonah, Joel, Malachi, Ezra, Daniel, Isaac, and David. The inner wheel depicts (clockwise, beginning at the top) John, Peter, Mark, Jude, Luke, James, Matthew, and Paul. The very centre of the wheel represents the mystery of God's essence (cf. Ezek. 1: 4).

Christ's coming, to 'extract' or 'separate' the spiritual meaning, the historical and spiritual had been interwoven from the outset. Or, to put it differently, the spiritual meaning was contained within the historical event: '*Christus in littera continetur* [Christ is contained in the letter]. *The spirit is not outside the history.* They are given together, inseparably, through the fact of a single inspiration. It is we who, after the event, separate them: "when they are expounded, they are broken".'[47]

De Lubac patterned the relationship between literal and spiritual meaning, and between Old and New Testaments, on the relationship between nature and the supernatural. In each case, the link was sacramental in character. Thus, when he expressed reservations about historical criticism, the reason was not an apprehension either of history or of critical scholarship as such. Rather, his objections to the actual functioning of much contemporary biblical scholarship rested on his Blondelian apprehension of 'historicism' or 'separated philosophy'.[48] In terms of biblical interpretation, De Lubac was convinced that problems arose if and when the historical meaning was treated as strictly autonomous and separate from the other levels of interpretation or perhaps was even regarded as providing the sole meaning of the text. What he objected to was the reduction of history to mere history and the restriction of Old Testament exegesis to its literal meaning. It is precisely at this point that de Lubac felt that the pre-modern understanding of history was illuminating:

Our ancient exegetes did not have any idea, thanks be to God, of that 'absolutized History' which is one of the principal idols invented by our age. On the other hand, they did have a sense of biblical history, or even of universal history, because they held on to its principle of discernment in the Mystery of Christ, the absolutely ultimate final cause. The doctrine of the four senses, through which this mystery has found its expression . . . thus appeared, in the very perspective which it engendered and which it kept alive for a long time, as providing the foundation for the objective sense of history and by that very fact *giving history its proper value*.[49]

The strength of medieval exegesis, in de Lubac's view, was that it held on to the centrality of Christ and rejected an 'absolutized' history.

Thus, when medieval authors contrasted 'letter' and 'spirit', and when they discussed the Pauline phrase that 'the letter kills' (2 Cor. 3: 6), de Lubac noted that they never maintained that history or the letter were problematic in and of themselves. It 'was not the "letter" that bothered them, but the "mere letter", the "mere surface of the letter", the "property of the letter alone", and those who

---

[47] De Lubac, *Medieval Exegesis*, ii. 26 (emphasis in original).
[48] Blondel's influence on de Lubac's critique of the historical critical method is widely recognized. See e.g. D'Ambrosio, 'Henri de Lubac and the Recovery of Traditional Hermeneutic', 41–4; Ignace de la Potterie, 'The Spiritual Sense of Scripture', *Comm* 23 (1996), 742; Kevin L. Hughes, 'The "Fourfold Sense": De Lubac, Blondel and Contemporary Theology', *HeyJ* 42 (2001), 451–62; Hollon, *Everything Is Sacred*, 97–100.
[49] De Lubac, *Medieval Exegesis*, ii. 71–2 (emphasis in original).

were aiming like "partisans of the letter" were in fact the "ones understanding according to the letter alone" '.[50] To view the letter in isolation from the spirit was precisely to ignore history because it was to deny the historical progress made through the event of the Incarnation. As de Lubac made clear:

Under the opposition of the letter and the spirit, or of the shadow and the truth, in its varied and sometimes, for us, paradoxical expressions, there is therefore always the opposition of two peoples, of two ages, of two regimes, of two states of faith, of two 'economies', which is affirmed. There are two peoples, two ages, two states, two régimes, two economies, which, however, are opposed to each other in a real contradiction properly speaking only once they have come to coexist, the first not having wished to disappear on the arrival of the one for which its whole task was to prepare, because it had not understood that it was merely the means of getting ready for it.[51]

For de Lubac, the Incarnation gave the history of the Old Testament its spiritual meaning and value. Properly understood, Old and New Testaments were not opposed to each other. Only the refusal of the letter to give way to the spirit would render the two economies irreconcilably opposed to each other.[52]

A Christological Hermeneutic

De Lubac objected to a historicism that reverted to the 'mere' letter and that ignored the radical historical progress made with the coming of Christ. The 'disappearance' of the letter, which de Lubac believed to be necessary, was not an absolute rejection of the letter.[53] Instead, it was a repudiation of a historicist isolation of the literal meaning, which was not just predicated on the illusion of independent and objective historical neutrality, but which also ignored the fact that the Christological fulfilment of the Old Testament illuminated its inner or spiritual meaning. Put differently, if and when critical scholarship denied that Christological and ecclesiological referents belonged intrinsically to the spiritual meaning of the text, it thereby undermined the sacramental structure of reality.

Allegorizing the biblical accounts was justified, de Lubac believed, strictly because of 'the Fact of Christ'. Origen, far from being merely a follower of the Jewish interpreter Philo of Alexandria (*c.*20 BC–*c.*AD 50), had justified allegory on the basis of Christology: 'At the summit of history, the Fact of Christ supposed history, and its radiance transfigured history.'[54] Origen had realized that 'through

---

[50] De Lubac, *Medieval Exegesis*, ii. 51. Cf. ibid. 55.   [51] Ibid. 54.

[52] Daniélou understood the relationship between pagan and Christian religions in a similar way. Only the refusal of the former to yield upon the arrival of the latter caused opposition between the two. Cf. Chap. 6, sect.: Cosmic and Christian Revelation.

[53] Thus, de Lubac could also comment that for Origen, with the coming of Christ, the law was no longer an 'ancient document' or 'outdated testament', precisely because it now had to be 'expounded in the evangelical sense' (*History and Spirit*, 194).

[54] De Lubac, *Medieval Exegesis*, ii. 105.

this Christian event the Old Law has become spiritual'.[55] David Grumett rightly observes, therefore, that for de Lubac Christology demanded a retroactive determination of the meaning of the biblical text: 'Faith in Christ cannot be lived out by the unspiritual observance of legal requirements. The law has not been rendered obsolete, however, but given a new deeper significance and fulfilment by Christ that is expressed allegorically.'[56] The reciprocity of nature and the supernatural, of history and spirit, and of Old and New Testaments implied for de Lubac that in each case the latter provided the former with deeper significance, and he was convinced that the Christ event warranted this retro-active signification.[57]

The centrality of Christology in de Lubac's sacramental hermeneutic was evident in the close link that he posited between Incarnation and the inspiration of Scripture:

Origen fought against Docetism. Now what he did not admit with respect to Christ, he was no more disposed to admit with respect to Christ's preparation in Israel. In his Scripture as in his earthly life, Origen thought, the Logos needs a body; the historical meaning and the spiritual meaning are, between them, like the flesh and the divinity of the Logos. All of Scripture is, so to speak, 'incorporated'; like the One whom it proclaims and prepares for, it is 'non in phantasia, sed in veritate' (not in fantasy, but in truth). Certainly, just as one must not stop in Christ at the man who is seen but, through the flesh that veils him to carnal eyes, perceive by faith the God who is in him, so one must go through the external history that is offered to us in the Holy Books, particularly in the Old Testament, in order to penetrate to the 'spiritual mystery' that is hidden there.[58]

In these remarks, de Lubac insisted on a parallel or analogy between Incarnation and inscripturation, concerned to avoid Docetism not only with regard to the doctrine of Christ, but also in connection with Scripture. In a very real sense, however, de Lubac went beyond positing a mere analogy. His comment that 'the Logos needs a body', whether that be the human body of Christ or the Scriptures, indicates that he believed that for Origen there was, through the Logos, a certain identity between Christ and the Scriptures. To be sure, at the human level—that of the text of Scripture and of the flesh of Christ—one could make no more than a comparison. But the medieval mindset had realized that at the divine level much more was at stake than just a comparison: '[F]rom the object of allegory to

---

[55] Id., *History and Spirit*, 310.

[56] David Grumett, *De Lubac: A Guide for the Perplexed* (London: T. & T. Clark/Continuum, 2007), 83. See e.g. de Lubac, *Catholicism*, 180–1: 'Yet the act of redemption is not a key which by unlocking the Old Testament reveals a meaning already present in it. This act in some sort creates the meaning. It is only for God, from the eternal point of view, that the Old Testament contains the New already in a mystery: *semel locutus est Deus et plura audita sunt* [God has spoken once and many things have been heard].'

[57] De Lubac recognized that his approach implied a 'vicious circle', since spiritual interpretation of the Old Testament rendered the insight of the need to view the relationship between the two Testaments in this fashion (*History and Spirit*, 195).

[58] Ibid. 104–5.

the divinity of the Word there is more than an analogy: there is, at the endpoint, coincidence. The divinity of the Word of God incarnate is in fact the central object of allegory.'[59] In a chapter entitled 'The Incorporations of the Logos', de Lubac detailed the various ways in which he believed the Logos was incorporated in history.[60] The working assumption mentioned at the outset was that 'there are not two Words any more than there are two Spirits'. The Word of Scripture was none other than the eternal Logos. De Lubac insisted that it was 'still the same word, the same biblical word, and there is no play on words in that'.[61]

De Lubac then proceeded to outline the various incorporations of that one eternal Word of God. In addition to the historical body of Christ, Origen had referred to the Word of Christ as embodied in Scripture, in the Eucharist, and in the Church.[62] De Lubac's thoughts here show how his study of Origen was determinative for his sacramental hermeneutic. Since Origen had portrayed Scripture as embodied (*incorporée*), one needed spiritual discernment 'to perceive the mystery of it'.[63] For example, when Origen had explained the allegorical meaning of the wells mentioned in the Book of Numbers, he had displayed no qualms about identifying them both with Christ and with the Scriptures: 'Word engendered by the Father with the Trinity, which is made manifest in somewhat the same way as particular wells in the different parts of the Holy Books in order to be found whole and unified again at the end, in that "delightful Well, superior to all the others", that is Christ Jesus.'[64] The word of God that is 'living and active, sharper than any two-edged sword' (Heb. 4: 12) received a similar dual interpretation: 'Here again, is this the biblical Word? Is this the person of Jesus? It is both, identically.'[65]

For de Lubac, the embodiments of the Logos in Scripture and in the Eucharist were intimately connected. Here de Lubac opposed the common view that Origen's allegorizing had led to a denial of the real presence in the Eucharist. The Alexandrian exegete had made the comment that

it is not this visible bread that he holds in his hands that the divine Logos said was his Body; but it was the Word in the mystery of which this bread was to be broken. And it was

---

[59] De Lubac, *Medieval Exegesis*, ii. 108. It is important to note that de Lubac stated that it was only 'at the endpoint' that there was a coincidence between the divinity of Christ and the spiritual meaning of the Scriptures. Since the anagogical meaning of Scripture would come to its completion only at the eschaton, it was only then that we could truly speak of a coincidence. Accordingly, de Lubac elsewhere gave the following commentary on Origen: 'In the literal meaning of Scripture, the Logos is thus not, properly speaking, incarnated as he is in the humanity of Jesus, and this is what allows us still to speak of comparison: he is, nevertheless, already truly incorporated there; he himself dwells there, not just some idea of him, and this is what authorizes us to speak already of his coming, of his hidden presence' (*History and Spirit*, 389).

[60] Id., *History and Spirit*, 385–426.

[61] Ibid. 385.

[62] Origen had also viewed both the human soul, imprinted with the 'image of God', and the entire universe as places inhabited by the eternal Word (ibid. 396–406).

[63] Ibid. 387.   [64] Ibid.   [65] Ibid. 390.

not this visible beverage that he designated as his Blood but the Word in the mystery of which this beverage was to be shed.[66]

This statement seemed to plead for a spiritual or allegorical understanding of the Eucharist while opposing the notion of a real presence. De Lubac countered this explanation by insisting that it relied on the erroneous notion that allegory excluded history. Origen had maintained that allegory presupposed history; likewise, in Eucharistic theology, the truth of the mystery took for granted the real presence of Christ's body and blood.[67] De Lubac argued that the 'fideist interpretation' of Origen overlooked the sacramental cast of his thought: Origen 'means here quite simply that the Body received in the Eucharist is still symbolic with respect to other more direct and more spiritual manifestations of the Logos'.[68]

Origen had regarded both Scripture and Eucharist as 'body of Christ', and he attributed a sacramental function to both. Both pointed to the Church, and in doing so made this 'third Body' present. In Chapter 7, I will elaborate in more detail on the close connection that de Lubac maintained between Eucharist and Church.[69] For now, I merely wish to make the point that he emphasized the 'efficacious sign' character of Scripture and Eucharist, both of them transforming the recipients into Christ himself: 'Scripture and Eucharist are thereby joined once again. Both never ceased to "build up" the Church.'[70] Both Scripture and Eucharist were thus meant to lead to a spiritual eating of the eternal Word and so to bring about the fullness of Christ in the Church.[71] As de Lubac put it:

As to this spiritual manducation of the Word, the effect of meditation on Scripture and of the sacrament received in the Church, it is itself, in the end, in reality, only still symbolic in relation to what it will become in the other life, or rather, what the other life will be: 'For it is manifest that it is in the kingdom of God that we will eat the true food and will drink the true drink, drawing from and strengthening there the true life.'[72]

In de Lubac's portrayal, Origen had regarded Scripture as one element in a 'trilogy' of 'incorporations' of the Word.[73] Scripture and Eucharist had both functioned as 'body of Christ' sacramentally pointing to the Church and, through the Church, to the completed body of Christ, the eternal Logos. Clearly, for de Lubac more was at stake than a mere parallel between Christology and the

---

[66] Origen, *Origenes Matthäuserklärung*, ed. Erich Klostermann (Leipzig: Hinrichs, 1933), 85 (pp. 196–7) (quot. de Lubac, *History and Spirit*, 410).

[67] De Lubac, *History and Spirit*, 409, 413.

[68] Ibid. 414.

[69] See Chap. 7, sect.: The Eucharist Makes the Church.

[70] De Lubac, *History and Spirit*, 418.

[71] De Lubac perceived in Origen a certain prioritizing of Scripture over the Eucharist, but insisted that when Origen exalted Scripture in this way he had in mind its sacramental reality (*res sacramenti*), 'the completed Body of Christ, the unique essence of the Word' (ibid. 425; cf. ibid. 419).

[72] Ibid. 422–3. The quotation is from Origen, *Origenes Matthäuserklärung*, 86 (pp. 198–9).

[73] De Lubac, *History and Spirit*, 425.

doctrine of Scripture. The sacramental move from letter to spirit had allowed
Origen to perceive in the Scriptures the very Word of God.[74]

An Arbitrary Hermeneutic?

Alexandrian and medieval allegorizing is commonly dismissed as an arbitrary
form of exegesis resulting from the unfortunate influence of Philo's Hellenizing
interpretive strategies. Since allegory reaches beyond the literal meaning of the
text, pre-modern interpretation of Scripture is seen as depending on the subjective disposition of the interpreter, rendering the exegetical results more or less
arbitrary in character. As we have already seen, the mere existence of differing
interpretations could not possibly be an issue for de Lubac. The very fact that the
literal meaning of the text was foundational for a number of additional levels of
interpretation implied multiplicity of meaning. And if *within* each of these levels
different commentators came to different conclusions, this too was to be
expected: the range of readers' horizons meant that each person would draw a
different meaning from the text. Multiplicity of meaning as such did not imply
arbitrariness.

De Lubac opposed the dismissal of Alexandrian and medieval interpretation
with the argument that Philo's Jewish allegorizing had lacked Christological or
sacramental characteristics and thus had not been the cause of the Christian
allegorical method.[75] Lacking a Christian sacramental hermeneutic, Philo had
been unable to give history the significant place that Origen and his medieval
followers had attributed to it.[76] De Lubac took exception to Lutheran portrayals
of Christian allegory as simply another instance of the general tendency that had
produced the philosophical allegorizing of the Homeric myths. He countered
that nothing short of an 'abyss' separated Christian commentary from the
allegorizing of pseudo-Heraclitus, Plotinus, Sallust, and others.[77] The Fourvière
theologian was not willing to acknowledge even a formal similarity between
Philonic and Christian allegorizing.[78] '[W]here would one find,' de Lubac asked
rhetorically,

in the facts of history, or only in the thought or imagination of the Greek allegorists, the
irruption of some 'new testament' analogous to that of the Christians, an irruption which

---

[74] Cf. William F. Murphy's comment: 'Thus, the allegorical sense, like the historical sense, refers
most properly to the event or reality disclosed through the text, but in a more adequate way. Such
language of "mediation" or "disclosure" recognizes both the priority of the salvific event, or the
underlying theological reality, and the sacramental character of the inspired text, with its unique
capacity to mediate divine reality' ('Henri de Lubac's Mystical Tropology', *Comm* 27 (2000), 181).
[75] De Lubac, *Medieval Exegesis*, i. 149–50; ii. 100–7.
[76] Id., *History and Spirit*, 21–2, 281.
[77] Id., *Medieval Exegesis*, ii. 9–17. De Lubac dealt in particular with the Lutheran theologians,
Samuel Friedrich Nathanael Morus (1736–92) and J. G. Rosenmüller (1736–1815), as well as with
the British Anglican scholar, Edwin Hatch (1835–89).
[78] Id., *Medieval Exegesis*, ii. 103.

one day would have turned the ancient exegesis of the Homeric poems upside-down by overturning the very being of their exegete? Where would one find, in Cornutus and the rest, anything even remotely resembling the opposition between the *oldness* of the letter and the *newness* of the spirit?[79]

A formal identity between Philonic and Christian exegesis would imply that the latter was interested in general 'metaphysical truths', without concern for historical events. Since it looked instead for the 'fact of Christ', Christian allegory— for which both Tertullian (*c*.160–*c*.225) and Origen had gone back to St Paul rather than to Philo —belonged to an entirely different category.[80]

This was not to deny that Origen's biblical interpretation had undergone any kind of Philonic influence at all. De Lubac did recognize similarities between Philo and Origen, such as the symbolism of numbers and names, the desire to explain morally shocking episodes, and the mystical rationalism that reserved inner truths to well-disposed minds.[81] De Lubac even granted that Origen had 'borrowed much too much' from Philo.[82] What disturbed de Lubac was the order in which Origen had dealt with the various meanings of Scripture. Origen had sometimes worked with a threefold method of interpretation, which moved from the historical, via the tropological or moral, to the allegorical sense. The more common medieval fourfold method—which formed the structure of de Lubac's own overview of medieval exegesis—had placed the tropological sense *after* the allegorical sense, so that one could only move to the Christian way of life via Christ and the Church.[83] De Lubac conceded that Philo's threefold method had unduly influenced Origen, and de Lubac was clearly apprehensive of the natural morality that this method appeared to assume.[84]

De Lubac took the edge off his criticism of Origen, however, by explaining that many commentators, including Origen himself, had fluctuated in the relative placement of tropology and allegory.[85] Origen had often presupposed prior knowledge of the Christian mysteries when he had set about his moral instructions.[86] An orientation to morality implied faithfulness to the mind of St Paul and to the realities of the Christian life:[87] Origen had 'conceived the

---

[79] Id., 104.
[80] Cf. id., 'Hellenistic Allegory and Christian Allegory', in *Theological Fragments*, 165–73.
[81] Id., *History and Spirit*, 183–5.
[82] Ibid. 186.
[83] De Lubac insisted that the fourfold understanding 'expresses authentic doctrine in both its fullness and its purity. It alone gives an adequate rendition of the Christian mystery' (*Medieval Exegesis*, i. 115). At the same time, he clarified that it would be erroneous sharply to distinguish the threefold and fourfold methods; they had never constituted two clearly distinct traditions (ibid. 82–115).
[84] Id., 'On an Old Distich', 112.
[85] Id., *History and Spirit*, 161–4. According to de Lubac, Origen had more often placed tropology after allegory than before (ibid. 169).
[86] Ibid. 206–7.   [87] Ibid. 208–14, 245–7.

Christian life above all as a combat initiated at baptism, and it is to this combat that he did not cease to exhort his listeners'.[88] And Philo had only known of *two* levels of meaning, corresponding to body and soul, while the Christian exegesis of Origen had introduced *three* levels of meaning, with the allegorical or mystical sense allowing him to move beyond Philo's lack of Christology:[89] 'Origen's third sense serves not merely to "modify" Philo's exegesis, or, to put it more broadly, Jewish exegesis in general. Jewish exegesis is really and truly surpassed, since what is at stake now is a new principle which owes nothing to it.'[90] This mitigated, for de Lubac, Philo's influence on Origen. De Lubac captured his position by commenting: 'Between Philo and Origen there is the whole Christian mystery.'[91] Origen's hermeneutic was stamped by the mystery of the Incarnation and, as a result, had been radically different from that of Philo.

De Lubac was nonplussed by examples of allegorical exegesis that to many others, including Jean Daniélou, appeared arbitrary in character. To be sure, de Lubac did recognize that excesses and arbitrary allegorizing had, on occasion, crept into pre-modern exegesis. He acknowledged 'arbitrary' exegesis,[92] 'abuse',[93] 'artificiality',[94] 'intemperate' use,[95] and 'debatable' spiritual meanings.[96] The 'transitory' and 'obsolescent' character of certain aspects of allegorical interpretation was due to the fact that it contained 'a lot of junk'.[97] De Lubac admitted that Origen's anti-Jewish apologetic and his desire to harmonize textual difficulties had tempted him to use the mystical sense as an 'expedient' to overcome such problems:[98] 'Processes, of course, that are very artificial, at the service of an exegesis that is often no less so. Dubious expedients. Annoying subtleties. Audacity that is at times worrisome.'[99] And de Lubac was particularly concerned with the excesses in allegory that he believed tied in with other negative developments starting in the High Middle Ages.[100] So, particular allegorical interpretations might well have to be rejected. But de Lubac regarded all this as simply a matter of disagreement about the *application* of the allegorical method, which itself was in no way affected by such disagreements.

De Lubac countered accusations of Origen's alleged arbitrariness by referring to the importance that the Alexandrian theologian had attached to the historical sense. The persistence of accusations of arbitrary exegesis was a matter of grave

---

[88] De Lubac, *History and Spirit*, 212.

[89] Ibid. 186. Origen's three levels of interpretation (historical, moral, and mystical) had corresponded to his tripartite anthropology (body–soul–spirit) (ibid. 172–90), though de Lubac remained unconvinced that the former had derived from the latter (ibid. 181).

[90] Id., *Medieval Exegesis*, i. 150.

[91] Id., *History and Spirit*, 187.

[92] Ibid. 330, 359.

[93] Id., *Medieval Exegesis*, ii. 6.

[94] Ibid. 32.   [95] Ibid. 56; id., *History and Spirit*, 349.

[96] Id., *History and Spirit*, 351.   [97] Id., *Medieval Exegesis*, ii. 211.

[98] Id., *History and Spirit*, 231.   [99] Ibid. 234.   [100] Id., *Medieval Exegesis*, ii. 56.

historical injustice. De Lubac was annoyed by the unfair treatment, often politically motivated, that Origen had undergone, first from the hand of Eustathius of Antioch (d. *c.*336), and then, through the Antiochian tradition, from many later theologians.[101] Usually, these criticisms had incorrectly assumed that Origen had in an unqualified fashion pitched the spirit against the letter. According to de Lubac, the examples of 'arbitrary' exegesis did not yield evidence of the mephitic influence of Philo; rather, they showed the sacramental cast of Christian allegorizing.

At the end of the day, de Lubac believed the 'analogy of faith'—the principle that Scripture required interpretation in light of the overall deposit of faith— warranted many of the allegorical interpretations that seemed out of place to the modern eye. The pre-modern tradition had boasted a keen sense of the unity of Scripture. This certainly had been the case with Origen:

> Placed finally by his faith before Scripture, not as before a book or a series of books, but before *the Book*, the exegete should first of all be aware of its unity. He should 'approach it as a single body, not tear or break apart the very continuous links of its structure, which make of it one harmonious whole'; that would be 'to tear apart the unity of the spirit that is spread everywhere'.[102]

This unity of Scripture justified interpreting the Old Testament in the light of the New, and it also allowed the reader to compare passages from different human authors within the Old Testament.[103] Such *congregatio in unum* (gathering into one) necessitated careful lexical analysis. Origen 'thus sheds light on some passages by means of others where it is a question, for example, of fate, trumpets, rocks, camels, "wine", shadow, clouds, the earth ... He observes a consistency in the symbolic use of the word "leaven". Mentions of glory, prudence, self-knowledge, salvation, and so on, are also noted.'[104] To be sure, de Lubac remained critical of Origen's textual comparisons, which did 'not take into account either the human contexts or lines of development'.[105] Still, the most important question was whether the spiritual meaning was based on the overall teaching of the Scriptures and so 'fruitful' for the believer.[106] As long as this was

---

[101] Id., *History and Spirit*, 225; id., 'Typology and Allegorization', *Theological Fragments*, 144–50.

[102] Id., *History and Spirit*, 353. De Lubac's quotations are from Origen, *Der Johanneskommentar*, ed. Erwin Preuschen (Leipzig: Hinrichs, 1903), 10, 13 (p. 189).

[103] De Lubac realized, of course, that this approach to the spiritual unity of the Scriptures implied a doctrine of inspiration that closely tied inspiration both to the divine contents and to the efficacious character of the Scriptures (*History and Spirit*, 340–4; cf. id., *Medieval Exegesis*, i. 81–2).

[104] Id., *History and Spirit*, 356. John J. O'Keefe and R. R. Reno also argue that this use of verbal association is central to understanding patristic exegesis (*Sanctified Vision: An Introduction to Early Christian Interpretation of the Bible* (Baltimore, Md.: Johns Hopkins University Press, 2005)).

[105] De Lubac, *History and Spirit*, 358. [106] Ibid. 360.

the case, the Church Fathers had felt they could freely use their imagination.[107] Thus, de Lubac asked:

Fundamentally, is what Origen recommends and practices anything other than recourse to the principle called, again according to an expression of Saint Paul, 'the analogy of faith'? Now, when we are truly governed by the analogy of faith, or again, when we submit our interpretation to 'the rule of piety', we never make the biblical text say what we wish: the meaning we discover in it is always in some way a biblical meaning. We still intend to 'sing the music written in the silent pages of the Holy Books'.[108]

The congruity between the piety of the believer and the harmony or unity of the biblical text provided sufficient reason, de Lubac was convinced, to maintain that Origen's interpretation had retained at least 'some objectivity'.[109] This objectivity did not, however, refer to an allegedly neutral, literal reading of the text. True objectivity, for de Lubac, resulted from the dialogical harmony between the Scriptures and the ecclesially shaped imagination of the believer.

JEAN DANIÉLOU'S RECOVERY OF TYPOLOGICAL INTERPRETATION

Daniélou as Student of de Lubac

The Lubacian dual interest in patristics and hermeneutics stamped the career of his student, Jean Daniélou, and the most foundational commonality between the two was undoubtedly their shared sacramental hermeneutic. Daniélou always remained indebted to de Lubac's patristic scholarship. He adopted his teacher's concern for the interpretation of the Scriptures, and agreed with de Lubac that patristic exegesis should continue to function as a model for contemporary interpretation.[110] Daniélou insisted that de Lubac's *Exégèse médiévale* was a

---

[107] Cf. De Lubac, *History and Spirit*, 374–5: 'If in fact the detail of their explanations, in so many instances, seems so fanciful, it is because that was not for them the essential thing. They spread out comfortably "in the vast field of divine Scriptures". They had no scruples about exercising their fertile imaginations there by freely using the "analogy of faith". Their sense of tradition did not command them to gather only exegeses already received and catalogued in the Church, but rather it commanded them to enrich and renew this collection with the same fidelity to the view of faith that had constituted it. This is because, they thought, "where the Spirit of the Lord is, there is the freedom to understand".'

[108] Ibid. 360. De Lubac's last quotation comes from Louis Massignon, 'L'Expérience mystique et les modes de stylisation littéraire', *Le Roseau d'or*, 20 (1927), 141–76.

[109] De Lubac, *History and Spirit*, 360. Cf. id., 'On an Old Distich', 122.

[110] Daniélou demurred that he did not mean 'to use the ancient texts as instruments to prove modern theses; I get quite annoyed by people who do this. When I devote myself to my historical studies, I try to understand, to see clearly, without preoccupying myself with contemporary implications' (*Et qui est mon prochain? Mémoires* (Paris: Stock, 1974), 122). As we will see, however, Daniélou rather strongly objected to some elements of patristic exegesis, while wholeheartedly embracing others. As in the case of de Lubac, so with Daniélou, his indebtedness to patristic interpretation was more evident than the manner in which he believed it to be superseded.

'great work' that remained 'foundational'.[111] To be sure, the Parisian student showed that he had an independent mind, and we will see that Daniélou was by no means a carbon copy of his erstwhile teacher. Their disagreement on the understanding of patristic exegesis and the validity of allegorical interpretation spilled over into public debate.[112] When compared to developments in modern biblical hermeneutics, however, these disagreements were relatively marginal. I will argue that although de Lubac was better able to do justice to the sacramental character of interpretation than his student, the two Jesuit scholars were none the less quite similar in their approach.

From beginning to end, Daniélou's reading of Scripture was based on the typological exegesis that he found in the Church Fathers.[113] Before looking at the sacramental structure of his approach, it may be good to highlight the centrality of typology throughout Daniélou's work. This began in 1942, with his introduction to Gregory of Nyssa's *The Life of Moses*, in which he traced Gregory's exegetical dependence on Philo, insisting that both Origen and Gregory had simply used the general framework of Philo's approach, while substituting a 'radically new reality', borrowed from the New Testament.[114] Gregory's 'typological' approach had regarded the events and institutions of the Exodus 'not first of all as figures of spiritual realties, but of another reality, historical and spiritual at the same time, which is Christ and the new order instituted by him'.[115] In his first book, *Le Signe du temple* (1942), Daniélou built on his patristic studies to trace the presence of God in the successive temples mentioned in Scripture.[116] Thus, the seven chapters of this booklet traced the cosmic temple, the temple of Moses, the temple of Christ, the temple of the Church, the temple of the prophets, the mystical temple, and the heavenly temple. Each of these was a

[111] Ibid. 92.
[112] Setting off the public discussion between de Lubac and Daniélou was the latter's essay, 'Traversée de la Mer Rouge et baptême aux premiers siècles', *RSR* 33 (1946), 402–30. De Lubac reacted in ' "Typologie" et "allégorisme" ', *RSR* 34 (1947), 180–226; English trans.: 'Typology and Allegorization', 129–64. Without mentioning de Lubac by name, Daniélou responded the next year with 'Les Divers Sens de l'Écriture dans la tradition chrétienne primitive', *ETL* 24 (1948), 119–26. Other theologians, such as Jean Leclercq, Louis Bouyer, A. M. Dubarle, Ceslas Spicq, Jacques Guillet, Robert Devreese, and Jean Gibromont also entered the discussion on spiritual interpretation in the late 1940s. For helpful accounts, see Walter J. Burghardt, 'On Early Christian Exegesis', *TS* 11 (1950), 78–116; Marie Anne Mayeski, 'Quaestio disputata: Catholic Theology and the History of Exegesis', *TS* 62 (2001), 140–53. Cf. also Daniélou, 'Autour de l'exégèse spirituelle', *DViv* 8 (1952), 123–6; Paul Lebeau, *Jean Daniélou* (Paris: Fleurus, 1967), 104–5.
[113] Cf. James M. Connolly, *The Voices of France: A Survey of Contemporary Theology in France* (New York: Macmillan, 1961), 142–6.
[114] Daniélou, Introduction to Gregory of Nyssa, *La Vie de Moïse ou Traité de la perfection en matière de vertu* (3rd edn, 1968; repr. Paris: Cerf, 2000), 22.
[115] Ibid.
[116] Id., *Le Signe du temple, ou de la présence de Dieu* (Paris: Gallimard, 1942); English trans.: *The Presence of God*, trans. Walter Roberts (Baltimore, Md.: Helicon, 1959). Daniélou later commented on his first book: 'I have the impression that in these sixty pages I said pretty much everything I have had to say and that, in my subsequent books, I have done nothing but give commentary or annotation on this booklet' (*Et qui est mon prochain?* 109).

typological foreshadowing of the next. As Daniélou put it, 'It is the property of these successive economies that each at the same time passes and preserves its predecessor'.[117] Daniélou based his own typological tracing of the temple theme in Scripture on the examples that he had encountered in his study of the Church Fathers.

His biblical and patristic reflections resulted in the latter half of the 1940s in a number of essays on the way in which the Fathers had developed certain biblical themes typologically. In 1945, he published an essay on the symbolism of baptismal rites, in which he looked at the way in which several Church Fathers, and especially Cyril of Jerusalem (*c.*315–86), had interpreted the various elements of the baptismal rite with the help of Old Testament themes.[118] This was followed the next year by two studies on Baptism, one connecting it to the patristic use of the Red Sea crossing, the other studying the relationship to the Flood narrative.[119] Then, focusing on the birth, sacrifice, and marriage of the Old Testament figure of Isaac, Daniélou discussed the interpretation of the patriarch in Palestinian Judaism, the New Testament, the later patristic catechetical tradition, Philo, the Alexandrian Fathers, and St Ambrose (*c.*340–97).[120] Around the same time, Daniélou also delved into the patristic understanding of history and the connection between typology and millenarianism in patristic thought, particularly in the second-century Church Father, St Irenaeus (d. *c.*202).[121] Finally, this was followed by two ecclesially oriented studies, one on the typology of Rahab as a figure of the Church and another on the typology of meals as foreshadowing the Eucharist.[122]

These biblical and patristic studies came to a climax with three major publications: *Origène* (1948), *Sacramentum futuri* (1950), and *Bible et liturgie* (1951).[123] The first was a general but carefully written introduction to Origen, which included a major section on the Alexandrian's interpretation of Scripture,

---

[117] Daniélou, *Presence of God*, 19.

[118] Id., 'Le Symbolisme des rites baptismaux', *DViv* 1 (1945), 15–43.

[119] Id., 'Traversée de la Mer Rouge'; id., 'Déluge, baptême, jugement', *DViv* 8 (1947), 97–112.

[120] Id., 'La Typologie d'Isaac dans le Christianisme primitif', *Bib* 28 (1947), 363–93.

[121] Id., 'Saint Irénée et les origines de la théologie de l'histoire', *RSR* 34 (1947), 227–31; id., 'La Typologie millénariste de la semaine dans le christianisme primitif', *VC* 2 (1948), 1–16. Unfortunately unaware of Daniélou's work on Irenaeus at the time, I explored the significance of Irenaeus's theology of recapitulation for spiritual interpretation in Boersma, 'Spiritual Imagination: Recapitulation as an Interpretive Principle', in Boersma (ed.), *Imagination and Interpretation: Christian Perspectives* (Vancouver: Regent College Publishing, 2005), 13–33.

[122] Daniélou, 'Rahab, figure de l'Eglise', *Irén* 22 (1949), 26–45; id., 'Les Repas de la Bible et leur signification', *LMD* 18 (1949), 7–33.

[123] Id., *Origène* (Paris: Table ronde, 1948); English trans.: *Origen*, trans. Walter Mitchell (New York: Sheed & Ward, 1955). For a discussion of this book, see Burghardt, 'On Early Christian Exegesis', 92–8; Daniélou, *Sacramentum futuri: Études sur les origines de la typologie biblique* (Paris: Beauchesne, 1950); English trans.: *From Shadows to Reality: Studies in the Biblical Typology of the Fathers*, trans. Wulstan Hibberd (London: Burns & Oates, 1960); id., *Bible et liturgie: La Théologie biblique des sacrements et des fêtes d'après les Pères de l'Église* (Paris: Cerf, 1951); English trans.: *The Bible and the Liturgy* (Notre Dame, Ind.: University of Notre Dame Press, 1956).

locating in Origen 'two streams of interpretation': on the one hand, the genuinely typological tradition as he had inherited it from Paul, Justin Martyr (*c*.100– *c*.165), and St Irenaeus, and, on the other hand, the allegorical method as influenced by Philo and Gnosticism.[124] The second book, *Sacramentum futuri*, studied typology in Scripture, Palestinian and Alexandrian Judaism, and the Church Fathers from the second to the fourth centuries. It did so in five parts, dealing with Adam and paradise, Noah and the Flood, the sacrifice of Isaac, Moses and the Exodus, and the Joshua cycle. One of Daniélou's stated purposes was to distinguish 'what in the Fathers belongs to ecclesiastical tradition and is strictly speaking typology, and what has its origin in extraneous sources, especially in the allegory of Philo'.[125] The third book, *Bible et liturgie*, while similar in approach, took its starting-point in the liturgy and the Church's sacraments, thus offering 'an interpretation of the symbolism of Christian worship according to the Fathers of the Church'.[126] Again discussing both biblical and patristic sources, Daniélou traced the typological antecedents of the sacraments of Baptism, Confirmation, and Eucharist, while also making a detailed study of the typology behind the celebration of the Sunday, Easter, Ascension, Pentecost, and the Feast of Tabernacles. This comprehensive volume showed again the continuity between biblical and patristic typology. Daniélou explained all this work as an attempt at *ressourcement*: the Fathers' 'sacramental theology is a biblical theology, and it is this biblical theology which we are to try to recover. We are to look for it in the Fathers of the Church inasmuch as they are the witnesses of the faith of primitive Christianity'.[127]

Typology and Christian Symbolism

Perhaps the best way to access Daniélou's guiding principles is to analyse briefly a chapter of his 1953 *Essai sur le mystère de l'histoire*,[128] a book that he later described as 'foundational for me'.[129] In the chapter entitled 'Symbolisme et histoire', Daniélou focused on 'symbolic theology', which, he insisted, was 'not to be regarded as a survival from a supposed "pre-logical" phase of mental development, and thus as something of purely archaeological interest, but on the contrary as a permanently valid category of religious thought'.[130] Drawing especially on Mircea Eliade's *Traité d'histoire des religions* (1949), Daniélou

---

[124] Daniélou, *Origen*, 132.   [125] Id., *From Shadows to Reality*, p. viii.
[126] Id., *Bible and the Liturgy*, 4. Geoffrey Wainwright discusses the liturgical lessons to be learned from Daniélou in ' "Bible et Liturgie": Daniélou's Work Revisited', *SL* 22 (1992), 154–62.
[127] Daniélou, *Bible and the Liturgy*, 8.
[128] Id., *Essai sur le mystère de l'histoire* (Paris: Seuil, 1953); English trans.: *The Lord of History: Reflections on the Inner Meaning of History*, trans. Nigel Abercrombie (1958; repr. Cleveland, Ohio: Meridian, 1968).
[129] Id., *Et qui est mon prochain?* 141.   [130] Id., *Lord of History*, 130–1.

argued that the 'nature-symbolism' found in paganism and in ancient religions had an objective basis:

Symbolism proves to be a definite, characteristic psychological attitude: it is substantially the effort of mind to extract the intelligible meaning contained within physical reality. This is not something purely subjective; the mind does not merely project its own pattern upon the world of things, but discovers a real content through the symbolic appearance: that which is revealed is from without.[131]

Eliade had referred to these 'symbolic appearances' as 'hierophanies', a term Daniélou adopted, as it indicated that even nature-symbolism was the result of objective revelation.[132] Symbolism was thus 'directed towards the discovery of analogies between the visible and invisible worlds' and 'a genuine mode of apprehension of the things of God'.[133] While aware that the 'debasement of hierophanies into idolatry' stunted the 'analogical apprehension of the transcendent Godhead',[134] Daniélou none the less maintained that in itself natural revelation was symbolic or analogical in character.

Christianity, however, was unlike nature-symbolism in regarding God as revealed not just in the rhythms of cosmic cycles, but also in the 'contingent singularity of historical events'.[135] Daniélou insisted on the significance and particularity of history. Whereas nature-symbolism tended to eliminate this particularity in favour of the changeless character of eternity, Christian symbolism did not 'ignore or mask' the 'individual existence and value' of historical events.[136] Daniélou captured his understanding of the analogical character of Christian symbolism as follows:

In the gradual unfolding of God's design, there appears a system of analogies between his successive works, for all their distinct self-sufficiency as separate creative acts. The Flood, the Passion, Baptism and the last Judgement, are closely linked together in one pattern. In each instance, though at different levels, there is a divine judgement on the sinful world, and a divine clemency whereby a man is spared to be the beginning of a new creation.

Hence arises a new kind of symbolism, which is characteristic of the Bible. Its specific difference is historicity, for it denotes a relationship between various events belonging to sacred history. It is called *typology*, from the wording of two passages in the New Testament: one where it is said of Adam that 'he was the type (τύπος) of him who was to come' [Rom. 5: 14]; and another where baptism is called the 'type (ἀντίτυπος)' of the Flood [1 Pet. 3: 21].[137]

---

[131] Daniélou, *Lord of History*, 133. See also id., *God and the Ways of Knowing*, trans. Walter Roberts (1956; repr. San Francisco, Calif.: Ignatius, 2003), 18–21.

[132] Id., *Lord of History*, 136. Cf. id., *Bible and the Liturgy*, 302. Daniélou was personally acquainted with Eliade, who invited him to conferences in Chicago (id., *Et qui est mon prochain?* 177).

[133] Id., *Lord of History*, 136.   [134] Ibid. 138.

[135] Ibid. 139.   [136] Ibid. 140.   [137] Ibid.

Daniélou argued that typology was a method of Christian interpretation capable of discovering analogical or symbolic relationships within history. In God's continuing involvement in historical developments, one could discern the symbolic or sacramental character of events, persons, and institutions. The transition from nature-symbolism to Christian symbolism, as well as from Old Testament types to New Testament antitypes, served as the key to the relationship between nature and the supernatural. Daniélou maintained that it was 'at the level of Christian symbolism that the interaction can be most clearly discerned between the natural and the supernatural apprehension of God'.[138]

The title of his *Sacramentum futuri* (1950)—*Sacrament of the Future*—captures well what Daniélou believed lay at the heart of both biblical and patristic typology: historical events, persons, and institutions functioned by way of sacramental signification. Daniélou explained that the *Contra Faustum* of St Augustine (354–430) had dealt with 'the story of creation, the sacrifice of Cain and Abel, the building of the Ark, Jacob's wrestling with the angel, and all the great *"sacramenta"* of the Old Testament'.[139] At the outset of his study on the typology of Adam, Daniélou made the programmatic comment: 'In the liturgical and catechetical tradition of the early Church the Law is a text charged with mysteries, *sacramenta*, which figuratively reveal to us the whole plan of the Gospel and the future Kingdom.'[140] Understandably, then, St Hilary of Poitiers (*c*.315–*c*.367) had regarded the sleep of Adam as the first of these Old Testament sacraments.[141] For Daniélou, Sunday, being the day after the Sabbath, was 'the perpetual sacrament of this eighth day'.[142] Daniélou also insisted that the analogical resemblances between the Flood, the descent into Hell, and Baptism were sacramental in character: 'Baptism is, then, a sacramental likeness to the descent into Hell, and both are prefigured by the Flood.'[143] And with regard to St Ambrose's discussion of the 'real analogies' between manna and Eucharist, Daniélou made clear that the Bishop's emphasis on the superiority of the latter 'should not cause us to misunderstand the fact that the manna of the Old Testament was already something other than an ordinary profane food, and constituted a true sacrament'.[144] Daniélou believed that Alexandrian allegorizing of the Old Testament did not do justice to the significance of history, and instead he argued in favour of typological exegesis: 'Traditional typology knows as privileged instances those that are the *sacramenta* of Scripture and that have been charged with a theological signification that helps us to understand the meaning of

---

[138] Ibid. 146. [139] Id., *From Shadows to Reality*, 200.
[140] Ibid. 11. [141] Ibid.
[142] Id., *Bible and the Liturgy*, 80. Cf. ibid. 293: Sunday 'is the commemoration of the Resurrection of Christ, the sacrament of His presence'.
[143] Id., *From Shadows to Reality*, 93. [144] Id., *Bible and the Liturgy*, 149.

certain mysteries of Christ, while at the same time the mysteries of Christ illuminate them retroactively.'[145] Daniélou regarded typological interpretation as constituting a sacramental hermeneutic, in that Old Testament events sacramentally prefigured their New Testament fulfilment.

Magnalia dei in History

Daniélou was interested not only in the historical character of the Christian faith or in a sacramental hermeneutic, but he was also motivated by a desire to bring these two aspects together. He was convinced that the link between sacrament, analogy, and typology had permitted the Church Fathers to combine history and sacramental interpretation, and that this model would serve in a contemporary context, as well. A closer look at Daniélou's understanding of the nature of typology will shed light on what exactly he was attempting to do. He defined typology as the 'mutual relationship' 'between past works and future works of God'.[146] A 'type' was an 'event which offers likeness to something in the future, but yet does not really fulfil this something'.[147] Daniélou could, therefore, also define typology as the 'science of similitudes between the two Testaments'.[148] He explained that the 'essence' of typology was 'to show how past events are a figure of events to come'.[149] The 'basic principle' of typology was the idea of 'an imperfect order which prepares for and prefigures an order of perfection'.[150] Daniélou argued that the historical basis of typology lay 'in showing that it is history itself which is figurative rather than in replacing history by allegory'.[151]

The key elements of typology for Daniélou, it appears, were (1) the reality of God's activity in the world; (2) the historical or event character of the figure as well as of the foreshadowed reality; (3) the similarity between the type and its fulfilment; and (4) the greater perfection of the New Testament reality over and above the Old Testament type. Daniélou often dealt with the first two elements in tandem, and so I will explore them together in this section (leaving the third and fourth elements to the next). Throughout his writings, he distinguished between various historical stages in typology. Old Testament prophecy was a form of 'eschatological typology', as it prophesied, by means of various types, the coming

---

[145] Daniélou, 'La Typologie d'Isaac', 369. See also Daniélou's discussion of the sacramental character of the story of Abraham in *The Advent of Salvation: A Comparative Study of Non-Christian Religions and Christianity*, trans. Rosemary Sheed (New York: Paulist, 1962), 36–50. Cf. Jemima Rosario Sullivan, 'The Contribution of Jean Daniélou to an Understanding of Biblical and Liturgical Typology in Liturgical Catechesis' (PhD diss., Catholic University of America, Washington, DC, 1999), 145.

[146] Daniélou, *Christ and Us*, trans. Walter Roberts (New York: Sheed & Ward, 1961), 72. English trans. of *Approches du Christ* (Paris: Grasset, 1960).

[147] Id., *From Shadows to Reality*, 125.

[148] Id., *Bible and the Liturgy*, 4. Cf. id., *Lord of History*, 214: 'Typology is the study of correspondences between the Old and the New Testaments.'

[149] Id., *From Shadows to Reality*, 12.

[150] Ibid. 31. Cf. id., *Christ and Us*, 72.

[151] Id., *From Shadows to Reality*, 52.

of the eschaton. This prophetic or eschatological typology found its fulfilment in Christ and in the Church. Christological fulfilment allowed one to speak of Old Testament figures as 'Christological typology', while 'sacramental typology', was a further fulfilment of prophetic typology in the Church's sacraments, notably Baptism and the Eucharist.[152] On at least one occasion, Daniélou spoke of a 'mystical typology', which applied the Old Testament types 'to the life of each individual soul, as *alter Christus*'.[153] Although he often listed prophetic or eschatological analogy first, Daniélou was convinced that the Incarnation was the central historical event, and that it was the historical fulfilment in Christ that allowed one to discern the eschatological analogy in the first place. 'We might say', commented Daniélou, 'that it was in the categories of the Old Testament that the First Fathers thought about the Fact of Christ'.[154] Therefore, when Daniélou spoke of typology's historical character, this included for him the historical fulfilment of all typology in the reality of Christ.

Typological interpretation was, for Daniélou, necessarily Christological in character. Thus, he began an essay in the first issue of the new journal *Dieu vivant* in 1945, with the comment:

The Christian faith has only one object, which is the mystery of Christ dead and crucified. But that unique mystery subsists in different modes: it was prefigured in the Old Testament; it has been accomplished historically in the earthly life of Christ; it is contained in mystery in the sacraments; it is experienced mystically in souls; it is accomplished socially in the church; it is achieved eschatologically in the heavenly kingdom.[155]

For Daniélou, Christ was the one and only historical mystery with which biblical interpretation concerned itself. Elsewhere, he called the Christological element the 'very hallmark of Christian typology, its basic and unique character'.[156] Clearly, the Christological element was central to Daniélou's understanding of typology.

If typology was Christological in character, it was also theocentric. Daniélou argued that the Old Testament described, on the one hand, the miraculous acts (*mirabilia*) or great acts (*magnalia*) of God, beginning with the creation of the world, moving on to his covenant with Moses and Israel's deliverance from Egypt, to the presence of God in the temple at Jerusalem and his kingship over

---

[152] For a discussion of the various levels of typology, see Rosario Sullivan, 'Contribution of Jean Daniélou', 108–19.

[153] Daniélou, *Lord of History*, 215.

[154] Id., *Bible and the Liturgy*, 307.

[155] Id., 'Le Symbolisme des rites baptismaux', 17. Cf. 'Les Divers Sens', 120: 'Thus, the typological sense only has Christ for its object. But it has for its object the whole Christ.' *Dieu vivant* was a lay journal that promoted religious dialogue. Although, as a priest, Daniélou was not in the journal's editorial committee, he was involved with it from the outset until its demise in 1955. See id., *Et qui est mon prochain?* 150–6; Lebeau, *Jean Daniélou*, 50–4.

[156] Daniélou, *From Shadows to Reality*, 24.

Israel. The Old Testament also showed, on the other hand, the key role played by human beings, such as Abraham, Moses, David, Elijah, and Isaiah, so that the eschatological fulfilment would involve a new Moses, a new David, a new Adam, and a new Jonah.[157] In the typological fulfilment in Christ, Daniélou maintained, these divine and human lines joined historically:

> He is the action of God coming towards man to save him and lead him to the Father. In Him, therefore, is revealed the fullness of the mystery of God's love. But He is also the Man who, raised up by God, mounts towards the Father and thus fulfils the vocation of man. He is at once—let us repeat—the movement of God towards man and the movement of man towards God.[158]

The historical character of typological interpretation justified for Daniélou the substantialist categories of Chalcedonian Christology. History showed that Christ was both divine and human. Chalcedon had done justice, Daniélou insisted, both to the divine and to the human element of prophetic typology.[159]

Jemima Rosario Sullivan rightly emphasizes the key role that salvation history played in the Jesuit's understanding of the Church Fathers, an emphasis that came to the fore particularly clearly in his 1953 *Essai sur le mystère de l'histoire*.[160] She explains that for Daniélou the Incarnation 'represents God's presence and actions in the historical process that effect a radical change in history. The substance of the Christian religion is the perception of God's activity on the scene of time and the effective interventions of divine activity in the world of human history.'[161] This historical character of the Christian faith countered the Platonic disregard for history and set Christianity apart from other religions.[162] In his *Essai sur le mystère de l'histoire*, Daniélou appealed to the Lutheran theologian Oscar Cullmann. In this book and elsewhere he probably quoted Cullmann more than any other contemporary author. Cullmann's book *Christus und die Zeit* (1946) brought home to Daniélou both the centrality of salvation history and the decisive nature of the historical event of the Resurrection of Christ, the one event in history that in its very nature was unsurpassable.[163] Alongside Cullmann, Daniélou took position against Albert Schweitzer's 'consequent eschatology', C. H. Dodd's 'realized eschatology', and Rudolf Bultmann's 'existential eschatology' in favour of an 'anticipated eschatology'. Cullmann's 'anticipated eschatology' regarded the resurrection of Christ as being of decisive importance while at the same time maintaining that many of its eschatological

[157] Daniélou, *Christ and Us*, 80.   [158] Ibid. 81.   [159] Id., *Lord of History*, 183–5.
[160] See Rosario Sullivan, 'The Contribution of Jean Daniélou', 139–51.
[161] Ibid. 142.
[162] Daniélou, *Lord of History*, 109–11.
[163] Ibid. 7. Cf. id., *From Shadows to Reality*, 92; id., *Christ and Us*, 71, 128. For Daniélou's dependence on Cullmann, see Mary C. Boys, *Biblical Interpretation in Religious Education: A Study of the Kerygmatic Era* (Birmingham, Ala.: Religious Education, 1980), 103–7.

effects were as yet unfulfilled.[164] God's intervention in and through Christ was the climax and the key to history. This explained typology's inherently Christological character: God's activities in the Old Testament came to typological fulfilment in what he had accomplished in Christ.

In addition to Christological typology, Daniélou spoke also of sacramental typology. The *mirabilia dei* continued in the Church's sacraments, particularly Baptism and the Eucharist. Again, Daniélou relied a great deal on Cullmann, notably his *Urchristentum und Gottesdienst* (1944), which had argued for an ecclesial setting for the Gospel of John and had elucidated its numerous sacramental allusions.[165] Thus, Daniélou could assert, in line with this Cullmannian understanding both of salvation history in general and of the sacraments in particular:

These eschatological times are not only those of the life of Jesus, but of the Church as well. Consequently, the eschatological typology of the Old Testament is accomplished not only in the person of Christ, but also in the Church. Besides Christological typology, therefore, there exists a sacramental typology, and we find it in the New Testament. The Gospel of St John shows us that the manna was a figure of the Eucharist; the first Epistle of St Paul to the Corinthians that the crossing of the Red Sea was a figure of Baptism. This means, furthermore, that the sacraments carry on in our midst the *mirabilia*, the great works of God in the Old Testament and the New: for example, the Flood, the Passion and Baptism show us the same divine activity as carried out in three different eras of sacred history, and these three phases of God's action are all ordered to the judgment at the end of time.[166]

Daniélou thus classified the sacraments among the *mirabilia dei* and, in doing so, believed himself to be in line with the great Tradition, including the writings of St Ambrose.[167]

This view of the sacraments implied that the life of the Church was also taken up into salvation history. The sacraments, Daniélou asserted, 'are pre-eminently the events which continue in the time of the Church, the great works of God in the Old and New Testaments. They have the same character'.[168] 'This time is that in which the great works of God are accomplished through those humble signs that are water, oil, and bread.'[169] Daniélou based the notion of the sacraments as the continuation of God's *mirabilia* on the unity between Christ and the Church. Although nothing essentially new happened in salvation history

---

[164] Daniélou, *Lord of History*, 270–2. Daniélou mildly criticized Cullmann as 'perhaps too exclusively concerned with the beginning and the end of the "last days", to the neglect of the interim in which our lives are spent', and he believed that Donatien Mollat's 'initiated eschatology' did better justice to the continual judgement in the interim period between Christ's resurrection and the final judgement (ibid. 272; cf. Connolly, *Voices of France*, 144–5).

[165] See Daniélou, *Lord of History*, 12, 225, 227; id., *From Shadows to Reality*, 153, 161, 185; id., *Christ and Us*, 137, 196.

[166] Id., *Bible and the Liturgy*, 5.   [167] Ibid. 199.

[168] Id., *Christ and Us*, 189.   [169] Ibid. 190.

after the eschaton-inaugurating moment of Christ's Resurrection, because the Church as *totus Christus* (the whole Christ) continued his life here on earth, the sacraments were rightly included among the *magnalia dei*.[170]

Typology as Doctrine of Analogy

Daniélou believed he had found the key to the Church Fathers' exegesis in the historical realities of the *magnalia dei* as well as in the event character of their Christological typology. As mentioned, in addition to these two key character-istics of typology, Daniélou pointed to two others: the similarity between type and fulfilment, and the greater perfection or dissimilarity of New Testament reality in relation to the Old. The element of similarity served to safeguard against the danger of arbitrary exegesis, while the element of dissimilarity high-lighted the newness and greater reality of the Christ event.

Daniélou consistently used the notion of 'analogy' to refer to this similarity and dissimilarity between type and antitype. This use of 'analogy' language is highly significant, as it points to the sacramental character of his hermeneutic. Daniélou observed that St Irenaeus's use of Adamic typology offered 'at one and the same time difference and similarity'.[171] Similarly, for Cyril of Jerusalem, Baptism, as an 'antitype' of Christ's passion and resurrection, was both 'like and unlike' its original.

And the text explains in what the likeness consists and in what the unlikeness. In the death and Passion of Christ, there are two aspects which must be distinguished: the historical fact, and the content of saving grace. The historical fact is only imitated: the sacramental rite symbolizes it, represents it. But the content of saving grace allows a true participation (*koinonia*).[172]

Daniélou explained the aspects of similarity and dissimilarity by making a distinction between 'illustrative' and 'theological' typology. He was keen to point out that the Church Fathers were generally not satisfied by observing a coincidence in terminology between typology and its historical fulfilment in Christ. So, one could not find allusions to Baptism in the Old Testament simply by looking there for references to water. The similarity in the mentioning of water was merely what Daniélou called an 'illustrative typology'. True typology went beyond such illustrative similarities. It contained also a 'theological analogy':

---

[170] Daniélou, *Christ and Us*, 157: 'Thus the era of the Church is simply the present form of the mighty works of the Trinity and the continuation of the mystery of the Incarnate word.' Cf. ibid. 182; id., 'Les Divers Sens', 120. Incidentally, since for Daniélou, God's power was at work primarily through the sacraments, he was always sceptical of political (especially Marxist) ideologies taking centre stage and of the Church being aligned with particular political, social, or economic causes. See e.g. id., *Lord of History*, 78, 83–4, 95.

[171] Id., *From Shadows to Reality*, 30.

[172] Id., *Bible and the Liturgy*, 45.

The first type of Baptism to be found in the most ancient catecheses is that of the primitive waters of Genesis. At first glance, this comparison may seem startling and artificial, but we must always be careful to look behind the 'illustrative' resemblances which are concerned with images for the theological analogies which constitute typology, properly speaking. Here the theological analogy is clear: the Prophets announced that God, at the end of time, would undertake a new creation.[173]

Daniélou insisted that where one saw illustrative and theological typology combined, a strong case for Christological typology could be made. Nowhere was God's activity in history more magnificent than in his action in Christ. Thus, the dissimilarity in the theological analogy highlighted typology's fourth ingredient: the greater perfection of the New Testament reality over and above its Old Testament type. At the end of time, God's acts were 'similar to these, but far surpassing them in splendour'.[174]

By using the discourse of 'analogy' and by explaining this in terms of similarity and dissimilarity, Daniélou appeared to invoke the traditional doctrine of *analogia entis*. We have already encountered this doctrine in connection with Henri Bouillard and Jean-Marie Le Blond, for whom it served to negotiate a non-conceptualist epistemology that would none the less do justice to the truthfulness of human discourse. We noticed also that Balthasar retained this doctrine in opposition to Karl Barth. In each case, the result was a sacramental ontology that could maintain both the similarity and the infinite dissimilarity between God and human beings. Unlike these other *nouvelle* theologians, however, Daniélou did not use the language of analogy to speak of the relationship between nature and the supernatural. Instead, the analogy that Daniélou developed was a *historical* analogy between types and their fulfilment by way of antitypes. We could also say that he used 'analogy' language to refer not to vertical but to horizontal connections. When speaking of Daniélou's 'sacramental hermeneutic', therefore, we do need to remember that he had in mind historical categories, in which the similarities and dissimilarities could be observed historically.

---

[173] Ibid. 71–2. Cf. ibid. 78: 'There are in fact two planes of comparison. On the one hand there is a *theological* resemblance between the Deluge, the Descent into the lower world, and Baptism, for here we see at work the same divine ways. In all three cases, there exists a sinful world which is to be annihilated by the punishment, and in all three cases a just man is spared: this just man, in the Deluge, is Noe; in the Descent into hell, Jesus Christ; in Baptism, the Christian by conformation to Jesus Christ. Thus Baptism is a sacramental imitation of the Descent into hell, both being prefigured by the Deluge. But, furthermore, in both the Deluge and Baptism, there is the element of water which might be called illustrative typology. This is not sufficient by itself to serve as a foundation for typology—and it became the error of certain exegetes to try to recognize a type of Baptism wherever water is mentioned in the Old Testament. But these illustrations have real meaning when they are the signs by which we can recognize theological analogies.' Cf. Daniélou's helpful exposition, 'The Sacraments and the History of Salvation', in A. G. Marimort (ed.), *The Liturgy and the Word of God* (Collegeville, Minn.: Liturgical, 1959), 21–32. This essay has recently been republished in *LS* 2 (2006), 203–15.
[174] Daniélou, *Christ and Us*, 79. Cf. id., *Advent*, 42–3.

Daniélou's historical, horizontal emphasis did not, however, imply a historicism that was limited to evolutionary cause and effect. In his later years, he expressed his deep worry that in the post-conciliar period the danger of Modernism had become more poignant than it had been at the beginning of the twentieth century, and he was quite troubled about contemporary Catholicism's accommodation to a modern, historicist mindset.[175] Thus, he made common cause with de Lubac, Balthasar, and others in opposing trends that he believed put into question the unalterable essence of the Christian faith.[176] Significantly, Daniélou expressed his apprehension of 'desacralizing' and 'secularizing' tendencies within Catholicism.[177] Notwithstanding his historical bent, Daniélou retained a sceptical attitude towards a reductionism focused solely on historical realities.

ALLEGORY OR TYPOLOGY? THE DISAGREEMENT BETWEEN DE LUBAC AND DANIÉLOU

Daniélou's 'Recent Scruples'

The question remains whether Daniélou, along with de Lubac, held to Gregory's notion of a 'wheel within a wheel'. We need to explore in more detail how exactly Daniélou saw the relationship between type and antitype, and what he meant to express about the relationship between the sacrament and its future reality with the title of his *Sacramentum futuri*. Put somewhat sharply, the question is whether Daniélou held to a 'real presence' that saw that the future (Christological and sacramental) reality as already present in its historical prefiguration or whether he regarded type and antitype, in nominalist fashion, as two separate historical realities. I will argue that in some ways Daniélou held to a truly sacramental hermeneutic, with the sacrament indeed containing the reality to which it pointed. At the same time, an ambiguity characterized his thinking on this point—an ambiguity which also characterized his philosophy of history.[178] Daniélou's consistent focus on the historical events themselves made it more difficult for him than for de Lubac to recognize the spiritual reality that history sacramentally contained.

As we have already noted, Daniélou emphasized the oneness of the mystery of Christ. As a result, he referred to the various historical figures and their fulfilments as different 'modes', 'registers', or 'dimensions' of the one Christological

---

[175] Daniélou, *Et qui est mon prochain?* 156–9, 189–202. Cf. ibid. 200: 'Personally, in the current situation, I reckon that we are threatened more by the Modernist danger than by the integrist danger and, after the great conciliar effort at adaptation to the modern world—an effort that must be pursued—I believe it is key to affirm the necessity of fidelity to fundamental values.'

[176] Ibid. 96–7, 195.   [177] Ibid. 137, 174, 210.

[178] See Chap. 6, sect.: Jean Daniélou: History and the Primacy of the Spiritual.

mystery.[179] Similarly, Daniélou commented: 'In the Exodus, in the death and resurrection of Christ, and in Baptism, it is the same redeeming action which is accomplished on different levels of history—that of the figure, of the reality, and of the sacrament.'[180] By referring to the 'same redeeming action' taking place at different moments in history, Daniélou seemed to suggest that at a deeper level both the Exodus and Baptism truly contained the redemption of Christ.[181] Daniélou could even go so far as to insist that the real significance of symbols was 'to afford us access through the visible world into a higher, transcendent plane of being',[182] and that symbolism was 'directed towards the discovery of analogies between the visible and the invisible worlds, and towards the formulation of their meaning'.[183] All of this fit with a theory of symbolism that looked to Old Testament occurrences as reality-filled sacraments of the future rather than as mere empty signs that pointed to future events. This understanding suited a sacramental understanding of analogy that involved a true participation of the type in its antitypical reality.

Daniélou's emphasis was none the less different from de Lubac's, a difference that came to the fore in their public disagreement about the terminology best used to describe spiritual interpretation. For Daniélou, typology was the legitimate heritage derived from Paul, Justin, and Irenaeus, while allegory showed the illegitimate influence of Philo and Gnosticism. As we have seen, however, de Lubac was quite at ease with the term 'allegory' and was not terribly concerned about individual instances where allegory seemed overly fanciful. He was convinced that the Fathers, including Origen and Gregory of Nyssa, had been correct in looking for the deeper meaning of history by means of allegory, tropology, and anagogy. Thus, when Daniélou expounded on the typological connection between the crossing of the Red Sea and Baptism, and insisted that the Alexandrian distinctive had been allegory, not typology, de Lubac reacted.[184] He showed that at least until the thirteenth century the term 'allegory' had been the standard term to refer to New Testament typological fulfilment.[185] 'The scruples regarding *allegoria*', he concluded, 'are completely recent'.[186] Besides Origen, Tertullian

---

[179] Daniélou, 'Le Symbolisme des rites baptismaux', 17.

[180] Id., *Bible and the Liturgy*, 87.

[181] Perhaps not quite as striking was Daniélou's comment about Justin Martyr's view of the *sphragis*, the sign of the Cross marked on the forehead: 'It is the sign of the Cross made with blood that preserved the Jews; it is this sign which saves the sinners who are marked with it in Baptism' (ibid. 164).

[182] Id., *Lord of History*, 135.

[183] Ibid. 136. These last two statements, with their vertical, almost Platonic, overtones, were rather uncharacteristic of Daniélou's generally quite historical approach.

[184] Daniélou made his comment in 'Traversée de la Mer Rouge', 416. In his book on Origen, Daniélou argued for a clear-cut distinction between typological and allegorical elements in the Alexandrian's exegesis: 'Only too often typology has been confused with allegory—historians have spoken as if in Origen's case the two things were the same' (*Origen*, 139).

[185] De Lubac, 'Typology and Allegorization', 130–41.

[186] Ibid. 141. Cf. also id., *Medieval Exegesis*, ii. 19. Cf. id., 'Spiritual Understanding', 10: 'The word [i.e., "typology"] is a neologism and has been barely a century in use.'

had also used the terminology of 'allegory', and de Lubac argued that it was much more likely that Origen had adopted this language from St Paul (Gal. 4: 24) than from Philo,[187] and that in this sense 'allegory means essentially what Father Daniélou and others call "typology"'.[188] As for Daniélou's charge that Origen had denied the historical basis of the text, 'nothing is farther from the truth'.[189] De Lubac acknowledged, in his response to Daniélou at least, that it might not be possible to revive the use of the term 'allegory' because of its negative connotations, and he willingly accepted the term 'typology'.[190] None the less, de Lubac insisted that Origen's allegorical or mystical sense had been quite different from his tropological meaning, for which he had indeed relied too much on Philo.[191] Furthermore, de Lubac remained unconvinced that Origen's allegorical exegesis was a form of esoteric teaching restricted to an elite who considered themselves beyond basic catechetical instruction: 'We fear that he [i.e., Daniélou] is still too much dominated by the current prejudices concerning Origen's esotericism. Moreover, is it not especially in his very simple, indeed vernacular, homilies that Origen multiplies his moral and spiritual applications from the sacred text?'[192] De Lubac was convinced that Origen had regarded allegory as something that benefited all Christians, regardless of their spiritual progress.

The argument between de Lubac and Daniélou was more than just a historical one about Origen's alleged grounding in Philo or about the place of history in the Alexandrian school. De Lubac's overall writings reflected his belief that the term 'typology' was incapable of fully grasping what went on in the interpretation of the great Tradition. He believed that the phrase remained strictly on the historical level and, while valuable, needed allegory as a spiritual foundation. Thus, de Lubac asserted that allegory had traditionally been a broader term, containing typology as one element among others. Moreover, he maintained, the term 'typology' itself did not yet indicate that spiritual interpretation involved a move from Old to New Testament. It did not sufficiently reflect the newness of the work accomplished by Christ.[193]

Although de Lubac believed history to be important, even foundational, to biblical exegesis, interpretation could not remain at this level. The typological or

[187] De Lubac, 'Typology and Allegorization', 141–4.
[188] Ibid. 144. Cf. Frances M. Young's comment: ' "Typology" is a modern construct. Ancient exegetes did not distinguish between typology and allegory, and it is often difficult to make the distinction, the one shading into the other all too easily' (*Biblical Exegesis*, 152).
[189] De Lubac, 'Typology and Allegorization', 145.
[190] Ibid. 151, 158.
[191] Ibid. 159–60.
[192] Ibid. 160.
[193] Id., *Medieval Exegesis*, i. 259. Marcellino D'Ambrosio deals with de Lubac's refusal to oppose typology to allegory in 'The Spiritual Sense in de Lubac's Hermeneutics of Tradition', *LS* 1 (2005), 150–2.

allegorical level was a way of moving beyond an absolutized understanding of 'mere history':

It will not be enough to 'allegorize' (still, of course, in the sense of Saint Paul) the events and persons of the Old Testament so as to see in them figures of the New if we continue to see in them only other events, other persons. Israel is the figure of spiritual things. In its turn, then, in order to be understood as it must be, in its newness, which is to say, in its spirit, in order to merit its name as New Testament, the content of this second Scripture must give way to a perpetual movement of transcendence. The spirit is discovered only through *anagogy*.[194]

De Lubac believed Origen had been right to insist that the spirit was not an additional letter.[195] The sacramental character of history implied that it pointed beyond itself not just in a horizontal, historical, but also in a vertical sense. The natural–supernatural relationship should provide the pattern for the relationship between history and spirit.

As a result, de Lubac often spoke of the inward character of the text. In a fascinating section of his *Exégèse médiévale*, he observed that in the great Tradition the historical meaning of the text had served as a sacrament of the future: 'There is an opposition of the "then" or *tunc* (past) to the "now" or *nunc*. An opposition within duration, at the same time as a relation of sign to thing signified.'[196] He then went on, however, to state:

Only, as history is not enough to contain the mystery, it is very true that Christian allegory is not contained by the historical dimension. To receive it totally and not to warp it, we must not restrict this reality 'to come' which is the New Testament within the bounds of the 'superficies historiae', the 'surface of history'. It overflows these boundaries. It involves another 'dimension'.[197]

According to de Lubac, Old Testament *history* prefigured New Testament *grace*. 'To misunderstand it would be to make out of the allegorical sense, which is a *spiritual* sense, a new literal sense; and this would practically negate the interiority of the Christian mystery.'[198] For the Church Fathers, the Christian mystery had reached beyond history, because they had been concerned with the interior sense of history, corresponding to an interior understanding. This interiority had obvious sacramental overtones. It 'is neither uniquely nor primarily what we today name "the interior life": it is, in the first place, the interiority of the mystery within the very object of the faith. Let us not be afraid of the pleonasm: it is a question of "internal mysteries" '.[199] Repeatedly, de Lubac made reference to the

---

[194] De Lubac, *History and Spirit*, 323. [195] Ibid. 324.
[196] Id., *Medieval Exegesis*, ii. 95. [197] Ibid.
[198] Ibid. 99.
[199] Ibid. 97. Cf. id., 'On an Old Distich', 117: 'The mystery is not only announced, prefigured or assured by the facts: the facts themselves have an interior that in diverse ways is already pregnant with the mystery. Therefore, it would be a great mistake to oppose allegory to history, as if the one denied or at least neglected the other in principle.'

'inner mystery' of 'outer facts'[200] and to the 'interior aspect' of the letter or of history.[201] He illustrated this with the point made so often throughout the Tradition that Scripture was like wax containing honey as its spiritual sense.[202] Needless to say, the mutual interpenetration of outer history and inner mystery explained de Lubac's attraction to Ezekiel's imagery of a wheel within a wheel.[203] Just as the outer wheel of Old Testament history derived its significance from the inner wheel of New Testament grace, so the external letter represented, in sacramental fashion, the internal mystery.

The Problem of Allegorical Detail

In his response to de Lubac, Daniélou eschewed the threefold and fourfold categorization, as well as the standard medieval terminology for the various levels of spiritual interpretation, restricting himself to the term 'typology', instead. He was convinced that the classification advocated by de Lubac did show the 'unfortunate influence exercised by Philo'[204] and he insisted:

There are, in the strict sense of the word, only two meanings of Scripture. The one is the literal meaning, which is that of the text. It is the meaning desired by the author and which the study of the text merely has to explain. Further, this meaning can either be its own or figured, depending on whether it concerns the literal meaning of history or a parable. The other is the typological meaning. It is not another meaning of the text. There is nothing in the text except what the author has wished to place there. But it is a meaning of the things themselves, of which the author speaks. It is a relation between the realities of the Old Testament and those of the New. The great patristic affirmation is that this meaning has Christ for its object. The personalities, the events, the institutions of the Old Testament first have their own historical reality, which is their literal meaning, and they are secondly a certain prefiguration of what Christ has accomplished at the end of time. Thus, throughout the Old Testament, little by little with various lines a figure is composed, so well, that when Christ arrives, he can only say, 'Ego sum' [I am]. The

---

[200] De Lubac, *Medieval Exegesis*, ii. 84, 86, 98. It is hard to avoid the impression that de Lubac had Daniélou's notion of 'analogy' in mind when he argued that it seemed 'clear that "the typology of the Red Sea" or that of the Cloud is not merely a comparison which is added on to the Pauline theology: it is an explicit part of it' (de Lubac, 'Spiritual Understanding', 8).

[201] De Lubac, *Medieval Exegesis*, ii. 79, 82, 201–2. Cf. id., 'Spiritual Understanding', 11.

[202] Id., *Medieval Exegesis*, ii. 162–5, 170.

[203] Or, as de Lubac piled on additional images: 'This honey in the wax was therefore the same thing as the pith [la moëelle (*sic*)] in the bark [Bede], or the nut in the shell [Honorius], or the grain in the ear [Rupert]' (ibid. 165; first square brackets, referring to *la moëlle*, in original).

[204] Daniélou, 'Les Divers Sens', 119. Daniélou's later publications continued to illustrate the same differences with his former teacher. Throughout his writings, he assailed the baleful influence of Philo of Alexandria, whose thought he carefully analysed. His work on Philo even led to a monograph on the Jewish interpreter (*Philon d'Alexandrie* (Paris: Fayard, 1958)). Here, too, Daniélou declared his allegorical interpretation as 'entirely deprived of a sense of history' (*Philon*, 119). Cf. id., *Origen*, 178–91; id., *From Shadows to Reality*, 57–65, 131–6. At the same time, however, Daniélou acknowledged that Gregory of Nyssa had adopted Philo's method of exegesis without accepting the contents provided by the latter (id., *From Shadows to Reality*, 224–6).

difference between the Old and the New Testaments is that between Christ represented and Christ present.[205]

Twice in this remarkable passage Daniélou stated unequivocally that only authorial intent determined the meaning of the text. This would seem to exclude any kind of spiritual interpretation as something that could properly determine the meaning of the text. None the less, with regard to the Christological fulfilment of the Old Testament, the passage continued to speak of typological *meaning*. This seemed to imply that there was an additional meaning, beyond that which the author himself had intended. Daniélou seemed to preclude the idea of a dual meaning, however, when he added that the typological meaning was 'not another meaning' and that the terminology of Christological 'typological meaning' simply referred to the foreshadowed New Testament realities (rather than to an additional meaning of the Old Testament passage itself). Thus, he reinforced the impression that he regarded the Old Testament types and their New Testament realities as separate historical events.

Insisting again that Scripture only had two meanings, one literal and the other Christological, Daniélou then criticized Origen 'with his doctrine of three senses', although he acknowledged that Origen's 'practice is much more worthwhile than his theory'.[206] Daniélou explained that, unlike Origen, the Western tradition had consistently followed St Matthew in looking to specific Old Testament passages as typologically foreshadowing Christ's life.[207] He then turned to the sacramental exegesis of John's Gospel, insisting that this, too, was a form of Christological interpretation, since 'Christ, as St Augustine often repeated, is the whole Christ, the head and the members'.[208] While recognizing that Origen had done justice to 'sacramental typology', Daniélou insisted that the Alexandrian's weakness had been his hostility to 'historical typology', the result of his attempt to combine biblical and Platonic categories.[209]

The attempt to move *beyond* history's surface in order to discover its inner, spiritual meaning constituted, for de Lubac, the attraction of allegory. This same attempt was Daniélou's reason for rejecting the term 'allegory' in favour of 'typology'.[210] To Daniélou, the sacramental link between two different events

---

[205] Id., 'Les Divers Sens', 119–20. It is perhaps worth noting that de Lubac agreed with Daniélou's observation that the various meanings of Scripture could be reduced to two: 'There are in Scripture, fundamentally, only two senses: the literal and the spiritual, and these two senses themselves are in continuity, not in opposition' (de Lubac, *History and Spirit*, 205). Daniélou insisted on 'only two meanings' also in *Origen*, 161.

[206] Daniélou, 'Les Divers Sens', 121.

[207] Ibid. 121–3. Cf. id., *Origen*, 161–2.

[208] Id., 'Les Divers Sens', 123. Cf. id., *Origen*, 162.

[209] Id., 'Les Divers Sens', 124–5.

[210] Daniélou saw Gnostic influence precisely in Origen's turning to the 'inner' meaning of Scripture: 'With its view that temporal events are an image of what takes place in the world of pure spirits, the method represents a special type of exegesis, different both from the rabbis' and from Philo's and not connected with the exegesis given by Catholic writers either, whether they interpreted Scripture of the Church or with reference to the Last Things. We can only call it

within history attracted him to typological interpretation. He argued that the typological similarity between historical events meant that a type was 'always an image of the future, a τύπος μέλλοντος, not a reflexion of some previous existence or one of a higher order'.[211] The Philonian attempt to escape history by means of allegorical exegesis was the cause, Daniélou believed, of its arbitrary character: 'The great weakness of Philo's exegesis was to find a symbolical meaning in every detail of Scripture. Further, like the Gnostic exegesis, it sought for correspondences between the world of the senses and the world of the intellect.'[212]

Daniélou was concerned about the arbitrary character of too much patristic and medieval interpretation, which he saw as the direct result of non-historical allegorizing.[213] And while he often singled out the Alexandrians, especially Clement (*c.*150–*c.*215) and Origen, Daniélou's criticism went further. He questioned the parallels St Cyril of Jerusalem had drawn between Jesus' crown of thorns and the thorns of Genesis 3: 18, and between the fig tree cursed by Jesus and the aprons of fig leaves Adam and Eve had made.[214] He was particularly critical of St Ambrose, who had undergone Philo's and Origen's influence, and whose 'moral allegorizing' of the Flood had gone well beyond that of his Alexandrian model. With Shem, Ham, and Japheth representing good, bad, and indifferent, the ark referring to the body with its dimensions and cavities, and the Flood speaking of the human passions, Daniélou noted a dependence 'not only on the method, but on the very details of Philo's exegesis' which, really, had 'left exegesis quite behind'.[215] Daniélou also observed this 'more allegorical line of thought' when Gregory of Nyssa interpreted the army of the Egyptians as a figure of the passions of the soul in *The Life of Moses*.[216] Moreover, while Daniélou was quite sympathetic to a Christological and sacramental reading of the Song of Songs, and especially of the invitation to the banquet in Canticles 5: 1,[217] he gave several examples from Ambrose and Augustine that were 'questionable'[218]

Gnostic. It occupies a prominent position in Origen's works, for in his view it represents the *innermost* meaning of Scripture' (*Origen*, 194; emphasis added).

[211] Daniélou, *From Shadows to Reality*, 30–1.

[212] Ibid. 288. In his book on Origen, Daniélou outlined five of Philo's hermeneutical principles, each of which had influenced Origen: (1) since Scripture is inspired by God, it can never mean anything that would be unworthy of God or useless to us; (2) every detail in Scripture has a figurative meaning; (3) a numerical symbolism needs to be sought behind the literal meaning of numbers; (4) Scripture contains allegories that should be applied to the moral life; and (5) the three meanings of Scripture correspond to the three parts of the soul and the three degrees of perfection (*Origen*, 178–91).

[213] For a similar contrast between allegory and typology, relying in part on Daniélou, see Joseph A. Galdon, *Typology and Seventeenth-century Literature* (The Hague: Mouton, 1975), 32–8.

[214] Daniélou, *From Shadows to Reality*, 42.

[215] Ibid. 111–12.

[216] Daniélou, *Bible and the Liturgy*, 90.

[217] Daniélou presented a beautiful chapter on the typological interpretation of the Song of Songs (ibid. 191–207).

[218] Ibid. 197.

or 'remarkable'.[219] And in response to a lengthy allegorical interpretation offered by the Alexandrian teacher Didymus the Blind (*c.*313–*c.*398) of Elijah making the axe head float on the surface of the Jordan (2 Kgs. 6: 1–7)—with Elijah prefiguring God, the iron in the dark abyss anticipating the power of sinful human nature, the wood symbolizing the Cross, and the Jordan alluding to Baptism by which, like the axe head, we return to our home country—Daniélou commented: 'Here we are in the full stream of allegorical development'.[220]

Eager to retain a typological foreshadowing in the Old Testament despite some of the problematic instances of patristic exegesis, Daniélou insisted that the problem lay with the way in which too many particular elements of the Scriptures were subjected to allegorizing exegesis. Thus, he criticized the 'detailed interpretations' that the Fathers had given of the Ascension Psalms (Pss. 22 [23], 109 [110], and 67 [68]),[221] all the while strongly maintaining, however, the validity of their Christological interpretation. The ancient tradition had 'adopted the Psalms, not because of their religious value nor because of their inspired character, but only because it thought that they were concerned with Christ'.[222] Much more important, therefore, than the detailed interpretations and their problems, was the fact that the Fathers were correct to see a general eschatological typology in the Psalms.[223]

Interestingly, Daniélou himself was willing to entertain a level of detail in typology that we rarely find reflected in contemporary commentaries. He was open, for instance, to the interpretation of the Flood given by the Antiochian preacher St John Chrysostom (*c.*347–407), in which the ark had referred to the Church, Noah to Christ, the dove to the Holy Spirit, and the olive branch to divine goodness: 'We have here the witness of an author little inclined to allegory, and it has the more importance for us since it shows us that we have here a common ecclesiastical tradition.'[224] The Fathers had rightly regarded Rahab's scarlet cord hanging out of her window as a memorial of the Passover and as a prophecy of the Passion.[225] And when Gregory of Nyssa had presented an exegesis of Psalm 22 [23] in which the details made reference to the outpouring of the Spirit, to Baptism, to the Eucharist, the inebriating chalice, and the blood of Christ,[226] Daniélou considered all this 'perfectly legitimate'.[227]

While his frequently voiced objection of 'detailed allegory' was no doubt genuine, Daniélou's underlying fears were probably more serious. Primarily, he was concerned about patristic attempts to find in the Old Testament accounts direct references to the human faculties (such as intellect, will, and passions) and their functioning. This had resulted in the moralizing nature of some

[219] Ibid. 198.   [220] Ibid. 109.   [221] Ibid. 317.
[222] Ibid. 315.   [223] Ibid. 317–18.   [224] Ibid. 85.
[225] Daniélou, 'Rahab', 44–5.
[226] Daniélou, *Bible and the Liturgy*, 178–90.
[227] Ibid. 190.

allegorizing practices, for which Origen and Ambrose had relied on Philo. As we have already seen, however, Daniélou was not alone in his objections to such moralizing allegory. De Lubac shared his apprehensions of the moralism that tended to come along with Origen's threefold method. On this point, de Lubac and Daniélou did not differ a great deal. Second, Daniélou was apprehensive about the Alexandrian philosophical tendency to move vertically *from* history *to* the spirit. This de-historicizing tendency allowed the Fathers, so he believed, to see spiritual references in all sorts of details of the Old Testament text—which in turn led to Daniélou's repeated objections to the 'detailed allegorizing' of the Fathers. On this score, de Lubac and Daniélou did, of course, have a genuine difference of opinion.

Analogy of Faith or Biblical Precedent

Neither of the two Jesuits articulated in detail when it might be warranted to press the spiritual sense of the text, whether in terms of allegory, tropology, or anagogy (de Lubac); or in terms of typological references to Christ and the sacraments (Daniélou). De Lubac, we saw, had recourse to the 'analogy of faith' and believed that the unity of Scripture was the justification for the various forms of spiritual interpretation, including allegory. De Lubac appeared to give the imagination relatively free reign, as long as the interpreter remained within the edifying teaching of the Scriptures. To specify exactly the cases in which allegory might be acceptable would probably have struck him as an attempt to limit the 'infinite forest of meanings'.

Daniélou was more circumspect. Although he never explained what would render a certain interpretation too detailed, he often referred to the biblical warrant, or the lack thereof, of particular typological readings. When the Bible itself already contained a typological link, Daniélou approved, but beyond this he was afraid to allow the imagination to go unchecked in determining the Christological and sacramental readings of Old Testament details.[228] Noting, for example, that the symbolism of the ark of Noah as a type of the Church might at first sight appear as 'a rather far-fetched allegory of Baptism', Daniélou set out to show that it was instead 'the natural development of the Biblical conception', highlighting the 'links which connect this interpretation with that which Scripture itself provides'.[229] Similarly, Daniélou defended Origen's 'typology' of Isaac and Christ with regard to the patriarch's birth and sacrifice, both of these being

---

[228] Whereas de Lubac restricted himself to the hermeneutics that he saw at work in the Tradition, Daniélou consistently went back to the typology of Scripture itself as background for what he found in the later Tradition. This difference goes some way to explaining Daniélou's concern for a biblical foundation in typological exegesis.

[229] Daniélou, *From Shadows to Reality*, 69.

grounded in Scripture,[230] but he was unable to find scriptural warrant for the 'allegory' of the marriage of Isaac as a type of the union between Christ and the Church:

In the first two *sacramenta* Origen bases himself on St Paul and works out the mystery in a spiritual sense. But for the third, St Paul afforded no help and Origen fell back on Philo. Origen borrowed from him the symbols, but gave them quite a different significance. We are here in the sphere not of typology, but of allegory, of Christian allegory.[231]

Daniélou's sole criterion for accepting or dismissing the typology of the various aspects of Isaac's life was the presence or absence of biblical precedent. In other cases, too, his defence of allegorical readings consisted of pointing to biblical background or precedence;[232] while he tended to object to allegorical readings as lacking in scriptural foundation.[233]

De Lubac and Daniélou certainly had their hermeneutical differences. First, de Lubac's emphasis on multiplicity of meaning ensured his openness to the free rein of a biblically shaped imagination in support of the edification of the Church. Daniélou tended to disqualify spiritual interpretation as 'allegorical' when he could not find a clear biblical precedent or foundation for a particular patristic Christological or sacramental reading of the text. Second, de Lubac insisted that while a historical foundation and a literal reading were indispensable the purpose of spiritual reading was to move beyond history. Daniélou was wary of such 'vertical' interpretation and insisted that typology was based on a prophecy-fulfilment scheme that was thoroughly historical in character. Third, and most significantly, de Lubac's sacramental hermeneutic regarded the spiritual meaning as internal to the historical event, so that one could never separate these two main levels of reality. The spiritual level was 'a wheel within a wheel'. Daniélou, while agreeing that spiritual interpretation was sacramental in

---

[230] Daniélou saw a Christological reference to Isaac's birth in Gal. 3: 16 and 4: 22–8 (*From Shadows to Reality*, 122); and to the sacrifice of Isaac in Rom. 8: 32 and Heb. 11: 17–19 (ibid. 120, 122–3).

[231] Ibid. 142–3. Interestingly, in his book on Origen, Daniélou acknowledged that the Church Fathers interpreted the patriarchs' marriages as typological 'figures of the mystery of Christ and the Church', and here he did not object to this view. Instead, he argued that the objectionable Philonian element in Origen was the individual moralizing, in which 'what had been figures of the Church become allegories of the soul' (*Origen*, 187). Cf. also Daniélou's discussion of the 'sacrament' of the marriage of Isaac and Rebecca in *Advent*, 48–50.

[232] The Fathers simply 'followed the teaching of the New Testament' in seeing Exodus fulfilled in Christ (Daniélou, *From Shadows to Reality*, 153). Eusebius' numerous parallels drawn from the Exodus account (Moses' and Jesus' forty days of fasting; the manna and the multiplication of the loaves; the Red Sea crossing and Jesus walking on the water; Moses and Jesus commanding the wind; the shining of Moses' face and the account of the Transfiguration; the call of Joshua and that of Simon Peter; the twelve spies and the twelve Apostles) were 'almost all such as the Evangelists themselves had in mind' (ibid. 199). The application of manna to the Eucharist 'rests upon Scripture itself' (ibid. 149). The Christological reading of the Ascension Psalms had 'its foundation in the Old Testament itself' (ibid. 316). Cf. id., *Bible and the Liturgy*, 193.

[233] Cf. id., *Bible and the Liturgy*, 205.

character, did not always make clear that he believed type and antitype to have such a 'perichoretic' relationship, emphasizing instead the temporal distance given with the historical development from the Old Testament to Christ and the Church.

At the same time, we should not exaggerate the differences between the two Jesuit scholars. Both purposely engaged in a project of *ressourcement*, convinced that the Fathers had contributed important exegetical insights to the Tradition, which to disregard would infinitely impoverish us today.[234] Both de Lubac and Daniélou were convinced of the importance of a historical foundation for spiritual interpretation and believed that without a careful literal reading of the text one could not move on to spiritual interpretation. Whether it be allegory or typology, both authors insisted that the Christological, sacramental, and eschatological fulfilment provided significant new horizons to the Old Testament text. The two theologians were thus allies in their common attempt to overcome a narrow modern preoccupation with the literal meaning of the text.

For both de Lubac and Daniélou, a sacramental hermeneutic of Scripture was the key element in the project of *ressourcement*. De Lubac, in particular, by insisting that the spiritual meaning of the text was the deeper level of the letter itself rather than merely a later imposition on the text, undermined the neo-scholastic separation between nature and the supernatural. The great Tradition, de Lubac was able to show, had demonstrated in its reading of the Bible that Christology, along with its moral and anagogical implications, was not an extrinsic addition to a purely autonomous natural realm. Spiritual interpretation was not just an unrelated addition to a historically established meaning of the text. Similarly, de Lubac and Daniélou were able to expose the excesses of higher biblical criticism, which had affected the Catholic Church through the impact of Modernism. Their forays into patristic exegesis made it abundantly clear that the Fathers had never been interested in simply establishing the literal meaning of the text, but had always looked to Old Testament figures as sacraments that pointed beyond themselves to spiritual fulfilment. Moreover, de Lubac would add, the great Tradition had regarded the text itself as already containing this infinite multiplicity of divine grace, and had thus witnessed to a sacramental hermeneutic.

---

[234] Daniélou commented in his memoirs: 'That which we have wanted, each in our own manner, Father de Lubac in his *Exégèse médiévale* and I in my various studies of typology, is to restore the exegesis of the Fathers to its position and, by doing so, recover a vision of a symbolic type more than a logical type' (*Et qui est mon prochain?* 135–6).

6

Living Tradition:
Recovering History for the Church

There flows in this garden a river of water which never runs dry.

St Hippolytus[1]

One of the distinctive elements of *nouvelle théologie* was its emphasis on history and historical development. But the realization that one had to do justice to history still left open the question: what exactly was its significance? The Modernist Crisis had exposed some of the difficulties involved in articulating the relationship between faith and history. If theological ideas could exist only within an actual historical context, one must consider how to avoid the kind of subjectivism and relativism that set the Christian faith adrift in a sea of human opinion. This was the main apprehension that neo-Thomism had about connecting theology to history. The *nouvelle* theologians, however, were convinced that a recovery of history was essential for the Church in order to retain and restore vitality to ecclesial life. They were well aware, of course, that not just any turn to history would do. To try and give an account of historical developments, particularly those of the Tradition of the Church, by inner-worldly cause and effect alone, would mean to grant absolute autonomy to natural historical developments. Such autonomy would run directly counter to *nouvelle théologie*'s project of trying to reintegrate nature and the supernatural. The task for *nouvelle théologie*, therefore, was to explore avenues that would restore history to its rightful place within theology, while at the same time doing justice to the fact that the eternal God was the origin, the centre, and the purpose of all historical development. The *nouvelle* theologians believed that only a sacramental ontology could enable a reintegration of the horizontal and vertical dimensions of history.

This chapter will open up three windows to look at *nouvelle théologie*'s sacramental view of history. The first one will look out on the attempt of Jean Daniélou to connect cosmic and Christian revelation, secular and sacred history, as well as earthly and heavenly cities. Daniélou attempted to do this in sacramental fashion: the similarities allowed him to take seriously the value of cosmic

---

[1] Hippolytus, *In Danielem*, i. 17 (quot. Congar, *Tradition and Traditions: The Biblical, Historical, and Theological Evidence for Catholic Teaching on Tradition*, trans. Michael Naseby and Thomas Rainborough (San Diego, Calif.: Basilica, 1966), 275).

revelation, secular history, and earthly city; the infinite dissimilarity meant that Christian revelation, sacred history, and heavenly city were the final end or sacramental reality to which all of history pointed. The second window will provide insight into the *nouvelle* theologians' attempts to provide a more historical explanation of doctrinal development, since they were convinced that the strictly intellectual categories of neo-Thomism did not adequately address the issue of development. After a brief account of some neo-scholastic theories of development of doctrine, I will analyse the attempts of Marie-Dominique Chenu, Louis Charlier, and Henri de Lubac to overcome the intellectualist approach of neo-Thomism. Chenu focused on the 'theandric mystery' of the Incarnation, Charlier insisted on development of doctrine by way of a 'continued Incarnation', and de Lubac saw this development as the historical 'cashing in' of the Christological treasury. Each of these Christological approaches to doctrinal development posited some kind of sacramental integration between the vertical and the horizontal, between homogeneity and historical development of the revealed deposit. The third window will open up on the broad horizon of Christian Tradition in the theology of Yves Congar. In this section, I will show that, for Congar, ecclesial time was sacramental in character, which implied that one could do justice to Scripture and Tradition only by treating them in sacramental fashion, since they served to realize the presence of Christ. It will become clear that Congar's sacramental ontology represents a serious challenge to both Catholic and Protestant traditions. To Congar—and in a real sense to each of the *nouvelle* theologians discussed in this chapter—the way to recover the centrality of history for the Church was by re-appropriating the 'living Tradition'.

JEAN DANIÉLOU: HISTORY AND THE PRIMACY OF THE SPIRITUAL

Cosmic and Christian Revelation

For the Parisian scholar Jean Daniélou history was a central category. As we saw in the previous chapter, his typological hermeneutic meant that an analogical relationship between historical events formed the basis for biblical exegesis. His apprehension of allegorical interpretation was at least in part the result of his view that Christianity was grounded in historical *mirabilia dei* (miraculous acts of God), most significantly the Incarnation, along with the preaching of the Word and the sacraments. This historically based view of spiritual interpretation raises several questions. Given his view of Christianity as a historical faith, how did Daniélou regard non-Christian religions? What was the relationship for Daniélou between secular and sacred history? And, immediately related to this, how did he value the temporal concerns of society, and how should the Church, in his opinion, relate to them?

Daniélou addressed these issues throughout his career, and behind each of them lay the question of the nature–supernatural relationship. Not surprisingly, therefore, Daniélou approached these issues by means of the sacramental ontology that characterized his overall theology. Whether he was discussing the relationship between cosmic and Christian revelation, between secular and sacred history, or between the earthly and heavenly cities, Daniélou emphasized their interrelatedness, while assigning relative value and autonomy to the former and insisting on the ultimate significance of the latter. Given the priority of Christian revelation, of sacred history, and of the heavenly city, Daniélou took his position squarely within the framework of the Christian faith in order to arrive at a true appreciation also of cosmic revelation, of secular history, and of the earthly city.

Unlike Henri de Lubac, Daniélou did not engage in an extensive discussion of theological notions such as pure nature (*pura natura*) or natural desire (*desiderium naturale*) for the beatific vision. His general framework, however, was very much that of his teacher. And, on occasion, he did make comments that reflected de Lubac's influence. For instance, Daniélou explained in *Les Saints païens de l'Ancien Testament* (1956) why he preferred the term 'cosmic religion' over the common expression 'natural religion', and he appealed to the second-century apologist Justin Martyr: 'Historically indeed man pertains to a supernatural order. The cosmic religion is not natural religion, in the sense that the latter means something outside the effective and concrete supernatural order. That is the reason we avoid the expression.'[2] Daniélou agreed with de Lubac that the actual historical natural order was never without grace. He developed this idea beyond what de Lubac would have been willing to accept, in referring to this actual state of affairs as a 'supernatural order'.[3] He then argued that the 'cosmic covenant' was also a 'covenant of Grace', though he acknowledged immediately that it was 'still imperfect, in the sense that God reveals Himself therein only through the cosmos, and it is very difficult to grasp by reason of the fact that it is addressed to an already weakened humanity'.[4] Daniélou clearly did not allow for a state of 'pure nature'. Instead, he argued that the various stages of historical development were all situated within the framework of supernatural revelation and of divine grace. No event in history was beyond the reach of God's supernatural embrace. All of history was predicated on the gracious initiative of God.

Daniélou denied any sharp distinction between secular and sacred history. He was quite aware that this raised the question of how the covenant of grace and the Christian faith could still be considered unique. If one were to agree with Church

---

[2] Daniélou, *Holy Pagans of the Old Testament*, trans. Felix Faber (London: Longmans, Green and Co, 1957), 20. Cf. also id., *God and the Ways of Knowing*, trans. Walter Roberts (1956; repr. San Francisco, Calif.: Ignatius, 2003), 9.

[3] Id., *Holy Pagans*, 20. Cf. ibid. 23: '[T]he cosmic covenant is itself a supernatural covenant. It is not of a different order from that of the Mosaic or the Christian covenant. It is the first shoot which will grow with the succeeding ages.'

[4] Ibid. 20.

Fathers such as Justin Martyr, Clement of Alexandria, and Origen in their fundamentally optimistic view of 'cosmic revelation' and of the salvation of non-Christians, how could one still uphold the centrality of Jesus Christ and of the Church? Or, as Daniélou himself rendered the words of his imaginary interlocutor in the introduction to *Le Mystère de l'Avent* (1948),

Then why not allow that there are a certain number of religions in the world, which we will not say are all equally valuable, but which all suit different temperaments, races or countries? After all, you agree that men of good will can be saved, even outside the Christian framework, in non-Christian religions. What, then, can this transcendence of Christianity mean?[5]

By insisting that there was only one historical order, which was supernatural in character, Daniélou obliged himself to give a more detailed account of the relationship between 'cosmic' and 'Christian' revelation.

Perhaps the best way into Daniélou's account is by way of the distinction that he made between a 'chronological relationship' and a 'dramatic relationship' between Christianity and other religions:

In fact, the relation of Christianity to other religions is in part historical—that is to say, there is a 'chronological' relationship between Christianity and the other religions insofar as it represents the end and fulfillment of all the rest; but it is at the same time a dramatic relationship—that is to say, that if it is true that Christianity fulfills, it is also true that it destroys, so that, on the one hand, pagan religions find their flowering in it, yet on the other they die to give it place.[6]

Daniélou wanted to maintain both elements of the relationship: the chronological element, which implied that Christianity was the fulfilment of pagan religions, and the dramatic element, which meant that paganism and Christianity were fundamentally opposed.

Daniélou's emphasis was on the chronological element. He was intent on retaining the overall unity of the one supernatural history of salvation. So, he often pointed to biblical instances of 'holy pagans' as well as to biblical texts that allowed for knowledge of God outside the Christian faith. Melchizedek was, for Daniélou, a key example of a 'holy pagan', whose religion was based on God's revelation in providence.[7] When, in Genesis 14, Melchizedek met Abram, 'the religion of the natural universe came for the first time, by the guidance of the Holy Spirit, to greet the religion of the Bible at its start and do homage to it'.[8] Melchizedek, Daniélou maintained, was high priest of the cosmic covenant that

---

[5] Daniélou, *The Advent of Salvation: A Comparative Study of Non-Christian Religions and Christianity*, trans. Rosemary Sheed (New York: Paulist, 1962), 5.

[6] Ibid. 6–7.

[7] Ibid. 58–9. Daniélou expressed his disagreement with the traditionalist notion that a primitive explicit and linguistic revelation accounted for the truths remaining in pagan religions (ibid. 58; id., *God and the Ways of Knowing*, 12–13). Instead, he appealed to divine providence and the human moral conscience to explain such positive elements.

[8] Id., *Advent of Salvation*, 63.

God had made with Noah (Gen. 9).[9] And Melchizedek was not the sole representative of cosmic religion in the biblical account. He was joined by Abel, Enoch, Danel, Noah, Job, Lot, and the Queen of Sheba, all of whom had served God outside the covenants made with Moses and Christ.[10] Further, Daniélou argued that according to a number of New Testament passages, as well, one could know the only true God both through his providence and through the universal moral conscience. Daniélou pointed to the comments of St Paul in Acts 14: 14–17 and 17: 25–7, as well as in Romans 1: 19–21 and 2: 14–15. He also appealed to Hebrews 11: 3–6.[11] Regarding the comment in verse 6 that 'he that cometh to God must believe that he is, and that he is a rewarder of them that diligently seek him', Daniélou wrote:

This text is perhaps the most important in the whole of Sacred Scripture bearing upon the religious status of the pagan world. It affirms in effect that there is a possibility of salvation for every man and lays down what are the conditions of his salvation. These conditions resolve themselves into faith in the living God. That faith is accommodated to the level of each of the covenants. For the Christian it is faith in the perfect covenant, made by God with human nature in Jesus Christ. For the Jew who could not have known Jesus Christ it is faith in the covenant made by Yahweh with Abraham and Moses. For the pagan who could not have known either Jesus Christ or Abraham, it is faith in the covenant made by God with the Gentiles.[12]

In these comments, Daniélou articulated the relationship between the 'cosmic' or Noahic covenant and later biblical covenants. While the latter superseded the former chronologically, Daniélou affirmed that God's grace was also at work within pagan religions.

Reconnecting with a patristic idea, Daniélou maintained that God had appointed angels for each of the nations and that it was their task to protect and assist the nations and to lead them to God.[13] Convinced that the Fathers had rightly followed both Old Testament and Jewish apocalyptic literature, Daniélou commented: 'This is a very fertile doctrine from the missionary point of view. The heathens are not entirely deprived of aid: the angels of God assist them, trying to lead them to the true God, preparing the way of the Lord.'[14] Gentiles were guided by angels to a constructive use of providence and of their moral

---

[9] Ibid. 66. Cf. id., *Holy Pagans*, 104.

[10] Daniélou discussed these various individuals, as well as Melchizedek, in *Les Saints païens*. The figure of Danel is not the same as the Daniel known from the biblical book named after him but is rather the figure mentioned in Ezek. 14: 14, 20.

[11] Daniélou, *Advent of Salvation*, 59–60; id., *Holy Pagans*, 14–18, 45–6, 80; id., *God and the Ways of Knowing*, 14–16.

[12] Id., *Holy Pagans*, 45–6.

[13] Daniélou appealed to Irenaeus, Hippolytus, Clement of Alexandria, Origen, Eusebius, Basil of Caesarea, John Chrysostom, and Denys (*The Angels and their Mission: According to the Fathers of the Church*, trans. David Heimann (1957; repr. Notre Dame, Ind.: Ave Maria, 1987)), 14–23). Cf. id., *Advent of Salvation*, 95–9.

[14] Id., *Angels and their Mission*, 17.

conscience. Thus, they could come to know God as the Creator of the world, as a God who was faithful to his cosmic covenant, and as a judge whose holiness was incompatible with sin.[15]

Daniélou did not ignore, however, that in addition to the 'chronological' relationship, Christianity also had a 'dramatic' relationship to other religions. Whenever he affirmed the possibility of the knowledge of God through cosmic revelation or discussed the Old Testament examples and New Testament passages that supported this notion, Daniélou acknowledged the strong tendency of pagan religions to subvert this knowledge of God into idolatry. He maintained, for example, that 'this first revelation appears everywhere and without exception to have been corrupted'.[16] Evil human inclinations as well as demonic influences, the negative counterpart of the positive angelic guidance of the Gentiles, were to blame for this.[17] Thus, although Daniélou highlighted the continuity between pagan religions and the Christian faith, he did not disregard the idolatrous claims and practices of the former.

Daniélou's strong historical sense led him to insist that one could look to pagan religions and their representative 'saints' as 'forerunners' to God's definitive revelation in Christ.[18] St Irenaeus (d. *c*.202) was one of Daniélou's favourite Church Fathers because of the Bishop of Lyons's sense of history. Irenaeus had insisted that God led the human race to maturity by way of an educational programme that would be completed in stages.[19] Daniélou repeatedly appealed to Irenaeus to support his own view that paganism had served a historical role and had to give way, first to Judaism and then to Christianity, simply because its role as forerunner had been completed.[20] Both pagan religions and Judaism should give way to the Christian faith, now that their role had come to completion. Daniélou insisted that one could not simply classify pagan religions as false, because they played a divinely ordained role in preparing the way for the Christian faith. Non-Christian religions were 'not so much false as essentially incomplete, unfinished'.[21] A forerunner, whether it was Melchizedek or Buddha, would be true to his role only if he was willing to yield in the presence of a new

[15] Daniélou, *Holy Pagans*, 12–13.

[16] Id., 'The Conception of History in the Christian Tradition', *JR* 30 (1950), 178. For similar comments, see id., *The Salvation of the Nations*, trans. Angeline Bouchard (New York: Sheed & Ward, 1950), 23; id., *Angels and their Mission*, 21; id., *Holy Pagans*, 4. Cf. James M. Connolly, *The Voices of France: A Survey of Contemporary Theology in France* (New York: Macmillan, 1961), 141.

[17] Daniélou, *Advent of Salvation*, 99–100; id., *Angels and their Mission*, 22.

[18] Daniélou borrowed the notion of 'forerunner' from Romano Guardini's *Der Herr* (1937); English trans.: *The Lord*, trans. Elinor Castendyk Briefs (1954; repr. Washington, DC: Gateway/Regnery, 1996), 22–9. See id., *Advent of Salvation*, 62; id., 'Conception of History', 178.

[19] For expositions on Irenaeus and his theology of history, see Daniélou, 'Saint Irénée et les origines de la théologie de l'histoire', *RSR* 34 (1947), 227–31; id., *Christ and Us*, trans. Walter Roberts (New York: Sheed & Ward, 1961), 94–102; id., *A History of Early Christian Doctrine before the Council of Nicaea*, ii *Gospel Message and Hellenistic Culture*, ed. and trans. John Austin Baker (London: Darton, Longman & Todd, 1973), 166–83, 221–34.

[20] Id., *Advent of Salvation*, 9, 18; id., 'Conception of History', 173, 176.

[21] Id., *Advent of Salvation*, 18.

stage in history: 'A forerunner is a man sent by God to lay down the road for someone else. When that someone himself appears, then the forerunner's mission is done and he must give way.'[22] The temptation of forerunners, argued Daniélou, was to refuse to yield.[23] The result of such refusal would inevitably be the 'dramatic' relationship of opposition between Christianity and pagan religions. Christianity was a category so unique, Daniélou argued, that, strictly speaking, it would be wrong to classify it as a religion among other religions. 'Too many people nowadays', he maintained, 'set Christianity on the same plane as "the religions", but it is not a religion amongst religions. It is a revelation and a phenomenon with which men of all religions are confronted.'[24]

For Daniélou, the relationship between cosmic and Christian revelation was similar to that between Old Testament type and New Testament antitype.[25] Both his understanding of biblical interpretation and his view of world religions were based on history. Just as in biblical interpretation he refused to ignore the specificity and constructive role of the historical Old Testament types, so he also insisted on the positive function of cosmic revelation within the one history of salvation. As a result, Daniélou was able to argue for the absolute and unique character of God's revelation in Christ while at the same time acknowledging the many similarities between pagan religion and Christianity.[26] Thus, we could say that his analogical sacramental view of typological interpretation also ruled his understanding of religion. Daniélou combined a 'chronological' relationship of continuity (or similarity) between cosmic and Christian revelation with a 'dramatic' relationship of discontinuity (or dissimilarity). It is true that Daniélou often accentuated similarity, which could at times give the impression of blurring the distinction between pagan religions and Christianity. But this was mitigated by the fact that in Daniélou's sacramental ontology both 'type' and 'cosmic revelation' functioned as historical forerunners to the reality that came with Christ and the Church. As a result, Daniélou's understanding of analogical sacramentality did justice to both similarity and dissimilarity.

The Two Cities

Daniélou's acknowledgement of similarity as well as dissimilarity was evident also in his articulation of the relationship between profane and sacred history. Just as a

---

[22] Ibid. 62.
[23] Ibid.; id., 'Conception of History', 178; id., *God and the Ways of Knowing*, 17.
[24] Id., *Holy Pagans*, 9. This distinction between 'religion' and 'revelation' did not stop Daniélou from routinely using the word 'religion' to designate also the Christian faith.
[25] Daniélou made the link explicit in 'Conception of History', 173.
[26] Daniélou saw the similarities especially in the symbols of water and sacred meal in the sacraments of Baptism and Eucharist (*Advent of Salvation*, 66–70). As in connection with spiritual interpretation, so in his discussion of world religions, Daniélou appealed to the work of Mircea Eliade on the role of symbolism in pagan religions (*God and the Ways of Knowing*, 17–33). Cf. Chap. 5, sect.: Typology and Christian Symbolism.

biblical antitype was already present within its type, and just as the true God was already worshipped by 'holy pagans', so Daniélou's theological disposition inclined him to stress the mutual penetration of sacred and profane history:

If we are to have an effective grasp of the whole problem, we must recognize a two-fold relationship between Christianity and history. On the one hand, Christianity falls within history. It emerged at a given point in the sequence of historical eventuation. It provides a constituent part of the fabric of recorded facts. To this extent, it belongs to the historian's province to describe its appearance in the chronicle of documented reality. But on the other hand, history falls within Christianity: all secular history is included in sacred history, as a part, a prolegomenon, a preparatory introduction. Profane history covers the whole period of this world's existence, but Christianity is essentially the next world itself, present here and now in a mystery.[27]

For Daniélou, there was a mutual penetration of Christianity and history: on the one hand, Christianity was part of history; on the other hand, history was included within Christianity.

If the supernatural reality of the Christian faith meant to Daniélou that historical developments could never be strictly autonomous, it also implied a strong relativizing of secular history, since its significance paled in comparison to sacred history. The centrality of the deliverance theme in Baptism and in its typological foreshadowing prompted Daniélou to maintain that God, rather than man, established the kingdom. There were forms of slavery worse than economic bondage,[28] and Baptism rather than economic justice brought about true deliverance.[29] Thus, Daniélou suggested: 'If anything is certain about the Christian view of economic and political values, it is that these are entirely relative. To treat them as absolute is a form of idolatry.'[30] Sacred history clearly was primary for Daniélou, and it served as the norm by which all profane historical developments were to be measured.

In this regard, the philosopher, Jacques Maritain (1882–1973), had a strong impact on Daniélou. Daniélou explained that in his *Primauté du spirituel* (1927), Maritain 'stated that politics must remain subordinated to the spiritual ends of man, that the rationality of the state is not the ultimate rationality. He made an appeal for the contemplative life and expressed the notion that the politicians that the world was going to need would be mystics, inspired by a profound sense of humanity'.[31] This emphasis on the ultimate value of the contemplative life fit hand in glove with Daniélou's sacramental understanding of history. While

---

[27] Daniélou, *The Lord of History: Reflections on the Inner Meaning of History*, trans. Nigel Abercrombie (1958; repr. Cleveland, Ohio: Meridian, 1968), 24. For some broad-ranging reflections on Daniélou's *Essai sur le mystère de l'histoire*, see Eric John, 'Daniélou on History', *DownR* 72/ 227 (1953), 2–15.

[28] Daniélou, *Lord of History*, 81, 83.

[29] Ibid. 83–4.

[30] Ibid. 100.

[31] Daniélou, *Et qui est mon prochain? Mémoires* (Paris: Stock, 1974), 65.

secular history and political involvement were to be valued, in Daniélou's mind they were always directed towards their greater, supernatural end.[32]

Sometimes Daniélou's desire to safeguard the priority of the Church's sacraments and his apprehension of secularizing developments within Catholicism caused him to separate secular and sacred history, and thus nature and the supernatural. He rejected 'providential' historiography—attempts like those of Eusebius of Caesarea (*c.*263–*c.*339) and Jacques-Bénigne Bossuet (1627–1704) to interpret the rise of empires in the light of revelation—and insisted that the growth of empires, as well as social and economic developments, were 'unrelated' to the kingdom of God and had 'no effect' on the latter: 'Thus profane history and sacred history appear to be perfectly independent of each other; at all events we cannot establish any relationship between them. Our knowledge of them derives from two incommensurable sources, since profane history is known by research, *historia* in its ancient meaning, while sacred history is only known by faith.'[33] This separation between secular and sacred history was not, however, characteristic of Daniélou's overall approach. Generally, he regarded the realities of secular history as fundamentally positive, while insisting that it ought not to take on complete autonomy in its relation to sacred history. Secular history served the supernatural end of sacred history. Sacred history, therefore, carried the greater weight.

Daniélou's belief that Christianity found its place within history convinced him of the need for an 'Incarnation' of the Christian faith, which he believed was of importance particularly in missionary contexts. He reflected on this theme in his 1946 book *Le Mystère du salut des nations*, in a chapter entitled 'Incarnation et transfiguration'. Daniélou rejected the 'error of certain missionaries to want to take their civilizations along with them', and he insisted that ecclesial use of the Latin language posed 'a serious problem'.[34] As the chapter title indicated, Daniélou was not simply concerned with the need to incarnate the Christian faith in today's social and cultural context, however important that might be. Instead, Christianity's penetration of its surroundings served a more ultimate purpose—namely, that of the transfiguration and deification of the world. Thus, Daniélou maintained that

---

[32] Cf. id., *Culture et mystère* (Brussels: Éditions universitaires, 1948), 35: 'History thus becomes the visible and progressive arrival [*traduction*] of a unique and invisible reality: the same mystery that is prefigured in the types of the Old Law and realized in the historical Christ subsists sacramentally in the Church and mystically in individual souls, while the forms of this mystery in turn prepare and prefigure the final fulfillment.'

[33] Id., *Lord of History*, 105. Daniélou's comments about the incommensurability of profane and sacred history occur in a discussion of Herbert Butterfield's and Karl Löwith's philosophies of history. Daniélou did add the cautionary comment that 'they both go rather too far in the direction of pessimism when they make an impassable gulf between sacred and profane history' (ibid. 106). Cf. id., 'Has History a Meaning?' *The Month*, 6 (1951), 44.

[34] Id., *Salvation of the Nations*, 58.

we must not forget that this [penetration of the real world] is merely the first step, that we must turn towards the world only in order to turn the world towards Christ, and that the Incarnation is the first stage of a process that is to reach fulfilment in the Transfiguration, that is, in the penetration of the world by the light of Christ.[35]

This 'Incarnation' of Christianity meant that for Daniélou technological advances could not be regarded as 'indifferent, or even diabolically hostile' to the kingdom of God.[36] In principle, one had to regard technology as something positive.[37] At the same time, Daniélou was ever conscious of the ambiguous character of technology, convinced that one of the greatest challenges of the modern age was to maintain (or, perhaps, to restore) the life of prayer and a sense of the sacred character of reality. The contemporary focus on the 'profane world' and its understanding of technological progress as separate from religion and the life of prayer was seriously problematic: '[I]f we accept a complete dissociation of the sacred and the profane worlds, we shall make access to prayer absolutely impossible to the mass of mankind.'[38] Our 'tragedy', insisted Daniélou, was that the bridges between technology and the sacred had been cut.[39] To overcome the separation between technology and the sacred, Daniélou pointed to the mediating role of art. Since art was tied both to technical change and to religious imagination it could position itself at the 'frontier' between technology and the sacred: 'While the artist as such is neither physicist nor metaphysicist, without him physics cannot lead to metaphysics.'[40] Daniélou looked to art as a bridge between technology and the sacred. If one would use art in this way, technology could serve as an example of an appropriate 'Incarnation' of the Christian faith.

St Augustine's reflections on the City of God served for Daniélou as a helpful example of a call for 'Incarnation' and 'Transfiguration'. For Augustine, 'the earthly city can be assimilated and taken up into the history of salvation', since '[n]o autonomous secular order can exist as part of God's ordinance without integration in the order of Christ and His Church'.[41] Christianity's place within history meant that the Church could not simply retreat from her responsibilities in the world. The Church had an interest in temporal society, 'for that also is subject to the law of God of which the Church is the interpreter'.[42] The integration of secular into sacred history meant, according to Daniélou, that

[35] Daniélou, *Salvation of the Nations*, 49–50. See further, id., *Lord of History*, 34–45; see esp. pp. 24, 35, 43–4 for the language of 'Incarnation'.

[36] Id., *Lord of History*, 30.

[37] Id., *Prayer as a Political Problem*, ed. and trans. J. R. Kirwan (New York: Sheed & Ward, 1967), 57–8.

[38] Ibid. 35. Cf. ibid. 72.

[39] Ibid. 71.

[40] Ibid.

[41] Id., *Lord of History*, 32.

[42] Id., *Prayer as a Political Problem*, 44. Cf. ibid. 119–20: 'Of course, there is a distinction of powers, and this world is not subject directly to the authority of the Church. But to say that this world is not directly subject to the Church's authority is not to say that it is not subject to the law of God, of which the *magisterium* of the Church is the interpreter.'

the state had a responsibility with regard to religion. Since religion, whether Christian or otherwise, was part of the 'temporal common good', it was the state's duty positively to recognize religious institutions.[43] A desacralized world, in which religion did not contribute in a positive way to civil society, would be 'inhuman'.[44] There would always be 'Christendoms' of one sort or another, because 'secular history is taken up and assimilated into sacred history'.[45] Just like secular and sacred history should not be separated, so a complete disjunction of Church and state would, according to Daniélou, be fatal for society as a whole. And state support was not only a moral obligation; it was also a practical necessity for the Church. Without political support, Daniélou did not believe Christianity would be able to function in the long run.[46] In short, Daniélou could not possibly regard Christendoms, the natural outcome of the incarnational principle, as problematic in and of themselves: '[C]ivilizations can also submit to God's law'.[47]

At the same time, Daniélou was aware of the danger that the Church might be co-opted by the earthly city.[48] After all, he refused to regard the temporal order as ultimate, and in line with his prioritizing of 'sacred history' Daniélou believed that the Church was the 'true society'.[49] Despite the positive role of successive Christendoms, they constituted 'only the outer garment', and the Church's primary task was not to 'humanize civilization'.[50] In his memoirs, Daniélou repeatedly expressed his apprehension about reducing Christianity to a force for social or political change, a tendency he believed had become all too common after the Second Vatican Council. In this context, he reiterated (not quite consistent with his overall sacramental ontology) that the spiritual and political domains were 'absolutely distinct'.[51] Beginning in the 1960s, Daniélou became

[43] Ibid. 18–21.

[44] Ibid. 22, 27, 83, 112.

[45] Id., *Lord of History,* 94. In similar vein, Daniélou expressed his appreciation for La Pira, Mayor of Florence, who had taught him not 'to separate the political domain from the moral domain' (*Et qui est mon prochain?* 171). In this context, Daniélou insisted: 'There is no civilization worthy of its name if the religious dimension is not visible in various forms, that of a mosque, a synagogue, a pagoda, or a cathedral' (ibid. 173–4).

[46] Id., *Prayer as a Political Problem,* 15.

[47] Id., 'Conception of History', 176.

[48] Daniélou expressed his concern also about the worker–priest movement: 'I regret to see the action of many priests turning aside from that [spiritual] finality to move into the social, political, and cultural domain, which does not directly result from their mission' (*Et qui est mon prochain?* 116; cf. ibid. 121–3, 193).

[49] Id., 'Conception of History', 177.

[50] Ibid.

[51] Id., *Et qui est mon prochain?* 40. This kind of comment obviated a sacramental understanding of history and lapsed into the dual problems of immanentism and extrinsicism that *nouvelle théologie* opposed. We need to keep in mind, however, the context in which Daniélou made his suggestions regarding a separation between the kingdom of God and the social, economic, and political domains. Each time, such comments served to underscore his belief that the Christian faith did not serve political or economic ends, as if they were more ultimate, but that instead it was the sacramental life of the Church that was central to God's activity on the world stage.

more and more wary of the privatizing of the Christian faith, which he saw as the outcome of the 'secularizing' and 'desacralizing' aspects of modernity.[52] This caused a certain tension in his thinking: while he mostly saw the need for an 'Incarnation' of the Christian faith in its historical context, at times he seemed to separate the spiritual and political domains. Despite this tension, Daniélou's overriding concern remained clear. He was convinced that when Christians served in the political or economic areas of life they were not subverting the faith into a crutch that served other, temporal ends; such activities were quite compatible with maintaining the primacy of the supernatural. For Daniélou, such 'incarnational' service aimed at the transfiguration of the world.

The centrality of historical categories in Daniélou's theology makes him a typical representative of *nouvelle théologie*. Our study of Daniélou also reveals why it is that the *nouvelle* theologians believed they could place such emphasis on the vicissitudes of history without endangering their sacramental ontology. For Daniélou, the fact that Christianity was a historical faith implied that it could integrate pagan religions into an overall sacramental vision of history. This vision did justice both to the similarities and to the great dissimilarity between paganism and the Christian faith. Daniélou's sacramental ontology caused him to argue for a mutual interpenetration between secular and sacred history, as well as earthly and heavenly cities. While Daniélou maintained the primacy of sacred history and of the heavenly city, his principle of the Incarnation meant that nature and the supernatural remained inseparable. For Daniélou, the light of Christ was meant to transform the world. Incarnation was meant for Transfiguration.

DEVELOPMENT OF DOCTRINE: FROM LOGICAL SYLLOGISM TO CHRISTOLOGICAL MYSTERY

Logical Theories of Development

Daniélou was not alone in turning history into a central category. All the *nouvelle* theologians were concerned to recover it. The notion of a *ressourcement* of the Church Fathers and the medieval tradition was based on the acknowledgement that historical considerations determined, at least in part, one's theological approach and position. So far, I have made the case that the historical embodiment of theological truth expressed a sacramental ontology that would enable the reintegration of nature and the supernatural—of history and theology. This reintegration had consequences for the way in which the *nouvelle* theologians approached the discipline of theology. Also here, they initiated a radical departure from neo-scholasticism. First, since the *nouvelle* theologians were convinced that

---

[52] This was the burden of Daniélou's argument in *L'Oraison, problème politique*. Cf. id., *Et qui est mon prochain?* 137, 174.

the truths of faith could be recognized only with 'eyes of faith' (Pierre Rousselot), they displayed a great deal more hesitancy than scholasticism in the use of logical arguments based on truths derived from nature rather than from revelation. Theology was not so much an attempt to arrive at conclusions by combining revealed and natural premises into syllogistic arguments. For the *ressourcement* scholars, theology was meant to be practised within the Church on the basis of the experience of faith. They believed that the dialectical argumentation of neo-scholasticism ignored the fact that the riches of Christian experience could not be expressed within the limited confines of dialectical argumentation. Second, since the *nouvelle* theologians' more experientially based approach to theology made them look with suspicion upon attempts to reach theological conclusions by means of rationally tight arguments, they could not accept that development of doctrine was a matter of building logical arguments leading to new theological insights. Such logical argumentation excluded the Spirit-guided development of faith experience from the contents of Christian doctrine. *Nouvelle théologie*'s approach to doctrinal development, therefore, wanted to take the historical character of truth seriously. To account for new doctrinal insights of the Church, one should look not to intellectual arguments but to the Spirit-guided sense of faith (*sensus fidei*) in history.

Daniélou never discussed these issues of the nature of theology and of development of doctrine in any detail.[53] Others, however, did. In 1924, Marie-Dominique Chenu published an essay on the development of doctrine in St Thomas Aquinas.[54] The nature of theology and the development of doctrine were also at stake in the controversy surrounding Louis Charlier and René Draguet in the late 1930s and early 1940s and in the debates, immediately thereafter, surrounding Henri Bouillard's dissertation on Thomas Aquinas.[55] And in 1948 de Lubac set out to discuss the problem of doctrinal development, sharply critiquing the neo-Thomist theologian Charles Boyer.[56]

[53] On one occasion, when Daniélou did broach the topic of doctrinal development, he commented: 'We have seen that progression is one of the characteristics of the Christian vision. Do we find this progress in church history? This question applies particularly to the progress of dogma. Clearly the object of the Revelation is immutable, and it is not a question of evolution in the modernist sense. But the development of dogma is something else. It consists in this: that, under the guidance of the Holy Spirit living in the church, certain aspects of the Revelation not explicitly expressed in the Scripture are defined by the church. These definitions of dogma, as Karl Thieme saw it, are like historical events, for they do not proceed only from the reasoning of the theologians or even from the conscience of the church, but they correspond to historical conjectures; they mark the great articulations in the life of the church. For Moehler and Newman this development is one of the characteristics of present sacred history' ('The Conception of History in the Christian Tradition', *JR* 30 (1950), 175).

[54] Chenu, 'La Raison psychologique du développement du dogme d'après Saint Thomas', *RSPT* 13 (1924), 44–51.

[55] For the historical background to these controversies, see Chap. 1, sects: Controversy over the Nature of Theology (1937–42); and Controversy over *Ressourcement* (1944–50). For Bouillard's views, see Chap. 3, sect.: Henri Bouillard: Analogy and Sacramental Ontology.

[56] De Lubac, 'Le Problème du développement du dogme', *RSR* 35 (1948), 130–60; English trans.: 'The Problem of the Development of Dogma', in *Theology in History*, trans. Anne Englund Nash (San Francisco, Calif.: Ignatius, 1996), 248–80.

Chenu, Charlier, Draguet, and de Lubac were all reacting against the scholastic approaches to doctrinal development that had become dominant since the Leonine revival of Thomism. Johann Baptist Franzelin (1816–86) was one of the most influential neo-Thomist theologians of the time, and he sketched a strictly logical view of the development of doctrine.[57] Franzelin was convinced that revelation had ceased with the death of the last apostles.[58] The fullness of divine truth revealed to the apostles implied, for Franzelin, that God had provided them with explicit knowledge of whatever doctrine the Church would later define. After the death of the apostles, much of this doctrine had been obscured, because the apostles had taught these truths only implicitly. Thus, the later development of doctrine was a slow, but sure, recovery of the teachings that the apostles had known explicitly, but that the Church as a whole now had to re-appropriate subjectively over time. This recovery of the full apostolic doctrine was, according to Franzelin, a purely logical or syllogistic process. Franzelin was careful to exclude non-revealed truths from this logical process of doctrinal development. Conclusions of 'illative' arguments—those in which natural premises (those known by reason apart from biblical revelation) influenced the material contents of the conclusion—were only 'virtually revealed' and as such could not be used to establish Christian dogma. For Franzelin, the only truths the Church could define as dogma were those that had been formally revealed. Only conclusions of 'explicative' arguments could be used to arrive at dogmatic definitions.[59]

Franzelin's scholastic distinctions served as powerful weapons in the anti-Modernist arsenal around the turn of the twentieth century. The next generation of scholastic theologians, however, were forced to consider whether Franzelin's position could adequately account for the actual developments that had taken place in Catholic doctrine, particularly the definitions of the Immaculate Conception (1854) and of papal infallibility (1870). Ambroise Gardeil (1859–1931) and Francisco Marín-Sola (1873–1932) were not convinced that one could reasonably maintain that these doctrines had been formally revealed in Scripture, even if only implicitly. While Franzelin's position was able to account for the unchangeable character of Christian dogma, it was not so clear that his theory fit the actual historical developments. Or, as Jan Walgrave puts it, 'With the best will in the world it seems impossible to fit the facts into the theory except by frankly Procrustean proceedings'.[60] As a result, Gardeil and Marín-Sola, while

---

[57] Johann Baptist Franzelin, *Tractatus de divina traditione et scriptura* (Rome: Collegio Romano, 1860–4); id., *Tractatus de Deo uno secundum naturam* (Rome: Taurini, 1870). For Franzelin, see Peter Walter, *Johann Baptist Franzelin (1816–1886): Jesuit, Theologe, Kardinal: Ein Lebensbild* (Bozen: Athesia, 1987).

[58] For my description of Franzelin's position, I rely on Gezinus Evert Meuleman, *De ontwikkeling van het dogma in de Rooms Katholieke theologie* (Kampen: Kok, 1951), 31–4.

[59] Franzelin did allow for the use of non-revealed premises in 'explicative' arguments, as long as these premises did not add materially to the revealed premise. See Meuleman, *De ontwikkeling van het dogma*, 33.

[60] Jan Hendrik Walgrave, *Unfolding Revelation: The Nature of Doctrinal Development* (Philadelphia, Pa.: Hutchinson, 1972), 166. Walgrave's comment refers to Reginald Maria Schultes, whose theory was closely patterned on that of Franzelin.

remaining firmly ensconced within the scholastic camp, attempted to create more room for the subjective elements in the process of doctrinal development and for the contribution of truths that had only been 'virtually revealed'.

Gardeil, the Dominican theologian from Le Saulchoir, confronted the anti-dogmatic character of the Modernists, in particular George Tyrrell's identification of revelation and experience.[61] On the basis of this identification, Tyrrell regarded doctrinal development as the evolution of symbolic structures that referred to subjective experiences. These underlying experiences were unaffected by the changing symbolic structures and thus remained constant.[62] In reaction to this position, Gardeil maintained the human ability to make absolute affirmations with regard to external realities.[63] And, insistent as he was on the role of the intellect, Gardeil was hesitant to subscribe to the organic understanding of development as Johann Adam Möhler had articulated it.[64] Gardeil compared dogmatic development to the development of scientific theories. Just as in scientific progress, so in the development of dogma, true development resulted from communal collaboration; and just as in scientific progress the object of the investigation did not change, so in doctrinal development the object of faith remained identical. In Christian doctrine, God was the object, and the Church arrived at dogmatic pronouncements with the definitive aid of the magisterium.[65] This comparison between science and doctrine created room for the initial, global intuition of faith, with which theological reflection was supposed cohere.[66] Doctrinal development could not be restricted to that which had been formally revealed, as Franzelin and others had erroneously maintained. Theological conclusions could play a role in the process of dogmatic development only if they were echoed in the living faith of the Church, which is to say, the social charism of the consent of the faithful (*consensus fidelium*).[67] Thus, Gardeil attempted to make room for the Spirit-guided, subjective element of the intuitive grasp of revelation, charting a course between the logical approach of the neo-scholastics and the organic approach of the Tübingen school.

Gardeil's student, Marín-Sola, likewise went beyond Franzelin's position.[68] He agreed with the common neo-Thomist view that the apostles had possessed explicit knowledge of whatever was formally included in divine revelation.

---

[61] Ambroise Gardeil, 'La Notion du lieu théologique', *RSPT* 2 (1908), 51–73, 246–76, 484–505; id., *Le Donné révélé et la théologie* (Paris: Lecoffre, 1910).

[62] Cf. Chap. 1, sect.: Modernism's Non-sacramental Mindset.

[63] Cf. Aidan Nichols, *From Newman to Congar: The Idea of Doctrinal Development from the Victorians to the Second Vatican Council* (Edinburgh: T. & T. Clark, 1990), 161–3.

[64] Ibid. 170–1.

[65] Ibid. 172.

[66] Ibid. 173–4.

[67] Meuleman, *De ontwikkeling van het dogma*, 39; Paul Gerard Crowley, 'Dogmatic Development after Newman: The Search for a Hermeneutical Principle in Newman, Marin-Sola, Rahner and Gadamer' (PhD diss., Graduate Theological Union, 1984), 110.

[68] Francisco Marín-Sola, *La evolución homogénea del dogma católico* (Madrid: La ciencia tomista, 1923). French trans: *L'Évolution homogène du dogme catholique*, 2 vols (2nd edn, Fribourg: St-Paul, 1924).

Dogmatic development could thus never go beyond the explicit knowledge of the apostles. Marín-Sola was aware, however, of the difficulties that Franzelin and others faced in explaining the logical connection between apostolic revelation and later dogmatic developments. Thus, he argued that in addition to formally revealed truth, also virtually revealed truth could become ecclesial dogma. This gave much greater scope to the use of natural premises than Franzelin had seen fit. As Nichols puts it: the 'magisterium works on the human formulae bequeathed by the apostles, formulae which are, according to Marín-Sola, "full of virtuality", jam-packed with latent meaning just waiting to be expressed'.[69] Marín-Sola insisted on a rational link between apostolic deposit and the truths virtually implicit in it. Since the latter were materially affected by natural premises, Marín-Sola believed there was a rational metaphysical connection between the initial deposit and the virtually implicit truths of revelation that did not come out into the open until later, in the course of doctrinal development. Although such virtually implicit truths could be expressed only by new concepts, Marín-Sola maintained that these later concepts did not add objectively new contents. Thus, he was able to walk a fine line. In one sense, he remained in continuity with the scholastic tradition, since he maintained that 'only those theological arguments are legitimate where the conclusion is entirely included in revelation'.[70] In other ways, however, he went beyond the scholastic tradition. His use of the concept of virtual revelation allowed for the greater conceptual developments that had obviously taken place over time and that were difficult to account for with the logical approach of the neo-Thomists.[71] Moreover, Marín-Sola added a subjective element by speaking of an experiential method (*via affectiva*) in addition to a speculative method (*via speculativa*). Since love directed the intellect towards its divine object, the believer had the infused capacity to discern that which was truly revealed.[72] In the end, Marín-Sola believed that it was the magisterium—

For discussion on Marín-Sola's position, see Meuleman, *De ontwikkeling van het dogma*, 39–47; Herbert Hammans, *Die neueren katholischen Erklärungen der Dogmenentwicklung* (Essen: Ludgerus, 1965), 135–63; Walgrave, *Unfolding Revelation*, 168–78; Crowley, 'Dogmatic Development, 85–130; Nichols, *From Newman to Congar*, 178–83.

69 Nichols, *From Newman to Congar*, 180.

70 Meuleman, *De ontwikkeling van het dogma*, 41.

71 Crowley helpfully outlines the four kinds of truths that Marín-Sola distinguished: (1) formally explicit truths were those that the apostles and prophets had directly entrusted to the Church; (2) formally implicit truths simply restated this revelatory contents in nominally different terms; (3) virtually implicit truths used non-revealed premises to draw conclusions, thereby allowing for conceptual development of doctrine; and (4) virtually non-implicit propositions included conceptual additions to revelation, thereby changing the actual meaning of the revealed formulas ('Dogmatic Development', 105–6).

72 Marín-Sola argued that the *via affectiva* verified the homogeneity of logical development and that it allowed the faithful initially to discern the truth of revelation. He none the less tended to reduce the affective sense of faith (*sensus fidei*) to logical argumentation, since only the latter was decisive. As Crowley puts it, 'Hence, dogmatic development must occur primarily by means of theological reasoning, for the affective life of faith arrives at nothing that cannot be demonstrated by speculative theology to be contained in the sources of revelation and in the defined formulas of faith' ('Dogmatic Development', 121). Marín-Sola's teacher, Gardeil, had been more open to the role of subjective elements like the *sensus ecclesiae*.

not theological argument or the believer's intuition—that determined whether or not a particular theological notion was included in the deposit of faith.[73]

Marie-Dominique Chenu: Development and the Theandric Mystery

The *nouvelle* theologians were uncomfortable with the neo-scholastic use of logical argumentation to protect the historical continuity of revealed truth. And, as we will see from the writings of Chenu, Charlier, and de Lubac, they all attempted to replace the logical method with a theological one, which relied, at least in part, on the approach of the nineteenth-century Tübingen theologian, Möhler.[74] This discomfort with the logical approach was first expressed in Chenu's 1924 essay on development. The essay took the form of an extensive review of a recent publication by Reginald Maria Schultes (1873–1928) on the development of doctrine, entitled *Introductio in historiam dogmatum* (1922).[75] One might expect Chenu to have sharply opposed Schultes' understanding of doctrinal development, considering the Dominican scholar from the Angelicum in Rome subscribed to Franzelin's neo-Thomist approach.[76] Instead, Chenu praised Schultes' book as 'truly an in-depth work, original and new, a little demanding in appearance and reception, but packed with stuff'.[77] The closest Chenu came to any criticism was in the final words of his essay, where he wrote that it was 'thanks to this investigation and analysis [of Schultes] that it has been possible in this article to relocate the true value of article 2 of IIa IIae Q. 1, somewhat forgotten by Fr Schultes, and to see here the psychological ground of the development of dogmatic formulas'.[78] Overall, Chenu seemed to be quite taken with Schultes' work.

Chenu's positive comments could not, however, hide the fact that his own approach was radically different from that of Schultes. Chenu's reference to one of the articles of the *Summa Theologica*, which had been 'somewhat forgotten' by Schultes, concerned a key question St Thomas had raised: 'Whether the Object of Faith is Something Complex by Way of a Proposition?'[79] In his discussion of

---

[73] Meuleman, *De ontwikkeling van het dogma*, 45–6; Crowley, 'Dogmatic Development', 122–4.

[74] Walgrave describes the logical and theological approaches to doctrinal development as follows: 'A theory of development is called "logical" because according to it the process of development is simply described in terms of logical inference and the criterion of its truth is the logical test, whereas the qualification *theological* means that the process is conceived of as partaking of the character of mystery that is proper to the object of theology, and that the criterion of its truth does not properly consist in a logical verification but in a charismatic decision accepted by faith' (*Unfolding Revelation*, 165).

[75] Chenu, 'La Raison psychologique'. Cf. Reginald Maria Schultes, *Introductio in historiam dogmatum: Praelectiones habitae in Collegio pontificio 'Angelico' de Urbe, 1911–1922* (Paris: Lethielleux, 1922). For Schultes' views on doctrinal development, see Meuleman, *De ontwikkeling van het dogma*, 34–6; Hammans, *Die neueren katholischen Erklärungen*, 121–8; Walgrave, *Unfolding Revelation*, 165–7.

[76] Cf. Meuleman, *De ontwikkeling van het dogma*, 34–6; Walgrave, *Unfolding Revelation*, 165–7.

[77] Chenu, 'La Raison psychologique', 44.

[78] Ibid. 51.

[79] *ST* II-II Q. 1, art. 2 ('Utrum objectum fidei sit aliquid complexum per modum enuntiabilis'). Cf. Chenu, 'La Raison psychologique', 46.

this question, Chenu explained that the psychological termination of the assent of faith was 'not a concept, a simple perception of a simple thing by way of simple intelligence [*per modum simplicis intelligentiae*] but a judgment, an operation by which the intellect synthesizes [*operatio qua intellectus componit*], a proposition'.[80] As a result, Chenu insisted that 'the act of the believer cannot free itself of the infirm complexity of human knowledge: it synthesizes and analyzes [*componit et dividit*]'.[81] Thus, Chenu explained that while dogma was indeed transcendent as object and infallible as proposition it could only ever be presented as a 'human statement' (*énontiable humain*).[82] Chenu quoted one of his favourite statements of the Angelic Doctor: 'The thing known is in the knower according to the mode of the knower.'[83] Whereas the object of faith itself was indeed simple, the human 'mode of the knower' (*modum cognoscentis*) meant that one could know the divine object of faith only by way of complex propositions.

This meant, according to Chenu, that one must take the historical development of human truth claims—including dogma—entirely seriously:

The knowledge of faith, which because of its human character is complex in nature, will thus, for the same reason, be progressive, through formulations more and more distinct, more and more 'explicit', through formulas more developed along with their successive refinements— this, moreover, without detracting either from the unity and immutability of the faith or from its 'reality'—because the act of the believer does not terminate in a proposition, but in a thing [*actus credentis non terminatur ad enuntiabile, sed ad rem*] (ad 2).[84]

For Chenu, complexity and simplicity, plurality and immutability, were in no way opposed to each other. One would expect to encounter 'varying formulas' throughout the ages, since 'dogma has a history because it is subject to the progress (homogeneous and infallible through the assistance of the Holy Spirit) of the human expression'.[85]

Chenu appealed to the analogy between doctrinal and scientific developments, which Ambroise Gardeil, his predecessor at Le Saulchoir, had used to explain the development of dogma. Expanding upon Gardeil's understanding, Chenu insisted: 'In reality, we should not speak of a simple analogy but of the same *principle* and of the *psychological ground* of the evolution, of the explication of dogmas: dogma develops because it really and truly presents itself as a human affirmation, of which it has the structure and dynamism.'[86] For Chenu, doctrinal development was subject to the same conditions as knowledge acquired in any

---

[80] Chenu, 'La Raison psychologique', 46.   [81] Ibid.   [82] Ibid.
[83] 'Cognita sunt in cognoscente secundum modum cognoscentis' (*ST* II-II Q. 1, art. 2). Chenu, 'La Raison psychologique', 46.
[84] Chenu, 'La Raison psychologique', 46.
[85] Ibid. 47.
[86] Ibid. 48–9. Cf. Mark Schoof, *A Survey of Catholic Theology 1800–1970*, trans. N. D. Smith (Paramus, NJ: Paulist Newman, 1970), 196.

other area. Doctrinal development escaped these human conditions only at the moment when the magisterium infallibly defined dogmas, according to Chenu. Any other attempt to restrict the development of doctrine in the name of the immutable object of faith seemed to him a wrongheaded confusion between the simple object of faith and the human mode of knowing.

Interestingly, in his essay, Chenu completely bypassed the scholastic distinctions that had been common in the commentatorial tradition. Chenu based the development of doctrine on the Thomist notion that knowledge comes only in the 'mode of the knower', and in doing so he ignored all questions as to how or by what criteria this development took place. Apart from his comment that the Holy Spirit guaranteed the homogeneity and infallibility of dogma, Chenu did not address issues such as whether continuity was guaranteed by logical or organic categories or what exactly the role of the magisterium might be.

When Chenu returned to the issue of doctrinal development a little over a decade later, he did go into more detail. In the third chapter of his controversial book *Une école de théologie: Le Saulchoir* (1937), he addressed the character of theology and, by way of corollary, the nature of the development of doctrine.[87] Again, Chenu emphasized what he had earlier called the 'psychological ground' of development, since he remained convinced that knowledge was possible only according to the mode of the knower (*modum cognoscentis*).[88] He was determined to uphold the tension between theology as reflection in faith on the 'revealed deposit' (*donné révélé*) and the scientific and intellectual character of the discipline. In doing so, he based doctrinal development on the sacramental ontology that characterized his overall theological approach.

Chenu's anti-intellectualism was markedly evident in his discussion of theology, especially in his appeals to the theologians of the Tübingen school. Chenu reiterated that theology had a legitimate place only within the context of faith and of the Church. He quoted Tübingen theologian Johann Evangelist Kuhn: 'No theology without new birth'.[89] Accordingly, Chenu emphasized that the Tradition did not exist to provide exterior 'proofs' for the truth of certain doctrines. Chenu echoed Möhler by holding the contrary position that Tradition was

proof in the sense that it is the permanent Christian conscience in the Church and serves as criterion to judge all renewal [*innovation*]. Not just a certain number of things to believe [*credenda*] according to an empirical and static conception of *loci*, but the presence of the Spirit in the social body of the Church, divine and human in Christ. Not just conservation of refined doctrines, of obtained results, or of decisions made in the past; but

---

[87] See Chenu, *Une école de théologie: Le Saulchoir*, with contributions by Giuseppe Alberigo, Étienne Fouilloux, Jean-Pierre Jossua, and Jean Ladrière (Paris: Cerf, 1985), 129–50.

[88] Ibid. 136–7.

[89] Ibid. 136. Chenu also used this quotation as an epigraph above his essay 'Position de la théologie', *RSPT* 24 (1935), 232–57; English trans.: 'What is Theology?' in *Faith and Theology*, trans. Denis Hickey (New York: Macmillan, 1968), 15–35.

chief creator of intelligibility and inexhaustible source of new life. The Tradition is not an aggregate of traditions, but a principle of organic continuity, of which the magisterium is the infallible instrument, in the theandric reality of the Church, the mystical body of Christ.[90]

Chenu's appeal to the Tübingen approach to Tradition was meant to counter the intellectualist understanding of theology and the logical view of development that characterized neo-scholasticism. For Chenu, neo-scholasticism failed to recognize the primacy of the revealed deposit for theology. It was 'not the "construct" that surrounds the "deposit" as its subtle framework; it is the "deposit" that, as spiritual milieu flowing from all parts, becomes the backbone from the inside and under its own pressure. It is contemplation that evokes a theology, not theology that leads to contemplation'.[91] Thus, for Chenu, theology was grounded in faith. He was apprehensive of the 'autonomous' logic of systematic constructs and of appeals to a 'catalogue of propositions filed in some Denzinger',[92] and he maintained that even the most perfect theological system would not add 'an ounce of light and truth to the gospel'.[93] Repeatedly, Chenu warned against an overconfident speculative theology.[94] To counter this overconfidence, he worked with a mystical theology based on the interior light of faith. As Robert Guelluy points out: 'Thinking of the complaints that will be made against him, one will note that Fr Chenu frequently employs terms that designate the affective element of the faith (which in no way is to say "sentimental"): "appetite" . . . "communion with divine thought" . . . "illumination" . . . "pious confidence" . . . "supernatural perception" . . . "pious theology".'[95]

While emphasizing the primacy of contemplation, Chenu did not disparage the intellectual aspect of theology. Thus, Guelluy immediately adds that Chenu did underline the coherence between religious perception, on the one hand, and objective dogmatic formulas, on the other hand.[96] In fact, towards the end of his chapter, Chenu waxed downright eloquent about theology as a science, and even about theological systems, readily agreeing that they were not all of equal value: 'We are Thomists. For a reason.'[97] Chenu would not, therefore, disregard theological argumentation as such. The divine–human or 'theandric mystery', which implied the definitive entry of the supernatural into the natural human realm, provided the justification for drawing rational theological conclusions, as long as faith provided the context.[98] The answer to both Modernist historicism

---

[90] Chenu, *Une école*, 141. Like Möhler, Chenu also employed the notion of 'continued Incarnation' (*incarnation prolongée*) (ibid. 142).

[91] Ibid. 131.

[92] Ibid. 132.

[93] Ibid. 131.

[94] Such scholastic theology, maintained Chenu, was characterized by Aristotelian 'commonplaces' [*lieux*] (ibid. 134), 'fixism' (ibid. 139), 'conceptualism' (ibid. 146), and 'extrinsicism' (ibid. 147).

[95] Robert Guelluy, 'Les Antécédents de l'encyclique "Humani Generis" dans les sanctions Romaines de 1942: Chenu, Charlier, Draguet', *RHE* 81 (1986), 432.

[96] Ibid. 432–3.   [97] Chenu, *Une école*, 148.   [98] Ibid. 137–8, 145.

(erroneously treating history as absolute) and scholastic theology (abandoning its supernatural character through its intellectualism) was a sacramental ontology that recognized the entry of the word of God *in* human words.[99]

Chenu's writings on doctrinal development simply applied the basic sacramental principle that one could know God only in a human manner (*modum cognoscentis*) and that the word of God came to us in human words: 'If the economy of revelation develops in time, if therefore faith finds its authentic expression in statements that are connected to history, the particular instance— which is all it is—of development of doctrine to the interiority of the new economy, in the life of the Church, does not worry the theologian: it is normal, and here the law of the Incarnation becomes manifest.'[100] For Chenu, the law of the Incarnation implied doctrinal development. He recognized that this opened the door to some degree of relativism.[101] But, he insisted, it was merely the relativism that inevitably accompanied the nature of human language. Chenu appealed to the doctrine of analogy to insist both on the truthfulness of human discourse and on its inadequacy.[102] Appealing to his renowned predecessor, Gardeil, Chenu wanted to retain the 'doctrine of analogical knowledge': 'With such a radical source of relativity, the historical contingencies and psychological complexities of dogmatic formulas can be considered in a level-headed way.'[103]

Since the 'theandric mystery' of Chenu's sacramental ontology allowed room not just for human history but also for intellectual argumentation and theological systems, it would seem that his view of doctrinal development would, at least in principle, also have a place for logical argumentation. After all, Chenu believed that both the spiritual and the scientific had a place within theology. Consistency would seem to demand a combination of theological and logical theories to explain development of doctrine. None the less, Chenu's antipathy to neo-scholasticism was probably the obstacle that prevented him from investigating the possibility of such a combination of theological and logical theories. When referring to doctrinal development, he preferred to focus, along with Möhler and others, on the faith-based character of theology and the Spirit-led organic development of doctrine within the Church. Progress in theology, maintained Chenu, did not consist in 'the utilization of an acquired system, in the proliferation of new conclusions at the edge of a more subtle dialectic'.[104] Instead, it had its origin in 'the insatiable appetite of faith, which holds to nothing less than the beatific vision—and not to some kind of conclusion'.[105]

---

[99] Chenu commented: 'The word of God is *in* the human word: the power of God reveals itself in this weakness' (ibid. 138).

[100] Ibid. 139.

[101] Ibid. 135, 140.

[102] Chenu's approach was similar to that of Bouillard. Cf. Chap. 3, the various sections under the heading 'Henri Bouillard: Analogy and Sacramental Ontology'.

[103] Chenu, *Une école*, 140. Throughout the chapter, Chenu shored up his arguments with appeals to Gardeil.

[104] Ibid. 149.   [105] Ibid.

Louis Charlier: Growth of the Revealed Deposit

Louis Charlier's 1938 book *Essai sur le problème théologique* was quite similar to Chenu's *Une école de théologie*. Charlier's evaluation of the current state of scholastic theology was equally negative.[106] He attempted to secure the support of St Thomas Aquinas for his own position, suggesting that Thomas's understanding of theology was more congenial to a theological than to a logical understanding of the development of doctrine. Charlier argued that by incorporating recent gains of theological progress he followed in the footsteps of the Angelic Doctor.[107] When Charlier discussed the relationship between theology and rational thought, he heaped encomium on Thomas's approach, maintaining that with Thomas one was 'far from rigorous deductions and from virtual revelation. We find ourselves in formal revelation and in the light of faith'.[108] Charlier argued that Thomas had regarded theology as an exercise of faith that operated within the Church, was centred on the mystery of God as the formal subject, and was primarily interested in exploring the revealed articles of faith.[109] Accordingly, Charlier insisted that 'demonstration, in the strict sense of the term, cannot be used in theology'.[110] While Charlier recognized that St Thomas had believed that revelation was closed and that he had not employed the notion of doctrinal development,[111] he argued that Thomas was a 'pliable [*souple*] and vigorous' force, 'susceptible to adaptation and progress'.[112] Further, he maintained that 'Saint Thomas has not said everything. He would consider as fools those who would claim that he had known everything and that theology... had not evolved and gained riches acquired after his writings'.[113] Thus, without claiming that Thomas had dealt with the same issues that the Church faced in the nineteenth and twentieth centuries, Charlier insisted that his own understanding of theology and doctrinal development was much more compatible with Thomas Aquinas's views than the approach of the neo-Thomists.

One of the main problems with scholastic theology, according to Charlier, was that its logical approach was unable to account for doctrinal development.[114] The root of the issue, Charlier was convinced, lay in the erroneous way in which scholastic thought had understood the connection between revelation and

---

[106] Charlier's views on development of doctrine are discussed in Meuleman, *De ontwikkeling van het dogma*, 70–5; Hammans, *Die neueren katholischen Erklärungen*, 180–5.

[107] Louis Charlier, *Essai sur le problème théologique* (Thuillies: Ramgal, 1938), 8.

[108] Ibid. 136. Cf. ibid. 149: '[T]he theological conclusion, in the sense that we hear about later, does not occur in the theological system of Saint Thomas.'

[109] Ibid. 84–150.

[110] Ibid. 137. It is this statement that Henri-Dominique Simonin set out to refute in 'De la nécessité de certaines conclusions théologiques', *Ang* 16 (1939), 72–82. Simonin highlighted several patristic controversies and concluded that the Fathers did not share Charlier's scruples about the use of natural reason in matters of faith. Marie-Rosaire Gagnebet also devoted a section of his essay to refuting this same statement ('Un essai sur le problème théologique', *RT* 45 (1939), 128–34).

[111] Charlier, *Essai sur le problème théologique*, 132, 149.

[112] Ibid. 7. Cf. ibid. 166.   [113] Ibid. 8.   [114] Ibid. 35.

theology. Charlier explained that the problem with Thomas Aquinas, and especially his successors, was the fact that they had excluded revelation from theology.[115] Theology had become a science originating in rational principles and leading to logical conclusions. In Thomas's Aristotelian philosophy, it had been possible to know something either by directly apprehending it—when the principles (*principia*) and the thing (*res*) were identical—or by apprehending the effects of the causes (or the conclusions of the principles), in which case one only had virtual knowledge (*science virtuelle*).[116] In this Aristotelian approach, therefore, theological conclusions were 'virtually' contained in the absolute, immutable, and eternal principles, and one could deduce these conclusions by way of 'rigorous demonstration'.[117]

This system, Charlier explained, was based on the distinction between revealed truths—the principles—and the science of theology, which had the task of drawing appropriate conclusions from revealed truths. Like any other science, theology took its principles from a higher, subalternating, science. As a subalternate science, theology thus depended for its work on principles alien to itself.[118] These principles—the articles of faith—were derived from the knowledge (*scientia*) of God and of the blessed departed. 'Revelation', Charlier commented, was 'thus in some way excluded from the domain reserved to the exploration of the theologian. No more than other sciences does theology have to prove its principles. It receives them from a knowledge that is superior in kind, namely, that of God and of the blessed departed'.[119] The result was 'a kind of verbalism and intemperate conceptualism almost empty of all reality'.[120] Theology, 'instead of investigating the revealed contents, trying to understand it within permissible bounds, adjusting itself to the revealed contents in its concepts and formulas as best as possible, while ever remaining in its light, distances itself and substitutes for it, more and more as its argumentation moves along, the light of natural reason'.[121] What concerned Charlier in the conceptualist scholastic understanding of theology was that it had severed the link between theology and revelation, and thus also between theology and the experiential reality of faith.

Charlier believed that it was mistaken to regard theology as a science like any other, taking its principles from a higher, subalternating, science.[122] Since in actuality revelation did not simply provide theology with its principles, scholastic

[115] Charlier discussed particularly the nature of theology according to John Capreolus (*c.*1380–1444), Thomas Cajetan (1469–1534), Dominic Bañez (1528–1604), and John of St Thomas (1589–1644) (ibid. 14–25).

[116] Ibid. 26–7.

[117] Ibid. 27.

[118] For Chenu's appropriation of the theory of subalternation, see Chap. 4, sect.: Theology as Initiation.

[119] Charlier, *Essai sur le problème théologique*, 29.

[120] Ibid. 32.

[121] Ibid.

[122] Cf. ibid. 148: 'St Thomas admits that theology is a science, but a science in the broad sense of the term.' Gagnebet, in his reaction, maintained that theology was a proper science ('Un essai', 122–8).

practice ended up relying on auxiliary disciplines, such as exegesis, history of doctrine, and the history of the Councils.[123] The result, Charlier, charged, was that theology outsourced the determination of its principles to these auxiliary disciplines, leading to a 'conflict of two methods, a conflict of two mentalities'— namely, between scholastic or speculative theology and positive or historical theology: 'In practice, experience so often shows us, each follows his way, the scholastic theologian buries himself in the depths of his speculations, while the exegete, the patrologist, the historian of doctrine, work on their own behalf, all this with great damage to the progress of theology.'[124] Charlier was convinced that this conflict showed up in the existence of positive theology and scholastic theology as two separate disciplines.[125] This division of labour overlooked, Charlier maintained, the fact that for the Angelic Doctor 'the world of natural things appeared as a world open to the world of the supernatural'.[126] Accordingly, an approach that was truly Thomist in character could never explore the positive sources of theology without concern for their speculative or systematic implications.

Scholasticism, wrongly convinced that it had access to absolute, eternal principles, could not but oppose the sense of relativity given with the history of doctrine. Echoing Chenu, Charlier insisted:

The antagonism between the mentalities asserts itself particularly in light of the thorny problem of the evolution of dogma. While the historian has the notion of the relative, the scholastic theologian has the notion of the absolute. The idea of development of dogma includes a certain relativism, which in no way undermines the inherent immutability of revelation, but which is difficult to accept by a mentality which, as we have put it, is used to considering principles from the point of view of rigid immutability. Also, since the problem of the evolution of dogma has successfully imposed itself, the scholastic conception is committed to resolve it—though, we readily acknowledge, perhaps with widely varying nuances—by means of the distinction between 'explicit' and 'implicit'... At bottom, they have recourse to logical methods to explain the evolution of dogma.[127]

---

[123] Charlier, *Essai sur le problème théologique*, 32.

[124] Ibid. 33.

[125] Charlier considered this separation a 'regrettable division of labour, which first compromises the unity of the sacred science and of its properly theological method, and which next, by removing from those two methods their purely auxiliary roles, ends up with a kind of schism between positive theologians and scholastic theologians. Two absolutely different mentalities are facing one another' (ibid. 165).

[126] Ibid. 97. Like de Lubac, Charlier rendered Thomas's view as follows: 'Just as, in fact, the entire natural universe is involved in the supernatural universe and is ordained, in itself and by itself, to the one end, so the entire order of natural truths is in subordination to the order of supernatural truths, as is in us reason to faith' (ibid. 148). Cf. ibid. 157: 'To be sure, there is a radical distinction between the order of nature and the order of grace... Seen within God, our adoptive filiation is what is essential of what God has wanted to make of us. Grace, then, does not appear to the theologian as an add-on [*surajoute*], indifferent in itself, to our nature. Isn't the primary plan of God, in effect, to turn us, his creatures, into his children, and to create for this a nature that is capable of receiving such a gift and that is itself ordained in every way to such a sublime end?'

[127] Ibid. 33–4.

Charlier underlined the inability of scholasticism to accept a real development of dogma by outlining the rise of positive theology in the sixteenth and seventeenth centuries.[128] The main concern of Catholic theology at that time, Charlier maintained, had been to prove the continuity of Catholic doctrine in the face of the Renaissance and the Reformation. By means of a 'brutal rupture with the ancient view of theology', Catholic scholasticism had begun to look to the positive sources of Scripture and Tradition as material that provided demonstrative proof of the continuity between these sources and the teaching of the infallible magisterium: 'Thus, since theology is a true science, it will have to demonstrate something. Thanks to the positive, it will no longer just demonstrate the conclusions, but also the principles or, if you will, the consistency of the principles, their immutability.'[129] In other words, Scripture and Tradition had been turned into apologetic tools. Once the magisterium had provided the faithful with the doctrine to be believed, the sources then had to be scoured for support. 'One might say', argued Charlier, 'that this is the vital problem of the positive: not simply to search the sources for what is contained here, but to prove that what is contained here is the same as that which has been defined in the proposition of the magisterium'.[130] Scholastic theology thus captured Scripture and Tradition within the scientific endeavour of demonstrating the revealed character of the Catholic faith. To Charlier, such attempts at shoring up Catholic truth demanded too much from historical investigation, since the contemporary state of Christian doctrine often simply could not be found back explicitly in the positive historical sources. Such apologetic attempts, therefore, could not do justice to the historical development of Christian doctrine.

Charlier then pointed to recent tendencies (*nouvelles tendances*) in French Catholic thought that had begun to take the historical development of doctrine more seriously, tendencies that reflected the influence of the Tübingen school of Drey and Möhler, as well as of John Henry Newman. The contemporary theologian was beginning to learn, Charlier explained, 'to discard his rigid dogmatic fixism and acquired a sense of the relative and the psychology of development. He began to see that dogma and history overlapped in a certain way, that the revealed contents and dogma thus allowed for the historical method, that one could set up a department of history, after all'.[131] In a book written by the Jesuit theologian August Deneffe (1875–1943) in 1931, Charlier noticed the recognition that the Tradition was more than a fixed collection of Aristotelian *loci* from which the life had been drained.[132] Deneffe employed a dual notion of Tradition. In one sense, it was the living and infallible preaching of the Church, which had begun with the apostles (*traditio constitutiva*) and continued in their successors (*traditio continuativa*).

128 Charlier discussed Melchor Cano, Gregory of Valencia, Dionysius Petavius, Louis Thomassin, Johann Baptist Franzelin, Gerard Cornelis van Noort, and Franz Diekamp (ibid. 37–47).
129 Ibid. 36.
130 Ibid. 48.
131 Ibid. 52–3.
132 Ibid. 63. Cf. August Deneffe, *Der Traditionsbegriff: Studie zur Theologie* (Münster: Aschendorff, 1931).

Tradition thus functioned as the 'proximate' rule of faith (*règle de foi prochaine*). In another sense, Tradition was constituted by the monuments that the preaching had left behind throughout the centuries. This Tradition Deneffe called the 'remote' rule of faith (*règle de foi éloignée*), since these monuments were the means by which one came to know the 'proximate' rule of faith. This distinction discarded the view that the role of positive theology was simply to provide historical evidence for the teaching of the magisterium. Instead, the most 'recent tendencies' of theology regarded the sources (Scripture and Tradition) as the first witnesses of the constitutive phase of the development of doctrine. This did not mean that previous historical stages were now regarded as irrelevant. But the purpose of positive theology had changed. One now 'returned to the past, not to look here for proofs, but to follow the course of the revealed contents in progress during the different periods of the Church'.[133]

Naturally, Charlier's approach raised the question of the role of the magisterium. If the positive sources no longer served to provide demonstrative proof of the current teaching of the Church, and if Scripture and Tradition were simply early 'phases' of doctrinal development, did this not give the magisterium a free hand in the determination of doctrine? Möhler had already faced this question, and it would always arise in connection with so-called 'theological' views of doctrinal development.[134] But Charlier denied that his views led to an arbitrary magisterium:

The magisterium must not be regarded as a simple exterior norm of faith, imposing on the faithful what they must believe; it is an organic function of the Church, emanating from her as one of her vital faculties. Doesn't this mean that the ecclesial preaching of the magisterium is the expression—official and infallible—that flows from the living faith of the Church? This presupposes the presence of the revealed contents in the Church; it is there that it develops, inasmuch as the Church assimilates it and permits it to grow in her.[135]

The magisterium served its purpose within the mystery of the Church. And because the magisterium was an expression of the Church's living faith Charlier argued that it could never function in a strictly juridical manner.[136]

---

[133] Charlier, *Essai sur le problème théologique*, 64.

[134] Cf. Charles Boyer's comment: 'Another aspect of the new methodology is the role attributed to the magisterium. In effect, that which Mr Draguet and Fr Charlier remove from the domain of reason, they give to the living magisterium of the Church' ('Qu'est-ce que la théologie: Réflexions sur une controverse', *Greg* 21 (1940), 262). Boyer proceeded to insist on a logical view of doctrinal development, arguing that the Immaculate Conception was based on the protevangelicum (Gen. 3: 15) and on the grandeur of the Mother of God and of Christ. Furthermore, he maintained that it was possible to be certain of the theological conclusion of the Virgin's Immaculate Conception prior to its official doctrinal definition in 1854 (ibid. 264).

[135] Ibid. 65. At the same time, Charlier did assign the magisterium the task of defining the progress of doctrine (ibid. 158–9).

[136] Cf. ibid. 71: 'The magisterium only defines, in terms that are precise and rigorous but always analogical and under the seal of infallibility, the exact range of this interior growth of revelation. Rule of

Charlier was concerned to overcome the dualism of a 'conflict of two methods', which tended to oppose the scholastic theologian (dealing with eternal, supernatural truths) to the historian or positive theologian (investigating natural events). The 'overlapping' of dogma and history, by means of which Charlier thought he could end the conflict, was indicative of an approach to doctrinal development that was sacramental in character. This sacramental character of doctrinal development showed up especially in Charlier's Christological mysticism and in his view of theological language as analogical in character. First, Charlier presented a Christological mysticism by insisting that one should look at the revealed deposit (*donné révélé*) not just from a 'conceptual' angle, but also from a 'real' (or experiential) point of view. Theology, which was nothing less than faith in action,[137] moved through concepts and formulas in order to reach the reality (*res*) of faith itself.[138] This given reality was God himself, who gave himself to us, and who by grace allowed us to participate in his nature and in his life.[139] This self-giving of God was entirely Christ-centred: 'God has predestined us to become his adopted children through Jesus Christ. Thus God gives himself to us, his children, in his unique incarnate Son. All of reality is in Christ. When he is given, his redemptive mission is realized, as is that of the Spirit who completes it; the revealed gift is acquired in its entirety.'[140]

While not explicitly appealing to Möhler on this point, Charlier strongly insisted that the Church was a continuation (*prolongement*) of the Incarnation.[141] This meant that the reality (*res*) of divine revelation—God revealed in Christ— came to us by means of the Church. One could say that 'the mystery of the Church goes back to the mystery of the *total being* of Christ, all of whose elements have already been acquired and predefined, once this divine personality has been given. And if there is development, this development will take place according to the natural law of this personality'.[142] Doctrinal development in the Church was legitimate since it was development within (the continuation of) Christ himself. The Church now contained the revealed deposit, seeing that the Church was an 'integral part of the mystery of Christ'.[143] This allowed for

faith, undoubtedly, but not, we insist, in the manner of a juridical and administrative role, imposing its dull statements as from the outside, with reference to its code of laws. As we have said: the magisterium stems from the mystery of the Church. It is the organ of the authentic expression of her preaching, as that in turn is the expression of her faith, in permanent contact with the revealed contents.'

[137] Ibid. 75.

[138] Ibid. 66. As a result, Charlier insisted that 'before anything else, the theologian must have a keen sense of the mystery of God' (ibid. 154).

[139] Ibid. 68.

[140] Ibid.

[141] Ibid.

[142] Ibid. 68–9.

[143] Ibid. 69. Chenu's use of the 'theandric mystery' highlighted the combination of divine *and* human elements in history, and so provided a rationale for taking time and place— including historical investigation according to the human manner of knowing (*modum cognoscentis*)—seriously in the science of theology. Charlier's Christology did not emphasize this human mode of knowing. Instead, he focused on 'continued Incarnation'. As a result, Charlier did not emphasize the historical context of theology nearly as much as Chenu. Jean-Claude

'real development' and 'real progress', for along with the growth of the Church came the growth of the entire mystery of God.[144] Because the Church developed and grew as the continuation of Christ, the revealed deposit necessarily developed and grew, as well.

Although he acknowledged that following the death of the apostles there could be no further public revelation,[145] Charlier pointedly refused to restrict development of doctrine to an increase in subjective appropriation. Instead, there was a mysterious development and growth of the revealed deposit in the Church.[146] This meant that the Incarnate Christ participated in particular historical vicissitudes: 'The Incarnation takes place at a precise moment in time. The mystical body of Christ—while realizing a unity that transcends time—takes shape successively through historical strands. Revelation has had a beginning and a final date. Development of dogma, in turn, starts off at a certain date and proceeds through chronological stages. How, then, would it not have a history?'[147] Development of doctrine meant, for Charlier, that as a result of the ecclesial continuation of the Incarnation, doctrine was wedded to historical developments. Through these historical developments, God enabled his Church to participate in the very reality of his own eternal life.

Second, Charlier's view of theological language fit his sacramental understanding of doctrinal development. Like Chenu, Charlier used the doctrine of analogy to insist both on the value and on the limitations of human language. The former accounted for the similarity, while the latter expressed the infinite dissimilarity between human language and the eternal reality (*res*) to which it referred. 'Here below,' Charlier maintained, 'God "informs" our spirit of the revealed deposit through the intervention of human words: authentic and official notification, sealed by God in certain signs of the given reality; true expression, undoubtedly, but inadequate to the reality which it can only translate analogically.'[148] Human language was sacramental in character: it contained the reality to which it pointed, while that reality also transcended human expressions. For Charlier, the doctrine of analogy was the way to express this sacramental understanding of truth.[149] In this view, the intellect could never claim to grasp the fullness of

---

Petit rightly observes that with Charlier the 'very careful attention to history does not go back to an awareness of the historicity of all thought, as that appeared to be the case with Chenu' ('La Compréhension de la théologie dans la théologie française au XX⁰ siècle: La Hantise du savoir et de l'objectivité; L'Exemple d'Ambroise Gardeil', *LTP* 45 (1989), 226).

[144] Charlier, *Essai sur le problème théologique*, 70.

[145] Ibid. 69.

[146] Ibid. 71. Gagnebet strongly opposed Charlier's position on this point, convinced that it implied continuing revelation. As Gagnebet put it: 'Dogmatic progress does not affect the mystery, the divine reality in itself. It affects dogma, for although the entire revealed teaching has been received with the death of the last of the apostles, it unveils itself little by little with regard to the Church, which proposes it to our faith' ('Un essai', 117). For a similar accusation, see Boyer, 'Qu'est-ce que la théologie', 264–5.

[147] Charlier, *Essai sur le problème théologique*, 72.

[148] Ibid. 68.   [149] Cf. ibid. 156.

divine truth. To discern the magisterium's role, therefore, 'Denzinger does not suffice'.[150] The logical view of doctrinal development went wrong by ignoring the 'relativism of the analogy of knowledge and the historical relativism of temporal conditions'.[151] As a result, Charlier insisted on appropriately valuing the 'human contingencies' of particular time periods which shaped the 'formulation' of Christian thought.[152] In short, a sacramental ontology underpinned Charlier's Christological mysticism as well as his analogical view of truth.

Henri de Lubac: 'Cashing in' Jesus

Six years after Chenu, Draguet, and Charlier had been disciplined for their views on theology and development of doctrine, Henri de Lubac returned to the latter issue and once more entered the debate surrounding Charlier's book, opposing Charles Boyer's objections to Charlier's theological approach.[153] In this 1948 essay 'Le Problème du développement du dogme' de Lubac expressed his amazement that Boyer had simply reiterated the earlier scholastic position of Marcolinus Maria Tuyaerts. In 1919, this Dominican theologian from Louvain had insisted, partially in reaction to the Modernist crisis, that all theological conclusions—and only theological conclusions—could be defined as dogma.[154] Since the time of Tuyaerts's publication, de Lubac explained, numerous theologians had repudiated such a strictly logical view of doctrinal development. They had argued instead that there was no absolute homogeneity between revelation and theology (Ambroise Gardeil);[155] that the prophetic instinct, reaching beyond historical and logical discourse, informed the magisterium (Léonce de Grandmaison);[156] that in its definitions the magisterium relied not just on theologians but also on the 'secret instinct' or 'Catholic sense' of the faithful

---

[150] Ibid. 77. Cf. Charlier's critical comment on scholastic theology's use of Denzinger (ibid. 165).

[151] Ibid. 80.

[152] Ibid.

[153] De Lubac, 'Le Problème du développement du dogme'. The reason de Lubac published this essay in 1948, long after the debate surrounding Charlier's book, is that as a result of the war, the 1940 volume of *Gregorianum*, containing Boyer's article, didn't reach France until 1946 (de Lubac, 'The Problem of the Development of Dogma', 255). Cf. Charles Boyer's reaction: 'Sur un article des Recherches de science religieuse', *Greg* 29 (1948), 152–4. For discussions of de Lubac's position on the development of doctrine, see Charles E. Sheedy, 'Opinions Concerning Doctrinal Development', *AER* 120 (1949), 19–32; John J. Galvin, 'A Critical Survey of Modern Conceptions of Doctrinal Development', in Proceedings of the Fifth Annual Meeting of the Catholic Theological Society of America (Washington, DC: n.p., 1950), 55–7; Meuleman, *De ontwikkeling van het dogma*, 63–8; Hammans, *Die neueren katholischen Erklärungen*, 192–6, 220–4; Nichols, *From Newman to Congar*, 195–213.

[154] De Lubac, 'Problem of the Development of Dogma', 248–9. Cf. Marcolinus Maria Tuyaerts, *L'Évolution du dogme: Étude théologique* (Louvain: Nova et vetera, 1919).

[155] De Lubac, 'Problem of the Development of Dogma', 249. Cf. Ambroise Gardeil, 'Introduction à la théologie', *RSPT* 9 (1920), 658; 11 (1922), 689.

[156] De Lubac, 'Problem of the Development of Dogma', 250–2. Cf. Léonce de Grandmaison, *Le Dogme chrétien: Sa nature, ses formules, son développement* (Paris: Beauchesne, 1928), 251–2, 255, 262–3.

(Jean-Vincent Bainvel);[157] that in addition to theological conclusions a *via affectiva* guided doctrinal development (Francisco Marín-Sola);[158] and that it was difficult to defeat heresy by means of a purely formal demonstration of errors (Henri-Dominique Simonin).[159] 'Under these conditions', de Lubac mused, 'the volume of the *Gregorianum* for the year 1940 . . . had a surprise in store for us'.[160] The surprise was Boyer's attack on Charlier, which basically returned to what de Lubac called the 'logicism' of Tuyaerts's position.

De Lubac's own view, which he juxtaposed to Boyer's, was similar to the positions held by Chenu and Charlier. Like his Dominican counterparts, de Lubac rejected the neo-Thomist limitation of development to theological conclusions. 'By what right', asked de Lubac, 'do we declare, so to speak, a priori and presuppose as if established in advance that the development of dogma is entirely circumscribed within these narrow limits?'[161] De Lubac insisted that the notion of development be broadened, since development often resulted from looking at the same problem from a different angle.[162] Such differences in approach over time meant that development did not always and necessarily mean progress, as logical theories of development insisted.[163] Thus, like Chenu and Charlier, de Lubac maintained that faith was indispensable for theology, since natural reason could never embrace revealed truth as it would other truths. Here, as in his views on spiritual interpretation, de Lubac showed his mystical bent:

Our natural logic is not going to be able to display itself in everything in its regard as it does with the objects of our reason. Not having *conceived* it, not having formed it in ourselves, we will never be the masters of it. To tell the truth, we do not possess it: it possesses us. We do not measure it: we are measured by it. We seek to penetrate into its understanding, and we do in fact reach it: the mystery is incomprehensible, it is not unintelligible. But the more we reach, the more we sense at the same time that this truth surpasses us, that it overflows us and disconcerts us.[164]

Theology, de Lubac was convinced, could not 'univocally' apply human logic to the mysteries of the Christian faith.[165] He did not seem to share Chenu's conviction that the theandric mystery implied a sanctioning of natural human

---

[157] De Lubac, 'Problem of the Development of Dogma,' 252. Cf. Jean-Vincent Bainvel, 'L'Histoire d'un dogme', *Études*, 101 (1904), 617, 620–1, 623–4, 625.

[158] De Lubac, 'Problem of the Development of Dogma', 253. Cf. Marín-Sola, *L'Évolution homogène*, i. 280, 368; ii. 57.

[159] De Lubac, 'Problem of the Development of Dogma', 254–5. Cf. Henri-Dominique Simonin, ' "Implicite" et "explicite" dans le développement du dogme', *Ang* 14 (1937), 134–5.

[160] De Lubac, 'Problem of the Development of Dogma', 255.

[161] Ibid. 257.

[162] Ibid. 257–8.

[163] Ibid. 258. De Lubac did not hold to a 'fall paradigm' of theology. But his critique of (neo-) scholasticism and his predilection for patristic and mystical theology implied that he did believe there were periods of theological decline in the Church. Cf. John Auricchio, *The Future of Theology* (Staten Island, NY: Alba, 1970), 281, 315.

[164] De Lubac, 'Problem of the Development of Dogma', 265.

[165] Ibid.

logic. To be sure, de Lubac was willing to allow for Boyer's insistence on a rational connection between the protevangelicum of Genesis 3: 15 and the Immaculate Conception of Mary.[166] De Lubac insisted, however, that one could only see this link

> provided that we adopt certain Christian value judgments, that we reason according to the analogy of faith, and particularly after the event, when we are guided by the unanimous Christian sentiment, itself canonized by the decision of the infallible Magisterium; when we have thereby attained the certitude that none of the objections raised is valid and that no other will ever be presented.[167]

In other words, for de Lubac, rational argumentation itself did not guide development. It was only possible to see the rational link a posteriori, and this rationality was not a neutral one but one that was guided by the 'analogy of faith', which would read Scripture in the light of the Church's faith. Just as de Lubac was convinced that it was the analogy of faith that ultimately justified allegorical interpretation, so he believed that only the analogy of faith enabled one to appreciate the rationality of doctrinal development.[168]

De Lubac did not shy away from the consequences of his position. Since he rejected the view that doctrinal development was the result of natural, logical arguments, he regarded development instead as a matter of the Church investigating what she actually believed. When the magisterium was called upon to define dogma, de Lubac maintained that this was the result of the Church examining her own conscience.[169] To de Lubac's neo-Thomist detractors, this theological approach was an abdication of human reason, and left the development of doctrine either to the subjective whim of an ill-defined *sensus ecclesiae* or to the arbitrary power of the magisterium. Either way, it was unclear to neo-scholastics like Boyer how de Lubac could possibly provide adequate criteria to assess the development of dogma.

Theological views like de Lubac's seemed to undermine the continuity or homogeneity of doctrine. De Lubac dealt with this problem in several ways, but most significantly by insisting on the Christological centrality and finality of revelation. As we have seen, Chenu and Charlier, too, made Christology central to doctrinal development. The 'theandric mystery' was central to Chenu's approach. It emphasized the integrity of time and space, and of human rationality. Charlier's view of a 'continued Incarnation' enabled him to posit growth of the 'revealed deposit'. His Christological identification of the Church meant that the mystery of

---

[166] Cf. above, n. 134.

[167] De Lubac, 'Problem of the Development of Dogma', 261–2.

[168] Cf. Chap. 5, sect.: An Arbitrary Hermeneutic? De Lubac alluded to the similarity between doctrinal development and interpretation in 'Problem of the Development of Dogma', 263 n. 35. Cf. Meuleman, *De ontwikkeling van het dogma*, 66–7.

[169] De Lubac, 'Problem of the Development of Dogma', 263. Cf. ibid. 262: 'What she [i.e., the Church] seeks to find is not if such a proposition is or is not correctly deduced but if such an assertion is or is not contained in her faith.'

Christ continued in history. While generally in agreement with the views of Chenu and Charlier, de Lubac employed Christology in a distinctive fashion. Unlike Chenu, he did not emphasize the Incarnation in order to point to the goodness of creation or of the human mode of knowing. And, although he was influenced by Möhler's notion of a 'continued Incarnation', for de Lubac this did not function in the way that it did for Charlier, as a concept explaining the development of doctrine. Instead, de Lubac pointed to the identity of the Person of Christ, whose fullness and mystery always eluded human beings. Development of doctrine was inevitable for de Lubac, given the fact that at no point in time could anyone grasp the fullness of the mystery of Christ. The development of doctrine was the story of 'cashing in', over time, the fullness of Christ (*monnayer Jésus*).

Several scholars have pointed out that de Lubac relied particularly on Pierre Rousselot for his Christological emphasis.[170] Like his Jesuit *confrère*, de Lubac looked to Christology to deal with the issue of the one and the many, of homogeneity and development. Revelation, for de Lubac, was not first of all a series of propositions, but a Person:

It would not be legitimate to believe...that revelation has been given to us without any intrinsic link with the one and total reality of Christ, that it has been delivered to us as a simple collection of formulas, in a series of propositions detached from that unique mystery and thereby separated from each other, like 'major premises', wholly ready for future reasoning.[171]

According to de Lubac, neither the 'logicism' of the neo-Thomists—the main target of his critique—nor the 'vitalism' of Newman and the Tübingen theologians did adequate justice to this Christological starting-point. The former replaced the unique Christological origin of development with 'principles' from which to draw conclusions, and the latter used the 'seed' analogy to explain development. 'In reality,' countered de Lubac,

concretely, what is first and that from which we must start without ever leaving it—what is first and last—is the redemptive Action; it is the gift that God makes us of himself in his Son...It is all that which, at first undivided, forms the total Object [*l'Objet global*], the incredibly rich Object of revelation. We can call it, to use an equivalent expression, 'the Whole of Dogma' [*le Tout du Dogme*]. And this 'Whole of Dogma' is, as its name

---

170 Nichols, *From Newman to Congar*, 195–213; Ulrich Kuther, *Kirchliche Tradition als geistliche Schriftauslegung: Zum theologischen Schriftgebrauch in Henri de Lubacs 'Die Kirche. Eine Betrachtung'* (Münster: Lit, 2001), 80–4. De Lubac published an essay of Rousselot on doctrinal development: Pierre Rousselot, 'Petite théorie du développement du dogme', ed. Henri de Lubac, *RSR* 53 (1965), 355–90. Nichols comments that de Lubac's 'positive remarks are hardly more than a re-statement of Rousselot's case, the latter being, of course, unknown since unpublished' (*From Newman to Congar*, 206). In his essay on development, de Lubac never mentioned Rousselot's influence with regard to his Christological starting-point, referring instead to Jules Lebreton, Étienne Hugueny, and Henri-Dominique Simonin ('Problem of the Development of Dogma', 276).

171 De Lubac, 'Problem of the Development of Dogma', 273 (translation adjusted).

indicates, not susceptible to any increase. It, too, like the Whole of the redemptive Action, is at once first and last. It is unsurpassable.[172]

De Lubac's Christological *Tout du Dogme* cleared away several thorny issues. First, there was no longer any need to posit, along with Franzelin and Marín-Sola, the unlikely notion that the apostles had explicitly known all propositional truths that the Church would later define as dogma. De Lubac was able to maintain that not only the apostles, but also the entire Tradition that followed them, did in fact have a grasp of all of dogma. Rather than knowing it as propositional truth, however, they knew it in a unitary fashion in Christ, since in him 'all has been both given and revealed to us at one stroke; and ... in consequence, all the explanations to come, whatever might be their tenor and whatever might be their mode, will never be anything but coins [*monnayage*] in more distinct parts of a treasure already possessed in its entirety', even if this possession was not necessarily by way of 'principles' and premises of logical arguments.[173] Second, by insisting that *le Tout du Dogme* was given in Christ, de Lubac was able to conclude that this revelation was 'unsurpassable'. Charlier's 'continued Incarnation' had been particularly vulnerable to the objection that it meant revelation continued in the Church. De Lubac protected the theological approach against this accusation by maintaining that development of doctrine was nothing but a 'cashing in' of the fullness of the treasury of the Christological mystery.

YVES CONGAR: TRADITION AND TRADITIONS

The 'Time of the Church' as Sacramental

Each in his own way, Daniélou, Chenu, Charlier, and de Lubac dealt with the question what it meant for theology to appropriate history as a theological category. It was up to Chenu's student, Yves Congar, to provide an overall theological framework for this historical focus by offering a profoundly learned exposition of the meaning of 'tradition'.[174] Congar's historical and theological

[172] Ibid. 274.

[173] Ibid. 275. Not only did de Lubac's overall position go back to Rousselot, but even his language of *monnayage* was reminiscent of Rousselot, who had used this metaphor throughout his essay 'Petite théorie'. Rousselot had commented, for example, 'Our explanation can be summarized as follows: we say that the entire tradition, the entire development of dogma and in general of Christian doctrine is simply a matter of itemizing, of cashing in Jesus (*monnayer Jésus*)' ('Petite théorie', 374).

[174] Yves Congar's three main publications on tradition were: (1) *La Tradition et les traditions*, i *Essai historique* (Paris: Fayard, 1960); (2) *La Tradition et les traditions*, ii *Essai théologique* (Paris: Fayard, 1963); English trans. in one vol.: *Tradition and Traditions: The Biblical, Historical, and Theological Evidence for Catholic Teaching on Tradition*, trans. Michael Naseby and Thomas Rainborough (San Diego, Calif.: Basilica, 1966); and (3) *La Tradition et la vie de l'Église* (Paris: Fayard, 1963); English trans.: *The Meaning of Tradition*, trans. A. N. Woodrow (San Francisco, Calif.: Ignatius, 2004). The last volume was largely a more popular and accessible summary of the two main volumes of *La Tradition et les traditions*.

overviews in *La Tradition et les traditions* (1960 and 1963) stemmed directly from his involvement in the World Council of Churches' Faith and Order Commission in the early 1960s and were the mature result of many years of ecumenical and ecclesiological study.[175] Ecumenism had been Congar's most passionate concern from the beginning of his career, and this was evident throughout his books on Tradition. Congar demonstrated his acquaintance with the Reformers' views on tradition, as well as with contemporary Protestant appraisals of the relationship between Scripture and Tradition. He particularly engaged Oscar Cullmann's work on the topic.[176] Deeply appreciative of the Lutheran's views on salvation history, Congar none the less remained unconvinced of Cullmann's insistence on *sola scriptura* and of his belief that the canonization of Scripture implied the end of Tradition as a criterion of truth.[177] Still, Congar set out to 'avoid all polemics',[178] and he concluded the theological exposition of his *Essai théologique* with an exploration of possible prospects for renewed dialogue with the churches of the Reformation.[179]

Not one to ignore theological differences in the interest of ecumenical dialogue, Congar investigated what he regarded as a central issue between Catholics and Protestants: the relationship between Scripture and Tradition. He believed that underneath this issue lurked the even more fundamental question of the Church's place within history. The disagreement with Protestants, Congar insisted in his 1962 book, *La Foi et la théologie*, concerned the 'time of the Church' (*le temps de l'Église*).[180] Explaining this expression, Congar posited the following thesis: 'The fact of a certain progress in the understanding of faith is based both on the nature of revelation itself and on the distinct character of the "time of the Church", which is a community of people on the way.'[181] One of the implications of the Church being a community of pilgrims (*viatores*) was that she had a dual place in time:

The time of the people of God can be reduced neither to astral or cosmic time, nor to the time of human history: it is not the time of the world in which the Church herself would live in a non-linear fashion. Placed in sidereal time and in that of history, the Church has

---

[175] Cf. Dulles, Foreword to Congar, *Meaning of Tradition* (pp. vii–viii). The Faith and Order consultations led to the 1963 Montreal report entitled 'Scripture, Tradition and Traditions'.

[176] Cf. Oscar Cullmann, *The Early Church*, ed. A. J. B. Higgins and trans. A. J. B. Higgins and S. Godman (London: SCM, 1956). Cullmann and Daniélou also engaged in a discussion on the topic of tradition. See Cullmann, 'Écriture et Tradition', *DViv* 23 (1952), 45–67; Daniélou, 'Réponse à Oscar Cullmann', *DViv* 24 (1953), 105–16.

[177] See esp. Congar, *Tradition and Traditions*, 38–42; id., *Meaning of Tradition*, 35–6.

[178] Id., *Meaning of Tradition*, 7.

[179] Id., *Tradition and Traditions*, 482–91.

[180] Id., *La Foi et la théologie* (Tournai: Desclée, 1962), 43. Congar also mentioned the Protestant denial of apostolicity of ministry. For a discussion of this book, which had its origins in a course taught at Le Saulchoir since the late 1930s, see Nichols, *From Newman to Congar*, 253–62.

[181] Congar, *La Foi et la théologie*, 99.

her own duration [*durée*], of which the value is positive from the point of view of salvation history, that is to say, of the plan of God.[182]

The Church had a place both in astral or cosmic time and in human or historical time. Congar maintained that the cosmic aspect of the *temps de l'Église*, given with the work of Christ and expressed in apostolic succession, guaranteed its 'permanence' or 'identity'; while the 'divine mission' of the Spirit brought this work to fulfilment in human history.[183] This latter temporal outworking of Christ's work came to expression in the numerous ecclesial activities throughout history, including later dogmatic declarations on the meaning of God's Word. In explaining historical maturation, Congar insisted, one should speak

neither of a simple coincidence with the past historical moment of Christ or with the text of Scripture, nor of new revelations, but of the actualizing *and the fulfilment*, in the duration, of the Deposit [*Donné*] given by God in Jesus Christ, which incorporates the living fidelity through which the Church herself incorporates this deposit: the shared banquet [*mutuum convivium*] of the Lord and his Spouse, who nourish and fulfil one another. (Cf. Rev. 3: 20 and the theme of 'fullness': Eph. 1: 23; 3: 19; 4: 10, 13, 15–16.) The *development* of the *deposit* joins together *Purity* and *Plenitude*.[184]

For Congar, the revealed deposit given in Christ was not simply a past body of texts, but was something that the Church was meant to 'actualize' or bring to 'fulfilment' so that purity and plenitude—the original deposit and its development—came together in the 'time of the Church'. This unique coincidence of the original deposit and its development was possible because of the coincidence of cosmic and historical time in the Church.

In *La Tradition et les traditions*, Congar elaborated on the unique character of ecclesial time, which the entrance of cosmic history into human history had created; he did so by referring to the time of sacred history as both divine and human.[185] In a 'sacramental ontology' (*ontologie sacramentelle*), explained Congar, past, present, and future flow together.[186] In the sacraments, 'past, present and future are not mutually exclusive, as in our chronological time'.[187] Sacramental time—the sacred history of the Church—allowed for a threefold presence: that of saving acts performed once for all, that of our present union with God, and that of the final end, which was already virtually present in seed-form today. 'We may call this', Congar maintained, 'the sacramental nature of the time of the Church'.[188]

Congar resonated both with Johann Adam Möhler and with Maurice Blondel.[189] A brief discussion of Congar's dependence on both these theologians

---

[182] Ibid. 105.   [183] Ibid. 105–6.   [184] Ibid. 107.

[185] Congar, *Tradition and Traditions*, 257–64.

[186] Ibid. 259. Cf. Johannes Bunnenberg, *Lebendige Treue zum Ursprung: Das Traditionsverständnis Yves Congars* (Mainz: Grünewald, 1989), 211–12.

[187] Ibid. 260.

[188] Ibid. 259.

[189] Throughout his work on tradition, Congar appealed a great deal to Blondel. None the less, in his preface to Charles MacDonald's book, Congar indicated that he felt MacDonald had over-emphasized his reliance on the French philosopher: '[Blondel] helped me to clarify and to expand

will serve to demonstrate their influence on his sacramental understanding of Tradition. The Tübingen theologians had employed the notion of 'living Tradition'. This expression, Congar explained, was first used at the time of the Reformation, and it had been one of the weapons with which to combat the Jansenist appeal to historical texts as opposed to the juridical authority of the magisterium.[190] For Möhler, the notion of 'living Tradition' drew attention to the fact that revelation concerned human subjects who were guided by the Holy Spirit.[191] Congar appreciated Möhler's historical mindset as well as his opposition to Enlightenment thought. He also found in the Romantic theologian an ally for his own opposition to a two-source theory of revelation that divided Scripture and Tradition, each containing different elements of the divine deposit.[192] Instead, according to Congar, living, active subjects received and passed on the divine deposit.[193] Thus, Congar believed that Möhler, as well as Newman, had been right to understand Tradition as reliant upon the Church's sense of faith (*sensus fidei ecclesiae*).[194] 'In this view', explained Congar, 'its [i.e., Tradition's] role in the Church would be similar to that played by awareness in a person's life: comprehension and memory, gauge of identity, instinct of what is fitting, witness and expression of personality.'[195] Möhler's 'living Tradition' was an expression of the sacramental unity in the Church of past, present, and future.

Maurice Blondel's philosophy of action contained two elements that, according to Congar, pointed in a similar direction as Möhler's view of 'living Tradition'. First, Congar appreciated Blondel's prioritizing of action over

---

my view of Tradition. But I do not regard this as my source. Moehler came before him, as well as my own experience of the Church' (*Church and World in the Plan of God: Aspects of History and Eschatology in the Thought of Père Yves Congar, OP* (Frankfurt: Lang, 1982), p. viii).

[190] Congar, *Tradition and Traditions*, 186, 189–91; id., *Meaning of Tradition*, 77.

[191] Congar was deeply indebted to Möhler for his pneumatological emphasis. For Congar's theology of the Holy Spirit, see Isaac Kizhakkeparampil, *The Invocation of the Holy Spirit as Constitutive of the Sacraments according to Cardinal Yves Congar* (Rome: Gregorian University Press, 1995); Elizabeth Theresa Groppe, *Yves Congar's Theology of the Holy Spirit* (Oxford: Oxford University Press, 2004); Patrick Mullins, 'The Spirit Speaks to the Churches: Continuity and Development in Congar's Pneumatology', *LouvStud* 29 (2004), 288–319; James Hanvey, 'In the Presence of Love; The Pneumatological Realization of the Economy: Yves Congar, *Le Mystère du temple*', *IJST* 7 (2005), 383–98; Richard P. McBrien, '*I Believe in the Holy Spirit*: The Role of Pneumatology in Yves Congar's Theology', in Gabriel Flynn (ed.), *Yves Congar: Theologian of the Church* (Grand Rapids, Mich.: Eerdmans, 2005), 303–27.

[192] Congar, *Tradition and Traditions*, 193.

[193] Mary was for Congar the clearest example of such welcoming of the Word (Luke 2: 19, 51) (*Tradition and Traditions*, 253–5).

[194] Ibid. 319; id., *Meaning of Tradition*, 79.

[195] Congar, *Meaning of Tradition*, 80. Cf. Congar's approach to development in 'Vie de l'Église et conscience de la catholicité', *BM* 18 (1938), 153–69; English trans.: 'The Life of the Church and Awareness of its Catholicity', in *The Mystery of the Church*, trans. A. V. Littledale (rev. edn, Baltimore, Md.: Helicon, 1965), 96–104. With an appeal to the Church's 'own interior law' and the animation of the Spirit, Congar argued here that, over time, the lived life of the Church elucidated the meaning of biblical texts, so that it was 'not enough to examine the relevant texts; the Church's own life is an indispensable *locus theologicus*' (ibid. 103).

understanding. Since for Blondel human actions were filled with implicit meaning, 'lived action' (*l'action vécue*) contained numerous elements of which the
acting person was unaware; these would come to the surface only by later
intellectual elaboration. For Congar, this Blondellian insight carried huge implications for the significance of the liturgy as one of the Tradition's monuments.[196]
If the Tradition was lived implicitly (*implicite vécu*) more than it was passed on by
way of deductive reflection, this meant that the liturgy was one of the most
powerful ways in which the Tradition was passed on.[197] Commented Congar:
'A large part of the Church's belief has become known to it through the holy
living-out of its faith, hope and love. Thus the liturgy is the privileged *locus* of
Tradition, not only from the point of view of conservation and preservation, but
also from that of progress and development.'[198] In this context, Congar again
emphasized the 'sacramental order' of reality, which the liturgy accomplished.
The liturgy efficaciously represented the mysteries of salvation 'at the present
moment of human and cosmic history'.[199] As such, the liturgy inserted the 'fact
of Christ' into the framework of the natural 'rhythm of seasons, weeks, days and
hours'.[200] For Congar, liturgical action was a concrete example that illustrated
the truth of Blondel's insistence on the priority and fecundity of human action.

Second, by opposing both the historicism of Modernism and the extrinsicism
of the neo-scholastics in his book *Histoire et dogme* (1904) Blondel had been able
to highlight the key role that Tradition played, both as a conserving and as a
conquering force in history. At several points, Congar's books on Tradition
summarized Blondel's opposition to the twin dangers of historicism and extrinsicism.[201] Echoing Blondel, Congar maintained that historicism and extrinsicism
both failed to appreciate the Church's living experience of the faith: 'Dogma,
though dependent on historical documents, draws upon another source: the
experience of an ever-present reality to which the documents bear witness at
their own level and in their own way.'[202] The living and experiential reality of the
faith was, for Congar, the 'living Tradition' itself. The result was a high view of
Tradition and of doctrinal development:

Tradition is not simply a thing of the past, an objective element in the deposit which has
not yet been written down; it is something more than a first sedimentation or an explicit
unwritten contribution...Tradition is the grasp, varying in the means and resources it
employs, of the treasure which living Christianity has possessed as a reality from the
beginning, and which passes progressively, as a result of reflection, from the level of the
implicit (*l'implicite vécu*) to that of the expressly known (*l'explicite connu*).[203]

[196] Congar, *Tradition and Traditions*, 359–61.
[197] Ibid. 354–61, 427–35; id., *Meaning of Tradition*, 134–9.
[198] Congar, *Tradition and Traditions*, 429.
[199] Ibid. 430.
[200] Ibid.
[201] Ibid. 215–16, 361–3.
[202] Ibid. 362.
[203] Ibid. 363. Cf. id., *La Foi et la théologie*, 109–10.

According to Congar, the Church's reflection on her lived faith allowed for the continuing growth of the Tradition. As a result, he believed with Blondel that Tradition was not just a conserving power but also had a renewing, forward-looking aspect.[204]

Scripture and Tradition as Sacraments

Congar's sacramental ontology lay at the basis of his understanding of biblical interpretation and of Tradition. Tradition itself, he maintained, was a 'sacramental deposit', since it contained more than could be 'expressed or grasped', and since its reality was gradually realized.[205] And to say that Tradition was sacramental was, for Congar, to say that Scripture was also sacramental. Both, after all, contained the same revealed deposit, and Scripture was the initial and most important element of the Tradition. Scripture, too, contained more than any one individual or any one time period could grasp. Accordingly, the Word of God was 'a *sign* of divine saving action, an *efficacious* sign, a sign of *grace*: and these are also the marks of a sacrament. Not surprisingly, then, the Word's sacramental nature has been traditionally recognized'.[206] Despite his high regard for Scripture, Congar repeatedly expressed his reluctance to identify it as the Word of God or as revelation itself.[207] Rather, he regarded Scripture as the external sign (*sacramentum tantum*), pointing to the uncreated Word as its sacramental reality (*sacramentum et res*), and intended to effect the presence of Christ in the believer as the saving fruit (*res tantum*).[208]

The sacramental character of Scripture meant that historical investigation could not possibly exhaust the meaning of the text. Congar found himself in fundamental agreement with the sacramental hermeneutic of de Lubac and Daniélou.[209] Scripture possessed its meaning 'outside itself' as 'the fruit of Scripture, its *res* (the spiritual reality resulting from the sacrament)'.[210] Congar included a lengthy section on typological exegesis as he discussed the views of the ante-Nicene Fathers on Tradition.[211] He maintained that since Scripture was not

---

[204] See on this point especially the careful discussion in Flynn, *Yves Congar's Vision of the Church in a World of Unbelief* (Burlington, Vt.: Ashgate, 2004), 198–211.

[205] Congar, *Tradition and Traditions*, 356.

[206] Ibid. 404.

[207] Ibid. 400–1, 452, 483–4.

[208] Ibid. 404; id., *Meaning of Tradition*, 90–1, 97. Cf. ibid. 102: 'Before being a critical reference or an argument, the sacred Text is a sort of sacrament conveying the Gospel so that we may live by it. The Fathers say that it is a means of grace and not only of information and knowledge. From another point of view, the same Fathers and the Catholic critics of the sixteenth-century Reformation came nowhere near to holding a book religion. The text as such is not the living Word of God, but only its sacrament (or sign). The decisive thing is the *act* accomplished by God and its actual operation within us.'

[209] To my knowledge, Congar never expressed explicit disagreement with de Lubac's views on interpretation. Congar was none the less more in line with Daniélou's 'typological' interpretation and expressed his apprehension of the excessive allegorizing and the lack of historical perspective among the Fathers (*Tradition and Traditions*, 69 n. 1, 440).

[210] Congar, *Meaning of the Tradition*, 91. Cf. id., *Tradition and Traditions*, 388–9; MacDonald, *Church and World*, 131–2.

[211] Congar, *Tradition and Traditions*, 64–85.

just human but also divine, the literary meaning did not exhaust its contents. The Scriptures witnessed to revelatory events that in turn referred to something 'beyond their immediate meaning, in a history which, while fully historical, is equally divine, the history of salvation: a history which is made by men *and the Holy Spirit*, together. Typological tradition is the fruit of this collaboration'.[212] Accordingly, the Fathers and medieval authors had 'unanimously' been of the conviction that 'the deeper meaning of a text was beyond the literal sense, although only to be reached *through* the literal sense'.[213] For Congar, interpretation of Scripture took place within the Church,[214] under the guidance of the Holy Spirit,[215] and always with reference to Christ.[216] Congar's view of theology took its sapiential aim and ecclesial context with utmost seriousness.[217] All of this resulted from his view of Scripture as sacramental in character, the reality of which Tradition unfolded over time, under the guidance of the Holy Spirit.

For Congar, the development of Tradition resulted from biblical interpretation guided by the 'analogy of faith' (*analogia fidei*). Biblical interpretation transcended purely historical investigation and followed the analogy of faith. We already encountered this category in de Lubac, who argued that it justified both allegorical interpretation and doctrinal development.[218] Congar not only made the notion central to his biblical hermeneutic, but he also maintained that the analogy of faith was the ultimate warrant for doctrinal development. He explained the *analogia fidei* by commenting:

This phrase, taken from St Paul (Rom. 12: 6) is taken to mean the proportion and relationships existing between the parts with one another, or between all the parts and

---

[212] Ibid. 75–6. [213] Ibid. 388.

[214] Ibid. 255, 382–6, 391–7; id., *Meaning of Tradition*, 87–9, 93–4.

[215] See esp. the sections on the Holy Spirit as the transcendent Subject of the Tradition in Congar, *Tradition and Traditions*, 338–46; id., *Meaning of Tradition*, 51–8.

[216] Congar, *Tradition and Traditions*, 389.

[217] See esp. Congar, *A History of Theology*, trans. and ed. Hunter Guthrie (Garden City, NY: Doubleday, 1968), 268–75. This book was the revised version of a dictionary article that Congar had initially written in 1939 ('Théologie', in A. Vacant, et al., *Dictionnaire de théologie catholique*, xv (Paris: Letouzey et Ané, 1946), 341–502). It is important to keep in mind that Congar was enough of a Thomist to take the intellectual side of theology seriously. In the article just mentioned, he expressed fairly strong reservations about Romantic tendencies that disparaged the intellect. See Kerr, 'Yves Congar and Thomism', in Flynn, *Yves Congar*, 67–97. Also, Congar was hardly persuaded by Charlier's affective approach, strongly insisting that for St Thomas deductive reasoning had a legitimate place in theology (id., review of R. Draguet, 'Méthodes théologiques d'hier et d'aujourd'hui'; J.-F. Bonnefoy, 'La Théologie comme science et l'explication de la foi selon saint Thomas d'Aquin'; L. Charlier, *Essai sur le problème théologique*; and R. Gagnebet, 'La Nature de la théologie spéculative', in *BT* 5 (1937–9), 490–505). Furthermore, Congar had no qualms about maintaining that there was a scientific side to theology, even if it was more than just a science (ibid. 498–500; id., *La Foi et la théologie*, 130–2; id., *History of Theology*, 221–6). And, while it is obvious that Congar did not hold to a logical view of doctrinal development, he did argue that intellectual arguments as well as historical documentation had a role to play alongside the (more significant) theological or ecclesial elements (id., *La Foi et la théologie*, 112–20).

[218] See Chap. 5, sect.: An Arbitrary Hermeneutic?; Chap. 6, sect.: Henri de Lubac: 'Cashing in' Jesus.

their common centre, which we may call the revelation of the covenant relation in Christ, the centre of the Christian mystery. This analogy of faith exists at the level of the dogmas or articles of faith. It is, thus, one of the main resources of theology. It exists also at the level of the scriptural texts and is in this way one of the main principles of theologico-biblical hermeneutics. This principle rests on the essential oneness of the Word of God, the covenant plan it communicates to us, and the unity that follows from this for Scripture.[219]

According to Congar, the analogy of faith, as the relationship of biblical data to Christ as well as to other scriptural data, naturally led to deepening insight into the biblical text and so to further development of the Tradition.[220] 'In this way', explained Congar, 'the Church gradually acquired an awareness, sometimes one that went beyond the explicit letter of the text, of the content of the Christian mystery by which it lives.'[221] A straightforward, historical reading of the text would not necessarily yield its richest meaning. Although the Christian Tradition did have to go back to Scripture, one had to keep in mind that 'from the standpoint of its present belief it *recognizes in the text* certain proofs not revealed by a simple reading of the text'.[222] As a result, Congar adopted the nineteenth-century distinction between 'historical tradition' and 'dogmatic tradition', where the former discussed the history of the Church without explicit appeal to theology or to the Church's doctrinal development, while the latter allowed for a reading of the Tradition in the light of the analogy of faith.[223]

The analogy of faith implied, according to Congar, that one could only interpret biblical texts in line with the deposit of faith as it had developed within the Church. Congar was quite aware of the fact that his Protestant interlocutors had difficulties especially with Marian doctrines that did not have explicit biblical support and had only recently been defined—the Immaculate Conception (1854) and the Assumption (1950)—and he often referred to the analogy of faith in defence of these particular dogmas.[224] Congar was convinced that his

---

[219] Congar, *Tradition and Traditions*, 406–7. Cf. ibid. 239, 403.

[220] Cf. Bunnenberg, *Lebendige Treue*, 222–4.

[221] Congar, *Tradition and Traditions*, 408.

[222] Congar, *Meaning of Tradition*, 126. Cf. ibid. 153.

[223] See e.g. Congar, *La Foi et la théologie*, 118; id., *Tradition and Traditions*, 189, 218-19, 454; id., *Meaning of Tradition*, 154. Congar made an analogous distinction between 'history of Christian doctrine' and 'positive theology', where only the latter was supposed to read the tradition in the light of later development and dogmatic definitions (*History of Theology*, 232–7). One can appreciate Congar's intent to do justice to the actual facts of history by means of the categories of 'historical tradition' and 'history of Christian doctrine', in order to avoid the temptation of bending or falsifying historical data for the sake of upholding the current teaching of the Church, something Congar feared in the manualist proofs *ex Scriptura* and *ex traditione*. I am not convinced, however, of Congar's solution. By allowing for a 'historical tradition' or a 'history of Christian doctrine' not shaped by the teaching of the Church, Congar seemed to lapse into a separation between nature and the supernatural that his sacramental ontology was meant overcome.

[224] Congar, *Tradition and Traditions*, 413: 'If we seek a critical justification of a particular article of faith by an express witness (for example, the bodily assumption of the Mother of God), we may, perhaps, not find this in Scripture, but only distant references, general outlines, which demand a long and subtle process of reasoning in the light of the analogy of faith before we can arrive at the

sacramental ontology—which included the sacramental character of Scripture and of Tradition—warranted these and other elaborations of the initial deposit of faith in the development of Christian doctrine.

Scripture, Tradition, and Church: The History of Juridicizing

At the same time, by studying the history of Christian doctrine, Congar became convinced that the sacramental ontology of the Fathers and the Early Middle Ages had lost some of its integrity. Two historical developments, in particular, had damaged the sacramental approach to salvation history. The result, Congar maintained, had been a weakening of the traditional unity between Scripture, Tradition, and Church. The first development that undermined this unity originated in the eleventh century. As Congar put it:

[T]he Gregorian Reform and its influence, decisive for an epoch as full of life as the twelfth century in the West, marked a definite turning-point: the transition from an appreciation of the ever active *presence of God* to that of *juridical powers* put at the free disposal of, and perhaps even handed over as its property to, 'the Church', i.e. the hierarchy. For the Fathers and the early Middle Ages, the sacred actions are performed *in* the Church, according to the forms of the Church, and are rigorously sacred as such. But their *subject is God*, in an actual and direct way... From the beginning of the twelfth century, a double process comes into operation, which will take nearly two centuries to have its full effect: a process of interpretation in terms of juridical realities and powers, a process of translation or construction of the Christian realities in terms of forms or nature and of causality, within the scholastic context, with its 'physicism' and its ontology.[225]

As a result of the Gregorian Reform, from the twelfth century onwards there had been an increasing emphasis on human and historical activities, on secondary causality, and on hierarchical juridical power in the Church.[226] All of this had

article in question.' Cf. ibid. 75, 353, 391, 413; id., *Meaning of Tradition*, 106, 120. See also the particularly clear treatment in id., 'Notes théologiques à propos de l'Assomption', *DViv* 18 (1951), 107–12; English trans.: 'Theological Notes on the Assumption', in *Faith and Spiritual Life*, trans. A. Manson and L. C. Sheppard (London: Darton, Longman, and Todd, 1969), 3–10.

[225] Congar, *Tradition and Traditions*, 135. While Congar did not mention the Lutheran scholar Rudolf Sohm in this context it seems clear that he depended at least in part on the latter's two-volume work, *Kirchenrecht* (1892–1923) and on his *Das altkatholische Kirchenrecht und das Dekret Gratians* (1918). Congar discussed Sohm's theory of the change from pneumatically based law to juridical law in *L'Église: De saint Augustin à l'époque moderne* (Paris: Cerf, 1970), 151–5 and 'R. Sohm nous interroge encore', *RSPT* 57 (1973), 263–94. While distancing himself from the particulars of Sohm's explanation, Congar agreed a change had taken place in the twelfth century: 'We (partially) step out of a Platonizing world, dominated by a heavenly exemplarism, so as to enter into a world interested in the nature and consistency of things. A certain juridicizing of the notion of Church seems to us incontrovertible: for nearly two centuries, it was simply placed alongside a vision that was still very theological and very sacramental, but it ended up prevailing by the beginning of the fourteenth century' (*L'Église*, 153).

[226] Cf. Congar, *L'Église*, 112; id., *Power and Poverty in the Church*, trans. Jennifer Nicholson (London: Chapman, 1965), 104–6; id., *Fifty Years of Catholic Theology: Conversation with Yves Congar*, ed. Bernard Lauret (Philadelphia, Pa.: Fortress, 1988), 40–4.

come at the cost of no longer being able to recognize the direct involvement of God and of the Spirit's free and unforeseen activities, and it had become steadily more difficult to identify ecclesial activities with divine action.[227] In short, juridical authority had come to be regarded as something extrinsic, more as externally imposed law than as the activity of God within the Tradition of the Church.

These desacralizing and juridicizing developments had influenced not only the way in which ecclesial authority functioned. A corresponding change in approach to Scripture had occurred. Up until the High Middle Ages, the mindset had been 'less historical than theological and sacramental'.[228] As a result, terms such as 'inspiration', 'revelation', and 'illumination' had consistently and freely been applied to the Fathers, councils, and canons of the Church.[229] Quite often, these words had been used 'to relate decisions taken by authority to an action of God'.[230] Thus, God's authority in the Church's Tradition had been inseparable from his authority in Scripture. Beginning in the thirteenth century, especially with Thomas Aquinas, theologians had begun to distinguish more sharply between the Spirit's 'inspiration' of the Bible and his mere 'assistance' in the life of the Church.[231] The distinction, Congar averred, had been indicative of an increasing separation between ordinary, human expressions of truth and biblical truth claims, or between nature and the supernatural.[232] Interestingly, Congar never criticized the change in terminology, agreeing instead that it was necessary to observe a 'qualitative difference' between the time of the prophets and that of the later Church.[233] Clearly, however, he looked at the change in vocabulary as inseparable from the juridicizing of ecclesial authority, the growing separation between nature and the supernatural, and the decline of the Church's sacramental ontology. The twelfth and thirteenth centuries had been responsible, in Congar's judgement, for a weakening of the bond between Church, Scripture, and Tradition.

The second major step in the process had taken place, according to Congar, in the fourteenth and fifteenth centuries. The weakening of the connection between Scripture and Tradition had made it possible to envisage a potential rivalry between

---

[227] Congar, *Tradition and Traditions*, 135–6, 179.   [228] Ibid. 339.

[229] See esp. the excursus, ibid. 119–37, which traces the terminology with numerous examples from the Tradition.

[230] Ibid. 120.

[231] Ibid. 93, 130.

[232] Ibid. 130.

[233] Ibid. 174. Congar indicated that earlier terminology was 'too naïvely "divinistic"' (ibid.). Elsewhere, he argued it was important to distinguish between 'inspiration' and 'assistance' of the Spirit (ibid. 208–9, 302, 314; id., *Meaning of Tradition*, 99–100), appealing at times to August Deneffe's distinction between *traditio constitutiva*, on the one hand, and *traditio continuativa* and *explicativa*, on the other hand (*Tradition and Traditions*, 208–9, 302; *History of Theology*, 232). Congar's adoption of these distinctions was in line with his acknowledgment that revelation itself had been 'closed since the death of the last apostle' (ibid. 21; cf. ibid. 266).

the two.[234] The growth in papal power had rendered inevitable the question which authority was supreme: scriptural or ecclesiastical. The relationship between Scripture and Church had become ever more tenuous, particularly once Henry of Ghent (*c*.1217–93) had posed the question directly: 'Must we believe the *auctoritates* (= the *dicta*, the texts) of sacred Scripture rather than those of the Church, or *vice versa?*'[235] John Duns Scotus had put further strain on this relationship, and William of Ockham (*c*.1288–*c*.1347) had perhaps been the most influential figure in this increasing rift between the two authorities, opting for Scripture (along with the Emperor) in his disagreement with the allegedly heretical views on the intermediate state advocated by Pope John XXII (1316–34).[236] Thus, with Henry of Ghent, Duns Scotus, and William of Ockham, the 'human and historical modalities' had been on the rise,[237] while the earlier sacramental mindset suffered correspondingly.

The Reformation was for Congar the logical result of this late medieval process. The potential of an antagonistic relationship between Scripture and Church had turned into reality in the rejection of ecclesial authority, first in John Wycliffe (*c*.1328–84) and John Hus (*c*.1369-1415), and then among the Reformers themselves. Wycliffe, Congar argued, 'prosecuted his demands for reform so radically that they constituted in effect the principle of *Sola scriptura* and the separation of Scripture from the Church. As a result, his orthodox critics felt obliged to defend the unwritten traditions *by arguing from the insufficiency of Scripture, and therefore, to a certain extent, by opposing them to it*—something which we can only regret, while recognizing that it was more or less inevitable.'[238] The Reformation slogan of *sola scriptura* was, for Congar, problematic because of its clear assertion of scriptural over against ecclesial authority.

Congar made clear, however, that he did not regard the Reformers as the initial or sole source of the weakening relationship of Scripture and Church. Nor did he believe that the Catholic Church had retained intact the vision of a sacramental universe in which the authorities of Church, Scripture, and Tradition functioned harmoniously. To be sure, the Reformation had opted unambiguously for Scripture rather than for the Church and her Tradition.[239] As the quotation of the previous paragraph indicates, however, Congar regretted the way in which the Catholic Church had tended to react to the Reformation by exacerbating the problems that had initially surfaced during the High and Late Middle Ages. The juridicizing of the Church, which had been underway since the Gregorian

---

[234] For this issue, Congar relied in part on George H. Tavard, *Holy Writ or Holy Church: The Crisis of the Protestant Reformation* (New York: Harper, 1959).

[235] Congar, *Tradition and Traditions*, 99.

[236] Ibid. 95. Congar sharply criticized Ockham's view of the Church and his insistence on individual freedom in *L'Église*, 290–5.

[237] Congar, *Tradition and Traditions*, 136.

[238] Ibid. 98.

[239] Cf. Congar's critique of the absolute value of the text, even to the detriment of the interior witness of the Spirit, in seventeenth-century Protestant scholasticism (ibid. 154–5).

Reform, had received an enormous impetus from the Counter-Reformation. The unanimity of Scripture, Church, and Tradition had become so damaged through the Reformation that the Catholic Church felt the need to insist much more strongly on the active role of the magisterium. Congar concluded his chapter on the Reformation with words that criticized developments in post-Tridentine Baroque theology: 'The duality of Scripture–Tradition has become a duality of Scripture-Church, with the emphasis, under the word "Church", very much on hierarchical authority, vested principally in papal authority.'[240]

Congar recognized that most theologians after the Council of Trent (1545–63) had interpreted the Council's decision on the relationship between Scripture and Tradition as if they constituted two independent and complementary sources of authority, each with its own distinct material contents.[241] And by reducing Tradition to the magisterium's decisions these post-Tridentine theologians had carried the juridicizing of authority to new heights:

> If the efforts of the Catholic doctors were concerned in the first place with the defence of traditions, that of the post-Tridentine theologians can be characterized as a moving away from a conception of tradition as content and deposit received from the apostles, to one of tradition considered from the point of view of the transmitting organism, seen as residing above all in the magisterium of the Church.[242]

As a result, the 'rule of faith' (*regula fidei*) came to be identified with the active Tradition of the magisterium rather than with the uncreated truth of divine revelation itself.[243] By opposing an identification of the magisterium with the rule of faith, Congar made the point that the magisterium did not have any kind of autonomous power to define the Tradition or to create the truth.[244] The magisterium was 'simply the servant, the purveyor of the rule', while it acted with authority that came from God.[245] The magisterium, therefore, always had to sift

---

[240] Congar, *Tradition and Traditions*, 155.

[241] In the text of its decree, the Council of Trent had replaced the earlier proposal of 'partly... partly' (*partim... partim*) with 'and' (*et*) to describe the relationship between Scripture and Tradition. Congar, after a careful study of the implications of the change, concluded that whatever the Council Fathers' intentions might have been, they had not gone so far as to canonize a two-source theory of revelation (ibid. 164–9).

[242] Ibid. 182.

[243] Congar criticized in particular his contemporary, Louis Billot, for distinguishing between the object of faith (i.e., Tradition) and the rule of faith (i.e., the magisterium's activity of transmitting the Tradition) (*Tradition and Traditions*, 210–13, 331; id., *Meaning of Tradition*, 69).

[244] Id., *Tradition and Traditions*, 188, 205, 269–70; id., *Meaning of Tradition*, 81, 152. In 1950, Congar had still been willing to acknowledge that, at least in a certain sense, the magisterium served as 'rule': 'The general principle is clear: the magisterium, which bears the responsibility and the charism of the apostolic witness, regulates [*règle*] the belief of the faithful; but the apostolic faith in the sense of the objective deposit of revealed truths regulates [*règle*] the witness of the magisterium and determines the competence within whose limits it has authority and grace' (*Vraie et fausse réforme dans l'Église* (Paris: Cerf, 1950), 523). See also id., *Divided Christendom: A Catholic Study of the Problem of Reunion*, trans. M. A. Bousfield (London: Bles, 1939), 185. Congar's overall position none the less never really changed.

[245] Id., *Meaning of Tradition*, 70.

and evaluate carefully what did or did not belong to the Tradition. The criterion that ought to guide this process, Congar insisted, was the 'mark of unanimity' (the Vincentian Canon), which the magisterium could discern by relying on the *sensus fidei* of the faithful and on the expertise of the theologians of the Church.[246] From personal experience, it seemed clear to Congar that the Roman hierarchy did not always live up to this ideal.[247]

Congar was apprehensive of the increasing focus on the 'active Tradition' of the magisterium and its corresponding extrinsicism of juridical authority.[248] The irony, Congar believed, was that to some extent Catholicism and Protestantism were both guilty of operating with a disjunction between Scripture, Church, and Tradition.[249] Reformation polemics had caused both traditions to rely increasingly on extrinsic, formal sources of authority. Protestants focused on Scripture, while Catholics looked to the magisterium of the Church; Protestants appropriated the purity of truth, while Catholics insisted on its plenitude.[250] Congar regretfully concluded that by separating purity and plenitude Protestants and Catholics both imperilled the 'living Tradition' itself.[251]

[246] See e.g. ibid. 71–2.

[247] For Congar's experiences, see *Journal d'un théologien (1946–1956)*, ed. Étienne Fouilloux (Paris: Cerf, 2000). Congar sometimes used harsh language to describe the functioning of the Roman hierarchy. For examples, see Alberto Melloni, 'Congar, Architect of the *Unam Sanctam*', *LouvStud* 29 (2004), 222–38; id., 'The System and the Truth in the Diaries of Yves Congar', in Flynn, *Yves Congar*, 277–302.

[248] Jonathan Robinson has argued—wrongly in my view—that Congar focused on active tradition (the process of transmission) at the cost of the contents of the deposit ('Congar on Tradition', in Flynn, *Yves Congar*, 329–55). Based on this misperception, Robinson jumps to the amazing charges that Congar's theology leads to process theology (ibid. 335) and liberal Catholicism (ibid. 355), and that the result of Congar's views on Tradition has been an increase in the importance of the magisterium at the expense of Tradition (ibid. 341, 343, 352). In actual fact, as we have seen, Congar expressed serious reservations about the juridicizing of authority. In similar vein, it simply does not do justice to Congar (or to Chenu) to state with Alberto Melloni that there were two intellectual 'dynasties', the one running from Blondel to de Lubac and the other from Loisy, via Chenu, to Congar ('Congar, Architect of the *Unam Sanctam*', 224–5). This assumes far too much of a cleavage between de Lubac and Congar. It also does not do justice to Congar's genuine disagreement with the historicism of Modernists like Loisy.

[249] To illustrate this point, when discussing the post-Tridentine Catholic focus on juridical authority rather than on the contents of the Tradition, Congar added in a footnote: 'We may note that a comparable development took place in Protestantism. Protestant orthodoxy laid special emphasis on the "formal principle" of *sola Scriptura*, while Luther had given the primacy to the content, the Gospel of salvation' (*Tradition and Traditions*, 181 n. 2).

[250] Congar often referred to the two principles of 'purity' and 'plenitude' as belonging together (e.g., ibid. 152–3, 270, 294; id., *Meaning of Tradition*, 83, 117, 160). Cf. the fine essay by John Webster, 'Purity and Plenitude: Evangelical Reflections on Congar's *Tradition and Traditions*', *IJST* 7 (2005), 399–413. The essay has been reprinted in Flynn, *Yves Congar,* 43–65.

[251] While discussing Protestant minimizing of the Church, Congar warned that Catholics should not put the magisterium in the place of the Holy Spirit: 'One one-sided emphasis should not be replaced by another' (*I Believe in the Holy Spirit*, trans. David Smith, i, *The Holy Spirit in the Economy: Revelation and Experience of the Spirit* (New York: Crossroad/Herder, 1997), 154; cf. ibid. 162–3).

Ressourcement: The Church Fathers and Holy Scripture

Congar was not satisfied simply to identify problematic developments in the history of the Church. He intended his contribution as a serious attempt to overcome problems inherited by Catholics and Protestants alike. Understandably, Congar sought a reintegration of Church, Scripture, and Tradition, to recover a more robust ontology founded on the sacramental character of each of these three authorities.[252] We have already encountered several aspects that Congar believed were central to such a reintegration: an acknowledgement of the supernatural presence of the Holy Spirit in the Church, a recovery of the typological interpretation of Scripture, and an appreciation of the role of the liturgy in passing on the Tradition. Another significant plank in Congar's platform of *ressourcement* was the role of the Church Fathers and of Scripture itself as normative monuments of the 'living Tradition'.

Congar regarded the witness of the Church Fathers as one of the most significant monuments in expressing and passing on the Tradition in the Church.[253] His view of the theological developments since the eleventh century did not allow him to accept the position that the Spirit's guidance of the Church meant uninterrupted progress of doctrinal insight. Like de Lubac, he made the point that historical developments included periods of decline.[254] His historical analysis may even give the impression of a 'fall' having occurred in the High Middle Ages, necessitating a return to the Church Fathers. Congar liberally drew on the Fathers throughout his writings. The historical period of the Church Fathers represented 'the moment when the deposit of apostolic faith was given an exact form with a view to excluding certain interpretations rejected as heretical'.[255] As a result, all the major doctrines of the Church were patristic in character: 'Our belief in the Trinity, the Person of the Holy Spirit, in Jesus Christ as true God and true man, in grace, the Eucharist, the Virgin Mary, and in the Church and its priesthood, is at once entirely biblical and entirely patristic. The same could be said for almost all the other matters we believe.'[256] The Fathers represented the 'undivided Church' for Congar.[257] What is more, he

---

[252] The next chapter will discuss Congar's sacramental ecclesiology.

[253] Congar saw the monuments of the Tradition as expressions of the gospel in the history of the Church; they passed on the contents of the Tradition. Thus, the Tradition was logically prior to its monuments, which were its expressions and the means of passing it on (*Tradition and Traditions*, 425; id., *Meaning of Tradition*, 151). Since Congar regarded Scripture itself as part of Tradition, he saw it, of course, as the most important monument of the Tradition. Congar considered the monument of the texts of the magisterium as 'next in importance immediately after the holy Scriptures' (ibid. 130), and he located these texts prior to the liturgy and the Fathers (ibid. 130–4; id., *Tradition and Traditions*, 426).

[254] 'History offers many expressions and developments that are doubtful, or simply less successful, in the realms of theology, devotion and government' (id., *Meaning of Tradition*, 56).

[255] Id., *Tradition and Traditions*, 444.

[256] Ibid. 445. Cf. id., *Meaning of Tradition*, 147–8.

[257] Id., *Tradition and Traditions*, 447.

considered the Fathers wonderful examples in terms of their pastoral approach. As pastors, they had been interested in building up the Church, committed to the exposition and defence of the Christian mystery, and concerned with the unity of faith and life.[258] Thus, the Fathers exercised a strong appeal to Congar.

At the same time, Congar was careful how he applied the principle of *ressourcement*. First, he did not accord the Fathers absolute value: 'It is the Church, not the Fathers, the consensus of the *Church* in submission to its Saviour which is the sufficient rule of our Christianity.'[259] Even the consent of the Fathers (*consensus Patrum*) did not, in itself, guarantee any particular doctrine.[260] Congar believed that neither logical nor historical evidence alone was sufficient to account for doctrinal development. Accordingly, he thought it was a weakness within the Orthodox tradition that it tended to restrict the Tradition to that of the Church Fathers.[261] Likewise, while he had high regard for the Vincentian Canon,[262] Congar was wary of 'too mechanical' an application of the rule.[263] Ultimately, he believed, it was the Church's faith, guided by the Spirit, which determined doctrine. Second, Congar resisted neglecting later Tradition in favour of the Church Fathers. His own theology was deeply indebted to later theology, particularly that of Thomas Aquinas and the Tübingen school.[264] And by conviction Congar believed that the Spirit had continued to work in the history of the Church. Thus, he commented, 'The tradition received by each one of us is not the quintessence of primitive Christianity, but the totality of what has been revealed about Christ over long ages. Nothing that is of value in past acquisitions has been lost.'[265] In short, Congar wanted a *ressourcement* of the entire Christian Tradition while according to the Church Fathers primacy of position.

Congar's project of *ressourcement* implied that Scripture was not the sole contributing factor to the life of the Church; Tradition also played a significant

---

[258] Ibid. 448–50.   [259] Ibid. 399.   [260] Ibid.
[261] Ibid. 441–3.
[262] Ibid. 4, 304; id., *Meaning of Tradition*, 71, 118–20. In his *Commonitorium* (AD 434), Vincent of Lérins had maintained that Catholic truth is that which has been believed 'everywhere, always, and by all' (*semper, ubique et ab omnibus*). Cf. Thomas G. Guarino, 'Tradition and Doctrinal Development: Can Vincent of Lérins Still Teach the Church?' *TS* 67 (2006), 34–72.
[263] Congar, *Tradition and Traditions*, 443; id., *Meaning of Tradition*, 71.
[264] Congar's indebtedness to St Thomas is evident throughout his writings. See e.g. Congar, 'Note sur la gnose ou l'enseignement religieux des savants et des simples selon S. Thomas', *BT* 1 (1931), 5*–7*; id., 'The Idea of the Church in St Thomas Aquinas', Thomist 1 (1939), 331–59; id., 'Saint Thomas: Serviteur de la vérité', in *Les Voies du Dieu vivant: Théologie et vie spirituelle* (Paris: Cerf, 1962), 289–308; id., 'St Thomas Aquinas and the Spirit of Ecumenism', *NBl* 55 (1974), 196–209. On this last essay, see Fergus Kerr, 'Yves Congar: From Suspicion to Acclamation', *LouvStud* 29 (2004), 273–87. See, further, Congar, *Thomas d'Aquin: Sa vision de théologie et de l'Église* (London: Variorum, 1984). Cf. Jean-Pierre Torrell, 'Yves Congar et l'ecclésiologie de Saint Thomas d'Aquin', *RSPT* 82 (1998), 201–42.
[265] Congar, *Tradition and Traditions*, 268.

role. As reflected in the title of his two volumes of *La Tradition et les traditions*, Congar distinguished between 'Tradition' (capital 'T') and 'traditions'.[266] The former was simply 'the transmission of the reality that is Christianity'.[267] The source of Tradition was the prophets and apostles and, in an eminent sense, Jesus Christ himself as the heart of the gospel.[268] Ultimately, Tradition had its origin in God the Father as 'the primordial Source' who had 'handed over' his Son to the world.[269] As Hippolytus of Rome (*c*.170–*c*.236) had explained in his commentary on Daniel, Christ was the life-giving river in the Garden of Eden, the Church:

There flows in this garden a river of water which never runs dry. *Four rivers* (Gen. 2: 10) flow from it, watering the whole earth. It is the same in the Church: Christ, who is the river, is announced throughout the world by the fourfold Gospel. He waters the earth and sanctifies those who believe in him, according to the word of the prophet: *Streams flow from his body* (John 7: 38). In Paradise there are *the tree of knowledge and the tree of life* (Gen. 2: 9), so, too, in our times two trees are planted in the Church: the Law and the Word. For *by the law comes knowledge of sin* (Rom. 3: 20), but by the Word we are given life and the forgiveness of sins.[270]

In early Christian iconography, the four rivers had soon turned from gospels into baptismal waters. Baptismal liturgies testified to the fact that the great Tradition was both noetic (the *traditio* of the Creed) and real (conversion through Baptism). 'The noetic *traditio* of the faith', commented Congar, 'was completed in a real *traditio* of the new life of Jesus Christ in the waters of which he is the source'.[271] Congar was attracted to the early Church's view of Christ as the source 'of Scripture, of the Gospels, of baptism, of saving knowledge, and of salvation, or life'.[272] This view of Christ as the source of Tradition naturally resulted in the notion of a 'living Tradition': 'It is clear that all this is of great importance for our idea of Tradition. Tradition is not only noetic but real. It is a handing over of salvation, of the Christian life, of the reality of the covenant.'[273]

---

[266] For explanations of the distinction, see Congar, *Tradition and Traditions*, 286–8; id., *Meaning of Tradition*, 157; id., *History of Theology*, 231. In several places, Congar presented elaborate overviews of the numerous distinctions that could be made with regard to the word 'tradition'. See id., *Tradition and Traditions*, 296–307; id., *Meaning of Tradition*, 45–6, 127–8.

[267] Id., *Meaning of Tradition*, 44. Cf. ibid. 127: 'It [i.e., Tradition] is the transmission of the whole Gospel, that is, of the Christian mystery, whatever form it takes: Scripture, preaching, profession of faith, sacraments and external forms of worship, customs and rules. And this is so in a twofold sense: first, objectively in the content of the deposit, and second, in the act of its transmission.' Cf. ibid. 125; id., *Tradition and Traditions*, 287.

[268] Id., *Meaning of Tradition*, 49–50, 121; id., *Tradition and Traditions*, 270–83. On what follows, cf. the helpful discussion in Aidan Nichols, *Yves Congar* (Wilton, Conn.: Morehouse/ Barlow, 1989), 33–6.

[269] Congar, *Meaning of Tradition*, 10.

[270] Hippolytus, *In Danielem*, i. 17 (quot. Congar, *Tradition and Traditions*, 275).

[271] Congar, *Tradition and Traditions*, 279.

[272] Ibid. 279.   [273] Ibid. 279–80.

Congar acknowledged the Scriptures to be the most important and authoritative among the monuments within this Tradition.[274] To be sure, he had great difficulties with the Protestant notion of *sola scriptura*. Regardless of his ecumenical concern, Congar would never ignore what he thought were real obstacles to unity. The difficulty with the Protestant position was that it separated Scripture from Tradition, much like the Catholic two-source theory did.[275] Congar criticized both views. He was fond of commenting that no doctrine was based either on Scripture independent of Tradition or on oral Tradition independent of Scripture.[276] The Protestant principle of *sola scriptura*, he believed, overlooked that the early Church had passed on numerous apostolic and ecclesiastical traditions that were not mentioned in Scripture.[277] The Scriptures, after all, were occasional writings written for specific purposes. Repeatedly, Congar made the point that we would hardly know anything about the central rite of the Christian faith, the Eucharist, had it not been for the controversy in the Church of Corinth.[278] The faith of the Church, he argued 'was formed and continues to be formed in the successive generations of Christians, from the Eucharist itself, taken as a present reality, celebrated in the Church according to tradition.'[279] Although the apostolic and ecclesial traditions did not add any material doctrinal contents beyond that of the Scriptures themselves, they were still significant carriers of the living Tradition. Congar used the example of the Cross to illustrate his point:

The whole of Christianity is contained in a sign of the cross; no theory of the Redemption expresses half as much as a simple crucifix hung on a wall, erected as a wayside shrine or put on a tomb or altar. A symbol contains a possibility of total communion, and its faithful repetition expresses something that escapes all conceptual analysis. This is why

[274] Aidan Nichols concludes from Congar's approach that since 'Scripture is the primary expression of tradition, there can be no sound theology which is not rooted in Scripture and irradiated by it' ('T. S. Eliot and Yves Congar on the Nature of Tradition', *Ang* 61 (1984), 484).

[275] For a comparison between Congar and a Protestant position quite sympathetic to the role of Tradition, see Hans Boersma, 'On Baking Pumpkin Pie: Kevin Vanhoozer and Yves Congar on Tradition', *CTJ* 42 (2007), 237–55.

[276] Congar, *Tradition and Traditions*, 168, 413; id., *Meaning of Tradition*, 39–40, 42, 106.

[277] As examples, Congar mentioned the Lenten fast, certain baptismal and Eucharistic rites, infant baptism, prayer facing the East, the validity of baptism by heretics, certain rules for the election and consecration of bishops, the sign of the Cross, prayer for the dead, and various liturgical feasts and rites (*Tradition and Traditions*, 50–64; id., *Meaning of Tradition*, 37–9). These 'traditions', as distinct from Tradition itself, mainly concerned worship and discipline, rather than doctrine (id., *Tradition and Traditions*, 287), and the monuments of the Tradition, especially the liturgy, passed on these traditions in the Church. The now common distinction between apostolic Tradition (capital 'T') and ecclesiastical (or confessional) traditions (small 't') is entirely different from Congar's distinction between apostolic tradition and ecclesiastical traditions. With regard to the latter, he was not thinking of the numerous confessional or denominational traditions that existed, but of the various practices instituted by the Catholic magisterium. Congar was, of course, aware also of the common distinction between 'Tradition' and (confessional) 'traditions' (see e.g. id., *Meaning of Tradition*, 166).

[278] Id., *Tradition and Traditions*, 350, 415; id., *Meaning of Tradition*, 34, 103–4, 139.

[279] Id., *Meaning of Tradition*, 20.

mere believers can transmit the whole of tradition even when they are quite ignorant of the terminology and subtleties of dogma.[280]

Congar maintained that the Cross expressed the heart of the gospel, and therefore the same material contents as the Scriptures themselves. The numerous apostolic and ecclesiastical traditions, passed on largely by liturgical celebration, did not just result in theological opinions or propositions. Rather, they shaped what Congar called the 'Catholic spirit' (*sensus catholicus*) or the 'mind of the Church' (*phronēma ekklēsiastikon*): 'It is the heritage of the Catholic communion, a heritage that is truly "catholic" and total, which greatly surpasses the part that is recorded, and even more the part that we have understood and are capable of explaining.'[281] Thus, to isolate the Scriptures from the other monuments of the Tradition would be to limit seriously the ability of its contents being passed on.

Despite this critique of Protestantism's isolation of Scripture, Congar left little doubt that his *ressourcement* project included a recovery of the centrality of Scripture. The written character of Scripture provided it with important advantages, such as its public character, its permanence and solidity, and its role as a fixed point of indisputable reference.[282] 'The Fathers', insisted Congar, 'did not regard Scripture only as a source of knowledge: for them it is the very principle of salvation and perfection, in short, of Christian living.'[283] Congar's assertions of the absolute authority of Scripture were explicit and numerous.[284] Its normative position was so firm that an appeal to Scripture could legitimately turn into a critique of elements of the Tradition:

> Exactly the same value, therefore, should not be attributed to tradition and to the holy Scriptures, even if they are paid the same respect. The holy Scriptures have an absolute value that tradition has not, which is why, without being the absolute rule of every norm, like the Protestant scriptural principle, they are the supreme guide to which any others there may be are subjected. If tradition or the Magisterium claimed to teach something contradicting the holy Scriptures, it would certainly be false, and the faithful ought to reject it.[285]

Comments like this revealed Congar's strong sense of the critical function of the canon over against the Church, even if it remained true that Scripture—being just one of several monuments of the Tradition—could not regulate the life of the Church by itself.

Even more important for ecumenical dialogue was Congar's unequivocal acceptance of Scripture's material sufficiency. For the Church Fathers,

---

[280] Congar, *Meaning of Tradition*, 74.
[281] Id., *Meaning of Tradition*, 33. Cf. ibid. 78.
[282] Id., *Tradition and Traditions*, 291–4.
[283] Ibid. 380.
[284] Congar showed no inhibition in his frequent commendations of Scripture as the ultimate norm of absolute authority. See e.g. ibid. 314, 380–2, 422; id., *Meaning of Tradition*, 4, 100–1, 111, 155, 160–1.
[285] Id., *Meaning of Tradition*, 100.

Tradition had simply been a matter of passing on the contents of the Scriptures, that is to say, the gospel or the apostolic rule of faith.[286] John Webster accurately captures Congar's intent:

In telegraphic form, Congar's argument goes something like this: scripture is materially sufficient (everything the church needs can be found in it) but formally insufficient because not perspicuous apart from the activity of the Holy Spirit in communicating the Word in the life of the church. Scripture and tradition cannot be separated because inspiration and illumination form a single trajectory of the Spirit's action in communicating divine truth and generating a form of common life bound together by 'an exegetical tradition'.[287]

Scripture was sufficient according to Congar, in the sense that the entire dogmatic contents of the faith could somehow be found there, either explicitly or implicitly.[288] This explains why Congar had precious little use for a two-source theory of revelation, which he typically described as the apostolic Tradition being 'handed down secretly through the ages, whispered in the ear'.[289] Traditions that one could not trace back to the Scriptures were never doctrinal in character; they always concerned only matters of liturgy, discipline, or custom.[290] The way to make the living Tradition one's own was not by elevating it as a separate source of revelation alongside Scripture. True *ressourcement*, Congar believed, meant a re-appropriation of the liturgy, the Church Fathers, and ultimately of Scripture itself. Only in this way could the unity of Church, Scripture, and Tradition be restored. For Congar, at stake was nothing less than the sacramental 'time of the Church'.

---

[286] Id., *Tradition and Traditions*, 32; id., *Meaning of Tradition*, 90.

[287] Webster, 'Purity and Plenitude', 407.

[288] Congar presented a lengthy list of passages from the Fathers and medieval theologians, proving that they had held to the material sufficiency of Scripture (*Tradition and Traditions*, 107–16; cf. ibid. 379–82; id., *Meaning of Tradition*, 108). He considered the difference with the Reformers to be that the latter went further by insisting also on the *formal* sufficiency of Scripture (id., *Tradition and Traditions*, 116–17) and he explained that while the Fathers and medieval theologians had accepted the material sufficiency of Scripture they had affirmed that 'Scripture by itself cannot adequately present its true meaning; it is only understood correctly in the Church and in its tradition' (ibid. 117).

[289] Id., *Tradition and Traditions*, 64. Cf. ibid. 167, 286, 414; id., *Meaning of Tradition*, 37, 169.

[290] Id., *Tradition and Traditions*, 50–64, 379.

7

Church as Sacrament: The Ecclesiology of de Lubac and Congar

> God gathered together as one all those who in faith look upon Jesus as the
> author of salvation and the source of unity and peace, and established them
> as the Church that for each and all it may be the visible sacrament of this
> saving unity.
>
> Second Vatican Council[1]

Few people have been as influential in the development of Catholic ecclesiology
as Henri de Lubac and Yves Congar. They are among the most significant
contributors to the rise of communion ecclesiology, for which the notion of
the Church as sacrament serves as one of the main theological pillars.[2] Officially
enshrined by the Second Vatican Council in *Lumen gentium* (1964) and
reaffirmed by the 'Final Report' of the Extraordinary Synod of Bishops (1985),
the sacramental character of the Church is one of the most significant elements in
much of contemporary Catholic ecclesiology.[3] De Lubac and Congar no doubt
influenced this new direction. In particular, Congar's role in the writing of *Lumen
gentium* meant that he was directly involved in recovering the sacramental cast of
Catholic ecclesiology.[4]

---

[1] *AAS* 57 (1965), 5–75, at 14; English trans.: *Lumen gentium*, 9 <http://www.vatican.va>.

[2] Cf. Dennis M. Doyle, 'Journet, Congar, and the Roots of Communion Ecclesiology', *TS* 58
(1997), 461–79; id., 'Henri de Lubac and the Roots of Communion Ecclesiology', *TS* 60 (1999),
209–27. For more general reflections on communion ecclesiology, see Matthäus Bernards, 'Zur
Lehre von der Kirche als Sakrament: Beobachtungen aus der Theologie des 19. und 20.
Jahrhunderts', *MTZ* 20 (1969), 29–54; Avery Dulles, 'The Church as Communion', in Bradley
Nassif (ed.), *New Perspectives on Historical Theology: Essays in Memory of John Meyendorff* (Grand
Rapids, Mich.: Eerdmans, 1996), 125–39; Dennis M. Doyle, *Communion Ecclesiology: Vision and
Versions* (Maryknoll, NY: Orbis, 2000); Susan K. Wood, 'The Church as Communion', in Peter C.
Phan (ed.), *The Gift of the Church: A Textbook on Ecclesiology in Honor of Patrick Granfield*
(Collegeville, Minn.: Glazier/Liturgical, 2000), 159–76.

[3] *Lumen gentium*, 1, 9, 48; Synod of Bishops, 'The Final Report', *Origins*, 15 (1985), 444–50.

[4] Congar was involved in drawing up many of the main documents of the Second Vatican
Council. Cf. Congar, *Mon journal du Concile*, ed. Éric Mahieu, 2 vols (Paris: Cerf, 2002); Alberto
Melloni, 'Yves Congar à Vatican II: Hypothèses et pistes de recherche', in André Vauchez (ed.),
Cardinal Yves Congar 1904–1995: Actes du colloque réuni à Rome les 3–4 juin 1996 (Paris: Cerf,
1999), 117–64; Gabriel Flynn, '*Mon journal du Concile*: Yves Congar and the Battle for a Renewed
Ecclesiology at the Second Vatican Council', *LouvStud* 28 (2003), 48–70; William Henn, 'Yves
Congar and *Lumen gentium*', *Greg* 86 (2005), 563–92; Michael Quisinsky, *Geschichtlicher Glaube in
einer geschichtlichen Welt: Der Beitrag von M.-D. Chenu, Y. Congar und H.-M. Féret zum
II. Vaticanum* (Berlin: Lit, 2007).

The sacramental approach to ecclesiology was one of the main fruits of the *ressourcement* of the great Tradition. The treatises on the Church (*De ecclesia*), the first of which was written just after 1300 by James of Viterbo (*c*.1255–1308), had consistently been juridical in nature, resulting in a static ecclesiology that engaged in polemical debates with non-Catholics and that seemed to have little interest in the life and eschatological aim of the Church.[5] The neo-scholastic manuals on ecclesiology against which de Lubac and Congar reacted—those of theologians like Louis Billot, Jean-Vincent Bainvel, Edmond Dublanchy, Timoteo Zapelena, and Joaquín Salaverri (1892–1992)[6]—seemed to be interested mainly in ascertaining the juridical validity of the sacraments, in defending the Church as a 'perfect society' (*societas perfecta*), in applying the four characteristics of the true Church (*notae ecclesiae*) to the Roman Catholic Church, and in upholding the supreme jurisdiction of the hierarchy and the pope in this 'unequal society' (*societas inaequalis*).[7] In reaction against these juridical approaches—dubbed by Congar as 'hierarchology'—de Lubac and Congar felt drawn to the Church Fathers and the period prior to the Late Middle Ages. There they found an understanding of the Church as sacrament, a view that had made ecclesial unity and fellowship its aim.[8] They found that the great Tradition had been more concerned with communion as the sacramental reality (*res*) of the Church than with her juridical, outward conditions (*sacramentum*).

The sacramental character of the Church was central in Henri de Lubac and Yves Congar.[9] My choice to highlight these two theologians is not intended to minimize the differences between the Jesuit from Lyons-Fourvière and the Dominican from Le Saulchoir. De Lubac was primarily a patristic scholar, who turned to ecclesiology by means of the Church Fathers. Congar's main interests were ecclesiology and ecumenism, and his main sources of inspiration were

---

⁵ Cf. Congar's expressions of displeasure with the treatises of *De ecclesia* as originating with James of Viterbo's *De regimine Christiano* in 'The Idea of the Church in St Thomas Aquinas', *Thomist* 1 (1939), 331, 358; id., *Lay People in the Church: A Study for a Theology of the Laity*, trans. Donald Attwater (rev. edn, London: Chapman, 1985), 43.

⁶ Louis Billot, *Tractatus de Ecclesia Christi sive continuatio theologiae de Verbo incarnate*, 2 vols (Rome: Gregorian University, 1898); Jean-Vincent Bainvel, *De ecclesia Christi* (Paris: Beauchesne, 1925); Edmond Dublanchy, 'Église', in A. Vacant, et al., *Dictionnaire de théologie catholique*, iv (Paris: Letouzey et Ané, 1927), 2108–223; Timoteo Zapelena, *De ecclesia Christi*, 2 vols (Rome: Gregorian University, 1950); Joaquín Salaverri, *Sacrae theologiae summa*, i (Madrid: Biblioteca de autores cristianos, 1950).

⁷ Cf. Congar's reflections in 'Moving towards a Pilgrim Church', in Alberic Stacpoole (ed.), *Vatican II by Those Who Were There* (London: Chapman, 1986), 129–52. Cf. also Avery Dulles, 'A Half Century of Ecclesiology', *TS* 50 (1989), 419–20; Cornelis Th. M. van Vliet, *Communio sacramentalis: Das Kirchenverständis von Yves Congar—genetisch und systematisch betrachtet* (Mainz: Matthias-Grünewald, 1995), 39–46.

⁸ This sacramental view of the earlier Tradition is highlighted in the marvellous exposition of Jean-Marie-Roger Tillard, *Flesh of the Church, Flesh of Christ: At the Source of the Ecclesiology of Communion*, trans. Madeleine Beaumont (Collegeville, Minn.: Liturgical, 2001).

⁹ Doyle uses the term 'sacramental ontology' to describe de Lubac's approach ('Henri de Lubac', 226–7). Van Vliet's *Communio sacramentalis* regards the sacramental structure of Congar's ecclesiology as the key to his approach.

Thomas Aquinas, Johann Adam Möhler, and slavophile Orthodox theologians like Alexei Khomiakov (1804–60). Although both de Lubac and Congar were interested in a *ressourcement* of the tradition, de Lubac was keenly aware of the horizontalizing impact of modern culture, while for Congar the need to 'adapt' to the developments of society was a central concern. The different emphases of these theologians led to differing evaluations of the post-conciliar situation. De Lubac became deeply disturbed by the secularizing developments, while Congar arguably moved in the opposite direction, questioning the way in which some of his own writings had distinguished between hierarchy and laity and criticizing his earlier theological views as insufficiently up to date.[10] In the years after the Council, the two scholars supported rival journals, Congar associating himself with *Concilium*, which advocated more radical change in the Church, and de Lubac supporting *Communio*.[11] Notwithstanding their differences, both theologians rejected the juridicized ecclesiology of the modern period, and they were united in their focus on the sacramental character of the Church. Together, de Lubac and Congar shaped the communion ecclesiology that became ensconced in the documents of the Second Vatican Council.

HENRI DE LUBAC: CHURCH AS SACRAMENTAL PRESENCE OF GOD

The Social Character of the Church

De Lubac's deep concern for the social character of the Church and his strong antagonism towards all forms of individualist Christianity were the most obvious and consistent elements of his ecclesiology. This communal concern tied in directly with his sacramental understanding of the relationship between nature and the supernatural, as was evident from the very opening words of his first book, *Catholicisme* (1938):

> The supernatural dignity of one who has been baptized rests, we know, on the natural dignity of man, though it surpasses it in an infinite manner: *agnoscere, christiane, dignitatem tuam—Deus qui humanae substantiae dignitatem mirabiliter condidisti.* [Recognize, O Christian, your dignity—God, who in a wonderful manner created and ennobled your human nature.] Thus, the unity of the Mystical Body of Christ, a supernatural unity, supposes a previous natural unity, the unity of the human race.[12]

---

[10] Cf. Congar's gentle personal reflections on his differences with de Lubac in *Une vie pour la vérité: Jean Puyo interroge le Père Congar*, ed. Jean Puyo (Paris: Centurion, 1975), 83–4.

[11] Although de Lubac was one of the founders of *Concilium* in 1965 he broke with it in order to join Hans Urs von Balthasar and Joseph Ratzinger in setting up the journal *Communio* in 1972. The difference in allegiance between de Lubac and Congar does not mean that Congar uncritically supported *Concilium*. Cf. his reservations as expressed in *Une vie pour la vérité*, 156–60.

[12] De Lubac, *Catholicism: Christ and the Common Destiny of Man*, trans. Lancelot C. Sheppard and Elizabeth Englund (San Francisco, Calif.: Ignatius, 1988), 25; English trans. of *Catholicisme: Les aspects sociaux du dogme* (Paris: Cerf, 1938).

Here de Lubac affirmed both the unity of and the distinction between our natural dignity, on the one hand, and our sacramentally conferred supernatural dignity, on the other hand. His reason for drawing a connection between the ecclesial question and the issue of the supernatural is that he wanted to affirm the unity of the human race as created with a view to the supernatural end of human life in fellowship with the triune God.[13] Laced from beginning to end with quotations from patristic and medieval sources, de Lubac's *Catholicisme* attempted to correct the misunderstanding, held among Catholics and non-Catholics alike, that Catholicism was only concerned with the salvation of individuals. Quite the contrary, de Lubac insisted. Catholicism was social 'not merely in its applications in the field of natural institutions but first and foremost in itself, in the heart of its mystery, in the essence of its dogma'.[14]

De Lubac focused, therefore, on the unity of all humanity, both in its origin and in its ultimate goal: 'Christ from the very first moment of his existence, virtually bears all men within himself—*erat in Christo Jesu omnis homo*. [Every human being was in Christ Jesus.] For the Word did not merely take a human body; his Incarnation was not simple *corporation* [embodiment], but, as St Hilary says, a *concorporatio* [shared embodiment].'[15] The Church's mission was to reveal to the world its pristine, organic unity, as well as to restore and complete this unity.[16] De Lubac quoted the French poet, Paul Claudel (1868–1955): 'The Bride of Christ never ceases to be aware of that total humanity whose destiny she carries in her womb.'[17] Understandably, de Lubac saw this social nature of Catholicism as intimately tied in with its historical character and as implying

---

[13] The subtitle of the English edition—*Christ and the Common Destiny of Man*—seems particularly well chosen since for de Lubac 'Christianity alone continues to assert the transcendent destiny of man and the common destiny of mankind' (*Catholicism*, 140–1). De Lubac linked this common destiny with our created nature: 'The human race is one. By our fundamental nature and still more in virtue of our common destiny we are members of the same body' (ibid. 222). For similar expressions of a 'common' or 'transcendent' destiny, see ibid. 232, 299, 353.

[14] Ibid. 15. De Lubac's emphasis on the unity of humanity, as well as his sacramental ontology, fit the Platonist–Christian synthesis that dominated the theological landscape until the Middle Ages. Indeed, Susan K. Wood comments that de Lubac's understanding of the relationship between Eucharist and Church—the latter being the real (*verum*) body—is very much Platonic ('The Church as the Social Embodiment of Grace in the Ecclesiology of Henri de Lubac' (PhD diss., Marquette University, Milwaukee, Wis., 1986), 146). De Lubac was aware of the Platonic affinities of his sacramental ontology (*Catholicism*, 307) and he lamented the 'fashionable anti-Platonism' (id., *The Splendor of the Church*, trans. Michael Mason (1956; repr. San Francisco, Calif.: Ignatius, 1999), 69; English trans. of *Méditation sur l'Église* (Paris: Montaigne, 1953)). None the less, he did not want to make too much of this affinity (*Catholicism*, 40) and remained careful to point out that Christianity rejected the Platonist 'individualist doctrine of escape' (ibid. 137; cf. 141) and its depreciation of the created order (*Splendor*, 180). He also had serious reservations about the Neoplatonic 'hierarchy of being' (*Catholicism*, 334). John Milbank seems too eager to draw de Lubac into his own Neoplatonic ontology (Milbank, *The Suspended Middle: Henri de Lubac and the Debate Concerning the Supernatural* (Grand Rapids, Mich.: Eerdmans, 2005), 18).

[15] De Lubac, *Catholicism*, 37.

[16] Ibid. 53.

[17] Id., *Splendor*, 184.

the necessity of the historic, visible Church for salvation. All of history, de Lubac insisted, and in particular that of the Old Testament, was taken up 'by the Church; the world made spiritual by man, and man consecrated by the Church'.[18]

Throughout his writings, de Lubac retained this emphasis on the social aspect of Catholicism. Individualist forms of Christianity struck at the root of the Church's identity: an 'individualist Christianity' was 'something unthinkable' due to the Pauline identity between redemption and the building up of the Church.[19] Even if, in the words of St Peter Damian (*c.*1007–72), the individual might have the appearance of a 'Church in miniature',[20] this did not mean that the individual could stand on his or her own: 'The kiss he [i.e., Christ] has for the Church is a kiss in which every one among the faithful will have a part "inasmuch as a member of the Church", for while each soul is loved individually, none is loved separately.'[21]

De Lubac cautioned, at the same time, that his emphasis on the social was not meant to minimize either individual personhood or the mysticism of the individual interior life. In the two concluding chapters of *Catholicisme*, de Lubac explained that he did not mean to 'diminish or dangerously obscure that other no less essential truth that salvation is a personal matter for every

[18] De Lubac, *Catholicism*, 274.
[19] Id., *Splendor*, 177 n. 47. Cf. de Lubac's critique of an individualism that rejected the institutional framework of the Church (*The Motherhood of the Church Followed by Particular Churches in the Universal Church and an Interview Conducted by Gwendoline Jarczyk*, trans. Sergia Englund (San Francisco, Calif.: Ignatius, 1982), 9, 12-13; English trans. of *Les Églises particulières dans l'Église universelle, suivi de La maternité de l'église, d'une interview rec. par G. Jarczyk* (Paris: Aubier Montaigne, 1971)).
[20] De Lubac, *Splendor*, 358.
[21] Ibid. 359. Paul McPartlan, while roundly acknowledging de Lubac's 'sustained attack upon individualism' (*The Eucharist Makes the Church: Henri de Lubac and John Zizioulas in Dialogue* (Edinburgh: T. & T. Clark, 1993), 14), argues that, none the less, in the end de Lubac fell prey to an individualist mysticism (ibid. 19, 48, 67, 302–3). The reason for de Lubac's return to individualism, McPartlan believes, was twofold: (1) for de Lubac, the Incarnation did not establish a corporate personality, since Christ's achievement was universalized only after the Ascension (ibid. 64–5); and (2) for de Lubac, the one (Christ) united the many (believers), while the many (believers) did not constitute the one (Christ) (ibid. 19, 67). With regard to the first point, it seems to me that de Lubac did insist on the universal embrace of the Incarnation itself (*Catholicism*, 37–40; cf. his quotation of Hilary of Poitiers above, n. 15). This more or less Platonic move seems to me to underlie his entire argument—namely, that the Incarnation has for its aim the redemption of the new humanity, not just of separate individuals. With regard to the second point, the reason for de Lubac's *ressourcement* of the medieval tradition lay in his attempt to recover the unity of the Eucharistic and ecclesial 'body of Christ' as one. This 'mystical body' is 'not only the "real body"', once born of the Virgin, but the "true body", the total and definitive body, the one for whose redemption the Saviour sacrificed his body of flesh' (*Corpus Mysticum; The Eucharist and the Church in the Middle Ages: Historical Survey*, trans. Gemma Simmonds, Richard Price, and Christopher Stephens and ed. Laurence Paul Hemming and Susan Frank Parsons (London: SCM, 2006), 68). The sacramental connection between the *sacramentum* of the Eucharist and the *res* of the Church's unity implied, for de Lubac, that the many (believers) constituted the one (Christ). I am grateful to Fr McPartlan for a stimulating email conversation on this point.

individual'.[22] He wholeheartedly accepted, even embraced, Christian mysticism, along with the importance of individual detachment and solitude:

> How indeed could Christian mysticism, the foretaste of the Beatific Vision, the 'novitiate' and the 'anteroom' of eternity, the secret entry into the City of God and, at the same time, the return to original purity, how could it be anything but the very opposite to Solipsism? The community supports the mystic with it, and in its turn is supported by him.[23]

De Lubac's emphasis on the historical and social character of Catholicism also did not imply a reductionist limitation of reality to the temporal present or a denial of the eternal and of God's unchanging transcendence. Rather, for de Lubac, the 'common destiny' was dependent on the supernatural character of divine transcendence.[24] Throughout his oeuvre, de Lubac insisted on the importance of acknowledging divine transcendence. Immanentism never held any appeal to the Jesuit scholar from Fourvière. It is true that during the early part of his career his pleas on behalf of divine transcendence were somewhat muted. His neo-Thomist antagonists consistently played the gratuity of the supernatural realm as their trump card, so de Lubac pressed back for social and historical embodiment and development. None the less, defence of divine transcendence and opposition to ill-conceived immanence were already part of his 1938 *Catholicisme*:

> 'Becoming', by itself, has no meaning; it is another word for absurdity. And yet, without transcendence, that is, without an Absolute actually present, found at the heart of reality which comes to be, working upon it, really making it move, there can only be an indefinite 'becoming'... If there is 'becoming' there must be fulfillment, and if there must be fulfillment there must have been always something else beside 'becoming'.[25]

De Lubac never regarded historical 'becoming' as ultimate. History had value only because of the mystery of divine transcendence that constituted both the origin and the end of all historical development. For de Lubac, the individual person and the journey of history were meant for a common destiny.

The Eucharist Makes the Church

De Lubac's concern for the 'social character' of the Church—'the common destiny of man'—was closely connected to his understanding of the Eucharist. For de Lubac, an interest in the social aspect of Catholicism *as such* would not overcome the dualism between nature and the supernatural. His monumental historical study, *Corpus mysticum* (1944), provided the Eucharistic and ecclesial

---

[22] De Lubac, *Catholicism*, 326.   [23] Ibid. 349.
[24] Ibid. 353.   [25] Ibid. 354–5.

dimension necessary for a full-orbed understanding of his social concerns.[26] This
study traced in detail the development of the meaning of the term 'mystical
body', but the book's purpose reached beyond purely historical interest. The
opponent, also in this study of the Eucharist, was the individualist understanding
of the Church that de Lubac perceived in the extrinsicism of neo-scholastic
theology. *Corpus mysticum*, we could say, looked at one key aspect of the social
character of the Church. It traced the connection between Eucharist and
Church.[27] De Lubac began his book by explaining that throughout the first
nine centuries of the Church Eucharist and Church had been closely connected:
'[T]he Eucharist corresponds to the Church as cause to effect, as means to end, as
sign to reality.'[28] The celebration of the sacrament had always had as its goal the
unity of the Church.[29] The *sanctorum communio* of the Creed had involved,
therefore, a twofold communion: 'For, in the same way that sacramental communion (*communion in the body and the blood* [*communio corporis et sanguinis*]) is
always at the same time an ecclesial communion (*communion within the Church,
of the Church, for the Church* . . . [*communio ecclesiastica, Ecclesiae, ad Ecclesiam*]),
so also ecclesial communion always includes, in its fulfilment, sacramental
communion.'[30] De Lubac averred that this close link—indeed, the identity—
between sacramental and ecclesial communion was also evidenced by the theologians of the Middle Ages, who had consistently emphasized the unity of the one
body of Christ. They highlighted this unity even when distinguishing the three
aspects (historical, sacramental, and ecclesial) of this threefold body (*corpus
triforme*).[31] Sacrament and the Church had always been regarded as one and
the same.

De Lubac demonstrated a common medieval usage of the term 'mystical
body', which had been different from the contemporary identification of the
Church as the mystical body. In the Eucharistic controversies of the ninth century

---

[26] De Lubac, *Corpus mysticum; L'Eucharistie et l'Église au moyen âge: Étude historique* (Paris:
Aubier, 1944); English trans.: *Corpus Mysticum*. Throughout, I will be quoting from the English
translation. For analyses of this book, see Wood, 'Church as the Social Embodiment', 102–18;
Christopher J. Walsh, 'Henri de Lubac and the Ecclesiology of the Postconciliar Church' (PhD diss.,
Catholic University of America, Washington, DC, 1993), 52–61; Lisa Wang, '*Sacramentum Unitatis
Ecclesiasticae*: The Eucharistic Ecclesiology of Henri de Lubac', *ATR* 85 (2003), 143–58, 150–4.

[27] Cf. the account of de Lubac in Catherine Pickstock, *After Writing: On the Liturgical
Consummation of Philosophy* (Malden, Mass.: Blackwell, 1998), 158–66.

[28] De Lubac, *Corpus Mysticum*, 13.

[29] 'Thus the *bread of the sacrament* [*sacramentum panis*] led them directly to the *unity of the body*
[*unitas corporis*]. In their eyes, the Eucharist was essentially, as it was already for St Paul and for the
Fathers, the *mystery of unity* [*mysterium unitatis*], it was the *sacrament of conjunction, alliance, and
unification* [*sacramentum conjunctionis, federationis, adunationis*]' (ibid. 17). Here, as well as elsewhere, I have added to the English translation de Lubac's Latin terminology as he provided it in the
original French edition.

[30] Ibid. 21.

[31] Ibid. 23–8. De Lubac explained that the term *corpus triforme* had originated in Amalarius of
Metz (d. *c*.850). See ibid. 24–5. De Lubac presented an extensive discussion of Amalarius's
'threefold body' and its development (ibid. 263–301).

between Paschasius Radbertus (d. 865), on the one hand, and Ratramnus (d. 868), Rabanus Maurus (d. 856), and Gottschalk (d. *c*.868), on the other hand, both parties had referred to the sacramental body, not the ecclesial body, as the *corpus mysticum*, an identification which they, in turn, had adopted from Hesychius of Jerusalem in the fifth century.[32] This usage was understandable, de Lubac maintained, against the background of the liberal use, throughout the Tradition, of the term 'mystical' in connection with the Eucharist.[33] The difference between *mysterium* and *sacramentum*, explained de Lubac, was that in the ancient sense of the term a mystery had been 'more of an action than a thing'.[34] Consequently, the term *mysterium* did not refer simply to either the sign or the intended reality, but instead denoted their mutual relationship and interpenetration. Therefore, 'mystery' had referred to 'the secret power [*virtus occulta*] by which the thing operates across the sign and through which the sign participates, here again in widely differing ways, in the higher efficacy of the thing'.[35]

De Lubac's message was that the Eucharist was something dynamic, not static. The active and ritual character of the term *mysterium* was to de Lubac an indication that the focus ought to move away from the neo-Thomists' extrinsicist approach, which had regarded the Eucharist too much as a supernatural intervention unconnected to the life of the Church. Instead, de Lubac wanted theology to recognize the Eucharist as an activity that created the unity of the Church.[36] He summarized his discussion by insisting that, at least in the ninth century, *corpus mysticum* had served as a technical term that distinguished the Eucharistic body both from the 'body born of the Virgin' and from the 'body of the Church', while keeping the three closely connected.[37]

According to de Lubac, this traditional unity of the *corpus triforme* had first begun to disintegrate in the early twelfth century with Gilbert of Nogent (1053–1124) and Rupert of Deutz (d. 1129). Gilbert had distinguished the historical body as *corpus principale* from the sacramental body as 'relative body' (*relativum corpus*), 'derived body' (*derivatum corpus*), or 'vicarious body' (*vicarium corpus*).[38] Although at this time Eucharist and Church had still been connected, the distinctions in terminology none the less betrayed an initial drifting apart of

---

[32] Ibid. 28–36.   [33] Ibid. 41–5.   [34] Ibid. 49.   [35] Ibid. 52.

[36] De Lubac distinguished three essential aspects in the Eucharistic mystery: (1) by way of presence, the body of Christ lay hidden in the element of the bread, *in mysterio panis*; (2) by way of memorial, the body of Christ was a mystery of commemoration, which rendered Christ's sacrifice present *in mysterio passionis*; and (3) by way of anticipation, the body of Christ was the reality of the hope of edification and unity of the Church, *in mysterio nostro*: '[The Eucharist] signifies us to ourselves—*our own mystery, a figure of ourselves* [*mysterium nostrum, figura nostra*]—in what we have already begun to be through baptism (*one baptism* [*unum baptisma*]), but above all in what we ought to become: in this sacrament of unity, *is prefigured what we will become in the future* [*praefiguratur quiddam quod futuri sumus*]' (ibid. 66–7).

[37] Ibid. 73.   [38] Ibid. 75.

the historical and sacramental body, on the one hand, and the ecclesial body, on the other hand. By the time of Peter Lombard (*c.*1095–*c.*1164), the expressions 'mystical flesh' (*caro mystica*) and 'spiritual flesh' (*caro spiritualis*) had come to be reserved for the Church to the exclusion of the Eucharist, which was now considered the 'proper flesh' (*caro propria*). Lombard, as well as the great scholastic theologians of the High Middle Ages, had clearly distinguished the Eucharistic body (as 'sacrament and reality' [*sacramentum-et-res*]) from the ecclesial body (as 'reality and not sacrament' [*res-et-non-sacramentum*]).[39] Soon the ecclesial meaning of 'mystical flesh' would induce theologians to transfer the expression 'mystical body' from the Eucharistic body to the body of the Church. As de Lubac put it: '*Mystical body* [*corpus mysticum*] would follow on closely from *mystical flesh* [*caro mystica*]. It was as if one called forth the other.'[40]

This widening gap between Eucharist and Church had made it possible, by the fourteenth century, to interpret the 'body of the Church' (*ecclesiae corpus*) by means of analogies with juridical, social, and political bodies.[41] These comparisons, de Lubac maintained, would in turn radically alter the meaning of the Church as *corpus mysticum*: it would become simply one body among many.[42] Thus, when the Reformation had started to dissociate the mystical body of Christ from the visible Church, the Catholic Church had been without adequate response: the common premise of both sides of the Reformation had been a separation between the Eucharistic body and the ecclesial body.[43]

At the same time that the unity of the *corpus triforme* had begun to disintegrate, the terminology used to describe the Eucharistic body had also altered. For most of the Tradition, de Lubac explained, the *corpus Christi* in the Eucharist had been regarded as a spiritual body (*corpus Christi spirituale*). This had been the

[39] De Lubac, *Corpus Mysticum*, 102.

[40] Ibid. 104.

[41] Ibid. 114–16. Cf. the analysis of the linguistic developments of *corpus mysticum* in Ernst H. Kantorowicz, *The King's Two Bodies: A Study in Mediaeval Political Theology* (2nd edn, Princeton, NJ: Princeton University Press, 1997), 193–232.

[42] De Lubac reiterated his displeasure with this understanding of the Church as simply one body among many in *Splendor*, 128–30. 'We no longer understand the Church at all if we see in her only her human merits, or if we see her as merely a means—however noble—to a temporal end; or if, while remaining believers in some vague sense, we do not primarily find in her a mystery of faith' (ibid. 215). Similarly, he commented elsewhere: 'People generally speak of "Christianity" as they do of "Catholicism". There is obviously nothing to condemn in this usage, which is as justified as it is old. It is nevertheless regrettable that it too often suggests the idea of one doctrine among others, or of one society among others, even if perfect adherence is accorded this doctrine or this society. In and of themselves these two words do not lead us much beyond this. Such an idea would not be false, but it would be entirely incomplete and superficial. It is a question of a life, of the divine life to which we are called. Into this life, the Church, the *Catholica mater*, gives us birth' (*Motherhood*, 120). Cf. also de Lubac's objections to 'man-made models' of collegiality in the Church (*The Church: Paradox and Mystery*, trans. James R. Dunne (New York: Ecclesia, 1969), 19; English trans. of *Paradoxe et mystère de l'Église* (Paris: Aubier Montaigne, 1967)).

[43] De Lubac, *Corpus Mysticum*, 114–17.

traditional Augustinian position.[44] But when Berengar of Tours (d. 1088) had started to contrast spiritual eating with corporeal eating, controversy had erupted.[45] Alger of Liège (1055–1131) and others had reacted strongly by insisting on bodily consumption of Christ.[46] And, de Lubac added, '[f]rom the affirmation of bodily reception, we are led by implication to the affirmation of a bodily presence'.[47] The result had been that '"spiritualist" vocabulary gradually became, if not suppressed, at least rare or translated [*transformé*]'[48] while all the emphasis had come to be placed on the real presence in the Eucharistic body of Christ. The theory of the threefold body had quickly turned into a theory of a twofold body: 'the historico-sacramental body and the ecclesial body'.[49]

The new emphasis on bodily feeding and on real presence in the Eucharist meant that the ecclesial body could no longer be regarded as true body (*corpus verum*). Prior to the Berengarian controversy, the identification of the ecclesial body as *corpus verum* had seemed fitting:

Given that the Eucharistic mystery was thought of as a spiritual meal destined to bring about the fulfilment of that body or of that 'plenitude of Christ', which constitutes the Church, it was doubly natural that the effect of such a mystery should be equally thought of as its 'truth', at the same time as its 'reality': *truth and reality* [*veritas et res*], *the truth of realities* [*rerum veritas*].[50]

Since the sacramental aim of the Eucharistic celebration had been the Church as the 'plenitude of Christ', this ecclesial aim had suitably been described as the truth (*veritas*) of the Eucharist. But the twelfth-century shift in emphasis from the ecclesial body to the Eucharistic body had made the identification of the unity of the Church as the 'true body' difficult to sustain. Instead, the elements had begun to take the place of the unity of the Church as *corpus verum*. The overall result of the massive shifts that had occurred through the Berengarian controversy, summarized de Lubac, was a 'slow inversion' of two expressions:

At first and for quite a long time, 'Corpus mysticum' meant the eucharistic body, as opposed to the 'corpus Christi quod est Ecclesia' [the body of Christ that is the Church], which was the 'verum corpus' par excellence. Was it not in fact quite natural to designate as 'mystical' that body whose hidden presence was due to 'mystical prayer' and which was received in a 'mystical banquet'? that body offered in forms which 'mystically' signified the Church? It is possible to trace the slow inversion of the two expressions.[51]

---

[44] Ibid. 138.   [45] Ibid. 143–4.   [46] Ibid. 146–54.
[47] Ibid. 155.   [48] Ibid. 161–2.   [49] Ibid. 162.
[50] Ibid. 189 (translation adjusted). De Lubac did acknowledge that *corpus verum* had also known a long history of association with the sacramental body (ibid. 187–8). Wood is correct, therefore, to observe that for de Lubac 'the realism of the eucharistic presence is never called into question' ('Church as the Social Embodiment', 103).
[51] De Lubac, *Catholicism*, 100 n. 68.

The end result of the 'slow inversion' of the two expressions had been that the Eucharist was now identified as *corpus verum*, while the Church was referred to as *corpus mysticum*. This reflected an increasing concern with the real presence of the Eucharist and thus a shift in focus from the sacramental reality (*res*) to the sacramental means (*sacramentum*).[52]

The final chapter of *Corpus mysticum* was in a sense the most significant one. Entitled 'From Symbolism to Dialectic', this chapter moved beyond the historical changes in Eucharistic and ecclesial vocabulary. Here de Lubac intimated that the changes in the eleventh and twelfth centuries had been part of a much larger shift—a shift in theological methodology from symbolism to dialectic. He was convinced that the separation between Eucharist and Church was the result of a rationalist mindset that transformed 'symbolic inclusions' into 'dialectical antitheses'.[53] Both Berengar and his orthodox opponents, de Lubac claimed, had taken the separation between the historical/Eucharistic body and the ecclesial body for granted, the Berengarians retaining the symbolism and his opponents the 'truth': 'Against *mystically, not truly* [*mystice, non vere*], was set, in no less exclusive a sense, *truly, not mystically* [*vere, non mystice*]. Perhaps orthodoxy was safeguarded, but on the other hand, doctrine was certainly impoverished'.[54] Berengar, maintained de Lubac, had introduced a dialectical approach to theology that had proved unable to affirm the mystery of the 'mutual immanence' between the presence of Christ in the Eucharist and in the unity of the Church.[55]

Thus, the understanding of the Eucharist was by no means the only issue at stake. Nor could the changes simply be reduced to Berengar's impact on the Church: 'It was not, in all honesty, a matter of one man's influence. More profoundly, more universally, it was a new mentality that was spreading, a new order of problem that was emerging and catching people's interest, a new way of thinking, the formulation of new categories.'[56] De Lubac pointed directly to St Anselm (d. 1109) and Peter Abelard (1079–1142) as changing the Augustinian symbolic approach, and he lamented the resulting Christian rationalism that approached the mysteries of faith only by means of intellectual demonstration.[57] In short, de Lubac did not just present a plea for a return to a more Eucharistic understanding of the Church; his concern was also for the restoration of a symbolic approach to theology, one that he felt had suffered greatly through the twelfth-century introduction of dialectical theology. And, as we know from de Lubac's appropriation of Blondel, he held this dialectical theology responsible for the later rise of the neo-scholastic approach to theology.

---

[52] Cf. William T. Cavanaugh's comment on this development: 'What concerned de Lubac about the inversion of *verum* and *mysticum* was its tendency to reduce the Eucharist to a mere spectacle for the laity. The growth of the cult of the host itself in the later medieval period (the feast of Corpus Christi began in the thirteenth century) was not necessarily an advance for Eucharistic practice' (*Torture and Eucharist: Theology, Politics, and the Body of Christ* (Oxford: Blackwell, 1998), 213).

[53] De Lubac, *Corpus Mysticum*, 226.

[54] Ibid. 223.   [55] Ibid. 226.   [56] Ibid. 228.   [57] Ibid. 236–8.

In his *Méditation sur l'Église* (1953), in a chapter entitled 'The Heart of the Church', de Lubac reiterated the close relationship between Eucharist and Church.[58] The chapter contained numerous echoes from his earlier *Corpus mysticum*. Here, however, de Lubac dealt less with historical details. Instead, he lucidly explained the theological implications of his earlier historical work. He reiterated the link between the Church as 'mystical body' and the Eucharist. The first theologians who had referred to the Church as *corpus mysticum* had meant 'the *corpus in mysterio*, the body mystically signified and realized by the Eucharist—in other words, the unity of the Christian community that is made real by the "holy mysteries" in an effective symbol (in the strict sense of the word "effective")'.[59] In short, the initial use of the term 'mystical body' to denote the Church had underscored the Eucharistic origin of the Church.

De Lubac's insistence on a sacramental relationship between Eucharist and Church raised the question of the clergy's role in this relationship. Here de Lubac was at pains to avoid two opposing errors. On the one hand, in opposition to immanentism, this later work introduced a cautionary comment. The Eucharist did make the Church, but de Lubac did not want this notion misunderstood in a secularist fashion. He did not want people to mistake his rejection of extrinsicism for a capitulation to immanentism. Thus, he also drew attention to the inverse notion that 'the Church produces the Eucharist'. De Lubac meant by this that the hierarchical priesthood produced the Eucharist. Without devaluing the priest-hood of all believers, de Lubac none the less cautioned that the hierarchical priesthood was not 'a sort of emanation from the community of the faithful'.[60] The priesthood had its own, divinely given role in producing the Eucharist.

On the other hand, in opposition to extrinsicism, de Lubac posited a close connection between the clergy and the Eucharist. The clergy ought not to impose its authority as something entirely exterior to the community. Since the Church produced the Eucharist, the priestly role of sanctification stood at the origin of the threefold hierarchical power of government, teaching, and sanctification. The centrality of the priestly role was a result of the significance of the Eucharist as the 'crucible of unity'.[61] And if the priestly role of sanctification

---

[58] This book, published in English in 1956 as *The Splendor of the Church*, was the outcome of a number of workshops between 1946 and 1949. De Lubac's silencing in 1950 delayed their publication in the form of a monograph for some time, which gave him the opportunity to supplement the quotations and add a few pages. In 1952, the book miraculously passed censorship, so that it was published the next year under the title *Méditation sur l'Église*. Later, de Lubac recalled how the book escaped the watchful eye of Father Janssens, the General of the Society of Jesus in France, commenting with some glee: 'When I saw him in Rome, in the spring of 1953, and thanked him for granting his authorization (the book was then at the printer), he paled and, very frankly, told me that there was no reason to thank him, that it was quite by chance' (*At the Service of the Church: Henri de Lubac Reflects on the Circumstances that Occasioned his Writings*, trans. Anne Elizabeth England (San Francisco, Calif.: Ignatius, 1993), 75). For a detailed analysis of de Lubac's *Méditation sur l'Église*, see Ulrich Kuther, *Kirchliche Tradition als geistliche Schriftauslegung: Zum theologischen Schriftgebrauch in Henri de Lubacs 'Die Kirche. Eine Betrachtung'* (Münster: Lit, 2001).

[59] De Lubac, *Splendor*, 132.   [60] Ibid. 141.   [61] Ibid. 147.

in the Eucharist had priority, this further implied that '[e]ach bishop constitutes the unity of his flock',[62] so that 'in each one of her parts' the Church was truly Church and was complete.[63] De Lubac thus continued to draw attention to the intrinsic connection between the Eucharistic life of the Church and ecclesial authority.

By insisting that the Eucharist made the Church, de Lubac was asserting an identity of sorts between Christ and the Church. Because Eucharist and Church were the same body of Christ, there was a 'mystical identification' between Christ and his Church.[64] While acknowledging the distinction between Bride and Groom, de Lubac none the less wished to emphasize the conviction of St Leo the Great (d. 461) that through the Eucharist 'we pass over unto that which we receive'.[65] Therefore, de Lubac concluded this discussion in *Méditation sur l'Église* with the comment: 'If the Church is thus the fullness of Christ, Christ in his Eucharist is truly the heart of the Church.'[66]

We need to place de Lubac's understanding of the Eucharist as making the Church in the context of his Blondelian opposition to the extrinsicism of neo-scholastic theology. De Lubac's historical study of the increasing focus on real presence and transubstantiation was clearly directed against the neo-Thomist neglect of the Church's identity as the body of Christ. By insisting that the Eucharist made the Church, de Lubac was able to oppose a 'separated theology'. As Susan Wood puts it:

---

[62] De Lubac, *Splendor*, 149

[63] Ibid. To be sure, de Lubac did emphasize that the bishops together formed one episcopate and that the bishops were in communion with the Bishop of Rome. Priests had consecrating power by sharing in that of the bishop (ibid. 150). Although de Lubac looked to the Eucharist as constituting the Church, he did not draw the conclusion that various local churches were merely 'federating' together to form the Catholic Church. Instead, there was—and here de Lubac quoted Yves Congar—a 'mutual interiority' between the particular and the universal Church (*Motherhood*, 201). Accordingly, de Lubac insisted that there was only *one* episcopacy and *one* Church. He refused, therefore, to describe his ecclesiology as a 'eucharistic ecclesiology': 'The weakness of an ecclesiology too narrowly (or rather we should say too incompletely) "eucharistic" would be in privileging the "dimension" of the particular church by seeming to forget this radical correlation' (ibid. 204; cf. id., *Church: Paradox and Mystery*, 36). In personal conversation with Paul McPartlan, de Lubac reiterated that the term 'Eucharistic ecclesiology' would be 'too short' (McPartlan, *Eucharist Makes the Church*, 98).

[64] De Lubac, *Splendor*, 157. Cf. ibid. 209–11.

[65] Ibid. 158.

[66] Ibid. 160. The emphasis on the Eucharist as providing the unity of the Church explains de Lubac's opposition to a more horizontally oriented liturgy. For de Lubac, such an approach would be a lapse into immanentism, which ignored the way in which Christ became sacramentally present in and through the Eucharist: 'In the present welcome efforts to bring about a celebration of the liturgy that is more "communal" and more alive, nothing would be more regrettable than a preoccupation with the success achieved by some secular festivals by the combined resources of technical skill and the appeal to man at his lower level. To reflect for a moment on the way in which Christ makes real the unity between us is to see at once that it is not by way of anything resembling mass hysteria or any sort of occult magic' (ibid. 155).

Both the Eucharist and Christ are the cause of the Church, not nominally or extrinsically, but intrinsically, for within the context of spiritual exegesis Christ and the Eucharist are eschatologically fulfilled or completed in the Church. The sacramental causation is intrinsic in the sense that the source of the Church is to be found in its relation to Christ and the Eucharist.[67]

De Lubac avoided neo-scholastic extrinsicism by insisting that the Eucharist was completed in the Church. At the same time, by adding that the Church, in turn, made the Eucharist, de Lubac also avoided the opposite error of an immanentism that might want to celebrate the community without regard for its divine origin. For de Lubac, the Eucharist provided an avenue for the mutual interpenetration of nature and the supernatural. In short, his Eucharistic theology served to counter the dualism between immanentism and extrinsicism and to reintegrate nature and the supernatural.

The Church as Sacrament

De Lubac's influence on later Catholic and ecumenical developments is most markedly evident in his idea that the Church herself was a sacrament. By referring to the Church as a sacrament, he remained true to the theology of Möhler.[68] De Lubac succinctly described the sacramentality of the Church at the beginning of an entire chapter on this topic:

> The Church is a mystery; that is to say that she is also a sacrament. She is 'the total *locus* of the Christian sacraments', and she is herself the great sacrament that contains and vitalizes all the others. In this world she is the sacrament of Christ, as Christ himself, in his humanity, is for us the sacrament of God.[69]

This remarkable statement established a sacramental link not only between the Church and Christ, but also between Christ and God. Since de Lubac regarded the Eucharist as the sacrament that made the Church, we may infer that for de Lubac there was a sacramental chain, as it were, that pointed from the Eucharist to the Church, from the Church to Christ, and from Christ to God. Put differently, through the sacramental means of Christ, the Church, and the Eucharist, God was present in the world.

    De Lubac's view that the Church herself was sacramental in character was, again, a way to avoid the extremes of neo-scholasticism's extrinsicism and of secularism's immanentism. In the Church, the transcendent Christ truly entered into the history of our world. So, in *Catholicisme*, de Lubac linked his rejection of extrinsicism and individualism to his notion of the Church as sacrament:

---

[67] Wood, 'Church as the Social Embodiment', 144. Cf. ibid. 104: '[T]he unity of the eucharistic body and the ecclesial body is never an extrinsic unity because the ecclesial body is not another body than the body of Christ, but the *totus Christus*, the fullness of Christ.'

[68] McPartlan, 'Eucharistic Ecclesiology', *OiC* 22 (1986), 317.

[69] De Lubac, *Splendor*, 202.

But the Church, the only real Church, the Church which is the Body of Christ, is not merely that strongly hierarchical and disciplined society whose divine origin has to be maintained, whose organization has to be upheld against all denial and revolt. That is an incomplete notion and but a partial cure for the separatist, individualist tendency of the notion to which it is opposed; a partial cure because it works only from without by way of authority, instead of effective union. If Christ is the sacrament of God, the Church is for us the sacrament of Christ; she represents him, in the full and ancient meaning of the term; she really makes him present. She not only carries on his work, but she is his very continuation, in a sense far more real than that in which it can be said that any human institution is its founder's continuation. The highly developed exterior organization that wins our admiration is but an expression, in accordance with the needs of this present life, of the interior unity of a living entity, so that the Catholic is not only subject to a power but is a member of a body as well, and his legal dependence on this power is to the end that he may have part in the life of that body.[70]

This statement reflected four significant elements of de Lubac's ecclesiology. First, de Lubac posited a sacramental link between Church, Christ, and God, which his overall sacramental ontology enabled him to do. Second, de Lubac maintained that as a sacrament of Christ the Church 'really makes him present'. In other words, as we have noted above, there was a mystical identity between Christ and the Church. This mystical or sacramental identity between the Church and Christ explains de Lubac's attraction to St Augustine's dictum, 'You will not change me into yourself like bodily food, but you will be changed into me'.[71] For de Lubac, this mystical or sacramental identity allowed the Church to continue Christ's very life in this world. ('[S]he is his very continuation.') This is reminiscent both of Möhler's idea of a continued Incarnation and of Blondel's insistence that we find Christ's life in the Tradition of devotion and adoration, not in a past to be accessed by means of historical reconstruction.[72] Christ's presence in the Tradition of the Church and through her sacraments overcame, for de Lubac, the false dilemma between extrinsicism and immanentism. Sacraments, after all, were not some kind of *tertium quid* occupying a distinct space in between nature and the supernatural. In de Lubac's words, they did not function as 'intermediates'. Instead, they were 'mediatory':

---

[70] De Lubac, *Catholicism*, 76.

[71] 'Nec tu me in te mutabis sicut cibum carnis tuae, sed tu mutaberis in me' (Augustine, *Confessions*, VII. 10). Cf. de Lubac's comment: 'When, with St Augustine, they heard Christ say to them: "I am your food, but instead of my being changed into you, it is you who shall be transformed into me", they unhesitatingly understood that by their reception of the Eucharist they would be incorporated the more in the Church' (*Catholicism*, 99–100). Cf. McPartlan, *Eucharist Makes the Church*, 67–74; id., '"You will be changed into me": Unity and Limits in de Lubac's Thought', *OiC* 30 (1994), 50–60.

[72] For Maurice Blondel, the latter would mean 'to immure [Christ] in the past, sealing him in his tomb beneath the sediments of history and to consider only the natural aspect of his work as real and effective; it would be to deprive him of the influence which every master communicates to his immediate disciples' ('History and Dogma', in *The Letter on Apologetics and History and Dogma*, trans. and ed. Alexander Dru and Illtyd Trethowan (Grand Rapids, Mich.: Eerdmans, 1994), 247).

sacraments were sensible bonds that united the transcendent to the immanent, the supernatural to the natural.[73]

Third, given the context of his 1938 publication of *Catholicisme*, de Lubac was primarily concerned with the extrinsicism of his neo-Thomist detractors. He was troubled less by historicist immanentism than by authoritarianism and individualism; the latter two the direct results of the sealing off of transcendence from any real connection with the historical and Eucharistic life of the Church. De Lubac wanted to ensure that authority not be construed in an extrinsicist fashion.[74] One of his greatest fears about authoritarian attitudes in the Church was precisely that they did not take seriously the close link between the Bishop and the Eucharistic life of the Church and therefore fell into the trap of extrinsicism: 'Although he is the Head of his Church, Christ does not rule her from without; there is, certainly, subjection and dependence between her and him, but at the same time she is his fulfillment and "fullness". She is the tabernacle of his presence, the building of which he is both Architect and Cornerstone.'[75] Christ ruled the Church from the inside, through clergy whose primary role was their priestly service of the Eucharist.

In no way did de Lubac intend to minimize the authority of the hierarchy or the need for obedience to the Church.[76] From the time of his earliest writings, de Lubac was deeply committed to the authoritative role of the magisterium. Even after he was forced to give up his teaching position, in 1950, he continued to insist on the imperative of love and obedience to the Church:

Even where he has a duty to act, and in consequence a duty to judge, he will on principle maintain a certain distrust with regard to his own judgment; he will take good care to have himself in hand, and if it so happens that he incurs disapproval, he will, far from becoming obstinate, if necessary accept the fact that he cannot clearly grasp the reasons for it.[77]

Although in his later years de Lubac emphasized more strongly the need to submit to the authority of the Church, this was not the result of any major shift in his thinking. Rather, when de Lubac observed that people misinterpreted the

---

[73] De Lubac, *Splendor*, 202. De Lubac took the distinction between 'mediation' and 'intermediaries' from Louis Bouyer (*Motherhood*, 93–4).

[74] Cf. Fergus Kerr, 'French Theology: Yves Congar and Henri de Lubac', in David F. Ford (ed.), *The Modern Theologians: An Introduction to Christian Theology in the Twentieth Century* (2nd edn, Cambridge: Blackwell, 1997), 115.

[75] De Lubac, *Splendor*, 209. Cf. de Lubac's discussion of papal infallibility as 'an infallibility that is not something *separate* from that of the whole Church' (ibid. 271; emphasis added). Cf. also ibid. 266.

[76] As we saw in the previous chapter (Henri de Lubac: 'Cashing in' Jesus), de Lubac's theological view of development meant that for him the magisterium was the final arbiter in making doctrinal decisions.

[77] De Lubac, *Splendor*, 264. Christopher Walsh points out that, after 1950, de Lubac probably added passages to his completed manuscript of *Méditation sur l'Église* in which he autobiographically reflected on his difficult circumstances in relationship to the Church ('Henri de Lubac', 35–8).

Second Vatican Council by democratizing the Church, he became convinced that the pendulum had swung from supernaturalist extrinsicism to naturalist immanentism.[78] While clergy were called to serve the Church, they still carried divine authority: '[I]n no case is it from the Christian people that these ministers hold their commission, nor, consequently, the authority necessary for its achievement.'[79] The activists of what he termed the 'underground council' (*para-concile*) were not satisfied with an *aggiornamento* that sought renewal in the Church by means of patristic *ressourcement*. Instead, what the underground council 'and its main activists wanted and demanded was a *mutation*: a difference not of degree but of nature'.[80] For de Lubac, the neo-scholastic overemphasis on hierarchical authority and the liberal critique of authority stemmed from one and the same source: a sharp disjunction between nature and the supernatural resulting in a 'separated theology' that failed to see how authoritative, supernatural means of grace played a divinely ordained role within the Eucharistic life of the Church. Both approaches, de Lubac insisted, failed to locate the clergy within the divine life of the Church and, therefore, undermined the true authority of the hierarchical priesthood.[81] Thus, throughout his career, de Lubac insisted that the hierarchy fulfilled a sacramental function in the Church.

Fourth and last, a key aspect of de Lubac's understanding of the sacramentality of the Church was his insistence that the hierarchical aspect of the Church was merely penultimate, 'in accordance with the needs of this present life'. From a purely historical perspective, as 'proper subject for sociological investigation', the Church was only a means, not an end: 'A necessary means, a divine means, but provisional as means always are.'[82] If the Church was provisional inasmuch as she was a 'means' of salvation, this implied that the sacramental character of the Church would not cross over into the eschaton: 'Insofar as she is visible and temporal, the Church is destined to pass away. She is a sign and a sacrament, and it is the peculiar quality of signs and sacraments to be re-absorbed in the reality

---

[78] At the same time, also after the Second Vatican Council, de Lubac continued to express his objections to extrinsic accounts of authority, warning against ecclesiologies that 'assume a positivist conception of the Church or that systematically confine themselves to her exterior aspects, without linking her structure to her underlying nature' (*Motherhood*, 21).

[79] Ibid. 99. De Lubac regarded the various methods of selecting bishops as 'contingent particulars' (ibid.).

[80] Id., *A Brief Catechesis on Nature and Grace*, trans. Richard Arnandez (San Francisco, Calif.: Ignatius, 1984), 236. Cf. his scathing critique of 'small pressure groups' engaging in 'an insidious campaign against the papacy—under the pretext of a fight against that eccentricity which is dogmatism, a rejection of dogmatics, which is to say a rejection of the Christian faith in its original twofold character comprising an objective content received from authority' (id., *Motherhood*, 26).

[81] By resorting to a view of ministry as 'an external, completely "sociological" function, a mere profession', we would turn it into 'an arbitrary law'. 'But besides the fact that all authority recognized in [priestly] ministry would in this case have lost its foundation, this would not only deny Catholic tradition but in actual fact repudiate the very reality of the Church by emptying the Christian mystery' (de Lubac, *Motherhood*, 139; cf. ibid. 353).

[82] Id., *Catholicism*, 70.

they signify.'[83] Again, de Lubac was concerned here to counter a view of the hierarchy that, obsessed with authority, forgot its limited, mediatory character. The hierarchy's authority was not eternal: 'With the idea of strengthening the authority of those who are in this world Christ's representatives and the Apostles' successors, they sometimes go so far as to want to make eternal not only the imprint of the sacred character they have received—which would be legitimate— but the exercise of their power.'[84] Such a focus on the hierarchy's authority ignored, de Lubac argued, that the 'exterior cultus' 'will subsist no longer in the Kingdom of Heaven, where nothing will take place in symbol but all in naked truth'.[85]

The eschatological disappearance of the hierarchy of the Church resulted from its sacramental and, therefore, mediatory function. The priest's role was to make present the Eucharistic body of Christ, which in turn made present the ecclesial body. Only the latter, the unity of the mystical body, would remain in the end: 'The sacramental element in the Church, being adapted to our temporal condition, is destined to disappear in the face of the definitive realm it effectively signifies; but this should not be thought of as one thing's effacing of another. It will be the manifestation of sacramentality's own proper truth; a glorious epiphany and a consummation.'[86]

De Lubac's distinction between two different aspects of the Church helps to identify what he regarded as sacramental and provisional and what he considered as eternal reality. De Lubac maintained that one could look at the one mystical body of Christ from two different angles: an active and a passive aspect. When considering the active aspect, one would look at the mystical body in its divine essence. Here the Church was the gathering Church (*ecclesia convocans, congregans*).[87] From this viewpoint, the Church was sheepfold, mother, and bride.[88] This was the institutional, this-worldly Church,[89] in which the clergy offered the sacraments (*communio sanctorum*),[90] so that here the Church produced the Eucharist.[91] Put differently, here the Church as Mother Mary gave birth to Christ in her members.[92] In its passive aspect, however, one would look at the same body of Christ in its human form. Here the Church was the gathered

---

[83] Id., *Church: Paradox and Mystery*, 53.

[84] Id., *Splendor*, 73.

[85] Ibid. 74.

[86] Ibid. 68. This quotation is again an indication that we should not misidentify de Lubac's cautioning against authoritarianism as a modern rejection of authority. He was merely concerned to point out the hierarchy's proper sacramental role vis-à-vis a neo-scholastic extrinsicist conception of authority. This explains why de Lubac balked at what he saw as a secularist and historicist democratization after the Second Vatican Council, which he believed was not true to the Council's intent.

[87] Id., *Splendor*, 104.

[88] Ibid. 106, 108. Cf. the beautiful collection of patristic passages on the motherhood of the Church in id., *Motherhood*, 47–58.

[89] Id., *Splendor*, 124.   [90] Ibid. 110, 106.

[91] Ibid. 133.   [92] Ibid. 321, 337–8.

Church (*ecclesia convocata, congregata*).[93] From this viewpoint, the Church was the flock of sheep, the people of God, and the daughter.[94] This was the mystical, other-worldly Church,[95] in which the laity formed the communion of saints (*communio sanctorum*),[96] so that here the Eucharist produced the Church.[97] Put differently, here the Church as Virgin Mary rendered the Church's *fiat*.[98] Keeping these two aspects of the Church together in paradoxical unity was important to de Lubac.[99] He refused to speak, therefore, of an invisible Church,[100] and he continually stressed that it was the *one* body of Christ that one should view in its two different aspects. At the same time, the ultimate reality of the Church was the unity established through communion. This meant that the institutional and hierarchical aspect of the Church was always the provisional means that served the mystical and communal aspect.[101]

The Church in the World

De Lubac's sacramental ontology influenced the way in which he viewed the place of the Church in the world. On the one hand, he was clearly aware that the Church might often find herself in conflict with the state. As a 'perfect society' (Pius IX), the Church 'in a sense duplicates civil society',[102] and the Church's power 'extends to all that is spiritual in every human affair in which it is engaged'.[103] Since the state 'always tends to overstep the domain it has inherited',[104] it should not be surprising that the Church 'must clash with the powers of this world'.[105] De Lubac cautioned Christians that the decline of anticlericalism in society could well be a sign that Christians had 'adapted themselves to it [i.e., the world]—to its ideas, its conventions, and its ways'.[106]

---

[93] De Lubac, *Splendor*, 104.   [94] Ibid. 106, 108.   [95] Ibid. 124.
[96] Ibid. 110, 106.   [97] Ibid. 133.   [98] Ibid. 321, 337–8.
[99] Ibid. 108. For de Lubac, 'paradox' was a key notion, intimately connected to the notion of 'mystery' (see id., *Church: Paradox and Mystery*, 1–29). For him the paradox of the Church went back to the paradox of the Incarnation, but in a sense the mystery of the Church was even more paradoxical than that of Christ: 'If a purification and transformation of vision is necessary to look on Christ without being scandalized, how much more is it necessary when we are looking at the Church!' (id., *Splendor*, 50).
[100] Id., *Splendor*, 88. For de Lubac, it was important to realize that the word 'mystical' was not to be 'taken as synonymous with "invisible", but that it refers rather to the sensible sign of a reality that is divine and hidden', so that it would be a serious misrepresentation 'to separate the *mystical* body from the *visible* Church' (ibid. 131–2). 'The Body of Christ is not an invisible Church or an invertebrate people' (id., *Motherhood*, 85).
[101] Cf. de Lubac's comment: 'Of the two intimately connected characteristics of the Church, institutional and mystical, hierarchical and communal, if the second is assuredly the principal in value, the more pleasant to contemplate and the one which alone will continue to exist, the first is its necessary condition...Communion is the objective—an objective which, from the first instant, does not cease to be realized in the invisible; the institution is the means for it—a means which even now does not cease to ensure a visible communion' (*Motherhood*, 34–5).
[102] Id., *Splendor*, 161.   [103] Ibid. 198.   [104] Ibid. 196.
[105] Ibid. 188.   [106] Ibid. 201.

On the other hand, de Lubac's oppositional logic was not absolute. His theological starting-point was again the relationship between nature and the supernatural: 'Man's nature is twofold—he is animal and spirit. He lives on this earth and is committed to a temporal destiny; yet there is in him something that goes beyond any terrestrial horizon and seeks the atmosphere of eternity as its natural climate.'[107] Nature and the supernatural, the temporal and the eternal, co-inhered. The two domains were not 'mutually extrinsic'.[108] The fact that divine revelation had taken historical form and had been conveyed to us through the Tradition meant, for de Lubac, that the Church could not ignore the temporal realm of the state as belonging to a different order. De Lubac cautioned, therefore, against 'an exaggerated or misguided critique of what is freely labelled "Constantinian Christianity" ',[109] insisting that those whom he called *spirituali* might dangerously restrict the Church's sphere of action, so that they ended up 'striking a compromise—without wishing to do so—with the forces that wished to suppress it [i.e., the gospel] by either suppressing or subjugating the Church'.[110] Charity, he reminded his readers, did not have to 'become inhuman in order to remain supernatural'.[111]

Despite this ecclesial interest in the affairs of the world, the Church should beware, de Lubac argued, of an immanentism that would close off the Church's horizons through the failure to recognize her eschatological calling. In this regard, the Council represented a turning point in de Lubac's intellectual development. More and more, he came to regard secular immanentism as the real threat to the Church.[112] No longer was the 'separated theology' of extrinsicism the main opponent. Now, de Lubac denounced a 'separated philosophy': 'In the past a theocratic temptation may have threatened; today, on the contrary (but because of a similar confusion, and with less excuse, given the historical context), the secularist temptation has come to the fore very strongly.'[113] Ironically, he believed, both temptations based themselves on the same separation of nature and the supernatural. Both immanentism and extrinsicism, in other words, failed to return to the sacramental ontology that had been integral to the theology of the Fathers and most of the medieval Church.[114]

[107] Ibid. 166.   [108] Ibid. 191.

[109] Ibid. 175. Cf. de Lubac's insistence that the papacy had maintained the independence and orthodoxy of the Church against semi-pagan emperors 'in the first few centuries of what is so often called in an appalling oversimplification the "Constantinian era" ' (*Motherhood*, 301).

[110] Id., *Splendor*, 175.

[111] Id., *Catholicism*, 365.

[112] Cf. the following characteristic passage: 'Christian faith does not exist piecemeal; and any effort to "adapt" this or that element in it to nonbelieving interlocutors in order to justify it to them runs the risk not only of remaining barren, but of producing the opposite effect' (de Lubac, *Brief Catechesis*, 130).

[113] Ibid. 110.

[114] Remarkably, considering the focus on late medieval nominalism, both in Radical Orthodoxy and in Louis Dupré's work (*Passage to Modernity: An Essay in the Hermeneutics of Nature and Culture* (New Haven, Conn.: Yale University Press, 1993)), de Lubac rarely discussed the nominalist turn in the

De Lubac regarded the secularizing impact of 'immanentism' as the result of a *mis*appropriation of the Second Vatican Council.[115] At the same, however, he was not entirely happy with some of the direction set by the Council itself. In particular, he questioned the centrality of the 'people of God' metaphor in *Lumen gentium*. While he considered this strictly 'a matter of stress and nuance',[116] de Lubac none the less regretted that the Church as Mother and as Spouse had been 'subordinated to that of the people of God'.[117] The result of this central place of the 'people of God', de Lubac believed, was a focus on history and on the Church as a pilgrim people. By emphasizing the temporal more than the eschatological aspect of the Church, *Lumen gentium* could not avoid 'a certain narrowing of the patristic horizons', insisted de Lubac.[118] The post-conciliar decline of a sacramental ontology coincided, he believed, with a utilitarian and technological society devoted to secular progress. Such a de-sacramentalized society offered 'no "way out" to our desire: refusing to know God, insensible to his revelation, it imprisons us in a closed world without love and without hope—and we are in danger of dying there, suffocated'.[119] Christopher Walsh accurately captures de Lubac's post-Second Vatican Council attitude by commenting that what he 'rejected was the "*secularism*" or *immanentism*, which separated the natural and supernatural orders in order to exalt the former while compromising or dismissing the latter'.[120]

De Lubac's new focus on the danger of immanentism was particularly evident in his *Petite catéchèse sur nature et grace* (1980). The structure of the book distinguished sharply between 'Nature and the Supernatural' (Part I) and the

---

Late Middle Ages as lying at the root of the separation between nature and the supernatural. To be sure, he showed his awareness of the serious impact that nominalism did have on ecclesiology (see de Lubac, *Splendor*, 129 n. 9). And, of course, de Lubac connected both his attempted recovery of spiritual interpretation of Scripture and his critique of the developments of Eucharistic theology to a move from symbolic to dialectical theology (id., *Scripture in the Tradition*, trans. Luke O'Neill (1968; repr. New York: Herder & Herder/Crossroad, 2000), 55–72; id., *Corpus Mysticum*, 221–47). For my critique of the late medieval abandonment of the Platonic–Christian synthesis in favour of a nominalist approach, see Hans Boersma, 'Theology as Queen of Hospitality', *EvQ* 79 (2007), 291–310.

[115] See de Lubac's repeated warnings after the Second Vatican Council against immanentism and accommodation to culture (*Brief Catechesis*, 22, 94–6, 110–12, 170–1), as well as his denunciations of the misappropriations of the Second Vatican Council (id., *Motherhood*, 165, 221–2; id., *Brief Catechesis*, 191–260; id., *L'Église dans la crise actuelle* (Paris: Cerf, 1969); abr. English trans.: 'The Church in Crisis', *TD* 17 (1969), 312–25; id., *Entretien autour de Vatican II: Souvenirs et réflexions*, ed. Angelo Scola (Paris: France catholique; Paris: Cerf, 1985), 33–40; abr. English trans.: de Lubac and Angelo Scola, *De Lubac: A Theologian Speaks* (Los Angeles, Calif.: Twin Circles, 1985), 14–15).

[116] De Lubac, *Church: Paradox and Mystery*, 46.

[117] Ibid. 55.

[118] Ibid. 51. Cf. ibid. 48.

[119] Id., *Motherhood*, 149.

[120] Christopher J. Walsh, 'De Lubac's Critique of the Postconciliar Church', *Comm* 19 (1992), 407. In his journal of the Vatican Council, de Lubac spoke of the 'atrophy of the supernatural' (*Carnets du Concile*, ed. Loïc Figoureux, 2 vols (Paris: Cerf, 2007), ii. 453).

'Consequences' of their relationship (Part II), on the one hand, and 'Nature and Grace' (Part III), on the other hand. This structure implied a differentiation between the supernatural and grace. It was necessary to distinguish these two clearly, de Lubac maintained, in order to take full account of human sinfulness. He recognized there were problems in discussing the relationship between nature and the supernatural without taking sin and grace into account. In his discussion, de Lubac linked the Incarnation with the supernatural, while he connected redemption to grace.[121] He was quite willing to acknowledge a sharp difference between the orders of nature and grace. While throughout Part I (on 'Nature and the Supernatural') he spoke of the supernatural as merely 'elevating', 'penetrating', and 'transforming' nature, his discourse changed in Part III (on 'Nature and Grace') to 'conversion' language:

There is an antagonism, violent conflict ('*natura filii irae*' [by nature children of wrath] says St Paul). Between grace and sin the struggle is irreconcilable. Consequently, the call of grace is no longer an invitation to a simple 'elevation', not even a 'transforming' one (to use the traditional words); in a more radical fashion it is a summons to a 'total upheaval', to a 'conversion' (of the 'heart', i.e., of all one's being).[122]

De Lubac's *Petite catéchèse* gave evidence of his renewed emphasis on the distinct character of divine transcendence and the supernatural, something that his neo-Thomist detractors had wanted him to accentuate in his earlier years.

De Lubac's rather sharp attack on Edward Schillebeeckx (b. 1914) was directly connected to this change in emphasis.[123] De Lubac's sacramental ontology entailed that he regarded the Church as *sacramentum Christi*. For de Lubac, the Eucharistically constituted body of Christ signified Christ and made him present in the world. The unity of the Church as the truth of the Eucharist was the embodiment of the eschatological unity of the whole Christ (*totus Christus*). While the Second Vatican Council adopted language identical to that of de Lubac by speaking of the Church as 'sacrament', it did not explicitly refer to the Church as 'sacrament *of Christ*', the way de Lubac had put it. *Lumen gentium* stated that in Christ the Church was 'like a sacrament or as a sign and instrument both of a very closely knit union with God and of the unity of the whole human race'.[124] Schillebeeckx had commented on this passage by saying: 'The Church is the "sacrament of the world". Personally, I consider this declaration as one of the most charismatic that have come from Vatican II.'[125] From this statement, de Lubac concluded that Schillebeeckx linked the Church more to the world than to Christ.

---

[121] De Lubac, *Brief Catechesis*, 122, 168.

[122] Ibid. 119.

[123] Ibid. 191–234. For analyses of de Lubac's attack on Schillebeeckx, see Wood, 'Church as the Social Embodiment', 179–89; Walsh, 'Henri de Lubac', 245–61.

[124] *AAS* 57 (1965), 5 (*Lumen gentium*, 1).

[125] Quot. de Lubac, *Brief Catechesis*, 191.

For de Lubac, Schillebeeckx's notion of the Church as sacrament of the world (*sacramentum mundi*) betrayed a foundational error in ecclesiology. De Lubac was willing to speak, along with Balthasar, of the Church as sacrament *for* the world, or as sacrament of the coming Kingdom of God.[126] He was also quite ready, in line with his sacramental ontology, to acknowledge that one could refer to the Church as *sacramentum mundi* in the sense that the world itself was a sacrament.[127] But to de Lubac it seemed that the Belgian theologian had given up on a truly sacramental ontology. He sensed in Schillebeeckx resistance to a 'theophanic world' and to 'sacralising religion', 'in order to return the "world" fully to its "worldly state"'.[128] For de Lubac, Schillebeeckx's focus on the *saeculum* made it impossible to retain a sacramental ontology. As Walsh puts it:

In de Lubac's view, the Christian mission is to bring the *lumen Christi* [light of Christ] into a world that does not know Christ, and thus to illuminate the darkness of the age with the splendor of him who abides, according to his promise, mysteriously, obscurely, yet really in his Body the Church. For him, this instrumental, mediatory role of the Church is intrinsic to what the council meant when it described the Church as sacrament: i.e., the Church is a sign that *effects* what it signifies.[129]

De Lubac was deeply suspicious of Schillebeeckx's understanding of the world as 'implicit Christianity', of his celebration of 'desacralizing secularization', and of his acceptance of liberation theology. He felt that Schillebeeckx had eliminated the distinction between nature and the supernatural by equating salvation with the pursuit of purely natural ends:

[D]oes the 'eschatological kingdom' not appear, in all this [i.e., in Schillebeeckx], as the culmination of our 'earthly expectations', as their supreme fulfillment and consummation? ... So, in practice, human history and salvation history would be one and the same. 'In this respect there is no difference between the Old and the New Testament.' Consequently, 'today's Christian reflection' eliminates 'the ancient problem of nature-supernature', traces of which, in the early days of the Council, could still be found in the first drafts of what was then called Schema 17. 'Creation and divinization together make up the unique supernatural order of salvation.'[130]

De Lubac was clearly afraid that Schillebeeckx was compromising the sacramental relationship between nature and the supernatural by collapsing the supernatural into a purely natural realm. De Lubac warned that we ought not 'to confuse the progress or the "construction" of the world with the new creation or even to

---

126   De Lubac, *Brief Catechesis*, 211.
127   Ibid. 213. As we will see, this was a strong emphasis in the later ecclesiology of Congar. Cf. below, sect.: Post-conciliar Development.
128   Id., *Brief Catechesis*, 215–16.
129   Walsh, 'Henri de Lubac', 261.
130   De Lubac, *Brief Catechesis*, 225–6. The quotation marks within this quote indicate statements made by Schillebeeckx.

suppose that the latter is an outgrowth of the former'.[131] He believed that Schillebeeckx had fallen into the trap of accepting nature as an isolated entity, which was exactly the problem Blondel had described as 'historicism'. The outcome of Schillebeeckx's position, de Lubac was convinced, would be an immanentist and secularist mindset, in which the Church would have nothing to convey to the world.[132] By describing the Church as sacrament of the world rather than of Christ, one would end up naturalizing and secularizing the Church. In short, de Lubac saw Schillebeeckx as undermining the very sacramental ontology that *nouvelle théologie* had worked so hard to restore.

YVES CONGAR: THE SACRAMENTAL UNITY OF STRUCTURE AND LIFE

Church as Return to the Trinity

Yves Congar's first main monograph, *Chrétiens désunis* (1937), turned out to be programmatic for his further career.[133] For the first time, the Dominican scholar entered the domain of ecumenical discussion among Catholics, Orthodox, and Protestants. Based on a sermon series preached at the Montmartre's Sacré Cœur Basilica during the Octave of Prayer for Christian Unity in 1936, the book cautiously opened the door to ecumenical dialogue, while critiquing—sharply at times—both Protestant theology and aspects of the ecumenical movement.[134] Congar theologically undergirded his approach in a chapter dealing with the unity of the Church. Here he grounded the Church in Trinitarian and Christological doctrine. The Church's oneness was grounded in the unity of God himself.[135] At the same time, to enter into the Church was to join the communion of the Trinitarian life. For Congar, the Church was constituted by people entering the divine life by faith and charity:

---

[131] Ibid. 228. I am not assessing here whether or not de Lubac interpreted Schillebeeckx correctly on this point. Walsh argues that this part of de Lubac's critique did not do justice to Schillebeeckx's position ('Henri de Lubac', 257–9).

[132] Wood captures the difference between the two theologians well when she comments that with Schillebeeckx it seemed that the Church was merely the visible embodiment of a prior unity of the human race, while for de Lubac the unity of the human race existed only *through* the Church ('Church as the Social Embodiment', 187–8).

[133] Congar, *Chrétiens désunis: Principes d'un 'oecuménisme' catholique* (Paris: Cerf, 1937); English trans.: *Divided Christendom: A Catholic Study of the Problem of Reunion*, trans. M. A. Bousfield (London: Bles, 1939).

[134] Congar's caution notwithstanding, Mariano Cordovani criticized the book in *L'Osservatore Romano*, as a result of which the Dominican Master General, Martin Stanislas Gillet, summoned Congar (Congar, *Une vie pour la vérité*, 100). In 1950, Congar was unable to obtain permission for a second edition of *Chrétiens désunis* from the new Master General, Emmanuel Suárez (ibid. 107).

[135] Congar, *Divided Christendom*, 48.

The Church is precisely this extension of the divine life to a multitude of creatures, not as a result of their own exertions to develop their religious sense or to lead a life similar to God's, but by the imparting to them of the very life of God itself, so that they actually share the life and participate in the purposes of God. The Church is not merely *a* society, men associated with God, but the divine *Societas* itself, the life of the Godhead reaching out to humanity and taking up humanity into itself.[136]

Since the Church was the society of those who had joined the Trinitarian life, she came from above: faith and charity were the outcome of the double procession of knowledge and love in the Trinity.[137] The Church was 'Church from the Trinity' (*ecclesia de trinitate*).

Christ, Congar maintained, provided the link between the Trinity and human beings. The Church was 'the visible Body of Christ, His σωμα [body], a Christophany: she is His own flesh, His Bride'.[138] Thus, the Church was also 'Church in Christ' (*ecclesia in Christo*): only by being incorporated into Christ could one join the Trinitarian life. At this point, Congar briefly discussed the sacraments: 'This incorporation in Christ is begun and effected—and this is all-important—by contact with Christ in the sacramental order.'[139] Thus, the sacraments were the means by which Christ's mediation was made actual. It was *because* of Baptism into Christ that we were formed into the body of Christ, and it was *because* there was one Eucharistic bread that the many became one body.[140]

Finally, the Church was also 'Church from the people' (*ecclesia ex hominibus*). In the present human condition, the divine life was given 'in a human mode adapted to the condition of sinful men'.[141] While in the heavenly beatific vision the divine life would be given perfectly, directly, spiritually, and in an interior manner, such was not yet the case today. Using the expression often employed also by his teacher, Marie-Dominique Chenu, Congar explained that the Church on earth followed the 'law of incarnation'.[142] This implied that the Church *ex hominibus* had to take tangible shape in an 'apostolic and hierarchic'[143] fashion: 'The Church is the Body of Christ, His glory, His human and collective visibility: the Christ, it has been said, needs the Church as a πνευμα [spirit] needs a σωμα [body].'[144] Congar expressed the link between 'spirit' and 'body' by describing the law of the Incarnation as follows: 'That most mystical and interior unity which makes us one body, as St Paul says, is in this manner interiorly caused and outwardly effected through the ministry of the apostles or the ministry derived from the apostles, and communicated by them, in celebrating under sacramental, sensible and collective forms the death and resurrection of the Lord.'[145] The organization or institution of the Church (*ecclesia ex hominibus*) provided the sacramental means of union with Christ (*ecclesia in Christo*), and so of spiritual

---

[136] Congar, *Divided Christendom*, 48.   [137] Ibid. 55–6.   [138] Ibid. 61.
[139] Ibid. 62.   [140] Ibid. 63.   [141] Ibid. 64.   [142] Ibid. 69, 73.
[143] Ibid. 70.   [144] Ibid. 70–1.   [145] Ibid. 73.

divinization (*ecclesia de trinitate*). Not surprisingly, Congar came to a conclusion similar to that of de Lubac: it was appropriate to regard the Church *ex hominibus* as a 'great sacrament in which everything is a sign and means of an inward unity of grace'.[146]

Congar drew up two columns further to elaborate on the distinction between the Church *de trinitate* as she came to share the divine life and the Church *ex hominibus* as she was in the world under human conditions. Juxtaposed in the two columns, he listed (1) divine unity or the communication of a simple principle versus social unity constituted in multiplicity by consensus; (2) organism versus organization; (3) a living body animated by faith and love versus a society involving commands and obedience; (4) a hierarchy of holiness and virtue (in which a pope 'may be much less near to Christ than a humble and ignorant woman'[147]) versus a social and juridical hierarchy in which clergy took a higher place because of their function; (5) communication of the life of God with Christ giving himself as he wanted versus a society organized for the common good with a visible head in Rome; (6) the Church as the Mystical Christ or the wholly realized union with God versus the Church as quantitative extension in various countries of the world; (7) the Church as vital body animated by the Holy Spirit as the interior principle of life versus the Church as an institutional or legal body with many activities and functions; and (8) the Church as existing eternally versus the Church on pilgrimage for the purpose of gathering together the members of Christ.[148]

Two elements are particularly worth noting in Congar's initial elaboration of the two aspects of the Church. First, as *aspects*, the characteristics mentioned in the two columns should not be separated. There were not two churches, Congar maintained.[149] He regarded the two aspects of the Church as related sacramentally. The *ecclesia ex hominibus* existed for the sake of the *ecclesia de trinitate*. Second, this meant that for Congar, the first column—the *ecclesia de trinitate*— had priority. The Church was a community or gathering of the faithful (*congregatio fidelium*), a dynamic process of entering the divine life by way of faith and charity as expressed in Baptism and Eucharist. This made the hierarchical or juridical elements radically subservient to the Church's spiritual life—a bold move in the face of the regnant ecclesiology of the manualist tradition. In Congar's understanding, the hierarchical structure was indispensable, to be sure; but in an important sense, it did not have theological priority.[150]

---

[146] Ibid. 87 (translation adjusted). Cf. Ibid. 84.

[147] Ibid. 77.

[148] Ibid. 76–80. Congar's two columns were similar to the two aspects of the Church distinguished by de Lubac (see in this Chapter, the sect. above: The Church as Sacrament.)

[149] Ibid. 80. Cf. the elaboration (ibid. 80–4).

[150] This point needs to be emphasized in the light of the common criticism that Congar prioritized the juridical or hierarchical element, especially in his earlier writings. To be sure, there was an obvious shift in Congar's thinking. But this shift in emphasis never involved a change in theological priority. From the very beginning, Congar related the two columns sacramentally,

Congar looked to St Thomas Aquinas for support for his dynamic view of a Church whose origin was the triune God and whose purpose was a deifying return (*reditus*) to him.[151] Congar's 1939 essay on Thomas's ecclesiology is particularly instructive, since it audaciously set out the sacramental purpose of the Church in reaction to the earlier reification of the outward elements.[152] The essay began by drawing attention to the fact that Thomas never wrote a treatise *De ecclesia*. The reason, Congar maintained, was that the entire *secunda pars* of Thomas's *Summa Theologica*, dealing with Christian faith and morals as the movement of human beings to God, had constituted his ecclesiology: 'To define the Church as a body having community of life with God is to conceive of it as humanity vitalized Godwards by the theological virtues, which have God for their object, and organized in the likeness of God by the moral virtues.'[153] Insisting that this return to God was thoroughly Christological—seeing that 'the Church, new life of humanity moving Godwards, is what she is only by participation in Christ, receiving from Him, yet adding nothing'[154]—Congar maintained that it was possible for the Church to be Christ's body since through his human nature he was 'homogeneous' with her.[155]

---

meaning that the juridical structure of the Church existed for the sake of the divine life. From today's perspective, it may well seem as though Congar's early writings highlighted the institutional aspect. But, such impressions are deceiving. Congar's neo-scholastic opponents did not get the same impression from his books on ecumenical dialogue, Church reform, and the laity—and rightly so. The sacramental character of the Church meant a rather fundamental reorientation in the function of the Church as social organization. For the common criticism of Congar's early emphasis on the Church's juridical structures, see Timothy I. MacDonald, *The Ecclesiology of Yves Congar: Foundational Themes* (Lanham, Md.: University Press of America, 1984), 130–3, 266; Victor Dunne, *Prophecy in the Church: The Vision of Yves Congar* (New York: Lang, 2000), 91–2; A. N. Williams, 'Congar's Theology of the Laity', in Gabriel Flynn (ed.), *Yves Congar: Theologian of the Church* (Grand Rapids, Mich.: Eerdmans, 2005), 135–59; Douglas M. Koskela, *Ecclesiality and Ecumenism: Yves Congar and the Road to Unity* (Milwaukee, Wis.: Marquette University Press, 2008), 79–80, 85–6.

151 For Congar's appropriation of Thomas's ecclesiology, cf. Jean-Pierre Torrell, 'Yves Congar et l'ecclésiologie de Saint Thomas d'Aquin', *RSPT* 82 (1998), 201–42.

152 Congar, 'The Idea of the Church in St Thomas Aquinas', *Thomist* 1 (1939), 331–59; French edn: 'L'Idée de l'Église chez saint Thomas', *RSPT* 19 (1940), 31–58. Cf. the more popular version, 'The Idea of the Church in St Thomas Aquinas', in *The Mystery of the Church*, trans. A. V. Littledale (rev. edn, Baltimore, Md.: Helicon, 1965), 53–74. I will be quoting from the 1939 essay.

153 Congar, 'Idea of the Church' [1939], 337. Cf. ibid. 339: 'For St Thomas, the Church is the whole economy of the return towards God, *motus rationalis creaturae in Deum* [the movement of the rational creature into God], in short, the *Secunda Pars* of his *Summa Theologica*.'

154 Ibid. 342.

155 Ibid. 347. The language of Christ's body being 'homogeneous' with the Church implied, for Congar, a close connection between Christ and his mystical body, something on which he elaborated by speaking of the Church as continued Incarnation, so that the Church was 'simply his [i.e., Christ's] visibility in extended and tangible form, it is a Christophany' ('The Church and its Unity', in *Mystery of the Church*, 27). Along these lines, Congar argued that we become the body of Christ through the Eucharistic body, so that 'body' and 'communion' denoted both Eucharist and Church (id., 'Eucharist and Church of the New Alliance', in *The Revelation of God*, trans. A. Mason and L. C. Sheppard (New York: Herder & Herder, 1968), 178). The body born of Mary, the Eucharistic body, and the ecclesial body were 'genuinely linked', since 'the first takes the form of the

Having made the argument that our return to God depended on our connection to Christ, Congar then drew out the sacramental implications. Since our union with Christ resulted from faith and the sacraments of faith, Thomas saw the institution of the Church as 'the Sacrament, the ministry, in short, the instrument of realization of the Mystical Body'.[156] The Church was not just the body of Christ, but was also 'the means of realization and construction of that Body'.[157] In short, the Church as sacrament mediated the unity of the body of Christ. As Congar put it:

The unity of the Mystical Body is the reality attained by that Sacrament which is the source, the end, the beginning and the consummation, of all the others, that by which and for which the Church—the Church the mystery of faith, of which we are speaking, as much as the Church building, the Cathedral, the Temple—that by which and for which the Church was created—the Eucharist. In numerous texts St Thomas asserts that the *Res hujus Sacramenti* [reality of this sacrament], that is, the thing attained by the effective symbolism of the Sacrament, is the *Unitas corporis mystici* [unity of the mystical body].[158]

His *ressourcement* of Thomas's theology enabled Congar to articulate his sacramental view of the Church—with the structure as the means of creating the unity of the mystical body. The conclusion that Congar drew from his engagement with the Angelic Doctor was that the deifying process of salvation constituted the Church.[159]

Reform without Schism

Congar's second programmatic book was his 1950 *Vraie et fausse réforme dans l'Église*.[160] Here he developed his earlier distinction between *ecclesia ex hominibus*

---

second so that it may exist in the third' (id., *The Mystery of the Temple, or, The Manner of God's Presence to His Creatures from Genesis to the Apocalypse*, trans. Reginald F. Trevett (London: Burns & Oates, 1962), 189). This position on the 'threefold body' was the same as de Lubac's. At the same time, Congar recognized limitations in the notion of a 'continued Incarnation'. See id., 'Dogme christologique et ecclésiologie: Vérité et limites d'un parallèle', in *Sainte Église: Études et approches ecclésiologiques* (Paris: Cerf, 1963), 69–104. These reservations were not just later developments; he already expressed them in *Chrétiens désunis* (1937). For scattered comments on 'continued Incarnation', see id., *Divided Christendom*, 58; id., 'The Mystical Body of Christ', in *Mystery of the Church*, 87, 94; id., 'The Holy Spirit and the Apostolic College, Promoters of the Work of Christ', in ibid. 129; id., 'The Church and Pentecost', in *Mystery of the Church*, 181, 186; id., *Christ, Our Lady and the Church: A Study in Eirenic Theology*, trans. Henry St John (London: Longmans Green, 1957), 5, 66–7; id., 'The Holy Spirit in the Church', in *Revelation of God*, 152; id., *Tradition and Traditions: The Biblical, Historical, and Theological Evidence for Catholic Teaching on Tradition*, trans. Michael Naseby and Thomas Rainborough (San Diego, Calif.: Basilica, 1966), 312, 345; id., *Ministères et communion ecclésiale* (Paris: Cerf, 1971), 12.

[156] Congar, 'Idea of the Church' [1939], 353.

[157] Ibid. 354.

[158] Ibid. 356.

[159] Cf. Elizabeth Teresa Groppe's comment: 'The eschatological mystery of deification is inseparable from the mystery of the church' (*Yves Congar's Theology of the Holy Spirit* (Oxford: Oxford University Press, 2004), 100).

[160] Congar, *Vraie et fausse réforme dans l'Église* (Paris: Cerf, 1950). Congar was prevented from republishing the book (which did not happen until 1968) and from having it translated. It was none

and *ecclesia de trinitate* by using the terminology of institution and community, of centre and periphery, and of structure and life, focusing throughout on the question of true and false reform. The institution–community distinction was for Congar a tool to approach the theological conundrum of the presence of sins and weaknesses in a holy and infallible Church. He set out to articulate in what sense one could maintain that the Church was infallible, while at the same time insisting that she needed reform. He began by distinguishing between two aspects of the Church.[161] The one aspect, most common among the Church Fathers, was that of the community of the faithful (*congregatio fidelium*). This was the Church as one experienced her in the daily life of the members. In this sense, the members made up the Church. The other aspect came to the fore by looking at the Church not from the perspective of the members but from that of the calling to make disciples and to baptize (Matt. 28: 19; Mark 16: 15–16): 'So, there is a sense or an aspect according to which the Church is made by her members and a sense or an aspect according to which she makes her members and is thus prior to them.'[162]

Congar then made a further distinction with regard to the second aspect, by which the Church was anterior to her members. He maintained that the Church made her members in two ways. First, he discussed the Church as mystery. He reiterated that one could speak of the Church in Christ (*l'Eglise dans le Christ*), both in the sense that God had elected people in his Son and in the sense that in the Incarnation the Son of God had espoused himself to human nature. In both ways, it was possible to speak of 'a reality of the Church *as mystery*, prior to its own reality as *congregatio (collectio) fidelium*'.[163] Next, Congar moved to the Church as institution. Here he was thinking of the elements that structured the Church as means of grace: 'the deposit of faith (and principally the revelation of the Holy Trinity), the sacraments of the faith instituted by Jesus Christ as means to unite oneself to the mystery of his passage to the Father, and, finally, the ministries or apostolic powers.'[164]

Congar explained that both elements of this second aspect—the Church as mystery (by way of election and Incarnation) and as institution—had to bear

---

the less translated into Spanish (see *Une vie pour la vérité*, 106–7) and small sections were translated into English ('Attitudes towards Reform in the Church', trans. Bernard Gilligan, *CC* 1/4 (1951), 80–102; 'Vraie et fausse réforme dans l'Église', trans. Lancelot Sheppard, *CC* 3/4 (1953), 358–65. A team of scholars is currently working on a complete English translation. For secondary literature on the book, see Joseph Famerée, *L'Ecclésiologie d'Yves Congar avant Vatican II; Histoire et Église: Analyse et reprise critique* (Louvain: Leuven University Press, 1992), 84–121; van Vliet, *Communio sacramentalis*, 100–19; Gabriel Flynn, 'Yves Congar and Catholic Church Reform: A Renewal of the Spirit', in Gabriel Flynn (ed.), *Yves Congar: Theologian of the Church* (Grand Rapids, Mich.: Eerdmans, 2005), 99–133; Joseph G. Mueller, 'Blindness and Forgetting: The Prophet–Reformer in Congar's *Vraie et fausse réforme dans l'Église*', *Comm* 34 (2007), 640–56; Avery Dulles, 'True and False Reform in the Church', in *Church and Society: The Laurence J. McGinley Lectures, 1988–2007* (New York: Fordham University Press, 2008), 401–13.

161 Congar, *Vraie et fausse réforme*, 94.
162 Ibid.   163 Ibid. 95.   164 Ibid. 95–6.

fruit in the sacramental realization of the first aspect: the Church as made by her members; believers joined themselves to the Church as *congregatio fidelium*:

> Ultimately, everything gets accomplished in it [i.e., the community of the faithful] which, once actualized, will be the *true* temple, the *true* spouse, the whole body of Christ. In relation to that reality of the work of God finally having borne fruit *in people*, all the rest is simply sacrament, in the patristic sense of the word, so auspiciously brought to light by Fr de Lubac in his *Corpus mysticum*. Eschatologically, when everything will have been completed—predestination, the mystery of the nuptial union, the faith, and the sacraments—all that will be left is one Church-communion.[165]

Whatever emphasis the early Congar may have placed on the Church as institution and as hierarchy, he was clearly at pains to recover the patristic, sacramental view, which had focused on the reality (*res*) of the Church. This reality was brought into being by way of election and incarnation (mystery), on the one hand, and through the structure of the Church (institution), on the other hand.[166]

Based on the distinction between Church as community (which the faithful make up) and as mystery and institution (which engenders the faithful), Congar then presented four meanings of the word 'Church'.[167] First, the Church as institution was charged (formally) with the faith deposit, the sacraments, and the apostolic powers of priesthood, teaching office, and government. This, Congar explained, was the *ecclesia de trinitate* of which he had spoken in *Chrétiens désunis*.[168] Second (materially), the *ecclesia ex hominibus* or the community of the faithful (*congregatio fidelium*) was the meaning Scripture often attributed to the word *ecclesia*.[169] Third, the hierarchy were those of the faithful who had been called to exercise certain hierarchical functions. In this sense, the first meaning of the term 'Church' had impacted the second: when members of the hierarchy acted in the name of the Church (*in persona ecclesiae*), they at the same time acted as believers belonging to the community.[170] Finally, the fourth meaning combined the formal, divine principle of the first meaning with the material, human element of the second: 'The word then takes on its fullness of meaning and

---

[165] Ibid. 97.

[166] Congar expressed himself strongly in a paper from around the same time (presented in 1949) which was published as 'L'Eucharistie et l'Église de la Nouvelle Alliance', *VSpir* 82 (1950), 347–72; English trans.: 'Eucharist and Church', in *Revelation of God*, 168–97. Here Congar argued that the Church as institution was meant for a journey, and as such was 'the sacrament of our crossing to the Father in Jesus Christ' (ibid. 180). As a sacrament, then, the Church was 'in no sense a terminus, but a means', while the temptation was 'to allow means to become ends or to obscure the end' (ibid. 181). Cf. id., *Lay People*, 184.

[167] After discussing the four meanings of the word 'Church' (Congar, *Vraie et fausse réforme*, 98–103), Congar then explained how one could or could not ascribe sins and weaknesses to the Church in each of these meanings (ibid. 103–30). Cf. the more detailed discussion in Gabriel Flynn, *Yves Congar's Vision of the Church in a World of Unbelief* (Burlington, Vt.: Ashgate, 2004), 163–70.

[168] Congar, *Vraie et fausse réforme*, 98.

[169] Ibid. 98–9.   [170] Ibid. 100.

designates synthetically the concrete Church in her totality: Church made up of people, but as these people have received Christ and put to work a new principle of being, organization, and activity.'[171]

Although *Vraie et fausse réforme* (1950) cross-referenced the earlier *Chrétiens désunis* (1937) several times,[172] a subtle but noteworthy shift took place. *Chrétiens désunis* had classified the hierarchy along with the organization of the Church as belonging to the human mode of being, adapted to our earthly, sinful existence. This meant that, according to the law of the Incarnation, the institution and the hierarchy belonged to the *ecclesia ex hominibus*. In *Vraie et fausse réforme*, however, the institution (the three elements of faith deposit, sacraments, and apostolic powers) was seen as coming from God. Since God worked by means of these elements, Congar now saw them as expressions of the *ecclesia de trinitate*. In effect, the institution had moved from the *ecclesia ex hominibus* to the *ecclesia de trinitate*. The hierarchy had moved along with it— at least in part. The hierarchy belonged not just to the community but also, perhaps even foremost, to the institution that came from God. By reworking the two columns of *Chrétiens désunis* in this way, Congar was able to do better justice to the divine origin of the institution of the Church and of the means of grace. At the same time, since the third meaning of the word 'Church' saw the hierarchy as acting *in persona ecclesiae*, Congar was also able to avoid a strict separation between hierarchy and laity.

In addition to the distinction between institution and community, however, Congar's *Vraie et fausse réforme* employed a second distinction, between centre and periphery, in order to deal with the conditions for a true reform 'without schism'.[173] One of these conditions, explained Congar, was that of remaining in communion with the whole body of the Church.[174] This implied the necessity of continuing in a living relationship with the hierarchy of the Church.[175] While this assumed an element of submission, this submission was not to be 'servile' or 'mechanical', but 'noble, loving and simple, like that of children'.[176] Thinking with the Church (*sentire cum ecclesia*) could not be reduced to 'pure obedience to the determinations of the authority'.[177] That kind of obedience, Congar averred, treated the body of the Church simply as 'a great administrative apparatus where everything is determined from above'.[178]

To counter such juridicism, Congar attempted to strike a balance between centre and periphery, above and below, city (*urbs*) and world (*orbis*), or hierarchy and laity. Acknowledging that at times reformist initiatives arose from the centre,[179] Congar none the less insisted that throughout history reform

---

[171] Congar, *Vraie et fausse réforme*, 100.   [172] Ibid. 98, 100.   [173] Ibid. 247.

[174] Ibid. 264–305. The title *Vraie et fausse réforme dans l'Église* deliberately contained the word *dans* ('in'), indicating that true reform excluded schism. Cf. ibid. 282–3; id., *Une vie pour la vérité*, 117.

[175] Id., *Vraie et fausse réforme*, 271.   [176] Ibid. 272.   [177] Ibid. 273.

[178] Ibid. 273–4.   [179] Ibid. 274–5. For the *orbis–urbs* distinction, see ibid. 287.

movements had usually originated with the periphery. And this was to be expected, considering the hierarchy's responsibility of ensuring the continuity of the Church's principles and essential structure.[180] Congar felt that the distinction in responsibilities explained why the periphery had usually been the cause of progress, while the hierarchy tended to ensure continuity: 'Altogether, initiatives and novelty come especially from the periphery, from the Church at her frontiers. The central organs have especially the function of holding to unity and continuity; they exercise particularly the charisms that assure apostolicity; they are in the body the criteria of life in the one and apostolic Church.'[181] Congar ensured that he was not misunderstood as advocating a revolutionary spirit. Reform movements could succeed only if they were broadly based,[182] and if they sought recognition from the centre: 'It is the centre that gives the initiative of the periphery the permission and sanctioning of unity.'[183] After all, the Spirit animated not just the periphery but also the centre. 'Thus', concluded Congar, 'some kind of tension is inscribed in our obedience to the Spirit, that is to say, an exchange or relationship between two equally necessary poles. And this obedience is only fully truthful if it reaches both poles and pervades everything in-between.'[184]

Although Congar was intent on safeguarding the unique task of the centre, his exposition was nevertheless meant to carve out more space for the periphery than agreed to by those who were apprehensive of the reforms advocated by *nouvelle théologie*. It may be necessary to criticize Congar's terminology of 'centre' and 'periphery'.[185] The laity, with their orientation to temporal matters, do not have a more tenuous attachment to the Church than do the hierarchy. And the responsibilities both of holding faithfully to the deposit of faith and of introducing necessary reforms are the domain of the entire Church, even if the roles within the Church may vary. At the same time, however, it is important to keep in mind the historical context and the way in which Congar employed this terminology of 'periphery' and 'centre'. His purpose was not to entrench or ossify but rather to enable lay movements like the JOC to bring about the reforms he believed were required.[186]

The final distinction that Congar made in *Vraie et fausse réforme* was that between structure and life. He understood this distinction to be identical to that between centre and periphery.[187] He used it much more frequently, however, than the centre–periphery distinction. Indeed, the structure–life distinction

---

[180] Ibid. 276.　　[181] Ibid.　　[182] Ibid. 181–2.
[183] Ibid. 282.　　[184] Ibid. 287.
[185] Joseph Famerée criticizes Congar's terminology as leading to a 'very polarized functioning' and questions the way in which Congar associated 'initiative' with the periphery and 'conservation' with the centre (*L'Ecclésiologie d'Yves Congar*, 116–17).
[186] Congar explicitly mentioned the JOC in *Vraie et fausse réforme*, 285.
[187] See the identification of the two sets of distinctions in ibid. 274, 276.

'provided a way for Congar to address the full reality of the Church in both its sacramental and its sociological aspects'.[188] Furthermore, this distinction, unlike that between centre and periphery, found its way into Congar's subsequent publications. His 1953 *Jalons pour une théologie du laïcat* contained a concise explanation of the structure–life distinction:

By *structure* we understand the principles which, because they come from Christ, representing with him and in his name the generative causes of the Church, are the things in her, as her *pars formalis* [formal part], that constitute men as Christ's Church. These are essentially the deposit of faith, the deposit of the sacraments of faith, and the apostolical powers whereby the one and the other are transmitted. Therein resides the Church's essence. By life we understand the activity which men, made Church by the said principles, exercise in order that the Church may fulfil her mission and attain her end, which is, throughout time and space, to make of men and a reconciled world the community-temple of God.[189]

This description was reminiscent of Congar's fourfold differentiation of the word 'Church'. 'Structure', as the Church's formal element, corresponded to the Church as institution (the first meaning), while 'life', as the material element, corresponded to the community of the faithful (the second meaning). Accordingly, in a 1952 essay, Congar argued that Christ accomplished his work on earth by way of two agents—the apostles and the Spirit—each with their own mission.[190] Congar connected the work of the apostles to the structure of the Church, while maintaining that the life of the Church was the work of the Spirit.[191] He further argued that the Spirit, while closely connected to Jesus Christ who had sent him, none the less retained a certain freedom or autonomy.[192] Said Congar: 'The Holy Spirit retains a kind of freedom of action which is immediate, autonomous and personal. In this way, there exists a kind of free sector which constitutes one of the most salient features of the life of the Church.'[193]

Congar's penchant for schematization may well have caused a difficulty at this point, since he reinforced the impression of a separation between hierarchy and laity. While he safeguarded the significance of the Spirit-guided life of the Church, the structure–life distinction none the less raised the question which connection the hierarchy had with the Spirit and with the rest of the Church. By imposing the structure–life distinction on the distinctions between centre and

[188] Douglas M. Koskela, 'The Divine–Human Tension in the Ecclesiology of Yves Congar', *Eccl* 4 (2007), 93.

[189] Congar, *Lay People*, 262 (English trans. of *Jalons pour une théologie du laïcat* (Paris: Cerf, 1953)).

[190] Id., 'Le Saint-Esprit et le corps apostolique, réalisateurs de l'œuvre du Christ', *RSPT* 36 (1952), 613–25; English trans.: 'Holy Spirit and the Apostolic College', in *Mystery of the Church*, 105–45.

[191] Id., 'Holy Spirit and the Apostolic College', 128. Congar distinguished between a 'Spirit-centred' 'life-ecclesiology' and a 'Christ-centred' 'structure-ecclesiology' (ibid. 142).

[192] Ibid. 132–45.   [193] Ibid. 138.

periphery and between the missions of the apostles and of the Spirit, Congar somewhat isolated the hierarchy from the community and from the Spirit.[194]

We need to keep in mind, however, Congar's sacramental understanding of the Church. He did not regard the two aspects of the Church as separate from each other. As Congar saw it, the structure was the sacrament (*sacramentum*) serving as the means to bring about life as the reality (*res*) of the Church. Thus, his purpose was in no way to focus on the hierarchy as such. His aim was precisely the opposite—namely, to point to the sacramental purpose of the hierarchy, that of facilitating the life of the Church.[195]

Congar was in many ways a traditional 'man of the Church' (*vir ecclesiasticus*). His insistence that the structure constituted the 'essence' of the Church was meant to safeguard an indispensable element of the Tradition. Throughout his career, including the post-Second Vatican Council period, Congar remained faithful to this insistence on the continuity of the faith, the sacraments, and the apostolic powers of the Church. They alone belonged to the Church's very being (*esse*). The way in which the changing life of the Church took shape was simply a matter of her well-being (*bene esse*).[196] Because he was concerned, however, with the neo-scholastic lack of attention to the sacramental aim of the Church's life, Congar pushed for changes in the way in which the life of the Church concretely took shape.[197]

Entre-deux: Combining Sacrament and History

The distinction between structure and life found its way into Congar's third main programmatic publication, his extended 1953 essay on the role of the laity, *Jalons pour une théologie du laïcat*. As the title indicated, Congar intended to present only some 'signposts' for a theology of the laity.[198] The book presented none the

[194] Cf. the criticism of Hans Urs von Balthasar, *The Office of Peter and the Structure of the Church*, trans. Andrée Emery (San Francisco, Calif.: Ignatius, 1986), 289–90. With appreciation to Bert Moes for alerting me to this reference.

[195] Furthermore, Congar was well aware that also the hierarchy had their place *within* the Church, along with the other faithful: '[W]e must state a very important truth that must never be lost sight of: a priest, a bishop, a pope is first of all a layman. He has to be baptized, to become a Christian, to offer his life as a spiritual sacrifice, to receive communion, to do penance, to be blessed, to work out his salvation. It is impossible to separate his personal religious life, that of layman, and the religious life of his office, that of priest or of bishop: the two are united in one single destiny, the destiny of one single person' (*Lay People*, 181).

[196] Congar, *Vraie et fausse réforme*, 540–1.

[197] Congar often spoke of 'structures' (plural), which he carefully distinguished from the inalterable 'structure' (singular) and instead classified with the 'life' of the Church. These 'structures' were not so much occasional elements of the Church's life but had obtained greater currency over time. Congar gave as examples the way in which the catechism was set up, the style and organizational structure of parishes, and the ordinary style of high masses (ibid. 57 n. 50).

[198] Cf. id., *Lay People*, p. xvi: 'In spite of the size of this book and the labour put into it, it is offered as no more than a first essay, simply "signposts", and it makes no claim to completeness or to the presentation of what is definitive.'

less a formidable foray into a topic that was beginning to attract more and more attention in the years surrounding the Second World War.[199] Congar's focus on the laity reflected his interest in overcoming the 'hierarchology' of the manualist tradition: as part of the life of the Church, the laity ought to be given their own, significant place in the Church. To this end, Congar supplemented the structure–life distinction with others, all of which had a similar focus.

As these distinctions proliferated, Congar increasingly emphasized the sacramental relationship between the two aspects of the Church. He explained, for instance, that the Church was not only a means of salvation (*Heilsanstalt*), but that she also served as the community of salvation (*Heilsgemeinschaft*). Highlighting the sacramental relationship between the two, Congar commented:

As the community of the faithful the Church is the *reality* of salvation (*Heilsgemeinschaft*); she is also the aggregate of the means of the calling to salvation—one may say, using the word in its wide sense, the *sacrament* of that reality (*Heilsanstalt*). In fact, according to their classical use in Western theology, the categories 'sacrament' and 'reality' are useful for showing the relationship between the two aspects of the Church that we have distinguished.[200]

For Congar, the *Heilsanstalt* (the hierarchical structure of the Church) served as the sacramental means to procure the reality of the *Heilsgemeinschaft* (the communal life of the faithful).

The *Heilsanstalt*, Congar was convinced, had its origin in the historical events of Christ's suffering, death, burial, and resurrection—his Pasch. Christ's actions and his suffering for us (*acta et passa pro nobis*) formed the starting-point for the role of the hierarchy. Their function was to mediate to the faithful what Christ had accomplished for them. The *Heilsgemeinschaft*, on the other hand, took its cue from Christ's return—his Parousia. Congar explained:

As regard the Pasch, we receive everything from the unique fact of Jesus Christ in his historical incarnation, his *acta et passa pro nobis*, a well-spring of holiness established outside ourselves at a certain moment in history. The Church is the aggregate of the means whereby these waters reach us (before she is the community in whom is the truth and grace of Jesus), and there we find the function of the apostolic hierarchy. As regards the Parousia, we, on the basis of what we have received, have to bring to God through Christ the modest riches of creation and of our free co-operation, or, if you will, the produce of the talents God has given us, 'the interests on his outlay'. Here is the lay state contributing actively to the building up of the Temple.[201]

Thus, in the 'time of the Church', the Pasch was the basis of the Church's structure, while the Parousia originated her life.

---

[199] Cf. Congar, *Lay People*, 54–8. Congar commented: 'In the ranks of Catholic Action there was a veritable "craze" for the doctrine of the mystical Body, for active participation of the faithful in the eucharistic liturgy, and so on' (ibid. 55).

[200] Ibid. 32. Cf. ibid. 110–11; van Vliet, *Communio sacramentalis*, 128.

[201] Congar, *Lay People*, 109–10. Cf. ibid. 116.

One could obtain this same overall view, Congar explained, by looking to Christ both as Alpha and as Omega. The former presented Christ in his suffering *for* us, while the latter meant Christ *with* us. The former was the historical Christ, born of the Virgin, while the latter was the fullness of Christ in his Parousia, including the entire *congregatio fidelium*. So, while Christ was 'Alpha only through all his *acta et passa in carne, for* us' he was 'Omega *with* us, not only in the body of flesh that was born of Mary and was crucified, but in his fellowship-body which we compose with him and in him—and he in us'.[202] This meant that in his Pasch Christ had done everything for our benefit without any contribution from our side, while the Parousia was the fullness of the Omega, that is to say, Christ in the fullness of the community, so that the eschaton would integrate our contribution with that of Jesus Christ.[203] The Pasch of Christ was thus the origin of the hierarchical, juridical mission of the apostles and their successors.[204] Theirs was a mission *ex officio*. But there was also a 'mission of life and love, a mission *ex spiritu*', which lay at the basis of the various tasks that Christ had assigned to the faithful.[205] In this mission, the faithful brought their sacrifices of praise to God. The distinction, Congar believed, had its origin in Christ's twofold relationship with his body, 'that of giving life through his Spirit, and that of authority and power'.[206]

Congar's juxtaposition of Pasch and Parousia, and of Alpha and Omega, was indicative of the central role that salvation history played in his thought.[207] Both the notion of the Church as the 'people of God' and the temple imagery allowed Congar to highlight the situation of the Church in the 'in-between' period between Pasch and Parousia. Congar was encouraged by the rediscovery of the notion of the 'people of God' between 1937 and 1942 through the work of theologians like Mannus Dominikus Koster (1901–81), Lucien Cerfaux (1883–1968), and others:[208] 'One of the greatest recoveries of contemporary Catholic theology has

---

[202] Ibid. 163.   [203] Ibid. 326–7.   [204] Ibid. 324–6.

[205] Ibid. 326. Cf. ibid. 354. Congar dealt with the *ex officio–ex spiritu* distinction in Chap. 7 of his book, examining the relationship between the laity and the Church's communal life. In the next chapter, he focused particularly on the role of Catholic Action, which Pius XI had organized with a view to 'the participation of the laity in the hierarchical apostolate' (ibid. 362). In his analysis of what lay 'participation' within the hierarchical apostolate might mean, Congar ended up explaining the mission of Catholic Action as 'a mission *quasi ex officio*': 'To their general mission *ex spiritu*—specified for each individual by his abilities and circumstances—there is added a certain juridical title, a mission *quasi ex officio*; and this apostolate being as it were "instituted", is recognized by the hierarchy, which makes use of it, directing and supervising it closely' (ibid. 371).

[206] Ibid. 325.

[207] Cf. Chap. 6, sect.: The 'Time of the Church' as Sacramental.

[208] Congar, *This Church that I Love*, trans. Lucien Delafuente (Denville, NJ: Dimension, 1969), 12–16. Congar referred, among others, to Mannes Dominikus Koster, *Ekklesiologie im Werden* (Paderborn: Bonifacius, 1940); Lucien Cerfaux, *La Théologie de l'Église suivant saint Paul* (Paris: Cerf, 1942). At the same time, Congar expressed reservations, insisting that the notion of the 'body of Christ' was equally important, since we should not ignore the radical newness that had come about through the Incarnation. Both the 'already' and the 'not yet' had to be done equal justice (*This Church that I Love*, 29–38).

been that of the eschatological sense, which implies a sense of history and of God's plan as leading everything to a consummation.'[209] The image of the 'people of God', with its background in the narratives of Israel's desert journey—highlighting the many shortcomings and failings of the Old Testament people of God—was particularly helpful, Congar believed, because it could accentuate the historical situation in which the Church found herself in the 'in-between' period.

The biblical imagery of the temple was attractive to Congar. While most of his books were of a historical theological nature, one notable exception was his extensive foray into biblical theology, *Le Mystère du temple* (1958).[210] The book elaborated on the temple theme in Scripture, beginning with God's calling of Abram (Gen. 12: 1) and ending with the New Jerusalem, whose temple was God himself (Rev. 21: 22). The biblical development of the temple imagery—synonym for the 'presence' of God—showed, according to Congar, that God's entire purpose was 'to make the human race, created in his image, a living, spiritual temple in which he not only dwells but to which he communicates himself and in turn receives from it the worship of a wholly filial obedience'.[211] Congar was convinced that the biblical story moved 'towards a definite end characterized by the highest possible degree of inward religion. Its stages are those of this increasing inwardness'.[212] The high point of the temple imagery, Congar argued, came with the Incarnation: 'Christ then has dwelt—and continues to dwell sacramentally—among us. Our temple is the Pasch of Jesus Christ, Jesus giving to the Father and taking up again that bodily life in which the fullness of the divinity resides'.[213]

Moving from biblical to speculative theology in his conclusion, Congar argued with Thomas Aquinas that the presence of God in Christ was greater than either his presence in creation or the presence of his gift of grace:

In Christ a human body truly becomes the temple of God, according to a mode of indwelling so intimate that there cannot be any greater, since this bond between man and God is that of personal existence, and when Jesus thinks and says: 'I am the temple of God', *the temple* is his body, but the *I* is no other than the Divine Person of the Word.[214]

---

[209] Congar, *This Church that I Love*, 18. See further van Vliet, *Communio sacramentalis*, 201–8, 219–24.

[210] Congar, *Le Mystère du temple, ou, L'Économie de la présence de Dieu à sa créature de la Genèse à l'Apocalypse* (Paris: Cerf, 1958); English trans.: *Mystery of the Temple*. Cf. James Hanvey, 'In the Presence of Love: The Pneumatological Realization of the Economy: Yves Congar, *Le Mystère du temple*', *IJST* 7 (2005), 383–98.

[211] Congar, *Mystery of the Temple*, p. ix. Cf. also id., *Vraie et fausse réforme*, 133–45.

[212] Congar, *Mystery of the Temple*, p. xi. Congar regularly referred to the 'inwardness' of the sacramental reality of God's grace or of heaven. See e.g. id., 'Idea of the Church' [1939], 336, 351, 357; id., 'Eucharist and Church', in *Revelation of God*, 181; id., *Lay People*, 168.

[213] Id., *Mystery of the Temple*, 142.

[214] Ibid. 241.

The sacraments, insisted Congar, incorporated believers into this body of Christ as the perfect temple: 'The Eucharist, the sacramental body of Christ, nourishes in our souls the grace through which we are God's spiritual temple.'[215]

Since the present dispensation was 'one of reality and also of anticipation',[216] the Church found herself in an 'in-between time' (*l'entre-deux*).[217] The hierarchical ministries and the sacraments were characteristic of the *entre-deux*, since they were the divinely intended means to lead believers to the fullness of Christ: 'The space between [*l'entre-deux*] these two moments [i.e., Christ as Alpha and as Omega] of the one fundamental mystery is the time of the Church, filled with the action of the Holy Spirit and of the ecclesial institution, sacraments and apostolic body.'[218] This connection between hierarchical Church and 'in-between' time implied that the visibility of the Church, her ministries, and her sacraments would disappear in the eschaton: 'The priesthood of holiness and the priesthood of authority will coincide exactly—or rather, the second will be swallowed up in the first, for it will no longer have to mediate grace, as it does in our present state of "exodus" as we journey from our Egypt to our Promised Land.'[219]

Congar used the notion of *entre-deux* to oppose what he saw as the ecclesiological weaknesses of neo-scholastic Catholic thought, as well as of Orthodox and of Protestant theology.[220] Congar boldly critiqued neo-scholastic ecclesiology in a 1949 presentation to the Eucharistic Congress:

Several years [*sic*] work have convinced me that this idea of an interim position is what is most lacking in the doctrine of the Church as set forth in the Counter-Reformation period, and in most contemporary manuals. That doctrine was most concerned with controversy; its main purpose was to establish the Church's credentials and it discussed the Church as an isolated phenomenon unrelated to the development of the historical movement, that movement whose progress permeates the Scriptures and indeed defines their purpose.[221]

---

[215] Ibid. 247. [216] Ibid. 246.
[217] Id., *Lay People*, 68, 164, 166. Cf. MacDonald, *Ecclesiology*, 99–102.
[218] Congar, *Lay People*, 164.
[219] Ibid. 168.
[220] Id., *Le Christ, Marie et l'Église* (Bruges: Desclée de Brouwer, 1952) was a fascinating instance where Congar took issue with both (extreme) sides in the Catholic–Protestant debate (English trans.: *Christ, Our Lady and the Church*). The book, written on the occasion of the fifteenth centenary of the Council of Chalcedon (451), argued that problems in Mariology and ecclesiology could be traced to problems in Christology. In Part I, Congar objected to Protestant (and especially Luther's) views, insisting that Protestants were unable to appreciate the principle of human mediation or creaturely cooperation, both in terms of Mariology and of ecclesiology (ibid. 25). In Christology, Congar argued, this led to a Nestorian separation of the two natures, in which God unilaterally acted from above (ibid. 30). Part II discussed Catholic Monophysite tendencies that overemphasized Christ's divinity at the cost of his humanity, refusing to acknowledge human weaknesses in the Church, and insisting on Mary as *mediatrix* to compensate for Christ's role as divine judge.
[221] Id., 'Eucharist and the Church', in *Revelation of God*, 169.

The scholastic approach of the manualist tradition lacked a sacramental perspective. It focused on the external sacramental means, ignoring that historical progression meant a two-stage realization and internalization of the sacramental reality of the presence of God.

Despite Congar's ecumenical interests, he did not refrain from critiquing his Protestant and Orthodox dialogue partners, particularly in his early years. Protestantism and Orthodoxy, he believed, suffered from a similar lack of historical and sacramental perspective—although in opposite ways. The Protestant weakness, Congar already observed in *Chrétiens désunis*, was, ironically, similar to that of his neo-Thomist detractors. Referring to the two aspects of the Church as institution and as mystical body, Congar commented: 'Extreme Protestants do not believe in the real and actual gift of the divine life to humanity: they believe that this life is only promised, albeit truly promised, and it is regarded as purely eschatological.'[222] The result, Congar argued, was that Protestants were reluctant to acknowledge God's activity in and through the institutional aspect of the Church: 'Logically, the institutional Church does not exist for them in the Christian sense, it is only the community of those who have heard the promise.'[223] This tendency to locate the true, invisible Church in the eschatological future led to Congar's accusation that Protestants tended to be stuck in the Old Testament.[224] Thus, although in their focus on the (future) Church of the elect, Protestants were quite unlike the neo-scholastic Catholics, they shared their lack of appreciation for the eschatological and sacramental reality in the *entre-deux*.

Orthodox theologians, in contrast, seemed to disregard the need for institutional and hierarchical mediation in favour of the already realized inward reality of grace: 'In a word, they regard the divine life as so completely given, and heaven so entirely descended to earth, that they almost look upon them as existing here below under their own ultimate condition of glory and the full possession of an enjoyment of God, and not according to the human mode, which is social, imperfect and militant.'[225] Orthodox theology thus suffered from impatience with the sacramental character of human mediation and temporary structures in the *entre-deux*.

One of Congar's most significant accomplishments was his combination of a sacramental ecclesiology with a salvation–historical focus. Sacramental ontology and history were not mutually exclusive categories for Congar. He maintained that whenever an ecclesiology focused unduly on the Pasch of Christ and on the institution of the Church, the result was a weakening of the sacramental reality (*res*) of the Church; at the same time, a single-minded focus on the Parousia and a corresponding neglect of the visible reality of the Church undermined the

---

[222] Congar, *Divided Christendom*, 91.
[223] Ibid.
[224] e.g., id., *This Church that I Love*, 29.
[225] Id., *Divided Christendom*, 92. Cf. ibid. 208–12.

historical and provisional character of the Church (*sacramentum*). Congar managed to develop this perhaps counter-intuitive combination of a sacramental and a historical perspective on the Church by identifying the sacramental reality (*res*) of grace as the inward, eschatological reality of the fullness of Christ.

Post-conciliar Development

Congar's theology constituted an attempt to join what he believed had too often been separated. Maintaining the sacramental character of the Church, he argued, was the way to keep together the institutional and communal aspects of the Church. Congar always retained this sacramental position. At the same time, in his later years, he did take his sacramental approach in a somewhat different direction.[226] In 1968, in *Cette Église que j'aime*, he gratefully picked up on some of the themes of the Second Vatican Council and continued to develop them.[227] Most strikingly, he elaborated here on the themes of the Church as the 'people of God' and as sacrament of salvation (*sacramentum salutis*), both of which *Lumen gentium* had highlighted. In a chapter on 'The Church, Universal Sacrament of Salvation',[228] he began by reiterating the 'Christological foundation' of the notion of Church as sacrament.[229] The only foundation of the sacramental character of the Church, Congar asserted, was Christ, who himself was the ultimate sacrament of salvation. He was 'the central and decisive event' in the history of salvation, who possessed 'grace with *absolute* plenitude'.[230] Thus, only by virtue of his accomplishments did grace inhabit the Church as his body, as well. Commented Congar: 'If the Church is the sacrament of salvation, we can say that Christ has that attribute prior to her, and that she has that attribute because He had it before her.'[231]

Congar also turned to the relationship between Church and world.[232] He briefly explained what he meant by the 'salvation' that the sacraments of Christ and the Church made present. Salvation was by no means an individual category. Human beings were linked to the cosmos, and God had in mind the salvation of

---

[226] Joseph Famerée rightly speaks of a 'profound continuity' between the early and later Congar, despite the developments in his thinking (*L'Ecclésiologie d'Yves Congar*, 437; id., 'Formation et ecclésiologie du "premier" Congar', in Vauchez, *Cardinal Yves Congar*, 52). For an excellent discussion of Congar's changing views, see Patrick Mullins, 'The Spirit Speaks to the Churches: Continuity and Development in Congar's Pneumatology', *LouvStud* 29 (2004), 288–319.

[227] Congar, *Cette Église que j'aime* (Paris: Cerf, 1968); English trans.: *This Church that I Love*.

[228] Cf. van Vliet, *Communio sacramentalis*, 208–14.

[229] Congar, *This Church that I Love*, 41–4.

[230] Ibid. 42.

[231] Ibid. 43.

[232] Starting in the late 1950s, Congar repeatedly turned to this topic. See e.g. his *Vaste monde, ma paroisse: Vérité et dimensions du salut* (Paris: Témoignage chrétien, 1959); English trans.: *The Wide World My Parish: Salvation and its Problems*, trans. Donald Attwater (Baltimore, Md.: Helicon, 1961); id., *Église catholique et France moderne* (Paris: Hachette, 1978). Cf. van Vliet, *Communio sacramentalis*, 192–6.

the entire cosmos: 'Salvation is not merely the rescue of some survivors, but the consummation in God of all his visible creation, together with man who is the crowning and the immanent goal.'[233] Likewise, Congar opposed a separation between nature and the supernatural. He showed himself uneasy with the noun 'supernature', 'as if there *existed* a "supernature" in the same way as there is a nature'.[234] Instead, Congar maintained, one should speak of 'a new condition of the realities of this world and of man, or a new relationship to God, the beginning and the end of everything'.[235]

Next, Congar moved to a discussion on the Church as sacrament. He defined sacraments as 'those forms under which God visibly approaches us as Grace, and through which, therefore, we can visibly and at the same time spiritually receive His action'.[236] The sacraments, particularly Baptism and Eucharist, constituted the reality of the Church. Thus, one could say that the Church 'represents the totality of sensible forms under which the historical coming of God for our salvation exists forever in the world'.[237] The Church was an efficacious sign of the appearance of God's grace in Christ and, therefore, the place in which past, present, and future collided.[238] To explain how this sacramentality of the Church functioned, Congar had recourse to his regular distinction between the Church as 'institution of salvation' and as 'people of God'.[239] As 'institution of salvation', Congar explained, the Church was 'an ensemble of means or mediations of grace, and being means or mediations, they have by the very fact a sacramental value: in them Christ, who originally instituted them, acts through his Spirit. It consists of a deposit of the Word of God, the sacraments and the corresponding services'.[240] As 'people of God', the Church was God-bearer (*theopher*) or Christ-bearer (*Christopher*), 'sacrament of the presence' of grace.[241] This meant that Congar no longer referred to the 'people of God' as the reality (*res*) that the sacrament of the institution made present. Instead, he now regarded the entire *communio fidelium* or 'people of God' as sacramentally representing Jesus Christ.[242]

---

[233] Congar, *This Church that I Love*, 44–5.   [234] Ibid. 45.

[235] Ibid. Both in his emphasis on the social aspect and in his approach to the supernatural, Congar sounded distinctly Lubacian.

[236] Ibid. 46.

[237] Ibid. 48.

[238] Ibid. 49–50. This approach was reminiscent of Congar's insistence that the 'time of the Church' was sacramental in character. See Chap. 6, sect.: The 'Time of the Church' as Sacramental.

[239] Congar, *This Church that I Love*, 51.

[240] Ibid.

[241] Ibid. 52.

[242] Congar appealed to *Lumen gentium*, 33: 'Thus, every lay person, through those gifts given to him, is at once the witness and the living instrument of the mission of the Church itself "according to the measure of Christ's bestowal" (Eph. 4: 7)' (id., *This Church that I Love*, 52). Cf. id., 'Le Diaconat dans la théologie des ministères', in P. Winninger and Y. Congar (eds), *Le Diacre dans l'église et le monde d'aujourd'hui* (Paris: Cerf, 1966), 131: 'The people of God is in its entirety and as such sign of the gospel, sacrament of salvation, mediator of life for the world, but it is structured organically.' Cf. id., *Un peuple messianique: L'Église, sacrement du salut; Salut et libération* (Paris: Cerf, 1975), 82: 'If the bearer of the sacrament of salvation is the people of God as such, this people is made up of persons, each one of whom has his gifts, his vocation, his place in the whole, which God knows.'

Not only did the entire people of God serve as a sacramental means to make God's grace present, but Congar went further by insisting that, in a sense, *all* people—humanity as such—were sacraments of divine grace. After all, Congar insisted, all people were objectively included in Christ's redemption.[243] While he was critical of Karl Rahner's use of the expression 'people of God' as including all of humanity, Congar nevertheless posed some daring questions:

[I]s it true that beyond the People of God in the strict sense . . . *every man* carries within himself a certain share of the sacrament of Christ, or of salvation? Some passages could lead us to answer in the affirmative: 'I was hungry and you gave me food, etc.' (Matt. 25: 35). Is not every man, in a sense, an encounter with Christ? Is it an exaggeration to talk about a 'sacrament of the neighbor?' Is it not there, in every man that we encounter a 'mystery' in the precise and traditional sense of the word—namely, something beyond that which is seen, where God operates and makes himself accessible? I personally believe so.[244]

Congar thus came to affirm that the Church as *whole*—rather than just the Church as institution—was sacramental in character, and he also maintained there was a sense in which *all* humanity was sacramental in character.[245]

As a result, Congar now abandoned the formula, 'Outside the Church there is no salvation' (*extra ecclesiam nulla salus*), replacing it with 'the Church, universal sacrament of salvation'.[246] To be sure, Congar immediately added several qualifiers. Only the Church was more than an *occasion* to find God, since only the Church was the carrier of positive revelation. Furthermore, only the Church was the 'public and universal sacrament of salvation', since individual non-Christians served merely as private and occasional 'sacraments'.[247] And although people could be saved without knowing the gospel, missionary activity was none the less of 'absolute necessity'.[248] Congar insisted that the Church was the divinely ordained means of salvation: 'From the point of view of individual salvation, the reality (*res* in the sense of classical analysis in sacramental theology) is sometimes bestowed independently of the *sacramentum*. But this unity of mankind, *as God wants it*, cannot be accomplished outside the Church, which is its sacrament.'[249] God had mandated only the Church to provide people with salvation in Christ.[250]

---

[243] Congar, *This Church that I Love*, 53.   [244] Ibid. 54.

[245] Cf. the discussion in Flynn, *Yves Congar's Vision*, 36–51.

[246] Congar, *This Church that I Love*, 59. In a 1956 essay on the topic, Congar had still maintained that there was no salvation outside the Church. Non-Catholics could share in the *res* of the sacrament without being members of the Church, so that 'the realities of grace that are found in them tend of themselves to their incorporation in the visible body of Jesus Christ, altogether *res* and *sacramentum*. Thus, the salvation that is ultimately assured to these non-Catholics is not given *extra ecclesiam*' ('Hors de l'Église, pas du salut', in *Sainte Église: Études et approches ecclésiologiques* (Paris: Cerf, 1963), 431).

[247] Id., *This Church that I Love*, 55.

[248] Ibid. 57–8.   [249] Ibid. 59.   [250] Ibid.

Not surprisingly, since he now thought that the entire people of God—not just the hierarchy—was the sacrament of salvation, Congar began to emphasize even more strongly than before the Church as community of the faithful. The Holy Spirit indwelt the entire people of God. As a result, Congar increasingly insisted that Christology not be separated from pneumatology and that the Spirit's work in the Church was of great ecclesiological significance. Congar's later work focused strongly on the role of the Holy Spirit. And in his three-volume work, *Je crois en l'Esprit Saint* (1979–80), he made sure to connect the work of the Spirit to that of Jesus Christ.[251]

Since Congar's views had changed and developed over the course of his career, he acknowledged that his earlier work had contained shortcomings. In a frank 1971 essay entitled 'Mon cheminement dans la théologie du laïcat et des ministères', he expressed several reservations about his earlier work.[252] He recognized that he had been tempted by a linear scheme that moved from Christ, via the hierarchy, towards the Church as community of the faithful. This, it now seemed to Congar, 'would in fact reduce the building of the community to the action of the hierarchical ministry'.[253] Congar regretted that he had once operated with the priesthood–laity distinction and wanted to replace it with the distinction between ministries or services, on the one hand, and community, on the other hand. Such a distinction, Congar argued, better reflected the fact that Christ had chosen the Twelve *within* the larger community.[254] Thus, one could speak of a 'structured community' (*communauté structuré*) that in its entirety was holy, priestly, prophetic, missionary, and apostolic, and within which certain ministries had their place.[255] Congar also agreed, in his 1984 book, *La Parole et le souffle*, that perhaps the structure–life distinction had not been entirely fortuitous,[256] and he indicated that his earlier approach to reform had placed too much emphasis on the requirement of obedience to hierarchical decisions. At the very least, he agreed with the growing ecumenical attention to the 'reception' of conciliar decisions.[257] This, Congar rightly perceived, brought him more in line with Orthodox views on the

---

[251] Congar, *Je crois en l'Esprit Saint*, 3 vols (Paris: Cerf, 1979–80); English trans.: *I Believe in the Holy Spirit*, trans. David Smith, 3 vols (New York: Crossroad/Herder, 1997).

[252] Id., 'Mon cheminement dans la théologie du laïcat et des ministères', in *Ministères*, 9–30; English trans.: 'My Path-findings in the Theology of Laity and Ministries', *Jur* 32 (1972), 169–88.

[253] Id., 'My Path-findings', 175.

[254] Ibid. 177. Cf. id., 'Le Diaconat', 130.

[255] Id., 'My Path-findings', 178.

[256] Id., *La Parole et le souffle* (Paris: Desclée, 1984); English trans.: *The Word and the Spirit*, trans. David Smith (London: Chapman, 1986), 81, where Congar mentioned that the Second Vatican Council had retained the distinction between the Church as a society and as a communion. He then added: 'I would not venture to draw attention now to the distinction which I have made in the past between structure and life, because it has been criticized for being inadequate.'

[257] See id., 'La "Réception" comme réalité ecclésiologique', *RSPT* 56 (1972), 369–403. Cf. id., *Word and the Spirit*, 81. Cf. also Monika-Maria Wolff, *Gott und Mensch: Ein Beitrag Yves Congars zum ökumenischen Dialog* (Frankfurt: Knecht, 1990), 304–22.

reception of conciliar decisions. The Orthodox notion of *sobornost*—a notion that is difficult to translate but carries overtones of spiritual unity and conciliarity—had always been intriguing to Congar,[258] and as he grew older he became increasingly intrigued by its ecumenical potential.

Congar also critiqued his earlier talk of a 'free sector' for the Holy Spirit, which, as we saw, weakened the link of the hierarchy with the community and the Spirit. In his second volume on the Holy Spirit he insisted that charism and institution should not be played out against each other, and he engaged in some self-criticism, acknowledging that he had worked 'too exclusively in a context of dualism' and had 'made too radical a distinction between the institution as derived from Christ and free interventions on the part of the Spirit'.[259] While still maintaining that something like a 'free sector' of the Spirit existed, he acknowledged that he had not been

sufficiently conscious of the unity that exists between the activity of the Spirit and that of the *glorified Christ*, since 'the Lord is the Spirit and where the Spirit of the Lord is, there is freedom' (2 Cor. 3: 17). According to Paul, the glorified Lord and the Spirit may be different in God, but they are functionally so united that we experience them together and are able to accept the one for the other: 'Christ in us', 'the Spirit in our hearts', '(we) in Christ', 'in the Spirit'—all of these are interchangeable.[260]

Congar came to recognize that the structure–life distinction—even though developed as a mechanism to counter an undue focus on the hierarchy itself—insufficiently highlighted the unity of the community of faith.

Congar's self-critique regarding a 'free sector' for the Holy Spirit was not meant to subordinate the Spirit to the ministries of the Church. Rather, since the hierarchy had its place *within* the overall community of faith, the entire community depended for its life on an epiclesis or invocation of the Spirit.[261] Eucharistic epiclesis, Congar insisted, was just one element of the overall epicletic character of the Church. At the conclusion of his three volumes on pneumatology, the mature Congar discussed the sacramental character of the Church and insisted again that the entire Church—rather than just the hierarchy—was sacramental in character: 'The whole Church—its people, its ministers, its treasure of the means of grace and its institution—is that sacrament of salvation.'[262] This sacramental character of the Church was not mechanical or

[258] See already Congar, *Divided Christendom*, 208–12. Despite his attraction to Orthodox ecclesiology, Congar criticized it for insufficiently recognizing the human, institutional side of the Church militant (ibid. 212–20). Van Vliet highlights the influence on Congar of the Russian slavophile theologian Alexei Khomiakov via the Russian émigrés Sergius Bulgakov and Nikolai Berdyaev (*Communio sacramentalis*, 62–4, 134–7).

[259] Congar, *I Believe in the Holy Spirit*, ii, *The Spirit Animates the Church*, trans. David Smith (New York: Crossroad/Herder, 1997), 11.

[260] Ibid. 12.

[261] Cf. Isaac Kizhakkeparampil, *The Invocation of the Holy Spirit as Constitutive of the Sacraments according to Cardinal Yves Congar* (Rome: Gregorian University Press, 1995).

[262] Congar, *I Believe in the Holy Spirit*, iii, *The River of the Water of Life (Rev 22:1) Flows in the East and in the West*, trans. David Smith (New York: Crossroad/Herder, 1997), 271.

automatic. The Church always had to rely on the supernatural gift of the Spirit. To say, therefore, that the Church was epicletic in character was 'to affirm that neither the "earthly means" nor the institution of the Church produces these by themselves. What we have here is an absolutely supernatural work that is both divine and deifying.'[263] The community of the Church, hierarchy or faithful, could not presume to control the sovereign work of the Spirit.

CONCLUSION

In his 1988 foreword to the English translation of *Catholicisme*, Joseph Cardinal Ratzinger drew attention to the immediate historical context of de Lubac's opposition to ecclesial individualism: 'The narrow-minded individualistic Christianity against which he strove is hardly our problem today.'[264] Instead, Ratzinger was convinced that 'we are now in danger of a sociological levelling down. Sacraments are often seen merely as celebrations of the community where there is no more room for the personal dialogue between God and the soul— something many greet with condescending ridicule. And so there has been a kind of reversal of the previous individualism'.[265] De Lubac would have had no difficulty in echoing these words. Over time, his emphasis shifted rather dramatically to a reaffirmation of transcendence and of the supernatural. Towards the end of his career, de Lubac began to express reservations regarding the immanentism of modern culture, which he believed was also infiltrating the Catholic Church.

In the post-conciliar period, de Lubac and Congar developed their ecclesiologies in opposite directions. De Lubac became wary of democratizing tendencies in the Church, grew anxious about the loss of a functioning authority in the Church, and became particularly apprehensive of the secularizing trends of the 1960s and beyond. He was concerned that the desire to be relevant to the surrounding culture hampered the authenticity of the Church's identity and message, so that efforts to 'adapt' elements of the Christian faith to the outside world ran the risk 'not only of remaining barren, but of producing the opposite effect'.[266] Congar, by contrast, reinforced his early attacks on the juridicizing tendencies of a static 'hierarchology'. He was much more content with the direction of the post-conciliar Church, and he even suggested that *aggiornamento*

---

[263] Congar, *I Believe in the Holy Spirit*, iii. 271. Congar had already insisted on the need for the Church's reliance on the Spirit by way of epiclesis in a 1953 essay republished in *Les Voies du Dieu vivant: Théologie et vie spirituelle* (Paris: Cerf, 1962); English trans.: 'Holy Spirit in the Church', in *Revelation of God*, 153. See also id., 'Holy Spirit and the Apostolic College', *Mystery of the Church*, 125.

[264] Joseph Ratzinger, foreword to de Lubac, *Catholicism*, 12.

[265] Ibid.   [266] De Lubac, *Brief Catechesis*, 130.

and 'adaptation' were insufficiently radical; in the face of the serious questions of the day, he believed it was necessary instead to call for a 'new creation'.[267]

Congar was truly Chenu's student in his deep, abiding desire to connect with the non-believing world. This desire was one of the main motivating factors behind his entire theological enterprise. The Dominican's intent to connect with his cultural context, however, may well have rendered him somewhat naive with regard to modernity's secularizing tendencies. While he agreed in principle with de Lubac's reintegration of nature and the supernatural, this issue did not dominate his writings, as it did de Lubac's. Instead, from the beginning, Congar focused on the importance of the laity who found themselves working in the trenches, and considered the possibilities of reforming the 'state of affairs' of the 'forms' or 'structures' of the Church.[268] Of course, both de Lubac and Congar believed that *ressourcement* of the Tradition should provide guidance for reform in the Church.[269] More so than for Congar, however, de Lubac's primary guiding principle for *ressourcement* was the Blondelian reintegration of nature and the supernatural. This guiding principle ensured that the Fourvière Jesuit was more keenly aware that *ressourcement* might clash with modern sensibilities.

Despite post-conciliar differences between the two theologians, their ecclesiologies were motivated by a shared opposition to neo-scholastic views of the Church. As a result, de Lubac and Congar ended up with positions quite similar to one another. Both sought to restore a sacramental view of the Church that would not only be concerned with the proper administration of the sacrament (*sacramentum*), but that would also keep its eye on the intended reality (*res*) of the sacrament: the unity of the Church, the community of the faithful, the fullness of Christ. By regarding the Church both as the sacramental means that passed on the faith (*ecclesia congregans*) and as the mystical body of believers (*ecclesia congregata*), de Lubac and Congar were able to avoid the extrinsicism of the manualist tradition as well as the immanentist historicism of secular modernity. As a result, they enriched the Tradition by means of a communion ecclesiology based on the Church as the great sacrament of the mystery of salvation.

---

[267] Congar, 'Renewal of the Spirit and Reform of the Institution', trans. John Griffiths, *Conc* 73 (1972), 47. Earlier, Congar had repeatedly used the word *adapter* to describe the changes that he advocated for the life (rather than the structure) of the Church (*Vraie et fausse réforme*, 48–50, 55, 149–52), while distinguishing 'adaptation as development' from 'adaptation as innovation' (ibid. 333–52).

[268] Congar used the language of *formes* (*Vraie et fausse réforme*, 48, 50, 52, 177), *structures* (ibid. 57, 187), *manières de faire* (ibid. 50), and *états de choses* (ibid. 186–7, 357) as belonging to the 'life' of the Church that could be revised.

[269] Cf. Congar's emphasis on *ressourcement* as the criterion by which to engage in Church reform (*Vraie et fausse réforme*, 43, 58, 189, 335–9).

8

Conclusion: The Future of *Ressourcement*

He who once felt the pain of shattered unity has no right to stop short, in his efforts for reunion, of the utmost of his loyalty, his courage, and his entire self-devotion.

Yves M.-J. Congar[1]

RECOVERY OF A SACRAMENTAL ONTOLOGY

It may be difficult to gauge the long-term ecclesial impact or success of the *ressourcement* movement. The careers of the *nouvelle* theologians discussed in this book spanned much of the twentieth century, and historically we are simply too close to take stock adequately. The task of analysing *nouvelle théologie*'s influence is further complicated by the momentous events surrounding the Second Vatican Council. On the one hand, the impact of the *nouvelle* theologians on the Council seems obvious. An in-depth comparison between the theology of the *ressourcement* scholars and the Council documents would reveal a remarkable degree of convergence in terms of the overall interest in *aggiornamento*, the understanding of divine revelation and of theology, the approach to the Scripture–Tradition relationship, the interpretation of Scripture, and the understanding of the Church. This would seem to indicate that *nouvelle théologie* was amazingly successful in steering theological developments in the Catholic Church. On the other hand, however, the markedly reserved attitude of most of the *nouvelle* theologians towards post-conciliar developments in the Catholic Church would seem to put into question the thesis that *nouvelle théologie* had a lasting influence on Catholic theology. Thus, the events surrounding the Council make it difficult to evaluate the lasting role that *nouvelle théologie* may or may not have had.

The theological differences among the *nouvelle* theologians add further difficulty to an assessment of their impact. I have tried to make clear throughout this book that the differences in nuance were at times rather pronounced. Marie-Dominique Chenu and Yves Congar are often branded as 'progressive', while Henri de Lubac, Jean Daniélou, and Hans Urs von Balthasar are considered

---

[1] Yves M.-J. Congar, *Divided Christendom: A Catholic Study of the Problem of Reunion*, trans. M. A. Bousfield (London: Bles, 1939), 3.

'conservative'. Although I have serious reservations about such sociological categorizations, they rightly indicate that there were differences in approach within the movement of *nouvelle théologie*. These theological differences must be accounted for in any study of *nouvelle théologie*'s lasting impact on post-conciliar Catholic thought. It will take time, therefore, before it will be possible to write a study of the overall impact of *nouvelle théologie*.

My purpose in writing this book has been more limited in scope. I have tried to describe the shared theological sensibility of the *ressourcement* movement. My research has made it increasingly evident to me, however, that this rather limited, descriptive task is by no means superfluous. My reading of *nouvelle théologie* has brought me to the conclusion that the shared sensibility of *nouvelle théologie* was its sacramental ontology—the conviction that historical realities of the created order served as divinely ordained, sacramental means leading to eternal divine mysteries. The interpenetration of sign (*signum*) and reality (*res*) meant, according to the *nouvelle* theologians, that external, temporal appearances contained the spiritual, eternal realities which they represented and to which they dynamically pointed forward. For *nouvelle théologie*, theology had as its task the dynamic exploration of the reality of the divine mystery: theology as a return to mystery. This interpretation of *nouvelle théologie* as advocating a sacramental ontology builds on several recent studies that have highlighted the sacramental cast of the theologies of Pierre Rousselot, de Lubac, Balthasar, and Congar.[2] Unfortunately, however, most studies of *nouvelle théologie* are still marked by the relative absence of sacramental ontology as a key to interpret the movement. For any future discussion of the impact of *nouvelle théologie*, it seems to me indispensable to take careful account of its shared sensibility of a sacramental ontology that served as a return to mystery. In other words, by clarifying the character of *nouvelle théologie*, this book will, I hope, have provided some clarification that is required for future discussion of the theological impact of *nouvelle théologie*.

My interpretation of *nouvelle théologie* as the recovery of a sacramental ontology implies that, in some sense, its theology was indeed new—at least against the backdrop of the movement's immediate historical context. As a result, I have resisted the temptation to locate *nouvelle théologie*, historically, between the Modernist Crisis of the early twentieth century and the theological pluralism of the post-Second Vatican Council period. The Modernist Crisis, with its turn to historical critical exegesis (Alfred Loisy) and to subjective human experience (George Tyrrell), had caused great upheaval within Catholicism during the first decade of the twentieth century. As a result, the ecclesiastical climate between 1907 and 1960 made it difficult for history and experience to function as theologically meaningful categories. The condemnation of Modernism ensured that theologians were careful not to give the impression that they were returning to the 'historicism' and 'subjectivism' of the Modernist movement. *Nouvelle*

---

[2] Cf. the studies mentioned in Chap. 1, n. 31.

théologie may thus appear as the one theological movement during this period that was not afraid to speak out against the dominant mindset, as the one exception to the rule of an overall submission to a climate of fear. The freedom of exploration and the theological pluralism following the Second Vatican Council may seem like a belated victory for the Modernist movement. Thus, on this understanding, the theological trajectory would run from Modernism, via *nouvelle théologie*, to post-conciliar pluralism.

This historical account is not without warrant. The *nouvelle* theologians were not afraid to speak up, sometimes at great personal cost. *Nouvelle théologie* had the same theological opponent that Modernism had faced: the intellectualism of neo-Thomism which, thanks to Pope Leo XIII's encyclical, *Aeterni Patris* (1879), had become the semi-official voice of Catholicism. This neo-Thomist establishment did suffer its most serious defeat at the Second Vatican Council, a loss that now seems irreversible, considering the indebtedness of the last two pontiffs to *nouvelle théologie*. And the neo-Thomist confidence in the ability of discursive reason to access and possess theological truth was not hospitable to the theological pluralism that characterized the years following the Council. In presenting a history of the decline of neo-Thomism, it would be quite appropriate to begin with Modernism and move, via *nouvelle théologie*, to the Second Vatican Council.

But it is, of course, possible for two quite disparate groups to face the same opponent. To give a historical account of the demise of neo-Thomism is not the same as to present a theological discussion of what motivated *nouvelle théologie*. In particular, the view of *nouvelle théologie* as a Modernism redivivus leaves unexplained the enigma of the remarkable change in attitude of most of the *nouvelle* theologians during the post-Vatican II years. One could perhaps argue that, faced with the consequences of their thinking, a number of them drew back and adopted a reactionary demeanour. There might be a psychological explanation for this—many Catholics found the liturgical, doctrinal, and social developments difficult to process—but the explanation fails to convince. That most of the *nouvelle* theologians, battle-hardened and seasoned scholars, would suddenly repudiate the consequences of their own theology seems unlikely. Indeed, my reading of these theologians has confirmed to me that we need to look deeper for an adequate interpretation of *nouvelle théologie*.

Interpreting *nouvelle théologie* as a movement in search of a sacramental ontology allows us to make sense of several important characteristics that would otherwise seem idiosyncratic. Most important, perhaps, is the characteristic of *nouvelle théologie* as a movement of *ressourcement*. The Fourvière monograph series Théologie, the republication of the Church Fathers in the Sources chrétiennes series, as well as the new, contextualized readings of Thomas Aquinas were intentional snubs of the neo-Thomist manualist tradition and attempts to locate within the great Tradition resources for a return to mystery. For the *ressourcement* scholars, the Church Fathers did not just provide positive, historical evidence supporting official Church doctrine. Instead, they were theologians with their own, distinct place in the overall development of doctrine, theologians whose sacramental approach to reality continued to make them fruitful dialogue partners. This *ressourcement* of the Tradition set *nouvelle théologie* apart from Modernists and neo-Thomists alike, which makes it difficult to interpret the movement as a historical step leading from Modernism to post-concilar pluralism.

The spiritual interpretation of Scripture was arguably the most important practice that the *ressourcement* scholars—de Lubac and Daniélou, in particular—learned from the Church Fathers. The patristic turn to allegory, tropology, and anagogy was an attempt to enter into the mystery of the text by regarding it as a sacramental deposit. In this book, I have highlighted this aspect of *nouvelle théologie* because one of their key concerns was a *ressourcement* of Scripture and so a restoration of the Bible as central to theological practice. This centrality of Scripture makes the question of its interpretation particularly significant. Moreover, *nouvelle théologie*'s recovery of the patristic sacramental hermeneutic renders the interpretation of *nouvelle théologie* as a second Modernist movement highly implausible. To be sure, *nouvelle théologie* shared Modernism's interest in history and in the human subject, and none of the *nouvelle* theologians were, in principle, opposed to historical critical exegesis. None the less, the *ressourcement* scholars' sacramental mindset deeply influenced their reading of Scripture, which I have styled a 'sacramental hermeneutic'. By regarding the relationship between the historical and spiritual levels of interpretation as sacramental in character, the *nouvelle* theologians made clear that they were interested in much more than adaptation or accommodation to contemporary culture.

The growing indifference to the Church and to the Christian faith in France in the years leading up to the Second World War was cause for deep concern among the *nouvelle* theologians. It is well known that de Lubac, Daniélou, and Balthasar were all suspicious of the secularizing tendencies of modernity. In this study, I have pointed to the influence of Maurice Blondel on the Fourvière theologians. His attempt at a sacramental reintegration of nature and the supernatural placed him in opposition not just to the neo-Thomist establishment but also to the secular academic world that rejected any connection between faith and history. The deeply engrained 'historicism' or 'immanentism' of modernity excluded a priori the possibility that supernatural horizons might impact the world of immanent cause and effect. The Fourvière theologians' programme of *ressource-ment* resulted from their rejection of a purely autonomous natural realm. And although the anti-modern sentiments were most pronounced among the Fourvière Jesuits, the Dominicans of Le Saulchoir also had concerns about militant secularism. Yves Congar's 1935 essay on the growing problem of unbelief identified the 'hiatus between faith and life' as the cause of the problem,[3]

---

[3] Congar, 'Une conclusion théologique à l'enquête sur les raisons actuelles de l'incroyance', *VInt* 37 (1935), 214–49; English trans.: 'The Reasons for the Unbelief of our Time: A Theological Conclusion', *Integr* (Aug. 1938), 13–21; (Dec. 1938), 10–26.

and he intended his subsequent ecclesiological and ecumenical endeavours as an attempt to counter the growing secularism of French society.[4] The worker–priest movement, in which Chenu was heavily involved, was likewise the result of concern about increasing secularization in France, which Henri Godin and Yvan Daniel had described in their 1943 book, *La France, pays de mission?*[5] To be sure, Chenu's work as a medievalist painted a remarkably positive picture of the developments towards the desacralizing and desacramentalizing of society in the twelfth and thirteenth centuries. His appropriation of the shared sensibility of a sacramental ontology is more ambiguous than that of the other *nouvelle* theologians. Overall, it none the less remains appropriate to characterize *nouvelle théologie* as an attempt to recover a sacramental ontology. The *nouvelle* theologians' post-conciliar expressions of concern about developments within Catholicism were not a sudden lapse into a 'conservative' mindset, but indicated the continued desire of these theologians to uphold a sacramental ontology. They were convinced, in other words, that a return to mystery could be endangered not just by neo-Thomist scholasticism but also by an adaptation to modern secularism. As heirs to the Blondelian approach, the *ressourcement* scholars continued the difficult task of trying to sail between the Scylla of extrinsicism and the Charybdis of immanentism—a task shared by Catholics and Protestants alike.

ECUMENICAL IMPLICATIONS

Genuine ecumenical theology, as Congar was undoubtedly aware, is an often difficult responsibility. Congar faced strong opposition from within the Catholic Church to his relative openness towards Orthodox and Protestant thought and to his sometimes sharp criticism of historical developments within the Catholic Church. At the same time, his genuine Catholic convictions meant that he was unwilling to ignore real, theological differences with his dialogue partners— although he became more and more convinced that there was much to learn from his Orthodox and Protestant fellow-believers. Undoubtedly, Congar must have felt exonerated by the Second Vatican Council's positive approach to ecumenical dialogue. It remains true, however, that Congar often felt compelled to speak out against tendencies in Catholicism as well as in Orthodoxy and Protestantism. Genuine ecumenical dialogue often presents challenges to both sides of the discussion.

I have come to the conclusion that a truly ecumenical discussion of *nouvelle théologie* is unable to avoid such a dual challenge. The rejection of neo-Thomism

---

[4] Cf. Chap. 1, sect.: Controversy over the Nature of Theology (1937–42).

[5] Henri Godin and Yvan Daniel, *La France, pays de mission?* (Paris: L'Abeille, 1943); English trans.: *France Pagan? The Mission of Abbé Godin*, trans. Maisie Ward (New York: Sheed & Ward, 1949).

in favour of a return to mystery implied a critical reappraisal of theological developments within Catholicism since the Late Middle Ages. According to *nouvelle théologie*, the desacramentalizing of Western society had resulted from a number of factors: (1) the juridicizing of ecclesial authority through the eleventh-century Gregorian Reform (Congar); (2) the increasing opposition between Scripture and Church as distinct authorities between 1100 and 1300 (Congar); (3) the loss of the sacramental unity between the Eucharistic and ecclesial bodies of Christ through the twelfth-century Berengarian controversy (de Lubac); (4) the 'discovery of nature' in the twelfth century and the growing autonomy of the natural realm among the mendicant orders in the thirteenth century (Chenu); and (5) the separation of nature and the supernatural in the sixteenth- and seventeenth-century reactions to Baianism and Protestantism (de Lubac).[6] Although the sacramental ontology of *nouvelle théologie* objected especially to the dominant theological paradigm within Catholic thought, each of these factors also influenced Protestantism. The decline of a sacramental ontology began well before the Reformation period. The tragic split of the Reformation was the result of theological developments that had been in the making for centuries.

It could be argued that the decline of a sacramental ontology has affected Protestantism more seriously than Catholicism.[7] In any ecumenical endeavour, one is most keenly and painfully aware of the challenges that the discussion presents to one's own tradition. In any case, it seems to me that true progress in ecumenical dialogue requires Protestants to re-appropriate the essentials of the sacramental ontology that characterized the great Tradition. This would imply a return to a sacramental hermeneutic (spiritual interpretation), going beyond authorial intent in order to gain an appreciation of the various spiritual levels of meaning. Such a re-appropriation would further require a reconnection of Scripture and Tradition, with Scripture as the most important and normative monument of the Tradition. And a positive reappraisal of the Tradition implies, in turn, the need to strengthen current attempts at evangelical *ressourcement* of the Tradition. Finally, a re-appropriation of a sacramental ontology would require an attempt to overcome the relative neglect of ecclesiology among Protestants. De Lubac and Congar forged their communion ecclesiology in the

[6] Interestingly, the *ressourcement* scholars did not focus on the nominalist and voluntarist shifts of the Late Middle Ages as causes of the desacramentalizing of modernity. For contemporary discussions of the detrimental influence of nominalism and voluntarism, see John Milbank, *Theology and Social Theory: Beyond Secular Reason* (Oxford: Blackwell, 1990); Catherine Pickstock, *After Writing: On the Liturgical Consummation of Philosophy* (Oxford: Blackwell, 1998); Louis Dupré, *Passage to Modernity: An Essay in the Hermeneutics of Nature and Culture* (New Haven, Conn.: Yale University Press, 1993); id., *Religion and the Rise of Modern Culture* (Notre Dame, Ind.: University of Notre Dame Press, 2008).

[7] Cf. the discussion of Andrew Greeley's *The Catholic Imagination* (Berkeley, Calif.: University of California Press, 2000) in Chap. 1, sect.: *Nouvelle théologie* and Catholic–Protestant Dialogue.

face of the neo-scholastic overemphasis on the real presence in the Eucharist. In reaction, they accentuated the sacramental purpose of the Church's unity as the reality (*res*) of the Eucharistic celebration. Of course, the Protestant temptation is not that of neo-Thomism. By focusing on the Eucharist as a fellowship meal, much contemporary Protestantism, and evangelicalism in particular, tends to ignore the sacramental basis (*sacramentum*) of the Church's unity. None the less, from the perspective of communion ecclesiology, both neo-Thomists and evangelical Protestants tend to separate the sacrament and its reality (though the former focus on the sacrament and the latter on the reality). Despite their different context, therefore, contemporary Protestants do have much to gain from an appropriation of de Lubac's and Congar's reintegration of the sacrament with its mystical reality. In short, spiritual interpretation, reintegration of Scripture and Tradition, and communion ecclesiology are among the most urgently required means to advance the unity of the Church. The re-appropriation of a sacramental ontology may provide a mindset that will open up avenues for a common return to mystery.

Bibliography

BIBLIOGRAPHIES

Henri Bouillard

Neufeld, Karl H., 'Bibliographie du P. Henri Bouillard: 1942–1981', in Henri Bouillard, *Vérité du christianisme*, ed. Karl H. Neufeld (Paris: Desclée de Brouwer, 1989), 357–61.

Scully, J. Eileen, 'Grace and Human Freedom in the Theology of Henri Bouillard' (PhD diss., University of St Michael's College, Toronto School of Theology, 1993).

Marie-Dominique Chenu

Potworowski, Christophe F., 'Bibliography of Marie-Dominique Chenu', *Contemplation and Incarnation: The Theology of Marie-Dominique Chenu* (Montreal: McGill–Queen's University Press, 2001), 237–321.

Yves Congar

Flynn, Gabriel, 'An Yves Congar Bibliography 1987–1995, with *Addenda*: 1996–2002', *Yves Congar's Vision of the Church in a World of Unbelief* (Burlington, Vt.: Ashgate, 2004), 229–33.

Nichols, Aidan, 'An Yves Congar Bibliography, 1967–1987', *Ang* 66 (1989), 422–66.

Quattrocchi, Pietro, 'General Bibliography of Yves Congar', in Jean-Pierre Jossua, *Yves Congar: Theology in the Service of God's People* (Chicago, Ill.: Priory, 1968), 185–241.

Jean Daniélou

'Bibliographie des travaux du Cardinal J. Daniélou sur le Judéo–Christianisme', *RSR* 60 (1972), 11–23.

Kannengiesser, Charles, 'Bibliographie patristique du cardinal Jean Daniélou', in Jacques Fontaine and Charles Kannengiesser (eds), *Epektasis: Mélanges patristiques offerts au Cardinal Jean Daniélou* (Paris: Beauchesne, 1972), 673–89.

Henri de Lubac

Neufeld, Karl H., and Michel Sales, 'Bibliographie de Henri de Lubac (corrections et compléments), 1942–1989,' in Henri de Lubac, *Théologie dans l'histoire*, ii, *Questions disputées et résistance au nazisme* (Paris: Desclée de Brouwer, 1990), 408–16.

—— —— *Bibliographie Henri de Lubac, 1925–1974* (2nd edn, Einsiedeln: Johannes, 1974).

Marie-Michel Labourdette

Donneaud, Henry, 'Bibliographie du Père M.-M. Labourdette, OP, 1935–1990', *RT* 92 (1992), 388–425.

Pierre Rousselot

McDermott, John M., *Love and Understanding: The Relation of Will and Intellect in Pierre Rousselot's Christological Vision*, Analecta Gregoriana, 229 (Rome: Università Gregoriana Editrice, 1983), 302–8.

Hans Urs von Balthasar

Capol, Cornelia (ed.), *Hans Urs von Balthasar: Bibliographie, 1925–1990* (Einsiedeln: Johannes, 1990).

PRIMARY LITERATURE[1]

Bainvel, Jean-Vincent, *De ecclesia Christi* (Paris: Beauchesne, 1925).
—— 'L'Histoire d'un dogme', *Études*, 101 (1904), 612–32.
Balthasar, Hans Urs von, *Cosmic Liturgy: The Universe according to Maximus the Confessor*, trans. Brian E. Daley (San Francisco, Calif.: Ignatius, 2003).
——*Explorations in Theology*, i *The Word Made Flesh*, trans. A. V. Littledale and Alexander Dru (San Francisco, Calif.: Ignatius, 1989).
—— 'The Fathers, the Scholastics, and Ourselves', trans. Edward T. Oakes, *Comm* 24 (1997), 347–96.
—— 'Geleitwort', in Henri de Lubac, *Der geistige Sinn der Schrift*, trans. Martha Gisi, Christ Heute, 2nd ser., 5 (Einsiedeln: Johannes, 1952), 7–12.
—— *The Glory of the Lord: A Theological Aesthetics*, trans. Erasmo Leiva-Merikakis, et al., 7 vols (San Francisco, Calif.: Ignatius, 1982–91).
—— 'Holy Scripture', trans. Jeremy Holmes, *NV* Eng 5 (2007), 707–24.
—— *Origen, Spirit and Fire: A Thematic Anthology of his Writings*, trans. Robert J. Daly (Washington, DC: Catholic University of America Press, 1984).
—— *Parole et mystère chez Origène* (Paris: Cerf, 1957).
—— *Presence and Thought: An Essay on the Religious Philosophy of Gregory of Nyssa*, trans. Mark Sebanc (San Francisco, Calif.: Communio/Ignatius, 1995).
—— (ed.), *The Scandal of the Incarnation: Irenaeus Against the Heresies*, trans. John Saward (San Francisco, Calif.: Ignatius, 1981).
—— *Test Everything; Hold Fast to What Is Good: An Interview with Hans Urs von Balthasar*, ed. Angelo Scola, and trans. Maria Shrady (San Francisco, Calif.: Ignatius, 1989).
—— *Theo-Drama: Theological Dramatic Theory*, trans. Graham Harrison, 5 vols (San Francisco, Calif.: Ignatius, 1988–98).
—— *Theo-Logic: Theological Logical Theory*, trans. Adrian J. Walker and Graham Harrison, 3 vols (San Francisco, Calif.: Ignatius, 2000–5).
—— *The Theology of Henri de Lubac: An Overview*, trans. Joseph Fessio and Susan Clements (San Francisco, Calif.: Communio/Ignatius, 1991).
—— *A Theology of History* (San Francisco, Calif.: Communio/Ignatius, 1994).

---

[1] This bibliography mostly omits (1) French and German originals where English translations are available; and (2) essays whose contents the authors included in subsequent monographs.

—— *The Theology of Karl Barth*, trans. Edward T. Oakes (San Francisco, Calif.: Communio/Ignatius, 1992).

Blondel, Maurice, *Action (1893): Essay on a Critique of Life and a Science of Practice*, trans. Olivia Blanchette (Notre Dame, Ind.: University of Notre Dame Press, 1984).

—— [alias François Mallet], 'La Foi et la science', *RCF* 47 (1906), 449–73, 591–605.

—— *The Letter on Apologetics and History and Dogma*, trans. and ed. Alexander Dru and Illtyd Trethowan (Grand Rapids, Mich.: Eerdmans, 1994).

—— 'Le Point de départ de la recherche philosophique', *APC* 151 (1906), 337–60; 152 (1906), 225–49.

—— 'Le Problème de la mystique', in Blondel, et al., *Qu'est-ce que la mystique? Quelques aspects historiques et philosophiques du problème*, Cahiers de la nouvelle journée, 3 (Paris: Bloud et Gay, 1925), 2–63.

Bonnefoy, Jean-François, *La Nature de la théologie selon saint Thomas d'Aquin* (Paris: Vrin; Bruges: Beyaert, 1939).

—— 'La Théologie comme science et l'explication de la foi selon Thomas d'Aquin', *ETL* 14 (1937), 421–46, 600–31; 15 (1938), 491–516.

Bouillard, Henri, *Blondel and Christianity*, trans. James M. Somerville (Washington, DC: Corpus, 1969).

—— *Conversion et grâce chez s. Thomas d'Aquin: Étude historique*, Théologie, 1 (Paris: Aubier, 1944).

—— 'L'Idée chrétienne du miracle', *Cahiers Laënnec* 8/4 (Oct. 1948), 25–37.

—— *Karl Barth*, 2 vols (Paris: Aubier/Montaigne, 1957).

—— *The Knowledge of God*, trans. Samuel D. Femiano (New York: Herder & Herder, 1968).

—— *The Logic of the Faith* (New York: Sheed & Ward, 1967).

—— 'Notions conciliaires et analogie de la vérité', *RSR* 35 (1948), 251–71.

—— 'Précisions', *RT* 47 (1947), 177–83.

—— 'La Preuve de Dieu dans le "Proslogion" et son interprétation par Karl Barth', in *Congrès international du IXe centenaire de l'arrivée d'Anselme au Bec*, Spicilegium Beccense, 1 (Le Bec-Hellouin: Abbaye Notre-Dame du Bec and Paris: Vrin, 1959), 190–207.

—— 'La Refus de la théologie naturelle dans la théologie protestante contemporaine', in Henri Birault, et al., *L'Existence de Dieu*, Cahiers de l'actualité religieuse, 16 (Tournai: Casterman, 1961), 95–108, 353–8.

—— 'The Thought of Maurice Blondel: A Synoptic Vision', *IPQ* 3 (1963), 392–405.

—— *Vérité du christianisme*, ed. Karl H. Neufeld (Paris: Desclée de Brouwer, 1989).

Boyer, Charles, 'Nature pure et surnaturel dans le *Surnaturel* du Père de Lubac', *Greg* 28 (1947), 379–96.

—— 'Qu'est-ce que la théologie: Réflexions sur une controverse', *Greg* 21 (1940), 255–66.

—— 'Sur un article des Recherches de science religieuse', *Greg* 29 (1948), 152–4.

Charlier, Louis, *Essai sur le problème théologique*, Section scientifique, 1 (Thuillies: Ramgal, 1938).

Chenu, Marie-Dominique, *Aquinas and his Role in Theology*, trans. Paul Philibert (Collegeville, Minn.: Liturgical, 2002).

—— *La 'Doctrine sociale' de l'église comme idéologie* (Paris: Cerf, 1979).

—— *Une école de théologie: Le Saulchoir*, with contributions by Giuseppe Alberigo, Étienne Fouilloux, Jean-Pierre Jossua, and Jean Ladrière (Paris: Cerf, 1985).

Chenu, Marie-Dominique, *Faith and Theology*, trans. Denis Hickey (New York: Macmillan, 1968).

——— 'Histoire et allégorie au douzième siècle', in Erwin Iserloh and Peter Manns (eds), *Festgabe Joseph Lortz*, ii (Baden-Baden: Grimm, 1958), 59–71.

——— *Is Theology a Science?*, trans. A. H. N. Green-Armytage (New York: Hawthorn, 1959).

——— *Nature, Man, and Society in the Twelfth Century: Essays on New Theological Perspectives in the Latin West*, trans. and ed. Jerome Taylor and Lester Little, Medieval Academy Reprints for Teaching, 37 (Toronto: University of Toronto Press, 1998).

——— *La Parole de Dieu*, 2 vols (Paris: Cerf, 1964).

——— *Peuple de Dieu dans le monde*, Foi vivante, 35 (Paris: Cerf, 1966).

——— 'Position de la théologie', *RSPT* 24 (1935), 232–57.

——— 'Pour lire saint Augustin', *VSpir* 24 (1930), 135–57.

——— 'La Raison psychologique du développement du dogme d'après Saint Thomas', *RSPT* 13 (1924), 44–51.

——— *La Théologie au XIIᵉ siècle*, Études de philosophie médiévale, 45 (Paris: Vrin, 2006).

——— *La Théologie comme science au XIIIᵉ siècle*, Bibliothèque thomiste, 33 (3rd edn, Paris: Vrin, 1957).

——— *Un théologien en liberté: Jacques Duquesne interroge le Père Chenu* (Paris: Centurion, 1975).

——— *The Theology of Work*, trans. Lilian Soiron (Chicago, Ill.: Henry Regnery, 1966).

——— *Toward Understanding Saint Thomas*, trans. Albert M. Landry and Dominic Hughes (Chicago, Ill.: Regnery, 1964).

——— 'Towards a Theology of Work', trans. Joseph Cunneen, *CC* 7/2 (1957), 175–83.

——— 'Vérité évangélique et métaphysique wolffienne à Vatican II', *RSPT* 57 (1973), 632–40.

Congar, Yves M.-J., 'Attitudes towards Reform in the Church', trans. Bernard Gilligan, *CC* 1/4 (1951), 80–102.

——— *Christ, Our Lady and the Church: A Study in Eirenic Theology*, trans. Henry St John (London: Longmans Green, 1957).

——— 'Le Diaconat dans la théologie des ministères', in P. Winninger and Y. Congar (eds), *Le Diacre dans l'église et le monde d'aujourd'hui*, Unam sanctam, 59 (Paris: Cerf, 1966), 121–41.

——— *Divided Christendom: A Catholic Study of the Problem of Reunion*, trans. M. A. Bousfield (London: G. Bles, 1939).

——— *L'Église: De saint Augustin à l'époque moderne*, Histoire des dogmes, 3 (Paris: Cerf, 1970).

——— *Église catholique et France moderne* (Paris: Hachette, 1978).

——— 'L'Esprit des Pères d'après Moehler', *VSpir* suppl., 55 (1938), 1–25.

——— *Faith and Spiritual Life*, trans. A. Manson and L. C. Sheppard (London: Darton, Longman, and Todd, 1969).

——— *Fifty Years of Catholic Theology: Conversation with Yves Congar*, ed. Bernard Lauret (Philadelphia, Pa.: Fortress, 1988).

——— *La Foi et la théologie* (Tournai: Desclée, 1962).

——— 'L'Hérésie, déchirement de l'unité', in Pierre Chaillet (ed.), *L'Église est une: Hommage à Moehler* (Paris: Bloud et Gay, 1939), 255–69.

—— *A History of Theology*, trans. and ed. Hunter Guthrie (Garden City: Doubleday, 1968.

—— *I Believe in the Holy Spirit*, trans. David Smith, 3 vols (New York: Crossroad/Herder, 1997).

—— 'The Idea of the Church in St Thomas Aquinas', *Thomist* 1 (1939), 331–59.

—— 'Johann Adam Möhler: 1796–1838', *TQ* 150 (1970), 47–51.

—— *Journal d'un théologien (1946–1956)*, ed. Étienne Fouilloux (Paris: Cerf, 2000).

—— *Lay People in the Church: A Study for a Theology of the Laity*, trans. Donald Attwater (rev. edn, London: Chapman, 1985).

—— *The Meaning of Tradition*, trans. A. N. Woodrow (San Francisco, Calif.: Ignatius, 2004).

—— *Ministères et communion ecclésiale* (Paris: Cerf, 1971).

—— *Mon journal du Concile*, ed. Éric Mahieu, 2 vols (Paris: Cerf, 2002).

—— 'Moving towards a Pilgrim Church', in Alberic Stacpoole (ed.), *Vatican II by Those Who Were There* (London: Chapman, 1986), 129–52.

—— 'My Path-findings in the Theology of Laity and Ministries', *Jur* 32 (1972), 169–88.

—— *The Mystery of the Church*, trans. A. V. Littledale (rev. edn, Baltimore, Md.: Helicon, 1965).

—— *The Mystery of the Temple, or, The Manner of God's Presence to His Creatures from Genesis to the Apocalypse*, trans. Reginald F. Trevett (London: Burns & Oates, 1962).

—— 'Note sur la gnose ou l'enseignement religieux des savants et des simples selon S. Thomas', *BT* 1 (1931), 5*–7*.

—— 'Notes théologiques à propos de l'Assomption', *DViv* 18 (1951), 107–12.

—— 'La Pensée de Möhler et l'ecclésiologie orthodoxe', *Irén* 12 (1935), 321–9.

—— *Un peuple messianique: L'Église, sacrement du salut; Salut et libération* (Paris: Cerf, 1975).

—— *Power and Poverty in the Church*, trans. Jennifer Nicholson (London: Chapman, 1965).

—— 'R. Sohm nous interroge encore', *RSPT* 57 (1973), 263–94.

—— 'The Reasons for the Unbelief of Our Time: A Theological Conclusion', *Integr* (Aug. 1938), 13–21; (Dec. 1938), 10–26.

—— 'La "Réception" comme réalité ecclésiologique', *RSPT* 56 (1972), 369–403.

—— 'Renewal of the Spirit and Reform of the Institution', trans. John Griffiths, *Conc* 73 (1972), 39–49.

—— *The Revelation of God*, trans. A. Mason and L. C. Sheppard (New York: Herder & Herder, 1968).

—— review of R. Draguet, 'Méthodes théologiques d'hier et d'aujourd'hui'; J.-F. Bonnefoy, 'La Théologie comme science et l'explication de la foi selon saint Thomas d'Aquin'; L. Charlier, *Essai sur le problème théologique*; and R. Gagnebet, 'La Nature de la théologie spéculative', in *BT* 5 (1937–9), 490–505.

—— 'Le Saint-Esprit et le corps apostolique, réalisateurs de l'œuvre du Christ', *RSPT* 36 (1952), 613–25.

—— *Sainte Église: Études et approches ecclésiologiques*, Unam sanctam, 41 (Paris: Cerf, 1963).

—— 'St Thomas Aquinas and the Spirit of Ecumenism', *NBl* 55 (1974), 196–209.

Congar, Yves M.-J., 'La Signification œcuménique de l'œuvre de Moehler', *Irén* 15 (1938), 113–30.

—— 'Sur l'évolution de l'interprétation de la pensée de Moehler', *RSPT* 27 (1938), 205–12.

—— 'Théologie', in A. Vacant, et al., *Dictionnaire de théologie catholique*, xv (Paris: Letouzey et Ané, 1946), 341–502.

—— *This Church that I Love*, trans. Lucien Delafuente (Denville, NJ: Dimension, 1969).

—— *Thomas d'Aquin: Sa vision de théologie et de l'Église* (London: Variorum, 1984).

—— *Tradition and Traditions: The Biblical, Historical, and Theological Evidence for Catholic Teaching on Tradition*, trans. Michael Naseby and Thomas Rainborough (San Diego, Calif.: Basilica, 1966).

—— 'Vie de l'Église et conscience de la catholicité', *BM* 18 (1938), 153–69.

—— *Une vie pour la vérité: Jean Puyo interroge le Père Congar* (Paris: Centurion, 1975).

—— *Les Voies du Dieu vivant: Théologie et vie spirituelle*, Cogitatio fidei, 3 (Paris: Cerf, 1962).

—— *Vraie et fausse réforme dans l'Église*, Unam sanctam, 20 (Paris: Cerf, 1950).

—— 'Vraie et fausse réforme dans l'Église', trans. Lancelot Sheppard, *CC* 3/4 (1953), 358–65.

—— *The Wide World My Parish: Salvation and its Problems*, trans. Donald Attwater (Baltimore, Md.: Helicon, 1961).

—— *The Word and the Spirit*, trans. David Smith (London: Chapman, 1986).

Cullmann, Oscar, *The Early Church*, ed. A. J. B. Higgins, and trans. A. J. B. Higgins and S. Godman (London: SCM, 1956).

—— 'Écriture et Tradition', *DViv* 23 (1952), 45–67.

Daniélou, Jean, *The Advent of Salvation: A Comparative Study of Non-Christian Religions and Christianity*, trans. Rosemary Sheed (New York: Paulist, 1962).

—— *The Angels and their Mission: According to the Fathers of the Church*, trans. David Heimann (1957; repr. Notre Dame, Ind.: Ave Maria, 1987).

—— 'Autour de l'exégèse spirituelle', *DViv* 8 (1952), 123–6.

—— *The Bible and the Liturgy*, Liturgical Studies, 3 (Notre Dame, Ind.: University of Notre Dame Press, 1956).

—— *Christ and Us*, trans. Walter Roberts (New York: Sheed & Ward, 1961).

—— 'The Conception of History in the Christian Tradition', *JR* 30 (1950), 171–9.

—— *Culture et mystère*, Chrétienté nouvelle, 16 (Brussels: Éditions universitaires, 1948).

—— 'Les Divers sens de l'Écriture dans la tradition chrétienne primitive', *ETL* 24 (1948), 119–26.

—— *Et qui est mon prochain? Mémoires* (Paris: Stock, 1974).

—— *From Shadows to Reality: Studies in the Biblical Typology of the Fathers*, trans. Wulstan Hibberd (London: Burns & Oates, 1960).

—— *God and the Ways of Knowing*, trans. Walter Roberts (1956; repr. San Francisco, Calif.: Ignatius, 2003).

—— 'Has History a Meaning?' *The Month*, 6 (1951), 41–4.

—— *A History of Early Christian Doctrine before the Council of Nicaea*, ii *Gospel Message and Hellenistic Culture*, ed. and trans. John Austin Baker (London: Darton, Longman & Todd, 1973).

—— *Holy Pagans of the Old Testament*, trans. Felix Faber (London: Longmans, Green and Co, 1957).

—— Introduction to Gregory of Nyssa, *La Vie de Moïse ou Traité de la perfection en matière de vertu* (3rd edn, 1968; repr. Paris: Cerf, 2000).

—— *The Lord of History: Reflections on the Inner Meaning of History*, trans. Nigel Abercrombie (1958; repr. Cleveland, Ohio: Meridian, 1968).

—— *Mythes païens, mystère chrétien* (Paris: Fayard, 1966).

—— 'Les Orientations présentes de la pensée religieuse', *Études*, 249 (1946), 5–21.

—— *Origen*, trans. Walter Mitchell (New York: Sheed & Ward, 1955).

—— *Philon d'Alexandrie, Les temps et les destines* (Paris: Fayard, 1958).

—— *Platonisme et théologie mystique: Doctrine spirituelle de Saint Grégoire de Nysse*, Théologie, 2 (Paris: Aubier, 1944).

—— *Prayer as a Political Problem*, ed. and trans. J. R. Kirwan (New York: Sheed & Ward, 1967).

—— *The Presence of God*, trans. Walter Roberts (Baltimore, Md.: Helicon, 1959).

—— 'Réponse à Oscar Cullmann', *DViv* 24 (1953), 105–16.

—— 'The Sacraments and the History of Salvation', in *The Liturgy and the Word of God*, ed. A. G. Marimort (Collegeville, Minn.: Liturgical, 1959), 21–32.

—— 'Saint Irénée et les origines de la théologie de l'histoire', *RSR* 34 (1947), 227–31.

—— *The Salvation of the Nations*, trans. Angeline Bouchard (New York: Sheed & Ward, 1950).

—— 'La Typologie millénariste de la semaine dans le christianisme primitif', *VC* 2 (1948), 1–16.

de Grandmaison, Léonce, *Le Dogme chrétien: Sa nature, ses formules, son développement* (Paris: Beauchesne, 1928).

de Lubac, Henri, *At the Service of the Church: Henri de Lubac Reflects on the Circumstances that Occasioned his Writings*, trans. Anne Elizabeth Englund (San Francisco, Calif.: Ignatius, 1993).

—— *Augustinianism and Modern Theology*, trans. Lancelot Sheppard (New York: Crossroad/Herder, 2000).

—— *A Brief Catechesis on Nature and Grace*, trans. Richard Arnandez (San Francisco, Calif.: Ignatius, 1984).

—— *Carnets du Concile*, ed. Loïc Figoureux, 2 vols (Paris: Cerf, 2007).

—— *Catholicism: Christ and the Common Destiny of Man*, trans. Lancelot C. Sheppard and Elizabeth Englund (San Francisco, Calif.: Ignatius, 1988).

—— *Christian Resistance to Anti-Semitism: Memories from 1940–1944*, trans. Elizabeth Englund (San Francisco, Calif.: Ignatius, 1990).

—— 'The Church in Crisis', *TD* 17 (1969), 312–25.

—— *The Church: Paradox and Mystery*, trans. James R. Dunne (New York: Ecclesia, 1969).

—— *Corpus Mysticum; The Eucharist and the Church in the Middle Ages: Historical Survey*, trans. Gemma Simmonds, Richard Price, and Christopher Stephens and ed. Laurence Paul Hemming and Susan Frank Parsons (London: SCM, 2006).

—— *De Lubac: A Theologian Speaks*, trans. Stephen Maddux and ed. Angelo Scola (Los Angeles, Calif.: Twin Circles, 1985).

—— *The Discovery of God*, trans. Alexander Dru, et al. (Grand Rapids, Mich.: Eerdmans, 1996).

—— *L'Église dans la crise actuelle* (Paris: Cerf, 1969).

de Lubac, Henri, *Entretien autour de Vatican II: Souvenirs et réflexions* (Paris: Cerf, 1985).

—— 'Esprit et liberté dans la tradition théologique', *BLE* 40 (1939), 121–50, 189–207.

—— *History and Spirit: The Understanding of Scripture According to Origen*, trans. Anne Englund Nash and Juvenal Merriell (San Francisco, Calif.: Ignatius, 2007).

—— Introduction to Origen, *Homélies sur l'Exode*, trans. P. Fortier, Sources chrétiennes, 16 (Paris: Cerf, 1947), 7–75.

—— Introduction to Origen, *Homélies sur la Genèse*, trans. Louis Doutreleau, Sources chrétiennes, 7 (Paris: Cerf, 1943), 5–62.

—— *Medieval Exegesis: The Four Senses of Scripture*, trans. Marc Sebanc and E. M. Macierowski, 2 vols (Grand Rapids, Mich.: Eerdmans, 1998–2000).

—— *More Paradoxes*, trans. Anne Englund Nash (San Francisco, Calif.: Ignatius, 2002).

—— *The Motherhood of the Church Followed by Particular Churches in the Universal Church and an Interview Conducted by Gwendoline Jarczyk*, trans. Sergia Englund (San Francisco, Calif.: Ignatius, 1982).

—— 'Le Mystère du surnaturel', *RSR* 36 (1949), 80–121.

—— *The Mystery of the Supernatural*, trans. Rosemary Sheed (New York: Crossroad/ Herder, 1998).

—— *Paradoxes of Faith*, trans. Anne Englund Nash (San Francisco, Calif.: Ignatius, 1987).

—— 'Le Problème du développement du dogme', *RSR* 35 (1948), 130–60.

—— *Scripture in the Tradition*, trans. Luke O'Neill (1968; repr. New York: Crossroad/ Herder, 2000).

—— 'Spiritual Understanding', trans. Luke O'Neill, in Stephen E. Fowl (ed.), *The Theological Interpretation of Scripture: Classic and Contemporary Readings* (Malden, Mass.: Blackwell, 1997).

—— *The Splendor of the Church*, trans. Michael Mason (1956; repr. San Francisco, Calif.: Ignatius, 1999).

—— *Surnaturel: Études historiques*, ed. Michel Sales (rev. edn, Paris: Desclée de Brouwer, 1991).

—— *Theological Fragments*, trans. Rebecca Howell Balinski (San Francisco, Calif.: Ignatius, 1989).

—— *Theology in History*, trans. Anne Englund Nash (San Francisco, Calif.: Ignatius, 1996).

de Solages, Bruno, 'Pour l'honneur de la théologie, les contre-sens du R. P. Garrigou-Lagrange', *BLE* 48 (1947), 64–84.

'Déclaration sur la liberté et la fonction des théologiens dans l'Église', *Conc* 41 (1969), 147–51.

Deneffe, August, *Der Traditionsbegriff: Studie zur Theologie* (Münster: Aschendorff, 1931).

Draguet, René, *L'Évolution des dogmes* (Saint-Dizier: Brulliard, 1937).

—— 'L'Évolution des dogmes', in Maurice Brillant and Maurice Nédoncelle (eds), *Apologétique: Nos raisons de croire, réponses aux objections* (Paris: Bloud et Gay, 1937), 1166–92.

—— *Histoire du dogme catholique* (Paris: Michel, 1941).

—— 'Méthodes théologiques d'hier et d'aujourd'hui', *RCIF* 15/42 (10 Jan. 1936), 1–7; 15/46 (7 Feb. 1936), 4–7; 15/47 (14 Feb. 1936), 13–17.

—— review of Louis Charlier, *Essai sur le problème théologique*, in *ETL* 16 (1938), 143–5.

Duméry, Henry, *La Philosophie de l'action: Essai sur l'intellectualisme blondélien* (Paris: Aubier/Montaigne, 1948).

Gagnebet, Marie-Rosaire, 'L'Amour naturel de Dieu chez saint Thomas et ses contemporains', *RT* 56 (1948), 394–446; 57 (1949), 31–102.

—— 'Un essai sur le problème théologique', *RT* 45 (1939), 108–45.

Gardeil, Ambroise, *La Crédibilité et l'apologétique* (Paris: Gabalda, 1908).

—— *Le Donné révélé et la théologie* (Paris: Lecoffre, 1910).

—— 'Introduction à la théologie', *RSPT* 9 (1920), 548–65; 11 (1922), 688–92.

—— 'La Notion du lieu théologique', *RSPT* 2 (1908), 51–73, 246–76, 484–505.

Garrigou-Lagrange, Réginald, *De gratia: Commentarius in Summam Theologicam S. Thomæ I^ae^ II^ae^ q. 109–114* (Turin: Berruti, 1947).

—— 'L'Immutabilité du dogme selon le Concile du Vatican, et le relativisme', *Ang* 26 (1949), 309–22.

—— 'Les Méthodes de l'apologétique', *RT* 21 (1913), 478–89.

—— 'Nécessité de revenir à la définition traditionnelle de la vérité', *Ang* 25 (1948), 185–98.

—— 'Les Notions consacrées par les Conciles', *Ang* 24 (1947), 217–30.

—— 'La Nouvelle Théologie, où va-t-elle?' *Ang* 23 (1946), 126–45.

—— *Reality: A Synthesis of Thomistic Thought*, trans. Patrick Cummins (St Louis, Mo: Herder, 1950).

—— 'Le Relativisme et l'immutabiltité du dogme', *Ang* 27 (1950), 219–46.

—— 'La Structure de l'encyclique "Humani generis"', *Ang* 28 (1951), 3–17.

—— 'Vérité et immutabilité du dogme', *Ang* 24 (1947), 124–39.

Gayraud, Hippolyte, 'Une nouvelle apologétique chrétienne', *APC* 35 (1896–7), 257–73, 400–8.

Gillon, Louis-Bertrand, 'Aux origines de la "puissance obédientielle"', *RT* 55 (1947), 304–10.

—— 'Théologie de la grâce', *RT* 46 (1946), 603–13.

Gilson, Étienne, *Being and Some Philosophers* (2nd edn, Toronto: Pontifical Institute of Mediaeval Studies, 1952).

Godin, Henri, and Yvan Daniel, *France Pagan? The Mission of Abbé Godin*, trans. Maisie Ward, Rencontres, 12 (New York: Sheed & Ward, 1949).

Guérard des Lauriers, Michel-Louis, 'La Théologie de s. Thomas et la grâce actuelle', *ATh* 6 (1945), 276–325.

Labourdette, Marie-Michel, 'La Théologie et ses sources', *RT* 46 (1946), 353–71.

—— and Marie-Joseph Nicolas, 'L'Analogie de la vérité et l'unité de la science théologique', *RT* 47 (1947), 417–66.

—— —— and R.-L. Bruckberger, *Dialogue théologique: Pièces du débat entre 'La Revue Thomiste' d'une part et les RR PP de Lubac, Daniélou, Bouillard, Fessard, von Balthasar, SJ, d'autre part* (Saint-Maximin: Arcades, 1947).

Ligeard, Hippolyte, 'La Crédibilité de la révélation d'après saint Thomas', *RSR* 5 (1914), 40–57.

Loisy, Alfred, *Autour d'un petit livre* (Paris: Picard, 1903).

—— *The Gospel and the Church*, introd. Bernard B. Scott (Philadelphia, Pa.: Fortress, 1976).

Maréchal, Joseph, *A Maréchal Reader*, ed. and trans. Joseph Donceel (New York: Herder & Herder, 1970).

—— *Le Point de départ de la métaphysique: Leçons sur le développement historique et théorique du problème de la connaissance*, v *Le Thomisme devant la philosophie critique* (Louvain: Museum Lessianum; Paris: Alcan, 1926).

Marín-Sola, Francisco, *La evolución homogénea del dogma católico*, Biblioteca de tomistas españoles, 1 (Madrid: La ciencia tomista, 1923).
—— *L'Évolution homogène du dogme catholique*, 2 vols (2nd edn, Fribourg: St-Paul, 1924).
Möhler, Johann Adam, *Athanasius der Grosse und die Kirche seiner Zeit, besonders im Kampfe mit dem Arianismus* (Mainz: Kupferberg, 1827).
—— *Symbolism: Exposition of the Doctrinal Differences between Catholics and Protestants as Evidenced by their Symbolical Writings*, trans. James Burton Robertson (New York: Crossroad, 1997).
—— *Unity in the Church, or the Principle of Catholicism: Presented in the Spirit of the Church Fathers of the First Three Centuries*, ed. and trans. Peter C. Erb (Washington, DC: Catholic University of America Press, 1996).
Parente, Pietro, 'Nuove tendenze teologiche', *L'Osservatore Romano* (9–10 Feb. 1942), 1.
Rousselot, Pierre, 'Amour spirituel et synthèse aperceptive', *RPh* 16 (1910), 225–40.
—— *Answer to Two Attacks*, trans. Avery Dulles (New York: Fordham University Press, 1990).
—— 'L'Être et l'esprit', *RPh* 16 (1910), 561–74.
—— *The Eyes of Faith*, trans. Joseph Donceel; *Answer to Two Attacks*, trans. Avery Dulles (New York: Fordham University Press, 1990).
—— *Intelligence: Sense of Being, Faculty of God*, ed. and trans. Andrew Tallon, Marquette Studies in Philosophy, 16 (Madison, Wis.: Marquette University Press, 1998).
—— 'Note sur le développement du dogme', *RSR* 37 (1950), 113–20.
—— 'Petite théorie du développement du dogme', ed. Henri de Lubac, *RSR* 53 (1965), 355–90.
—— *The Problem of Love in the Middle Ages: A Historical Contribution*, trans. Alan Vincelette, Marquette Studies in Philosophy, 24 (Madison, Wis.: Marquette University Press, 2001).
Schultes, Reginald Maria, *Introductio in historiam dogmatum: Praelectiones habitae in Collegio pontificio 'Angelico' de Urbe, 1911–1922* (Paris: Lethielleux, 1922).
Schwalm, Marie-Benoît, 'Les Illusions de l'idéalisme et leurs dangers pour la foi', *RT* 4 (1896), 413–41.
Simonin, Henri-Dominique, 'De la nécessité de certaines conclusions théologiques', *Ang* 16 (1939), 72–82.
—— '"Implicite" et "explicite" dans le développement du dogme', *Ang* 14 (1937), 126–45.
—— 'La Théologie et ses sources: Réponse', *RSR* 33 (1946), 385–401.
Tuyaerts, Marcolinus Maria, *L'Évolution du dogme: Étude théologique* (Louvain: Nova et vetera, 1919).
Tyrrell, George [alias Hilaire Bourdon], *L'Église et l'avenir* (priv. pub., 1903).
—— *Through Scylla and Charybdis; or, The Old Theology and the New* (London: Longmans, Green, and Co, 1907).

SECONDARY LITERATURE

Arnal, Oscar L., 'A Missionary "Main Tendue" toward French Communists: The "Témoignages" of the Worker–Priests, 1943–1954', *FHS* 13 (1984), 529–56.

——— *Priests in Working-Class Blue: The History of the Worker–Priests (1943–1954)* (New York: Paulist, 1986).

——— 'Theology and Commitment: Marie-Dominique Chenu', *CC* 38 (1988), 64–75.

Aubert, Roger, *Le Problème de l'acte de foi* (2nd edn, Louvain: Warny, 1950).

——— *La Théologie catholique au milieu du XXe siècle* (Tournai: Casterman, 1954).

Auricchio, John, *The Future of Theology* (Staten Island, NY: Alba, 1970).

Ayres, Lewis, 'The Soul and the Reading of Scripture: A Note on Henri de Lubac', *SJT* 61 (2008), 173–90.

Baum, Gregory, 'The Blondelian Shift', in *Man Becoming: God in Secular Experience* (1970; repr. New York: Crossroad/Seabury, 1979), 1–36.

Bernards, Matthäus, 'Zur Lehre von der Kirche als Sakrament: Beobachtungen aus der Theologie des 19. und 20. Jahrhunderts', *MTZ* 20 (1969), 29–54.

Blankenhorn, Bernhard, 'Balthasar's Method of Divine Naming', *NV* Eng 1 (2003), 245–68.

Boersma, Hans, 'Accommodation to What? Univocity of Being, Pure Nature, and the Anthropology of St Irenaeus', *IJST* 8 (2006), 266–93.

——— ' "*Néoplatonisme belgo-français*": *Nouvelle théologie* and the Search for a Sacramental Ontology', *LouvStud* (2007), 333–60.

——— 'On Baking Pumpkin Pie: Kevin Vanhoozer and Yves Congar on Tradition', *CTJ* 42 (2007), 237–55.

——— 'A Sacramental Journey to the Beatific Vision: The Intellectualism of Pierre Rousselot', *HeyJ* 49 (2008), 1015–34.

——— 'Sacramental Ontology: Nature and the Supernatural in the Ecclesiology of Henri de Lubac', *NBl* 88 (2007), 242–73.

——— 'Spiritual Imagination: Recapitulation as an Interpretive Principle', in Boersma (ed.), *Imagination and Interpretation: Christian Perspectives* (Vancouver: Regent College Publishing, 2005), 13–33.

——— 'Theology as Queen of Hospitality', *EvQ* 79 (2007), 291–310.

——— *Violence, Hospitality, and the Cross: Reappropriating the Atonement Tradition* (Grand Rapids, Mich.: Baker Academic, 2004).

Boey, Koen, 'Blondels metafysica van de wil', *Bijdragen* 62 (2001), 317–38.

Bonino, Serge-Thomas, et al., *Saint Thomas au XXe siècle* (Paris: St-Paul, 1994).

Boys, Mary C., *Biblical Interpretation in Religious Education: A Study of the Kerygmatic Era* (Birmingham, Ala.: Religious Education, 1980).

Bradley, Denis J. M., *Aquinas on the Twofold Human Good: Reason and Human Happiness in Aquinas's Moral Science* (Washington, DC: Catholic University of America Press, 1997).

Bramwell, Bevil, 'Hans Urs von Balthasar's Theology of Scripture', *NBl* 86 (2005), 308–22.

Bunnenberg, Johannes, *Lebendige Treue zum Ursprung: Das Traditionsverständnis Yves Congars*, Walberger Studien, 14 (Mainz: Grünewald, 1989).

Burghardt, Walter J., 'On Early Christian Exegesis', *TS* 11 (1950), 78–116.

——— review of *Origène: Homélies sur la Genèse*, ed. and trans. Louis Doutreleau, *TS* 9 (1948), 262–6.

Carabine, Deidre, 'The Fathers: The Church's Intimate, Youthful Diary', in Bede McGregor and Thomas Norris (eds), *The Beauty of Christ: An Introduction to the Theology of Hans Urs von Balthasar* (Edinburgh: T. & T. Clark, 1994), 73–91.

Castro, Michel, 'Henri Bouillard (1908–1981): Éléments de biographie intellectuelle', *MSR* 60/4 (2003), 43–58; 63/2 (2006), 47–59.

Cavanaugh, William T., *Torture and Eucharist: Theology, Politics, and the Body of Christ* (Oxford: Blackwell, 1998).

Chadwick, Owen, *From Bossuet to Newman: The Idea of Doctrinal Development* (2nd edn, Cambridge: Cambridge University Press, 1987).

Chantraine, Georges, *Henri de Lubac*, i *De la naissance à la démobilisation (1896–1919)*, Études Lubaciennes, 6 (Paris: Cerf, 2007).

Colin, Pierre, *L'Audace et le soupçon: La Crise du modernisme dans le catholicisme français 1893–1914* (Paris: Desclée de Brouwer, 1997).

Connolly, James M., *The Voices of France: A Survey of Contemporary Theology in France* (New York: Macmillan, 1961).

Conticello, Carmelo Giuseppe, '*De contemplatione* (Angelicum 1920): La Thèse inédite du P. M.-D. Chenu', *RSPT* 75 (1991), 363–422.

Conway, Michael A., 'A Positive Phenomenology: The Structure of Blondel's Early Philosophy', *HeyJ* 47 (2006), 579–600.

Cottier, Georges P., *Le Désir de Dieu: Sur les traces de saint Thomas* (Paris: Parole et Silence, 2002).

——'Désir naturel de voir Dieu', *Greg* 78 (1997), 679–98.

Crowley, Paul Gerard, 'Dogmatic Development after Newman: The Search for a Hermeneutical Principle in Newman, Marin-Sola, Rahner and Gadamer' (PhD diss., Graduate Theological Union, 1984).

D'Ambrosio, Marcellino, 'Henri de Lubac and the Critique of Scientific Exegesis', *Comm* 19 (1992), 365–88.

——'Henri de Lubac and the Recovery of the Traditional Hermeneutic' (PhD diss., Catholic University of America, Washington, DC, 1991).

——'*Ressourcement* Theology, *Aggiornamento*, and the Hermeneutics of Tradition', *Comm* 18 (1991), 530–55.

——'The Spiritual Sense in de Lubac's Hermeneutics of Tradition', *LS* 1 (2005), 147–57.

Daley, Brian E., 'Balthasar's Reading of the Church Fathers', in Edward T. Oakes and David Moss (eds), *The Cambridge Companion to Hans Urs von Balthasar* (Cambridge: Cambridge University Press, 2004), 187–206.

——'The *Nouvelle Théologie* and the Patristic Revival: Sources, Symbols and the Science of Theology', *IJST* 7 (2005), 362–82.

Daly, Gabriel, *Transcendence and Immanence: A Study in Catholic Modernism and Integralism* (Oxford: Clarendon Press, 1980).

de la Potterie, Ignace, 'The Spiritual Sense of Scripture', *Comm* 23 (1996), 738–56.

de Lavalette, Henri, 'Le Théoricien de l'amour', *RSR* 53 (1965), 462–94.

de Moulins-Beaufort, Éric, *Anthropologie et mystique selon Henri de Lubac: 'L'Esprit de l'homme' ou la présence de Dieu en l'homme*, Études Lubaciennes, 3 (Paris: Cerf, 2003).

de Schrijver, Georges, *Le Merveilleux Accord de l'homme et de Dieu: Étude de l'analogie de l'être chez Hans Urs von Balthasar*, BETL, 63 (Louvain: Leuven University Press, 1983).

Desmazières, Agnès, 'La "Nouvelle théologie", prémisse d'une théologie herméneutique? La controverse sur l'analogie de la vérité (1946–1949)', *RT* 104 (2004), 241–72.

Dickens, W. T., *Hans Urs von Balthasar's Theological Aesthetics: A Model for Post-critical Biblical Interpretation* (Notre Dame, Ind.: University of Notre Dame Press, 2003).

Dietrich, Donald J., and Michael J. Himes (eds), *The Legacy of the Tübingen School: The Relevance of Nineteenth-century Theology for the Twenty-first Century* (New York: Crossroad, 1997).

Donneaud, Henry, 'Une vie au service de la théologie', *RT* 92 (1992), 17–51.

Donnelly, Philip J., 'On the Development of Dogma and the Supernatural', *TS* 8 (1947), 471–91.

Doré, Joseph, and Jacques Fantino (eds), *Marie-Dominique Chenu: Moyen-âge et modernité*, Les cahiers du Centre d'études du Saulchoir, 5 (Paris: Cerf, 1997).

Doyle, Dennis M., *Communion Ecclesiology: Vision and Versions* (Maryknoll, NY: Orbis, 2000).

—— 'Henri de Lubac and the Roots of Communion Ecclesiology', *TS* 60 (1999), 209–27.

—— 'Journet, Congar, and the Roots of Communion Ecclesiology', *TS* 58 (1997), 461–79.

—— 'Möhler, Schleiermacher, and the Roots of Communion Ecclesiology', *TS* 57 (1996), 467–80.

Dulles, Avery, 'The Church as Communion', in Bradley Nassif (ed.), *New Perspectives on Historical Theology: Essays in Memory of John Meyendorff* (Grand Rapids, Mich.: Eerdmans, 1996), 125–39.

—— 'A Half Century of Ecclesiology', *TS* 50 (1989), 419–42.

—— 'True and False Reform in the Church', in *Church and Society: The Laurence J. McGinley Lectures, 1988–2007* (New York: Fordham University Press, 2008), 401–13.

Dunne, Victor, *Prophecy in the Church: The Vision of Yves Congar*, European University Studies, 23 (New York: Lang, 2000).

Dupré, Louis, 'Hans Urs von Balthasar's Theology of Aesthetic Form', *TS* 49 (1988), 299–318.

—— *Passage to Modernity: An Essay in the Hermeneutics of Nature and Culture* (New Haven, Conn.: Yale University Press, 1993).

—— *Religion and the Rise of Modern Culture* (Notre Dame, Ind.: University of Notre Dame Press, 2008).

Durand, Jean-Dominique (ed.), *Henri de Lubac: La Rencontre au cœur de l'Église* (Paris: Cerf, 2006).

English, Adam C., *The Possibility of Christian Philosophy: Maurice Blondel at the Intersection of Theology and Philosophy* (London: Routledge, 2007).

Famerée, Joseph, *L'Ecclésiologie d'Yves Congar avant Vatican II: Histoire et Église: Analyse et reprise critique*, BETL, 107 (Louvain: Leuven University Press, 1992).

Feingold, Lawrence, *The Natural Desire to See God according to St Thomas Aquinas and his Interpreters* (Rome: Apollinaris, 2001).

Flynn, Gabriel, '*Mon journal du Concile*: Yves Congar and the Battle for a Renewed Ecclesiology at the Second Vatican Council', *LouvStud* 28 (2003), 48–70.

—— 'The Role of Unbelief in the Theology of Yves Congar', *NBl* 85 (2004), 426–43.

—— (ed.), *Yves Congar: Theologian of the Church* (Grand Rapids, Mich.: Eerdmans, 2005).

Flynn, Gabriel, *Yves Congar's Vision of the Church in a World of Unbelief* (Burlington, Vt.: Ashgate, 2004).

Foley, Brian, 'The Catholic Critics of Karl Barth: In Outline and Analysis', *SJT* 14 (1961), 136–55.

Ford, David F. (ed.), *The Modern Theologians: An Introduction to Christian Theology in the Twentieth Century* (2nd edn, Cambridge: Blackwell, 1997).

—— and Rachel Muers (eds), *The Modern Theologians: An Introduction to Christian Theology since 1918* (3rd edn, Oxford: Blackwell, 2005).

Fouilloux, Étienne, *La Collection 'Sources chrétiennes': Éditer les Pères de l'Église au XXᵉ siècle* (Paris: Cerf, 1995).

—— 'La "Dialogue théologique" selon Marie-Joseph Nicolas', *BLE* 103 (2002), 19–32.

—— *Une Église en quête de liberté: La pensée catholique française entre modernisme et Vatican II (1914–1962)* (Paris: Desclée de Brouwer, 1998).

—— 'Friar Yves, Cardinal Congar, Dominican: Itinerary of a Theologian', *USCath Hist* 17/2 (1999), 63–90.

—— 'Henri de Lubac au moment de la publication de *Surnaturel*', *RT* 101 (2001), 13–30.

Franz Franks, Angela, 'Trinitarian *analogia entis* in Hans Urs von Balthasar', *Thomist* 62 (1998), 533–59.

Franzelin, Johann Baptist, *Tractatus de Deo uno secundum naturam* (Rome: Taurini, 1870).

—— *Tractatus de divina traditione et scriptura* (Rome: Collegio Romano, 1860–4).

Galdon, Joseph A., *Typology and Seventeenth-century Literature* (The Hague: Mouton, 1975).

Galvin, John J., 'A Critical Survey of Modern Conceptions of Doctrinal Development', in Proceedings of the Fifth Annual Meeting of the Catholic Theological Society of America (Washington, DC: n.p., 1950), 45–63.

Geffré, Claude, 'Le Réalisme de l'incarnation dans la théologie du Père M.-D. Chenu', *RSPT* 69 (1985), 389–99.

Geiselmann, Josef Rupert, *Die katholische Tübinger Schule: Ihre theologische Eigenart* (Freiburg: Herder, 1965).

Gilmore, George B., 'J. A. Möhler on Doctrinal Development', *HeyJ* 19 (1978), 383–98.

Greeley, Andrew, *The Catholic Imagination* (Berkeley, Calif.: University of California Press, 2000).

Groppe, Elizabeth Teresa, *Yves Congar's Theology of the Holy Spirit* (Oxford: Oxford University Press, 2004).

Grumett, David, *De Lubac: A Guide for the Perplexed* (London: T. & T. Clark/Continuum, 2007).

Guarino, Thomas G., 'Fundamental Theology and the Natural Knowledge of God in the Writings of Henri Bouillard' (PhD diss., Catholic University of America, Washington, DC, 1984).

—— 'Henri Bouillard and the Truth-status of Dogmatic Statements', *ScEs* 39 (1987), 331–43.

—— 'Tradition and Doctrinal Development: Can Vincent of Lérins Still Teach the Church?' *TS* 67 (2006), 34–72.

Guelluy, Robert, 'Les Antécédents de l'encyclique "Humani Generis" dans les sanctions Romaines de 1942: Chenu, Charlier, Draguet', *RHE* 81 (1986), 421–97.

Guillet, Jacques, *La Théologie catholique en France de 1914 à 1960* (Paris: Médiasèvres, 1988).

Hammans, Herbert, *Die neueren katholischen Erklärungen der Dogmenentwicklung* (Essen: Ludgerus, 1965).

Hankey, Wayne J., *One Hundred Years of Neoplatonism in France: A Brief Philosophical History*, Studies in Philosophical Theology, 32 (Louvain: Peeters, 2006).

Hanson, R. P. C., *Allegory and Event: A Study of the Sources and Significance of Origen's Interpretation of Scripture* (London: SCM, 1959).

Hanvey, James, 'In the Presence of Love: The Pneumatological Realization of the Economy: Yves Congar, *Le Mystère du temple*', *IJST* 7 (2005), 383–98.

Harent, S., 'Foi', q.v. A. Vacant, E. Mangenot, and E. Amann (eds), *Dictionnaire théologie catholique*, vi (Paris: Letouzey et Ané, 1920), 55–514.

Henn, William, 'Yves Congar and *Lumen gentium*', *Greg* 86 (2005), 563–92.

Henry, Patrick, 'The French Catholic Church's Apology', *FrR* 72 (1999), 1099–105.

Hill, Harvey, 'Loisy's *L'Évangile et l'église* in Light of the "Essais"', *TS* 67 (2006), 73–98.

—— 'Loisy's "Mystical Faith": Loisy, Leo XIII, and Sabatier on Moral Education and the Church', *TS* 65 (2004), 73–94.

Himes, Michael J., *Ongoing Incarnation: Johann Adam Möhler and the Beginnings of Modern Ecclesiology* (New York: Crossroad, 1997).

Hollon, Bryan C., *Everything Is Sacred: Spiritual Exegesis in the Political Theology of Henri de Lubac*, Theopolitical Visions, 3 (Eugene, Ore.: Cascade-Wipf & Stock, 2008).

Holstein, Henri, 'Le Théologien de la foi', *RSR* 53 (1965), 422–61.

Howsare, Rodney A., *Hans Urs von Balthasar and Protestantism: The Ecumenical Implications of His Theological Style* (London: T. & T. Clark/Continuum, 2005).

Hughes, Kevin L., 'The "Fourfold Sense": De Lubac, Blondel and Contemporary Theology', *HeyJ* 42 (2001), 451–62.

Hütter, Reinhard, '*Desiderium Naturale Visionis Dei—Est autem duplex hominis beatitudo sive felicitas*: Some Observations about Lawrence Feingold's and John Milbank's Recent Interventions in the Debate over the Natural Desire to See God', *NV* Eng 5 (2007), 81–132.

Jeffrey, David Lyle, *Houses of the Interpreter: Reading Scripture, Reading Culture* (Waco, Tex.: Baylor University Press, 2003).

—— review of John Milbank, *The Suspended Middle: Henri de Lubac and the Debate concerning the Supernatural*, *JAAR* 75 (2007), 715–17.

Jenkins, John I., *Knowledge and Faith in Thomas Aquinas* (Cambridge: Cambridge University Press, 1997).

Jodock, Darrell (ed.), *Catholicism Contending with Modernity: Roman Catholic Modernism and Anti-modernism in Historical Context* (Cambridge: Cambridge University Press, 2000).

John, Eric, 'Daniélou on History', *DownR* 72/227 (1953), 2–15.

Jolivet, Jean, 'M.-D. Chenu, médiéviste et théologien', *RSPT* 81 (1997), 381–94.

Jossua, Jean-Pierre, 'Théologie et vie spirituelle chez saint Thomas selon le Père Chenu', *VSpir* 147 (1993), 747–55.

—— *Yves Congar: Theology in the Service of God's People*, trans. Mary Jocelyn (Chicago, Ill.: Priory, 1968).

Kantorowicz, Ernst H., *The King's Two Bodies: A Study in Mediaeval Political Theology* (2nd edn, Princeton, NJ: Princeton University Press, 1997).

Kasper, Walter (ed.), *Logik der Liebe und Herrlichkeit Gottes: Hans Urs von Balthasar im Gespräch* (Ostfildern: Matthias-Grünewald, 2006).

Kerr, Fergus, 'Chenu's Little Book', *NBl* 66 (1985), 108–12.

—— 'A Different World: Neoscholasticism and its Discontents', *IJST* 8 (2006), 128–48.

—— *Twentieth-century Catholic Theologians: From Neoscholasticism to Nuptial Mysticism* (Malden, Mass.: Blackwell, 2007).

—— 'Yves Congar: From Suspicion to Acclamation', *LouvStud* 29 (2004), 273–87.

Kizhakkeparampil, Isaac, *The Invocation of the Holy Spirit as Constitutive of the Sacraments according to Cardinal Yves Congar* (Rome: Gregorian University Press, 1995).

Knasas, John F. X., *Being and Some Twentieth-century Thomists* (New York: Fordham University Press, 2003).

Komonchak, Joseph A., 'Returning from Exile: Catholic Theology in the 1930s', in Gregory Baum (ed.), *The Twentieth Century: A Theological Overview* (New York: Orbis, 1999), 35–48.

—— 'Theology and Culture at Mid-century: The Example of Henri de Lubac', *TS* 51 (1990), 579–602.

Koskela, Douglas M., 'The Divine–Human Tension in the Ecclesiology of Yves Congar', *Eccl* 4 (2007), 88–106.

—— *Ecclesiality and Ecumenism: Yves Congar and the Road to Unity*, Marquette Studies in Theology, 61 (Milwaukee, Wis.: Marquette University Press, 2008).

Kuther, Ulrich, *Kirchliche Tradition als geistliche Schriftauslegung: Zum theologischen Schriftgebrauch in Henri de Lubacs 'Die Kirche. Eine Betrachtung'*, Studies in Tradition Theory, 5 (Münster: Lit, 2001).

Le Blond, Jean-Marie, 'L'Analogie de la vérité: Réflexion d'un philosophe sur une controverse théologique', *RSR* 34 (1947), 129–41.

Lebeau, Paul, *Jean Daniélou*, Théologiens et spirituels contemporains, 4 (Paris: Fleurus, 1967).

Leonard, Ellen, *George Tyrrell and the Catholic Tradition* (London: Darton, Longman and Todd, 1982).

Levering, Matthew, 'Balthasar on Christ's Consciousness on the Cross', *Thomist*, 65 (2001), 567–81.

—— *Participatory Biblical Exegesis: A Theology of Biblical Interpretation* (Notre Dame, Ind.: University of Notre Dame Press, 2008).

Lindsay, Austin J., 'De Lubac's Images of the Church: A Study of Christianity in Dialogue' (PhD diss., Catholic University of America, Washington, DC, 1974).

Long, Stephen A., 'On the Possibility of a Purely Natural End for Man', *Thomist*, 64 (2000), 211–37.

Losinger, Anton, *Relative Autonomy: The Key to Understanding Vatican II* (Frankfurt: Lang, 1997).

Louth, Andrew, *The Origins of the Christian Mystical Tradition: From Plato to Denys* (Oxford: Oxford University Press, 1981).

McCool, Gerald A., *Catholic Theology in the Nineteenth Century: The Quest for a Unitary Method* (New York: Crossroad/Seabury, 1977).

—— *From Unity to Pluralism: The Internal Evolution of Thomism* (New York: Fordham University Press, 1989).

McDermott, John M., 'De Lubac and Rousselot', *Greg* 78 (1997), 735–59.

—— *Love and Understanding: The Relation of Will and Intellect in Pierre Rousselot's Christological Vision*, Analecta Gregoriana, 229 (Rome: Università Gregoriana Editrice, 1983).

MacDonald, Charles, *Church and World in the Plan of God: Aspects of History and Eschatology in the Thought of Père Yves Congar, OP*, Regensburger Studien zur Theologie, 27 (Frankfurt: Lang, 1982).

MacDonald, Timothy I., *The Ecclesiology of Yves Congar: Foundational Themes* (Lanham, Md.: University Press of America, 1984).

McGregor, Bede, and Thomas Norris (eds), *The Beauty of Christ: An Introduction to the Theology of Hans Urs von Balthasar* (Edinburgh: T. & T. Clark, 1994).

McInerny, Ralph, *Praeambula fidei: Thomism and the God of the Philosophers* (Washington, DC: Catholic University of America Press, 2006).

McKenzie, John L., 'A Chapter in the History of Spiritual Exegesis: De Lubac's *Histoire et esprit*', *TS* 12 (1951), 365–81.

McNally, Robert E., 'Medieval Exegesis', *TS* 22 (1961), 445–54.

McNeill, John J., *The Blondelian Synthesis: A Study of the Influence of German Philosophical Sources on the Formation of Blondel's Method and Thought* (Leiden: Brill, 1966).

McPartlan, Paul, *The Eucharist Makes the Church: Henri de Lubac and John Zizioulas in Dialogue* (Edinburgh: T. & T. Clark, 1993).

—— 'Eucharistic Ecclesiology', *OiC* 22 (1986), 314–31.

—— ' "You will be changed into me": Unity and Limits in de Lubac's Thought', *OiC* 30 (1994), 50–60.

Maggiolini, Allessandro, 'Magisterial Teaching on Experience in the Twentieth Century: From the Modernist Crisis to the Second Vatican Council', trans. Andrew Matt and Adrian Walker, *Comm* 23 (1996), 225–43.

Mansini, Guy, 'Henri de Lubac, the Natural Desire to See God, and Pure Nature', *Greg* 83 (2002), 89–109.

Marty, Élie, *Le Témoignage de Pierre Rousselot, SJ, 1878–1915: D'après ses écrits et sa correspondance* (Paris: Beauchesne, 1940).

Matteo, Anthony M., *Quest for the Absolute: The Philosophical Vision of Joseph Maréchal* (DeKalb, Ill.: Northern Illinois University Press, 1992).

Mayeski, Marie Anne, 'Quaestio disputata: Catholic Theology and the History of Exegesis', *TS* 62 (2001), 140–53.

Melloni, Alberto, 'Congar, Architect of the *Unam Sanctam*', *LouvStud* 29 (2004), 222–38.

Mettepenningen, Jürgen, 'L'Essai de Louis Charlier (1938): Une contribution à la *nouvelle théologie*', *RTL* 39 (2008), 211–32.

—— 'Truth as Issue in a Second Modernist Crisis? The Clash between Recontextualization and Retrocontextualization in the French-speaking Polemic of 1946–47', in M. Lamberigts, L. Boeve, and T. Merrigan (eds), *Theology and the Quest for Truth:*

Historical and Systematic Theological Studies, BETL, 202 (Louvain: Leuven University Press, 2006), 119–42.

Meuleman, Gezinus Evert, *De ontwikkeling van het dogma in de Rooms Katholieke theologie* (Kampen: Kok, 1951).

Milbank, John, *The Suspended Middle: Henri de Lubac and the Debate Concerning the Supernatural* (Grand Rapids, Mich.: Eerdmans, 2005).

—— *Theology and Social Theory: Beyond Secular Reason* (Oxford: Blackwell, 1990).

Mongrain, Kevin, *The Systematic Thought of Hans Urs von Balthasar: An Irenaean Retrieval* (New York: Crossroad/Herder, 2002).

—— 'Von Balthasar's Way from Doxology to Theology', *TTod* 64 (2007), 58–70.

Mueller, Joseph G., 'Blindness and Forgetting: The Prophet–Reformer in Yves Congar's *Vraie et fausse réforme dans l'Église*', *Comm* 34 (2007), 640–56.

Mullins, Patrick, 'The Spirit Speaks to the Churches: Continuity and Development in Congar's Pneumatology', *LouvStud* 29 (2004), 288–319.

Murphy, William F., 'Henri de Lubac's Mystical Tropology', *Comm* 27 (2000), 171–201.

Nédoncelle, Maurice, 'L'Influence de Newman sur les "Yeux de la foi" de Rousselot', *RSR* 27 (1953), 321–32.

Neufeld, Karl-Heinz, 'Fundamentaltheologie in gewandelter Welt: H. Bouillards theologischer Beitrag', *ZKT* 100 (1978), 417–40.

Nichols, Aidan, *From Newman to Congar: The Idea of Doctrinal Development from the Victorians to the Second Vatican Council* (Edinburgh: T. & T. Clark, 1990).

—— *Reason with Piety: Garrigou-Lagrange in the Service of Catholic Thought* (Naples, Fla.: Sapientia Press of Ave Maria University, 2008).

—— 'T. S. Eliot and Yves Congar on the Nature of Tradition', *Ang* 61 (1984), 473–85.

—— *Yves Congar* (Wilton, Conn.: Morehouse/Barlow, 1989).

Nienaltowski, Henry Raphael, *Johann Adam Möhler's Theory of Doctrinal Development: Its Genesis and Formulation*, Catholic University of America Studies in Sacred Theology, 113 (Washington, DC: Catholic University of America Press, 1959).

O'Connell, Marvin R., *Critics on Trial: An Introduction to the Catholic Modernist Crisis* (Washington, DC: Catholic University of America Press, 1994).

O'Hanlon, Gerard F., *The Immutability of God in the Theology of Hans Urs von Balthasar* (Cambridge: Cambridge University Press, 1990).

O'Meara, Thomas, '"Raid on the Dominicans": The Repression of 1954', *America*, 107/4 (5 Feb. 1994), 9–18.

O'Regan, Cyril, 'Balthasar and Gnostic Genealogy', *MTh* 22 (2006), 609–50.

—— 'Von Balthasar and Thick Retrieval: Post-Chalcedonian Symphonic Theology', *Greg* 77 (1996), 227–60.

Oakes, Edward T., *Pattern of Redemption: The Theology of Hans Urs von Balthasar* (New York: Continuum, 1994).

—— and David Moss (eds), *The Cambridge Companion to Hans Urs von Balthasar* (Cambridge: Cambridge University Press, 2004).

Peddicord, Richard, *The Sacred Monster of Thomism: An Introduction to the Life and Legacy of Reginald Garrigou-Lagrange* (South Bend, Ind.: St Augustine's, 2005).

Petit, Jean-Claude, 'La Compréhension de la théologie dans la théologie française au XXᵉ siècle: La Hantise du savoir et de l'objectivité: L'Exemple d'Ambroise Gardeil', *LTP* 45 (1989), 379–91.

—— 'La Compréhension de la théologie dans la théologie française au XXᵉ siècle: Vers une nouvelle conscience historique: G. Rabeau, M.-D. Chenu, L. Charlier', *LTP* 47 (1991), 215–29.

Potworowski, Christophe F., *Contemplation and Incarnation: The Theology of Marie-Dominique Chenu* (Montreal: McGill–Queen's University Press, 2001).

—— 'Dechristianization, Socialization and Incarnation in Marie-Dominique Chenu', *ScEs* 93 (1991), 17–54.

—— 'History and Incarnation in the Theology of Marie-Dominique Chenu', *ScEs* 92 (1990), 237–65.

Poulat, Émile, *Critique et mystique: Autour de Loisy ou la conscience catholique et l'esprit moderne* (Paris: Centurion, 1984).

—— *Histoire, dogme et critique dans la crise moderniste* (3rd edn, Paris: Albin Michel, 1996).

Quisinsky, Michael, *Geschichtlicher Glaube in einer geschichtlichen Welt: Der Beitrag von M.-D. Chenu, Y. Congar und H.-M. Féret zum II. Vaticanum*, Dogma und Geschichte: Historische und begriffsgeschichtliche Studien zur Theologie, 6 (Berlin: Lit, 2007).

Robinson, Jonathan, 'Congar, Architect of the *Unam Sanctam*', *LouvStud* 29 (2004), 224–5.

Rowland, Tracey, *Culture and the Thomist Tradition after Vatican II* (London: Routledge, 2003).

—— *Ratzinger's Faith: The Theology of Pope Benedict XVI* (Oxford: Oxford University Press, 2008).

Russo, Antonio, *Henri de Lubac; Teologia e dogma nella storia: L'Influsso di Blondel* (Rome: Edizioni Studium, 1990).

St Hilaire, Robert N., 'Desire Divided: Nature and Grace in the Neo-Thomism of Pierre Rousselot' (PhD diss., Harvard Divinity School, 2008).

Schillebeeckx, Edward, *Revelation and Theology*, ii *The Concept of Truth and Theological Renewal*, trans. N. D. Smith (London: Sheed & Ward, 1968).

Schindler, David L. (ed), *Hans Urs von Balthasar: His Life and Work* (San Francisco, Calif.: Communio/Ignatius, 1991).

Schmitt, Jean-Claude, 'L'Œuvre de médiéviste du Père Chenu', *RSPT* 81 (1997), 395–406.

Schmutz, Jacob, 'Escaping the Aristotelian Bond: The Critique of Metaphysics in Twentieth-century French Philosophy', *Dionysius*, 17 (1999), 169–200.

Schoof, Mark, *A Survey of Catholic Theology 1800–1970*, trans. N. D. Smith (Paramus, NJ: Paulist Newman, 1970).

Schultenover, David G., *George Tyrrell: In Search of Catholicism* (Shepherdstown, W.Va.: Patmos, 1981).

Scully, J. Eileen, *Grace and Human Freedom in the Theology of Henri Bouillard* (Bethesda, Md.: Academica, 2006).

Sesboüé, Bernard, 'Le Surnaturel chez Henri de Lubac: Un conflit autour d'une théologie', *RSR* 80 (1992), 373–408.

Sheedy, Charles E., 'Opinions Concerning Doctrinal Development', *AER* 120 (1949), 19–32.

Sicouly, Pablo, 'Yves Congar und Johann Adam Möhler: Ein theologisches Gespräch zwischen den Zeiten', *Cath* 45 (1991), 36–43.

Smart, Ninian, et al. (eds), *Nineteenth-century Religious Thought in the West*, ii (Cambridge: Cambridge University Press, 1985).

Smith, James K. A., *Introducing Radical Orthodoxy: Mapping a Post-secular Theology* (Grand Rapids, Mich.: Baker Academic, 2005).

Sullivan, Jemima Rosario, 'The Contribution of Jean Daniélou to an Understanding of Biblical and Liturgical Typology in Liturgical Catechesis' (PhD diss., Catholic University of America, Washington, DC, 1999).

Synod of Bishops, 'The Final Report', *Origins* 15 (1985), 444–50.

Tallon, Andrew, 'Doctrinal Development and Wisdom: Rousselot on "Sympathetic Knowing" by Connaturality', *PT* 15 (2003), 353–83.

Tillard, Jean-Marie-Roger, *Flesh of the Church, Flesh of Christ: At the Source of the Ecclesiology of Communion*, trans. Madeleine Beaumont (Collegeville, Minn.: Liturgical, 2001).

Torrell, Jean-Pierre, 'Yves Congar et l'ecclésiologie de Saint Thomas d'Aquin', *RSPT* 82 (1998), 201–42.

Tortorelli, Kevin M., 'Balthasar and the Theodramatic Interpretation of St Irenaeus', *DownR* 11 (1993), 117–26.

van Vliet, Cornelis Th. M., *Communio sacramentalis: Das Kirchenverständis von Yves Congar–genetisch und systematisch betrachtet* (Mainz: Matthias-Grünewald, 1995).

Vauchez, André (ed.), *Cardinal Yves Congar 1904–1995: Actes du colloque réuni à Rome les 3–4 juin 1996* (Paris: Cerf, 1999).

Verhoeven, Jan, *Dynamiek van het verlangen: De godsdienstfilosofische methode van Rahner tegen de achtergrond van Maréchal en Blondel* (Amsterdam: Thesis Publishers, 1996).

Voderholzer, Rudolf, *Meet Henri de Lubac: His Life and Work*, trans. Michael J. Miller (San Francisco, Calif.: Ignatius, 2008).

Voss, Gustav, 'Johann Adam Möhler and the Development of Dogma', *TS* 4 (1943), 420–44.

Wagner, Jean-Pierre, *Henri de Lubac* (Paris: Cerf, 2001).

Wainwright, Geoffrey, '"Bible et Liturgie": Daniélou's Work Revisited', *SL* 22 (1992), 154–62.

Walgrave, Jan Hendrik, *Unfolding Revelation: The Nature of Doctrinal Development* (Philadelphia, Pa.: Hutchinson, 1972).

Walker, Adrian J., 'Love Alone: Hans Urs von Balthasar as a Master of Theological Renewal', *Comm* 32 (2005), 1–24.

Walsh, Christopher J., 'De Lubac's Critique of the Postconciliar Church', *Comm* 19 (1992), 404–32.

—— 'Henri de Lubac and the Ecclesiology of the Postconciliar Church' (PhD diss., Catholic University of America, Washington, DC, 1993).

Wang, Lisa, '*Sacramentum Unitatis Ecclesiasticae*: The Eucharistic Ecclesiology of Henri de Lubac', *ATR* 85 (2003), 143–58.

Wang, Stephen, 'Aquinas on Human Happiness and the Natural Desire for God', *NBl* 88 (2007), 322–34.

Webster, John, 'Purity and Plenitude: Evangelical Reflections on Congar's *Tradition and Traditions*', *IJST* 7 (2005), 399–413.

Weigel, Gustave, 'Gleanings from the Commentaries on *Humani Generis*', *TS* 12 (1951), 520–49.

—— 'The Historical Background of the Encyclical *Humani Generis*', *TS* 12 (1951), 208–30.

Widmer, Gabriel, 'Karl Barth vu par le P. Bouillard', *RTP* 3rd ser., 9 (1959), 166–76.

Williams, A. N., 'The Future of the Past: The Contemporary Significance of the *Nouvelle Théologie*', *IJST* 7 (2005), 347–61.

Wolff, Monika-Maria, *Gott und Mensch: Ein Beitrag Yves Congars zum ökumenischen Dialog*, Frankfurter theologische Studien, 38 (Frankfurt: Knecht, 1990).

Wood, Susan K., 'The Church as the Social Embodiment of Grace in the Ecclesiology of Henri de Lubac' (PhD diss., Marquette University, Milwaukee, Wis., 1986).

—— *Spiritual Exegesis and the Church in the Theology of Henri de Lubac* (Grand Rapids, Mich.: Eerdmans, 1998).

Worgul, George S., 'M. Blondel and the Problem of Mysticism', *ETL* 61 (1985), 100–22.

Young, Frances M., *Biblical Exegesis and the Formation of Christian Culture* (Cambridge: Cambridge University Press, 1997).

Scripture Index

General Index

Index